Contents

KT-504-079

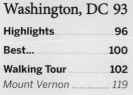

Contents

On the Road

Glen
Nate
Ned
Mariella Kr
Kevin   ....ea Schulte-Peevers,
Ryan ver Berkmoes, John A Vlahides, Karla Zimmerman

The Pacific Northwest **p333**

Boston & New England **p153**

New York City **p51**

Chicago **p123**

Washington, DC **p93**

California **p367**

The Grand Canyon & the Southwest **p287**

New Orleans & the South **p197**

Florida **p247**

● New York City

- Central Park
- Statue of Liberty & Ellis Island
- Metropolitan Museum of Art
- Times Square & Broadway
- Brooklyn Bridge

● Washington, DC

- National Mall
- Capitol Hill
- The White House
- U Street Corridor
- Dupont Circle
- Georgetown

● Chicago

- Millennium Park
- Art Institute of Chicago
- Lincoln Park
- Deep-Dish Pizza
- John Hancock Center
- Wrigley Field

● Boston & New England

- Freedom Trail
- Fall Foliage
- Lighthouses
- Cape Cod
- Martha's Vineyard
- Acadia National Park

● New Orleans & the South

- New Orleans
- Great Smoky Mountains National Park
- Graceland & Memphis
- Nashville
- Savannah
- Cajun Country

● Florida

- Walt Disney World
- Miami Beach
- Key West
- The Everglades
- Aquatic Adventures
- Little Havana

In Focus

Survival Guide

●●●

The Best
of the Rest   421

This Is the USA

Enormous in size and staggeringly diverse, America harbors an astounding collection of natural and cultural wonders, from teeming city streets to mountains, coastlines and forests covering vast swaths of the continent.

America: home to Los Angeles, Las Vegas, Chicago, Miami, Boston and New York City. Each is a brimming metropolis whose name alone conjures a million different notions of culture, cuisine and entertainment. Look more closely, and the American quilt unfurls in all its surprising variety: the red-hot music scene of Memphis, the easygoing charms of antebellum Savannah, the eco-consciousness of free-spirited Portland and the magnificent waterfront of San Francisco.

This is a country of road trips and great open skies. It's a country where four million miles of highways lead past red-rock deserts, below towering mountain peaks and across fertile wheat fields that roll off toward the horizon. The scenic country lanes of New England, the lush rainforests of the Pacific Northwest and the Spanish moss–draped backdrop of the Deep South are a few fine starting points for the great American road trip.

Cuisine is another illumination of the American experience. New York locals get their fix of bagels and lox at a century-old deli on Manhattan's Upper West Side, while several states away, pancakes and fried eggs disappear under the clatter of cutlery at a 1950s-style diner. Plates of fresh lobster served off a Maine pier, oysters and champagne in a wine bar in California, beer and deep-dish pizza at a Chicago pub – just a few of the ways to dine à la Americana.

The world's third-largest nation has made tremendous contributions to the arts. Cities like Chicago and New York have become veritable drawing boards for the great architects of the modern era. Musically speaking, America has few peers on the world stage. From the jazz of New Orleans to the country of Nashville, plus bluegrass, hip-hop and rock and roll, America has invented sounds that are integral to modern music.

Grand Canyon National Park (p298)

> " Look closely, and the American quilt unfurls in all its surprising variety "

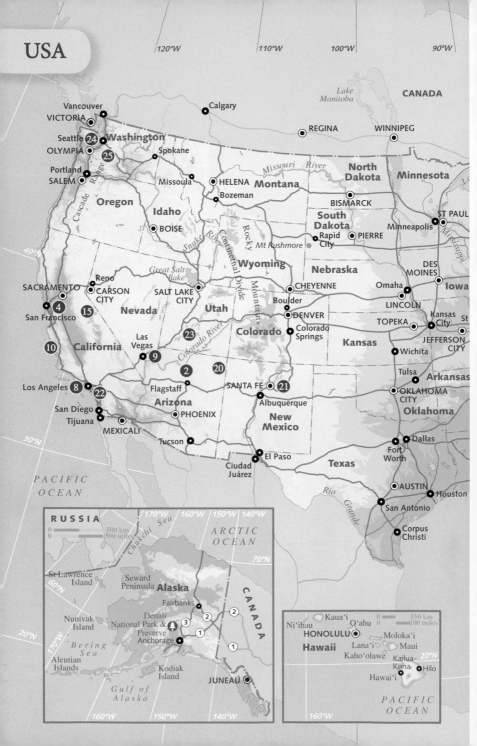

25

Top Experiences

1. New York City
2. Grand Canyon National Park
3. New Orleans
4. San Francisco & Wine Country
5. Fall Colors, New England
6. Disney World
7. Chicago
8. Los Angeles
9. Las Vegas
10. Pacific Coast Highway
11. Washington, DC
12. Nashville
13. Deep South
14. Miami
15. Yosemite National Park
16. Coastal Maine
17. Memphis & Graceland
18. Boston & Cape Cod
19. Everglades National Park
20. Native American Sites
21. Santa Fe
22. Disneyland
23. Zion & Southern Utah National Parks
24. Seattle
25. Mt Rainier National Park

ELEVATION

16,000ft
12,000ft
9000ft
5000ft
2000ft
1000ft
500ft
Sea Level
-500ft

25 USA's Top Experiences

New York City

Home to striving artists, hedge-fund moguls and immigrants from every corner of the globe, New York City (p62) is constantly reinventing itself. It remains a world center for fashion, theater, food, music, publishing, advertising and finance. A staggering number of museums, parks and ethnic neighborhoods are scattered through the five boroughs, so do as every New Yorker does: hit the streets. Every block reflects the character and history of this dizzying kaleidoscope, and on even a short walk here you can cross continents.

1

WITOLD SKRYPCZAK/LONELY PLANET IMAGES ©

②

Grand Canyon National Park

You've seen pictures and heard about it from everyone else – is it worth the hype? The answer is a resounding yes. The Grand Canyon (p298) is vast and nearly incomprehensible in age: it took six million years for the canyon to form, while some rocks exposed along its walls are two billion years old. Peer over the edge to confront the great power and mystery of this earth we live on. Once you've seen it, no other natural phenomenon will quite compare.

New Orleans

While the rest of us eat to live, New Orleanians live to eat. The French, Spanish, Filipinos, Haitians, former Yugoslavians, Irish and Lord-knows-who-else have all contributed to the gastro amalgamation here, making New Orleans (p208) one of the USA's most food-centric cities. Sure, there's unique history, gorgeous architecture and amazing music, but a visit here inevitably ends up being all about the food. For the true taste of N'awlins, eat with the locals in Riverbend, Uptown, Faubourg Marigny and the Bywater. Cajun cuisine: ham hock with sweet potatoes, pickled greens and black-eye peas

The Best...
Wine Regions

NAPA VALLEY
With over 200 vineyards, Napa is synonymous with world-class winemaking. (p414)

WILLAMETTE VALLEY
This fertile region outside of Portland, Oregon, produces superb pinot noirs. (p360)

RUSSIAN RIVER VALLEY
Home to scores of wineries in a scenic setting northwest of Napa. (p415)

SANTA YNEZ & SANTA MARIA VALLEYS
Head north of Santa Barbara in Southern California to the rolling hills of vineyards made famous in the film *Sideways*. (p415)

The Best...
National Parks

OLYMPIC NATIONAL PARK
A sprawling wilderness of temperate virgin rainforest and rugged coastline, with adventure activities galore. (p354)

GREAT SMOKY MOUNTAINS NATIONAL PARK
A much-loved and bio-diverse woodland in southern Appalachia. (p237)

YELLOWSTONE NATIONAL PARK
Geysers, geothermal springs, giant moose and towering peaks: prepare to be awed. (p431)

CANYONLANDS NATIONAL PARK
Go for hiking, rafting or four-wheel driving amid stunning red-rock scenery. (p320)

JERRY ALEXANDER/LONELY PLANET IMAGES ©

San Francisco & Wine Country

4

Amid the clatter of old-fashioned trams and thick fog that sweeps in by night, the diverse neighborhoods of San Francisco (p400) invite long days of wandering, with indie shops, world-class restaurants and bohemian nightlife. If you can tear yourself away, the lush, rolling vineyards of Napa, Sonoma and the Russian River Valley lie just north of the city. Touring wineries, drinking great wine and lingering over farm-to-table meals – it's all part of the great Wine Country experience.

PETER PTSCHELINZEW/LONELY PLANET IMAGES ©

New England in Fall

5

Watching the leaves change color is an epic event in New England (p158). See autumn's fire light up Boston and Cambridge, up through Portsmouth, New Hampshire, and all the way to Maine's Acadia National Park. Or head inland to Vermont, where entire hillsides blaze in brilliant crimsons, oranges and yellows. Covered bridges and white-steeple churches form the backdrop to leaf-peeping heaven.

Walt Disney World

Walt Disney World (p282), the self-styled 'Happiest Place on Earth,' pulls out all the stops to deliver the exhilarating sensation that *you* are the most important character in the show. Despite all the rides and entertainment, the real magic is watching your own child swell with belief after they've made Goofy laugh, been curtsied to by Cinderella and guarded the galaxy with Buzz Lightyear.

Chicago

The Windy City (p123) will blow you away with its cloud-scraping architecture, lakefront beaches and world-class museums – but its true mojo is its blend of high culture and earthy pleasures. Is there another metropolis that dresses its Picasso sculpture in local sports-team gear? Where residents are as likely to queue for hot dogs as for some of North America's top restaurants? While the winters are long and brutal, come summer Chicago fetes the arrival of warm days with a magnificent array of food and music festivals that make fine use of its striking waterfront. *Cloud Gate* sculpture by Anish Kapoor, Millennium Park

Los Angeles

The entertainment capital of the world, Los Angeles (p378) is much more than a two-dimensional movie town. To start, this is the city of oddball-haven Venice Beach; art galleries and dining in Santa Monica; indie-loving neighborhoods like Los Feliz and Silverlake; surf-loving beaches like Malibu and rugged and wild Griffith Park. Dig even deeper and you'll find an assortment of museums displaying all kinds of ephemera, a cultural renaissance happening downtown and vibrant multi-ethnic 'hoods where great food lies just around the corner.

8

The Best...
Scenic Drives

BLUE RIDGE PARKWAY
Mountainous scenery plus great hiking and wildlife-watching in the southern Appalachian Mountains. (p238)

OVERSEAS HIGHWAY
An engineering masterpiece, this highway traverses the Florida Keys, with splendid scenery along the way. (p272).

NATCHEZ TRACE PARKWAY
An incredibly lush drive between Tennessee and Mississippi, sprinkled with historic sites. (p237)

PACIFIC COAST HIGHWAY
Wild and remote beaches with clifftop views overlooking crashing waves. (p418)

RICHARD CUMMINS/LONELY PLANET IMAGES ©

Las Vegas

Sin City (p309) is a neon-fueled ride through the nerve center of America's strike-it-rich fantasies. See billionaires' names gleam from the marquees of luxury hotels. Hear a raucous soundscape of slot machines, clinking martini glasses, and the hypnotic beats of DJs spinning till dawn. Sip cocktails under palm trees and play blackjack by the pool. Visit Paris, the Wild West and a tropical island, all in one night. It's all here and it's all open 24 hours – all for the price of a poker chip and a little luck. Neon signs at the Fremont Street Experience

The Best...
Historic Sites

NEW YORK CITY
Discover surprising sights (like an 1811 fortress) in Lower Manhattan, then head to immigrant gateway Ellis Island. (p62)

BOSTON
The ghosts of the past live on in the cobblestone streets and house museums of historic Boston. (p164)

SANTA FE
Time-travel to the 1600s amid adobe buildings and scenic public squares. (p322)

WASHINGTON, DC
See where history was made in the White House, on Capitol Hill and on the National Mall. (p104)

DOUG MCKINLAY/LONELY PLANET IMAGES ©

(10)

Pacific Coast Highway

Stunning coastal highways (p418) wind their way down the US's West Coast, from Canada all the way to the Mexican border, offering dramatic scenery that's hard to match anywhere in the world. You'll get clifftop views over crashing waves, and pass sunlit rolling hills, fragrant eucalyptus forests and lush redwoods, wild and remote beaches, idyllic towns and fishing villages, and primeval rainforest. Amid the remote natural beauty you can mix things up with big-city adventures, dipping into Seattle, Portland, San Francisco and Los Angeles.

Washington, DC (11)

A city of soaring monuments, wide boulevards and neoclassical architecture, Washington, DC (p93), was built to grand scale after America's independence. Besides being the political nexus of the US, it has some of the nation's finest museums (many with free admission), packed with fine art, Native American lore, spacecraft, dinosaurs and straight-up Americana. DC also offers great options for dining, drinking and exploring, in areas such as historic Georgetown and verdant Rock Creek Park. US Capitol Building

Nashville

Nicknamed 'Music City,' Nashville (p230) is home to a head-spinning variety of sounds – from homespun country ballads to hands-in-the-air Southern rock and wide-eyed jazz improvisations, from toe-stomping bluegrass and down-and-dirty blues – all found in the honky-tonks, college bars and nightclubs littering town. Even restaurants and cafes host live music, so you won't have to go far to hear the local (or even international) talent. Come for the love of music, and bring an appetite: hearty Southern cooking is a Nashville specialty. Tootsie's Orchid Lounge

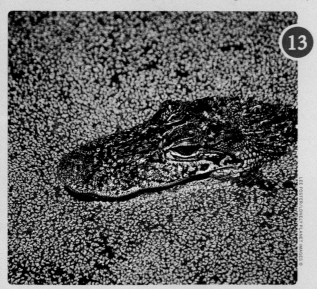

Deep South

Steeped in history and complex regional pride, the Deep South (p197) is America at its most fascinating, from the moss-draped Georgia swamps to the juke joints of the Mississippi Delta to the French-speaking enclaves of the Louisiana bayou. Famous for its slow pace, the Deep South is all about enjoying life's small pleasures: nibbling on Cajun crawfish at an old-school New Orleans eatery, strolling Savannah's antebellum alleys or sipping sweet tea on a Charleston porch with new friends. Swamp alligator

Miami

How does one city get so lucky? Most cities content themselves with one or two admirable attributes, but Miami (p258) seems to have it all. Beyond the stunning beaches and Art Deco Historic District, there's culture at every turn. In smoky dance halls, Havana expats dance to Cuban music, while in fashionable nightclubs fiery-eyed Brazilian models move to Latin beats. Old men clack dominos in the park, and to top it off, street vendors and restaurants dish out flavors from the Caribbean, Cuba, Argentina and Spain.

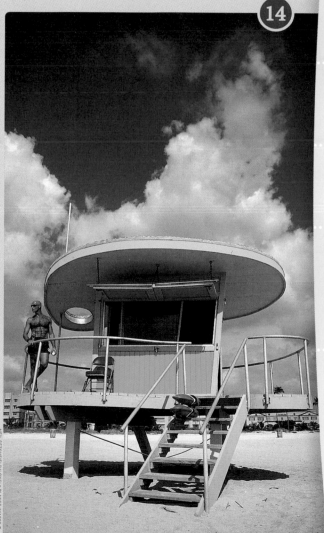

14

NEIL SETCHFIELD/LONELY PLANET IMAGES ©

The Best...
Museums

NEW YORK CITY
Spend days ploughing through the city's museums and you'll barely even scratch the surface. (p62)

WASHINGTON, DC
Treasured halls dedicated to outer space, history and art – plus woolly mammoths. (p104)

SAN FRANCISCO
Cutting-edge exhibits at San Francisco Museum of Modern Art, futuristic design at the MH de Young and American counterculture at the Beat Museum. (p400)

CHICAGO
Home to a treasure trove of great art, including the spectacular Art Institute of Chicago, plus loads of small galleries. (p134)

The Best...
Hiking

SOUTH KAIBAB
Stupendous panoramas along one of the prettiest hikes inside the Grand Canyon. (p301)

MARIN COUNTY
Hike amid towering redwoods, then watch the sun set over the Pacific. (p413)

WONDERLAND TRAIL
The 93-mile jewel of Mt Rainier National Park, with lush alpine scenery and abundant wildlife. (p359)

ACADIA NATIONAL PARK
Maine's coastal beauty offers sea cliffs, craggy shorelines and boulder-strewn peaks. (p193)

15

JUDY BELLAH/LONELY PLANET IMAGES ©

EMILY RIDDELL/LONELY PLANET IMAGES ©

Yosemite National Park

The iconic glacier-carved valley in Yosemite National Park (p416) never fails to get the heart racing, even when the crowds are bumper-to-bumper in summer. In springtime, get drenched by the spray of thundering snowmelt waterfalls, then twirl to your mental score of *The Sound of Music* in high-country meadows awash with wildflowers and enlivened by the occasional bear. Yosemite's scenery is intoxicating, with dizzying rock walls and formations, and ancient giant sequoia trees. It's also a place of solitude, space and nary an exhaust pipe – 1100 sq miles of utter wilderness for you to roam and explore. **Left:** Yosemite Falls; **Right:** Chipmunks at Glacier Point

Coastal Maine

Marked by fingerlike peninsulas and picturesque inlets, the rugged Maine coast offers ample rewards for travelers. The charming harbor city of Portland (p190) is home to decadent seafood restaurants, colorful nightlife and plentiful opportunities to get out on the water. Drive further north, stopping at seaside villages and feast-worthy lobster shacks en route to photogenic Boothbay Harbor, before heading to Acadia National Park (p193), a magnificent reserve whose coastal mountains and craggy shores are paradise for hikers and kayakers. Acadia National Park

Memphis & Graceland

In the early 1900s, Memphis (p224) became a major hub for the emerging and utterly transfixing sound of what came to be known as 'the blues'; fifty years later, American rock and roll was born there. Today the music lives on in the carnivalesque riot of Beale St, with rock, blues, jazz and country playing late into the night. By day, see where musical history was made at Sun Studio, and check out the kitschy extravagance of Elvis' Graceland. Sun Studio

Boston & Cape Cod

Start by tracing the footsteps of early tea partiers like
Paul Revere and Sam Adams on Boston's famed Freedom
Trail (p156). After following the road through American
Revolutionary War history, romp around the campus of
Harvard University and do a little 'rebel'-rousing yourself
at one of the city's famed clubs. Then cool off by hitting
the beaches of the Cape Cod National Seashore (p181),
joining a whale-watching cruise and getting lost in the wild
dunes of Provincetown. Humpback whale

The Best...
Live Music

CHICAGO
World-class blues and jazz
players, plus huge events
like the Chicago Blues Fest.
(p149)

NEW ORLEANS
The Big Easy has a sound-
track as intoxicating as
the city itself – room-filling
big-band jazz, funk, blues,
zydeco and indie rock.
(p219)

NASHVILLE
You'll find country croon-
ing, heart-pounding rock
and jazz, bluegrass and
blues on the bright stages
of Nashville. (p235)

NEW YORK CITY
Big, rock-loving venues,
downstairs jazz clubs and
countless other music
venues. (p88)

BRANDON COLE MARINE PHOTOGRAPHY/ALAMY ©

Everglades National Park

Not quite the fetid swamp full of people-eating alligators as you might have heard, the Everglades (p269) is actually a rich ecosystem of eight distinct habitats – including cypress groves, coastal prairies and mangrove systems – with a great variety of wildlife, from bottlenose dolphins and manatees to snowy egrets and bald eagles. The best viewing is during the dry season (December to April). You can visit on foot or by kayak, bicycle or guided boat tour, and it makes an easy add-on to a trip to Miami or the Keys.

Shark Valley Observation Tower

WITOLD SKRYPCZAK/LONELY PLANET IMAGES ©

The Best...
Architecture

NEW YORK CITY
There's as much happening overhead as there is on the streets, from the spiraling Guggenheim to the majestic Brooklyn Bridge. (p62)

CHICAGO
Birthplace of the skyscraper and home to the nation's tallest buildings. (p130)

MIAMI
Miami's Art Deco Historic District is a Technicolor dream come true, with the world's largest collection of deco buildings. (p258)

LOS ANGELES
Frank Gehry's Walt Disney Concert Hall and the hilltop Getty Center are scene-stealers. (p378)

(20) Native American Sites

The Southwest is Native American country, with a fantastic array of sites covering both the distant past and the present. In New Mexico (p328), you can visit the ancient clifftop homes of the Puebloan peoples who lived among this dramatic and rocky landscape before mysteriously abandoning it. For living cultures, pay a visit to the Navajo Nation (p320), where you can hire a guide and trek to the bottom of the sacred Canyon de Chelly, stay overnight on reservation land and buy handicrafts directly from Native American artisans.

Cliff dwellings at Mesa Verde National Park

EMILY RIDDELL/LONELY PLANET IMAGES ©

Santa Fe

For a glimpse back in time in this 400-year-old city (p322), start at the central plaza (a former bullfighting ring), fronted by the striking 17th-century Palace of Governors and a slew of relic-filled history museums. Nearby, Santa Fe unfolds in all its captivating variety: galleries, celebrated art museums (including the Georgia O'Keeffe Museum), Spanish Colonial churches, shops selling finely wrought Native American crafts and jewelry, plus cafes, bars and restaurants, some of which are tucked inside historic adobe buildings.

ANN CECIL/LONELY PLANET IMAGES ©

RICHARD CUMMINS/LONELY PLANET IMAGES ©

Disneyland

No matter what your age, it's hard not to be swept away by the Disneyland (p391) experience. You can stroll through Main Street, an idyllic turn-of-the-century town with barbershop quartets, penny arcades and old-fashioned ice-cream parlors, then delve deeper into the fantasy world by mingling with princesses beneath Sleeping Beauty Castle or hurtling through utter darkness at frightening speeds on Space Mountain. There's an Old West theme town, adventure-style outings à la Indiana Jones, and nightly fireworks in summer, plus pirates aplenty.

Zion & Southern Utah National Parks

With red-rock canyons, sculpturelike rock formations and towering massifs, Southern Utah has some of the most memorable scenery in the Southwest. Zion National Park (p317) is home to 85% of Utah's flora and fauna, though it's better known for towering canyon walls and dramatic hikes through gallery-like tunnels and up to majestic heights. Bryce Canyon National Park (p316), with its strange, spirelike rock formations, is mesmerizing beneath the amber glow of sunset. There are other great geological wonders inside the aptly named Arches (p319) and Canyonlands (p320) National Parks. Hiking in Zion National Park

The Best...
Foodie Cities

NEW YORK CITY
Whether you crave steak *frites*, sushi or gourmet hot dogs, globe-trotting Gotham has you covered. (p81)

CHICAGO
Great Greek, Thai and molecular gastronomy, famous deep-dish pizzas and much more. (p81)

SAN FRANCISCO
Real-deal taquerias and trattorias, sprawling farmers markets and critically acclaimed California cooking. (p408)

NEW ORLEANS
Down-home cooking served just right, with jambalaya, beignets, gumbo and Cajun crawfish. (p217)

Seattle

Seattle (p344) is a cutting-edge Pacific Rim city with an uncanny habit of turning locally hatched ideas into global brands. It's earned its place in the pantheon of US metropolises, with a world-renowned music scene, a mercurial coffee culture and a penchant for internet-driven innovation. But while Seattle's trendsetters rush to unearth the next big thing, city traditionalists guard its soul with distinct urban neighborhoods, a home-grown food culture and what is arguably the nation's finest public market at Pike Place.

Space Needle, Seattle Center

LAWRENCE WORCESTER/LONELY PLANET IMAGES ©

The Best...
Beaches

MALIBU
Great surf and lovely scenery abound in this iconic SoCal spot. (p384)

SOUTH BEACH
Famous the world over, Miami's South Beach has pretty sands adorned with beautiful bodies. (p258)

CAPE COD NATIONAL SEASHORE
Massive sand dunes, picturesque lighthouses and cool forests invite endless exploring. (p181)

SAN DIEGO
Coronado for white sand, Pacific and Mission Beaches for people-watching and fish tacos. (p393)

RICHARD CUMMINS / LONELY PLANET IMAGES ©

㉕ Mt Rainier National Park

Visible from Seattle and unobstructed by other peaks, Mt Rainier's (p359) overwhelming presence has long enraptured the many inhabitants who live in its shadow. Encased in a 368-sq-mile national park, the mountain's forested foothills harbor numerous hiking trails and huge swaths of flower-carpeted meadows. When the clouds magically disappear during long, clear days in July and August, it becomes one of Washington's most paradisiacal playgrounds. Native Americans called it Tahoma, or 'Mother of Waters,' while Seattleites refer to it reverently as 'the Mountain.'

USA's
Top Itineraries

NYC to Washington, DC Urban Exploring

7 DAYS

Short visit? Focus on two of America's most fascinating cities, NYC and Washington, DC, for their world-class museums, iconic buildings and top-notch food and entertainment options.

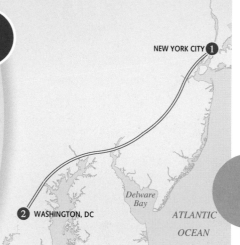

NEW YORK CITY ①

② WASHINGTON, DC

Delware Bay

ATLANTIC OCEAN

① New York City (p62)

The great dynamo of art, fashion and culture, New York City is America at her most urbane. Spend four days exploring the metropolis, visiting memorable people-watching 'hoods such as Chinatown, the West and East Villages, the Lower East Side, SoHo, Nolita and the Upper West Side, then museum-hop down the Upper East Side. Have a ramble in Central Park, stroll the High Line and take a detour across the Brooklyn Bridge (go early in the morning or at sunset). Prioritize iconic sights, including the Statue of Liberty, Ellis Island and the Metropolitan Museum. Catch a Broadway show or a concert at legendary venues like Carnegie Hall or Lincoln Center. Set aside at least one evening for a big night, taking in downtown's nightlife. And plan a few memorable meals at some of New York's classic eateries: bagels and lox at a Jewish deli, dim sum in Chinatown and a slice of thin-crust from one of the city's ubiquitous pizzerias.

② Washington, DC (p104)

Take a train or a bus down to Washington, DC, for a look at the nation's capital. With three days here, you can take in the city highlights. Spend a day on the National Mall, taking in iconic sights like the Washington Monument, the Lincoln Memorial and the Vietnam Veterans Memorial. Visit a few nearby Smithsonian museums, and end the day with dinner and drinks at Dupont Circle. On the next day, head to Georgetown for shopping, cafe-hopping and strolling along atmospheric tree-lined streets. Catch a show at the Kennedy Center, then explore the nightlife on the U Street Corridor. On your last day, hop across the Potomac River (via metro) to Virginia for a look at Arlington Cemetery, then take a stroll through old-world Alexandria.

NEW YORK CITY ➲ WASHINGTON, DC

🚃 **Four hours** On Amtrak from NYC's Penn Station to Washington's Union Station.
🚌 **Four hours** Numerous inexpensive operators including BoltBus, Megabus and Greyhound.

The High Line (p69), New York City
GRAHAM CROUCH/LONELY PLANET IMAGES ©

10 DAYS

Washington, DC, to Provincetown
East Coasting

This exploration along the East Coast takes in three cities with distinct personalities – politically charged Washington, DC, cosmopolitan New York City and historic and heady Boston. Cap it off with a jaunt out to Provincetown for a look at Cape Cod's lovely seaside.

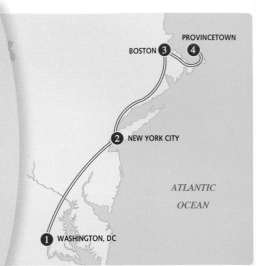

PROVINCETOWN

BOSTON **3** **4**

2 NEW YORK CITY

ATLANTIC OCEAN

1 WASHINGTON, DC

❶ Washington, DC (p104)

Spend two days in the nation's capital. Stroll around the Tidal Basin and the National Mall, then delve into recent history at the Newseum. Feast on fresh seafood at the Maine Avenue Fish Market and have drinks at the Eighteenth Street Lounge. On day two, have a look at the White House, grab lunch in Dupont Circle and take walk in Rock Creek Park. That night go bar-hopping in Adams Morgan.

WASHINGTON, DC ➲ NEW YORK CITY
🚃 **Four hours** On Amtrak from Washington's Union Station to NYC's Penn Station.
🚌 **Four hours** By BoltBus, Megabus or Greyhound.

❷ New York City (p62)

Start downtown, visiting Wall Street, the National September 11 Memorial & Museum and the Hudson River Park. Explore immigrant history at the Lower East Side Tenement Museum, then have dinner in nearby East Village. The next day, visit the Whitney Museum of American Art, Solomon R Guggenheim Museum or Metropolitan Museum of Art. Have a meal at the Central Park Boathouse, then head to a jazz club. On your last day, take a boat to Sandy Hook for a seashore frolic before dinner and drinks in the Meatpacking District.

NEW YORK CITY ➲ BOSTON
🚃 **Four hours** On Amtrak from NYC's Penn Station to Boston's South Station.
🚌 **Four hours** By BoltBus, Megabus or Greyhound.

❸ Boston (p164)

Follow in the footsteps of America's revolutionary founders on the Freedom Trail. In the afternoon, hit the stellar Museum of Fine Arts, then have dinner in the North End. On day two stroll along the Charles River, then go over to Cambridge to poke around Harvard Square. On day three, go gallery hopping on Newbury St and watch the sunset from the Prudential Center Skywalk.

BOSTON ➲ PROVINCETOWN
⚓ **1½ hours** Bay State Cruise Company sails from Boston's World Trade Center Pier.
🚌 **3½ hours** Plymouth and Brockton buses connect Boston and Provincetown.

❹ Provincetown (p181)

In Provincetown, visit galleries and shops in the town center then head out for a walk among dunes and crashing waves on Race Point Beach. That night have a feast at the Lobster Pot. On your last day, go for a bike ride along the Cape Cod National Seashore, followed by waterfront drinks at Ross' Grill.

Museum of Fine Arts (p170), Boston

10 DAYS

New Orleans to Miami Southern Explorer

Cajun cooking, Southern hospitality and sparkling beaches all play starring roles in this ramble through New Orleans, Nashville, Savannah, Orlando and Miami. You'll also find otherworldly theme parks, antebellum architecture and decadent down-home fare.

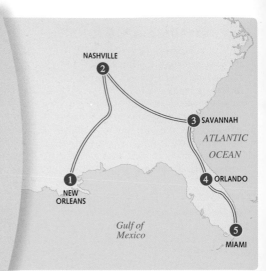

NASHVILLE
2

3 SAVANNAH

ATLANTIC OCEAN

1
NEW ORLEANS

4 ORLANDO

Gulf of Mexico

5
MIAMI

❶ New Orleans (p208)

With two days in the Big Easy, spend your first day exploring the French Quarter, taking in Jackson Square, the scenic riverfront and the history-packed Louisiana State Museum. At night, hear live jazz at a club on Frenchman St. The next day learn about New Orleans' deep African American roots in the Tremé, then go gallery-hopping in the Warehouse District and have a Cajun feast at Coop's or GW Fins.

NEW ORLEANS ➡ NASHVILLE

🚗 **Nine hours** Along ❶-59 and ❶-65.

❷ Nashville (p230)

It's all about the music when you come to Nashville. Spend two nights drinking up the scene, hitting at least one boot-stompin' honky-tonk and a smokin' blues club. By day, learn more about Nashville's soul at the Country Music Hall of Fame and spend time exploring the District. Make at least one meal Nashville's famous Southern fried chicken.

NASHVILLE ➡ SAVANNAH

🚗 **Eight hours** Along ❶-24, ❶-75 and ❶-16.

❸ Savannah (p241)

After long, music-filled nights in Nashville, recharge in picture-perfect Savannah. Base yourself in one of the city's heritage B&B's and spend two days taking in the historic district, visiting antebellum mansions, strolling the riverfront and indulging in rich low-country cooking.

SAVANNAH ➡ ORLANDO

🚗 **Five hours** Along ❶-95.

❹ Orlando (p280)

Following the Savannah recharge, it's time for a bit of Walt Disney World–style adventure. With just two days, you'll have to make some tough choices. The safe bet: spend day one in the Magic Kingdom, seeing Cinderella's Castle, Pirates of the Caribbean and nightly fireworks. On day two go on safari at Animal Kingdom and see a show in the Tree of Life. Epcot, with its world showcase of global fare and cultural attractions, is another top option.

ORLANDO ➡ MIAMI

🚗 **Four hours** Along Florida's Turnpike (a toll road).

❺ Miami (p258)

End your southern journey with two days in body-beautiful Miami. Spend time strolling the Technicolor backdrop of the Art Deco Historic District, delving into the contemporary art scene in Wynwood and connecting with Miami's Latin roots in Little Havana. Set aside plenty of downtime for playing in the waves, and for long walks on Miami Beach, and plan at least one night out in South Beach.

Ocean Drive, Miami Beach (p258)
WITOLD SKRYPCZAK/LONELY PLANET IMAGES ©

2 WEEKS

Las Vegas to Seattle
Sin City & the Left Coast

The West Coast has an array of mesmerizing attractions: picturesque beaches, verdant scenery and beautifully sited cities with some of America's best dining and nightlife. This itinerary starts in Vegas and heads west to five must-see coastal destinations.

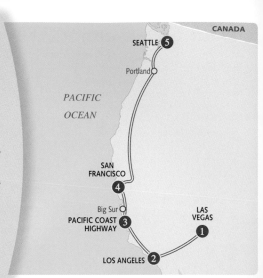

CANADA

SEATTLE **5**

Portland

PACIFIC OCEAN

SAN FRANCISCO **4**

Big Sur

PACIFIC COAST HIGHWAY **3**

LAS VEGAS **1**

LOS ANGELES **2**

❶ Las Vegas (p309)

Spend two days in Sin City, aka Las Vegas, checking out the surreal and over-the-top design of this casino kingdom, where you can travel from ancient Rome to the South Pacific without leaving the Strip. By day bask by lovely pools and visit curiosities like the Atomic Testing Museum. By night, dine at celebrated restaurants like Sage, see top-notch shows and take in the city's riotous nightlife.

LAS VEGAS ➲ LOS ANGELES

🚗 **4½ hours** Along ❶-15.
✈ **One hour** Frequent flights.

❷ Los Angeles (p378)

After Las Vegas, spend three days in Los Angeles. Take in the beachside neighborhoods of tony Santa Monica and eccentric Venice. Spend a day wandering around Hollywood and ever-evolving Downtown. Eat your way around the globe in Little Tokyo and other ethnic enclaves. Snap the Hollywood sign from the Griffith Observatory and celebrity-spot, or play in the waves off Malibu.

LOS ANGELES ➲ BIG SUR

🚗 **5½ hours** Along Hwy 101 and CA 1.

❸ Pacific Coast Highway (p418)

Although you could fly up to San Francisco in an hour, instead hire a car and take a breathtakingly scenic drive along the Pacific Coast Highway. The long and winding road traverses cliffs with the crashing sea to your left and rolling green hills to your right. Stop at Big Sur to admire the rugged, untrammeled beauty of this coastline and at the Monterey Aquarium for a look at what lies offshore.

BIG SUR ➲ SAN FRANCISCO

🚗 **Three hours** Along CA 1.

Alamo Square Park (p406), San Francisco
THOMAS WINZ/LONELY PLANET IMAGES ©

❹ San Francisco (p400)

Leave plenty of time for San Francisco (we've allowed four days). This is a city with great museums – like the avant-garde-loving San Francisco Museum of Modern Art and the head-turning MH de Young Fine Arts Museum – as well as Victorian-lined neighborhoods packed with treasures (of the shopping, eating and drinking variety) just waiting to be unearthed. San Francisco also makes a fine base for memorable day trips: walks among the towering redwoods at Muir Woods, vineyard-hopping in Napa Valley and gazing at the panorama from the Marin Headlands.

SAN FRANCISCO ➲ SEATTLE

🚗 **14 hours** Along ❶-5.

❺ Seattle (p344)

After San Francisco, head up through Portland (p358) to Seattle, the gateway to the lush Pacific Northwest. Spend two days here, shopping at Pike Place Market, stepping back in time at Pioneer Square, and moving into the future via the Space Needle, the monorail and the Experience Music Project at the Seattle Center. Don't miss the cafe culture, microbreweries and locavore dining (seafood is tops).

Chicago to LA
The Great American Road Trip

Fill up the tank, roll down the windows and crank the radio as you drive toward the Southwest's sunbaked landscapes and all the way to California. Beneath great open skies, you'll pass red-rock deserts, Spanish-colonial towns and one awe-inspiring canyon.

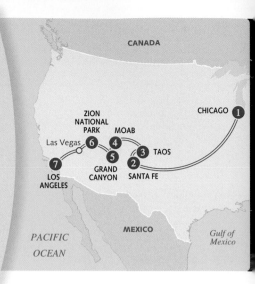

1 Chicago (p125)

Start in broad-shouldered Chicago, whose skyscrapers and big-city culture provide a dramatic contrast to the wild landscapes of the Southwest. Visit the venerable Art Institute of Chicago, eat deep-dish pizza, take an architectural walking tour, stroll through the sculptural wonderland of Millennium Park, visit the ocean-like lakefront and hit a few of Chicago's legendary blues clubs.

CHICAGO ➔ SANTA FE
🚗 **22 hours** Along ❶-55, ❶-44 and ❶-40.
✈ **Three hours** Nonstop to nearby Albuquerque.

2 Santa Fe (p322)

Gateway to the Southwest, Santa Fe is an arts-loving city set against the photogenic backdrop of the Sangre de Cristo Mountains. Centuries-old adobe neighborhoods, relic-filled museums and fine art galleries provide a fine introduction to this culturally rich region. Don't miss tasty Spanish-influenced Southwestern fare, sunset drinks from one of Santa Fe's enticing watering holes and a surreal performance at the open-air Santa Fe Opera.

SANTA FE ➔ TAOS
🚗 **1½ hours** Along Hwy 68.

3 Taos (p328)

A short but scenic drive from Santa Fe, Taos boasts a magnificent mountain setting that has long attracted artists, writers and assorted arts-minded bohemians eager to bask in the scenery. You can spend your time browsing art museums or hiking the great outdoors, or checking out the creative restaurants and eco-friendly lodgings. Nearby sights worth a day trip include the ancient clifftop dwellings of Bandelier, and Georgia O'Keeffe's adobe house in Abiquiu.

TAOS ➔ MOAB
🚗 **Seven hours** Along Hwys 64, 160, 184 and 191.

4 Moab (p318)

The drive to Moab is long, but the stunning scenery more than makes up for it. Once there, you can unwind with a microbrew and a first-rate meal, and make plans for the activities ahead: hiking, biking, rafting and horseback riding. Moab is an adventure-

lovers mecca, and well positioned near the spectacular scenery of Arches National Park and Canyonlands National Park.

MOAB ➲ GRAND CANYON, NORTH RIM
🚗 7½ hours Along Hwys 191. ⓘ -70, 89 and 67.

⑤ Grand Canyon (p298)

The jewel of the Southwest is the Grand Canyon, whose age and vast size simply boggles the imagination. Plan ahead so that you can stay in the lodge at the North Rim. Go for hikes and revel in the experience of standing atop one of Earth's great wonders. The road to the North Rim is often closed in winter so check before you go.

GRAND CANYON ➲ ZION NATIONAL PARK
🚗 Three hours Along Hwys 67 and 89.

⑥ Zion National Park (p317)

Although few places can compare with the sheer immensity of the Grand Canyon, Zion National Park will also leave you breathless – particularly if you ascend to the eagles' nest perch at the end of the Angels Landing Trail. Ideally book well in advance at the onsite Zion Lodge, set in the middle of Zion Canyon. There are also decent places to stay in nearby Springdale.

ZION NATIONAL PARK ➲ LOS ANGELES
🚗 Seven hours Along ⓘ -15. Detour via Las Vegas (p309).

⑦ Los Angeles (p378)

When you can see the Pacific, your epic road trip has come to an end. Dust off and recharge in palm-tree lined Los Angeles. After days in the wilderness get a dose of culture – high and low – at the Los Angeles County Museum of Art, the Paley Center for Media and the Grammy Museum. Treat yourself to dinner and drinks at a hotspot in West Hollywood, go beachcombing at Santa Monica and tour a few film studios.

Zion National Park.

USA Month by Month

Top Events

 Mardi Gras, February or March

 National Cherry Blossom Festival, March

 Chicago Blues Festival, June

 Independence Day, July

 Art Basel, December

 January

The New Year starts off with a shiver, as snowfall blankets large swaths of the country. Ski resorts kick into high gear, while sun-lovers seek refuge in warmer climes (especially Florida).

Chinese New Year

In late January or early February, look for colorful celebrations anywhere there's a Chinatown. NYC and San Francisco throw parades with elaborate floats, firecrackers, music, food and plenty of merriment.

February

Many Americans dread February for its long dark nights and frozen days. But this can be the cheapest time for visitors to travel, with ultra-discounted rates for flights and hotels.

Mardi Gras

Held in late February or early March on the day before Ash Wednesday, Mardi Gras (Fat Tuesday) is the finale of Carnival. New Orleans' celebrations are legendary as colorful parades, masquerade balls, feasting and plenty of hedonism rule the day.

March

The first blossoms of spring arrive in the south, while the north still shivers. In the mountains, it's still high season for skiing, while rowdy students descend on Florida for their spring break.

St Patricks Day

On March 17, the patron saint of Ireland is honored with brass bands and ever-flowing pints of Guinness; there are huge parades in New York, Boston and Chicago (which even dyes its river green).

(left) June Gay Pride parade, San Francisco
RICK GERHARTER/LONELY PLANET IMAGES ©

National Cherry Blossom Festival

(www.nationalcherryblossomfestival.org) The brilliant blooms of Japanese cherry blossoms around DC's Tidal Basin are celebrated with concerts, parades, taiko drumming, kite-flying and 90 other events during the five-week fest. More than one million people attend each year, so be sure to book ahead.

 ### South by Southwest

(www.sxsw.com) Every year Austin, Texas, becomes ground zero for one of the biggest music fests in North America. Over 2000 performers play at nearly 100 venues. SXSW is also a major film festival and interactive fest – a platform for groundbreaking ideas.

 # April

The weather is warming up, but April can still be unpredictable, with chilly weather up north mixed with a few teasingly warm days. It's a fine time to travel down south.

 ### Jazz Fest

(www.nojazzfest.com) On the last weekend in April, New Orleans hosts the country's best jazz jam, with top-notch acts (local resident Harry Connick Jr often headlines) and plenty of good cheer. In addition to world-class jazz, there's also great food and crafts.

 # May

May is true spring and one of the best times to travel, with blooming wildflowers and generally mild, sunny weather – before summer crowds and high prices arrive.

 ### Cinco de Mayo

Across the country, celebrate Mexico's victory over the French with salsa music and

pitchers of margaritas. Denver throws one of the best Cinco de Mayos, with music on three stages and dozens of food and craft stalls (www.cincodemayodenver.com).

 # June

Summer is here. Americans spend time at outdoor cafes and restaurants, and head to the shore or to national parks. School is out, and vacationers fill the highways and resorts, resulting in higher prices.

 ### Gay Pride

In some cities, gay pride celebrations last a week, but San Francisco has a month-long party, with giant parades on the last weekend in June. You'll find other great pride events at major cities across the country.

 ### Chicago Blues Festival

(www.chicagobluesfestival.us) It's the globe's biggest free blues fest, with three days of the music that made Chicago famous. More than 640,000 people unfurl blankets by the multiple stages that take over Grant Park in early June.

 ### Mermaid Parade

(www.coneyisland.com) In Brooklyn, Coney Island celebrates summer's steamy arrival with a kitsch-loving parade. Skimpily attired but brilliantly imaginative mermaids and horn-blowing mermen march through Coney Island. Afterwards, everyone (at least those not afraid of NY Harbor water) takes a dip in the ocean.

 # July

With summer in full swing, Americans break out the backyard barbecues or head for the beach. The prices are high and the crowds can be fierce, but it's one of the liveliest times to visit.

 # September

With the end of summer, cooler days arrive, making for pleasant outings nationwide. The kids are back at school, and concert halls, gallery spaces and performing arts venues kick off a new season.

Burning Man Festival

(www.burningman.com) Over one week, some 50,000 revelers, artists and other assorted free spirits descend on Nevada's Black Rock Desert to create a temporary metropolis of art installations, theme camps and environmental curiosities, culminating in the burning of a giant stick figure.

New York Film Festival

(www.filmlinc.com) Just one of many big film fests in NYC (Tribeca Film Fest in late April is another), this one features world premiers from across the globe, plus Q&As with indie and prominent directors alike. Lincoln Center plays host.

Independence Day

The nation celebrates its birthday with a bang as nearly every town and city stages a massive fireworks show. Quick to the draw, Chicago goes off on July 3. Washington, DC, New York, Philadelphia and Boston are all great spots to celebrate.

Oregon Brewers Festival

(www.oregonbrewfest.com) The beer-loving city of Portland pulls out the stops and pours a heady array of handcrafted perfection, with 80 different beers from around the country.

Lollapalooza

(www.lollapalooza.com) This once-traveling raucous rock fest now lives permanently in Chicago. Over 125 bands, including A-listers, spill off eight stages in Grant Park on the first weekend in August.

October

Temperatures are falling as autumn brings fiery colors to northern climes. It's high season where the leaves are most brilliant (New England); elsewhere has lower prices and fewer crowds.

Halloween

It's not just for kids; adults celebrate Halloween at masquerade parties. In NYC, you can don a costume and join the Halloween parade up Sixth Ave. Los Angeles is the place to see California's most outrageous outfits.

Fantasy Fest

(www.fantasyfest.net) Key West's answer to Mardi Gras

brings more than 100,000 revelers to the subtropical enclave in the week leading up to Halloween. Expect parades, colorful floats, costume parties and plenty of (alcohol-fueled) merriment.

November

No matter where you go, this is generally low season, with cold winds discouraging visitors, and lower prices (although airfares skyrocket around Thanksgiving). There's a lot happening culturally in the cities.

 ### Thanksgiving

On the fourth Thursday in November, Americans gather with family and friends over day-long feasts featuring roast turkey, sweet potatoes, cranberry sauce, wine, pumpkin pie and loads of other dishes (and pro football on TV). New York City hosts a huge parade.

December

Winter arrives as ski season kicks off in the Rockies (out east, conditions aren't usually ideal until January). Unless you're involved in winter sports, December means heading inside and curling up by the fire.

 ### Art Basel

(www.artbaselmiamibeach.com) This massive arts fest offers four days of cutting-edge art, film, architecture and design. Over 250 major galleries from across the globe come to the event, with works by 2000 artists, plus much hobnobbing with a glitterati crowd in Miami Beach.

 ### New Year's Eve

Americans are of two minds when it comes to ringing in the New Year. Some celebrate in festive crowds, others get away to escape the mayhem. Whichever you choose, plan well in advance. Expect high prices (especially in NYC).

Far left: May Traditional Mexican dancing at a Cinco de Mayo celebration, Los Angeles **Left: September** A painter at the Burning Man Festival, Nevada

What's New

For this first edition of Discover USA, *we've hunted down America's newest things to do and see: the fresh, the hot and the happening. These are some of our favorites. For up-to-the-minute recommendations, see lonelyplanet.com/usa.*

1 FOOD TRUCK CITY
Food trucks are taking America by storm, with diverse gourmet fare such as lobster rolls, *banh mi* (Saigon-style sandwiches), Colombian *arepas* (cornmeal cake) and more. Look for trucks in NYC, LA, San Francisco, Austin and Portland.

2 THE HIGH LINE
NYC's much-loved new greenway, the High Line, has opened stage two. Now you can walk for almost a mile peacefully above the traffic, following former railroad tracks (p69).

3 ART-LOVING BOSTON
Boston's Museum of Fine Arts has opened a spectacular multimillion-dollar Art of the Americas wing, with over 50 galleries of American art covering everything from pre-Columbian to contemporary American works (p170).

4 BIKE-FRIENDLY NATION
Cities across the country have added hundreds of miles of bike lanes. Boston and DC also have bike-sharing programs, making it easy to go for a pedal.

5 NAPA IS NOW
Downtown Napa is popping, with enticing new restaurants and the now fully functioning Oxbow Public Market, with artisinal bakers, cheesemongers and yet more sustainable restaurants (p414).

6 A MOVING MEMORIAL
On the 10th anniversary of the terrorist attacks, the National September 11 Memorial & Museum opened in NYC. It pays moving tribute to those who lost their lives (p63).

7 WIZARDS & SUCH
In Florida, Universal Orlando opened the Wizarding World of Harry Potter in 2010, to great acclaim. It's the hottest theme park experience of the moment (p283).

8 A REBORN DOWNTOWN
For decades, Downtown LA was dead after offices cleared out. But no more – artists, loft living, bars, restaurants and entertainment venues have brought new life to the neighborhood.

9 DESTINATION DINING
At Chicago's Next restaurant, chef Grant Achatz chooses a place and time period – say Paris 1906 – and serves a multicourse meal from that era. Every three months he changes everything (p147).

10 GREENING NYC
NYC is all about parks and green living these days, with new waterfront parks in Brooklyn (near the Brooklyn Bridge) and all along Manhattan's West Side.

Get Inspired

Books

o **Huckleberry Finn** (Mark Twain, 1884) A moving tale of journey and self-discovery.

o **The Color Purple** (Alice Walker, 1982) Powerful portrait of life for African Americans in the 1800s.

o **On the Road** (Jack Kerouac, 1957) A Beat Generation classic of post-WWII America.

o **Travels with Charley** (John Steinbeck, 1962) Steinbeck's trek across America with his poodle for company.

o **On the Rez** (Ian Frazier, 2000) Portrait of modern life on Native American reservations.

Films

o **Singin' in the Rain** (Stanley Donen & Gene Kelly, 1952) One of the best American musicals, with a timeless score.

o **The Godfather Trilogy** (Francis Ford Coppola, 1972–90) A classic look at American society through the story of immigrants and organized crime.

o **Unforgiven** (1992) Clint Eastwood's searing Western drama.

o **Easy Rider** (Dennis Hopper, 1969) Bikers on a journey through a nation in turmoil.

o **The Blues Brothers** (John Landis, 1980) Cult comedy of Belushi and Aykroyd finding musical redemption.

Music

o **Kind of Blue** (Miles Davis, 1959) One of most beautifully conceived jazz albums of all time.

o **Highway 61 Revisited** (Bob Dylan, 1965) The finest of road music by a folk-singing legend.

o **What's Going On** (Marvin Gaye, 1971) Groundbreaking work by one of Motown's finest native sons.

o **Off the Wall** (Michael Jackson, 1979) MJ's grooviest album still rocks after all these years.

o **Nevermind** (Nirvana, 1991) Launched the fist-pumping grunge movement.

Websites

o **Festivals.com** (www. festivals.com) America's best celebrations, live music, dance and more.

o **New York Times Travel** (http://travel. nytimes.com) Travel news, practical advice and engaging features.

o **Roadside America** (www.roadsideamerica. com) For all things weird and wacky.

 **Short on time?**

This list will give you an instant insight into the country.

Read *State by State: A Panoramic Portrait of America* (2008) A collection of 50 essays about the 50 states, many by well-known literary personalities.

Watch *Forrest Gump* (Robert Zemeckis, 1994) Feel-good Oscar-winning film spanning America's major events of the late 20th century.

Listen *Best of John Lee Hooker* (1962) First-rate blues by an all-time great.

Log on www.away.com has boundless ideas for outdoor and urban adventure travel across the 50 states.

Monument Valley Navajo Tribal Park (p321)

Need to Know

Currency
US dollar ($)

Language
English

ATMS
Widely available.

Credit Cards
Accepted at most hotels, restaurants and shops.

Visas
Visitors from many countries don't need visas for up to 90 days, but others do. See http://travel.state.gov for details.

Mobile Phones
Only tri- or quad-band foreign phones will work. Or buy a cheap phone with a top-up plan on arrival.

Wi-Fi
Common in hotels, cafes and some public squares.

Internet Access
Internet cafes are rare; get online at public libraries.

Driving
Drive on the right; steering wheel is on the left.

Tipping
Tip restaurant servers 15–20%, bartenders 10–15% per round (minimum per drink $1) and taxi drivers 10–15%.

When to Go

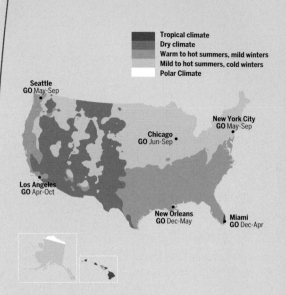

Tropical climate
Dry climate
Warm to hot summers, mild winters
Mild to hot summers, cold winters
Polar Climate

Seattle
GO May-Sep

New York City
GO May-Sep

Chicago
GO Jun-Sep

Los Angeles
GO Apr-Oct

New Orleans
GO Dec-May

Miami
GO Dec-Apr

High Season (Jun-Aug)
○ Warm days across the country (except San Francisco), with high temperatures

○ Crowds are bigger and accommodation prices are higher

○ For skiing, January to March is high season

Shoulder Season (Oct, Apr & May)
○ Milder temperatures and fewer crowds

○ Blooming spring flowers (April); fiery autumn colors (October), especially in New England

Low Season (Nov-Mar)
○ Dark, wintry days, with snowfall in the north, and heavier rains in some regions

○ Lowest prices for accommodation (except ski resorts and winter getaway destinations)

Advance Planning

○ **Six months before** Reserve accommodation at popular sites like the Grand Canyon and Walt Disney World.

○ **Three months before** Reserve internal flights and/or train travel.

○ **One month before** Book tickets to Broadway shows and big-name concerts. Reserve a table at popular restaurants like Chez Panisse.

○ **One week before** Peruse entertainment listings and eating and nightlife reviews of cities you'll visit. Book walking and outdoor adventure tours.

Set Your Budget

Budget less than $100

○ Dorm bed $20–30; campground $15–30; budget motel from $60

○ Free activities (beach days, concerts, museums)

○ Travel off-season; avoid resort areas

Midrange $150-250

○ Double room in midrange hotel $100–200

○ Dinner in decent restaurant $50–80 for two

○ Car hire from $30 per day

Top End over $250

○ Lodging in a resort from $250

○ Dining in top restaurant $60–100 per person

○ Night out (theatre, concert, clubs) $60–200

Exchange Rates

Australia	A$1	US$1.03
Canada	C$1	US$0.98
Euro	€1	US$1.28
Japan	¥100	US$1.30
New Zealand	NZ$1	US$0.79
UK	UK£1	US$1.53

For current exchange rates see www.xe.com

What to Bring

○ **Driver's license** Your standard home license should be sufficient.

○ **Dress clothes** Essential for top restaurants or big nights out on the town.

○ **A half-empty suitcase** You'll need room for the clothes, jewelry, books and other souvenir temptations.

○ **Raincoat** Have handy for unexpected thunderstorms on the East Coast and very expected drizzle in the northwest.

○ **Binoculars** A must-have for spotting wildlife in national parks.

○ **Travel insurance** Check the policy for coverage on adventure sports (skiing, diving, climbing), luggage loss and healthcare.

Arriving in the USA

○ **JFK International Airport, New York**

Airtrain/LIRR – $12 to $14 (45 minutes)

Airtrain/Subway – $7.25 (90 minutes)

Taxi – $45 to Manhattan, plus toll and tip (45 minutes)

○ **Los Angeles International Airport (LAX)**

LAX Flyaway Bus – $7 to Union Station

Shared-ride vans – $16–28

Taxi – $47 to Downtown

○ **Miami International Airport**

Express Bus – $2.35 to South Beach (36 minutes)

Shared-ride vans – $26 to South Beach

Taxi – $32 to Miami Beach (25 minutes)

Getting Around

○ **Train** Decent network (on Amtrak) along the East Coast (Miami up to Boston) and West Coast (San Diego to Seattle) and a few spots in between (New Orleans, Chicago).

○ **Bus** Private companies cover the whole country. Cheaper and usually faster than trains.

Accommodations

○ **National Parks** Old-fashioned lodges and rustic inns with simple rooms. Essential to reserve well ahead.

○ **B&Bs** Character-filled guesthouses across the country, some set in historic buildings.

○ **Hotels** Everything from luxury boutique hotels to soulless (but cheap!) chain hotels along the Interstate.

Be Forewarned

○ **Summertime** Big crowds and busy highways wherever you go.

○ **Heat** Can be relentless in the summer. Plan indoor activities.

○ **Crime** Keep your wits about you and avoid deserted urban areas.

New York City

Loud, fast and pulsing with energy, New York City is symphonic, exhausting and always evolving. Coming here is like stepping into a movie, one that contains all imagined possibilities. From the southern reaches of Manhattan to the outer rim of Queens, New York City is a vertiginous mix of beauty and grit, with people from every corner of the globe mixing on the teeming city streets. One of the city's greatest attributes is its astounding diversity, which manifests itself in great ethnic restaurants, music-filled clubs and colorful storefronts.

The New York City experience is about so many things: wandering the people-packed streets of Chinatown, fine dining in the West Village, gallery-hopping in Chelsea, catching an award-winning show off Broadway or sipping cocktails in the Lower East Side. This is just the beginning, and there really is no end.

Central Park as seen from Top of the Rock (p71)

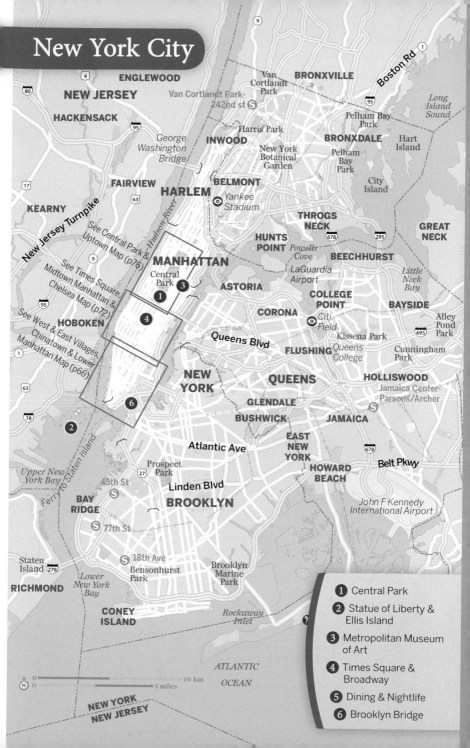

New York City

ENGLEWOOD
NEW JERSEY
HACKENSACK

BRONXVILLE
Boston Rd

Van Cortlandt Park
Long Island Sound

Van Cortlandt Park–242nd st
Pelham Bay Park

George Washington Bridge
INWOOD
Harris Park
BRONXDALE
Hart Island

New York Botanical Garden
Pelham Bay Park
City Island

FAIRVIEW
BELMONT
KEARNY
HARLEM
Yankee Stadium
THROGS NECK
GREAT NECK

New Jersey Turnpike
HUNTS POINT
Powells Cove
BEECHHURST

See Central Park & Uptown Map (p76)
MANHATTAN
LaGuardia Airport
Little Neck Bay

See Times Square, Midtown Manhattan & Chelsea Map (p72)
Central Park
❶
❸
ASTORIA
COLLEGE POINT
BAYSIDE

See West & East Villages, Chinatown & Lower Manhattan Map (p66)
HOBOKEN
❹
CORONA
Citi Field
Alley Pond Park

Queens Blvd
Kissena Park
Cunningham Park

FLUSHING
Queens College

NEW YORK
QUEENS
HOLLISWOOD
Jamaica Center–Parsons/Archer

❻
GLENDALE
BUSHWICK
JAMAICA

❷
Atlantic Ave
EAST NEW YORK
Belt Pkwy

HOWARD BEACH

Upper New York Bay
Prospect Park
Linden Blvd
John F Kennedy International Airport

Ferry to Staten Island
45th St
BROOKLYN

BAY RIDGE
77th St

Staten Island
18th Ave
Bensonhurst Park
Brooklyn Marine Park

RICHMOND
Lower New York Bay

CONEY ISLAND
Rockaway Inlet

ATLANTIC OCEAN

0 10 km
0 5 miles

NEW YORK
NEW JERSEY

❶ Central Park
❷ Statue of Liberty & Ellis Island
❸ Metropolitan Museum of Art
❹ Times Square & Broadway
❺ Dining & Nightlife
❻ Brooklyn Bridge

New York City's Highlights

HUW JONES/LONELY PLANET IMAGES ©

1 Central Park

This majestic 843-acre wonderland in the middle of Manhattan offers New Yorkers an oasis from the rigors of urban life, with lush lawns, cool forests, flowering gardens, glassy lakes and meandering, wooded paths. This 'people's park' is one of the city's most popular year-round attractions, with boating and outdoor concerts in summer and sledding and ice skating in winter.

Need to Know

LOCATION 59th St to 110th St, between Fifth and Eighth Aves **SURVIVAL TIP** Buy your picnic fare at Whole Foods in the Time Warner building (59th St & Eighth Ave) **For more, see p74.**

Central Park Don't Miss List

BY ROBERT REID, LONELY PLANET TRAVEL EDITOR AND CREATOR OF THE 76-SECOND TRAVEL SHOW

1 SHEEP MEADOW

The heart of the park is this 15-acre expanse of lawn (below left), with the best vantage points of New York's skyline from inside the park. Dozens of movies have been shot here, including the iconic scene in *Wall Street* where Michael Douglas bloodies Charlie Sheen. Don't bring a sheep – they've been a no-no since 1934.

2 BOATHOUSE

Every time I make it to Central Park's lake (above left) for a snack at the Loeb Boathouse (p84), I realize I don't come here often enough. It's a superb spot to rest and enjoy the city's backyard. Venetian gondola rides are on offer, but it's nice enough just lazing at the boathouse (first built in 1874, then rebuilt after a fire in 1950).

3 CONCERTS IN CENTRAL PARK

One of my favorite NYC moments was when Mayor Rudy Giuliani declared August 7, 1997 'Garth Brooks Day' in New York. Garth Brooks, *here?* But that's the power of the Central Park stage. Perhaps best known as the setting for Simon and Garfunkel's legendary 1981 concert, the park's at its most intimate for smaller deals throughout the summer. Hit one.

4 GREAT VIEWS

Central Park is filled with spots where, save for a distant honk, you'll forget you're in the city. But the best view from above is on the rooftop terrace of the Metropolitan Museum of Art (p79; far left). A sea of trees lies just below you, lipped in the distance by buildings across the way – such as the Dakota, where John Lennon died in 1980.

5 THE ZOO

New York's oldest zoo was an accident. The park's builders were gifted a few animals in the 1860s, which were caged in the park; it later grew into a proper zoo. The Bronx Zoo gets more attention, deservedly, but this is ultimately New York's zoo. Its convenience and quaintness strike a chord with Manhattanites: Simon and Garfunkel wrote a song about it, and Holden Caulfield took his sister Phoebe here in *The Catcher in the Rye*.

Statue of Liberty & Ellis Island

In a city full of icons, the Statue of Liberty (p62) – gazing majestically from her harbor island perch – is magnificent. Over her left shoulder lies Ellis Island, the fabled gateway to America for millions of immigrants from 1892 to 1954. The interactive Immigration Museum, housed in a beautifully detailed red-brick building, provides a fascinating journey back in time.

2

SCOTT BARROW/CORBIS ©

3 ## Metropolitan Museum of Art

The 'Met' (p79) is a self-contained, cultural city-state of 17 acres, with two million individual objects in its collection.

Its staggering list of departments – covering Ancient Greece, Rome and the Near East up to the present – can thrill, confound, inspire and exhaust. A stroll through the galleries provides an impressive record of the achievements of the human imagination.

MICHELLE BENNETT/LONELY PLANET IMAGES ©
ARTWORK © CHUCK CLOSE, COURTESY THE PACE GALLERY.

Times Square & Broadway

Smack in the middle of Midtown Manhattan, the always crowded and ever colorful Times Square (p70) is the quintessential stop for first-time visitors who want to take the pulse of the throbbing metropolis. Its glittery marquees and billboards also demarcate the epicenter of NYC's renowned Theater District, where much-loved revivals, over-the-top musicals and critically acclaimed dramas draw big crowds every night of the week.

Dining & Nightlife

The range of international cuisine you'll find in NYC is staggering. Get ready to plunge your chopsticks into authentic Cantonese or Korean, slurp down fresh oysters, nibble on Spanish tapas or Turkish mezes, and feast on Indian, Thai, Greek, French or even just classic American fare. Or spend your calories on liquid refreshment, drinking in New York's heady bar scene. The live music and clubs are sustenance enough for some. Pouring cocktails at Bemelman's Bar (p86)

Brooklyn Bridge

Walking across the grand Brooklyn Bridge (p65) is a rite of passage for New Yorkers and visitors alike, and an inspiration for poets and photographers. Just after sunrise is magical – you'll have the bridge mostly to yourself. Or go at sunset for golden-lit views of the skyscrapers of Lower Manhattan and the Statue of Liberty.

New York City's Best...

Neighborhoods

○ Chinatown (p64)
Head here for sensory overload: fragrant markets, overflowing shops and pan-Asian restaurants.

○ Tribeca & SoHo (p64)
Browse boutiques and eateries in cast-iron buildings along brick streets in these trendy neighborhoods.

○ East Village (p65) Find alternative shops, cafe culture and great nightlife in this bohemian 'hood.

○ West (Greenwich) Village (p65) Meandering, tree-lined streets hide an array of intimate dining and drinking spots.

Modern Art

○ Museum of Modern Art (p75) Features innovative multimedia exhibits, a sculpture garden and film screenings.

○ Solomon R Guggenheim Museum (p78) The architectural icon is big in the contemporary art scene, with excellent retrospectives.

○ Chelsea Galleries (p69) Dozens of galleries pack the western streets of this once-industrial neighborhood.

○ Whitney Museum of American Art (p78) Cutting-edge exhibits of the most important contemporary American artists; renowned for its Biennial.

Ethnic Eats

○ Katz's Delicatessen (p82) A long-popular, old-school deli with much-celebrated pastrami sandwiches.

○ Momofuku Noodle Bar (p82) David Chang's brilliantly inventive eatery, with superb ramen and steamed buns.

○ Veselka (p82) Atmospheric Ukrainian diner with tasty pierogi, blintzes and other classic fare.

○ Eataly (p83) Feast on all things Italian at this sprawling food market.

Need to Know

Night Spots

o **Village Vanguard** (p87) A venerable jazz spot that's hosted legends for 50 years, and counting.

o **Cielo** (p87) A great spot for dancing in the club-lined Meatpacking District.

o **KGB Bar** (p85) A watering hole for the literary-minded in drink-loving East Village.

o **Bemelman's Bar** (p86) Uber-classy lounge complete with white-coated waiters and giant *Madeline* murals.

ADVANCE PLANNING

o **One month before** Call to book tables at trendy restaurants; reserve seats at popular shows.

o **One week before** Buy and print tickets to visit the Empire State Building, Top of the Rock and other popular sights.

RESOURCES

o **New York magazine** (www.nymag.com/visitorsguide) Up-to-date tips for culture savvy visitors.

o **NYC** (www.nycgo.com) Comprehensive site run by the city's tourism department.

o **Time Out New York** (http://newyork.timeout.com) Key site for eating, drinking and entertainment listings.

o **Gothamist** (www.gothamist.com) Quirky news and NYC gossip.

GETTING AROUND

o **Airports** (www.panynj.gov/airports) Key airports are JFK and LaGuardia (both in Queens) and Newark in New Jersey. Each has loads of transport links to the city.

o **Bicycle** Always wear a helmet; riding on the sidewalks is illegal. For maps of bike lanes and other pedal resources, see www.nycbikemaps.com.

o **Subway** Purchase MetroCards (usable on local buses too) from station vending machines or subway attendants.

o **Taxi** Only hail one if the taxi's roof light is on (otherwise it's taken).

o **Walking** Manhattan is divided into east and west sides, with Fifth Ave the dividing line.

BE FOREWARNED

o **Public restrooms** Few and far between; your best bet is to pop into a Starbucks.

o **Restaurants** Many places don't take reservations; some places only take cash.

o **Smoking** Banned in all enclosed public places including bars and restaurants, plus most parks.

o **Subways** Because of constant track work, weekend schedule changes are confusing (see www.mta.info).

Left: A brownstone in Brooklyn (p88);
Above: Solomon R Guggenheim Museum (p78).

New York City Walking Tour

Manhattan's most unruly maze of streets can be found in Greenwich Village, historically a hotbed for freedom-seeking upstarts, radicals, bohemians, poets, folk singers, feminists and gays and lesbians.

WALK FACTS

- **Start**
  Christopher Park
- **Finish**
  Weatherman House
- **Distance** 1.5 miles
- **Duration** 1½ hours

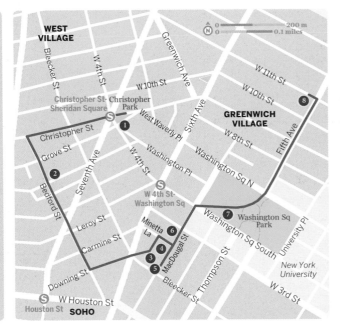

① Christopher Park

Disembark the subway at Christopher St and stop at tiny Christopher Park, where two white, life-sized statues of same-sex couples (*Gay Liberation,* 1992) stand guard. On the park's north side is the legendary Stonewall Inn, where a clutch of fed-up drag queens rioted for their civil rights in 1969, signaling the start of the gay revolution.

② Chumley's

Cross Seventh Ave South and continue west along Christopher St, still known as the pulse of gay life here. Turn left onto quaint Bedford St; stop and peer into Chumley's, the site of a prohibition-dodging, socialist-run speakeasy.

③ Fat Black Pussycat

Continue along Bedford St for several blocks, make a left on Downing St and cross Sixth Ave. Continue east on the crooked Minetta St, home to the unremarkable Pan-chito's Mexican Restaurant, which recently painted over the faded sign for the Fat Black Pussycat – called the Commons in 1962 when a young Bob Dylan wrote and first performed 'Blowin' in the Wind' here.

④ Minetta Tavern

Turn right on Minetta Lane and right on MacDougal St to find the historic Minetta Tavern, which opened as a speakeasy in 1922. Its walls are lined with photos of celebs who have visited.

5 Folklore Center

Also on this block is the former site of the Folklore Center, where Izzy Young established a hangout for folk artists including Dylan, who found his first audience at the music venue Cafe Wha? (115 MacDougal St).

6 Cafe Reggio

Return up MacDougal St to reach the cozy Cafe Reggio (119 MacDougal St). Its original owners claimed to be the first to bring cappuccino from Italy to the US in 1927.

7 Washington Square Park

Continue up MacDougal St to Washington Square Park, which has a long history as a magnet for radicals hosting anti-war, pro-marijuana and dyke pride demonstrations, among others. It's pure theater on warm days when the square brings buskers, chess players, sunbathers and strollers.

8 Weatherman House

Exit the park beneath the iconic arch; head up Fifth Ave and turn left on W 11th St, where you'll pass the infamous Weatherman House (18 W 11th St), used in 1970 as a hideout and bomb factory for an anti-government group until an explosion killed three members and destroyed the house. It was rebuilt in its current form in 1978.

New York City in....

TWO DAYS

Spend your first day exploring Chinatown, SoHo, Nolita, and the West and East Villages. In the evening, visit Times Square, see a Broadway show and end with drinks in Midtown.

On day two, museum-hop your way up Fifth Avenue, starting with the Metropolitan Museum of Art. Stroll through Central Park and have lunch at the Boathouse. Then head downtown for a ferry ride to the Statue of Liberty and Ellis Island or visit the National September 11 Memorial & Museum. Take a sunset walk along the Brooklyn Bridge, then have dinner in Chinatown.

FOUR DAYS

On day three, grab a bite at the Chelsea Market, then take a stroll on the High Line. Stop for lunch in the Meatpacking District before visiting some art galleries in Chelsea. In the evening, see a performance at Lincoln Center. On day four, visit Midtown landmarks: the Empire State Building, the MoMA and Rockefeller Center. Go window-shopping up Fifth Ave then catch a live band downtown at Joe's Pub or the Highline Ballroom.

Chelsea Market (p83)

Discover
New York City

Empire State Building as seen from Top of the Rock (p71)
RICHARD I'ANSON/LONELY PLANET IMAGES ©

◉ Sights

Lower Manhattan

STATUE OF LIBERTY Monument
(Map 53; ☎212-363-3200; www.nps.gov/stli; New York Harbor, Liberty Island; ⏰9:30am-5pm) One of the world's most famous sculptures, the Statue of Liberty was conceived as early as 1865 by French intellectual Edouard Laboulaye as a monument to the republican principals shared by France and the USA; it's still generally recognized as a symbol for the ideals of opportunity and freedom to many. French sculptor Frédéric-Auguste Bartholdi traveled to New York in 1871 to select the site, then spent more than 10 years in Paris designing and making the 151ft-tall figure *Liberty Enlightening the World*. It was then shipped to New York, erected on a small island in the harbor and unveiled in 1886.

The island, reached via ferry, is usually visited in conjunction with nearby Ellis Island. **Ferries** (Map p66; ☎201-604-2800, 877-523-9849; www.statuecruises.com; adult/child $13/5; ⏰every 30min 9am-5pm, extended summer hours) leave from Battery Park. South Ferry and Bowling Green are the closest subway stations. Ferry tickets (additional $3 for crown admission) include admission to both sights and reservations can be made in advance.

ELLIS ISLAND Museum
(Map p53) The way-station from 1892 to 1954 for more than 12 million immigrants who were hoping to make new lives in the United States, Ellis Island conjures the humble and sometimes miserable

beginnings of the experience of coming to America – as well as the fulfillment of dreams. Ferries to the Statue of Liberty make a second stop at the **immigration station** on Ellis Island. The handsome main building has been restored as the **Immigration Museum** (☏ 212-363-3200; www.ellisisland.org; New York Harbor; audio guide $8; ◷ 9:30am-5pm), with fascinating exhibits and a film about immigrant experiences, the processing of immigrants and how the influx changed the USA.

NATIONAL SEPTEMBER 11 MEMORIAL & MUSEUM   Memorial

(Map p66; www.national911memorial.org) After a decade of cost overruns, delays and politicking, the redevelopment of the World Trade Center site destroyed by the attacks of September 11, 2001, is finally coming to fruition. Its focus is two large pools with cascading waterfalls set in the footprints of the north and south towers. Bronze parapets surrounding the pools are inscribed with the names of those killed in the attacks. Visitor passes (free) can be reserved through the memorial's website. The museum is scheduled to open in September 2012.

SOUTH STREET SEAPORT   Neighborhood

Known more for the large commercial mall jutting out over the East River on Pier 17 than for its history, this 11-block enclave of cobblestoned streets and restored historic buildings has been revitalized into an area worthy of a walk. The combination of residents and tourists mix in a handful of bars and restaurants housed in restored mid-19th-century buildings.

Wall Street & the Financial District

BATTERY PARK & AROUND   Neighborhood

The southwestern tip of Manhattan Island has been extended with landfill over the years to form Battery Park, so-named for the gun batteries that used to be housed at the bulkheads. **Castle Clinton** (Map p66), a fortification built in 1811 to protect Manhattan from the British, was originally 900ft offshore but is now at the edge of Battery Park, with only its walls remaining. Battery Place is also the start of the stunning **Hudson River Park** (www. hudsonriverpar.org), which incorporates renovated piers, grassy spaces, gardens,

People contemplating 'Ground Zero' (the former World Trade Center site)

basketball courts, a trapeze school, food concessions and, best of all, a bike/skate/running path that stretches 5 miles up to 59th St.

Tribeca & SoHo

The 'TRIangle BElow CAnal St,' bordered roughly by Broadway to the east and Chambers St to the south, is the more downtown of these two sister 'hoods. It has old warehouses, very expensive loft apartments and chichi restaurants.

SoHo, like Tribeca, takes its name from its geographical placement: SOuth of HOuston St. SoHo is filled with cast-iron industrial buildings that date to just after the Civil War, when this was the city's leading commercial district. It had a bohemian/artsy heyday that had ended by the 1980s, and now this super-gentrified area is a major shopping destination, home to chain stores, boutiques and hordes of consumers, especially on weekends.

Nearby are two small areas, **NoHo** ('North of Houston') and **Nolita** ('North of Little Italy'), both known for excellent shopping – lots of small, independent and stylish clothing boutiques for women – and dining.

Chinatown & Little Italy

The best reason to visit Chinatown is to experience a feast for the senses – it's the only spot in the city where you can simultaneously see whole roasted pigs hanging in butcher-shop windows, get whiffs of fresh fish and hear the twangs of Cantonese and Vietnamese rise over the chatter of visitors from every corner of the globe.

Once known as a truly authentic pocket of Italian people, culture and eateries, Little Italy is a barely-there remnant that's constantly shrinking (Chinatown keeps encroaching). Still, loyal Italian Americans, mostly from the suburbs, flock here to gather around red-and-white-checked tablecloths at one of a handful of longtime red-sauce restaurants. Join them for a stroll along **Mulberry Street**, and take a peek at the **Old St Patrick's Cathedral** (Map p66; 263 Mulberry St), which became the city's first Roman Catholic cathedral in 1809.

Lower East Side

First came the Jews, then the Latinos, and now, of course, the hipsters. Today the Lower East Side, once the densest neighborhood in the world, is focused on being cool – by cramming into low-lit lounges, live-music clubs and trendy bistros.

LOWER EAST SIDE TENEMENT MUSEUM Museum (Map p66; ☎ 212-982-8420; www.tenement.org; 90 Orchard St, at Broome St; tours $17; ☺visitor center 10am-5:30pm, tours 10:15am-5pm) To keep the humble past in perspective, this museum puts the neighborhood's

A hot-dog stand on Broadway
MERTEN SNIJDERS/LONELY PLANET IMAGES ©

Don't Miss **Brooklyn Bridge**

Marianne Moore's description of the world's first suspension bridge – which inspired poets from Walt Whitman to Jack Kerouac even before its completion – as a 'climatic ornament, a double rainbow' is perhaps most evocative. No visit to New York City is complete without a stroll across it, but it's just as popular with locals, so walk no more than two abreast or else you're in danger of colliding with runners and speeding cyclists. With an unprecedented span of 1596ft, it remains a compelling symbol of US achievement and a superbly graceful structure, despite the fact that its construction was plagued by budget overruns and the deaths of 20 workers. The bridge and the smooth pedestrian/cyclist path, beginning just east of City Hall, afford wonderful views of Lower Manhattan and Brooklyn.

THINGS YOU NEED TO KNOW
Pedestrian & Bicycle Path Entrance **(Map p66)**

heartbreaking heritage on full display in several reconstructed tenements. Visits are available only as part of variously themed scheduled tours, which typically operate every 40 or 50 minutes.

East Village
Bordered roughly by 14th St, Lafayette St, E Houston St and the East River, the East Village has gentrified rapidly in the last decade or so, much to the horror of longtime tenants and punk-kid squatters,

who have been floating around here for decades. These days real-estate developers have the upper hand – although the 'hood has not yet shaken its image as an edgy, radical, be-yourself kind of place, which it still is, mostly.

West (Greenwich) Village
Once a symbol for all things artistic, outlandish and bohemian, this storied and popular neighborhood – the birthplace of the gay-rights movement as well as

66

West & East Villages, Chinatown & Lower Manhattan

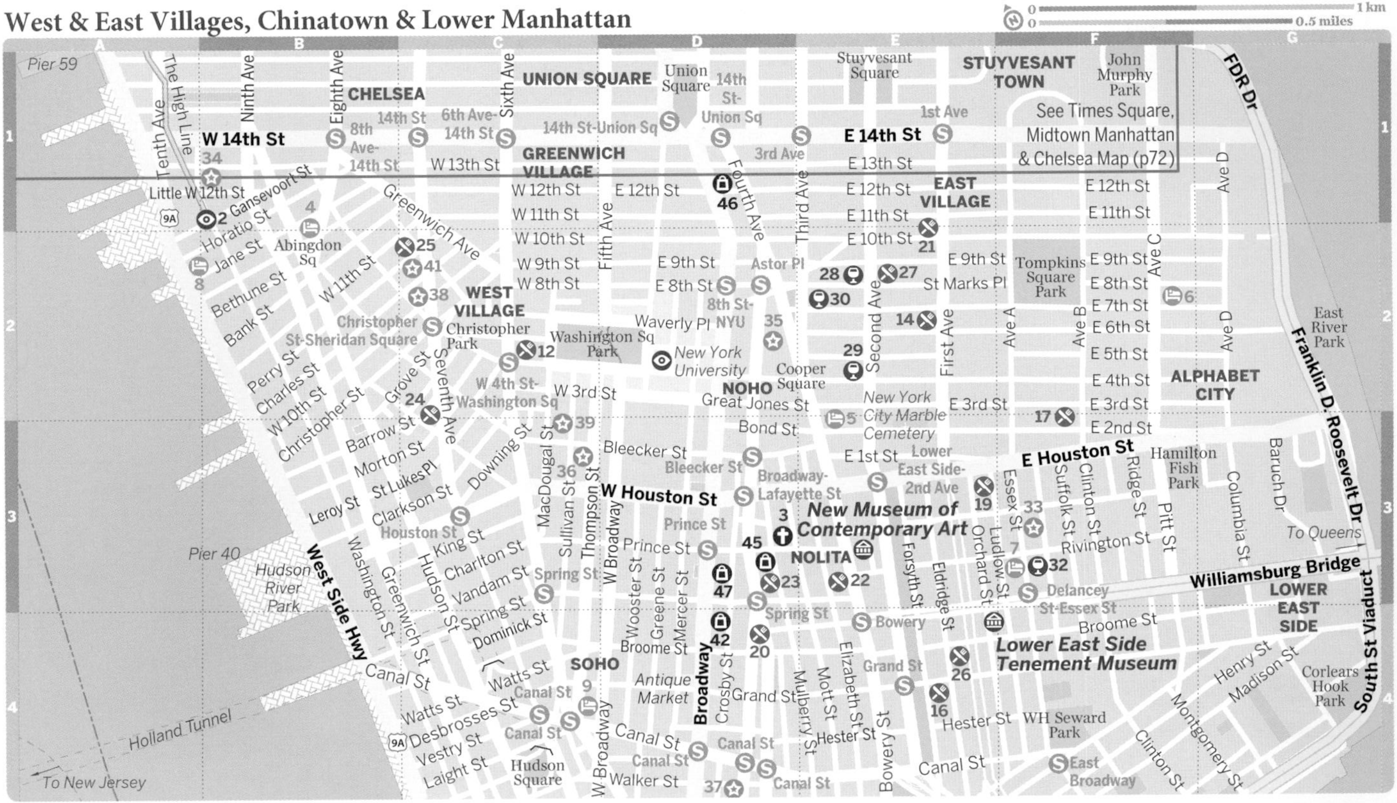

0.5 miles
1 km

Pier 59

The High Line

Little W 12th St
Gansevoort St

CHELSEA

UNION SQUARE

GREENWICH VILLAGE

EAST VILLAGE

STUYVESANT TOWN

ALPHABET CITY

NOHO

NOLITA

SOHO

WEST VILLAGE

LOWER EAST SIDE

Lower East Side Tenement Museum

New Museum of Contemporary Art

See Times Square, Midtown Manhattan & Chelsea Map (p72)

FDR Dr

Franklin D. Roosevelt Dr

Williamsburg Bridge

South St Viaduct

Holland Tunnel

West Side Hwy

Hudson River Park

To New Jersey

To Queens

East River Park

John Murphy Park

Baruch Dr

Stuyvesant Square

Washington Square Park

Abingdon Sq

Sheridan Square

Christopher Park

Union Square

Tompkins Square Park

New York Marble Cemetery

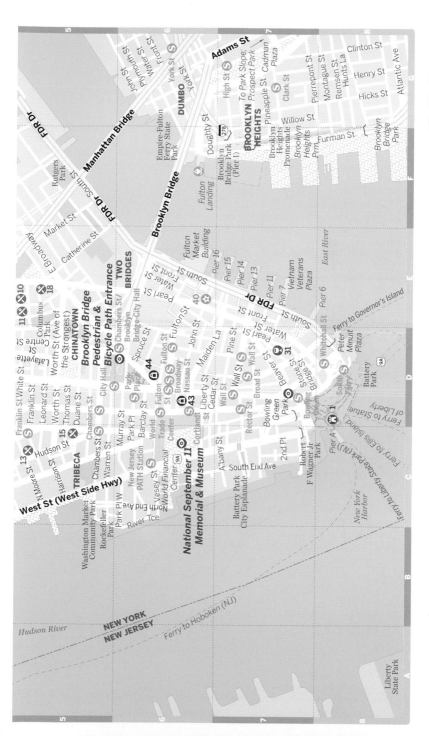

Hudson River

NEW YORK
NEW JERSEY
Ferry to Hoboken (NJ)

Liberty
State Park

Ferry to Liberty State Park (NJ)

New York Harbor

Ferry to Ellis Island

Ferry to Statue of Liberty

FDR Dr

FDR Dr

Manhattan Bridge

Rutgers Park

E Broadway

Market St

Catherine St

FDR Dr

DUMBO

Adams St

High St
278

To Park Slope; Prospect Park
Cadman Plaza

BROOKLYN HEIGHTS

Pineapple St
Clinton St
Henry St
Clark St
Hicks St
Willow St
Montague St
Pierrepont St
Rensen La
Hunts La
Atlantic Ave

Brooklyn Heights Promenade
Brooklyn Heights Prm

Furman St

Brooklyn Bridge Park

Doughty St

Empire-Fulton Ferry State Park

Brooklyn Bridge Park (Pier 1)

Fulton Landing

Brooklyn Bridge

Fulton Market Building

York St

John St
Plymouth St
Water St
Front St

East River

Pier 16
Pier 15
Pier 14
Pier 13
Pier 11
Pier 7
Pier 6

Vietnam Veterans Plaza

South St
Water St
Front St
FDR Dr

TWO BRIDGES

Pearl St
Front St
Water St
South St

40

Fulton St
John St
Maiden La
Pine St
Wall St

Brooklyn Bridge Pedestrian & Bicycle Path Entrance

CHINATOWN

Columbus Park

10
18
11

Lafayette St
Centre St
Worth St (Ave of the Strongest)
White St
Franklin St
Leonard St
Worth St
Thomas St
Duane St

13
15

N Moore St
Hudson St
Harrison St

TRIBECA

West St (West Side Hwy)

Washington Market Community Park

Rockefeller Park

River Tce
Park Pl W
North End Ave 9A

New Jersey PATH Station

Vesey St
World Financial Center

National September 11 Memorial & Museum

World Trade Center

Cortlandt St

Liberty St
Cedar St

Rector St

A'Bany St

South End Ave

Battery Park City Esplanade

2nd Pl

Robert F Wagner Jr Park

Pier A

Battery Park
9A

Whitehall St

Peter Minuit Plaza

Ferry to Governor's Island

31

Bowling Green Park

Stone St
Broad St
Beaver St

Bowling Green

Pearl St
Water St

43
44

Chambers St
Brooklyn Bridge-City Hall
Park Pl
Spruce St

City Hall

Murray St
Park Pl
Barclay St
Fulton
Broadway
Nassau St
Fulton St
Broadway

Warren St
Chambers St

West & East Villages, Chinatown & Lower Manhattan

former home of Beat poets and important artists – feels worlds away from busy Broadway; in fact it feels almost European. Known by most visitors as 'Greenwich Village,' although that term is not used by locals, it has narrow streets lined with well-groomed and high-priced real estate, as well as cafes and restaurants, making it an ideal place to wander.

WASHINGTON SQUARE PARK & AROUND Park
(Map p66) This park began as a 'potter's field' – a burial ground for the penniless – and its status as a cemetery protected it from development. It is now a completely renovated and an incredibly well-used park, especially on the weekend.

Meatpacking District

This neighborhood was once home to 250 slaughterhouses – today only eight butchers remain – and was best known for its groups of tranny hookers, racy S&M sex clubs and, of course, its sides of beef. These days, the hugely popular High Line park has only intensified an every increasing proliferation of trendy wine bars, eateries, nightclubs, high-end designer clothing stores, chic hotels and high-rent condos.

DISCOVER NEW YORK CITY SIGHTS

GRAHAM CROUCH/LONELY PLANET IMAGES ©

Don't Miss The High Line

With the completion of the High Line – a 30ft-high abandoned stretch of elevated railroad track transformed into a long ribbon of parkland – there's finally some greenery amid the asphalt jungle. It's only three stories above the streetscape, yet this thoughtfully and carefully designed mix of contemporary, industrial and natural elements is a refuge and escape from the ordinary. A glass-front amphitheater with bleacher-like seating sits just above 10th Ave – bring some food and join the local workers on lunch break. Rising on concrete stilts over the High Line, the Standard is one of the celebrated destinations of the moment, with two choice drinking spots and a grill (plus hotel rooms where high-paying guests sometimes expose themselves in front of their floor-to-ceiling windows in a towel – or less).

The second phase, a half-mile stretch from 20th to 30th Sts (the northern end not far from Penn Station) opened in the summer of 2011. The Whitney Museum of American Art (long located on the Upper East Side) has broken ground on construction of its new Meatpacking District home on Gansevoort St, scheduled for a 2015 opening.

THINGS YOU NEED TO KNOW

Map p66; www.thehighline.org; Gansevoort St to W 34th St, entrances at Gansevoort, 14th, 16th, 18th, 20th & 30th Sts; elevator access at all but 18th St; 7am-10pm

Chelsea

This 'hood is popular for two main attractions: one, the parade of gorgeous gay men (known affectionately as 'Chelsea boys') who roam Eighth Ave, darting from gyms to trendy happy hours; and two, it's one of the hubs of the city's art-gallery scene – it's currently home to nearly 200 modern-art art spaces, most of which are clustered west of Tenth Ave.

Flatiron District

At the intersection of Broadway, Fifth Ave and 23rd St, the famous 1902 **Flatiron Building** has a distinctive triangular shape to match its site. Its surrounding district is a fashionable area of boutiques, loft apartments and a growing high-tech corridor, the city's answer to Silicon Valley between here and neighboring Chelsea. Peaceful **Madison Square Park** bordered by 23rd and 26th Sts, and Fifth and Madison Aves, has an active dog run, rotating outdoor sculptures, shaded park benches and a popular burger joint.

Union Square

A true town square, albeit one with a grassy interior, Union Square is a hive of activity with all manner of New Yorkers rubbing elbows, sharing hacky sacks and eyeing each other.

GREENMARKET FARMERS MARKET   Food Market
(Map p72; ☎212-788-7476; www.grownyc.org; 17th St, btwn Broadway & Park Ave S; ☺8am-6pm Mon, Wed, Fri & Sat) Four days a week, Union Square's north end hosts the most popular of the nearly 50 greenmarkets throughout the five boroughs, where even celebrity chefs come for just-picked rarities including fiddlehead ferns, heirloom tomatoes and fresh curry leaves.

Midtown

The classic NYC fantasy – shiny skyscrapers, teeming mobs of worker bees, Fifth Ave store windows, taxi traffic – and some of the city's most popular attractions can be found here.

TIMES SQUARE & THEATER DISTRICT   Neighborhood
(Map p72) There are few images more universally iconic than the glittering orb dropping from Times Square on New Year's Eve – the first one descended 100 years ago. Near the intersection of

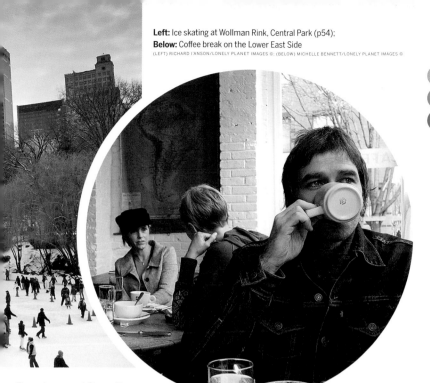

Broadway and Seventh Ave, 'the Crossroads of the World' draws 35 million visitors annually.

The Times Square area is at least equally famous as New York's official **Theater District**, with dozens of Broadway and off-Broadway theaters located in an area that stretches from 41st to 54th Sts, between Sixth and Ninth Aves.

ROCKEFELLER CENTER
Historic Building

(Map p72) The 360-degree views from the tri-level observation deck of the **Top of the Rock** (☎ 212-698-2000; www.topoftherocknyc.com; main entrance 50th St, btwn Fifth & Sixth Aves; adult/child $22/15; ⏰ 8am-midnight) are absolutely stunning and should not be missed; on a clear day you can see quite a distance across the river into New Jersey. In winter the ground floor outdoor space is abuzz with ice-skaters and Christmas tree gawkers. Within the complex is the 1932, 6000-seat **Radio City Music Hall** (☎ 212-247-4777; www.radiocity.com; Sixth Ave at 50th St; tours adult/child $22.50/16; ⏰ tours 11am-3pm Mon-Sun).

EMPIRE STATE BUILDING
Historic Building

(Map p72; ☎ 212-736-3100; www.esbnyc.org; 350 Fifth Ave, at E 34th St; adult/child $20/15; ⏰ 8am-2am) One of New York's most famous members of the skyline is this limestone classic built in just 410 days during the depths of the Depression at a cost of $41 million. You can ride the elevator to observatories on the 86th and 102nd floors (for the latter it's an additional $17), but be prepared for crowds. Try to come very early or very late (and purchase your tickets ahead of time, online or pony up for more expensive 'express passes') for an optimal experience.

Times Square, Midtown Manhattan & Chelsea

See Central Park & Uptown Map (p76)

57th St-7th Ave 🔵 ⭐22

W 57th St

Eighth Ave

W 55th St

✕17

Hudson River Park

Dewitt Clinton Park

Eleventh Ave

Tenth Ave

Ninth Ave

W 53rd St

New York City & Company 7th Ave 🔵 ℹ

20 🔴

W 51st St

19 🔴

15 🔵 ✕

Seventh Ave

50th St 🔵

Worldwide Plaza

49th St 🔵

W 49th St

W 47th St

27 ⭐ TIMES SQUARE ℹ

25 ⭐

THEATER DISTRICT

New York City & Company (Times Square) 🔳 11

W 45th St

HELL'S KITCHEN

42nd St-Port Authority

42nd St-Times Sq 🔵🔵 ⭐21

Pier 83 🔴6

W 42nd St

🔵

Broadway

Pier 81

W 40th St

🔳

495 Lincoln Tunnel

Port Authority Bus Terminal

W 38th St

Jacob Javits Convention Center

GARMENT DISTRICT

W 36th St

34th St-Penn Station 🔵

31 🔒

W 34th St

Bolt Bus 🔳🔳 Mega Bus

W 33rd St

🔳

24 ⭐ 🔳 Penn Station

Hudson River

KOREATOWN

W 30th St

Eleventh Ave

W 28th St Chelsea Park

28th St 🔵

W 26th St

Chelsea Waterside Park

23rd St 🔵

23rd St 🔵

High Line

Eleventh Ave (West Side Hwy)

W 23rd St 🔵

CHELSEA

Tenth Ave

Ninth Ave

12 ✕

W 21st St

Eighth Ave

Seventh Ave

Chelsea Piers

9 🔳 W 19th St

18th St 🔵

🔒29

See West & East Villages, Chinatown & Lower Manhattan Map (p66)

W 17th St

23 ⭐

13 ✕

8th Ave-14th St 🔵

14th St 🔵

28 🔒 W 14th St 🔵

72

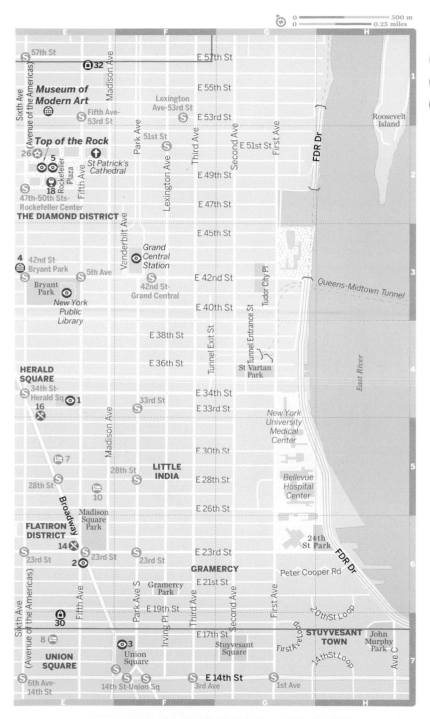

0   500 m
0   0.25 miles

57th St Ⓢ

🔒32

E 57th St

Museum of
Modern Art 🏛

Fifth Ave-
53rd St Ⓢ

Lexington
Ave-53rd St Ⓢ

E 55th St

E 53rd St

Roosevelt
Island

Top of the Rock 🎦

E 51st St

5 ◉◉

St Patrick's
Cathedral 🜚

E 49th St

26 ☆

18 Ⓢ
Rockefeller
Plaza

Fifth Ave

E 47th St

Ⓢ 47th-50th Sts-
Rockefeller Center

THE DIAMOND DISTRICT

Vanderbilt Ave

E 45th St

4 🏛
42nd St-
Bryant Park

Grand
Central
Station ◉

5th Ave Ⓢ

E 42nd St

Queens-Midtown Tunnel

Bryant
Park ◉

42nd St-
Grand Central

E 40th St

New York
Public
Library

Tunnel Exit St

E 38th St

E 36th St

Tunnel Entrance St

Tudor City Pl

St Vartan
Park

East River

HERALD
SQUARE

34th St-
Herald Sq Ⓢ

◉1

16 🍴

33rd St Ⓢ

E 34th St

E 33rd St

New York
University
Medical
Center

🛍7

E 30th St

28th St Ⓢ

LITTLE
INDIA

28th St Ⓢ

🏨10

E 28th St

Bellevue
Hospital
Center

E 26th St

Madison
Square
Park

FLATIRON
DISTRICT

14 🍴

Broadway

E 23rd St

Ⓢ 23rd St

2 ◉

23rd St Ⓢ

23rd St

GRAMERCY

24th
St Park

FDR Dr

Peter Cooper Rd

Sixth Ave
(Avenue of the Americas)

Fifth Ave

Park Ave S

Gramercy
Park

Irving Pl

E 21st St

E 19th St

Second Ave

20thSt Loop

🔒30

E 17th St

STUYVESANT
TOWN

John
Murphy
Park

8 🛍

◉3

Union
Square

Stuyvesant
Square

First Ave Loop

Ave C

UNION
SQUARE

14thSt Loop

Ⓢ 6th Ave-
14th St

14th St-Union Sq

Ⓢ E 14th St
3rd Ave

Ⓢ 1st Ave

DISCOVER NEW YORK CITY

73

Times Square, Midtown Manhattan & Chelsea

**INTERNATIONAL CENTER OF
PHOTOGRAPHY** Museum
(Map p72; ☎212-857-0000; www.icp.org; 1133
Sixth Ave, at 43rd St; adult/child $12/free;
☺10am-6pm Tue-Sun, to 8pm Fri) The city's
most important showcase for major
photographers, especially photojournal-
ists. Its past exhibitions have included
work by Henri Cartier-Bresson, Matthew
Brady and Robert Capa.

**HERALD SQUARE &
AROUND** Neighborhood
This crowded convergence of Broadway,
Sixth Ave and 34th St is best known as
the home of **Macy's** department store,
where you can still ride some of the
remaining original wooden elevators to
floors ranging from home furnishings to
lingerie.

Upper West Side

Shorthand for liberal, progressive and
intellectual New York, this neighborhood
comprises the west side of Manhattan from Central Park to the Hudson
River. Here you'll find massive, ornate
apartments and a diverse mix of stable,
upwardly mobile folks (with a number
of actors and classical musicians
sprinkled throughout); and some lovely
green spaces – **Riverside Park**, which
stretches for 4 miles between W 72nd St
and W 158th St along the Hudson River,
is a great place for strolling, running,
cycling or simply gazing at the sun as it
sets over the Hudson River.

CENTRAL PARK Park
(Map p76; ☎212-310-6600; www.centralpark
nyc.org; btwn 57th & 110th Sts & Fifth Ave &
Central Park; ☻) This enormous wonderland of a park, sitting right in the middle
of Manhattan, provides both metaphori-
cal and spiritual oxygen to its residents.
The park's 843 acres were set aside
in 1856 on the marshy northern fringe
of the city. The landscaping (the first
in a US public park), by Frederick Law
Olmsted and Calvert Vaux, was innova-

PHOTOGRAPHER: HUW JONES/LONELY PLANET IMAGES © / ARTWORK: © THE ANDY WARHOL FOUNDATION FOR THE VISUAL ARTS, INC/ARS, LICENSED BY VISCOPY, 2012

Don't Miss **Museum of Modern Art**

A veritable art universe of more than 100,000 pieces, the 75-year old Museum of Modern Art (MoMA) houses one of the more significant collections of works in the world. Most of the big hitters – including Matisse, Picasso, Cézanne, Rothko and Pollock – are housed in the central five-story atrium. Be prepared for long entrance queues and crowds.

THINGS YOU NEED TO KNOW

Map p72; ☎212-708-9400; www.moma.org; 11 W 53rd St, btwn Fifth & Sixth Aves; adult/child $20/free, free 4-8pm Fri; ☉10:30am-5:30pm, to 8pm Fri, closed Tue

tive in its naturalistic style, with forested groves, meandering paths and informal ponds.

A favorite tourist activity is to rent a **horse-drawn carriage** (Map p76; 30min tour plus generous tip $35) at 59th St (Central Park South) or hop in one of the **pedicabs** (30min tours $30) that congregate at Central Park West and 72nd St.

LINCOLN CENTER　　　　Arts Center (Map p76; ☎212-875-5456; www.lincolncenter. org; cnr Columbus Ave & Broadway) The world's largest performing arts center is the home of the lavishly designed **Metropolitan Opera House** (Met), the largest opera house in the world, seats 3900 people. Fascinating one-hour **tours** (☎212-875-5350; adult/child $15/8; ☉10:30am-4:30pm) of the complex leave from the lobby of Avery Fisher Hall daily; these tours vary from architectural to backstage tours.

AMERICAN MUSEUM OF NATURAL HISTORY　　　　Museum (Map p76; ☎212-769-5100; www.amnh. org; Central Park West, at 79th St; suggested admission adult/child $16/9, extra for space shows, IMAX shows & special exhibits; ☉10am-5:45pm; ⊞) Founded in 1869, this museum includes more than 30 million

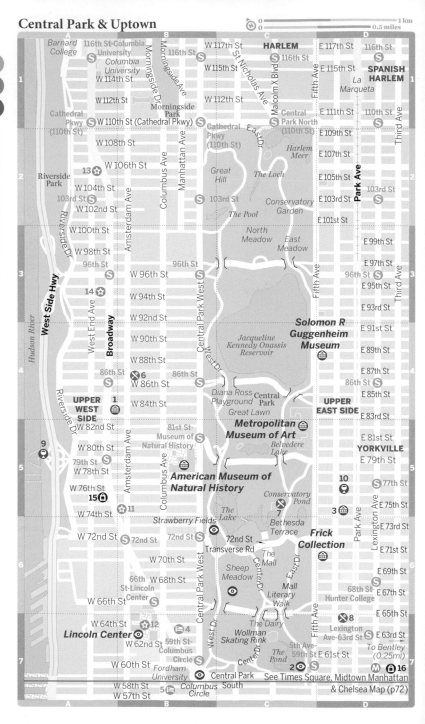

0   1 km
0   0.5 miles

HARLEM

SPANISH HARLEM

Barnard College

116th St-Columbia University

Columbia University

W 117th St

E 117th St

116th St

W 114th St

116th St

W 115th St

E 115th St

W 112th St

Morningside Park

W 112th St

E 111th St

110th St

Cathedral Pkwy (110th St)

W 110th St (Cathedral Pkwy)

Cathedral Pkwy (110th St)

Central Park North (110th St)

E 109th St

La Marqueta

W 108th St

Harlem Meer

E 107th St

W 106th St

13

E 105th St

103rd St

Riverside Park

W 104th St

Great Hill

The Loch

Park Ave

103rd St

W 102nd St

E 103rd St

103rd St

W 100th St

103rd St

The Pool

Conservatory Garden

E 101st St

W 98th St

North Meadow

East Meadow

E 99th St

96th St

96th St

E 97th St

96th St

W 96th St

96th St

E 95th St

14

W 94th St

E 93rd St

Third Ave

W 92nd St

Jacqueline Kennedy Onassis Reservoir

Solomon R Guggenheim Museum

E 91st St

W 90th St

E 89th St

W 88th St

E 87th St

6

86th St

86th St

86th St

W 86th St

Diana Ross Playground

Central Park

E 85th St

UPPER WEST SIDE 1

W 84th St

Great Lawn

UPPER EAST SIDE

W 82nd St

81st St-Museum of Natural History

Metropolitan Museum of Art

E 83rd St

9

W 80th St

Belvedere Lake

E 81st St

YORKVILLE

79th St

W 78th St

E 79th St

W 76th St

American Museum of Natural History

10

77th St

15

Conservatory Pond

7

3

E 75th St

11

W 74th St

The Lake

Strawberry Fields

Bethesda Terrace

E 73rd St

W 72nd St

72nd St

72nd St

72nd St

72nd St Transverse Rd

Frick Collection

E 71st St

W 70th St

The Mall

E 69th St

66th St-Lincoln Center

W 68th St

Sheep Meadow

68th St

E 67th St

Hunter College

W 66th St

Mall Literary Walk

E 65th St

W 64th St

12

8

Lincoln Center

W 62nd St

The Dairy

59th St-Columbus Circle

4

Wollman Skating Rink

Lexington Ave-63rd St

E 63rd St

To Bentley (0.25mi)

W 60th St

Fordham University

West Dr

Center Dr

5th Ave-59th St

E 61st St

2

16

W 58th St

5

Columbus Circle

Central Park South

See Times Square, Midtown Manhattan & Chelsea Map (p72)

W 57th St

Riverside Park

Hudson River

West Side Hwy

Riverside Dr

West End Ave

Amsterdam Ave

Broadway

Columbus Ave

Manhattan Ave

Morningside Dr

Morningside Ave

Central Park West

West Dr

East Dr

Fifth Ave

Malcolm X Blvd

St Nicholas Ave

Park Ave

Lexington Ave

Third Ave

The Pond

Central Park & Uptown

artifacts, interactive exhibits and loads of taxidermy. It's most famous for its three large dinosaur halls, an enormous (fake) blue whale that hangs from the ceiling above the Hall of Ocean Life and the elaborate **Rose Center for Earth & Space**, with space-show theaters and the planetarium.

Upper East Side

The Upper East Side (UES) is home to New York's greatest concentration of cultural centers, including the grand dame that is the Metropolitan Museum of Art (p79); Fifth Ave above 82nd St is officially known as Museum Mile. Home to ladies who lunch as well as frat boys who drink, the high-rent neighborhood becomes decidedly less chichi the further east you go.

FRICK COLLECTION   Museum
(Map p76; ☑212-288-0700; www.frick.org; 1 E 70th St; admission $18; ⊙10am-6pm Tue-Sat, 11am-5pm Sun) This spectacular art collection sits in a mansion built by businessman Henry Clay Frick in 1914. The 12 richly furnished rooms on the ground floor display paintings by Titian, Vermeer, El Greco, Goya and other masters.

 Tours

Big Onion Walking Tours   Walking
(☑212-439-1090; www.bigonion.com; tours $15) Popular and quirky guided tours specializing in ethnic and neighborhood tours.

Circle Line   Boat
(Map p72; ☑212-563-3200; www.circleline42.com; Pier 83, W 42nd St; tickets $16-34) Ferry boat tours, from semicircle to a full island cruise with guided commentary.

Gray Line Sightseeing   Bus
(☑212-445-0848; www.newyorksightseeing.com; adult/child from $42/$32) Hop-on, hop-off double-decker multilingual guided bus tours of all the boroughs (except Staten Island).

 Sleeping

A cluster of national chains, including Sheraton, Ramada and Holiday Inn, have affordably priced rooms in hotels right around 39th Ave in Long Island City, Queens, from where it's just a quick N, Q or R train ride across the river into midtown Manhattan.

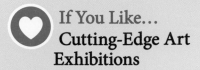

If You Like…
Cutting-Edge Art Exhibitions

If you like the Museum of Modern Art (p75), pay a visit to New York's other three world-class contemporary art galleries.

1 SOLOMON R GUGGENHEIM MUSEUM
(Map p76; www.guggenheim.org; 1071 Fifth Ave; adult/child $18/free; ⏰10am-5:45pm Sat-Wed, to 7:45pm Fri) This Frank Lloyd Wright–designed museum holds paintings by 20th-century artists, including Picasso, Pollock, Chagall and Kandinsky. Its sweeping spiral staircase a superb sculpture in its own right.

2 WHITNEY MUSEUM OF AMERICAN ART
(Map p76; www.whitney.org; 945 Madison Ave, at 75th St; admission $18; ⏰11am-6pm Wed, Thu, Sat & Sun, to 9pm Fri) One of the few places to concentrate on American works of art, this museum specializes in 20th-century and contemporary art, with works by Hopper, Pollock and Rothko, as well as special shows, such as the much-ballyhooed Biennial.

3 NEW MUSEUM OF CONTEMPORARY ART
(Map p66; www.newmuseum.org; 235 Bowery, at Prince St; adult/child $12/free; ⏰11am-6pm Wed, Fri, Sat & Sun, to 9pm Thu) Housed in an architecturally ambitious building on a formerly gritty Bowery strip, this is the city's sole museum dedicated to contemporary art.

SoHo

SOHO GRAND HOTEL   Boutique Hotel **$$$**
(Map p66; ☎212-965-3000; www.sohogrand. com; 310 W Broadway; d $195-450; ❄@🛜) The original boutique hotel of the 'hood still reigns, with its striking glass-and-cast-iron lobby stairway, and 367 rooms with cool, clean lines plus Frette linens, plasma flat-screen TVs and Kiehl's grooming products. The lobby's Grand Lounge buzzes with action.

Lower East Side & East Village

BOWERY HOTEL   Boutique Hotel **$$$**
(Map p66; ☎212-505-9100; www.thebowery hotel.com; 335 Bowery, btwn E 2nd & 3rd Sts; r from $325; ❄@🛜) Perhaps as far as you can get from the Bowery's gritty flophouse history, this stunningly stylish hotel is all 19th-century elegance. Rooms come equipped with lots of light and sleek furnishings mixed with antiques.

HOTEL ON RIVINGTON   Boutique Hotel **$$**
(Map p66; ☎212-475-2600; www.hotel onrivington.com; 107 Rivington St, btwn Essex & Ludlow Sts; r from $160; ❄@🛜) This shimmering 20-floor tower has glass-enclosed rooms with stunning views of the East River and downtown's spread. The ground-floor restaurant is a scenester hot spot.

EAST VILLAGE BED & COFFEE   B&B **$$**
(Map p66; ☎212-533-4175; www.bedand coffee.com; 110 Ave C, btwn 7th & 8th Sts; r with shared bath from $115; ❄🛜) The 10 airy rooms sport different well-executed themes and the common areas are lovely, from the high-ceilinged kitchen to the leafy back garden.

West (Greenwich) Village

ABINGDON GUEST HOUSE   B&B **$$**
(Map p66; ☎212-243-5384; www.abingdon guesthouse.com; 21 Eighth Ave, at Jane St; r from $159; ❄@🛜) Don't look out the window and you'll swear you've landed in a New England B&B. Elegant, comfortable rooms feature four-poster beds, (non-working) fireplaces, scads of exposed brick, and billowing curtains. There's also a lovely little garden out back.

JANE HOTEL   Hotel **$$**
(Map p66; ☎212-924-6700; www.thejanenyc. com; 113 Jane St; r with shared bath from $100; ❄🛜) Originally built for sailors, then a temporary refuge for survivors of the Titanic, a YMCA and rock-and-roll venue, the single bunk rooms feature flat-screen TVs and the communal showers are more than adequate.

MICHELLE BENNETT/LONELY PLANET IMAGES ©

Don't Miss **Metropolitan Museum of Art**

The Metropolitan Museum of Art (aka 'the Met') is a self-contained cultural city-state, with two million individual objects in its collection and an annual budget of over $120 million. With more than five million visitors a year, it's New York's most popular single-site tourist attraction.

Highlight rooms include Egyptian Art, American Paintings and Sculpture, Arms and Armor, Modern Art, Greek and Roman Art and European Paintings. Its 19th-century European paintings and sculpture galleries have been greatly expanded and refurbished.

Don't miss the gorgeous rooftop, which offers bar service and spectacular views throughout the summer.

THINGS YOU NEED TO KNOW

Map p76; ☎212-535-7710; www.metmuseum.org; 1000 Fifth Ave, at 82nd St; suggested donation adult/child $25/free; ⊙9:30am-5:30pm Tue-Thu & Sun, to 9pm Fri & Sat

Chelsea

ACE HOTEL NEW YORK CITY
Boutique Hotel **$$**
(Map p72; ☎212-679-2222; www.acehotel.com/newyork; 20 W 29th St; r $99-369; ❄🛜) This hotel, the outpost of a hip Pacific northwest chain, sits on the northern edge of Chelsea. Clever touches such as vintage turntables and handwritten welcome notes elevate the Ace beyond the standard.

CHELSEA LODGE
B&B **$$**
(Map p72; ☎212-243-4499; www.chelsealodge.com; 318 W 20th St, at Eighth Ave; s/d $124/134; ❄) Housed in a landmark brownstone, the European-style, 20-room Chelsea Lodge has homey, well-kept though small rooms.

Union Square & the Flatiron District

CHELSEA INN
B&B **$$**
(Map p72; ☎212-645-8989; www.chelseainn.com; 46 W 17th St, near Sixth Ave; r from $100; ❄🛜) This funky-charming hideaway

made up of two adjoining 19th-century four-story, walk-up townhouses has small but comfortable rooms that look like they were furnished entirely from flea markets or grandma's attic.

GERSHWIN HOTEL
Hotel **$$**

(Map p72; 212-545-8000; www.gershwinhotel. com; 7 E 27th St, at Fifth Ave; dm/d/ste from $45/109/299; ❄ @ 🛜) This popular and funky spot is half youth hostel, half hotel, and buzzes with original pop art, touring bands and a young, artsy European clientele.

Midtown

HUDSON
Hotel **$$$**

(Map p76; 212-554-6000; www.hudsonhotel. com; 356 W 58th St, btwn Eighth & Ninth Aves; r from $240; ❄ @ 🛜) This delicious marriage between designer Phillipe Starck and hotelier Ian Schrager is an absolute jewel. Part hotel and part nightclub, this beauty has several lounge bars that are always jammin', and the teensy rooms are highly stylized, with lots of glass, bright wood and gossamer scrims.

ROOM-MATE GRACE
Boutique Hotel **$$**

(Map p72; 212-354-2323; www.room-mate hotels.com; 125 W 45th St; r incl breakfast from $185; ❄ 🛜 🏊) Part of a Spanish chain, this ultra-hip hotel is good value when you consider you're steps from the Midtown action. A steam-room, sauna and lively pool-bar are reasons to choose the Mate over others.

Upper West Side

EMPIRE HOTEL
Hotel **$$$**

(Map p76; 212-265-7400; www.empirehotelnyc. com; 44 W 63rd St; r from $225; ❄ @ 🛜 🏊) An uptown version of the W, the Empire is a chic hotel directly across the street from the Lincoln Center. The decor is all classy earth tones and of decent size – for NYC. There's a rooftop pool deck with fabulous views, and it's a nighttime hot spot.

Upper East Side

BENTLEY
Boutique Hotel **$$$**

(off Map p76; 888-664-6835; www.nychotels. com; 500 E 62nd St, at York Ave; r from $200; ❄ 🛜) Featuring great East River views, the Bentley overlooks FDR Dr, as far east as you can go. Formerly an office building,

A hands-on broadcasting exhibit at the Children's Museum of Manhattan

ANGUS OBORN/LONELY PLANET IMAGES ©

New York City for Children

New York is a pretty child-friendly city. Cutting-edge playgrounds abound from Union Square to Battery Park, and the city's major parks, including Central Park, have playgrounds in abundance. There are at least as many attractions that would appeal to toddlers and tweens as there are for adults, including the **Children's Museum of Manhattan** (Map p76; ☏212-721-1223; www.cmom.org; 212 W 83rd St, btwn Broadway & Amsterdam Ave; admission $10; ⏱10am-5pm Tue-Sun) and the **Brooklyn Children's Museum** (☏718-735-4400; www.brooklynkids.org; 145 Brooklyn Ave, Prospect Heights; admission $7.50; ⏱11am-5pm Wed-Fri, from 10am Sat & Sun), the Central Park and Bronx zoos, and the Coney Island aquarium.

Times Square's themed megastores and kid-friendly restaurants are also good options.

the hotel has shed its utilitarian past in the form of chic boutique-hotel styling, a swanky lobby and sleek rooms.

 Eating

Tribeca, SoHo & NoHo

EDWARD'S　　　American $$
(Map p66; 136 W Broadway, btwn Thomas & Duane Sts; mains $13; ⏱9am-midnight) Located on a busy block in Tribeca, Edward's has the feel of a casual European bistro – high ceilings, mirrored walls and dark wood booths. The menu offers everything from pasta to burgers.

LA ESQUINA TAQUERIA　　Mexican $
(Map p66; 114 Kenmare St, at Cleveland Pl; mains $6; ⏱8am-1:45am, from noon Sat & Sun) This Mexican hot spot, whose only marking is a huge neon sign that blares 'The Corner' (hence *la esquina*), bustles night and day for good reason. Delectable, authentic treats are served at the counter or in the mellow cafe around the corner.

BUBBY'S PIE COMPANY　　American $$
(Map p66; 120 Hudson St, at N Moore St; mains $12-25; ⏱noon-1am Mon, 8am-midnight Tue, 24hr Wed-Sun) This kid-friendly Tribeca standby is *the* place for simple, big, delicious food: slow-cooked BBQ, grits, matzo-ball soup, buttermilk potato salad, fried okra and big fat breakfasts, all melt-in-your-mouth good.

Chinatown, Little Italy & Nolita

PEASANT　　　Italian $$$
(Map p66; ☏212-965-9511; 194 Elizabeth St, btwn Spring & Prince Sts; mains $20-30; ⏱6-11pm Tue-Sat, to 10pm Sun) A warm dining area of bare oak tables is structured around a brick hearth and open kitchen, which lovingly turns out hearty, pan-Italian, mostly meat-based fare. After dinner, head downstairs to the dark, cozy cellar wine bar.

RUBY'S　　　American $$
(Map p66; 219 Mulberry St; mains $12; ⏱10am-11pm) Tuck in those elbows for a seat at one of the picnic tables at this unpretentious tiny nook serving healthy salads, paninis and an Aussie-style burger (topped with fried egg, beet and roasted pineapple).

Lower East Side

SPITZER'S CORNER　　Modern American $$
(Map p66; ☏212-228-0027; 101 Rivington St; mains $9-19; ⏱noon-4am Mon-Sat, 10am-midnight Sun) The corner location offers an open-air gastropub experience with a concise menu designed by a Michelin-starred chef, with more than 40 different beers on tap.

Best Eats in Chinatown

With hundreds of restaurants, from holes-in-the-wall to banquet-sized dining rooms, Chinatown is wonderful for exploring cheap eats on an empty stomach. One of the best places to lunch for Cantonese cuisine is **Amazing 66** (Map p66; 66 Mott St, at Canal St; mains $7; ☉11am-11pm). The best of the dumpling joints is **Vanessa's Dumpling House** (Map p66; 118 Eldridge St, at Broome St; 4 dumplings for $1; ☉7:30am-10:30pm). Head to **Big Wong King** (Map p66; 67 Mott St, at Canal; mains $5-20; ☉7am-9:30pm) for chopped meat over rice and reliable congee (sweet or savory soft rice soup). Always busy **Joe's Shanghai** (Map p66; 9 Pell St; mains $10; ☉11am-11pm) is tourist-friendly and does good noodle and soup dishes. And finally, the **Egg Custard King** (Map p66; Natalie Bakery Inc; 271 Grand St; custards $1; ☉7am-9:30pm) is the place for the eponymous dessert.

KATZ'S DELICATESSEN   Deli **$$**
(Map p66; 205 E Houston St; sandwiches $13; ☉8am-9:45pm Mon & Tue, to 10:45pm Wed, Thu & Sun, to 2:45am Fri & Sat) One of the few remaining Jewish delicatessens in the city, Katz's attracts locals, tourists and celebrities whose photos line the walls. Massive pastrami, corned beef, brisket, and tongue sandwiches are throwbacks, as is the payment system: hold on to the ticket you're handed when you walk in and pay cash only.

East Village

St Marks Place and around, from Third Ave to Second Ave, has turned into a little Tokyo with loads of Japanese sushi and grill restaurants. Cookie-cutter Indian restaurants line Sixth St between First and Second Aves.

MOMOFUKU NOODLE BAR   Japanese **$$**
(Map p66; 171 First Ave, at 11th St; mains $9-16; ☉noon-4pm & 5:30-11pm Sun-Thu, to midnight Fri & Sat) Ramen and steamed buns are the name of the game at this infinitely creative Japanese eatery, part of the growing David Chang empire. Seating is on stools at a long bar or at communal tables.

COUNTER   Vegetarian **$$**
(Map p66; ☎212-982-5870; 105 First Ave, btwn E 6th & 7th Sts; mains $15-25; ☉5pm-midnight Mon-Thu, to 1am Fri, 11am-1am Sat, to 4pm Sun; ✔) This unique eatery manages to mix infused-vodka martinis with organic vegetarian cuisine with outlandish success.

IL BAGATTO   Italian **$$**
(Map p66; ☎212-228-0977; 192 E 2nd St, near Ave B; mains $18; ☉5:30pm-midnight, closed Mon) A bustling yet romantic little nook, this spot has thoroughly delicious Italian creations at exceptionally reasonable prices – plus an excellent wine list.

Veselka   Eastern European **$$**
(Map p66; 144 Second Ave, at 9th St; mains $12; ☉24hr) Generations of East Villagers have been coming to this bustling institution for blintzes and breakfast regardless of the late hour.

West (Greenwich) Village

BLUE HILL   Modern American **$$$**
(Map p66; ☎212-539-1776; 75 Washington Pl, btwn Sixth Ave & MacDougal St; mains $22-50; ☉5:30-11pm Mon-Sat, to 10pm Sun) A place for high-rolling Slow Food junkies, Blue Hill is a low-key, high-class dining spot where you can be certain that everything on your plate is fresh and seasonal. Expect barely seasoned veggies as centerpieces for dishes with poultry and fish. The below-street-level space is sophisticated and serene.

SNACK TAVERNA   Greek **$$**
(Map p66; 63 Bedford St; mains $15-25; ☉noon-11pm Mon-Sat, to 10pm Sun) If you can't make it out to the Greek restaurants in Astoria, Queens, try this West Village place. The

menu goes beyond the standard gyro and moussaka – the small plates like the smoked trout with barley rusks, tomato, cheese and balsamic vinaigrette are excellent.

Taïm Middle Eastern **$**
(Map p66; 222 Waverly Pl, btwn Perry & W 11th Sts; mains $7-9; ⏰noon-10pm) This tiny little falafel joint serves smoothies, salads and tasty falafel which range from the traditional to those spiced up with roasted red pepper or hot harissa.

Chelsea, Union Square, Flatiron District & Gramercy Park

BRESLIN Modern American **$$**
(Map p72; 16 West 29th St; mains $18; ⏰7am-midnight) Attached to the uber-trendy Ace Hotel, the Breslin has a pub-influenced menu by widely celebrated chef April Bloomfield that doesn't disappoint.

EATALY Italian **$**
(Map p72; www.eataly.com; 200 Fifth Ave at 23rd St; mains $7; ⏰noon-10pm) With a handful of specialty dining halls, all with a different focus (pizza, fish, vegetables, meat, pasta) and the *pièce de résistance*, a rooftop beer garden, not to mention a coffee shop, gelatería and grocery, there's enough choices to overwhelm even a blogging gourmand.

BLOSSOM Vegan **$$$**
(Map p72; 📞212-627-1144; 187 Ninth Ave, btwn 21st & 22nd Sts; mains $25-35; ⏰noon-10:30pm Fri, Sat & Sun, 5-10pm Mon-Thu; 🌱) A creative and elegant vegan restaurant, housed in a Chelsea townhouse, where menu items span the globe and enliven the taste buds. Try the flaky seitan empanada, mojo-marinated tempeh or portobello mushroom stuffed with cashew-tahini sauce.

Chelsea Market Market **$$**
(Map p72; www.chelseamarket.com; 75 Ninth Ave, btwn W 15th & 16th Sts; ⏰7am-10pm Mon-Sat, 8am-8pm Sun) Will thrill gourmet food fans with its 800ft-long shopping concourse.

Midtown

KUM GANG SAN Korean **$$**
(Map p72; 49 W 32nd St, at Broadway; mains $12-26; ⏰24hr) One of Koreatown's larger and more extravagant restaurants, Kum Gang San serves standout barbecue –

Le Verdure, a dining space at Eataly

you do it at your table. As in most Korean restaurants, the side dishes that accompany the mains are delicious meals in and of themselves.

ELLEN'S STARDUST DINER   Diner $$
(Map p72; 1650 Broadway, at 51st St; mains $15; ⊙7am-midnight Mon-Thu, to 1am Fri & Sat, to 11pm Sun) No New Yorker would be caught dead here, but this '50s theme diner/ dinner theater is a super-fun place to head after a show. When the talented waitstaff belt out show tunes and pop songs while picking up your checks, you can't help but applaud.

Patsy's   Italian $$$
(Map p72; 236 W 56th St, btwn Broadway & Eight Ave; mains $23; ⊙noon-9:30pm) Sinatra used to eat at this old-school Italian restaurant.

Upper West Side & Morningside Heights

BARNEY GREENGRASS   Deli $$
(Map p76; 541 Amsterdam Ave, at W 86th St; mains $8-17; ⊙8:30am-4pm Tue-Fri, to 5pm Sat & Sun) Old-school Upper Westsiders and pilgrims from other neighborhoods crowd this century-old 'sturgeon king' on weekends. It serves a long list of traditional if pricey Jewish delicacies, from bagels and lox to sturgeon scrambled with eggs and onions.

Upper East Side

DANIEL   French $$$
(Map p76; ☎212-288-0033; 60 E 65th St, btwn Madison & Park Aves; 3-course prix fixe dinners $105; ⊙5:30-11pm Mon-Sat) This chichi French palace features floral arrangements and wide-eyed foodies who gawk over plates of peekytoe crab and celery-root salad, foie gras terrine with gala apples, and black truffle-crusted lobster – and that's just the first course.

CENTRAL PARK BOATHOUSE RESTAURANT   American $$$
(Map p76; ☎212-517-2233; Central Park Lake, enter Fifth Ave, at 72nd St; mains $15-40; ⊙noon-9:30pm) The historic Loeb Boathouse, perched on the shores of the park's

Left: Lower East Side mainstay Katz's Delicatessen (p82);
Below: Large pretzels on a street vendor's cart
(LEFT) HUW JONES/LONELY PLANET IMAGES ©; (BELOW) LEE FOSTER/LONELY PLANET IMAGES ©

lake, is one of the city's more incredible settings for a serene and romantic meal.

🍷 Drinking

Downtown

DECIBEL
Bar

(Map p66; 240 E 9th St; ⏰6pm-3am) Just nod your head and sip. Hearing is a challenge even when you're crammed in a corner touching knees. Nevertheless, this cozy and dark downstairs hideaway feels like an authentic Tokyo dive, from the sake varieties to the delicious snacks.

KGB BAR
Bar

(Map p66; ☎212-505-3360; 85 E 4th St, at 2nd Ave; ⏰7pm-3:30am) The East Village's own grungy Algonquin roundtable has been drawing literary types to its regular readings since the early 1990s. Even when there's no artist in residence the heavily worn wood bar is good for kicking back.

MCSORLEY'S OLD ALE HOUSE
Bar

(Map p66; 15 E 7th St, btwn Second & Third Aves; ⏰11am-1am) Around since 1854 – it has the cobwebs and sawdust floors to prove it – McSorley's feels far removed from the East Village veneer of cool: you're more likely to drink with firemen, Wall St refugees and a few tourists.

WELCOME TO THE JOHNSONS
Bar

(Map p66; 123 Rivington St; ⏰3pm-4am) Looking like a set from *The Brady Bunch* or *That '70s Show,* this Lower East Side theme bar can be enjoyed with or without irony. Wash down the free Doritos with a Jack Daniel's and root beer.

Ulysses
Cocktail Bar

(Map p66; 58 Stone St; ⏰11am-4am) Big with old-school financial types, Ulysses is an Irish/modern hybrid, with a long bar, a kitchen serving oysters and sandwiches and picnic tables out on cobbled Stone St.

If You Like...
Performing Arts

If you like the Lincoln Center (p75), don't pass up an opportunity to see a great show at one of these celebrated venues:

1 CARNEGIE HALL
(Map p72; ☎212-247-7800; www.carnegiehall.org; 154 W 57th St, at Seventh Ave) Since 1891 the historic Carnegie Hall has hosted performances by the likes of Tchaikovsky, Mahler and Prokofiev and more recently Stevie Wonder, Sting and Tony Bennett. Its three halls also host visiting philharmonics, the New York Pops orchestra and various world-class musicians. Note that it's mostly closed in July and August.

2 SYMPHONY SPACE
(Map p76; ☎212-864-5400; www.symphony space.org; 2537 Broadway, at W 95th St) A multigenre space with several facilities in one, this Upper West Side gem is home to many performance series, as well as theatre, cabaret, comedy, dance and world-music concerts throughout the week.

3 BROOKLYN ACADEMY OF MUSIC
(BAM; ☎718-636-4100; www.bam.org; 30 Lafayette Ave) Like an edgier version of Lincoln Center, the spectacular Academy hosts everything from modern dance to opera, cutting-edge theater and music concerts.

Midtown

RUSSIAN VODKA ROOM Bar
(Map p72; 265 W 52nd St, btwn 8th Ave & Broadway; ⊙4pm-2am) The lighting is dark and the corner booths intimate, but more importantly the dozens of flavored vodkas, from cranberry to horseradish, are fun to experiment with. Eastern European dishes such as latkes, smoked fish and schnitzel can quiet a rumbling stomach.

MORRELL WINE BAR & CAFÉ Wine Bar
(Map p72; 1 Rockefeller Plaza, W 48th St, btwn Fifth & Sixth Aves; ⊙11:30am-midnight Mon-Sat, noon-6pm Sun) The list of vinos at this pioneering wine bar is over 2000 long, with a whopping 150 available by the glass. The airy, split-level room is equally intoxicating.

THERAPY Gay Bar
(Map p72; 348 W 52nd St, btwn Eighth & Ninth Aves; ⊙5pm-2am, to 4am Fri & Sat) Multi-leveled, airy and sleekly contemporary, Therapy is a longstanding gay Hell's Kitchen hot spot. Theme nights abound, from stand-up comedy to musical shows.

Uptown

79TH STREET BOAT BASIN Bar
(Map p76; W 79th St, in Riverside Park; ⊙noon-11pm) A covered, open-sided party spot under the ancient arches of a park overpass, this is an Upper West Side favorite once spring hits. Order a pitcher, some snacks and enjoy the sunset view over the Hudson River.

BEMELMAN'S BAR Bar
(Map p76; Carlyle Hotel, 35 E 76th St, at Madison Ave; ⊙11am-1am) Waiters wear white jackets, a baby grand piano is always being played and Ludwig Bemelman's *Madeline* murals surround you. It's a classic spot for a serious cocktail, and the kind of place that could easily turn up in a Woody Allen film.

 Entertainment

New York magazine and the weekend editions of the *New York Times* are great guides for what's on once you arrive.

Nightclubs

Most nightclubs are open from 10pm to 4am but some open earlier.

SANTOS PARTY HOUSE Club
(Map p66; ☎212-584-5492; www.santos partyhouse; 96 Lafayette St; cover $5-15) Shaggy rocker Andrew WK created this bi-level 8000-sq-ft cavernous bare-bones dance club.

BEAUTY & ESSEX Club
(Map p66; ☎212-614-0146; www.beautyand essex.com; 146 Essex St) This newcomer's glamour is concealed behind a pawnshop front space and memories of its former incarnation as a furniture store. Now, there's 10,000 sq ft of sleek lounge space

And All That Jazz

From bebop to free improvisation in classic art-deco clubs and intimate jam sessions, you'll find a stunning array of talent in NYC.

Smalls (Map p66; 212-252-5091; www.smallsjazzclub.com; 183 W 4th St; cover $20) is a subterranean jazz dungeon that rivals the world-famous **Village Vanguard** (Map p66; 212-255-4037; www.villagevanguard.com; 178 Seventh Ave, at W 11th St) in terms of sheer talent. **BB King Blues Club & Grill** (Map p72; 212-997-4144; www.bbkingblues.com; 237 W 42nd St), in the heart of Times Square, offers old-school blues along with rock, folk and reggae acts.

Heading uptown, **Dizzy's Club Coca-Cola: Jazz at Lincoln Center** (Map p76; 212-258-9595; www.jalc.org/dccc; 5th fl, Time Warner Bldg, Broadway, at W 60th St), one of Lincoln Center's three jazz venues has stunning views overlooking Central Park and nightly shows featuring top lineups. Further north on the Upper West Side, check out the **Smoke Jazz & Supper Club-Lounge** (Map p76; 212-864-6662; www.smokejazz.com; 2751 Broadway, btwn W 105th & 106th Sts), which gets crowded on weekends.

filled with a mix of well-dressed 20- and 30-somethings.

SULLIVAN ROOM
Club

(Map p66; 212-505-1703; www.sullivanroom.com; 218 Sullivan St, btwn Bleecker & W 3rd Sts; ☾Wed-Sun) An eclectic downtown mix and top-flight DJs make Sullivan Room one of the best places to dance the night away.

CIELO
Club

(Map p66; 212-645-5700; www.cieloclub.com; 18 Little W 12th St, btwn Ninth Ave & Washington St; cover $5-20) Known for its intimate space and kick-ass sound system, this space age–looking Meatpacking District staple packs in a fashionable, multiculti crowd nightly for its blend of tribal, old-school house and soulful grooves.

PACHA
Club

(Map p72; 212-209-7500; www.pachanyc.com; 618 W 46th St, btwn Eleventh Ave & West Side Hwy)

A massive and spectacular place, this is 30,000 sq ft and four levels of glowing, sleek spaces and cozy seating nooks that rise up to surround the main dancefloor atrium. Big-name DJs are always on tap.

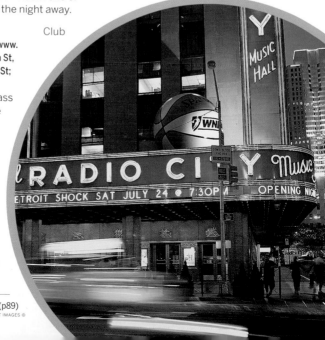

Radio City Music Hall (p89)
COREY WISE/LONELY PLANET IMAGES ©

Detour:
Brooklyn

Brooklyn is a world in and of itself. With 2.5 million people and growing – with everyone from well-to-do new parents seeking stately brownstones in Park Slope to young band members wanting cheap rents near gigs in Williamsburg – this borough has long been considered cooler and more liveable than Manhattan in many people's minds. With sandy beaches and breezy boardwalks at one end and foodie destinations at the other, and with a massive range of ethnic enclaves, world-class entertainment, stately architecture and endless shopping strips in between, Brooklyn is a rival to Manhattan's attractions.

Here's a quick rundown of the top neighborhoods for exploring:

○ **Williamsburg** Young, alternative scene with loads of art galleries, record stores, bars and eateries.

○ **Brooklyn Heights** Gorgeous tree-lined streets and a promenade with stellar Lower Manhattan views (at the end of Montague St).

○ **Dumbo** Atmospheric brick streets on the waterfront with art galleries, shops, cafes and picture-postcard Manhattan views.

○ **Fort Greene** Pretty and racially diverse 'hood, and home of the famed Brooklyn Academy of Music (p86), a highly respected performing arts complex and cinema.

○ **Boerum Hill, Cobble Hill & Carroll Gardens** Tree-lined streets, attractive brownstones and restaurant-lined Smith and Court Sts.

○ **Park Slope** Classic brownstones, loads of great eateries and boutiques (along Fifth Ave and Seventh Ave), lush 585-acre **Prospect Park** (www.prospectpark.org) and the **Brooklyn Botanic Garden** (www.bbg.org; 1000 Washington Ave; adult/child $8/ free, free Tue; ⏰8am-6pm Tue-Fri, from 10am Sat & Sun).

○ **Coney Island** Old-fashioned boardwalk, amusement park and **aquarium** (www.nyaquarium.com; Surf Ave btwn 5th & W 8th Sts; adult/child $15/11; ⏰10am-6pm Mon-Fri, to 7pm Sat & Sun; 👪).

Live Music

LE POISSON ROUGE　　Live Music
(Map p66; ☎212-796-0741; www.lepoisson rouge.com; 158 Bleecker St, at Sullivan St) This Bleecker St basement club is one of the premier venues for experimental contemporary, from classical to indie rock to electro-acoustic.

JOE'S PUB　　Live Music
(Map p66; ☎212-967-7555; www.joespub.com; Public Theater, 425 Lafayette St, btwn Astor Pl & E 4th St) Part cabaret theater, part rock and new-indie venue, this small and lovely supper club has hosts a wonderful variety of styles, voices and talent.

HIGHLINE BALLROOM　　Live Music
(Map p72; ☎212-414-5994; www.highline ballroom.com; 431 W 16th St, btwn Ninth & Tenth Aves) A classy Chelsea venue with an eclectic lineup, from Mandy Moore to Moby.

BEACON THEATRE　　Concert Venue
(Map p76; ☎212-465-6500; www.beacon theatre.com; 2124 Broadway, btwn W 74th & 75th Sts) This Upper West Side venue hosts big acts for folks who want to see shows in an environment that's more intimate than that of a big concert arena.

MADISON SQUARE
GARDEN   Concert Venue

(Map p72; ☎212-465-5800; www.thegarden.com; Seventh Ave, btwn W 31st & W 33rd Sts) For the biggest shows like Green Day and Andrea Bocelli, this place draws stadium-sized crowds.

RADIO CITY MUSIC
HALL   Concert Venue

(Map p72; ☎212-247-4777; www.radiocity.com; Sixth Ave at W 50th St) In the middle of Midtown, the architecturally grand concert hall hosts the likes of Barry Manilow and Cirque de Soleil and of course the famous Christmas spectacular.

Theater

Choose from current shows by checking print publications or a website such as **Theater Mania** (www.theatermania.com). You can purchase tickets through **Telecharge** (☎212-239-6200; www.telecharge.com) and **Ticketmaster** (www.ticketmaster.com) for standard ticket sales, or **TKTS ticket booths** (www.tkts.com; Downtown Map p66; Front St, at John St, South St Seaport; ☉11am-6pm; Midtown Map p72; under the red steps, 47th St, at Broadway; ☉3-8pm) for same-day tickets to Broadway and off-Broadway musicals at up to 50% off regular prices.

Sports

In 2009 the city's two major-league baseball teams, the uber-successful **New York Yankees** (www.yankees.com), who play at **Yankee Stadium** (Map p53; cnr 161st St & River Ave, the Bronx), and the more historically beleaguered **New York Mets** (www.mets.com), who play at **Citi Field** (Map p53; 126th St, at Roosevelt Ave, Flushing, Queens), inaugurated long-anticipated brand-new stadiums.

For basketball, you can get courtside with the NBA's **New York Knicks** (www.nba.com/knicks) at **Madison Square Garden** (btwn Seventh Ave & 33rd St). The cross-river rivals, **New Jersey Nets** (www.nba.com/nets) are scheduled to move to the Atlantic Yards, a large complex in downtown Brooklyn some time in 2012.

New York City's NFL (pro-football) teams, the **Giants** (www.giants.com) and **Jets** (www.newyorkjets.com), share the **New Meadowlands Stadium** in East Rutherford, New Jersey.

Times Square (p70)

JEAN-PIERRE LESCOURRET/LONELY PLANET IMAGES ©

🔒 Shopping

While chain stores have proliferated, NYC is still the best American city for shopping. It's not unusual for shops – especially downtown boutiques – to stay open until 10pm or 11pm.

Downtown

Strand Bookstore Bookstore
(Map p66; 828 Broadway, at E 12th St; ⏰9:30am-10:30pm Mon-Sat, from 11am Sun) The city's preeminent bibliophile warehouse, selling new and used books.

Century 21 Department Store
(Map p66; 22 Cortlandt St, at Church St) A four-level department store beloved by New Yorkers of every income, is shorthand for designer bargains.

J&R Music & Computer World Electronics
(Map p66; 15-23 Park Row) Every electronic need, especially computer- and camera-related, can be satisfied here.

Bloomingdale's SoHo Department Store
(Map p66; 504 Broadway) The smaller, younger

outpost of the Upper East Side legend, focuses on designer fashion.

Uniqlo Clothing
(Map p66; 546 Broadway) Japanese retailer, has moderately priced men's and women's fashion.

McNally Jackson Books Bookstore
(Map p66; 📞212-274-1160; 52 Prince St; ⏰10am-10pm Mon-Sat, to 9pm Sun) A Nolita refuge with a nice cafe and regular author readings.

Idlewild Books Bookstore
(Map p72; 📞212-414-8888; 12 W 19th St; ⏰11:30am-8pm Mon-Fri, noon-7pm Sat & Sun) Fiction and nonfiction are uniquely organized by country and regions of the world. Near Union Sq.

Apple Store Electronics
(Map p72; 401 W 14th St, at Ninth Ave) Pilgrims flock here for shiny new gadgets.

Midtown & Uptown

TIFFANY & CO Jewelry
(Map p72; 727 Fifth Ave) This famous jeweler, with the trademark clock-hoisting Atlas over the door, has become synonymous with NYC luxury. It carries fine diamond rings, watches, necklaces etc, as well as crystal and glassware.

Main Hall, Grand Central Terminal

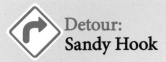

Detour:
Sandy Hook

At the northernmost tip of the Jersey Shore is the **Sandy Hook Gateway National Recreation Area**, a 7-mile-long sandy barrier beach at the entrance to New York Harbor. You can see the city skyline from your beach blanket on clear days, which only heightens the sense of pleasure and feeling of dislocation. The ocean side of the peninsula has wide, sandy beaches (including a nude beach, the only legal one in New Jersey, at **Gunnison Beach**) edged by an extensive system of bike trails, while the bay side is great for fishing or wading. The brick buildings of the abandoned coastguard station, **Fort Hancock** (🕒1-5pm **Sat & Sun**) houses a small museum. The **Sandy Hook Lighthouse**, which offers guided tours, is the oldest in the country. Bug spray is recommended as biting flies can be a nuisance at dusk.

A fast ferry service, the **Seastreak** (📞800-262-8743; www.seastreak.com; return trip adult/child $43/16), runs between Sandy Hook and Pier 11 (in downtown Manhattan) or East 35th St, in about an hour.

Macy's   Department Store
(Map p72; 151 W 34th St) The grande dame of midtown department stores, sells everything from jeans to kitchen appliances.

Bloomingdale's   Department Store
(Map p76; 1000 3rd Ave, at E 59th St) Uptown, the sprawling, overwhelming Bloomingdale's is akin to the Metropolitan Museum of Art for shoppers.

Barney's Co-op   Clothing
(Downtown Map p72; 236 W 18th St; Uptown Map p76; 2151 Broadway) Offers hipper, less-expensive versions of high-end fashion.

ℹ Information

New York City & Company (Map p72; 📞212-484-1222; www.nycgo.com; 810 Seventh Ave, at 53rd St; 🕒8:30am-6pm Mon-Fri, 9am-5pm Sat & Sun) is the official information service of the Convention & Visitors Bureau has helpful multilingual staff and various branches around town.

ℹ Getting Around

To & From the Airport

Taxis charge a $45 flat rate (plus toll and tip) from JFK to anywhere in Manhattan. Fares are metered from Newark (approximately $50 to $70) and LaGuardia ($35 to $45).

A cheaper and pretty easy option to/from JFK is the AirTrain ($5 one way), which connects to subway lines into the city ($2.25; coming from the city, take the Far Rockaway-bound A train) or to the LIRR (about $7 one way) at Jamaica Station in Queens (this is probably the quickest route to Penn Station in the city).

To/from Newark, the AirTrain links all terminals to a New Jersey Transit train station, which connects to Penn Station in NYC ($12.50 one way combined NJ Transit/Airtrain ticket).

The New York Airport Service Express Bus (www.nyairportservice.com), which serves all three airports, leaves every 15 minutes for Port Authority, Penn Station (NYC) and Grand Central Terminal.

Public Transportation

The Metropolitan Transport Authority (MTA; www.mta.info) runs both the subway and bus systems ($2.25 per ride). To board, you must purchase a MetroCard, available at windows and self-serve machines, which accept change, dollars or credit/debit cards; purchasing many rides at once works out cheaper per trip.

Washington, DC

No matter your politics, it's hard not to fall for the nation's capital. Washington, DC, is a proud and complicated city of grand boulevards, iconic monuments, and idyllic vistas over the Potomac River. Its museums and historic sites bear tribute to both the beauty and the horrors of years past and, even on a short visit, you can delve into the world of Americana – from moving artworks by Native American painters to memorable moonwalks from the likes of Neil Armstrong and Michael Jackson.

Of course DC is much more than a mere museum piece or marble backdrop to nightly news reports. It is a city of tree-lined neighborhoods and a vibrant theater scene, with ethnically diverse restaurants and a dynamism percolating just beneath the surface. It has a number of markets, historic cobblestone streets and a rich African-American heritage.

Lincoln Memorial (p97 & p108)

The Washington Monument (p105) and the US Capitol (p110)
JEAN-PIERRE LESCOURRET/LONELY PLANET IMAGES ©

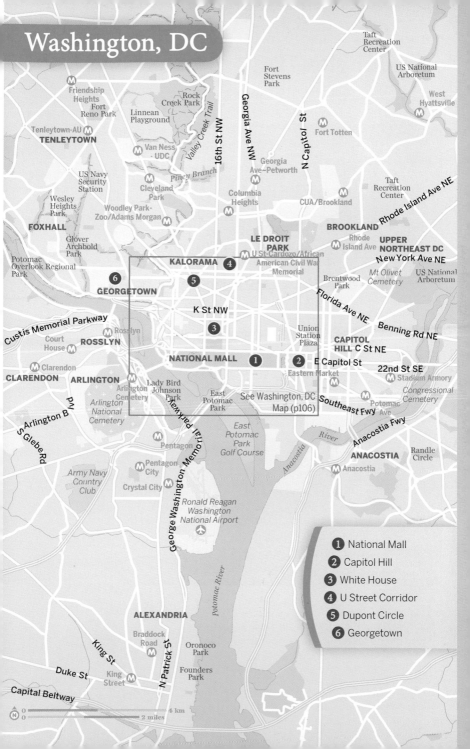

Washington, DC's Highlights

1
National Mall

Marble buildings that resemble Greek temples, Abe Lincoln and a reflecting pool, hallowed memorials and staggering museums – the Mall (p104) is all this and more. It is America's great public space, where citizens come to visit iconic sights, protest their government, go for scenic runs and commune with the country's most revered icons.

Need to Know
BEST VIEWS Go early for great views from the Washington Monument
TOP TIP The National Mall demands several visits; don't try to see everything at once **For more, see p104.**

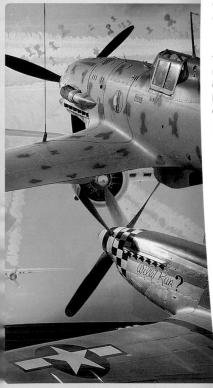

National Mall Don't Miss List

BY STEPHEN PICKHARDT, TOUR
GUIDE, DC BY FOOT WALKING TOURS

1 US CAPITOL

The US Capitol (p110) is an unmatched location to see the federal government in action, from lawmakers and staffers to lobbyists and constituents. Everything is abuzz, even during non-session days. Visitors can tour the Capitol building or meet with their representatives or their staff, or even take in a committee meeting.

2 LINCOLN MEMORIAL

From here there's a great view over the Mall and of the Washington Monument. I've been here a thousand times and never tire of it. The memorial (p108) is powerful – the scale and grandeur; the subtle symbolism, with one of Lincoln's feet placed slightly forward, showing freedom on the march.

3 VIETNAM VETERANS MEMORIAL

This memorial (far left & above left; p108), which lists the names of those who died in the Vietnam War, does the most with the least out of all the memorials. Maya Lin's design seems so minimalist when you're actually there, but when you leave you can feel like you've had a huge, overpowering experience. When you're looking at the names, you can see yourself reflected behind them in the polished wall. People really connect with it.

4 NATIONAL AIR & SPACE MUSEUM

One of DC's most unique museums (below left; p104) charts American exploration: the Wright brothers' plane, Charles Lindbergh's *Spirit of St Louis* and the rockets from the Gemini and Mercury missions are all here. It's about new frontiers and our yearning to understand the universe. Some of the museum volunteers have worked in national defense, and you can learn a lot by talking to them.

5 NATIONAL MUSEUM OF AMERICAN HISTORY

This museum (p104) is loaded with an impressive diversity of American treasures. You can see Kermit the Frog, C-3PO from *Star Wars* and props from *The Wizard of Oz*, then get serious and take in powerful Civil Rights exhibits, like the lunch counter where the Greensborough Four staged their historic sit-in. This is really shared cultural history for all Americans.

Capitol Hill

Looming large over DC and America's political landscape, the magnificent Capitol Building (p110), with its massive 285ft cast-iron dome, is both the geographic heart of the city and the political center of the US government. It is also the nexus of the fascinating Capitol Hill neighborhood, home to a vibrant restaurant and cafe scene, picturesque tree-lined streets lined with elegant townhouses and a fabulous food market. Rotunda interior, US Capitol

3 The White House

The home of every US president for the last 200 years, the White House (p114) is an instantly recognizable landmark and symbol of American power. It has survived both fire (the Brits torched it in 1814 – only a storm saved its complete destruction) and insults (Jefferson groused that it was 'big enough for two emperors, one Pope and the grand Lama'), and although getting inside is tricky, it's one iconic sight not to be missed.

MTU/IMAGEBROKER

U Street Corridor

④

Home to eclectic galleries, boutiques and cafes, the U Street Corridor has seen dramatic changes since its days of urban decay in the late 20th century. By night, live music spills out of clubs and bars, while restaurant-goers pack stylish, low-lit dining rooms. This is Washington at her most diverse – whether black, white, straight or gay – and an obligatory stop when exploring the capital. Mural of Miles Davis at a U Street jazz club

⑤

Dupont Circle

A well-heeled splice of gay community and DC diplomatic scene, this is city life at its best. Great restaurants, bars, bookstores, cafes, captivating architecture and the electric energy of a lived-in, happening neighborhood make Dupont worth a linger. The local historic mansions have largely been converted into embassies, and Embassy Row (on Massachusetts Ave) runs through DC's thumping gay heart. Afterwords cafe (p118), Dupont Circle

⑥

JASON COLSTON/LONELY PLANET IMAGES ©

Georgetown

Historical buildings are thick on the ground and dripping antebellum charm in Washington's most aristocratic neighborhood. Leafy Georgetown (p112) is older than the city itself and home to the prestigious university that fuels the neighborhood's intellectual and nocturnal excesses. Great shopping and top-notch dining, plus scenic walks along both the Potomac River and the picturesque C&O Canal begin here. Bridge over the C&O Canal

Washington, DC's Best...

Activities for Kids

○ **National Zoological Park** (p112) Home to 2000 animals, including gorillas, cheetahs and pandas.

○ **National Museum of Natural History** (p104) Woolly mammoths, dinosaur bones and prehistoric sea creatures are always a crowd pleaser.

○ **National Mall** (p104) Kids can run free on the great open lawns, ride a carousel and then go paddle-boating on the nearby Tidal Basin.

○ **International Spy Museum** (p111) Indulge budding spymasters at this fun, gadget-filled showcase.

Restaurants

○ **Etete** (p117) Serving some of the city's best Ethiopian fare.

○ **Busboys & Poets** (p117) Feed your body and soul at this restaurant, cafe, bookshop and stage.

○ **Jaleo** (p116) An artistic atmosphere is the perfect setting for some of DC's best tapas.

○ **Eastern Market** (p116) Sumptuous food market with legendary crab cakes.

Museums

○ **National Museum of American History** (p104) A treasure chest of glorious Americana.

○ **National Museum of the American Indian** (p104) Fascinating overview of America's great indigenous cultures.

○ **Newseum** (p109) Delve into the momentous events that have shaped our times.

○ **US Holocaust Memorial Museum** (p105) A moving journey into the darkest days of the 20th century.

Architectural Gems

- **Jefferson Memorial** (p111) Thoughtful quotes by the great American president, plus sublime views over the Tidal Basin.

- **Union Station** (p109) A magnificent beaux-arts building.

- **Washington National Cathedral** (p112) A Gothic masterpiece that seems straight out of old Europe.

- **Library of Congress** (p109) An inspiring monument to human knowledge, including a grand reading room complete with 160ft-high dome.

Need to Know

ADVANCE PLANNING

- **Three to six months before** Book a tour of the Capitol and try to book in to visit the White House.

- **One month before** Reserve a table at popular restaurants and book tickets to concerts and plays.

- **One week before** Purchase online tickets to get a guaranteed line-free admission to popular sights including the Washington Monument, Ford's Theatre and the US Holocaust Memorial Museum.

RESOURCES

- **Washington, DC** (www.washington.org) Official tourism site with useful links.

- **Washingtonian** (www.washingtonian.com) Excellent insight into dining, shopping, entertainment and local luminaries.

- **Washington City Paper** (www.washingtoncitypaper.com) Edgy weekly with handy listings.

- **DCist** (www.dcist.com) Insider look at all things DC.

GETTING AROUND

- **Airports** Key airports are Ronald Reagan Washington National (www.metwashairports.com), easily accessible by metro; Washington Dulles International (www.metwashairports.com), best reached by shuttle or taxi; and BWI (www.bwiairport.com), reachable by shuttle, train or taxi.

- **Bicycle** Capital Bikeshare (www.capitalbikeshare) has over 100 quick-hire stations.

- **Metro** Fast, safe and convenient; buy fare cards from self-service machines (www.wmata.com).

- **Taxi** Widely available.

- **Walking** Washington is divided into Northeast, Northwest, Southeast and Southwest, with the Capitol at the center. Letters go east–west, numbers north–south.

BE FOREWARNED

- **Planning** The Mall is packed with museums, but don't try to see it all. Prioritize your must-see spots and take your time.

- **Museum entry** Security checks (through metal detectors) are common at many museums. Arrive early to beat the queues.

- **Crime** Be cautious late at night, particularly in nightlife hot spots such as U St and Adams Morgan, where muggings on lonely side streets can occur.

Left: National Museum of the American Indian (p105); **Above:** Jefferson Memorial (p111)

Georgetown Walking Tour

Founded in 1751, this neighborhood is older than Washington, DC, itself. It's home to a world-class university, garden-lined streets, fantastic shopping and dining, and idyllic scenery along the Potomac River and old C&O Canal.

WALK FACTS

- **Start**
  37th & O Sts NW
- **End**
  Washington Harbor
- **Distance**
  2.7 miles
- **Duration**
  2½ hours

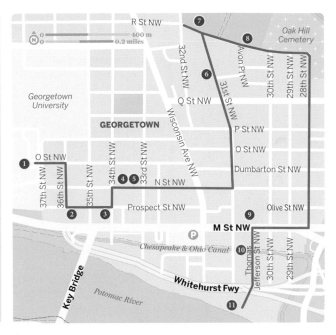

1 Georgetown University

Begin at stately Georgetown University (founded 1789). Enter the campus through the iron gates at 37th and O Sts NW to admire the Gothic spires of the Healy Building.

2 Exorcist Stairs

From the gates, walk one block east on O St and turn right on 36th St. Two blocks on, you'll pass the spot where demonically possessed Reagan of *The Exorcist* sent victims to their screaming deaths.

3 Halcyon House

Turn left and walk two blocks east on Prospect St. The private Halcyon House (3400

Prospect St) dates back to 1786; in 1900 the eccentric Albert Clemens (nephew of Mark Twain) purchased the property and, believing constant renovation would extend his life, added countless rooms.

4 Cox's Row

Turn left on 34th St and right on N St. On the left, the five Federal houses from 3327 to 3339 are known as Cox's Row, built by the fashionable Georgetown mayor John Cox (served 1823–45).

5 Marbury House

Further down the block, the formal, red-brick Marbury House (3307 N St) was the home of John and Jacqueline Kennedy before Kennedy became president and they moved into the White House.

6 Tudor Place

Continue along N St and turn left on 31st St. Five blocks up you'll find Tudor Place, the gracious urban estate of the prominent Custis Peter clan (descendants of George Washington).

7 Dumbarton Oaks

Continue further up 31st St to one of Georgetown's hidden highlights, the eclectic museum and gorgeous gardens of Dumbarton Oaks.

8 Montrose Park

Turn right and walk east on R St. The cobblestone trail on the left was years ago dubbed Lovers' Lane. It leads down into lush Dumbarton Oaks Park. Further along R St, tamer Montrose Park hosts the requisite dogs chasing balls and kids on swings.

9 Old Stone House

Continue on R St, turn right on 28th St and right again on M St. After two blocks, you'll pass the Old Stone House. It was built in 1765, making it the oldest standing building in Washington.

10 C&O Canal

Turn left onto Jefferson St and cross over the C&O Canal, a bucolic waterway with a picturesque cobbled lane running alongside it. The canal, one of the civil engineering feats of the 19th century, runs 185 miles from here to Cumberland, MD.

11 Washington Harbor

End your saunter at Washington Harbor, a riverside complex with loads of outdoor restaurants and bars. There are great views over the Potomac River, with Roosevelt Island in front and the Kennedy Center to the left.

Washington, DC In...

TWO DAYS

Start at the **Air & Space Museum**, followed by the **National Museum of Natural History**. Around lunchtime visit the **National Museum of the American Indian**, for aboriginal lore and a great meal. Wander down to the **Lincoln Memorial** and **Vietnam Veterans Memorial**. That night, go to **U Street** for dining and drinks.

Next day, head to the **US Holocaust Memorial Museum**; stroll alongside the **Tidal Basin** and see the new **Martin Luther King Jr National Memorial**. At twilight pass by the **White House**, then have dinner around **Capitol Hill**.

FOUR DAYS

On day three, take our walking tour around **Georgetown**, followed by lunch at **Martin's Tavern**. Afterwards, take a hike in **Rock Creek Park**. Head to **Dupont Circle** for dinner, followed by drinks at **Eighteenth Street Lounge**.

On the last day, visit the **Newseum**, **Capitol** and **Library of Congress**, then walk to **Eastern Market** for a meal. That evening, go to bohemian H Street NE; **Granville Moore's** is a good place to start off the night.

Library of Congress (p109)

Discover
Washington, DC

At a Glance

- **National Mall** (p104) Iconic museums and monuments, sparse eating options.

- **Capitol Hill** (p116) Architectural gems and a foodie-loving market.

- **Tidal Basin** (p110) Cherry blossoms, picturesque memorials.

- **Downtown** (p110) People-packed streets, shopping, dining.

- **Adams Morgan, Shaw & U Street** (p119) Washington's best nightlife.

- **Dupont Circle** (p118) Trendy eating and drinking spots.

- **Georgetown** (p112) Historic university district with diverse shops and eateries.

Sights

National Mall

The 1.9-mile-long lawn is anchored at one end by the Lincoln Memorial, at the other by Capitol Hill, intersected by the reflecting pool and WWII memorial, and centered by the Washington Monument.

SMITHSONIAN INSTITUTION Museums (☎202-633-1000; www.si.edu) Massive in size and ambition, the 19 Smithsonian museums, galleries and zoo – all admission free – comprise the world's largest museum and research complex. Massive dinosaur skeletons, lunar modules and artworks from every corner of the globe are all part of the Smithsonian largesse.

All the museums are free and open daily (except Christmas Day) from 10am to 5:30pm unless otherwise noted. Some have extended hours in summer.

NATIONAL AIR & SPACE MUSEUM
(cnr 6th St & Independence Ave SW) The Air & Space Museum is the most popular Smithsonian museum; everyone flocks to see the Wright brothers' flyer, Chuck Yeager's *Bell X-1*, Charles Lindbergh's *Spirit of St Louis* and the *Apollo 11* command module. An IMAX theater, planetarium and ride simulator are all here (adult/child $9/7.50 each).

NATIONAL MUSEUM OF NATURAL HISTORY
(cnr 10th St & Constitution Ave SW) A favorite of the kids, the Museum of Natural History showcases dinosaur skeletons, a fantastic archaeology/anthropology

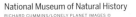

National Museum of Natural History
RICHARD CUMMINS/LONELY PLANET IMAGES ©

collection, wonders from the ocean, and unusual gems and minerals, including the 45-carat Hope Diamond.

NATIONAL MUSEUM OF AMERICAN HISTORY (cnr Constitution Ave & 14th St NW) The Museum of American History is accented with the daily bric-a-brac of the American experience – synagogue shawls, protest signs and cotton gins – plus an enormous display of the original Star-Spangled Banner and icons such as Dorothy's slippers from *The Wizard of Oz* (1939) and Kermit the Frog.

NATIONAL MUSEUM OF THE AMERICAN INDIAN (cnr 4th St & Independence Ave SW) The Museum of the American Indian provides a fine introduction to the indigenous people of the Americas, with an array of costumes, video and audio recordings, and cultural artifacts. Don't miss the regionally specialized menu of Native-inspired dishes at Cafe Mitsitam on the ground floor.

HIRSHHORN MUSEUM & SCULPTURE GARDEN (cnr 7th St & Independence Ave SW; ⏱museum 10am-5:30pm, garden 7:30am-dusk) The doughnut-shaped Hirshhorn Museum &

Sculpture Garden houses a huge collection of modern works, including pieces by Rodin, O'Keeffe, Warhol, Man Ray and de Kooning.

FREE **NATIONAL GALLERY OF ART** Museum (www.nga.gov; Constitution Ave NE, btwn 3rd & 4th Sts NW; ⏱10am-5pm Mon-Sat, 11am-6pm Sun) Set in two massive buildings, the National Gallery of Art houses a staggering art collection (over 100,000 objects), spanning the Middle Ages to the present.

FREE **US HOLOCAUST MEMORIAL MUSEUM** Museum (www.ushmm.org; 100 Raoul Wallenberg Pl; ⏱10am-5:20pm) For a deep understanding of the Holocaust – its victims, perpetrators and bystanders – this harrowing museum is a must-see. Only a limited number of visitors are admitted each day, so go early.

FREE **WASHINGTON MONUMENT** Monument (⏱9am-10pm Jun-Aug, to 5pm Sep-May) Just peaking at 555ft (and 5in), the Washington Monument is the tallest building in

The National Gallery of Art's East Wing, designed by IM Pei

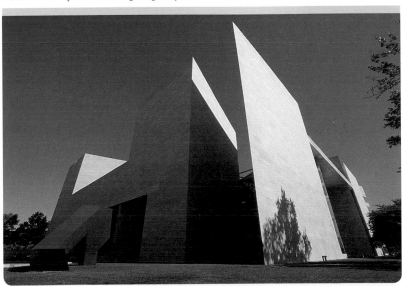

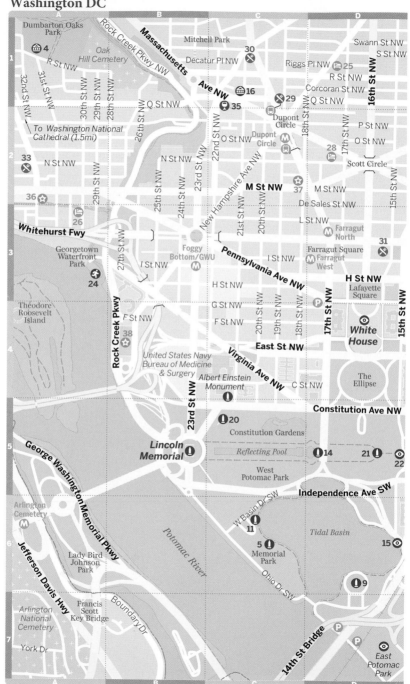

Dumbarton Oaks
Park

Oak
Hill Cemetery

Mitchell Park

Decatur Pl NW

Swann St NW
S St NW

Riggs Pl NW

R St NW

Corcoran St NW

Q St NW

P St NW

O St NW

16th St NW

Rock Creek Pkwy NW

Massachusetts

Ave NW

R St NW

31st St NW
30th St NW
29th St NW
28th St NW
26th St NW

32nd St NW

Q St NW

To Washington National
Cathedral (1.5mi)

N St NW

N St NW

N St NW

25th St NW
24th St NW
23rd St NW
22nd St NW

New Hampshire Ave NW

Dupont
Circle

Dupont
Circle

18th St NW

17th St NW

15th St NW

Scott Circle

M St NW

M St NW

De Sales St NW

L St NW

Farragut
North

Whitehurst Fwy

Georgetown
Waterfront
Park

27th St NW

I St NW

Foggy
Bottom/GWU

Pennsylvania Ave NW

21st St NW
20th St NW

I St NW

H St NW

G St NW

F St NW

20th St NW
19th St NW
18th St NW

Farragut
West

Farragut Square

H St NW
Lafayette
Square

17th St NW

15th St NW

White
House

Théodore
Roosevelt
Island

Rock Creek Pkwy

F St NW

United States Navy
Bureau of Medicine
& Surgery

Albert Einstein
Monument

23rd St NW

Virginia Ave NW

East St NW

C St NW

The
Ellipse

Constitution Ave NW

Lincoln
Memorial

Constitution Gardens

Reflecting Pool

West
Potomac Park

Independence Ave SW

George Washington Memorial Pkwy

Arlington
Cemetery

Jefferson Davis Hwy

Lady Bird
Johnson
Park

W Basin Dr SW

Ohio Dr SW

Tidal Basin

Potomac River

Arlington
National
Cemetery

Francis
Scott
Key Bridge

Boundary Dr

14th St Bridge

East
Potomac
Park

York Dr

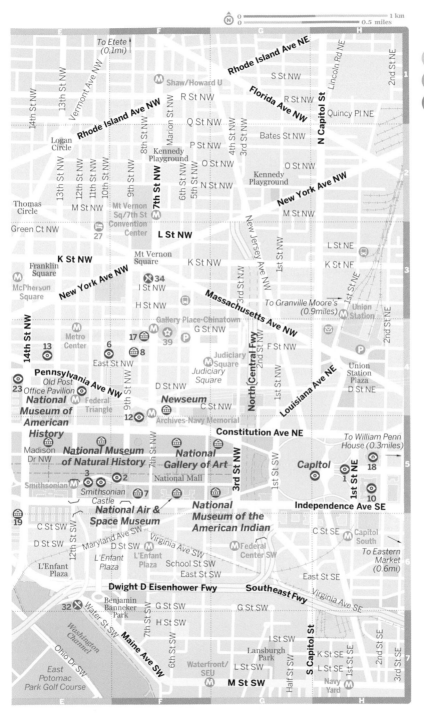

0 1 km
0 0.5 miles

To Etete (0.1mi)

Rhode Island Ave NE

Rhode Island Ave NW

Florida Ave NW

Shaw/Howard U

S St NW

R St NW
R St NW

Lincoln Rd NE

Quincy Pl NE

2nd St NE

Q St NW

Bates St NW

N Capitol St

13th St NW
14th St NW
Vermont Ave NW

8th St NW
Marion St NW

P St NW
O St NW

4th St NW
3rd St NW

Logan
Circle

Kennedy
Playground

N St NW

Kennedy
Playground

O St NW

New York Ave NW

M St NW

13th St NW
12th St NW
11th St NW
10th St NW
9th St NW

6th St NW
5th St NW

7th St NW

Thomas
Circle

M St NW

Mt Vernon
Sq/7th St

Convention
Center
27

L St NW

Green Ct NW

Franklin
Square

K St NW

Mt Vernon
Square

K St NW

L St NE

K St NE

McPherson
Square

New York Ave NW

34
I St NW

Massachusetts Ave NW

3rd St NW

New Jersey Ave NW

1st St NW

14th St NW

H St NW

To Granville Moore's
(0.9miles)

Union
Station

2nd St NE

Gallery Place-Chinatown

G St NW

1st St NE

Metro
Center

13

17
6

East St NW

8

39

Judiciary
Square

F St NW

North Central Fwy
2nd St NW

1st St NW

Union
Station
Plaza

D St NE

Pennsylvania Ave NW

Judiciary
Square

D St NW

Louisiana Ave NE

Old Post
Office Pavilion
23

National
Museum of
American
History

Federal
Triangle

9th St NW

Newseum

12

C St NW

Archives-Navy Memorial

Constitution Ave NE

Madison
Dr NW

National Museum
of Natural History

3

National
Gallery of Art

7th St NW

National Mall

Capitol

3rd St NW

1st St SW

18

1st St NE

Smithsonian

2

Smithsonian
Castle

7

National Air &
Space Museum

National
Museum of the
American Indian

1

10

Independence Ave SE

19

C St SW

Maryland Ave SW

D St SW

12th St SW

Virginia Ave SW

School St SW

Federal
Center SW

C St SE

Capitol
South

L'Enfant
Plaza

L'Enfant
Plaza

East St SW

East St SE

To Eastern
Market
(0.6mi)

Dwight D Eisenhower Fwy

Southeast Fwy

Virginia Ave SE

32

Water St SW

Benjamin
Banneker
Park

7th St SW

G St SW

G St SW

6th St SW

H St SW

1st St SW

Lansburgh
Park

S Capitol St

K St SE

1st St SE
2nd St SE

Washington Channel

Maine Ave SW

Waterfront/
SEU

L St SW

L St SE

3rd St SE

Ohio Dr SW

East
Potomac
Park Golf
Course

M St SW

Half St SW

Navy
Yard

To William Penn
House (0.3miles)

To Etete (0.1mi)

Washington DC

the district. Tickets are free but must be reserved from the **kiosk** (15th St, btwn Madison St & Jefferson Dr SW; ☉8:30am-4:30pm), or you can order them in advance by calling the **National Park Service** (☎877-444-6777; www.recreation.gov; tickets $1.50).

FREE LINCOLN MEMORIAL   Monument
(☉24hr) Anchoring the Mall's west end is the hallowed shrine to Abraham Lincoln, who gazes peacefully across the reflecting pool beneath his neoclassical Doric-columned abode.

FREE VIETNAM VETERANS
MEMORIAL   Monument
(Constitution Gardens; ☉24hr) The opposite of DC's white, gleaming marble edifices, the country's Vietnam war memorial is a black, low-lying 'V' – a physical expression of the psychic scar wrought by the Vietnam War. The monument follows a slow descent deeper into the earth, with the names of the 58,267 dead soldiers – listed in the order in which they died – chiseled into the dark, reflective wall.

LEE FOSTER/LONELY PLANET IMAGES ©

Don't Miss **Newseum**

Although you'll have to pay up, this massive, highly interactive news museum is well worth the admission price. You can delve inside the major events of recent years (the fall of the Berlin Wall, September 11, Hurricane Katrina), and spend hours watching film footage, perusing Pulitzer Prize–winning photographs and reading moving works by journalists killed in the line of duty.

THINGS YOU NEED TO KNOW
www.newseum.org; 555 Pennsylvania Ave NW; adult/child $22/13; ☺9am-5pm

It's a subtle, but remarkably profound monument – and all the more surprising as it was designed by 21-year-old undergraduate student Maya Lin in 1981.

FREE LIBRARY OF
CONGRESS   Landmark
(www.loc.gov; 1st St SE; ☺8:30am-4:30pm Mon-Sat) To prove to Europeans that America was cultured, John Adams plunked the world's largest library on Capitol Hill. The visitor center and tours of the reading rooms are both located in the **Jefferson Building**, just behind the Capitol building.

FREE SUPREME COURT   Landmark
(www.supremecourt.gov; 1 1st St NE; ☺9am-4:30pm Mon-Fri) Even nonlaw students are impressed by the highest court in America. Arrive early to watch arguments (periodic Mondays through Wednesdays October to April). You can visit the permanent exhibits and the building's seven-spiral staircase year-round.

UNION STATION   Landmark
(www.unionstationdc.com; 50 Massachusetts Ave) Greets train visitors to the capital with a gorgeous 1908 beaux-arts building. Its great hall was modeled on the Roman baths of Diocletian.

JOHN NEUBAUER/LONELY PLANET IMAGES ©

Don't Miss **The Capitol**

Since 1800, this is where the legislative branch of American government – ie Congress – has met to write the country's laws. The lower House of Representatives (435 members) and upper Senate (100 members) meet respectively in the south and north wings of the building.

A visitor center showcases the exhaustive background of a building that fairly sweats history. If you book in advance you can go on a free tour of the building, which is as daunting as the exterior, if a little cluttered with the busts, statues and personal mementos of generations of Congress members.

To watch Congress in action, US citizens can request visitor passes from their representatives or senators; foreign visitors need to show their passport at the House gallery. Congressional committee hearings are actually more interesting (and substantive) if you care about what's being debated; check for a schedule, locations and to see if they're open to the public (they often are) at www.house.gov and www.senate.gov.

THINGS YOU NEED TO KNOW

Visitor Center (202-224-3121; www.visitthecapitol.gov; 1st & E Capitol Sts NE; 8:30am-4:30pm Mon-Sat)

Tidal Basin

It's magnificent to stroll around this man-made inlet and watch the monument lights wink across the Potomac. The blooms are loveliest during the Cherry Blossom Festival, the city's annual spring rejuvenation, when the basin bursts into a pink and white floral collage. **Paddleboat rentals** (1501 Maine Ave SW; 2-person boat per hr $12) are available at the boathouse.

Downtown

FREE **NATIONAL ARCHIVES** Landmark (www.archives.gov; 700 Constitution Ave NW; 10am-7pm mid-Mar–early Sep, to 5:30pm

Sep–mid-Mar) It's hard not to feel a little in awe of the big three documents in the National Archives. The Declaration of Independence, the Constitution and the Bill of Rights, plus one of four copies of the Magna Carta: taken together, it becomes clear just how radical the American experiment was for its time.

FREE **REYNOLDS CENTER FOR AMERICAN ART** Museum
(cnr F & 8th Sts NW) Don't miss the Reynolds Center for American Art, which combines the **National Portrait Gallery** (www.npg.si.edu) with the **American Art Museum** (http://americanart.si.edu). From haunting depictions of the inner city and rural heartland to the self-taught visions of itinerant wanderers, the center has dedicated itself to capturing the relentless optimism and critical self-appraisal of American art, and succeeds in a big way.

INTERNATIONAL SPY MUSEUM Museum
(www.spymuseum.org; 800 F St NW; adult/child $18/15; ⊘10am-6pm Sep–mid-Apr, 9am-7pm mid-Apr–Aug) You like those bits in the Bond movies with Q? Then you'll like the immensely popular International Spy Museum. All the undercover tools of the trade on display make this place great for (secret) history buffs. Get there early.

FREE **FORD'S THEATRE** Historic Site
(www.fordstheatre.org; 511 10th St NW; ⊘9am-4pm) On April 14, 1865, John Wilkes Booth assassinated Abraham Lincoln in his box seat here. The theater still operates today; you can take a tour of the theater, and learn about the events that transpired on that fateful April night. There's also a newly restored **Lincoln Museum** devoted to Lincoln's presidency that you can see as part of the tour. Arrive early to get a ticket, as limited numbers are admitted each day.

If You Like…
Evocative Memorials

If you like the Lincoln Memorial (p103), pay a visit to Washington's other awe-inspiring memorials, which celebrate visionaries, statesmen and courageous commoners alike.

1 **JEFFERSON MEMORIAL**
(900 Ohio Drive, SW, south side of Tidal Basin; admission free; ⊘24hr) This domed memorial is etched with the founding father's most famous writings.

2 **MARTIN LUTHER KING JR NATIONAL MEMORIAL**
(www.mlkmemorial.org; 1964 Independence Ave SW, northwest side of Tidal Basin; admission free; ⊘24hr) New in 2011, this memorial pays moving tribute to one of the world's great peace advocates.

3 **FDR MEMORIAL**
(Memorial Park; admission free; ⊘24hr) A 7.5-acre tribute to the longest-serving president in US history and the era he governed.

4 **NATIONAL WWII MEMORIAL**
(17th St, btwn Constitution & Independence Aves; admission free; ⊘24hr) Occupying one end of the reflecting pool, the National WWII Memorial honors the 400,000 Americans who died in WWII, along with the 16 million US soldiers who served.

Dupont Circle
PHILLIPS COLLECTION Museum
(www.phillipscollection.org; 1600 21st St NW; permanent collection admission free, special exhibitions adult/child $12/free; ⊘10am-5pm Tue-Sat, to 8:30pm Thu summer, 11am-6pm Sun) The first modern-art museum in the country (opened in 1921) houses a small but exquisite collection of European and American works – including pieces by Gauguin, Van Gogh, Matisse, Picasso, O'Keefe, Hopper and many other greats. It's partially set in a beautifully restored Georgian Revival mansion.

Georgetown

Thousands of the bright and beautiful, from Georgetown students to ivory-tower academics and diplomats, call this leafy, aristocratic neighborhood home. At night, shop-a-block M St becomes congested with traffic, turning into a weird mix of high-school cruising and high-street boutique.

DUMBARTON OAKS Gardens
(www.doaks.org; cnr R & 31st Sts NW) A free museum featuring exquisite Byzantine and pre-Columbian art is housed within this historic mansion. More impressive, are the 10 acres of beautifully designed formal **gardens** (adult/child $8/5 Apr-Oct, free Nov-Mar; ☺2-6pm Tue-Sun), which are simply stunning during the springtime blooms. Visit on weekdays to beat the crowds.

Upper Northwest DC

FREE NATIONAL ZOOLOGICAL PARK Zoo
(http://nationalzoo.si.edu; 3000 Connecticut Ave NW; ☺10am-6pm Apr-Oct, to 4:30pm Nov-Mar) Home to over 2000 individual animals (400 different species) in natural habitats, this 163-acre zoo is famed for its giant pandas Mei Xiang and Tian Tian.

WASHINGTON NATIONAL CATHEDRAL Church
(☎202-537-6200; www.nationalcathedral.org; 3101 Wisconsin Ave NW; suggested donation $5; ☺10am-5:30pm Mon-Fri, to 4:30pm Sat, 8am-5pm Sun) This Gothic cathedral, as dramatic as its European counterparts, blends both the spiritual and the profane in its architectural treasures.

 **Activities**

The 1754 acres of **Rock Creek Park** follow Rock Creek as it winds through the northwest of the city. There are miles of bicycling, hiking and horseback-riding trails, and even a few coyotes. The C&O Canal offers bicycling and hiking trails in canalside parks.

Thompson Boat Center Boat Rental
(☎202-333-9543; www.thompsonboatcenter.com; cnr Virginia Ave & Rock Creek Pkwy NW;

Street scene, Georgetown

DAN HERRICK/LONELY PLANET IMAGES ©

DOUGLAS STEAKLEY/LONELY PLANET IMAGES ©

Don't Miss **Arlington National Cemetery**

Just across the Potomac River from DC, Arlington County was once part of Washington until it was returned to Virginia in 1847. Today it's best known as the somber final resting place for more than 300,000 military personnel and their dependents, with veterans of every US war from the Revolution to Afghanistan. Much of the cemetery, which spreads over 612 hilly acres, was built on the grounds of **Arlington House**, the former home of Robert E Lee and his wife Mary Anna Custis Lee, a descendant of Martha Washington. When Robert left to lead Virginia's army in the Civil War, Union troops confiscated the property to bury their dead.

The **Tomb of the Unknowns** contains the remains of unidentified American servicemen from both World Wars and the Korean War; military guards retain a round-the-clock vigil and the changing of the guard (every half-hour March to September, every hour October to February) is one of Arlington's most moving sights. An eternal flame marks the **grave of John F Kennedy**, next to those of Jacqueline Kennedy Onassis and two of her infant children.

Tourmobiles are a handy way to visit the cemetery's memorials; they depart from the visitor center.

THINGS YOU NEED TO KNOW

Arlington Cemetery (www.arlingtoncemetery.org; ⊙8am-7pm Apr-Sep, to 5pm Oct-Mar); Tourmobiles (☏202-554-5100; www.tourmobile.com; adult/child $8.50/4.25)

⊙8am-5pm) At the Potomac River end of Rock Creek Park, it rents canoes (per hour $12), kayaks (per hour single/double $10/17) and bikes (per hour/day $7/28).

Big Wheel Bikes Bicycle Rental
(☏202-337-0254; www.bigwheelbikes.com; 1034 33rd St NW; per hr/day $7/35; ⊙11am-7pm Tue-Fri, 10am-6pm Sat & Sun) A good bike-rental outfitter.

JEAN-PIERRE LESCOURRET/LONELY PLANET IMAGES ©

Don't Miss **The White House**

The White House has survived both fire (the Brits torched it in 1814 – only a thunderstorm saved its complete destruction) and insults (Jefferson groused that it was 'big enough for two emperors, one Pope and the grand Lama'). Although its facade has changed little since 1924, its interior has seen frequent renovations. Franklin Roosevelt added a pool; Truman gutted the whole place (and simply discarded many of its historical features – today's rooms are thus historical replicas); Jacqueline Kennedy brought back antique furnishings and historic details; Nixon added a bowling alley; Carter installed solar roof panels, which Reagan then removed; Clinton added a jogging track; and George W Bush installed a T-ball field. Cars can no longer pass the White House on Pennsylvania Ave, clearing the area for posing school groups and round-the-clock peace activists.

A self-guided tour will lead you through the ground and 1st floors, but the 2nd and 3rd floors are off-limits. These tours must be arranged up to six months in advance. Americans must apply via one of their state's members of Congress, and non-Americans must apply through either the US consulate in their home country or their country's consulate in DC. If that sounds like too much work, pop into the White House visitor center; it's not the real deal, but hey, there's executive paraphernalia scattered about.

THINGS YOU NEED TO KNOW

Self-guided tours (📞202-456-7041; admission free, advance booking required; ⏱7:30am-11am Tue-Sat); White House visitor center (www.whitehouse.gov; cnr 15th & E Sts NW; ⏱7:30am-4pm)

Tours

DC METRO FOOD TOURS
Walking
(☎ 800-979-3370; www.dcmetrofoodtours.com; per person $27-60) These walking tours take in the culinary riches of DC, exploring various neighborhoods and stopping for bites along the way.

DC BY FOOT
Walking
(www.dcbyfoot.com) Guides for this free, tip-based walking tour dispense intriguing stories and historical details on different walks around town, covering the National Mall, Arlington Cemetery and Lincoln's assassination.

 **Sleeping**

Downtown & White House Area

MORRISON-CLARK INN
Boutique Hotel $$$
(☎ 202-898-1200; www.morrisonclark.com; 1015 L St NW; r from $220; P ❄ ☎) Listed on the Register of Historic Places, this elegant inn comprises two 1864 residences filled with fine antiques, chandeliers, richly hued drapes and other features evocative of the antebellum South.

Capitol Hill

WILLIAM PENN HOUSE
Hostel $
(☎ 202-543-5560; www.williampennhouse.org; 515 E Capitol St SE; dm incl breakfast from $40; ❄ @) On a peaceful street five blocks east of the Capitol, this friendly Quaker-run guesthouse with garden offers clean, well-maintained dorms, but it could use more bathrooms.

Dupont Circle

CARLYLE SUITES
Hotel $$$
(☎ 202-234-3200; www.carlylesuites.com; 1731 New Hampshire Ave NW; r from $220; ❄ @ ☎) Inside this all-suites art-deco gem, you'll find sizable, handsomely furnished rooms with crisp white linens, luxury mattresses and full kitchens.

TABARD INN
Hotel $$
(☎ 202-785-1277; www.tabardinn.com; 1739 N St NW; r with shared/private bath from $120/165; P ❄ ☎) Set in a trio of 19th-century row houses, the Tabard Inn has attractive, antique-filled guest rooms sprinkled with unique flourishes – iron bedframes,

---

Washington, DC for Children

Top destination for families is undoubtedly the (free!) zoo (p112). The wide-open spaces of the Mall are perfect for outdoor family fun, whether you want to throw a Frisbee, have a picnic, ride the old-fashioned **carousel** (tickets $2.50) or stroll through museums.

Kids like things that go squish and/or make other things go squish; they can find both in the dinosaurs and insects of the National Museum of Natural History (p104). The National Air & Space Museum (p104) has moon rocks, IMAX films and a wild simulation ride.

The **National Theatre** (☎ 202-628-6161; www.nationaltheatre.org; 1321 Pennsylvania NW) offers free Saturday-morning performances, from puppet shows to tap dancers (reservations required). **Discovery Theater** (☎ 202-633-8700; www.discoverytheater.org; 1100 Jefferson Dr SW; adult/child $6/5), in the basement of the Ripley Center, stages entertaining shows for young audiences.

wing-backed chairs, decorative fireplaces. There's an excellent restaurant here, with garden.

Adams Morgan

ADAM'S INN B&B **$$**
(☎202-745-3600; www.adamsinn.com; 1746 Lanier Pl NW; r with shared/private bath from $109/139; [P][❄][@]) On a pretty, tree-lined street near Adams Morgan, this town-house has small but nicely decorated rooms; thin walls mean you might hear your neighbor.

Georgetown

HOTEL MONTICELLO Hotel **$$$**
(☎202-337-0900; www.monticellohotel.com; 1075 Thomas Jefferson St NW; r from $220; [P][❄][🛜]) In the heart of Georgetown, the Hotel Monticello has spacious rooms, with brass-and-crystal chandeliers, colonial-reproduction furniture, comfortable high-end mattresses and tasteful flower arrangements. Helpful staff.

Eating

Capitol Hill

GRANVILLE MOORE'S Modern American **$$**
(1238 H St NE; mains $12-16; ☺5pm-midnight Sun-Thu, to 3am Fri & Sat) One of the anchors of the bohemian Atlas District (which runs along H St NE), Granville Moore's bills itself as a gastropub with a Belgian fetish. Indeed you'll find more than 70 Belgian beers by the bottle and at least seven on tap. There's also good pub fare (and recommended mussels), a lively happy hour and fun crowds most nights.

EASTERN MARKET Market **$**
(225 7th St SE; ☺7am-7pm Tue-Fri, to 6pm Sat, 9am-5pm Sun) One of the icons of Capitol Hill, this covered arcade sprawls with de-lectable produce and good cheer on the weekends. The crab cakes at the Market Lunch stall are divine.

Downtown & White House Area

PING PONG Asian **$$**
(☎202-506-3740; 900 7th St NW; dim sum $5-7; ☺11:30am-11pm Mon-Sat, 11am-10pm Sun) At Ping Pong you can enjoy delectable dim sum anytime. The pan-Asian menu features delicate steamed dump-lings, honey-roasted pork buns, seafood clay pots and other hits, plus tasty libations like plum wine and elderflower saketini.

JALEO Spanish **$$**
(☎202-628-7949; 480 7th St NW; tapas $7-12, dinner mains $16; ☺11:30am-11:30pm Tue-Sat, to 10pm Sun & Mon) Amid vintage murals and buzzing ambience, Jaleo serves some of DC's best tapas.

Produce stands at Eastern Market

Detour:
Alexandria

The charming colonial village of Alexandria is just 5 miles and 250 years away from Washington. Once a salty port town, Alexandria – known as 'Old Town' to locals – is today a posh collection of red-bricked colonial homes, cobblestoned streets, flickering gas lamps and a waterfront promenade. King St is packed with boutiques, outdoor cafes, and neighborhood bars and restaurants.

Gadsby's Tavern Museum (www.gadsbystavernmuseum.us; 134 N Royal St; adult/child $5/3; ⏱10am-5pm Tue-Sat, from 1pm Sun & Mon) has exhibits on colonial life and is still a working pub and restaurant; past guests include George Washington and Thomas Jefferson. Near the waterfront, the **Torpedo Factory Art Center** (www.torpedofactory.org; 105 N Union St; admission free; ⏱10am-6pm Fri-Wed, to 9pm Thu) is a former munitions factory that today houses dozens of galleries and studios.

To get to Alexandria from downtown DC, get off at the King St Metro station. A free trolley (every 20 minutes, 11:30am to 10pm) makes the 1-mile journey between the Metro station and the waterfront.

GEORGIA BROWN'S   Southern **$$**
(☎202-393-4499; 950 15th St NW; mains $16-32; ⏱11:30am-10pm Mon-Thu, noon-11pm Fri & Sat, 10am-2:30pm & 5-10pm Sun) Georgia Brown's elevates the humble ingredients of the South (shrimp, cornmeal, catfish, grits and sausage) to high art in dishes like fried green tomatoes stuffed with herbed goat's cheese, and fried chicken marinated in sweet tea.

MAINE AVENUE FISH MARKET   Seafood **$**
(1100 Maine Ave SW; ⏱8am-9pm) If you're a seafood-lover, this sprawling and bustling fish market should take high priority on your itinerary. Big plump oysters ($7 for six), crab cakes, soft-shell crabs, steamed crabs and peel-and-eat shrimp are just the beginning...

Adams Morgan, Shaw & U Street

BUSBOYS & POETS   International **$$**
(☎203-387-7638; www.busboysandpoets.com; 2021 14th St NW; mains $8-16; ⏱8am-midnight Mon-Fri, from 9am Sat & Sun; 🛜) A cultural icon, Busboys (named for a Langston Hughes poem) attracts an eclectic crowd that gathers for coffee, bistro fare (pizzas, burgers, crab cakes) and a progressive line-up of events – book signings, poetry readings, film screenings.

ETETE   Ethiopian **$$**
(☎202-232-7600; 1942 9th St NW; mains $10-20; ⏱11:30am-11pm; 🖊) In the small ethnic enclave sometimes called 'Little Ethiopia,' Etete serves authentic and high-quality food – fiery *yebeg wat* (spicy lamb stew), tender golden *tibs* (marinated short beef ribs), bountiful vegetarian platters and tangy *injera* (spongy flatbread) for soaking it all up.

TRYST   Cafe **$**
(2459 18th St NW; ⏱6:30am-late; 🛜) In Adams Morgan, stylish Tryst with its smattering of tables and sofas attracts the laptop crowd by day (free wi-fi) and a more garrulous gathering by night; there's live jazz Monday to Wednesday (from 8pm), an early happy hour (3pm to 5:30pm) and decent coffees, small plates and desserts.

BEN'S CHILI BOWL   Fast Food **$**
(1213 U St NW; mains $4-9; ⏱11am-2am Mon-Thu, to 4am Fri & Sat, to 11pm Sun) One of DC's landmarks, Ben's has been going strong for over 50 years, doling out burgers, fries and the well-loved chili-smothered half-smokes (pork and

beef sausages) from its old-school U St storefront.

Dupont Circle

BISTRO DU COIN   French $$
(📞202-234-6969; 1738 Connecticut Ave NW; mains $12-27; 🕐11:30am-11pm Sun-Wed, to 1am Thu-Sat) For a quick culinary journey across the Atlantic, the lively and much-loved Bistro Du Coin delivers the goods.

AFTERWORDS   American $$
(📞202-387-3825; 1517 Connecticut Ave NW; mains $12-20; 🕐7:30am-1am Sun-Thu, 24hr Fri & Sat; 📶) Not your average bookstore cafe, this buzzing spot overflows with good cheer at its packed cafe tables and outdoor patio.

Georgetown

MARTIN'S TAVERN   American $$
(📞202-333-7370; 1264 Wisconsin Ave NW; lunch mains $12-15, dinner $13-30; 🕐from 11:30am) Martin's is a favorite with Georgetown students and US presidents, who all enjoy the tavern's old-fashioned dining room and unfussy classics like thick burgers, crab cakes and prime rib.

🍷 Drinking & Entertainment

See the weekly *Washington City Paper* (www.washingtoncitypaper.com) or *Washington Post* (www.washingtonpost.com) weekend section for comprehensive listings. Conveniently located at the Old Post Office Pavilion, **Ticketplace** (http://culturecapital.tix.com; 407 7th St NW; 🕐11am-6pm Wed-Fri, 10am-5pm Sat) sells same-day concert and show tickets at half-price.

Bars & Nightclubs

CAPITOL HILL & DOWNTOWN

HAWK & DOVE   Bar
(329 Pennsylvania Ave SE; 🕐from 10am) The quintessential Capitol Hill bar is a hot spot for political junkies, with intimate corner booths perfect for sipping pints and creating the next District scandal.

RED PALACE   Live Music
(📞202-399-3201; http://redpalacedc.com; 1212 H St NE; 🕐from 5pm) A pillar of the frenzied

Madam's Organ

JUSTIN MATHEWS/LONELY PLANET IMAGES ©

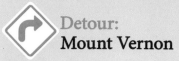

Detour:
Mount Vernon

One of the most visited historic shrines in the nation, **Mount Vernon** (📞703-780-2000; www.mountvernon.org; adult/child $15/7; ⏰9am-5pm Mar-Oct, to 4pm Nov-Feb) was the beloved home of George and Martha Washington, who lived here from their marriage in 1759 until George's death in 1799. Now owned and operated by the Mount Vernon Ladies Association, the estate offers glimpses of 18th-century farm life and the first president's life as a country planter.

In the warmer months, you can take a 40-minute **sightseeing cruise** (adult/child $9/5; ⏰Tue-Sun May-Aug, Sat & Sun Apr & Sep).

Mount Vernon is 16 miles south of DC off the Mount Vernon Memorial Hwy. **Tourmobile** (📞202-554-5100; www.tourmobile.com; adult/child incl admission $32/16; ⏰mid-Jun–Aug) offers one trip a day to Mount Vernon from Arlington National Cemetery. **Grayline** (📞202-289-1995; www.grayline.com; adult/child incl admission from $55/30) departs daily from DC's Union Station year-round.

Several companies offer seasonal boat trips from DC and Alexandria; the cheapest is **Potomac Riverboat Company** (📞703-684-0580; www.potomac riverboatco.com; adult/child incl admission $40/20). A healthy alternative is to take a lovely bike ride along the Potomac River from DC (18 miles from Roosevelt Island).

H St scene, Red Palace books a mix of live bands and burlesque shows, with an abundance of indie rock and experimental sounds.

ADAMS MORGAN, SHAW & U STREET

MARVIN   Lounge
(2007 14th St NW; ⏰5:30pm-2am) Stylish but unpretentious, Marvin has a low-lit lounge with vaulted ceilings where DJs spin soul and rare grooves to a mixed 14th St crowd. The upstairs roof deck is a draw both on summer nights and in winter, when folks huddle under roaring heat lamps sipping cocktails and Belgian beers.

MADAM'S ORGAN   Live Music
(www.madamsorgan.com; 2461 18th St NW; cover $3-7; ⏰5pm-2am Sun-Thu, to 3am Fri & Sat) The Organ is a well-loved standby, with lively crowds, cheap drinks, a rambling interior and roof deck, free pool and bands playing nightly.

DUPONT CIRCLE
EIGHTEENTH STREET
LOUNGE   Lounge
(www.eighteenthstreetlounge.com; 1212 18th St NW; cover $5-15; ⏰from 9:30pm Sat & Sun, from 5:30pm Tue-Fri) Chandeliers, velvet sofas, antique wallpaper and an attractive dance-loving crowd adorn this multi-floored mansion.

BIER BARON   Bar
(1523 22nd St NW; ⏰from 11:30am Thu-Sun, from 4:30pm Mon-Wed) Since changing name and ownership, the former Brickskeller serves better food and has better service, with the same dark, pubby ambience and venerable selection of bottled and draft beer (over 500 brews!).

GEORGETOWN

TOMBS   Bar
(1226 36 St, at P St NW; ⏰from 11:30am Mon-Sat, from 9:30am Sun) If it looks familiar, think back to the '80s; this was the

setting for *St Elmo's Fire*. Today this cozy, windowless bar is a favorite with Georgetown students and teaching assistants boozing under crew regalia.

Live Music

BLUES ALLEY   Live Music
(www.bluesalley.com; 1073 Wisconsin Ave NW; ⏰from 8pm) The classy Georgetown jazz supper club attracts some big-name players, as well as some forgettable proponents of smooth jazz. Enter through the alley just off M, south of Wisconsin.

Performing Arts

KENNEDY CENTER   Performing Arts
(📞800-434-1324; www.kennedy-center.org; 2700 F St NW) Perched on 17 acres along the Potomac, the magnificent Kennedy Center hosts a staggering array of performances. The Millennium Stage puts on free performances at 6pm daily.

Sports

Washington Redskins   Football
(📞301-276-6800; www.redskins.com) The city's football team plays at **FedEx Field** (1600 Fedex Way, Landover, MD; tickets $40-500), east of DC in Maryland.

Washington Nationals   Baseball
(📞202-675-6287; http://washington. nationals.mlb.com) DC's baseball team plays at **Nationals Park** (1500 S Capitol St SE), along the Anacostia riverfront in southeast DC. The season runs from April through October.

Washington Wizards   Basketball
(📞202-661-5050; www.nba.com/wizards) NBA season runs from October through April, with home games played at the **Verizon Center** (601 F St NW).

ℹ Information

Destination DC (📞202-789-7000; www. washington.org; 901 7th St NW, 4th fl) Doles out loads of information online, over the phone or in person at a handy downtown location.

Left: Main hall of Union Station (p109);
Below: Brass band, Dupont Circle
(LEFT) RICHARD CUMMINS/LONELY PLANET IMAGES ©; (BELOW) LEE FOSTER/LONELY PLANET IMAGES ©

Getting There & Away

Bus

There are numerous cheap bus services to New York (four to five hours); most charge around $20 one-way.

Greyhound (☎800-231-2222, 202-589-5141; www.greyhound.com; 1005 1st St NE)

Bolt Bus (☎877-265-8287; www.boltbus.com; 📶) Leaves from the upper level of Union Station.

Train

Amtrak (☎800-872-7245; www.amtrak.com) Trains depart from Union Station.

Getting Around

To/From the Airport

Supershuttle (☎800-258-3826; www.supershuttle.com) A door-to-door shuttle that connects downtown DC with Dulles ($29), National ($14) and BWI ($37).

Metrobus 5A (www.wmata.com) Runs from Dulles to Rosslyn Metro station (35 minutes) and central DC (L'Enfant Plaza, 48 minutes). The combo bus/Metro fare is about $8.

Metrorail (www.wmata.com) National airport has its own Metro rail station, which is fast and cheap (around $2.50).

Washington Flyer (www.washfly.com) Runs every 30 minutes from Dulles to West Falls Church Metro ($10).

Taxi

Try **Capitol Cab** (☎202-636-1600), **Diamond** (☎202-387-6200) or **Yellow Cab** (☎202-544-1212).

121

Chicago

There's something about this cloud-scraping city that bewitches. Well, maybe not during the six-month winter, when the 'Windy City' gets slapped by snowy blasts. However, come May, when the weather warms and everyone dashes for the outdoor festivals, ballparks, lakefront beaches and beer gardens – nowhere tops Chicago. And we mean it literally, as the skyscrapers here are among the nation's tallest.

Beyond its mighty architecture, Chicago is a city of Mexican, Polish, Vietnamese and other ethnic neighborhoods, great for wandering through. It's a city of blues, jazz and rock clubs, with music on every night of the week. And it's a chowhound's town, where diners queue for everything from down-home hot dogs to some of North America's top restaurants.

Forgive us, but it has to be said: the Windy City will blow you away with its low-key, cultured awesomeness.

Crown Fountain, Millennium Park (p134)

Facade and neon sign of the Chicago Theatre
RICHARD CUMMINS/LONELY PLANET IMAGES ©

Chicago

W Peterson Ave

Rosehill Cemetery

East River Park

LINCOLN SQUARE

EDGEWATER

Loyola
Morse
Granville
Thorndale
Bryn Mawr

ANDERSONVILLE

W Foster Ave

UPTOWN

North Branch Chicago River

To O'Hare International Airport (10mi)

Kedzie
Kimball
Francisco
Rockwell
Western
Damen

Waveland Park

Irving Park

W Irving Park Rd

Addison
W Addison St
Horner Park

Graceland Cemetery

6

LAKEVIEW

Belmont
W Belmont Ave

N Western Ave

N Milwaukee Ave

John F Kennedy Expwy

Logan Square

LINCOLN PARK

W Fullerton Ave

LOGAN SQUARE

BUCKTOWN

California
Western

North Ave Beach

Lake Michigan

Clybourn Station (Metra)

OLD TOWN

3

Lincoln Park

W North Ave

Damen

W North Ave

HUMBOLDT PARK

WICKER PARK

Division

Goose Island

Chicago

W Grand Ave

UKRAINIAN VILLAGE

Garfield Park

Cicero
Pulaski

California

Ashland

Grand

5

Grand

4

Medical Center

Kedzie-Homan

GREEKTOWN

THE LOOP

1 Millennium Park

2

Pulaski
Kedzie
Western
Racine
Polk

LITTLE ITALY

EisenhowerExpressway

W Roosevelt Rd

Douglas Park

Central Park
Kedzie
California

18th St

12th St Beach

Kildare
Pulaski
W Cermak Rd
Western
Hoyne

See Downtown Chicago Map (p136)

Hawthorne Race Track

Ashland
McGuane Park
Halsted

CHINATOWN

Cermak-Chinatown

27th St Station (Metra)
31st St Beach

Sanitary Drainage & Ship Canal

Adlai Stevenson Expwy

35th St/Archer
McKinley Park

BRIDGEPORT

Sox-35th St

35th St-Bronzeville-IIT

BRONZEVILLE

Woodland Park

S Cicero Ave

W Pershing Rd

Indiana
43rd St

S Archer Ave

Kedzie
Western

47th St

KENWOOD

Pulaski

47th St
51st St

55th-56th-57th St Station (Metra)
51st-53rd St Station (Metra)

Sherman Park

W Garfield Blvd
Garfield

Dan Ryan Expressway

Garfield

HYDE PARK

57th St Beach

0 ___ 4 km
0 ___ 2 miles

See Downtown Chicago Map (p136)

1 Millennium Park
2 Art Institute of Chicago
3 Lincoln Park
4 Deep-Dish Pizza
5 John Hancock Center
6 Wrigley Field

Chicago's Highlights

1

Millennium Park

Chicago's showpiece (p134) shines with whimsical public art. Where to start amid the mod designs? Pritzker Pavilion, Frank Gehry's swooping, silver bandshell? Jaume Plensa's Crown Fountain, with its human gargoyles? Anish Kapoor's silvery *Cloud Gate* sculpture (aka 'The Bean'). Summertime concerts and winter ice skating add to the fun.

Need to Know
FREE AUDIO TOUR
Downloadable from www.
millenniumpark.org **FREE**
WALKING TOURS Daily at
11:30am and 1pm from the
park's Welcome Center
**For more, see
p134.**

Millennium Park Don't Miss List

BY KATIE LAW, MANAGER, CHICAGO GREETER AND VOLUNTEER SERVICES

1 'THE BEAN'

It's a mirror reflecting the city (above left). Everyone wants to take a picture of it. Most people stand in the front courtyard, but there are good vantage points at the sculpture's north and south ends, too. For great people-watching, go up the stairs on Washington St, on the Park Grill's north side, where there are shady benches.

2 CROWN FOUNTAIN

The faces of one thousand local Chicagoans appear on the two glass-block towers' video displays, blowing out water from their lips. Kids love it – it's like a water park.

3 SECRET GARDEN

People often overlook the Lurie Garden, because it's hidden behind a big hedge. It's planted with all native Midwest grasses, trees and flowers, and there's a little river to dangle your feet in. On weekends volunteers give free tours of the grounds. Another thing visitors miss is walking all the way across the snaky BP Bridge to Daley Bicentennial Plaza, which is a quiet little area.

4 MUSICAL VIEWS

Sitting at an evening concert at Pritzker Pavilion (far left), on the lawn looking up through the grid Frank Gehry put up, and seeing all the architecture at the corner of Randolph and Michigan while hearing the music – there's nothing like it. When summer hits, there are free concerts almost every night, including jazz, world music and youth-oriented bands on Monday.

5 CYCLING & ICE SKATING

You can rent bikes at the McDonald's Cycle Center, which is a popular thing to do. In winter you can go ice skating at the McCormick Tribune Rink. In summer, the rink converts into a beer garden operated by the **Park Grill** (☎ 312-521-7275; www.parkgrillchicago.com; 11 N Michigan Ave). It's a great place to sit outside and take a break.

Art Institute of Chicago

The second-largest art museum in the country, the Art Institute (p134) houses treasures and masterpieces from around the globe, including a fabulous selection of Impressionist and post-Impressionist paintings. The Modern Wing, dazzling with natural light, hangs Picassos and Mirós on its 3rd floor. An added bonus is the mod, pedestrian Nichols Bridgeway arching from here into Millennium Park.

Lincoln Park

Lincoln Park (p140) is Chicago's largest green space, an urban oasis spanning 1200 leafy acres along the lakefront. Lincoln Park is also the name for the abutting neighborhood. Both are alive day and night with people jogging, walking dogs, pushing strollers and driving in circles looking for a place to park. Highlights include a family-friendly zoo, a lush conservatory filled with exotic blooms and the Southern California–style North Avenue Beach.

Deep-Dish Pizza

Chicago's iconic dish boasts a thick, buttery crust that rises two or three inches above the plate and cradles a molten pile of toppings. One gooey piece is practically a meal. It was invented back in 1943 at Pizzeria Uno (p144), and is required eating for any self-respecting pizza lover visiting the Windy City. Top contenders for Chicago's best pizza are Gino's East, Giordano's and of course, the deep-dish birthplace, Uno's.

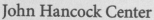

John Hancock Center

The 100-story John Hancock Center (p140) has unrivaled views over the lake and the city beside it. Those needing a city history lesson should ascend to the 94th-floor observatory and listen to the edifying audio tour that comes with admission. Those secure in their knowledge should shoot up to the 96th-floor Signature Lounge, where the view is free if you buy a drink.

Wrigley Field

Ivy-covered Wrigley Field (p141), which dates from 1914, is an old-school slice of Americana, with a hand-turned scoreboard, havoc-wreaking wind patterns blowing off the lake and an iconic neon sign. It's home to the much-loved but perpetually losing Chicago Cubs. If they're playing a game, you can peep in the 'knothole,' a garage door-sized opening on Sheffield Ave, to watch the action for free.

Chicago's Best...

Museums

o **Field Museum of Natural History** (p135) Delve far into the past while exploring these eye-opening collections.

o **Shedd Aquarium** (p135) Whales, dolphins, sharks and other fascinating creatures from the deep.

o **Adler Planetarium & Astronomy Museum** (p138) Journey to the nether regions of outer space at this lakeside gem.

o **Museum of Science & Industry** (p141) Geek out at the largest science museum in the western hemisphere.

Architecture

o **Willis Tower** (p134) Breathtaking views from the 103rd-floor Skydeck.

o **Rookery** (p139) Floating staircases feature in Frank Lloyd Wright's light-filled atrium.

o **Chicago Board of Trade** (p139) An art-deco, photogenic classic.

o **Robie House** (p141) Frank Lloyd Wright's masterpiece in Hyde Park.

Dining

o **Frontera Grill** (p144) A famed, sustainable Mexican restaurant that's a favorite of Barack Obama's.

o **Alinea** (p145) New American cooking reaches high art at this futuristic restaurant.

o **Next** (p147) An extraordinary dining experience that changes radically from season to season.

o **Hot Doug's** (p146) The humble hot dog receives the star treatment at this uber-popular Wicker Park eatery.

Need to Know

Live Music

- **Buddy Guy's Legends** (p149) Top music club where you can catch some of the world's best blues players.

- **Kingston Mines** (p149) A Lincoln Park favorite with two stages and smokin'-hot blues.

- **Green Mill** (p149) Al Capone's former hangout is a great spot to hear top-notch jazz and other fare.

- **Hideout** (p149) A rambling indie-rock club near Bucktown.

Left: Chicago Board of Trade Building (p139);
Above: Live music at the Hideout (p149)

ADVANCE PLANNING

- **Two months before** Chowhounds who crave dinner at top-end restaurants such as Alinea, Next or Topolobampo should make reservations.

- **One month before** Browse for half-price tickets to theater, sports events and concerts at www.goldstar.com.

- **One week before** Buy online discount cards (try www.gochicagocard.com or www.citypass.com) if you're planning to do a lot of sightseeing.

RESOURCES

- **Explore Chicago** (www.explorechicago.org) The city's official tourism site has loads of info.

- **Chicagoist** (www.chicagoist.com) Quirky take on news, food, arts and events.

- **Gapers Block** (www.gapersblock.com) News and events site with Chicago attitude.

- **Chicago Gluttons** (www.chicagogluttons.com) Entertaining, unvarnished restaurant reviews by a group of foul-mouthed 'regular Joes.'

- **Time Out Chicago** (www.timeoutchicago.com) Weekly magazine with all-encompassing listings.

GETTING AROUND

- **Airport** O'Hare International Airport (ORD; www.ohare.com) is the main airport; the CTA Blue Line offers a quick trip to downtown ($2.25). Airport shuttles are $29 per person, cabs about $45. From Midway Airport (www.flychicago.com) take the CTA Orange Line.

- **Public Transport** The CTA offers an extensive network of elevated/subway train cars (aka the El). Purchase a Transit Card from train station vending machines. Rides cost about $2.25.

- **Taxi** Cabs are plentiful in the Loop, north to Andersonville and west to Wicker Park/Bucktown.

- **Train** Amtrak trains depart at least once daily for San Francisco, Seattle, New York City and New Orleans.

BE FOREWARNED

- **Planning** Pre-booking accommodation during summer is a good idea, especially when festivals are on.

- **Weather** Winter, running from late November into April, can be long and brutal.

Chicago Walking Tour

This tour swoops through the Loop, highlighting Chicago's revered art and architecture, with a visit to Al Capone's dentist thrown in for good measure.

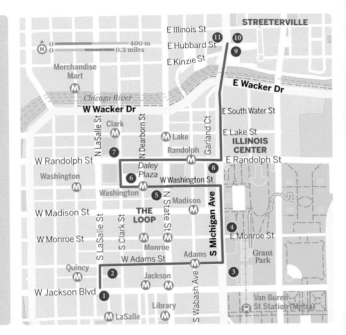

1 Chicago Board of Trade

Start at the Chicago Board of Trade, where fast-talking guys in Technicolor coats traffic corn and pork bellies inside a stunning art-deco building.

2 Rookery

A few blocks north, step into the Rookery – a historic 1888 landmark building, with a lobby remodeled by Frank Lloyd Wright in 1905. Pigeons used to roost here, hence the name.

3 Art Institute of Chicago

Head east on Adams St to the Art Institute of Chicago, one of the city's most-visited attractions. The lion statues out front make for a classic, keepsake photo.

4 Millennium Park

Walk a few blocks north to avant-garde Millennium Park and saunter in to explore the famous *Cloud Gate* (aka 'The Bean'), human-gargoyle fountains and other contemporary designs.

5 Hotel Burnham

When you depart Millennium Park, head west on Washington St to Hotel Burnham. It's housed in the Reliance Building, which was the precursor to modern skyscraper design; Capone's dentist drilled teeth in what's now room 809.

⑥ Untitled

Just west, the *Untitled*, created by Pablo Picasso, is ensconced in Daley Plaza. Bird, dog, woman? You decide.

⑦ Monument with Standing Beast

Head north on Clark St to Jean Dubuffet's *Monument with Standing Beast*, another head-scratching sculpture.

⑧ Cultural Center

Walk east on Randolph St through the theater district. Pop into the Cultural Center and have a look at the exquisite interior; its rooms are modeled on the Doge's Palace in Venice and Palazzo Vecchio in Florence.

⑨ Wrigley Building

Walk north on Michigan Ave and cross the Chicago River. Just north of the bridge you'll pass the Wrigley Building, a 1920s-era building that ranks among one of Chicago's finest architectural works.

⑩ Tribune Tower

Nearby is the Gothic, eye-popping Tribune Tower. Have a close look when passing to see chunks of the Taj Mahal, Parthenon and other famous structures embedded in the lower walls.

⑪ Billy Goat Tavern

To finish your tour, visit Billy Goat Tavern, a vintage Chicago dive that spawned the Curse of the Cubs. Just look around at the walls and you'll get the details, but in short, the tavern's owner, Billy Sianis, once tried to enter Wrigley Field with his pet goat. The smelly creature was denied entry, so Sianis called down a mighty curse on the baseball team in retaliation. They've stunk ever since.

Chicago in...

TWO DAYS

On your first day take our walking tour through the **Loop**, then stop for a deep-dish pizza at **Giordano's**. In the afternoon, catch the sunset from the **John Hancock Center**. On day two explore the **Art Institute of Chicago** or **Field Museum of Natural History**. Browse boutiques and grab a stylish dinner in **Wicker Park** before heading north to the **Green Mill** for an evening of jazz.

FOUR DAYS

On your third day, rent a bicycle, dip your toes in Lake Michigan at **North Avenue Beach** and cruise through **Lincoln Park**, making stops at the zoo and conservatory. If it's baseball season, head to **Wrigley Field** for a Cubs game. A blues club, such as **Buddy Guy's Legends**, is a fine way to finish the day.

Pick a neighborhood on your fourth day to eat, shop and soak up the culture: murals and mole sauce in **Pilsen**, pagodas and Vietnamese sandwiches in **Uptown**, or Frank Lloyd Wright architecture in **Hyde Park**. Then see a play at one of Chicago's 200 theaters, or a comedy at **Second City**.

Dinosaur skeleton outside the Field Museum (p135)
RICHARD CUMMINS/LONELY PLANET IMAGES ©

Discover Chicago

At a Glance

- **The Loop** (p134) City center; home to great architecture and top museums.

- **South Loop** (p135) Home to lakefront park-and-museum district, aka Museum Campus.

- **Near North** (p138) Shopping on the Magnificent Mile and amusement on Navy Pier

- **Lincoln Park** (p140) Lush park and adjoining hood with a zoo, conservatory and popular beach.

- **Uptown** (p145) 'Little Saigon' with Vietnamese, Thai and Chinese restaurants and shops.

- **Wicker Park, Bucktown & the Ukrainian Village** (p148) Galleries, boutiques and music clubs.

Cyclists riding along the lakefront
PETER PTSCHELINZEW/LONELY PLANET IMAGES ©

 Sights

The Loop

FREE **MILLENNIUM PARK**   Park
(Map p136; www.millenniumpark.org; Welcome Center, 201 E Randolph St; ⊙6am-11pm; 👪)
Rising boldly by the lakefront, Millennium Park is a treasure trove of free and arty sights. Frank Gehry's 120ft-high swooping silver band shell anchors what is, in essence, an outdoor modern design gallery. It includes Jaume Plensa's 50ft-high **Crown Fountain**, which projects video images of locals spitting water, gargoyle style; the Gehry-designed **BP Bridge** that spans Columbus Dr and offers great skyline views; and the **McCormick Tribune Ice Rink** that fills with skaters in winter (and al fresco diners in summer). The park's biggest draw is 'the Bean' – officially titled **Cloud Gate** – Anish Kapoor's ridiculously smooth, 110-ton, silver-drop sculpture.

ART INSTITUTE OF CHICAGO   Museum
(Map p136; ☎312-443-3600; www.artic.edu/aic; 111 S Michigan Ave; adult/child $18/free; ⊙10:30am-5pm, to 8pm Thu; 👪) The Art Institute has a magnificent collection, and you could easily spend a full day exploring the vast galleries. Its standout works include Grant Wood's *American Gothic,* the pointillist classic *A Sunday on La Grande Jatte* by Georges Seurat, Edward Hopper's *Nighthawks,* Picasso's *The Old Guitarist* and Monet's *Stacks of Wheat.*

WILLIS TOWER   Tower
(Map p136; ☎312-875-9696; www.the-skydeck.com; 233 S Wacker Dr; adult/child $17/11; ⊙9am-10pm Apr-Sep, 10am-8pm Oct-Mar)

Willis Tower was the Sears Tower until mid-2009, when insurance broker Willis Group Holdings bought the naming rights. No matter what you call it, it's still the USA's tallest building (1454ft), and its 103rd-floor Skydeck puts visitors way up in the clouds.

FREE **CHICAGO CULTURAL CENTER** Cultural Building
(Map p136; ☎ 312-744-6630; www.chicago culturalcenter.org; 78 E Washington St; ⏱8am-7pm Mon-Thu, 8am-6pm Fri, 9am-6pm Sat, 10am-6pm Sun; 🛜) The block-long, beaux arts building houses art exhibitions, foreign films, and jazz and world music concerts at 12:15pm on weekdays. It also contains the world's largest Tiffany stained-glass dome and Chicago's main visitor center.

GRANT PARK Park
(Map p136; Michigan Ave btwn 12th & Randolph Sts; ⏱6am-11pm) Grant Park hosts the city's mega-events, such as Taste of Chicago, Blues Fest and Lollapalooza. **Buckingham Fountain (cnr Congress Pkwy & Columbus Dr)** is Grant's centerpiece. It lets loose on the hour every hour between 10am and 11pm mid-April to mid-October, accompanied at night by multicolored lights and music.

South Loop

FIELD MUSEUM OF NATURAL HISTORY Museum
(Map p136; ☎ 312-922-9410; www.fieldmuseum. org; 1400 S Lake Shore Dr; adult/child $15/10; ⏱9am-5pm; 🚻) The mammoth Field Museum houses everything but the kitchen sink – beetles, mummies, gemstones, Bushman the stuffed ape. The collection's rockstar is Sue, the largest *Tyrannosaurus rex* yet discovered. Special exhibits, like the 3D movie, cost extra.

SHEDD AQUARIUM Aquarium
(Map p136; ☎ 312-939-2438; www.shedd aquarium.org; 1200 S Lake Shore Dr; adult/child $29/20; ⏱9am-6pm Jun-Aug, to 5pm Sep-May; 🚻) Top draws at the kiddie-mobbed Shedd Aquarium include the Oceanarium, with its beluga whales and frolicking white-sided dolphins, and the shark exhibit, where there's just 5in of Plexiglas between you and two dozen fierce-looking swimmers.

Caribbean Reef display, Shedd Aquarium

Downtown Chicago

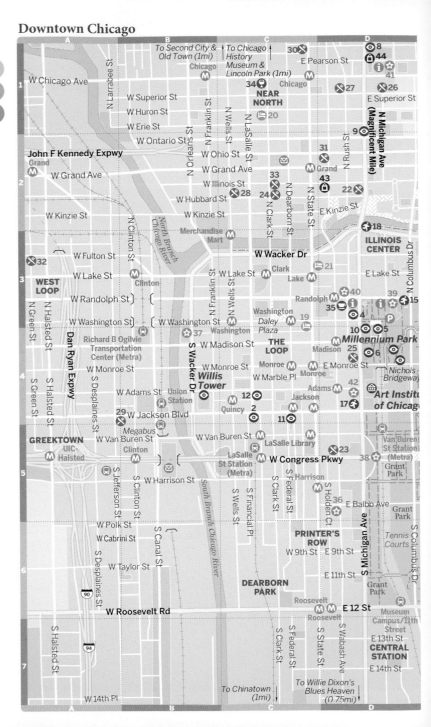

0   1 km

0   0.5 miles

Lake Shore Park
E Chicago Ave

Lakefront Path

Water Filtration Plant

Olive Park

E Ontario St

Ohio St Beach

STREETERVILLE

N Lake Shore Dr

Navy Pier

E Grand Ave
E Illinois St

3

13

16

14

Shoreline Water Taxi to Museum Campus

E North Water St

River Esplanade

E Wacker Dr

N Lake Shore Dr

E Randolph St

Daley Bicentennial Plaza

Butler Field
ute

7
1

S Lake Shore Dr

Lakefront Path

Lake Michigan

Hutchinson Field

Shedd Aquarium

MUSEUM CAMPUS

Adler Planetarium & Astronomy Museum

Solidarity Dr

Field Museum of Natural History

Burnham Park

Burnham Harbor

S Lynn White Dr

Downtown Chicago

**ADLER PLANETARIUM & ASTRONOMY
MUSEUM** Museum
(Map p136; ☎312-922-7827; www.adlerplanet
arium.org; 1300 S Lake Shore Dr; adult/child
$12/8; ☺9:30am-6pm Jun-Aug, 10am-4pm
Sep-May; 👶) Space enthusiasts will get a
big bang (pun!) out of the Adler. There
are public telescopes from which to view
the stars, 3D lectures where you can
learn about supernovas, and the Planet
Explorers exhibit where kids can 'launch'
a rocket.

Near North

FREE NAVY PIER Waterfront
(Map p136; ☎312-595-7437; www.navypier.com;
600 E Grand Ave; ☺10am-10pm, to midnight Fri
& Sat; 👶) Half-mile-long Navy Pier is Chicago's most-visited attraction, sporting a
150ft Ferris wheel (per ride $6), an IMAX
theater, a beer garden and gimmicky
chain restaurants. The fireworks displays
on summer Wednesdays (9:30pm) and
Saturdays (10:15pm) are a treat too.

RICHARD CUMMINS/LONELY PLANET IMAGES ©

Don't Miss Famous Loop Architecture

Ever since it presented the world with the first skyscraper, Chicago has thought big with its architecture and pushed the envelope of modern design. The Loop is a fantastic place to roam and gawk at these ambitious structures. The **Chicago Architecture Foundation** runs tours that discuss many of these buildings, including the following (Map p136):

○ **Chicago Board of Trade** A 1930 art deco gem with a small visitors center where you can learn about the traders at work. Or stay outside and check out the giant statue of Ceres, the goddess of agriculture, that tops the building.

○ **Rookery** The 1888 Rookery (pictured) looks fortress-like outside, but the inside of this office building is light and airy thanks to Frank Lloyd Wright's atrium overhaul. Pigeons used to roost here, hence the name.

○ **Monadnock Building** Architectural pilgrims get weak-kneed when they see the Monadnock Building, which is two buildings in one. The north is the older, traditional design from 1891 while the south is the newer, mod half from 1893. See the difference?

THINGS YOU NEED TO KNOW

Chicago Architecture Foundation (☎ 312-922-3432; www.architecture.org; 224 S Michigan Ave; tours $5-40); Chicago Board of Trade (141 W Jackson Blvd); Rookery (209 S LaSalle St); Monadnock Building (53 W Jackson Blvd)

The Chicago Children's Museum (p147) and gorgeous **Smith Museum of Stained Glass Windows** (Map p136; ☎ 312-595-5024; admission free; Festival Hall; ☼ 10am-10pm, to midnight Fri & Sat) are also on the pier, as are several boat-cruise operators. Try the **Shoreline water taxi** (Map p136; www.shorelinesightseeing.com; ☼ 10am-7pm late May–early Sep) for a fun ride to the Museum Campus (adult/child $7/4).

PETER PTSCHELINZEW/LONELY PLANET IMAGES ©

Don't Miss John Hancock Center

Get high in Chicago's third-tallest skyscraper. In many ways the view here surpasses the one at Willis Tower, as the Hancock is closer to the lake and a little further north. Those needing a city history lesson should ascend to the 94th-floor observatory and listen to the archaic audio tour that comes with admission. Those secure in their knowledge should shoot up to the 96th-floor Signature Lounge, where the view (pictured) is free if you buy a drink ($6 to $14).

THINGS YOU NEED TO KNOW

Map p136; ☎888-875-8439; www.hancockobservatory.com; 875 N Michigan Ave; observatory adult/child $15/10; ☺9am-11pm

MAGNIFICENT MILE   Street
(Map p136; www.themagnificentmile.com; N Michigan Ave) Spanning Michigan Ave between the river and Oak St, the Mag Mile is the much-touted upscale shopping strip, where Bloomingdales, Neiman's and Saks will lighten your wallet.

Lincoln Park

FREE LINCOLN PARK ZOO   Zoo
(☎312-742-2000; www.lpzoo.org; 2200 N Cannon Dr; ☺10am-4:30pm Nov-Mar, to 5pm Apr-Oct, to 6:30pm Sat & Sun Jun-Aug; 👪) It's a local family favorite, filled with gorillas,

lions, tigers and other exotic creatures in the shadow of downtown.

FREE LINCOLN PARK CONSERVATORY   Gardens
(☎312-742-7736; 2391 N Stockton Dr; ☺9am-5pm) Near the zoo's north entrance, the magnificent 1891 hothouse coaxes palms, ferns and orchids to flourish.

NORTH AVENUE BEACH   Beach
(1600 N Lake Shore Dr; 👪) Chicago's most popular and amenity-laden stretch. You can rent bikes, kayaks, volleyballs and

lounge chairs, as well as eat and drink at the party-orientated beach house.

CHICAGO HISTORY MUSEUM   Museum
(off Map p136; ☎312-642-4600; www.chicago history.org; 1601 N Clark St; adult/child $14/free; ◷9:30am-4:30pm Mon-Sat, noon-5pm Sun) Multimedia displays cover the history of the Windy City, from the Great Fire to 1968 Democratic Convention.

Lakeview

WRIGLEY FIELD   Stadium
(Map p125; www.cubs.com; 1060 W Addison St) The Chicago Cubs last won the World Series in 1908, but their fans still pack baseball's most charming stadium, which dates from 1914 and is one of America's most picture-perfect ballparks. For tickets, check the website for deals or try the box office two to three hours before game time. To get there take the CTA Red Line to Addison; it's 4.5 miles north of the Loop.

Hyde Park & South Side

MUSEUM OF SCIENCE & INDUSTRY   Museum
(☎773-684-1414; www.msichicago.org; 5700 S Lake Shore Dr; adult/child $15/10; ◷9:30am-5:30pm Jun-Aug, reduced Sep-May) This colossal play-palace will overstimulate the serenest of souls with its flashy exhibits. Highlights include a WWII German U-boat nestled in an underground display ($8 extra to tour it) and the 'Science Storms' exhibit with a mock tornado.

ROBIE HOUSE   Architecture
(☎708-848-1976; www.gowright.org; 5757 S Woodlawn Ave; adult/child $15/12; ◷11am-4pm Thu-Mon) Of the numerous buildings that Frank Lloyd Wright designed around Chicago, none is more famous or influential than Robie House. The resemblance of its horizontal lines to the flat landscape of the Midwestern prairie became known as the Prairie style. Inside are 174 stained-glass windows and doors, which you'll see on the hour-long tours.

Activities

Cycling

Riding along the 18.5-mile lakefront path is a fantastic way to see the city. Rental bikes cost roughly $10 per hour, or $35 per day.

Bike Chicago   Cycling
(Map p136; ☎888-245-3929; www.bikechicago. com; 239 E Randolph St; ◷6:30am-8pm Mon-Fri, from 8am Sat & Sun, closed Sat & Sun Nov-Mar) Multiple locations, including Millennium Park and Navy Pier.

Bobby's Bike Hike   Cycling
(Map p136; ☎312-915-0995; www. bobbysbikehike.com; 465 N McClurg Ct; ◷8:30am-7pm Jun-Aug, closed Dec-Feb) At the River East Docks' Ogden Slip.

Blues Fans' Pilgrimage

From 1957 to 1967, the humble building at 2120 S Michigan Ave was Chess Records, the seminal electric blues label. Muddy Waters, Howlin' Wolf and Bo Diddley cut tracks here, and paved the way for rock 'n' roll with their sick licks and amped-up sound. The studio is now called **Willie Dixon's Blues Heaven** (off Map p136; ☎312-808-1286; www.bluesheaven.com; 2120 S Michigan Ave; tours $10; ◷11am-4pm Mon-Fri, noon-2pm Sat), named for the bassist who wrote most of Chess's hits. Staff give tours that take in the reception area and main studio. Free blues concerts rock the side garden on summer Thursdays at 6pm. The building is near Chinatown, and about a mile south of the Museum Campus.

Tours

For DIY tours check out **Chicago Blues Tour** (www.downloadchicagotours.com/blues media) and **Chicago Movie Tour** (www. onscreenillinois.com).

FREE **CHICAGO GREETER** Walking tour (Map p136; ☎312-744-8000; www.chicago greeter.com) This outfit pairs you with a local city dweller who will take you on a personal tour customized by theme or neighborhood. Reserve seven business days in advance.

CHICAGO ARCHITECTURE FOUNDATION Boat tour, Walking tour (Map p136; ☎312-922-3432; www.architecture. org; 224 S Michigan Ave; tours $5-40) The gold-standard boat tours ($35) sail from Michigan Ave's river dock, while the popular Rise of the Skyscraper walking tours ($16) leave from the downtown address. There are also many more options.

Sleeping

Loop & Near North

HOTEL BURNHAM Hotel $$$
(Map p136; ☎312-782-1111; www.burnham hotel.com; 1 W Washington St; r from $189; P ⊖ ✳ @ 🛜) Housed in the Loop's landmark 1890s Reliance Building (precedent for the modern skyscraper), its super-slick decor woos architecture buffs. The bright, butter-colored rooms are furnished with mahogany writing desks and chaise lounges.

HOTEL FELIX Hotel $$
(Map p136; ☎312-447-3440; www.hotel felixchicago.com; 111 W Huron St; r $139-189; P ⊖ ✳ @ 🛜) Opened in 2009 in the Near North, the 225-room, 12-story Felix is downtown's first hotel to earn ecofriendly LEED certification. The earthtoned, mod-furnished rooms are small but efficiently and comfortably designed.

Left: Live jazz at the Green Mill (p149);
Below: Exhibits at the Adler Planetarium (p138)
(LEFT) CHARLES COOK/LONELY PLANET IMAGES ©; (BELOW) RICHARD CUMMINS/LONELY PLANET IMAGES ©

WIT Hotel **$$$**
(Map p136; 312-467-0200; www.thewithotel.com; 201 N State St; r from $229;) Viewtastic rooms, a rooftop bar and an on-site movie theater draw holidaying hipsters and business travelers to the design-savvy, green-glass Wit.

Lakeview & Wicker Park/ Bucktown

WILLOWS HOTEL Hotel **$$**
(773-528-8400; www.willowshotelchicago.com; 555 W Surf St; r incl breakfast $169-229;) Small and stylish, the Willows wins an architectural gold star. The chic little lobby provides a swell refuge of overstuffed chairs by the fireplace, while the 55 rooms, done up in shades of peach, cream and soft green, evoke a 19th-century French countryside feel.

WICKER PARK INN B&B **$$**
(773-486-2743; www.wickerparkinn.com; 1329 N Wicker Park Ave; r incl breakfast $149-199;) This classic brick row house is steps away from Chicago's most rockin' bar-restaurant scene. The sunny rooms aren't huge, but all have hardwood floors, soothing pastel colors and small desk spaces.

LONGMAN & EAGLE Inn **$$**
(773-276-7110; www.longmanandeagle.com; 2657 N Kedzie Ave; r $75-200;) Check in at the Michelin-starred gastropub downstairs, then head to your wood-floored, vintage-stylish accommodation on the floor above. The six rooms aren't particularly soundproofed, but after using your whiskey tokens in the bar, you probably won't care.

Detour:
Oak Park

Located 10 miles west of the Loop and easily reached via CTA train, Oak Park has spawned two famous sons: novelist Ernest Hemingway was born here, and architect Frank Lloyd Wright lived and worked here from 1889 to 1909.

During Wright's 20 years in Oak Park, he designed many houses. Stop at the **visitors center** (✆888-625-7275; www.visitoakpark.com; 158 N Forest Ave; ⏰10am-5pm) and buy an architectural site map ($4) that gives their locations. To actually get inside a Wright-designed dwelling, you'll need to visit the **Frank Lloyd Wright Home & Studio** (✆708-848-1976; www.gowright.org; 951 Chicago Ave; adult/child $15/12; ⏰11am-4pm). Tour frequency varies, from every 20 minutes on summer weekends to every hour or so in winter. The Studio also offers guided neighborhood walking tours, as well as a self-guided audio version.

Despite Hemingway calling Oak Park a 'village of wide lawns and narrow minds,' the town still pays homage to him at the **Ernest Hemingway Museum** (✆708-848-2222; www.ehfop.org; 200 N Oak Park Ave; adult/child $10/8; ⏰1-5pm Sun-Fri, 10am-5pm Sat). Admission includes access to **Hemingway's birthplace** (339 N Oak Park Ave) across the street.

From downtown Chicago, take the CTA Green Line to its terminus at the Harlem stop, which drops you about four blocks from the visitors center. The train traverses some bleak neighborhoods before emerging into Oak Park's wide-lawn splendor.

Eating

The Loop & South Loop

GAGE   Pub $$$
(Map p136; ✆312-372-4243; www.thegage chicago.com; 24 S Michigan Ave; mains $16-32; ⏰11am-11pm, to midnight Fri) This gastropub dishes up Irish-tinged grub with a fanciful twist, such as Guinness-battered fish and chips, and fries smothered in curry gravy.

PIZZERIA UNO   Pizza $$
(Map p136; www.unos.com; 29 E Ohio St) One of Chicago's great culinary gifts to the world, the deep-dish pizza has been served with panache since its inception here in 1943.

LOU MITCHELL'S   Breakfast $
(www.loumitchellsrestaurant.com; 565 W Jackson Blvd; mains $6-11; ⏰5:30am-3pm Mon-Sat, 7am-3pm Sun) A relic of Route 66, Lou's old-school waitresses deliver double-yoked eggs and thick-cut French toast just west of the Loop by Union Station.

CAFECITO   Cuban $
(Map p136; www.cafecitochicago.com; 26 E Congress Pkwy; sandwiches $4-6; ⏰6am-9pm Mon-Fri, 10am-6pm Sat & Sun; 🛜) Cafecito serves killer Cuban sandwiches layered with citrus-garlic-marinated roasted pork and ham.

Near North

This is where you'll find Chicago's mother lode of restaurants.

🍃FRONTERA GRILL   Mexican $$$
(Map p136; ✆312-661-1434; www.rickbayless. com; 445 N Clark St; mains $18-30; ⏰lunch Tue-Fri, dinner Tue-Sat, brunch Sat) Celebrated chef Rick Bayless uses seasonal, sustainable ingredients for his jump-off-the-tongue Mexican creations. Sister restaurant **Topolobampo**, in an adjoining room, is sleeker and pricier, with similar hours.

XOCO — Mexican $$

(Map p136; www.rickbayless.com; 449 N Clark St; mains $8-13; ⏰8am-9pm Tue-Thu, 8am-10pm Fri & Sat) Next door to Frontera Grill, crunch into warm *churros* (spiraled dough fritters) for breakfast, meaty *tortas* (sandwiches) for lunch and rich *caldos* (soups) for dinner at Rick Bayless' Mexican street-food joint.

BILLY GOAT TAVERN — Burgers $

(Map p136; www.billygoattavern.com; lower level, 430 N Michigan Ave; burgers $4-6; ⏰6am-2am Mon-Fri, 10am-2am Sat & Sun) Order a 'cheezborger' and Schlitz, then look around at the newspapered walls to get the scoop on infamous local stories.

Lincoln Park & Old Town

Halsted, Lincoln and Clark Sts are the main veins teeming with restaurants and bars.

ALINEA — New American $$$

(☎312-867-0110; www.alinea-restaurant.com; 1723 N Halsted St; multicourse tastings $150-225; ⏰5:30-9:30pm Wed-Sun) Superstar chef Grant Achatz is the guy behind Alinea's

'molecular gastronomy.' If you secure a coveted reservation, prepare for roughly 12 to 24 courses of mind-bending, space-age cuisine.

Lakeview & Wrigleyville

Clark, Halsted, Belmont and Southport are fertile streets.

CRISP — Asian $

(www.crisponline.com; 2940 N Broadway; mains $7-12; ⏰11:30am-9pm Tue-Thu & Sun, to10:30pm Fri & Sat) Music pours from the stereo, and cheap, delicious Korean fusions arrive from the kitchen at this cheerful cafe.

MIA FRANCESCA — Italian $$

(☎773-281-3310; www.miafrancesca.com; 3311 N Clark St; mains $13-27; ⏰5-10pm Sun-Thu, to 11pm Fri & Sat) Local chain Mia's buzzes with regulars who come for the trattoria's Italian standards.

Andersonville & Uptown

For 'Little Saigon' take the CTA Red Line to Argyle. For the European cafes in Andersonville, go one stop further to Berwyn.

The Chicago River

145

If You Like...
Chicago Pizza

If you like the classic deep-dished decadence served up at Pizzeria Uno (p144), don't miss these other places, all of which have their own die-hard fan base. All are open from 11am to 10pm or so daily, and a large pizza will set you back on average around $20.

1 GINO'S EAST
(Map p136; www.ginoseast.com; 162 E Superior St) The classic stuffed cheese-and-sausage pie oozes cheese over its crispy cornmeal crust. Write on the walls while you wait for your pie.

2 LOU MALNATI'S
(Map p136; www.loumalnatis.com; 439 N Wells St) One of the original deep-dish pizza makers, famous for its 'buttercrust' pizzas.

3 GIORDANO'S
(Map p136; www.giordanos.com; 730 N Rush St) Perfectly tangy tomato sauce. For a slice of heaven, try the stuffed pizza with sausage, mushroom, green pepper and onions.

4 PIZANO'S
(Map p136; www.pizanoschicago.com; 864 N State St) Oprah's favorite Chicago pizza; also has great thin-crust pies for those not yet won over to deep-dish.

HOPLEAF European $$
(☏773-334-9851; www.hopleaf.com; 5148 N Clark St; mains $10-17; ⏱5pm-11pm Mon-Thu, to midnight Fri & Sat, 4-10pm Sun) A cozy, European-style tavern, Hopleaf draws crowds for its Montréal-style smoked brisket, house-specialty *frites*, ale-soaked mussels and 200 types of brew.

BA LE BAKERY Vietnamese $
(☏773-561-4424; 5016 N Broadway; sandwiches $3-5; ⏱7:30am-8pm) Ba Le serves Saigon-style *banh mi* sandwiches, with steamed pork, shrimp cakes or meatballs on fresh baguettes made right here.

Wicker Park, Bucktown & Ukrainian Village

Trendy restaurants open almost every day in these 'hoods.

HANDLEBAR BAR & GRILL International $$
(☏773-384-9546; www.handlebarchicago.com; 2311 W North Ave; mains $9-14; ⏱10am-midnight Mon-Thu, to 2am Fri & Sat, to 11pm Sun; ▨) Local cyclists congregate around the eclectic, vegetarian-friendly menu (ie West African groundnut stew) and summertime patio to quaff from the well-curated beer list.

BIG STAR TAQUERIA Mexican $
(www.bigstarchicago.com; 1531 N Damen Ave; tacos $3-4; ⏱11:30am-2am) This honky-tonk gets packed, but damn, the tacos are worth the wait. Cash only.

Logan Square & Humboldt Park

Several eats and drinks ring the intersection of Milwaukee, Logan and Kedzie Blvds.

HOT DOUG'S American $
(☏773-279-9550; www.hotdougs.com; 3324 N California Ave; mains $3-8; ⏱10:30am-4pm Mon-Sat) Doug's the man to fulfill all your hot-dog fantasies. He serves multiple dog styles (Polish, bratwursts, Chicago) cooked multiple dog ways (char-grilled, deep-fried, steamed). Doug also makes gourmet 'haute dogs,' such as blue-cheese pork with cherry cream sauce. It's sublime, but a heck of a haul unless you're traveling by car. Cash only.

Near West Side & Pilsen

Greektown extends along S Halsted St (take the Blue Line to UIC-Halsted), and the Mexican Pilsen enclave centers around W 18th St (take the Pink Line to 18th). The West Loop holds several stylish eateries along Randolph and Fulton Market Sts.

Chicago for Children

Chicago is a kid's kind of town. **Time Out Chicago Kids** (www.timeoutchicagokids.com) and **Chicago Parent** (www.chicagoparent.com) are indispensible resources. Top choices for toddlin' times include:

○ **Chicago Children's Museum** (Map p136; ☎312-527-1000; www.chicagochildrensmuseum.org; 700 E Grand Ave; admission $12, free Thu evening; ⊙10am-5pm, to 8pm Thu) Climb, dig and splash in this educational playland on Navy Pier; follow with an expedition down the carnival-like wharf itself, including spins on the Ferris wheel and carousel.

○ **Chicago Children's Theater** (☎773-227-0180; www.chicagochildrenstheatre.org) See a show by one the best kids' theater troupes in the country. Performances take place at venues around town.

○ **North Avenue Beach** (p140) Pint-sized waves, soft sand, lifeguards, snack bar and bathrooms.

○ **Lincoln Park Zoo** (p140) The African exhibit and the Farm-in-the-Zoo are always young-crowd pleasers.

○ **Museum of Science & Industry** (p141) A huge interactive museum.

NEXT Eclectic $$$
(☎312-226-0858; www.nextrestaurant.com; 953 W Fulton Market; multicourse meal avg $100; ⊙5:30-9:30pm Wed-Sun) Grant Achatz's West Loop restaurant, which opened in 2011, is the hottest ticket in town. It started by serving an eight-course French meal from 1906 Paris, but every three months the whole thing changes: new era, new menu, new decor.

PUBLICAN American $$$
(Map p136; ☎312-733-9555; www.thepublicanrestaurant.com; 837 W Fulton Market; mains $16-30; ⊙3:30-10:30pm Mon-Thu, to 11:30pm Fri & Sat, 10am-2pm & 5-10pm Sun) Set up like a swanky beer hall, Publican specializes in oysters, hams and fine suds – all from small family farms and microbrewers.

Exhibits at the
Chicago Children's Museum
CHARLES COOK/LONELY PLANET IMAGES ©

Drinking

The Loop & Near North

SIGNATURE LOUNGE   Lounge
(Map p136; www.signatureroom.com; John Hancock Center, 875 N Michigan Ave; ☺from 11am) Take the elevator up to the 96th floor and order a drink while looking out over the city.

CLARK STREET ALE HOUSE   Bar
(Map p136; 742 N Clark St; ☺from 4pm) Midwestern microbrews are the main draw; order a three-beer sampler for $5.

INTELLIGENTSIA COFFEE   Cafe
(Map p136; www.intelligentsia.com; 53 E Randolph St; ☺from 6am Mon-Fri, 7am Sat & Sun) The local chain roasts its own beans and percolates strong stuff.

Old Town & Wrigleyville

OLD TOWN ALE HOUSE   Bar
(www.oldtownalehouse.net; 219 W North Ave; ☺from 8am Mon-Sat, from noon Sun) This unpretentious neighborhood favorite lets you mingle with beautiful people and grizzled regulars, seated pint by pint under the nude-politician paintings.

GINGERMAN TAVERN   Bar
(3740 N Clark St; ☺from 3pm Mon-Fri, from noon Sat & Sun) The pool tables, good beer selection and pierced-and-tattooed patrons make Gingerman wonderfully different from other Wrigleyville sports bars.

Wicker Park, Bucktown & Ukrainian Village

MAP ROOM   Pub
(www.maproom.com; 1949 N Hoyne Ave; ☺from 6:30am Mon-Fri, 7:30am Sat, 11am Sun; 🛜) At this map-and-globe-filled 'travelers' tavern' artsy types sip coffee by day and suds from the 200-strong beer list by night.

DANNY'S   Bar
(1951 W Dickens Ave) Danny's comfortably dim and dog-eared ambience is perfect for conversations over a pint. A poetry-reading series and occasional DJs add to the scruffy artiness.

West Loop

AVIARY   Cocktail Bar
(www.twitter.com/@aviarycocktails; 955 W Fulton Market; ☺from 6pm Wed-Sun) The lounge's bar shakes and stirs one-of-kind drinks such as Buttered Popcorn (tastes as advertised); they cost around $16 each.

 Entertainment

For same-day theater seats at half-price, try **Hot Tix** (www.hottix.org). You can buy them online, or in person at booths in the **Chicago Tourism Center** (Map p136; 72 E Randolph St) and **Water Works Visitor Center** (Map p136; 163 E Pearson St).

Check the **Reader** (www.chicagoreader.com)

Behind the bar at Buddy Guy's Legends

and **Time Out Chicago** (www.timeoutchicago. com) for listings.

Dreamboat old theaters that host various touring shows cluster at State and Randolph Sts. **Broadway in Chicago** (☎800-775-2000; www. broadwayinchicago.com) handles tickets for most.

Live Music, Comedy & Theatre

BUDDY GUY'S LEGENDS   Blues
(Map p136; www.buddyguys.com; 700 S Wabash Ave) Top local and national acts wail on the stage of local icon Buddy Guy. The man himself usually plugs in his axe in January.

SECOND CITY   Comedy
(Off Map p136; ☎312-337-3992; www. secondcity.com; 1616 N Wells St) It's the cream of the crop, where Bill Murray, Stephen Colbert, Tina Fey and many more honed their sharp, biting wits. Bargain: turn up after the evening's last show (Friday excluded), and watch the comics improv a performance for free.

STEPPENWOLF THEATRE   Theater
(☎312-335-1650; www.steppenwolf.org; 1650 N Halsted St) Drama club of Malkovich, Sinise and other Hollywood stars; 2 miles north of the Loop in Lincoln Park.

Clubs

Clubs in the Near North and West Loop tend to be cavernous and luxurious (with dress codes). Clubs in Wicker Park-Ukrainian Village are usually more casual.

LATE BAR   Club
(www.latebarchicago.com; 3534 W Belmont Ave; ☺Tue-Sat) Owned by a couple of DJs, Late Bar's weird, new wave vibe draws fans of all stripes. It's off the beaten path in a forlorn stretch of Logan Sq, though easily reachable via the Blue Line train to Belmont.

If You Like...
Live Music

If you like blues, hit Buddy Guy's Legends, then check out some of these other venerable spot. Blues and jazz have deep roots in Chicago, and indie-rock clubs slouch on almost every corner. Cover charges range from $5 to $20.

1 KINGSTON MINES
(www.kingstonmines.com; 2548 N Halsted St) Two stages, seven nights a week, ensure somebody's always on. It's noisy, hot, sweaty, crowded and conveniently located in Lincoln Park.

2 GREEN MILL
(www.greenmilljazz.com; 4802 N Broadway) The timeless Green Mill earned its notoriety as Al Capone's favorite speakeasy (the tunnels where he hid the booze are still underneath the bar), and you can feel his ghost urging you on to another martini. Local and national artists perform six nights per week; Sundays are for the nationally acclaimed poetry slam.

3 HIDEOUT
(www.hideoutchicago.com; 1354 W Wabansia Ave) Hidden behind a factory at the edge of Bucktown, this two-room lodge of indie rock and alt-country is well worth seeking out. The owners have nursed an outsider, underground vibe, and the place feels like the downstairs of your grandma's rumpus room. Music and other events (bingo, literary readings etc) take place nightly.

Performing Arts

FREE GRANT PARK ORCHESTRA   Classical Music
(Map p136; ☎312-742-7638; www.grantpark musicfestival.com) The beloved group puts on free classical concerts in Millennium Park throughout the summer.

SYMPHONY CENTER   Classical Music
(Map p136; ☎312-294-3000; www.cso.org; 220 S Michigan Ave) The Chicago Symphony Orchestra plays in the Daniel Burnham–designed hall.

CIVIC OPERA HOUSE
Opera

(Map p136; ☎312-332-2244; www.lyricopera.org; 20 N Wacker Dr) The renowned Lyric Opera of Chicago hits high Cs in this chandeliered venue.

HUBBARD STREET DANCE CHICAGO
Dance

(☎312-850-9744; www.hubbardstreetdance.com) Chicago's preeminent dance company performs at the **Harris Theater for Music and Dance** (Map p136; www.harristheaterchicago.org; 205 E Randolph St).

Shopping

The shoppers' siren song emanates from the N Michigan Ave, along the Magnificent Mile. **Water Tower Place** (Map p136; 835 N Michigan Ave) is among the large vertical malls here.

CHICAGO ARCHITECTURE FOUNDATION SHOP
Souvenirs

(Map p136; www.architecture.org/shop; 224 S Michigan Ave) Skyline posters, Frank Lloyd Wright note cards, skyscraper models and more for those with an edifice complex.

STRANGE CARGO
Clothing

(www.strangecargo.com; 3448 N Clark St) The retro store stocks kitschy iron-on T-shirts featuring Ditka, Obama and other renowned Chicagoans.

JAZZ RECORD MART
Music

(Map p136; www.jazzmart.com; 27 E Illinois St) One-stop shop for Chicago jazz and blues CDs and vinyl.

Information

Tourist Information

The Chicago Office of Tourism (☎312-744-2400; www.explorechicago.org) operates two well-stocked visitors centers, each with a staffed information desk, ticket outlet, cafe and free wi-fi. Check the website for excellent free neighborhood maps and guides. Also runs a Twitter feed of free events each day at twitter.com/explorechicago.

Chicago Cultural Center Visitors Center (77 E Randolph St; ☺8am-7pm Mon-Thu, 8am-6pm Fri, 9am-6pm Sat, 10am-6pm Sun)

Water Works Visitors Center (163 E Pearson St; ☺8am-7pm Mon-Thu, 8am-6pm Fri, 10am-6pm Sat, 10am-4pm Sun)

BP Bridge, designed by Frank Gehry, Millennium Park (p134)

RICK GERHARTER/LONELY PLANET IMAGES ©

Detour:
Galena

Galena draws hordes of Chicagoans to its perfectly preserved, Civil War–era streets. It spreads across wooded hillsides near the Mississippi River, amid rolling, barn-dotted farmland. Red-brick mansions in Greek Revival, Gothic Revival and Queen Anne styles – left over from Galena's heyday in the mid-1800s, when local lead mines made it rich – line the streets. Throw in cool kayak trips, foodie farm tours and winding backroad drives, and you've got a lovely, slow-paced getaway.

The **visitors center** (✆877-464-2536; www.galena.org; 101 Bouthillier St; ☉9am-5pm) in the 1857 train depot is a good place to start. Get a map, leave your car in the lot ($5 per day) and explore on foot.

Elegant old Main St curves around the hillside and the historic heart of town. Among numerous sights is the **Ulysses S Grant Home** (✆815-777-3310; www. granthome.com; 500 Bouthillier St; adult/child $4/2; ☉9am-4:45pm Wed-Sun Apr-Oct, reduced hours Nov-Mar), where Grant lived until he became the country's 18th president.

Head to **Fever River Outfitters** (✆815-776-9425; www.feverriveroutfitters.com; 525 S Main St; ☉10am-5pm, closed Tue-Thu early Sep-late May), which rents canoes, kayaks, stand up paddleboards, bicycles and snowshoes. It also offers guided tours, such as two-hour kayak trips ($45 per person, equipment included) on the Mississippi River's backwaters.

Galena brims with quilt-laden B&Bs, like the charming **DeSoto House Hotel** (✆815-777-0090; www.desotohouse.com; 230 S Main St; r $128-200; ❄✳🛜), which dates from 1855.

Galena is 165 miles west of Chicago (a three-hour drive), and is best reached with your own wheels.

ℹ Getting There & Around

To/From the Airport

CHICAGO MIDWAY AIRPORT 11 miles southwest of the Loop, connected via the CTA Orange Line ($2.25). Other options include shuttles (per person $24) and cabs ($30 to $40).

O'HARE INTERNATIONAL AIRPORT 17 miles northwest of the Loop. The cheapest, and often the quickest, way to/from O'Hare is by the CTA Blue Line ($2.25), but the station is a long walk from the flight terminals. Airport Express shuttles run between the airport and downtown hotels (per person $29). Cabs to/from downtown cost about $45.

Public Transportation

The Chicago Transit Authority (CTA; www. transitchicago.com) operates the city's buses and the elevated/subway train system (aka the El). Standard fare is $2.25 (bus $2) with a Transit Card, sold from vending machines at train stations. Day passes (one-/three-day pass $5.75/14) can be purchased at airports and various drug stores and currency exchanges.

Taxi

Recommended companies:

Flash Cab (✆773-561-1444)

Yellow Cab (✆312-829-4222)

Train

Chicago's classic Union Station (Map p136; www. chicagounionstation.com; 210 S Canal St) is the hub for Amtrak's (✆800-872-7245; www.amtrak. com) national and regional service.

Boston & New England

New England may look small on a map, but don't let that fool you. From big-city Boston – the cradle of the American experiment – to the rugged shores of Maine, New England packs a dazzling array of attractions. Historical sites, world-class restaurants and age-old fishing villages are all part of the vibrant mix.

On the coast you'll find sandy beaches begging a dip and pristine harbor towns sprinkled with old mansions, wide lawns and quaint antique shops and galleries. The joys here are simple but amply rewarding – from cracking open a lobster at a weathered seafood shack by the water, to hiking a coastal trail past tranquil ponds and along seacliffs to magnificent views. And if you're lucky enough to be here in autumn, you'll be rewarded with the most brilliant fall foliage you'll ever see.

Frenchman Bay, Bar Harbor (p195), Maine
PETER PTSCHELINZEW/LONELY PLANET IMAGES ©

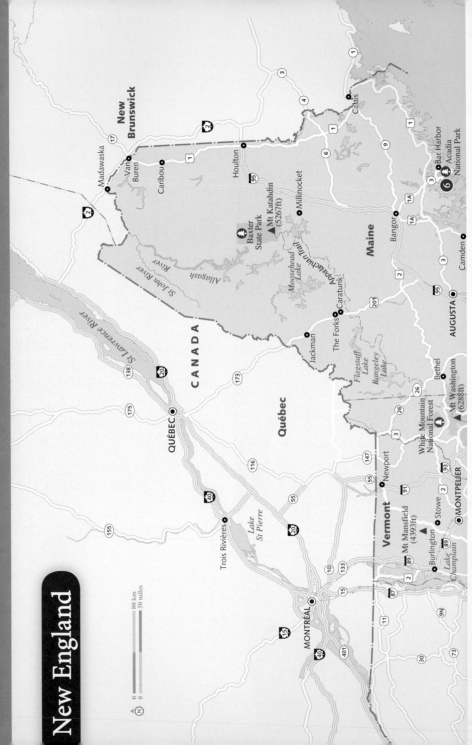

New England

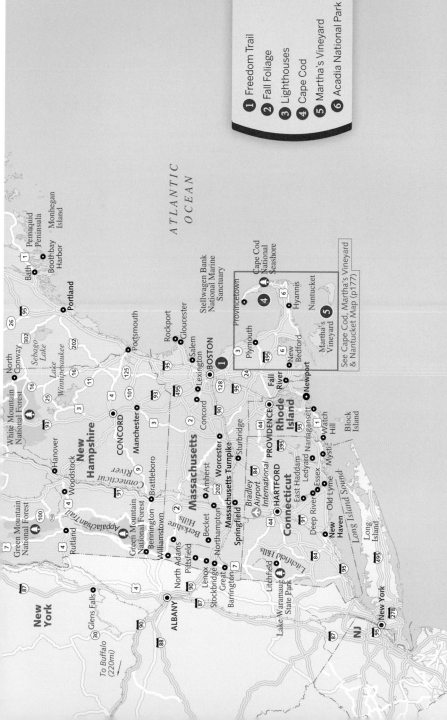

1 Freedom Trail
2 Fall Foliage
3 Lighthouses
4 Cape Cod
5 Martha's Vineyard
6 Acadia National Park

ATLANTIC OCEAN

New York

To Buffalo (220mi)

Glens Falls

ALBANY

Vermont

Green Mountain National Forest

Rutland

Appalachian Trail

Bennington
Williamstown
Green Mountain National Forest

North Adams
Pittsfield
Lenox
Stockbridge
Great Barrington

Berkshire Hills

Becket
Northampton
Amherst

Massachusetts

Springfield
Massachusetts Turnpike

Sturbridge
Worcester

Concord

Lexington
BOSTON 1

Salem
Gloucester
Rockport

Portsmouth

New Hampshire

CONCORD
Manchester

Hanover
Woodstock

Connecticut River

Brattleboro

White Mountain National Forest

North Conway

Lake Winnipesaukee
Sebago Lake

Portland

Boothbay Harbor
Bath
Pemaquid Peninsula
Monhegan Island

Stellwagen Bank National Marine Sanctuary

Provincetown
4
Cape Cod National Seashore

Plymouth
Hyannis
Nantucket

New Bedford
Martha's Vineyard 5

See Cape Cod, Martha's Vineyard & Nantucket Map (p177)

Fall River

Newport
Watch Hill
Block Island

Rhode Island
PROVIDENCE
Narragansett

Mystic
Connecticut
HARTFORD
Bradley International Airport
East Haddam
Ledyard
Essex
Deep River
Old Lyme
New Haven

Litchfield Hills
Litchfield
Lake Waramaug State Park

Long Island Sound
Long Island

New York
New York
NJ

Boston & New England's Highlights

① Freedom Trail

Following in the footsteps of Colonial rebel rousers, the Freedom Trail takes in pivotal sights giving an insight into the birth of the USA. While the main landmarks are easy to find, an insider's perspective will help you break from the crowds and dig deeper.

Need to Know

LOCATION Boston Common to Bunker Hill **BEST PHOTO OP** Paul Revere statue and Old North Church **BEST LUNCH SPOT** North End Italian cafes **For more, see p168.**

Freedom Trail Don't Miss List

BY GRETCHEN GROZIER,
BOSTON BY FOOT TOUR LEADER

1 STATE HOUSE

A lot of people see the outside of the State House (below left; p165), but never enter. Inside it's magnificent, with artwork and historic treasures. The Civil War collection includes the tattered flag of the 54th Massachusetts, the African American regiment featured in the movie *Glory*. Don't miss the Robert Gould Shaw Memorial, opposite the State House, honoring the regiment.

2 KING'S CHAPEL

Colonists were not thrilled with the building of the king's Anglican church on the edge of the Puritan cemetery (at the corner of Tremont and School Sts), so the exterior was purposely built plain. But inside it's very elaborate with a wine-glass pulpit, a fantastic organ and a canopy over the royal governor's pew. Paul Revere called the church bell, which he cast, 'the sweetest bell I ever made.'

3 FANEUIL HALL

Most people just walk through the ground-floor shops at Faneuil Hall (p168) and wonder what the building is. You have to go upstairs. Colonial town meetings, including pivotal debates leading to the American Revolution, were held on the 2nd floor. The first utterance of speech about separating from England occurred here. In later years, abolitionists took to the floor and JFK made speeches here. Even today, Faneuil Hall is used for the same purpose for which it was built in 1742.

4 OLD NORTH CHURCH

History students offer behind-the-scenes tours of the church (above left; p168) during summer for a fee (it's worth it), going down into the crypt, where 1000 people are buried, and up into the bell tower. The eight bells are pealed so mathematically that the bell-ringers guild is staffed by students from the Massachusetts Institute of Technology.

5 USS CONSTITUTION

The oldest commissioned warship (far left; p168) in the US Navy is definitely worth a visit. It's a great stop for kids. You can go on the ship and see the cannon, then go into the museum, which has fake swords, props and sailor uniforms that kids can dress up in.

Fall Foliage

From late September to mid-October, New England becomes a fiery blaze of color, with leaves of red, orange, yellow and gold covering the rolling forests and hillsides. A well-planned road trip beneath crisp autumn skies is the best way to take in the cinematic beauty – stopping for fresh cranberries, hot apple cider and other goodies at orchards and farmers markets along the way. Autumn leaves, Vermont (p188)

2

3 Lighthouses

New England is graced with scores of highly photogenic lighthouses. Wild and rugged coasts, idyllic beaches and serene islands form the backdrop to these historic guideposts, some of which date back to the late 1700s. With more than 60 lighthouses, Maine has the lion's share. You can spy one of its most famous variants, the 1827 Pemaquid Point Light, on the back of the Maine quarter. Portland Head Light (p190), Maine

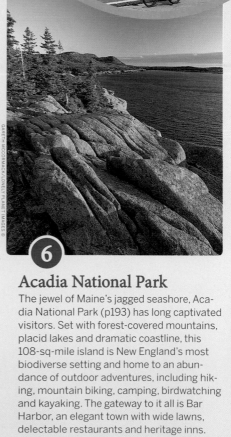

Cape Cod

4

From clambering across the National Seashore (p181) dunes, cycling the Cape Cod Rail Trail (p178) or eating oysters at Wellfleet Harbor (p180), this sandy peninsula serves up a bounty of local flavor. Fringed with 400 miles of sparkling shoreline, the Cape (p176) rates as New England's top beach destination. When you've had your fill of sun and sand, get out and explore artist enclaves, take a cruise or join the free-spirited street scene in Provincetown (right; p181).

5

Martha's Vineyard

New England's biggest island (p186) is also one of its premier vacation destinations, with picture-perfect harbor towns, decadent restaurants and wildlife-filled reserves. Days can be spent beachcombing, wave-frolicking, bike riding, gallery hopping and exploring the island's fascinating maritime history. Kayaking, windsurfing and drinking the fine quaffs at the Vineyard's own vineyard are other fine ways to spend a sun-drenched afternoon.

6

Acadia National Park

The jewel of Maine's jagged seashore, Acadia National Park (p193) has long captivated visitors. Set with forest-covered mountains, placid lakes and dramatic coastline, this 108-sq-mile island is New England's most biodiverse setting and home to an abundance of outdoor adventures, including hiking, mountain biking, camping, birdwatching and kayaking. The gateway to it all is Bar Harbor, an elegant town with wide lawns, delectable restaurants and heritage inns.

GARETH MCCORMACK/LONELY PLANET IMAGES ©

Boston & New England's Best...

Lobster

o **Brewster Fish House** (p180) A humble spot serving some of the Cape's best seafood and lobster bisque.

o **Lobster Pot** (p183) Fantastic place in Provincetown for chowing on lobster.

o **Portland Lobster Co** (p192) A harborside shack serving up some of Maine's finest produce.

o **Trenton Bridge Lobster Pound** (p195) Pull up a picnic table and crack open a lobster at this buzzing eatery near Acadia National Park.

Historic Sites

o **Beacon Hill** (p165) This leafy Boston neighborhood, complete with gold-domed 18th-century State House, is packed with history.

o **North End** (p168) Littered with picturesque narrow streets and colonial buildings.

o **Strawbery Banke Museum** (p188) Portsmouth's sprawling living-history museum is a great spot to delve into the past.

o **Edgartown** (p186) Grand homes (some dating back to the 1600s) line the streets of this maritime-rich town on Martha's Vineyard.

Coastal Resorts

o **Provincetown** (p181) Heritage inns and a lively atmosphere at the Cape's northern tip.

o **Nantucket** (p184) Picturesque and landmarked village with gorgeous beaches nearby.

o **Oak Bluffs** (p186) Sunny summertime fun at the gateway to Martha's Vineyard.

o **Bar Harbor** (p195) A coastal gem in Maine with elegant homes and inns, good restaurants and plenty of waterside adventures.

Left: Coopering demonstration, Strawbery Banke Museum (p188);
Above: Kayakers near a covered bridge, Vermont (p188)

Need to Know

Outdoor Activities

- **Hiking** (p194) Hike and bike the trails of the awe-inspiring Acadia National Park.

- **Cycling** (p178) Cycle the scenic 22-mile Cape Cod Rail Trail.

- **Whale watching** (p182) Go eye-to-eye with giants of the deep on a whale-watching cruise from Provincetown.

- **Kayaking** (p195) Hop in a kayak and paddle around the islands of Frenchman Bay, near Bar Harbor.

ADVANCE PLANNING

- **Six months before** Reserve accommodation if traveling during busy times, including summer and peak leaf-season in autumn.

- **One month before** Browse online for tickets to theater, sporting events and concerts.

- **One week before** Book walking tours, cruises and other activities.

RESOURCES

- **Discover New England** (www.discovernewengland.org) Official tourism site with info on destinations throughout New England.

- **Boston.com** (www.boston.com/travel/explorene) Listings of travel tips and itineraries.

- **Yankee** (www.yankeemagazine.com) Excellent general-interest site with classic things to see, destination profiles and events.

- **Visit New England.com** (www.visitnewengland.com) One of many online travel resources, with a comprehensive listing of hotels and attractions.

GETTING AROUND

- **Airport** Boston's Logan International Airport (BOS) is New England's main hub. From the airport, take the 'T' (subway) downtown (30 minutes).

- **Bike** Boston's bike-sharing scheme (www.thehubway.com) allows quick and inexpensive rides across the city.

- **Bus** Greyhound (www.greyhound.com) provides service between major towns.

- **Hire car** You'll need a car if you want to explore the region thoroughly, though in Boston it's easier to rely on public transit.

- **Train** Amtrak (www.amtrak.com) connects Boston with New York City.

BE FOREWARNED

- **Opening days** Some museums are closed on Monday.

- **Crowds** Traffic can be hellish during summer; if possible, avoid traveling on weekends to popular destinations like Cape Cod, Martha's Vineyard and Bar Harbor.

- **Cold** Prepare for brisk ocean temperatures, even during the height of summer. Come in winter and brace yourself for snow and icy winds.

Boston & New England Itineraries

*Stunning coastline, historic towns, outdoor adventure –
New England has all this and more. Its relatively compact size means you can cram a lot into a short trip and
take in more than a few of the region's many highlights.*

5 DAYS

BOSTON TO CAPE COD

A Captivating Threesome: City, Cape & Island

Spend a day exploring **(1) Boston**. Stroll through Boston Common, visit the historic sites of Beacon Hill and enjoy a first-rate meal in a North End trattoria.

On day two, rise early for the drive east. First stop: **(2) Sandwich**, Cape Cod's oldest village. Take in the historic center with its swan pond and colorful museums, then take a stroll along Sandy Neck Beach. Next, head to **(3) Brewster** for a lobster feast and a visit to the idyllic Nickerson State Park. Wander through **(4) Chatham** and have a splash on Lighthouse Beach then check out **(5) Wellfleet**, with its lovely beaches,

tony art galleries and famous oysters. In **(6) Provincetown**, book a whale-watching cruise, enjoy a seafood feast and take in the riotous cabaret scene.

On day four, head to Woods Hole for the vehicle ferry to **(7) Martha's Vineyard**. Check out the pretty cottages of **(8) Oak Bluffs**, take a scenic bike trail along the coast, get out on the water at **(9) Vineyard Haven**, explore historic Edgartown, and stroll among the birdlife-filled marshes and ponds of **(10) Felix Neck Wildlife Sanctuary**. From here, head back to the mainland for a final night in Boston.

BOSTON TO BAR HARBOR
Cruising Up the Coast

7 DAYS

Start in **(1) Boston**, taking in the scenic waterfront, heady Cambridge and the historic Freedom Trail walk. From here, go north to **(2) Salem**, rich in maritime history and the infamous site of the Witch Trials. The New Hampshire coast is tiny, but don't miss **(3) Portsmouth**, an old shipbuilding center with heritage homes, fog-filled evenings and a lively eating and drinking scene. Leaving Portsmouth, you'll quickly cross into Maine. Stop in the vibrant waterside city of **(4) Portland**. Explore the lamplit lanes of the Old Port, take in the art-gallery scene, and dine at one of the city's award-winning restaurants. Continue north to **(5) Boothbay**

Harbor for fresh-off-the-boat lobster and scenic cruises (or kayak paddles) out on the harbor. To get away from it all, take a boat out to **(6) Monhegan Island** for walks along the seacliffs and an overnight stay in an ocean-fronting guesthouse. Near trip's end, book a night at a historic B&B in **(7) Bar Harbor**. Rise early the next day to take in the natural splendor of inspiring **(8) Acadia National Park**. You can go for a hike up Cadillac Mountain, cycle along miles of former carriage roads and explore the surf-pounded beaches and dramatic cliffs of the island.

Man sitting near lobster buoys, Provincetown (p181)

Discover Boston & New England

BOSTON

One of America's oldest cities is also one of its youngest. A score of colleges and universities add a fresh face to Massachusetts' historic capital and feed a thriving arts and entertainment scene. But don't think for a minute that Boston is all about the literati. Grab a seat in the bleachers at Fenway Park and join the fanatical fans cheering on the Red Sox.

◉ Sights & Activities

Boston Common & Public Garden

BOSTON COMMON Park
(Map p166) The heart of Boston since 1634, the 50-acre common, bordered by Tremont, Beacon and Charles Sts, was the nation's first public park. In years past it was a pasture for cattle grazing, a staging ground for soldiers of the American Revolution and the site of chastising pillory-and-stocks for those who dared defy Puritan mores. These days, it's a gloriously carefree scene, especially at the **Frog Pond**, where waders cool off on hot summer days and ice-skaters frolic in winter.

PUBLIC GARDEN Gardens
(Map p166) Adjoining the Common, the 24-acre Public Garden provides an inviting oasis of bountiful flowers and shady trees. Its centerpiece, a tranquil lagoon with old-fashioned pedal-powered **Swan Boats**, has been delighting children for generations.

Baseball player, Fenway Park (p175), Boston
LOU JONES/LONELY PLANET IMAGES ©

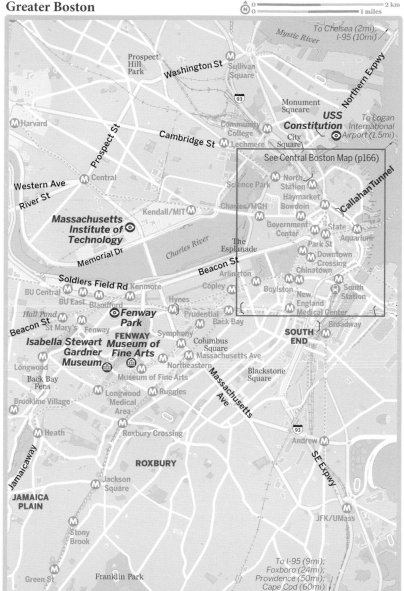

Beacon Hill & Downtown

Rising above Boston Common is Beacon Hill, Boston's most historic and affluent neighborhood.

FREE **STATE HOUSE** Historic Building
(Map p166; 617-727-3676; Beacon St, at Park St; 8am-5pm Mon-Fri) Crowning Beacon Hill is the golden-domed capitol building, the seat of Massachusetts' government

Central Boston

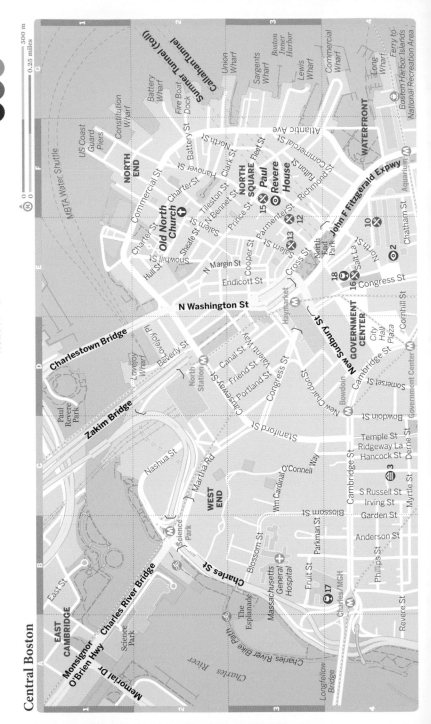

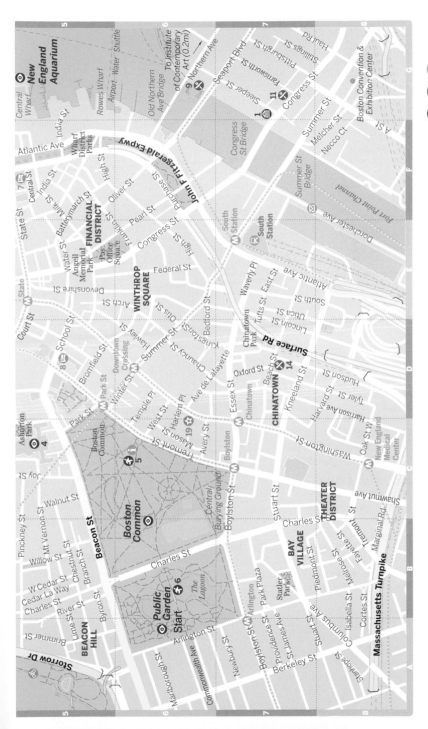

New England
Aquarium

Central
Wharf

To Institute
of Contemporary
Art (0.2mi)

Northern Ave

Seaport Blvd

Sleeper St

Farnsworth St

Pittsburgh St

Stillings St

Haul Rd

Congress St

Boston Convention &
Exhibition Center

A St

Summer St

Melcher St

Necco Ct

Rowes Wharf

Airport Water Shuttle

Old Northern
Ave Bridge

Congress
St Bridge

Summer St
Bridge

Fort Point Channel

Dorchester Ave

Atlantic Ave

India St

Wharf
District
Parks

High St

Oliver St

Purchase St

John Fitzgerald Expwy

Central St

Milk St

State St

Batterymarch St

FINANCIAL
DISTRICT

Pearl St

Congress St

High St

South
Station

South
Station

Atlantic Ave

East St

Waverly Pl

Water St

Angell Memorial Park

Post
Office
Square

Franklin St

Pearl St

Federal St

South St

Utica St

Lincoln St

Tufts St

Devonshire St

WINTHROP
SQUARE

Arch St

Otis St

Bedford St

Chinatown
Park

Surface Rd

Court St

State

School St

Bromfield St

Kingston St

Summer St

Hawley St

Downtown
Crossing

Chauncy St

Ave de Lafayette

Essex St

Oxford St

Beach St

CHINATOWN

Kneeland St

Harvard St

Hudson St

Tyler St

Harrison Ave

Washington St

New England
Medical
Center

Oak St W

Winter St

Temple Pl

West St

Hamlet Pl

Mason St

Avery St

Chinatown

Boylston

Park St

Boston
Common

Ashburton
Park

Joy St

Park St

Tremont St

Stuart St

Central
Burying Ground

Boylston St

Charles St

THEATER
DISTRICT

Shawmut Ave

Pinckney St

Mt Vernon St

Walnut St

Beacon St

Boston
Common

Charles St

BAY
VILLAGE

Tremont St

Fayette St

Melrose St

Marginal Rd

Massachusetts Turnpike

Willow St

W Cedar St

Chestnut St

Cedar La Way

Charles St

BEACON
HILL

River St

Byron St

Public
Garden

The
Lagoon

Arlington

Arlington St

Park Plaza

Statler
Park

Piedmont St

Stuart St

Isabella St

Cortes St

Columbus Ave

Stanhope St

Brimmer St

Lime St

Storrow Dr

Commonwealth Ave

Marlborough St

Newbury St

Boylston St

Providence St

St James St

Berkeley St

Boylston St

Arlington

167

Central Boston

since 1798. Volunteers lead free 40-minute **tours** from 10am to 3:30pm.

FANEUIL HALL Historic Site
(Map p166; Congress St) This landmark red-brick hall, topped with its famed grasshopper weathervane, has been a market and public meeting place since 1742. Today the hall, Quincy Market and North and South Market buildings make up the Faneuil Hall Marketplace chock-full of small shops and eateries.

MUSEUM OF AFRO-AMERICAN HISTORY Museum
(Map p166; www.afroammuseum.org; 46 Joy St; adult/child $5/3; ☺10am-4pm Mon-Sat) Illustrating the accomplishments of Boston's African American community, this museum includes the adjacent **African Meeting House**, where former slave Frederick Douglass recruited African American soldiers to fight in the Civil War.

North End & Charlestown

An old-world warren of narrow streets, the Italian North End offers visitors an irresistible mix of colorful period buildings and mouthwatering eateries.

PAUL REVERE HOUSE Historic Building
(Map p166; www.paulreverehouse.org; 19 North Sq; adult/child $3.50/1; ☺9:30am-5:15pm) The oldest house (1680) still standing in Boston is the former home of Paul Revere, a leader of the colonial militia, the Minutemen.

FREE **OLD NORTH CHURCH** Church
(Map p166; www.oldnorth.com; 193 Salem St; tours adult/child $8/5; ☺9am-6pm Jun-Oct, 9am-5pm Nov-May) It was at this church, built c 1723, that two lanterns were hung in the steeple on that pivotal night of April 18, 1775, signaling to a waiting Paul Revere that British forces were setting out by sea ('one if by land, two if by sea').

FREE **USS CONSTITUTION** Battleship
(Map p165; www.history.navy.mil/uss constitution; Charlestown Navy Yard; ☺10am-6pm Tue-Sun Apr-Oct, 10am-4pm Thu-Sun Nov-Mar; ♿) Clamber the decks of this legendary warship, built in 1797. Its oak-timbered hull is so thick that cannonballs literally bounced off it, earning it the nickname 'Old Ironsides.'

Back Bay

Extending west from Boston Common, this well-groomed neighborhood boasts graceful brownstone residences, grand edifices and the tony shopping mecca of Newbury St.

COPLEY SQUARE　　　　　Plaza
(Map p165) Here you'll find a cluster of handsome historic buildings, including the ornate French-Romanesque **Trinity Church** (www.trinitychurchboston.org; cnr Boylston & Clarendon Sts; adult/child $7/free; ⏰9am-5pm Mon-Sat, 1-6pm Sun). Across the street, the classic **Boston Public Library** (www.blp.org; 700 Boylston St; ⏰9am-9pm Mon-Thu, 9am-5pm Fri & Sat; 📶), you can pick up a self-guided tour brochure and wander around, noting gems like the murals by John Singer Sargent and sculpture by Augustus Saint-Gaudens.

Prudential Center Skywalk　　Viewpoint
(📞617-859-0648; 800 Boylston St; adult/child $12/8; ⏰10am-10pm) For a stunning 360-degree bird's-eye view of the city, head to this tower's 50th-floor observation deck.

Waterfront & Seaport District

Boston's waterfront offers an ever-growing list of attractions, all connected by the Harborwalk, a dedicated pedestrian path.

NEW ENGLAND AQUARIUM　　Aquarium
(Map p166; 📞617-973-5200; www.neaq.org; Central Wharf; adult/child $22/14; ⏰9am-5pm Mon-Fri, 9am-6pm Sat & Sun; ♿) Centering on a four-story tank teeming with sharks and colorful tropical fish, the New England Aquarium is a magnet for kids. Also popular are the aquarium's **whale-watching cruises** (adult/child $40/32; ⏰Apr-Oct), led by naturalists.

Chinatown, Theater District & South End

Compact and easy to stroll, Chinatown offers up enticing Asian eateries cheek-by-jowl, while the adjacent Theater District is clustered with performing-arts venues. The sprawling South End boasts one of America's largest concentrations of Victorian row houses, a burgeoning art scene and terrific neighborhood cafes.

Skyline over the Charles River, Boston

JEAN-PIERRE LESCOURRET/LONELY PLANET IMAGES ©

If You Like...
Art Museums

If you like Boston's celebrated Museum of Fine Arts (p170), it's well worth visiting these other captivating galleries.

1 INSTITUTE OF CONTEMPORARY ART
(off Map p166; www.icaboston.org; 100 Northern Ave; adult/child $15/free; ⏱10am-5pm Tue, Wed, Sat & Sun, to 9pm Thu & Fri) This dazzling museum snags rave exhibits by the likes of street artist Shepard Fairey. The building's striking cantilevered architecture defines modern, and its floor-to-ceiling glass walls pop with Boston's most dramatic harbor view. Admission is free after 5pm on Thursday.

2 ISABELLA STEWART GARDNER MUSEUM
(Map p165; www.gardnermuseum.org; 280 The Fenway; adult/child $12/free; ⏱11am-5pm Tue-Sun) Gardner assembled her vast collection – which includes Rembrandts and portraits by Bostonian John Singer Sargent – a century ago, and lived in the magnificent Venetian-style palazzo that houses it all. Seeing the mansion itself, with its garden courtyard, is worth the admission price alone.

Fenway & Kenmore Square

With world-class museums and America's oldest ballpark, the Fenway neighborhood is a destination in itself.

MUSEUM OF FINE ARTS   Museum
(MFA; Map p165; ☎617-267-9300; www.mfa.org; 465 Huntington Ave; adult/child $20/7.50; ⏱10am-4:45pm Sat-Tue, 10am-9:45pm Wed-Fri) One of the country's finest art museums just got better with the opening of its spectacular new Art of the Americas wing, whose 53 galleries showcase everything from pre-Columbian art to Paul Revere silver and Winslow Homer paintings. Admission is free after 4pm on Wednesdays.

Cambridge

On the north side of the Charles River lies politically progressive Cambridge, home to academic heavyweights Harvard University and Massachusetts Institute of Technology (MIT). Some 30,000 students make for a diverse, lively scene. Its central **Harvard Square** overflows with cafes, bookstores and street performers.

HARVARD UNIVERSITY   College Campus
Along Massachusetts Ave, opposite the Harvard T station (Map p165), lies the leafy campus of Harvard University. Dozens of Nobel laureates and eight US presidents are among its graduates – for other chewy tidbits join a free student-led campus tour at the **Harvard University Information Center** (☎617-495-1573; www.harvard.edu/visitors; 1350 Massachusetts Ave; ⏱1hr tours 10am, noon & 2pm Mon-Sat).

MASSACHUSETTS INSTITUTE OF TECHNOLOGY   College Campus
(MIT; Map p165) Nerds rule ever so proudly at America's foremost tech campus. Stop at the **MIT Information Center** (☎617-253-4795; www.mit.edu; 77 Massachusetts Ave; ⏱free 90min tours 11am & 3pm Mon-Fri) for the scoop on where to see campus art, including Henry Moore bronzes and cutting-edge architecture by the likes of Frank Gehry.

Tours

BOSTON DUCK TOURS   Adventure
(☎617-723-3825; www.bostonducktours.com; adult/child $32/22; ⏱9am-dusk mid-Mar–mid-Nov; 👶) Ridiculously popular tours using WWII amphibious vehicles that cruise the downtown streets before splashing into the Charles River. Tours leave from the Prudential Center and the Museum of Science.

FREEDOM TRAIL FOUNDATION   Walking
(Map p166; ☎617-357-8300; www.thefreedomtrail.org; adult/child $12/6; ⏱10:30am-5pm; 👶) Guides dressed in Colonial garb lead 90-minute walking tours of the Freedom Trail, departing from the visitor center at the Boston Common.

Boston for Children

Boston's small scale makes it easy for families to explore. A good place to start is the **Public Garden**, where you can paddle the lagoon in a Swan Boat. Across the street at the **Boston Common**, kids can cool their toes in the Frog Pond and romp on playground swings and jungle gyms.

Boston Children's Museum (Map p166; ☏ 617-426-6500; www.bostonchildrensmuseum.org; 300 Congress St; admission $12; ⏱ 10am-5pm Sat-Thu, 10am-9pm Fri) offers oodles of fun for the younger ones. Hits at the **New England Aquarium** include petting cool creatures at the touch pool, watching seals being fed and hopping aboard a whale-watching tour.

 Sleeping

OMNI PARKER HOUSE
Historic Hotel **$$$**

(Map p166; ☏ 617-227-8600; www.omniparkerhouse.com; 60 School St; r $219-419; ❄ 🛜 👪)
If the walls could talk, this historic hotel overlooking the Freedom Trail would fill volumes. Employees have included Malcolm X and Ho Chi Minh, the guest list Charles Dickens and JFK. Despite its well-polished elegance, dark woods and chandeliers, there's nothing stodgy about the place. And you couldn't be more in the thick of things; it's just a stroll to many of Boston's top sights.

🖉 HARDING HOUSE
B&B **$$**

(☏ 617-876-2888; www.cambridgeinns.com/harding; 288 Harvard St; r incl breakfast $165-265; ❄ 🛜 👪)
A classic Victorian, blending comfort and artistry in spacious, bright rooms. Old wooden floors toss back a warm glow and lovely antique furnishings complete the inviting atmosphere.

CHARLESMARK HOTEL
Boutique Hotel **$$**

(☏ 617-247-1212; www.thecharlesmark.com; 655 Boylston St; r incl breakfast $189-219; ❄ @ 🛜) This smart boutique hotel packs it all from an unbeatable Copley Sq location to cheery rooms graced with artwork, Italian tile and high-tech amenities.

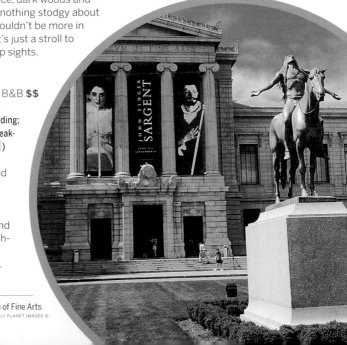

Museum of Fine Arts

HARBORSIDE INN
Hotel $$$

(Map p166; ☎617-723-7500; www.harborside innboston.com; 185 State St; r $189-269; ❄@🛜) This renovated 19th-century warehouse-turned-inn offers cozy rooms just steps from Faneuil Hall and Boston's waterfront.

Eating

Head to Chinatown for affordable Asian fare, to the South End for the cafe scene. And when the sun sets, there's no place like the Italian North End, where the narrow streets are thick with trattorias and ristorantes.

Beacon Hill & Downtown

YE OLDE UNION OYSTER HOUSE
Seafood $$$

(Map p166; ☎617-227-2750; www.union oysterhouse.com; 41 Union St; mains $16-28; ⊙11am-9:30pm) Slurp up fresh-shucked oysters and a heaping of history at Boston's oldest restaurant (1826).

DURGIN PARK
American $$

(Map p166; ☎617-227-2038; 340 Faneuil Hall Marketplace; lunch mains $9-30; ⊙11:30am-10pm Mon-Sat, 11:30am-9pm Sun; 👫) Durgin Park's been dishing out New England staples like Yankee pot roast, Indian pudding and slow-cooked Boston baked beans since 1827.

North End

POMODORO
Italian $$

(Map p166; ☎617-367-4348; www.pomodoro boston.com; 319 Hanover St; mains $15-25; ⊙3pm-11pm Tue-Fri, 11am-11pm Sat & Sun) This cozy place is one romantic setting for homestyle Italian cuisine. The food is simply but perfectly prepared. Reserve ahead or be prepared to wait.

Modern Pastry Shop
Bakery $

(Map p166; www.modernpastry.com; 257 Hanover St; snacks $2-4; ⊙8am-10pm Sun-Fri, 7am-midnight Sat) Not the biggest bakery on Hanover St, but certainly the best. Chocolate ganache and decadent cannoli filled to order in front of your eyes.

Left: Houses along Acorn St, Beacon Hill (p165);
Below: Bust on windowsill, Beacon Hill

Neptune Oyster
Seafood **$$$**

(Map p166; ☏617-742-3474; www.
neptuneoyster.com; 63 Salem St; mains $20-32;
⌚11:30am-11pm) Barely bigger than a clam, this
snappy place has the North End's best raw bar
and good Italian-style seafood.

Waterfront & Seaport District

FLOUR BAKERY & CAFE
Bakery **$**

(Map p166; www.flourbakery.com; 12 Farns-
worth St; light eats $3-10; ⌚7am-7pm Mon-Fri,
8am-6pm Sat, 9am-4pm Sun; 🚼) This bakery
makes awesome pecan sticky buns and
wildly innovative sandwiches and pizzas.

BARKING CRAB
Seafood **$$**

(Map p166; ☏617-426-2722; www.thebarking
crab.com; 88 Sleeper St; mains $12-34;
⌚11:30am-10pm; 🚼) A waterfront landmark, this brightly painted and ever-
bustling seafood shack serves big
buckets of steaming crabs, authentic
New England clambakes and good ol'
beer-battered fish and chips.

Chinatown, Theater District & South End

MYERS + CHANG
Asian Fusion **$$**

(☏617-542-5200; www.myersandchang.com;
1145 Washington St; mains $10-18; ⌚11:30am-
10pm Sun-Wed, 11:30am-11pm Thu-Sat) The re-
sult of a marriage between two South End
top chefs, this smokin' multiethnic joint
dishes up eclectic taste treats, blending
Thai, Chinese and Vietnamese influences
with an urban New England tweak.

NEW JUMBO SEAFOOD
Chinese **$$**

(Map p166; www.newjumboseafoodrestaurant.
com; 5 Hudson St; mains $6-30; ⌚11am-1am
Sun-Thu, to 4am Fri & Sat) A wall of tanks
crawling with lobster, crabs and eels
constitute the decor at this Chinatown
classic renowned for its fresh seafood and
Cantonese cuisine.

🍷 Drinking

ALIBI — Lounge
(Map p166; www.alibiboston.com; 215 Charles St) The quirkiest place to have a drink in Boston is in the former Charles Street Jail, now renovated into the upscale Liberty Hotel.

BELL IN HAND TAVERN — Pub
(Map p166; www.bellinhand.com; 45 Union St) A gaggle of bars lines historic Union St, just north of Faneuil Hall, including this one, which opened in 1795, making it the oldest tavern in the USA.

Top of the Hub — Lounge
(www.topofthehub.net; 800 Boylston St) A truly head-spinning city view is on tap at this chic restaurant-lounge on the 52nd floor of the Prudential Center.

Sonsie — Cafe
(www.sonsieboston.com; 327 Newbury St) Overlooking the action on trendy Newbury St, Sonsie is where the beautiful people go to see and be seen.

☆ Entertainment

For up-to-the-minute listings, grab a copy of the free *Boston Phoenix*.

Live Music

CLUB PASSIM — Folk
(☎617-492-7679; www.clubpassim.org; 47 Palmer St) Folkies flock to this venerable Cambridge club, which has been a haunt of up-and-coming folk singers since the days of Dylan and Baez.

PARADISE ROCK CLUB — Rock
(☎617-562-8800; www.thedise.com; 967 Commonwealth Ave) Top bands – like U2, whose first gig in the USA was on this stage – rock at this edgy landmark club.

Classical Music & Opera

Symphony Hall — Music
(☎888-266-1200; www.bso.org; 301 Massachusetts Ave) The celebrated Boston Symphony Orchestra and Boston Pops perform here.

Boston Symphony Orchestra, Symphony Hall

Detour: Plymouth

Proclaiming itself 'America's hometown,' Plymouth (41 miles south of Boston) celebrates its heritage as the region's first permanent European settlement. **Plymouth Rock**, a weather-worn chunk of granite on the harborfront, is said to mark the place the Pilgrims came ashore in 1620.

These days, people make their pilgrimage to **Plimoth Plantation** (508-746-1622; www.plimoth.org; MA 3A; adult/child $29.50/19; ⏰9am-5pm mid-Mar–Nov; 👫), an authentically re-created 1627 Pilgrim village. Everything – the houses, the crops, the food cooked over wood stoves and even the vocabulary used by the costumed interpreters – is meticulously true to the period. Equally insightful are the home sites of the Wampanoag tribe, who helped the Pilgrims through their first difficult winter. If you're traveling with kids, or you're a history buff, don't miss it. The admission price includes entry to the *Mayflower II,* a replica of the Pilgrims' ship, at Plymouth Harbor.

Opera House   Theater
(Map p166; 617-880-2442; www.boston operahouseonline.com; 539 Washington St) Restored to its 1920s grandeur, this extravagant theater hosts Broadway productions.

Sports

Boston is a huge sports city with top-rated pro teams. From April to September join the fans cheering on the **Boston Red Sox** (🕿617-267-1700; www.redsox.com), at **Fenway Park (Map p165)**, major-league baseball's oldest and most storied ballpark (1912).

🔒 Shopping

Head to fashionable Newbury St, Boston's version of New York's Fifth Ave, for the city's most interesting shopping stroll. Its highbrow east end is all Armani, Brooks Brothers and Cartier, but by the time you reach the west end you'll find offbeat shops and funky bookstores.

Copley Place (Map p165; www.shopcopleyplace.com; 100 Huntington Ave) and the **Prudential Center** (Map p165; www.prudentialcenter.com; 800 Boylston St), both in the Back Bay, are the city's main indoor shopping malls.

ⓘ Information

Greater Boston Convention & Visitors Bureau (www.bostonusa.com) has visitor centers at Boston Common (Map p166; 🕿617-426-3115; 148 Tremont St; ⏰8:30am-5pm Mon-Fri, 9am-5pm Sat & Sun) and the Prudential Center (800 Boylston St; ⏰9am-5pm).

ⓘ Getting There & Away

The train and bus stations are conveniently side by side, and the airport is a short subway ride away.

AIR Logan International Airport (BOS; www.massport.com/logan), just across Boston Harbor from the city center.

BUS South Station (Map p166; 700 Atlantic Ave) is the terminal for Greyhound (www.greyhound.com), and for Fung Wah Bus Company (www.fungwahbus.com), which runs buses between South Station and New York City for just $15 each way.

TRAIN The Amtrak (www.amtrak.com) terminal is at South Station.

ⓘ Getting Around

SUBWAY The MBTA (www.mbta.com; single ride $2, day/week pass $9/15; ⏰5:30am-12:30am) operates the 'T'. Five color-coded lines radiate 'outbound' from the downtown stations of Park St, Downtown Crossing and Government Center.

DELLA HUFF/ALAMY ©

TAXI Flag taxis on the street, find them at major hotels or call **Metro Cab** (☎617-242-8000) or **Independent** (☎617-426-8700).

Salem

Salem, 20 miles northeast of Boston, burned itself an infamous place in history with the 1692 hysteria that put innocent people to death for witchcraft. The tragedy has proven a boon for operators of numerous Salem witch attractions, some serious, others just milking witchy-wacky-woo for all it's worth.

The exceptional **Peabody Essex Museum** (☎978-745-9500; www.pem.org; East India Sq; adult/child $15/free; ☺10am-5pm Tue-Sun) reflects Salem's rich maritime history. The museum was founded upon the art, artifacts and curios collected by Salem traders during their early expeditions to the Far East.

The most poignant site in Salem is the **Witch Trials Memorial** (Charter St), a quiet park behind the Peabody Essex Museum, where simple stones are inscribed with the names and final words of the victims, decrying the injustice befallen them.

CAPE COD

'The Cape', as it's called by locals, lures vacationers with its 400 miles of wondrous Massachusetts shoreline. It's fringed with dune-studded beaches, dotted with fishing harbors and graced with scores of old sea captain's homes, many of which have been turned into inviting B&Bs. In addition to long ambles on the shore, Cape Cod is a great place for a boat trip, browsing galleries and old-fashioned antique shops, and taking in the culinary bounty of lively Provincetown.

Sandwich

The Cape's oldest village wraps its historic center around a picturesque swan pond with a c 1654 grist mill and several small museums.

◉ Sights & Activities

If you're ready for salt spray, head to **Sandy Neck Beach** (Sandy Neck Rd), found off MA 6A, a 6-mile dune-backed strand (parking $15) ideal for beachcombing and a bracing swim.

Cape Cod, Martha's Vineyard & Nantucket

Ⓝ 0 ▬▬▬▬▬▬ 10 km
0 ▬▬▬▬▬▬ 6 miles

Hingham
Cohasset

To Boston
(25mi)

Stellwagen Bank
National Marine
Sanctuary

ATLANTIC
OCEAN

Hanover

Pembroke
Marshfield
(14)
(53)
(3)
(3A)

Plymouth
Bay

(106)

Plymouth
Plymouth
Plimoth Plantation
Plympton
Manomet
(44)

(58)

Race Point
Beach
Provincetown
Herring Cove
Beach
North
Truro

Truro
(6)

Wellfleet

Cape Cod National Seashore

Wellfleet
Harbor
Wellfleet Beaches

South
Middleboro
Myles Standish
State Forest
(3)
(3A)

Cape Cod
Bay

Cape Cod
Rail Trail
Eastham
Rock
Harbor

(495)

Cape Cod
Canal
Cedarville
Shawme-Crowell
State Forest
(25)
(6)

Sandy Neck
Beach

Brewster
Orleans
Nickerson
State Park
Pleasant
Bay

Sagamore
Sandwich
Buzzards
Bay
Bourne
(6A)
West Yarmouth
Barnstable
Dennis
East
Dennis
(6A)
(137)

Rochester

(28)
(130)
Mid-Cape Hwy
Chatham

Marstons
Mills
(28)
Hyannis
(134)
(6)
Harwich
Port
Lighthouse
Beach

(195)

North
Falmouth
Mashpee
Hyannisport
South
Yarmouth
Monomoy
National
Wildlife
Refuge

Old Silver
Beach

East
Falmouth

Buzzards
Bay

Falmouth
Woods
Hole
Falmouth
Heights

Vineyard Sound

Monomoy
Island

Elizabeth Islands

Vineyard Sound

Vineyard
Haven
Tisbury
Oak
Bluffs
Felix Neck
Wildlife Sanctuary

Nantucket
Sound

Cedar Tree
Neck Sanctuary
Edgartown

Menemsha
West Tisbury
Chappaquiddick
Island
Great Point
Light

Aquinnah
Chilmark
Katama
Beach
Muskeget
Island
Coskata
Wauwinet

Martha's
Vineyard

Nantucket
Madaket
Cisco
Surfside
Siasconset

ATLANTIC
OCEAN

Nantucket

HERITAGE MUSEUMS & GARDENS
Museum

(☎508-888-3300; www.heritagemuseums
andgardens.org; cnr Grove & Pine Sts; adult/
child $12/6; ⏱10am-5pm; 👫) The 76-acre

site sports a terrific **vintage automobile
collection**, folk-art exhibits and one of
the finest **rhododendron gardens** in
America. Kids will love riding the classic
1912 carousel.

Cycling the Rail Trail

A poster child for the rails-to-trail movement, the **Cape Cod Rail Trail** follows a former railroad track for 22 glorious miles past cranberry bogs and along sandy ponds ideal for a dip. There's a hefty dose of Olde Cape Cod scenery en route and you can detour into quiet villages for lunch or sightseeing. The path begins in Dennis on MA 134 and continues all the way to South Wellfleet. If you have time to do only part of the trail, begin at Nickerson State Park in Brewster and head for the Cape Cod National Seashore in Eastham. Bicycle rentals are available at the trailhead in Dennis, at Nickerson State Park and opposite the National Seashore's Salt Pond Visitor Center.

Sleeping & Eating

BELFRY INNE & BISTRO B&B $$
(☎ 508-888-8550; www.belfryinn.com; 8 Jarves St; r incl breakfast $189-255; ❄ 🛜) Ever fall asleep in church? Then you'll love the rooms, some with the original stained-glass windows, in this creatively restored former church, now an upmarket B&B.

SEAFOOD SAM'S Seafood $$
(www.seafoodsams.com; 6 Coast Guard Rd; mains $10-20; ⏱ 11am-9pm; 🚻) Sam's is a good family choice for fish and chips, clams and lobster. Dine at picnic tables overlooking Cape Cod Canal and watch the fishing boats sail by.

Falmouth

Crowd-pleasing beaches and a seaside bicycle trail highlight the Cape's second-largest town.

 Sights & Activities

SHINING SEA BIKEWAY Bike Trail
Cyclists won't want to miss this 10.7-mile beaut that runs along the entire west coast of Falmouth, offering unspoiled views of salt ponds and seascapes. **Corner Cycle** (☎ 508-540-4195; www.cyclecorner.com; 115 Palmer Ave; per day $17; ⏱ 9am-6pm) rents bicycles near the trail.

OLD SILVER BEACH Beach
(off MA 28A, North Falmouth; parking $20; 🚻) Deeply indented Falmouth has 70 miles of coastline, none finer than this long, sandy stretch with calm water.

Sleeping & Eating

FALMOUTH HEIGHTS MOTOR LODGE Motel $$
(☎ 508-548-3623; www.falmouthheightsresort.com; 146 Falmouth Heights Rd; r incl breakfast from $149; ❄ ♨ 🚻) All 28 rooms are a cut above the competition. The beach and the Martha's Vineyard ferry are minutes away.

CASINO WHARF FX Seafood $$
(☎ 508-540-6160; www.casinowharf.weebly.com; 286 Grand Ave; mains $10-30; ⏱ 11:30am-10:30pm) Just grab a deck table and let the feast begin.

Hyannis

Cape Cod's commercial hub, Hyannis is best known to visitors as the summer home of the Kennedy clan and a jumping-off point for passenger ferries to Nantucket and Martha's Vineyard.

 Sights & Activities

The town's mile-long Main St is fun to stroll and the place for dining, drinking and shopping. **Kalmus Beach** (Ocean St) is popular for windsurfing, while **Craigville Beach** (Craigville Beach Rd) is where the college set goes; parking at either costs $15.

JOHN F KENNEDY HYANNIS MUSEUM
Museum

(508-790-3077; www.jfkhyannismuseum.org; 397 Main St; adult/child $5/2.50; 9am-5pm Mon-Sat, noon-5pm Sun) Celebrates the USA's 35th president with photos, videos and exhibits.

HY-LINE CRUISES
Harbor Cruise

(508-790-0696; www.hylinecruises.com; Ocean St Dock; adult/child $16/8; mid-Apr–Oct) Offers an hour-long harbor cruise aboard an old-fashioned steamer that circles past the compound of Kennedy family homes.

 Sleeping & Eating

ANCHOR-IN
Hotel $$

(508-775-0357; www.anchorin.com; 1 South St; r incl breakfast $139-259; ❋ @ 🛜 ☲) Bright airy rooms with harbor-view balconies separate this family-run, boutique hotel from all the chains back on the highway.

SEACOAST INN
Motel $$

(508-775-3828; www.seacoastcapecod.com; 33 Ocean St; r incl breakfast $108-158; ❋ @ 🛜) The rates are a bargain, but it's no Plain Jane. Rooms are spacious with perks aplenty, from free wi-fi to kitchenettes.

RAW BAR
Seafood $$

(www.therawbar.com; 230 Ocean St; lobster rolls $18-25; 11am-7pm) Come here for the mother of all lobster rolls – it's like eating an entire lobster in a bun.

Brewster

Woodsy Brewster, on the Cape's bay side, makes a good base for outdoorsy types.

 Sights & Activities

CAPE COD MUSEUM OF NATURAL HISTORY
Museum

(508-896-3867; www.ccmnh.org; 869 MA 6A; adult/child $8/3.50; 9:30am-4pm; ♿) Come here for exhibits on the Cape's creatures and a cool boardwalk trail that tromps across a saltmarsh to a remote beach.

New England Clam Chowder

BON APPETIT/ALAMY ©

Sleeping & Eating

OLD SEA PINES INN — B&B $$
(📞508-896-6114; www.oldseapinesinn.com; 2553 MA 6A; r incl breakfast $85-165; @ 📶) A former girls' school dating to 1840, the inn's 21 rooms retain a simple yesteryear look: antique fittings, sepia photographs, clawfoot bathtubs.

BREWSTER FISH HOUSE — Seafood $$
(www.brewsterfish.com; 2208 MA 6A; mains $12-30; ⏱11:30am-3pm & 5-9:30pm) Not an eye-catcher from the outside, but inside you'll find some of the best seafood on the Cape. Start with the lobster bisque, naturally sweet with chunks of fresh lobster. Just 11 tables, and no reservations, so think lunch or early dinner to avoid long waits.

Chatham

Upscale inns and tony shops are the hallmarks of the Cape's most genteel town. Start your exploring on Main St, with its old sea captains' houses and cool art galleries. At **Chatham Fish Pier** (Shore Rd) watch fishermen unload their catch and spot seals basking on nearby shoals. A mile south on Shore Rd is **Lighthouse Beach**, an endless expanse of sea and sandbars.

Sleeping & Eating

BOW ROOF HOUSE — B&B $$
(📞508-945-1346; 59 Queen Anne Rd; r incl breakfast $100-115) This homey, six-room, c 1780 house is delightfully old-fashioned in price and offerings, and within walking distance of the town center and beach.

CHATHAM SQUIRE — Pub $$
(www.thesquire.com; 487 Main St; mains $8-22; ⏱11:30am-10pm) This perky pub is the busiest place in town. The menu's piled high with Monomoy steamers, raw oysters and other briny local delights.

Wellfleet

Art galleries, primo beaches and those famous Wellfleet oysters lure visitors to this little seaside town.

 Sights & Activities

WELLFLEET BEACHES — Beach
Marconi Beach has a monument to Guglielmo Marconi, who sent the first wireless transmission across the Atlantic from this site, and a beach backed by undulating dunes. The adjacent **White Crest Beach** and **Cahoon Hollow Beach** offer high-octane surfing. **SickDay Surf Shop** (📞508-214-4158; www.sickdaysurf.com; 361 Main St; half-/full day $18/25; ⏱9am-9pm Mon-Sat) rents surfboards.

 Sleeping & Eating

STONE LION INN OF CAPE COD — B&B $$
(📞508-349-9565; www.stonelioncapecod.com; 130 Commercial St; r incl breakfast $150-220; ❄📶) This 1871 Victorian is the finest place in Wellfleet to tuck in. Pine floors, antique decor and handcrafted furnishings set the tone.

MAC'S SEAFOOD MARKET — Seafood $$
(www.macsseafood.com; Wellfleet Town Pier, takeout $6-20; ⏱7:30am-11pm) Head here for market-fresh seafood at bargain prices.

Drinking & Entertainment

BEACHCOMBER — Dance Club
(📞508-349-6055; www.thebeachcomber.com; 1120 Cahoon Hollow Rd) 'Da Coma' is the coolest summertime hangout on the entire Cape. Set in a former lifesaving station right on Cahoon Hollow Beach, you can enjoy the surf action till the sun goes down. At night local bands take to the stage.

KIM GRANT/LONELY PLANET IMAGES ©

Don't Miss Cape Cod National Seashore

Cape Cod National Seashore (also see p182) extends some 40 miles around the curve of the Outer Cape and encompasses most of the shoreline from Eastham to Provincetown. It's a treasure-trove of unspoiled beaches, dunes, salt marshes and forests. The **Salt Pond Visitor Center** has exhibits and films on the area's ecology and the scoop on the park's numerous cycling and hiking trails, some of which begin right at the center.

Coast Guard Beach, just down the road from the visitor center, is a stunner that attracts surfers and beachcombers alike. Summertime parking passes cost $15 per day or $45 for the season, and are valid at all Cape Cod National Seashore beaches including Provincetown.

THINGS YOU NEED TO KNOW

Cape Cod National Seashore (www.nps.gov/caco); Salt Pond Visitor Center (☎508-255-3421; cnr US 6 & Nauset Rd, Eastham; admission free; ⏰9am-5pm)

WELLFLEET DRIVE-IN　　　　Drive-In
(☎508-349-7176; www.wellfleetcinemas.com; US 6; 🚻) Enjoy an evening of nostalgia at this old-fashioned drive-in theater.

Provincetown

This is it: as far as you can go on the Cape, and more than just geographically. The draw is irresistible. Fringe writers and artists began making a summer haven in Provincetown a century ago. Today this sandy outpost has morphed into the hottest gay and lesbian destination in the Northeast. Flamboyant street scenes, brilliant art galleries and unbridled nightlife paint the town center. Provincetown's untamed coastline and vast beaches also beg exploring.

⊙ Sights & Activities

CAPE COD NATIONAL
SEASHORE   National Seashore
The **Province Lands Visitor Center** (www.
nps.gov/caco; Race Point Rd; admission free;
⊙9am-5pm) has displays on dune ecology
and a rooftop observation deck with a
360-degree view of the outermost reaches of Cape Cod. The deck stays open to
midnight, offering stellar stargazing.

The nearby **Race Point Beach** is
a breathtaking stretch of sand with
crashing surf and undulating dunes as
far as the eye can see. Swimmers favor
the calmer though equally brisk waters
of **Herring Cove Beach**; nude (though
illegal) sunbathers head to the left,
families to the right. Also see p181.

⌖ DOLPHIN FLEET WHALE
WATCH   Whale-Watching
(☎508-240-3636; www.whalewatch.com; Mac-
Millan Wharf; adult/child $39/31; ⊙Apr-Oct; ⊛)

Offers up to nine tours daily in peak season, each lasting three to four hours.

PROVINCETOWN ART ASSOCIATION &
MUSEUM   Museum
(PAAM; www.paam.org; 460 Commercial St;
adult/child $7/free; ⊙11am-8pm Mon-Thu, 11am-
10pm Fri, 11am-5pm Sat & Sun) This superb
museum displays the works of artists who
have found inspiration in Provincetown
over the past century. On Friday evenings,
admission is free.

CYCLING   Cycling
Eight exhilarating miles of bike trails
crisscross the forest and undulating
dunes of the Cape Cod National Seashore and lead to Herring Cove and Race
Point Beaches.

The best place to rent bicycles is
at **Ptown Bikes** (☎508-487-8735; www.
ptownbikes.com; 42 Bradford St; per day $22;
⊙9am-6pm).

Left: Gaily painted house, Oak Bluffs (p186), Martha's Vineyard;
Below: A North Atlantic Humpback whale breaches off the Massachusetts coast
(LEFT) GLENN VAN DER KNIJFF/LONELY PLANET IMAGES ©; (BELOW) VICKI BEAVER/ALAMY ©

Sleeping

CARPE DIEM Inn $$$
(☎ 508-487-4242; www.carpediemguesthouse.
com; 12 Johnson St; r incl breakfast $175-359;
✳ @ 🛜) Sophisticated and relaxed, with
smiling buddhas, orchid sprays and a
European-style spa. Each room's decor
is inspired by a different gay literary gen-
ius; the room themed on poet Raj Rao,
for example, has sumptuous embroi-
dered fabrics and hand-carved Native
American furniture.

CHRISTOPHER'S BY THE BAY B&B $$
(☎ 508-487-9263; www.christophersbythebay.
com; 8 Johnson St; r with shared/private bath
from $105/155; ✳ 🛜) Tucked away on a
quiet side street, this welcoming inn is
top value. The 2nd-floor rooms are the
largest and snazziest, but the 3rd-floor
rooms, which share a bathroom, get the
ocean view.

Eating

LOBSTER POT Seafood $$$
(☎ 508-487-0842; www.ptownlobsterpot.com;
321 Commercial St; mains $20-35; ⏱ 11:30am-
10pm) True to its name, this bustling fish
house overlooking the ocean is *the* place
for lobster. Best way to beat the crowd is
to come mid-afternoon.

MEWS RESTAURANT & CAFÉ Bistro $$
(☎ 508-487-1500; www.mews.com; 429 Com-
mercial St; mains $12-18; ⏱ 6-10pm) Skip the
excellent but pricey restaurant and go
upstairs to the bar for a fab view, great
martinis and scrumptious bistro fare.

**FANIZZI'S BY THE
SEA** Family Restaurant $$
(☎ 508-487-1964; www.fanizzisrestaurant.com;
539 Commercial St; mains $10-25; ⏱ 11:30am-
10pm; 🚼) Consistent food, an amazing wa-

183

ter view and reasonable prices make this restaurant at the east end of Province-town a sure winner. The extensive menu has everything from fresh seafood to salads and fajitas.

Drinking & Entertainment

PATIO Cafe
(www.ptownpatio.com; 328 Commercial St) Grab yourself a sidewalk table and order a ginger-lime cosmo at this umbrella-shaded cafe hugging the pulsating center of Commercial St.

Ross' Grill Bistro
(www.rossgrille.com; 237 Commercial St) A fab water view and 75 different wines by the glass.

Crown & Anchor Nightclub
(www.onlyatthecrown.com; 247 Commercial St) The queen of the scene, this multiwing complex has a nightclub, a leather bar and a steamy cabaret that takes it to the limit.

🛈 Getting There & Away

Plymouth & Brockton buses (www.p-b.com) connect Boston and Provincetown ($35, 3½ hours). From mid-May to mid-October, **Bay State Cruise Company** (☎877-783-3779; www.baystatecruises.com) runs a ferry (round-trip $79, 1½ hours) between Boston's World Trade Center Pier and MacMillan Wharf.

NANTUCKET

Once home port to the world's largest whaling fleet, Nantucket's storied past is reflected in its period homes and cobbled streets. When whaling went bust in the mid-19th century the town plunged from riches to rags. The population dwindled, and its grand old houses sat idle until wealthy urbanites discovered Nantucket made a fine place to summer. High-end tourism has been Nantucket's mainstay ever since.

Harbor buildings, Nantucket

ALLAN MONTAINE/LONELY PLANET IMAGES ©

Sights & Activities

Step off the boat and you're in the only place in the USA where the entire town is a National Historic Landmark. It's a bit like stepping into a museum – wander around, soak up the atmosphere. Start your explorations by strolling up Main St, where you'll find the grandest whaling-era mansions lined up in a row.

NANTUCKET WHALING MUSEUM   Museum
(www.nha.org; 13 Broad St; adult/child $17/8; ☺10am-5pm) A top sight is this evocative museum in a former spermaceti (whale-oil) candle factory.

NANTUCKET BEACHES   Beach
If you have young 'uns head to **Children's Beach**, right in Nantucket town, where the water's calm and there's a playground. **Surfside Beach**, 2 miles to the south, is where the college crowd heads for an active scene and bodysurfing waves. The best place to catch the sunset is **Madaket Beach**, 5.5 miles west of town.

CYCLING   Cycling
No destination on the island is more than 8 miles from town and thanks to Nantucket's relatively flat terrain and dedicated bike trails, cycling is an easy way to explore. For a fun outing, cycle to the picturesque village of **Siasconset** ('Sconset), known for its rose-covered cottages. A couple of companies rent bikes ($30 a day) right at the ferry docks.

Sleeping

PINEAPPLE INN   B&B $$$
(☏508-228-9992; www.pineappleinn.com; 10 Hussey St; r incl breakfast $200-375; ❄@🛜)
The 12 guest rooms at this 1838 whaling captain's house have been completely restored with understated elegance. Run by restaurateurs, the inn is justifiably famous for its breakfast.

NESBITT INN   B&B $$
(☏508-228-0156; nesbittinn@comcast.net; 21 Broad St; s incl breakfast $105, d $125-170)
Operating as an inn since 1872, Nesbitt's a bit faded but it has damn good prices and plenty of old-fashioned character. The finest room, the Captain's Quarters, has a bay window overlooking bustling Broad St and a cavernous bathroom with a real-deal clawfoot tub. Most other guest rooms share bathrooms.

Eating

CENTRE STREET BISTRO   Cafe $$
(www.nantucketbistro.com; 29 Centre St; lunch $7-12, dinner $20-30; ☺11:30am-9:30pm; 🖊)
Settle in at a parasol-shaded sidewalk table and watch the traffic trickle by at this relaxed cafe. The chef-owners make everything from scratch from the breakfast granola to the warm goat's cheese tarts.

BROTHERHOOD OF THIEVES   Pub $$
(www.brotherhoodofthieves.com; 23 Broad St; mains $7-25; ☺11:30am-1am) Nantucketers come here for the friendly tavern atmosphere – all brick and dark woods – and the island's best burgers. Good fresh seafood too, including sweet Nantucket scallops.

BLACK-EYED SUSAN'S   Cafe $$
(www.black-eyedsusans.com; 10 India St; mains $8-30; ☺7am-1pm daily & 6-10pm Mon-Sat)
Snag a seat on the back patio and try the sourdough French toast topped with caramelized pecans and Jack Daniels butter. At dinner the fish of the day with black-eyed peas takes top honors.

🛈 Getting There & Around

BOAT The **Steamship Authority** (☏508-477-8600; www.steamshipauthority.com; round-trip adult/child slow ferry $35/18, fast ferry $67/34) runs ferries throughout the day between Hyannis and Nantucket. The fast ferry takes an hour; the slow ferry 2¼ hours.

BUS The **NRTA Shuttle** (www.shuttlenantucket.com; rides $1-2, day pass $7; ☺late May-Sep) operates buses around town and to 'Sconset, Madaket and the beaches. Buses have bike racks, so cyclists can bus one way and pedal back.

MARTHA'S VINEYARD

New England's largest island is a world unto itself. Home to 15,500 year-round residents, its population swells to 100,000 in summer. The towns are charming, the beaches good, the restaurants chef-driven. And there's something for every mood here – fine-dine in gentrified Edgartown one day and hit the cotton candy and carousel scene in Oak Bluffs the next.

Oak Bluffs

Odds are this ferry-port town, where the lion's share of boats arrive, will be your introduction to the island. Welcome to the Vineyard's summer fun mecca – a place to wander with an ice-cream cone in hand, poke around honky-tonk sights and go clubbing into the night.

 Sights & Activities

BIKE TRAIL Cycling
A flat, scenic bike trail runs along the coast connecting Oak Bluffs, Vineyard Haven and Edgartown. Rent bicycles at **Anderson's Bike Rental** (508-693-9346; 1 Circuit Ave Extension; per day $18; 9am-6pm) near the ferry terminal.

 Sleeping & Eating

NASHUA HOUSE Hotel $$
(508-693-0043; www.nashuahouse.com; 30 Kennebec Ave; r with shared bath $69-219;) You'll find suitably simple and spotlessly clean accommodations at this small inn right in the center of town.

NARRAGANSETT HOUSE B&B $$
(508-693-3627; www.narragansetthouse.com; 46 Narragansett Ave; r incl breakfast $140-275;) On a quiet residential street, this B&B occupies two adjacent Victorian gingerbread-trimmed houses.

SLICE OF LIFE Cafe $$
(www.sliceoflifemv.com; 50 Circuit Ave; mains $8-20; 8am-9pm Tue-Sat;) The look is casual, the fare is gourmet: portobello mushroom omelets, roasted cod with sun-dried tomatoes and luscious desserts.

 **Drinking & Entertainment**

OFFSHORE ALE CO Microbrewery
(www.offshoreale.com; 30 Kennebec Ave) This popular microbrewery is the place to enjoy a pint of Vineyard ale while soaking up live jazz and Irish music on weekday nights.

Edgartown

Perched on a fine natural harbor, Edgartown has a rich maritime history and a patrician air. At the height of the whaling era it was home to more than 100 sea captains, whose fortunes built the grand old homes that line the streets today.

 Sights

KATAMA BEACH Beach
(Katama Rd) One of the Vineyard's best beaches is just 4 miles south of Edgartown center. Also called South Beach, Katama stretches for three magnificent miles. Rough surf is the norm on the ocean side, but there are protected salt ponds on the inland side.

Sleeping & Eating

EDGARTOWN INN Guesthouse $$
(508-627-4794; www.edgartowninn.com; 56 N Water St; r with shared bath $100-125, with private bath $150-300;) The Inn's best bargain in town with straightforward rooms spread across three adjacent buildings. The oldest dates to 1798 and claims Nathaniel Hawthorne and Daniel Webster among its early guests.

LOU JONES/LONELY PLANET IMAGES ©

Don't Miss Up-Island

Known as Up-Island, the rural western half of Martha's Vineyard is a patchwork of rolling hills, small farms and open fields frequented by wild turkeys and deer. Feast your eyes and your belly at the picturesque fishing village of **Menemsha**, where you'll find seafood shacks with food so fresh the boats unload their catch at the back door. They'll shuck you an oyster and steam you a lobster while you watch, and you can eat alfresco on a harborside bench.

The coastal **Aquinnah Cliffs**, also known as the Gay Head Cliffs, are so special they've been declared a National Natural Landmark. The 150ft-high cliffs glow with an amazing array of colors that can be best appreciated in the late-afternoon light. You can hang out at **Aquinnah Beach**, just below the multi-hued cliffs, or walk 1 mile north along the shore to an area that's popular with nude sunbathers.

Cedar Tree Neck Sanctuary, off State Rd, has an inviting 2.5-mile hike across native bogs and forest to a coastal bluff with views of Cape Cod. The Massachusetts Audubon Society's **Felix Neck Wildlife Sanctuary** is a birder's paradise, with 4 miles of trails skirting marshes and ponds. Outdoor dining at the Aquinnah Cliffs

THINGS YOU NEED TO KNOW

Cedar Tree Neck Sanctuary (www.sheriffsmeadow.org; Indian Hill Rd, West Tisbury; admission free; ⊙8:30am-5:30pm); Felix Neck Wildlife Sanctuary (www.massaudubon.org; Edgartown-Vineyard Haven Rd; adult/child $4/3; ⊙dawn-dusk)

DÉTENTE French **$$$**
(☎508-627-8810; www.detentemv.com; 3 Nevin Sq; mains $28-40; ⊙5-10pm) Détente's French-inspired fare includes a rave rendition of 'ahi tartare served with vanilla-lychee puree. Local organic greens, island-raised chicken and Nantucket bay scallops get plenty of billing on the innovative menu.

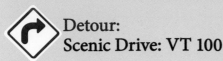

Detour:
Scenic Drive: VT 100

Running up the rugged backbone of Vermont, VT 100 meanders through the rural heart of the state. This quintessential country road rambles past rolling pastures speckled with cows, through tiny villages with white-steepled churches, and along green mountains crossed with hiking trails and ski slopes. It's the perfect sidetrip for those who want to slow down, inhale pine-scented air and soak up the bucolic country life that forms the very soul of Vermont. Think farm stands, century-old farmhouses converted to small inns, pottery shops, country stores and home-style cafes. The road runs north to south all the way from Massachusetts to Canada. It has some tranquil moments but never a dull one – jump on at any point for a taste of it.

ⓘ Getting There & Around

Boat

Frequent ferries operated by the Steamship Authority (☎508-477-8600; www.steamshipauthority.com; round-trip adult/child/car $16/8.50/135) link Woods Hole to both Vineyard Haven and Oak Bluffs, a 45-minute voyage. If you're bringing a car, book well in advance.

From Hyannis, Hy-Line Cruises (☎508-778-2600; www.hylinecruises.com; Ocean St Dock; round-trip adult/child slow ferry $45/free, fast ferry $71/48) operates a slow ferry (1½ hours) once daily to Oak Bluffs and a high-speed ferry (55 minutes) five times daily.

Bus

Martha's Vineyard Regional Transit Authority (www.vineyardtransit.com; 1-/3-day pass $7/15) operates a bus network with frequent service between towns.

PORTSMOUTH

America's third-oldest city (1623), Portsmouth wears its history on its sleeve. Its roots are in shipbuilding, but New Hampshire's sole coastal city also has a hip, youthful energy. The old maritime warehouses along the harbor now house cafes and boutiques. Elegant period homes built by shipbuilding tycoons have been converted into B&Bs.

◉ Sights & Activities

STRAWBERY BANKE
MUSEUM   Museum
(☎603-433-1100; www.strawberybanke.org; cnr Hancock & Marcy Sts; adult/child $15/10; ⊙10am-5pm May-Oct) Encompassing an entire neighborhood of 40 period buildings, Strawbery Banke is an eclectic living-history museum depicting the town's multilayered past. Visit the old general store, watch the potter throw his clay then treat yourself to a scoop of homemade ice cream.

USS ALBACORE   Museum
(☎603-436-3680; www.ussalbacore.org; 600 Market St; adult/child $5/3; ⊙9:30am-5pm Jun–mid-Oct, 9:30am-4pm Thu-Mon mid-Oct–May) Like a fish out of water, this 205ft-long submarine is now a beached museum on a grassy lawn.

ISLES OF SHOALS STEAMSHIP
COMPANY   Cruise
(☎603-431-5500; www.islesofshoals.com; 315 Market St; adult/child $28/18; 🚹) From May to September you can hop aboard a replica 1900s ferry for a leisurely harbor cruise that takes in three lighthouses, nine islands and countless harbor sights.

 Sleeping

ALE HOUSE INN   Inn **$$**
(☎603-431-7760; www.alehouseinn.com; 121
Bow St; r $140-239, ❄ 🛜) Portsmouth's
snazziest boutique inn occupies an at-
mospheric c 1880 brewery. The building's
period character of brick and wood fuses
flawlessly with the rooms' clean contem-
porary design.

INN AT STRAWBERY BANKE   B&B **$$**
(☎603-436-7242; www.innatstrawberybanke.
com; 314 Court St; r incl breakfast $160-170)
Friendly innkeepers, cozy rooms and a
delicious homemade breakfast are the
hallmarks of this Colonial-era B&B.

 Eating & Drinking

**BLACK TRUMPET
BISTRO**   International **$$$**
(☎603-431-0887; www.blacktrumpetbistro.
com; 29 Ceres St; mains $17-35; ⏱5:30-9pm)
Chef-driven and oozing sophisticated
ambience, Portsmouth's top bistro whips
up inventive dishes like *baharat*-crusted
scallops over whipped parsnips.

**JUMPIN' JAY'S FISH
CAFÉ**   Seafood **$$$**
(☎603-766-3474; www.jumpinjays.com; 150
Congress St; mains $20-26; ⏱5:30-10pm) Fish-
fanciers book tables at this sleek contemporary seafooder, which features a wide
range of fresh pan-seared fish spiced with
delicious sauces.

Portsmouth Brewery   Microbrewery **$**
(www.portsmouthbrewery.com; 56 Market St;
light eats $7-12; 🛜) This lively microbrewery
serves specialty beers like Smuttynose
Portsmouth Lager along with light eats,
including the best fish sandwich in town.

COASTAL MAINE

Maine is New England's frontier – a land so
vast it could swallow the region's five other
states with scarcely a gulp. The sea looms
large with mile after mile of sandy beaches, craggy sea cliffs and quiet harbors.
Time-honored fishing villages and seaside
lobster joints are the fame of Maine.

Buoy-adorned lobster restaurant, Bar Harbor (p195)

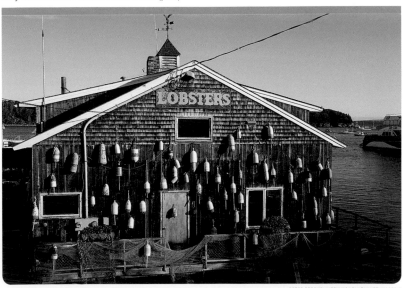

Portland

The 18th-century poet Henry Wadsworth Longfellow referred to his childhood city as the 'jewel by the sea,' and thanks to a hefty revitalization effort, Portland once again sparkles. Its lively waterfront, burgeoning gallery scene and manageable size add up to great exploring. Foodies, rev up your taste buds: cutting-edge cafes and chef-driven restaurants have turned Portland into the hottest dining scene north of Boston.

Sights

OLD PORT   Neighborhood
Portland's heart thumps from the Old Port, where salt-scented breezes, brick sidewalks and gas-lamp-lit streets just beg for poking about. This restored waterfront district centers on the handsome 19th-century buildings lining Commercial St and the narrow side streets extending a few blocks inland. What to do here? Eat some wicked fresh seafood, down a local microbrew and peruse the numerous galleries.

PORTLAND MUSEUM OF ART   Museum
(☎207-775-6148; www.portlandmuseum.org; 7 Congress Sq; adult/child $10/4, 5-9pm Fri free; ☺10am-5pm Sat-Thu, 10am-9pm Fri, closed Mon mid-Oct–May) Showcasing works of Maine painters Winslow Homer, Edward Hopper and Andrew Wyeth, Maine's finest art museum also boasts solid contemporary collections and a brilliant collection of art glass. If you enjoy period homes, be sure to stroll through the restored 1801 **McLellan House**, entered through the museum and included in the ticket price.

FORT WILLIAMS PARK   Lighthouse
(admission free; ☺sunrise-sunset) Up for a picnic in an unbeatable setting? Head 4 miles south of central Portland to Cape Elizabeth and this 90-acre park where you'll find **Portland Head Light** (☎207-799-2661; www.portlandheadlight.com; 1000 Shore Rd, Cape Elizabeth; lighthouse museum adult/child $2/1; ☺10am-4pm Jun-Oct), New England's

Left: Lakeside autumn colors, Maine;
Below: Pemaquid Point lighthouse (p193)

(LEFT) GARETH MCCORMACK/LONELY PLANET IMAGES ©: (BELOW) EDDIE BRADY/LONELY PLANET IMAGES ©

most photographed lighthouse and the oldest (1791) of Maine's more than 60 lighthouses.

LONGFELLOW HOUSE
Historic Building

(☏207-879-0427; www.mainehistory.org; 489 Congress St; adult/child $12/3; ⏰10am-5pm Mon-Sat, noon-5pm Sun May-Oct) The childhood home of Henry Wadsworth Longfellow (1807–82) retains its original character, complete with the poet's family furnishings.

 **Activities**

For a whole different angle on Portland and Casco Bay, hop one of the boats offering narrated scenic cruises out of Portland Harbor.

CASCO BAY LINES
Cruise

(☏207-774-7871; www.cascobaylines.com; 56 Commercial St; adult $13-24, child $7-11) This outfit tours the Portland coast and Casco Bay islands on a variety of cruises that last from 1¾ to six hours.

MAINE ISLAND KAYAK COMPANY
Kayaking

(☏207-766-2373; www.maineislandkayak.com; 70 Luther St, Peaks Island; tour $70; ⏰May-Nov) You can have Casco Bay Lines drop you off at Peaks Island and then hook up with this outfit for a half-day kayak tour of the bay.

 Sleeping

MORRILL MANSION
B&B $$

(☏207-774-6900; www.morrillmansion.com; 249 Vaughan St; r incl breakfast $149-239; ❄ 🛜) This B&B has seven handsome guest rooms furnished in a trim, classic style. Little extras like a generous home-cooked breakfast and afternoon cookies add a welcoming touch.

191

INN AT ST JOHN
Inn $$

(☎207-773-6481; www.innatstjohn.com; 939 Congress St; r incl breakfast $79-169; ❄@ 🛜) Built in 1897 to accommodate train passengers arriving at the old Union Station, this Victorian hotel retains its period character with style. Light sleepers should request a room away from noisy Congress St.

Portland Harbor Hotel
Hotel $$$

(☎207-775-9090; www.portlandharborhotel.com; 468 Fore St; r from $269; 🛜) Portland's finest hotel radiates period appeal from the coiffed lobby to the classically fitted rooms with sunny gold walls and pert blue toile bedspreads.

 Eating & Drinking

GREEN ELEPHANT
Vegetarian $$

(☎207-347-3111; www.greenelephantmaine.com; 608 Congress St; mains $9-13; 🕚11:30am-2:30pm Tue-Sat & 5-9:30pm Tue-Sun; 🍴) Even carnivores shouldn't miss the brilliant vegetarian fare at this Zen-chic, Thai-inspired cafe. Start with the crispy spinach wontons, then move on exotic soy creations like gingered 'duck' with shiitake mushrooms.

HUGO'S
Fusion $$$

(☎207-774-8538; www.hugos.net; 88 Middle St; mains $24-30; 🕔5:30-9pm Tue-Sat) Award-winning chef Rob Evans presides over this temple of molecular gastronomy, and masterfully fuses California influences with fresh New England ingredients.

✒ Standard Baking Co
Bakery $

(75 Commercial St; snacks $2-4; 🕖7am-6pm Mon-Fri, 7am-5pm Sat & Sun) For a sweet breakfast treat, head to this Old Port bakery and order a blueberry cream scone and chocolate croissant.

Portland Lobster Co
Seafood $$

(www.portlandlobstercompany.com; 180 Commercial St; mains $10-23; 🕚11am-9pm) Lobster stew, lobster rolls and lobster dinners shore up the menu at this harborfront shack.

Great Lost Bear
Pub $$

(www.greatlostbear.com; 540 Forest Ave; mains $8-16; 🕛noon-11pm; 🛜) Decked out in flea-market kitsch, this boisterous cave of a bar and restaurant is a Portland institution.

Gritty McDuff's
Brewpub

(www.grittys.com; 396 Fore St; 🕚11am-1am) This Old Port brewpub has it all: harbor views, high energy, good pub grub and award-winning ales.

Coastal view, Acadia National Park

FRANK WING/LONELY PLANET IMAGES ©

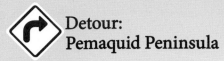

Detour: Pemaquid Peninsula

Adorning the southernmost tip of the Pemaquid Peninsula, **Pemaquid Point** is one of the most wildly beautiful places in Maine, with its tortured igneous rock formations pounded by treacherous seas. Perched atop the rocks in the 7-acre **Lighthouse Park** (207-677-2494; www.bristolparks.org; Pemaquid Point; adult/child $2/free; sunrise-sunset) is the 11,000 candle power **Pemaquid Light**, built in 1827. A climb to the top will reward you with a fine coastal view. The keeper's house now serves as the **Fishermen's Museum** (9am-5:15pm mid-May–mid-Oct) displaying period photos, old fishing gear and lighthouse paraphernalia.

Pemaquid Peninsula is 15 miles south of US 1 via ME 130.

Information

The Greater Portland Convention & Visitors Bureau (207-772-5800; www.visitportland. com; 14 Ocean Gateway Pier; 9am-5pm Mon-Fri year-round, 9am-4pm Sat & Sun Jul & Aug) has free guides to Portland.

Getting There & Around

AIR Portland International Jetport (PWM; www. portlandjetport.org) has nonstop flights to cities in the eastern US.

BUS Greyhound (www.greyhound.com) buses and Amtrak (800-872-7245; www.amtrak.com) trains connect Portland and Boston; both take about 2½ hours and charge $20 to $24 one way.

Boothbay Harbor

On a fjord-like harbor, this achingly picturesque fishing village with narrow, winding streets is thick with tourists in the summer. Other than eating lobster, the main activity here is hopping on boats. **Balmy Days Cruises** (207-633-2284; www.balmydayscruises.com; Pier 8) runs one-hour harbor tours (adult/child $15/8) and day trips to **Monhegan Island** (adult/child $32/18). **Cap'n Fish's Boat Trips** (207-633-3244; www.mainewhales. com; Pier 1;) offers four-hour whale-watching trips (adult/child $38/25). **Tidal Transit** (207-633-7140; www.kayak boothbay.com; 18 Granary Way) leads three-hour kayak tours ($40 to $50) up coastal waters where wildlife abounds.

Sleeping & Eating

TUGBOAT INN Hotel $$
(207-633-4434; www.tugboatinn.com; 80 Commercial St; r incl breakfast $100-240;) Wings of this hotel, literally hanging over the water, are on piers, offering the most amazing water views you'll ever experience without being on a boat.

LOBSTER DOCK Seafood $$
(www.thelobsterdock.com; 49 Atlantic Ave; mains $10-25; 11:30am-8:30pm) From chunky lobster stew to boiled lobster in the shell, this seaside place perfects everything that can be done with Maine's signature shellfish.

ACADIA NATIONAL PARK

The only national park in New England, **Acadia National Park** (www.nps.gov/acad) encompasses an unspoiled wilderness of undulating coastal mountains, towering sea cliffs, surf-pounded beaches and quiet ponds. The dramatic landscape offers a plethora of activities for both leisurely hikers and adrenaline junkies. The park covers over 62 sq miles, including most of mountainous Mount Desert Island, and is home to moose, puffins and bald eagles.

ASGEIR WHITNEY/ALAMY ©

Don't Miss Park Loop Road

Park Loop Road is the main sightseeing jaunt through Acadia National Park, and takes you to several of its highlights. For a bracing swim or a stroll on Acadia's longest beach, stop at **Sand Beach**. About 1 mile beyond is **Thunder Hole** (above), where wild Atlantic waves crash into a deep, narrow chasm with such force that it creates a thundering boom, loudest during incoming tides. Look to the south to see **Otter Cliffs**, a favorite rock-climbing spot rising vertically from the sea. At **Jordan Pond** choose from a 1-mile nature trail loop around the south side of the pond or a 3.5-mile trail that skirts the entire perimeter. When you've worked up an appetite, relax with some afternoon tea on the lawn of **Jordan Pond House**. Near the end of Park Loop Rd, a side road leads up to Cadillac Mountain.

THINGS YOU NEED TO KNOW
Jordan Pond House (www.thejordanpondhouse.com; afternoon tea $9, mains $10-25; ⏱11:30am-9pm mid-May–Oct)

👁 Sights & Activities

Acadia National Park's majestic center-piece is **Cadillac Mountain** (1530ft), the highest coastal peak in the eastern US, reached by a 3.5-mile spur road off Park Loop Rd. Four **trails** lead to the summit should you prefer hiking boots to car tires.

Some 125 miles of **hiking trails** crisscross Acadia National Park, from easy half-mile nature walks and level rambles to mountain treks up steep and rocky terrain. A standout is the 3-mile round-trip **Ocean Trail**, which runs between Sand Beach and Otter Cliffs and takes in the most interesting coastal scenery in the park.

The park's 45 miles of carriage roads are the prime attraction for **cycling**. You can rent quality mountain bikes at **Acadia Bike** (📞207-288-9605; www.acadiabike.com; 49 Cottage St, Bar Harbor; per day $22; ⏱8am-8pm).

Rock climbing on the park's sea cliffs and mountains is breathtaking. Gear up with

Acadia Mountain Guides (☎207-288-8186; www.acadiamountainguides.com; 228 Main St, Bar Harbor; half-day outing $75-140; ⊗May-Oct).

 Information

The park is open year-round, though Park Loop Rd and most facilities are closed in winter. An admission fee is charged from May 1 to October 31. The fee, which is valid for seven consecutive days, is $20 per vehicle between mid-June and early October, $10 at other times, and $5 on bike or foot.

 Getting There & Around

The convenient Island Explorer (www.exploreacadia.com; rides free; ⊗late Jun-early Oct) runs eight shuttle bus routes throughout Acadia National Park and to adjacent Bar Harbor.

BAR HARBOR

Set on the doorstep of Acadia National Park, this alluring coastal town once rivaled Newport, Rhode Island, as a trendy summer destination for wealthy Americans. Today many of the old mansions have been turned into inviting inns and the town has become a magnet for outdoor enthusiasts.

Sights & Activities

BAR HARBOR WHALE WATCH Cruise (☎207-288-2386; www.barharborwhales.com; 1 West St; adult $32-62, child $20-32; ⊗mid-May-Oct; 🚸) This outfit has a wide variety of sightseeing cruises, including whale-watching and puffin trips.

COASTAL KAYAKING TOURS Kayaking (☎207-288-9605; www.acadiafun.com; 48 Cottage St; 2½/4hr tours $38/48; ⊗8am-8pm) Kayaking tours generally go to the islands in Frenchman Bay or the west side of Mount Desert Island, depending on the wind.

 Sleeping

HOLLAND INN B&B $$
(☎207-288-4804; www.hollandinn.com; 35 Holland Ave; r incl breakfast $95-175; ❄🛜)

Nine cheery rooms with frill-free decor, a hearty breakfast and innkeepers who make you feel at home are in store just a short stroll from the town center and waterfront.

ANNE'S WHITE COLUMNS INN B&B $$
(☎207-288-5357; www.anneswhitecolumns.com; 57 Mount Desert St; r incl breakfast $75-165; ❄) Once a Christian Scientist church, this B&B's name refers to its dramatic columned entrance. Rooms have a quirky Victorian charm, with plenty of florals and bric-a-brac.

AYSGARTH STATION INN B&B $$
(☎207-288-9655; 20 Roberts Ave; www.aysgarth.com; r incl breakfast $115-155; ❄) On a quiet side street, this 1895 B&B has six cozy rooms with homey touches. Request the Tan Hill room, which is on the 3rd floor, for a view of Cadillac Mountain.

 Eating & Drinking

CAFE THIS WAY American $$
(☎207-288-4483; www.cafethisway.com; 14½ Mount Desert St; mains breakfast $6-9, dinner $15-24; ⊗7-11:30am Mon-Sat, 8am-1pm Sun, 5:30-9pm nightly; 🍴) *The* place in Bar Harbor for breakfast. Vegans will love the scrambled tofu chock-full of veggies, old-schoolers the eggs Benedict with smoked salmon. Solid seafood menu at dinner.

MCKAYS American $$
(☎207-288-2002; www.mckayspublichouse.com; 231 Main St; mains $10-20; ⊗4:30-9:30pm Tue-Sun) One of Maine's buy-local and organic-when-possible restaurants, this pub-style eatery dishes up Maine crab cakes, farm-raised chicken and good ol' beer-battered fish and chips.

Trenton Bridge Lobster Pound Seafood $$
(ME 3, Ellsworth; lobsters $10-15; ⊗10:30am-8pm Mon-Sat) Sit at a picnic table and crack open a boiled lobster at this traditional lobster pound bordering the causeway that connects Mount Desert Island to mainland Maine.

New Orleans & the South

More than any other part of the country, the South has an identity all its own: a musical way of speaking, a complicated political history and a pride in a shared culture that cuts across state lines.

Nurtured by deep roots yet shaped by hardship, the South has produced some of America's most important culture, from novelists such as William Faulkner and Flannery O'Connor, to foodstuffs like barbecue, bourbon and Coca-Cola, to music like blues and rock and roll. The cities of the South are some of the country's most fascinating, with antebellum beauties like New Orleans and Savannah, and musical legends including Nashville and Memphis.

But it's the legendary Southern hospitality that makes travel in the region such a pleasure. People round here love to talk. Stay long enough and you'll no doubt be invited for dinner.

Bayou tour guide, Cajun Country (p220)

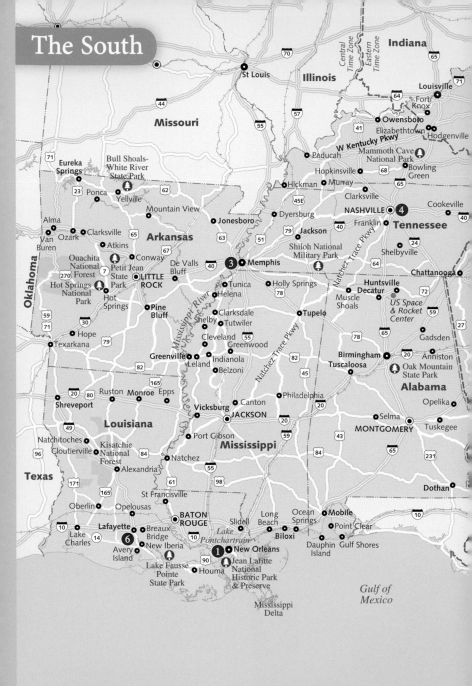

The South

Indiana

Louisville
Fort Knox
Elizabethtown
Hodgenville
Owensboro

Illinois

St Louis

Missouri

W Kentucky Pkwy
Mammoth Cave National Park
Bowling Green
Paducah
Hopkinsville
Clarksville
Hickman
Murray
Cookeville

Central Time Zone
Eastern Time Zone

Eureka Springs
Bull Shoals-White River State Park
Ponca
Yellville
Mountain View
Jonesboro
Dyersburg
NASHVILLE ④
Franklin
Tennessee
Shelbyville
Chattanooga

Alma
Ozark
Van Buren
Clarksville
Arkansas
Atkins
Conway
Jackson
Shiloh National Military Park
Huntsville
Decatur
Muscle Shoals
US Space & Rocket Center

Ouachita National Forest
Petit Jean State Park
LITTLE ROCK
De Valls Bluff
③ Memphis
Tunica
Helena
Holly Springs
Tupelo
Gadsden
Anniston

Hot Springs National Park
Hot Springs
Pine Bluff
Clarksdale
Tutwiler
Shelby
Cleveland
Greenwood
Indianola
Belzoni
Birmingham
Tuscaloosa
Oak Mountain State Park
Alabama
Opelika

Hope
Texarkana
Greenville
Leland
Philadelphia
Selma
MONTGOMERY
Tuskegee

Shreveport
Ruston
Monroe
Epps
Canton
JACKSON
Mississippi

Louisiana
Natchitoches
Kisatchie National Forest
Cloutierville
Vicksburg
Port Gibson
Natchez
Alexandria

Texas
Oberlin
Opelousas
St Francisville
BATON ROUGE
Slidell
Long Beach
Ocean Springs
Mobile
Point Clear

Lake Charles
Lafayette
Breaux Bridge
New Iberia
⑥
Avery Island
Lake Fausse Pointe State Park
Houma
① New Orleans
Jean Lafitte National Historic Park & Preserve
Biloxi
Dauphin Island
Gulf Shores
Lake Pontchartrain

Dothan

Mississippi Delta

Gulf of Mexico

Mississippi River
Natchez Trace Pkwy

0   200 km
0   100 miles

New Orleans & the South's Highlights

1
New Orleans

A clash of cultures and storied history makes New Orleans (p208) what it is today: the most culturally rich, gastronomically delectable, inherently beautiful city in America. History, cuisine, music and architecture combine seamlessly in the Big Easy, weaving a unique kaleidoscopic web of tradition that's so very, very easy to love.

Need to Know
TOP TIP Don't limit your visit to the French Quarter **PACKING LIST** Comfortable walking shoes, hearty appetite **GETTING AROUND** Walk or take streetcars **For more, see p208.**

New Orleans Don't Miss List

BY GRACE WILSON, DIRECTOR OF COMMUNICATIONS, NEW ORLEANS MUSEUM OF ART

1 PRESERVATION HALL

New Orleans has amazing culture, architecture and cuisine, but what really sets this city apart is that it's the birthplace of America's truest art form: jazz. Hear authentic, traditional jazz every night at Preservation Hall (above left; p219), which offers 'pure musical experiences' nightly. No food. No drinks. Just jazz.

2 CITY PARK

Recently described as 'one of the greatest comeback stories of New Orleans', City Park (p215) is one of the largest city parks in any major US city. The red Canal St streetcar stops just steps away from the New Orleans Museum of Art (NOMA; p215). Near the museum, around Big Lake, rent a bike or a paddleboat. Or hire a gondola, which ventures into the park's lagoons and NOMA's Sculpture Garden.

3 ARNAUD'S FRENCH 75 BAR

Just a few steps off bawdy Bourbon St is a bastion of authentic, historic New Orleans: the relaxing, cozy **Arnaud's French 75 Bar** (813 Rue Bienville) and its classic cocktails. It's famous for its French 75s, but mixologist Chris Hannah will make you the best Ramos Gin Fizz, Sazerac, Pimm's Cup or any other libation your heart desires.

4 ST CHARLES AVENUE STREETCAR

The French Quarter is the cultural core of New Orleans, but there's a whole lot more city to see. Hop on the St Charles streetcar (below left; p214) at Bourbon and Canal Sts. As you chug along under the canopy of oaks, you can snap pictures of the mansions along St Charles Ave. Hop off at different spots for an easy walk to Magazine St (a 6-mile shopping stretch), Audubon Zoo and trendy Oak St.

5 SECONDLINES

The name 'secondline' comes from the second line of paraders that follow a jazz funeral, behind the deceased's family and friends. You don't have to wait for someone to pass over to the other side to enjoy a secondline: these parades generally happen every Sunday. The Backstreet Cultural Museum (p212) in the Tremé neighborhood has information on which clubs parade and when.

201

Great Smoky Mountains National Park

Called 'land of the blue smoke' by the Cherokee, this territory (p237) is in the Appalachians, the world's oldest mountain range, featuring miles of cool, humid deciduous forest. There's superb hiking throughout the park, intriguing relics left by early settlers and magnificent vistas that seem to lurk around every bend.

2

3 Graceland & Memphis

Memphis (p224) has a wild spirit fueled by its burgeoning music scene. Roll along the streets of downtown – a jumble of Victorian mansions and eerie abandoned factories – to Beale St, birthplace of the blues and home to smokin'-hot music joints. Then pay your respects to the king at the palatial wonderland of kitsch, Graceland (p225). BB King's Blues Club, Memphis

Nashville

4

For country-music fans, there's no place like Nashville (p230). Since the 1920s the city has been attracting musicians who have taken the country genre from the 'hillbilly music' of the early 20th century to the slick 'Nashville sound' of the 1960s to the punk-tinged alt-country of the 1990s. Boot-stompin' live-music bars, historic sites, theme parks and a big friendly welcome are all part of the Nashville experience.

5

Savannah

With its gorgeous mansions, cotton warehouses, beautiful squares and Colonial public buildings, Savannah (p241) preserves its past with pride and grace. However, unlike its sister city of Charleston, SC, which retains its reputation as a dignified and refined cultural center, Savannah isn't clean-cut – the town has been described as 'a beautiful lady with a dirty face.'

6

Cajun Country

Getting out and around the waterways, villages and ramshackle roadside taverns really drops you straight into Cajun living. It's hard to find a bad meal here; jambalaya (a rice-based dish with tomatoes, sausage and shrimp) and crawfish *étouffée* (a thick Cajun stew) are prepared slowly with pride (and cayenne!). If folks aren't fishing, then they are probably dancing. Don't expect to sit on the sidelines...*allons danson* (let's dance). Shrimp *étouffée*

NEW ORLEANS & THE SOUTH'S HIGHLIGHTS ● ● ●

New Orleans & the South's Best...

Southern Cookin'

○ **Cochon** (p218) Award-winning brasserie serving heavenly pulled pork, best washed down with moonshine.

○ **Mrs Wilkes'** (p243) A southern feast with all the fixings served family style in lovely Savannah.

○ **City House** (p234) Inventive fusion fare that melds Italian and New South cooking, plus great cocktails, at a hidden Nashville gem.

○ **Cozy Corner** (p229) The humble plate of barbecue becomes high art at this classic Memphis spot.

Live Music

○ **Wild Bill's** (p230) Smokin'-hot blues in a well-worn Memphis juke joint.

○ **Tootsie's Orchid Lounge** (p235) This honky-tonk club, with plenty of hollerin' and boot-stompin', is a Nashville classic.

○ **Preservation Hall** (p219) Legendary New Orleans club that's a mecca for lovers of traditional and Dixieland jazz.

○ **Blue Moon Saloon** (p222) In the heart of Cajun country, this backyard jamfest is a great spot to hear homegrown talent.

Historic Sites

○ **National Civil Rights Museum** (p226) Located on the site of Martin Luther King Jr's tragic assassination is this tribute to his enduring legacy.

○ **Charleston Historic District** (p238) This beautifully preserved center is sprinkled with antebellum mansions.

○ **Louisiana State Museum** (p209) Delve into the past with fascinating exhibits set in heritage buildings (the oldest dating to 1813).

○ **Hermitage** (p232) See what 19th-century life was like for folks working on this 1000-acre plantation.

Left: Statue in the garden of a Charleston mansion;
Above: Waterfall, Graveyard Fields, Blue Ridge Parkway (p238)

Need to Know

Scenery

- **Swamp tours** (p221) Take a ride into the bayou on a swamp tour just outside of New Orleans.

- **Okefenokee National Wildlife Refuge** (p245) Rich wetland area with gators and migratory birds a few hours south of Savannah.

- **Natchez Trace Parkway** (p237) A lush roadway near Nashville, lined with historic sites.

- **Blue Ridge Parkway** (p238) Travel the spine of the southern Appalachians, with stunning views on either side.

ADVANCE PLANNING

- **Six months before** Book accommodation well in advance if you're going to Mardi Gras or Jazzfest.

- **Two months before** Browse upcoming shows and festivals in New Orleans and Nashville; snag tickets to big events.

- **Two weeks before** Reserve a table at top restaurants like New Orleans' Cochon.

- **One week before** Book tours, river cruises and other activities.

RESOURCES

- **Gambit** (www.bestofneworleans.com) Free weekly hot sheet of music, culture, politics and classifieds.

- **Arts Council of New Orleans** (www.artsneworleans.org) Great site for up-to-date info on gigs, gallery openings and other happenings in the Big Easy.

- **Off Beat** (www.offbeat.com) Free monthly specializing in New Orleans' music scene.

- **Metromix** (www.nashville.metromix.com) Handy music and entertainment listings for Nashville.

- **Memphis Flyer** (www.memphisflyer.com) Free Memphis weekly with all the entertainment goings-on.

- **Visit Savannah** (www.savannahvisit.com) Handy reference on Savannah, including upcoming events.

GETTING AROUND

- **Airports** Nashville Airport (www.nashintl.com) is a $25 taxi ride from downtown; New Orleans (www.flymsy.com) is a $33 taxi ride to its central district. Savannah (www.savannahairport.com), Memphis (www.mscaa.com) and Charleston (www.chs-airport.com) are other options.

- **Bus** Greyhound (www.greyhound.com) operates between major towns.

- **Hire car** Essential for exploring beyond big cities.

- **Train** Routes include New Orleans–Chicago via Memphis, New Orleans–LA and Miami–NYC via Savannah and Charleston.

BE FOREWARNED

- **Crime** New Orleans and Memphis have high crime rates; neighborhoods go from good to ghetto very quickly. Catch a cab to avoid walks at night.

- **Museums** Some are closed on Mondays.

New Orleans & the South Itineraries

Great music, mouth-watering feasts and eye-popping scenery are yours for the taking on these memorable journeys. Revel in the cultural riches of New Orleans; if time allows, tack on a grand tour around the South.

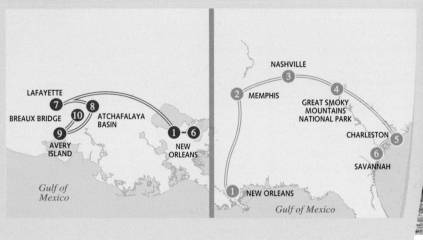

5 DAYS

NEW ORLEANS TO LAFAYETTE
Around the Big Easy & Cajun Country

Spend the first day exploring the picturesque streets of the **(1) French Quarter**. That night, have a bang-up meal at Bayona, followed by live jazz at Preservation Hall.

On day two explore the historic mansions of the **(2) Garden District** and browse the boutiques and galleries along Magazine St. Catch the St Charles Ave streetcar back to the **(3) Warehouse District** and go museum-hopping in the afternoon. That night, have dinner at fabulous Cochon. The next day, head out on a morning **(4) swamp tour**, where you can spy alligators, birds and other creatures amid the bio-rich wetlands. In the afternoon

catch the Canal St streetcar out to lush **(5) City Park** and the notable New Orleans Museum of Art. That evening drink in the music joints along Frenchmen St in **(6) Faubourg Marigny**.

On your fourth day, take a road trip to **(7) Lafayette** in the heart of Cajun Country. Browse exhibits at Vermilionville. That night, hit one of Lafayette's jumpin' dance halls. On the final day, explore the Cajun Wetlands near Lafayette. Take in the swampy scenery of the **(8) Atchafalaya Basin**, look for wildlife on **(9) Avery Island** and chow down on crawfish in **(10) Breaux Bridge** before heading back to New Orleans.

NEW ORLEANS TO SAVANNAH

Greatest Hits of the South

Start in **(1) New Orleans**. Explore the French Quarter, take a riverfront stroll and then drink in the fantastic live music scene along Faubourg Marigny's Frenchmen St.

Next up is **(2) Memphis**, a 6½ hour drive north. Visit the National Civil Rights Museum, Sun Studio and Graceland; in the evening, stroll along carnivalesque Beale St before hitting a Memphis blues joint.

After Memphis, go 3½ hours east to **(3) Nashville**. Check out the Country Music Hall of Fame & Museum, have a peak at the state capitol, and leafy Vanderbilt University. That night join the fray at a country-music-loving honky-tonk.

From Nashville drive four hours' east to the **(4) Great Smoky Mountains National Park**, where you can hike amid craggy peaks and waterfalls.

Next, drive southeast 350 miles (six hours) to **(5) Charleston**. Its Historic District has beautifully preserved antebellum mansions, Lowcountry cuisine and antique-filled B&Bs. Last stop is **(6) Savannah**, a 2¼ hour drive southwest. Take in the pretty parks and riverfront, browse historic 19th-century homes and feast at one of its farm-to-table gems.

Cades Cove, Great Smoky Mountains National Park (p237)

Discover New Orleans & the South

NEW ORLEANS

When it comes to having a good time, New Orleanians are kind of like Manhattanites on a deadline. Just one more beer? Nah son, have a shot with that. You want a burger? How's about we put peanut butter and bacon on top? And throw in a huge baked potato with sour cream on the side. And hell, some crawfish.

Tolerating everything and learning from it is the soul of this Louisiana city. Social tensions and divisions of race and income keep New Orleans jittery, but when its citizens aspire to that great Creole ideal – a mix of all influences into something better – we get: jazz; Nouveau Louisiana cuisine; storytellers from African *griots* (West African storyteller) to Seventh Ward rappers to Tennessee Williams; French town houses a few blocks from Foghorn Leghorn mansions groaning under sweet myrtle and bougainvillea; Mardi Gras celebrations that mix pagan mysticism with Catholic pageantry.

New Orleans may take it easy, but it takes it – the whole hog.

Sights & Activities

French Quarter

Elegant, Caribbean-colonial architecture, lush gardens and wrought-iron accents are the visual norm in the French Quarter. The 'Vieux Carré' (Old Quarter, first laid out in 1722) is the focal point of much of this city's culture and in the quieter back lanes and alleyways there's a sense of faded time shaken and stirred with joie de

Jazz musicians playing on the street, New Orleans
JON DAVISON/LONELY PLANET IMAGES ©

Renewed Orleans

New Orleans is back. The 'Katrina Tattoo,' the line on thousands of buildings that marked the top elevation of 2005's Hurricane Katrina floodwaters, has faded, and talk of 'the Storm' is slowly but surely fading into the history books. Sure, there are still buildings left scarred with international rescue codes and plenty of rebuilding to do, but it's business as usual, especially on the 'sliver by the River' extending from the blocks of Riverbend down in a curve along Uptown and Magazine St, up into the CBD, French Quarter and Faubourg Marigny.

There are new hot spots as well, from art gallery row on St Claude Ave, recently made-over Oak St in Riverbend and the Tremé neighborhood of HBO fame. Thanks to the thousands of new arrivals, affectionately nicknamed YURPs – Young, Urban Rebuilding Professionals (they've even got a website: www.nolayurp.com) – who came to carve the city back to life from the sludge and muck, as well as returnees, the city's population now stands at 70% of pre-Katrina levels. There are also signs of renewed life in the embattled Ninth Ward, Gentilly, Lakeview and Broadmoor neighborhoods, where young, idealistic folk are buying property and starting new businesses.

Another litmus test for new frontiers of urban planning is Brad Pitt's Make It Right campaign (p213), which has turned much of the Lower Ninth Ward into a model sustainable neighborhood with a retro futuristic vibe so cool that it's worth a visit just to gawk at the homes.

vivre – the quintessential romance this town imparts – that's so rich your head goes fuzzy.

Jackson Square is the heart of the Quarter. Sprinkled with lazing loungers, surrounded by fortune-tellers, sketch artists and traveling showmen and overlooked by cathedrals, offices and shops plucked from a Parisian fantasy, this is one of America's great green spaces. The identical, block-long **Pontalba Buildings** overlook the square, and the nearly identical **Cabildo** and **Presbytère** structures flank **St Louis Cathedral**, the square's masterpiece. Designed by Gilberto Guillemard, this is one of the finest examples of French ecumenical (church) architecture in America.

LOUISIANA STATE MUSEUM Museum (http://lsm.crt.state.la.us; adult/child per bldg $6/free; ☺10am-4:30pm Tue-Sun) This institution operates several museums across the state. The standouts here include the 1911 **Cabildo** (701 Chartres St), on the left of the cathedral, a Louisiana history museum located in the old city hall where Plessy vs Ferguson (which legalized segregation) was argued. The huge amount of exhibits inside can easily eat up half a day, the remainder of which can be spent in the Cabildo's sister building, on the right of the church, the 1813 **Presbytère** (751 Chartres St). Inside is an excellent **Mardi Gras museum**, with displays of costumes, parade floats and royal jewelry; and a poignant new **Katrina & Beyond** exhibit, chronicling the devastating storm.

HISTORIC NEW ORLEANS COLLECTION Museum (www.hnoc.org; 533 Royal St; admission free, tours $5; ☺9:30am-4:30pm Tue-Sat, 10:30am-4:30pm Sun) In several exquisitely restored buildings are thoughtfully curated exhibits, such as the original transfer documents of the Louisiana Purchase. Separate home, architecture/courtyard

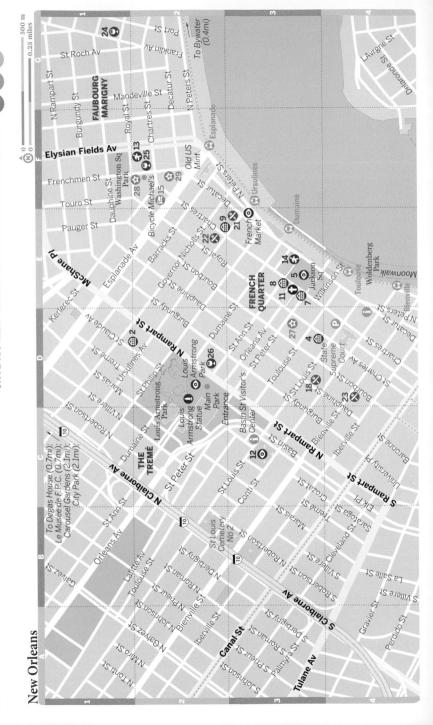

New Orleans

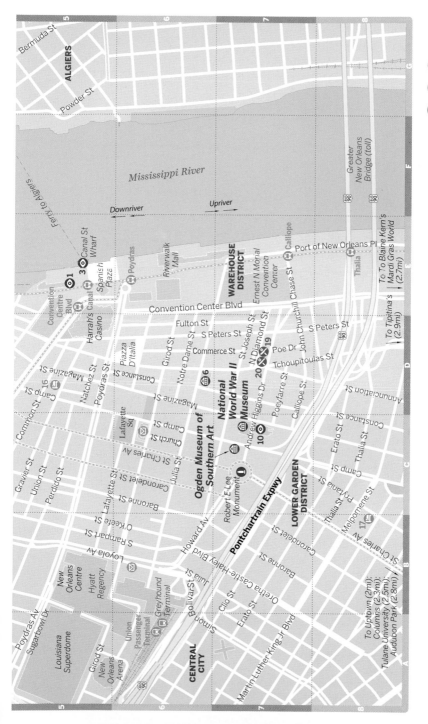

ALGIERS

Bermuda St

Powder St

Ferry to Algiers

Mississippi River

Downriver

Upriver

Greater
New Orleans
Bridge (toll)

To To Blaine Kern's
Mardi Gras World
(2.7mi)

To Tipitina's
(2.9mi)

Port of New Orleans Pl

Calliope

Thalia

Convention
Centre
Blvd

Harrah's Canal
Casino

Spanish
Plaza

Canal St
Wharf

Poydras

Riverwalk
Mall

WAREHOUSE
DISTRICT

Ernest N Morial
Convention
Center

John Churchill Chase St

S Peters St

Convention Center Blvd

Fulton St

S Peters St

Girod St

Commerce St

Notre Dame St

St Joseph St

N Diamond St

Poe Dr

Tchoupitoulas St

Poeyfarre St

Calliope St

Annunciation St

Piazza
D'Italia

Natchez St

Poydras St

Constance St

Magazine St

National
World War II
Museum

Andrew Higgins Dr

Ogden Museum of
Southern Art

Lafayette
Sq

Church St

Camp St

Julia St

St Charles Av

Carondelet St

Constance St

Erato St

Thalia St

Camp St

Pontchartrain Expwy

LOWER GARDEN
DISTRICT

Robert E Lee
Monument

Carondelet St

Baronne St

Thalia St

Pytania St

Melpomene St

St Charles Av

Common St

Camp St

Magazine St

Gravier St

Union St

Perdido St

Lafayette St

Baronne St

O'Keefe St

S Rampart St

Loyola Av

Howard Av

Oretha Castle Haley Blvd

Julia St

Clio St

Simon Bolivar Av

Erato St

Thalia St

Martin Luther King Jr Blvd

CENTRAL
CITY

New Orleans
Centre

Hyatt
Regency

Greyhound
Terminal

Union
Passenger
Terminal

Poydras Av
Sugarbowl Dr

Louisiana
Superdome

Girod St
New
Orleans
Arena

To Uptown (2mi);
Columns (2.3mi);
Tulane University (2.5mi);
Audubon Park (2.8mi)

1

3

6

10

19

20

17

New Orleans

and history tours also run at 10am, 11am, 2pm and 3pm, the home being the most interesting.

OLD URSULINE CONVENT Historic Building

(1112 Chartres St; adult/child $5/3; ⊗tours 10am-4pm Mon-Sat) In 1727, 12 Ursuline nuns arrived in New Orleans to care for the French garrison's 'miserable little hospital' and to educate the young girls of the colony. Between 1745 and 1752 the French colonial army built what is now the oldest structure in the Mississippi River Valley and the only remaining French building in the Quarter. The self-guided tour takes in various rotating exhibits and the beautiful St Mary's chapel.

The Tremé

The oldest African American neighborhood in the city is obviously steeped in a lot of history.

BACKSTREET CULTURAL MUSEUM Museum

(www.backstreetmuseum.org; 1116 St Claude Ave; admission $8; ⊗10am-5pm Tue-Sat) This is the place to see one facet of this town's distinctive customs – its African American side – and how they're expressed in daily life. If you have any interest in Mardi Gras Indian suits (African Americans who dress up in Carnivalesque Native American costume), second lines and the activities of social aid and pleasure clubs (the local African American community version of civic associations), you need to stop by.

LE MUSÉE DE FPC Museum

(Free People of Color Museum; www.lemuseede fpc.com; 2336 Esplanade Ave; adult/child $10/5; ⊗11am-4pm Wed-Sat or by appointment) Inside a lovely 1859 Greek Revival mansion in the Upper Tremé, this newcomer showcases a 30-year collection of artifacts, documents, furniture and art telling the story of a forgotten subculture: the 'free people of color' before the Civil War. The small but fascinating collection includes original documentation of slaves who became free, either by *coartación* (buying their own freedom) or as a reward for particularly good service.

ST LOUIS CEMETERY NO 1   Cemetery
(Basin St; ⏰9am-3pm Mon-Sat, to noon Sun)
This cemetery received the remains of
most early Creoles. The shallow water
table necessitated aboveground burials,
with bodies placed in the family tombs
you see to this day.

Faubourg Marigny, the Bywater & the Ninth Ward

North of the French Quarter are the
Creole suburbs ('faubourgs,' which more
accurately means 'neighborhoods') of the
Marigny and the Bywater. The Marigny is
the heart of the local gay scene. Frenchman Sreet, which runs through the center
of the 'hood, is a fantastic strip of live-
music goodness – what Bourbon St used
to be before the strip clubs and daiquiri
factories took over. The Bywater is an
edgier area, where a good mix of white,
African American working class and artists are straddling the edge of urban cool.

📷 **MAKE IT RIGHT**   Neighborhood
(www.makeitrightnola.org; N Clairborne at Tennessee St) Brad Pitt's futuristic green building project in the Lower Ninth Ward, Make
It Right, dots the former devastated landscape like *Jetsons*-style living quarters.
Some 75 sustainable, storm-resistant
homes had been built at time of writing
(45 of which are LEED-certified platinum),
giving the neighborhood a beautiful kaleidoscopic aura that is in striking contrast
to the despairing images beamed around
the world during Katrina.

CBD & Warehouse District

The CBD and Warehouse District comprise the commercial section established
after the Louisiana Purchase. Several outstanding museums anchor the
Warehouse District and local art galleries
cluster along Julia St.

NATIONAL WORLD WAR II
MUSEUM   Museum
(www.nationalww2museum.org; 945 Magazine
St; adult/child $18/free, with film $23/12/5;
⏰9am-5pm) The museum presents an ad-
mirably nuanced analysis of the biggest
war of the 20th century. Of particular
note is the **D-Day exhibition**, arguably
the most in-depth of its type in the country. The new 4-D *Beyond All Boundaries*
film, narrated by Tom Hanks and shown
on a 120ft-wide immersive screen in the

Botanical gardens, City Park (p215)

new **Solomon Victory Theater**, is a loud, proud and awesome extravaganza well worth the extra $5.

OGDEN MUSEUM OF
SOUTHERN ART
Art Gallery

(www.ogdenmuseum.org; 925 Camp St; adult/child $10/5; 10am-5pm Wed-Mon, 6-8pm Thu) New Orleans entrepreneur Roger Houston Ogden has assembled one of the finest collections of Southern art anywhere, which includes huge galleries ranging from Impressionist landscapes to outsider folk-art. There's live music from 6pm to 8pm Thursday for $10.

BLAINE KERN'S MARDI GRAS
WORLD
Museum

(www.mardigrasworld.com; 1380 Port of New Orleans Pl; adult/child $20/13; tours 9:30am-4:30pm;) This garish and good-fun place houses (and constructs) many of the greatest floats used in Mardi Gras parades. You can see them being built or on display any time of the year by popping by the facilities.

Aquarium of the Americas
Aquarium

(www.auduboninstitute.org; 1 Canal St; adult/child $20/13; 10am-5pm;) Simulates an eclectic selection of watery habitats – look for the rare white alligator. You can buy combination tickets to the IMAX theater next door or the Audubon Zoo in Uptown.

Canal Street Ferry
River

(pedestrian & cyclist/car free/$1; 6:15am-12:15am) Departing from the foot of Canal St is a fast and fabulous ride across the Mississippi to Algiers, an attractive historic neighborhood just across the river, and back.

Garden District & Uptown

The main architectural division in New Orleans is between the elegant town houses of the Creole and French northeast and the magnificent mansions of the American district, settled after the Louisiana Purchase. Magnificent oak trees arch over St Charles Ave, which cuts through the heart of this sector and where the supremely-picturesque **St Charles Avenue streetcar** (per ride $1.25;) runs.

Left: Preservation Hall (p219);
Below: Mardi Gras float
(LEFT) JUDY BELLAH/LONELY PLANET IMAGES ©; (BELOW) WITOLD SKRYPCZAK/LONELY PLANET IMAGES ©

The boutiques and galleries of **Magazine Street** form the best shopping strip in the city.

Further west, **Tulane University** and **Loyola University** occupy adjacent campuses alongside expansive **Audubon Park**.

AUDUBON ZOOLOGICAL GARDENS Zoo (www.auduboninstitute.org; 6500 Magazine St; adult/child $15/10; ☺10am-5pm Tue-Sun) Among the country's best zoos. It contains the ultracool **Louisiana Swamp** exhibit, full of alligators, bobcats, foxes, bears and snapping turtles.

City Park & Mid-City

CITY PARK Park (www.neworleanscitypark.com) The Canal streetcar makes the run from the CBD to City Park. Three miles long, 1 mile wide, stroked by weeping willows and Spanish moss and dotted with museums, gardens, waterways, bridges, birds and the oc-casional alligator, City Park is the nation's fifth-largest urban park (bigger than

Central Park in NYC) and New Orleans' prettiest.

NEW ORLEANS MUSEUM OF ART Art Gallery (www.noma.org; 1 Collins Diboll Circle; adult/child $10/6; ☺10am-5pm Tue-Thu, Sat & Sun, to 9pm Fri) Inside the park, the elegant museum was opened in 1911 and is well worth a visit both for its special exhibitions and top-floor galleries of African, Asian, Native American and Oceanic art.

 Tours

Check the *New Orleans Official Visitors Guide* for a full selection of the myriad of-ferings. Some companies now give post-Katrina devastation/rebuilding tours.

CONFEDERACY OF CRUISERS Cycling (☎504-400-5468; www.confederacyofcruisers. com; tour $45) Get yourself out of the

215

New Orleans for Children

Many of New Orleans' daytime attractions are well suited for kids: the Audubon Zoological Gardens (p215), Aquarium of the Americas (p214) and Mardi Gras World (p214), for example.

Carousel Gardens (www.neworleanscitypark.com; admission $3) The 1906 carousel is a gem of vintage carny-ride happiness inside City Park.

Louisiana Children's Museum (www.lcm.org; 420 Julia St; admission $8; ⏰9:30am-4:30pm Tue-Sat, noon-4:30pm Sun) Offers great hands-on exploratory exhibits and a toddler area.

Quarter and on two wheels – this super informative, laid-back bike tour takes you through Nola's non-Disneyland neighborhoods – Faubourg Marigny, Esplanade Ridge, the Tremé – often with a bar stop and the occasional jazz funeral pop-in along the way.

FRIENDS OF THE CABILDO   Walking
(📞504-523-3939; 1850 House Museum Store, 523 St Ann St; adult/child $15/free; ⏰tours 10am & 1:30pm Tue-Sun) Volunteers lead the best available walking tours of the Quarter.

🛏 Sleeping

COLUMNS   Historic Hotel $$
(📞504-899-9308; www.thecolumns.com; 3811 St Charles Ave; r incl breakfast weekend/weekday from $160/120; ❄🛜) This stately 1883 Italianate mansion in the Garden District is both elegant and relaxed, boasting all sorts of extraordinary original features: a stained-glass-topped staircase, elaborate marble fireplaces, richly carved woodwork throughout, etc. To top it off, there's a lovely 2nd-floor porch overlooking oak-draped St Charles Ave and a damn inviting bar.

**LOFT 523**   Boutique Hotel $$$
(📞504-200-6523; www.loft523.com; 523 Gravier St; r low/high season $79/299; @🛜) The hip industrial-minimalist style of Loft 523's 16 lodgings is a jarring change

of pace for New Orleans. Whirligig-shaped fans circle over low-lying Mondo beds and polished concrete floors and that half-egg-shaped tub is about as inviting as the Pearly Gates themselves. The sustainable angle – keys made from corn, partially-used toiletries being shipped off to countries in need – are mere bonuses.

PRYTANIA PARK HOTEL   Hotel $
(📞504-524-0427; www.prytaniaparkhotel.com; 1525 Prytania St; r from $49-69; P❄🛜) This great-value complex of three separate hotels offers friendly, well-located bang-for-your-buck. It's a perfect spot for folks of all budgets bouncing between the Quarter and the Garden District and/or Uptown.

LAMOTHE HOUSE   Historic B&B $$
(📞504-947-1161; www.lamothehouse.com; 621 Esplanade Ave; r incl breakfast $109-189, ste incl breakfast $209-399; ❄🛜🏊) Splashes of blue or green have lightened up the grand rooms in this 1839 mansion complete with gilt accents, rococo carvings and delicate oil paintings. Starker rooms in the outbuildings adjoin easily for families, and the spacious courtyard lets you all spread out.

DEGAS HOUSE   Historic Hotel $$
(📞504-821-5009; www.degashouse.com; 2306 Esplanade Ave; r incl breakfast from $199; P❄🛜) Edgar Degas, the famed French Impressionist, lived in this 1852 Italianate house when visiting his mother's family

in the early 1870s. Arty rooms recall the painter's stay with reproductions of his work and period furnishings.

 Eating

French Quarter

GW FINS Seafood, Cajun **$$$**
(📞504-581-3467; www.gwfins.com; 808 Bienville St; mains $26-36; ⏰5-10pm Sun-Thu, to 10:30pm Fri & Sat) Fins focuses almost entirely on fish: fresh caught and prepped so the flavor of the sea is always accented and never overwhelmed. And it's not your average dishes served here, either: wood-grilled mangrove snapper, parmesan-crusted sheep's head, and bourbon-and-vanilla mashed potatoes.

BAYONA Modern American **$$$**
(📞504-525-4455; www.bayona.com; 430 Dauphine St; mains $27-32; ⏰11:30am-2pm Mon-Fri & 6-10pm Mon-Thu, 6-11pm Fri & Sat) Bayona is a great splurge in the Quarter. Expect fish, fowl and game on the daily-changing menu divided between long-time classics and daily specials (about four of each).

COOP'S Cajun, Creole **$$**
(1109 Decatur St; mains $8-17.50; ⏰11am-3am) For a cheap but thoroughly satisfying meal in the Quarter, this Cajun country shack disguised as a divey bar is as good as it gets: try the rabbit and sausage jambalaya or the red beans and rice for a taste of Cajun heaven.

CROISSANT D'OR PATISSERIE Cafe **$**
(617 Ursulines Ave; pastries $1.50-5.75; ⏰6:30am-3pm Mon & Wed-Sun) This ancient and spotlessly clean pastry shop is where many Quarter locals start their day.

Faubourg Marigny & the Bywater

BACCHANAL Cafe **$$**
(www.bacchanalwine.com; 600 Poland Ave; mains $8-14, cheese per piece from $5; ⏰11am-midnight) Grab a bottle of wine, let the folks behind the counter prep your *fromage* into a work of art, then kick back in a backyard of overgrown garden green scattered with rusted-out lawn chairs set up for whoever showed up to play live that day.

ELIZABETH'S Cajun, Creole **$$$**
(www.elizabeths-restaurant.com; 601 Gallier St; mains $16-26; ⏰8am-2:30pm & 6-10pm Tue-Sat, 8am-2:30pm Sun) Elizabeth's is deceptively divey, but the food tastes as good as the best haute New Orleans chefs can offer. Be sure to order some praline bacon, no matter the time of day: fried up in brown sugar and, as far as we can tell, God's own cooking oil.

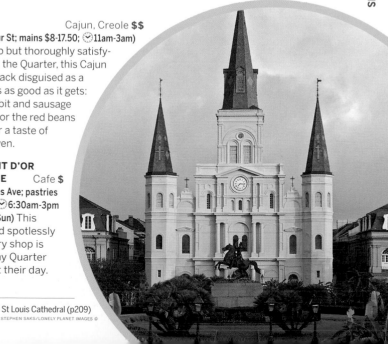

St Louis Cathedral (p209)
STEPHEN SAKS/LONELY PLANET IMAGES ©

CBD & Warehouse District

COCHON   Contemporary Cajun **$$$**
(504-588-2123; www.cochonrestaurant.
com; 930 Tchoupitoulas St; mains $19-25;
11am-10pm Mon-Fri, 5:30-10pm Sat) James
Beard Award–winning chef Donald Link's
fabulous brasserie serves up gourmet
Southern comfort food in such curious
and intriguing ways, you won't know
what to do with yourself. The housemade
Louisiana *cochon* (moist, pulled pork) –
heaven on the inside, crusty, pan-seared
perfection on the outside – is probably
the best swine you will ever have. Reser-
vations essential.

BUTCHER   Cajun, Southern **$$**
(www.cochonbutcher.com; 930 Tchoupitoulas St;
sandwiches $9-12; 10am-10pm Mon-Thu, to
11pm Fri & Sat, to 4pm Sun) Around the corner
from Cochon, Chef Donald Link makes
his in-house cured meat philosophy accessible to all budgets at this don't-miss
butcher shop–deli and bar.

Garden District & Uptown

**COMMANDER'S
PALACE**   Contemporary Creole **$$$**
(504-899-8221; www.commanderspalace.
com; 1403 Washington Ave; dinner mains $28-45;
11:30am-2pm Mon-Fri, to 1pm Sat, 10:30am-
1:30pm Sun & 6:30-10pm Mon-Sat) This New
Orleans grand dame is outstanding
across the board. Chef Tory McPhail's
shrimp-and-tasso appetizer swimming
in Louisiana hot sauce and the hickory-
grilled pork are explosively satisfying
dishes. It's an impeccable mainstay
of Creole cooking and knowledgeable,
friendly service, in the heart of the Garden
District. No shorts allowed.

BOUCHERIE   New Southern **$$**
(504-862-5514; www.boucherie-nola.com; 8115
Jeannette St; large plates $12-15; 11am-3pm
& 5:30-9pm Tue-Sat) Just when you thought
a Krispy Kreme doughnut was already
perfection personified, Boucherie comes
along and turns it into a bread pudding.
For dinner, blackened shrimp-and-grits
cakes are darkly sweet and savory, garlic

Bourbon St bar, French Quarter

RICHARD CUMMINS/LONELY PLANET IMAGES ©

parmesan fries are gloriously stinky and gooey, and the smoked Wagyu beef brisket just melts in your mouth.

 Drinking

Skip loutish Bourbon St and get into the neighborhoods, where you can experience some of the best bars in America. The kinder, gentler strip runs along Frenchmen St in Faubourg Marigny.

SPOTTED CAT   Live Music
(www.spottedcatmusicclub.com; 623 Frenchmen St) A throwback retro cool permeates through this excellent Frenchman staple that you might recognize from numerous episodes of *Tremé*.

MIMI'S IN THE MARIGNY   Bar
(2601 Royal St; ⏰til 5am) Great bi-level bar (pool downstairs, music upstairs) serving up excellent Spanish tapas ($5 to $8), casual neighborhood jazz (most nights) and DJs on the weekend (Swamp Pop every other Friday, Retro Soul otherwise).

TONIQUE   Bar
(www.bartonique.com; 820 Rampart St) If you're going to drink in the Quarter (on the edge of it, anyway), this serious cocktail bar is the place, where cool folks who appreciate an excellent concoction gather over the best Sazerac in town.

 Entertainment

PRESERVATION HALL   Jazz
(www.preservationhall.com; 726 St Peter St; ⏰8-11pm) A veritable museum of traditional and Dixieland jazz, Preservation Hall is a pilgrimage. But like many religious obligations, it ain't necessarily easy, with no air-conditioning, limited seating and no refreshments.

THREE MUSES   Jazz
(www.thethreemuses.com; 536 Frenchman St; ⏰4-10pm Wed-Thu & Sun-Mon, to 2am Fri & Sat) This newcomer was an instant hit with both musicians and foodies – they've

If You Like...
Live Music

If you like Preservation Hall (p219) and Three Muses (p219), check out these other top music spots.

1 **SNUG HARBOR**
(www.snugjazz.com; 626 Frenchmen St; cover $15-25) In the Marigny, the city's best contemporary jazz venue is all about world-class music and a variety of acts. If you can't afford the show, sit downstairs at the bar and watch on close-circuit TV.

2 **MAPLE LEAF BAR**
(☎504-866-9359; 8316 Oak St; cover $10-20) Riverbend's pride and joy. The pressed-tin ceiling and close atmosphere get especially heated late at night. Big nights are Papa Grows Funk and Rebirth Brass Band, plus Monday and Tuesday.

3 **TIPITINA'S**
(www.tipitinas.com; 501 Napoleon Ave; cover $8-37) Always drawing a lively crowd, this legendary Uptown club rocks out like the musical mecca it is. Offers local jazz, blues, soul and funk stop in, as well as national touring bands.

managed to happily marry an excellent soundtrack with gourmet cuisine in a more intimate room than most on Frenchman. There's loads of great local art to peruse between acts and courses.

ℹ Information

Tourist Information

Basin St Visitors Center (☎504-293-2600; www.neworleanscvb.com; 501 Bason St; ⏰9am-5pm) This interactive tourist info center has loads of helpful info and maps as well as an historical overview film and a small rail museum component. It's next door to St Louis Cemetery No 1.

Louisiana Visitors Center (☎504-566-5661; www.louisianatravel.com; 529 St Ann St; ⏰8:30am-5pm) Provides lots of free information and maps for Nola and the state.

ℹ Getting There & Away

AIR Louis Armstrong New Orleans International Airport (MSY; www.flymsy.com; 900 Airline Hwy), 11 miles west of the city, handles primarily domestic flights.

BUS The Union Passenger Terminal (☎504-299-1880; 1001 Loyola Ave) is home to Greyhound (☎504-525-6075) and Amtrak (☎504-528-1610).

ℹ Getting Around

To/From the Airport

The Airport Shuttle (☎866-596-2699; www.airportshuttleneworleans.com; one way per person $20) runs to downtown hotels.

Taxis downtown cost $33 for one or two people, $14 more for each additional passenger.

Taxi

For a taxi, call United Cabs (☎504-522-9771; www.unitedcabs.com) or White Fleet Cabs (☎504-822-3800).

Bicycle

Rent bicycles at Bicycle Michael's (☎504-945-9505; www.bicyclemichaels.com; 622 Frenchmen St; rentals per day $35; ⏰10am-7pm Mon, Tue & Thu-Sat, to 5pm Sun), in Faubourg Marigny.

Around New Orleans

Barataria Preserve

This section of the **Jean Lafitte National Historical Park & Preserve**, south of New Orleans near the town of Marrero, provides the easiest access to the dense swamplands that ring New Orleans. The 8 miles of platform trails are a stunning way to tread lightly through the fecund, thriving swamp where you can check out gators and other fascinating plant life and creatures.

Start at the **NPS Visitors Center** (☎504-589-2330; www.nps.gov/jela; Hwy 3134; admission free; ⏰9am-5pm; 👥), 1 mile west of Hwy 45 off the Barataria Blvd exit, where you can pick up a map or join a guided walk or canoe trip (most Saturday mornings and monthly on full-moon nights; call to reserve a spot). To rent canoes or kayaks for a tour or an independent paddle, go to **Bayou Barn** (☎504-689-2663; www.bayoubarn.net; canoes per person $20, 1-person kayak per day $25; ⏰10am-6pm Thu-Sun) on the Bayou de Familles just outside the park entrance.

CAJUN COUNTRY

One of the truly unique parts of the US, Acadiana is named for French settlers exiled from L'Acadie (now Nova Scotia, Canada) by the British in 1755. As they lived alongside Native Americans and Creoles, 'Acadian' eventually morphed into 'Cajun.' The harrowing journey to Louisiana and the fight for survival in its swamplands are points of cultural pride for modern-day Cajuns, and do a lot to explain their combination of toughness and absolute ease.

Cajuns are the largest French-speaking minority in the US – prepare to hear it on radios and in the sing-song lilt of their English.

Lafayette

At its edges Lafayette looks like Anytown USA, but venture into its nucleus and you'll find an unsung jewel, especially if you like to shake your moneymaker. Surprisingly, its incredibly vibrant music scene remains relatively under the radar. Around the university town, bands are rocking most nights, and you'll drink a beer next to genuine, life-lovin', laid-back folks looking for a dance or to kick back and appreciate the show. Between venues, there are some of the best restaurant and bars in Louisiana outside New Orleans, set in the compact and cool historic downtown.

◉ Sights & Activities

VERMILIONVILLE Cultural Building
(www.vermilionville.org; 300 Fisher Rd; adult/child $10/6; ⏰10am-4pm Tue-Sun; 👥) A tranquil restored/re-created 19th-century Cajun village wends along the bayou near the airport. Friendly costumed

LEE FOSTER/LONELY PLANET IMAGES ©

Don't Miss **Swamp Tours**

You haven't experienced Louisiana until you've been out on its waterways, and the easiest way to do it is to join a swamp tour. Arrange a tour from New Orleans or go on your own and contract directly with a bayou-side company.

Annie Miller's Son's Swamp & Marsh Tours (☏985-868-4758; www.annie-miller.com; 3718 Southdown Mandalay Rd, Houma; adult/child $15/10; ✿) The son of legendary swamp guide Annie Miller now follows in his mom's footsteps.

Westwego Swamp Adventures (☏504-581-4501; www.westwegoswampadventures.com; 501 Laroussini St, Westwego; adult/child with transport $49/24; ✿) One of the closest to New Orleans; also offers a pick-up service in the Quarter.

docents explain Cajun, Creole and Native American history; local bands perform on Sundays. They also offer guided **boat tours** (☏337-233-4077; adult/child $12/8; ✿10:30am Tue-Sat Mar-May & Sep-Nov) of Bayou Vermilion.

 ## Sleeping & Eating

BLUE MOON GUEST
HOUSE   Guesthouse $
(☏337-234-2422, 877-766-2583; www.blue moonguesthouse.com; 215 E Convent St; dm $18,

r $73-94; P❄@☎) This tidy old home is one of Louisiana's travel gems, an upscale hostel-like hangout, walking distance from downtown. Snag a bed and you'll be on the guest list for Lafayette's most popular down-home music venue, located in the backyard.

BUCHANAN
LOFTS   Boutique Apartments $$
(☏337-534-4922; www.buchananlofts.com; 403 S Buchanan; r per night/week from $100/600; P❄@☎) These tragically hip lofts could be in New York City if they weren't so big: doused in contemporary cool

art and design – all fruits of the friendly owner's globetrotting.

JOHNSON'S BOUCANIÈRE   Cajun **$**
(1111 St John St; mains $5-8; ☉10am-5pm Thu-Fri, 7am-3pm Sat) This resurrected 70-year-old family prairie smoker business turns out detour-worthy *boudin* (Cajun-style pork and rice sausage) and an unstoppable smoked pork-brisket sandwich topped with smoked sausage.

 Entertainment

Lafayette specializes in big ol' dance halls that offer one-stop entertainment, dancing and local cuisine. Some standout Cajun music and dance joints:

BLUE MOON SALOON   Live Music
(www.bluemoonpresents.com; 215 E Convent St; cover $5-8) This intimate venue on the back porch of the accompanying guesthouse is what Louisiana is all about: Good music, good people and good beer.

Mulate's   Dance
(325 Mills Ave, Breaux Bridge) On the way to Breaux Bridge.

Randol's   Dance
(www.randols.com; 2320 Kaliste Saloom Rd, Lafayette; ☉5-10pm Sun-Thu, to 11pm Fri & Sat) South of town.

Prejean's   Dance
(www.prejeans.com; 3480 NE Evangeline Thruway/I-49, North Lafayette) Two miles north of town.

❶ Getting There & Away

BUS Greyhound (☎337-235-1541; 315 Lee Ave) operates from a hub beside the central commercial district, making several runs daily to New Orleans (3½ hours).
TRAIN Amtrak's (133 E Grant St) *Sunset Limited* goes to New Orleans three times a week.

Cajun Wetlands

In 1755, *le Grande Dérangement*, the British expulsion of the rural French settlers from Acadiana, created a homeless

Left: Louisiana bayou; **Below:** Jambalaya with andouille sausage

population of Acadians who searched for decades for a place to settle. In 1785, seven boatloads of exiles arrived in New Orleans. By the early 19th century, 3000 to 4000 Acadians occupied the swamplands southwest of New Orleans. Native American tribes such as the Allakapas helped them learn to eke out a living based upon fishing and trapping, and the aquatic way of life is still the backdrop to modern living.

East and south of Lafayette, the **Atchafalaya Basin** is the preternatural heart of the Cajun wetlands. Stop in to the **Atchafalaya Welcome Center** (☎337-228-1094; Butte La Rose; 🕙8:30am-5pm), at Exit 121 from I-10, to learn how to penetrate the dense jungle protecting these swamps, lakes and bayous from the casual visitor. They'll fill you in on exploring the **Sherburne Wildlife Management Area**, as well as the exquisitely situated **Lake Fausse Pointe State Park**.

Eleven miles east of Lafayette in the sleepy, crawfish-lovin' town of **Breaux Bridge**, you'll find sophisticated **Café des Amis** (www.cafedesamis.com; 140 E Bridge St; mains $14-24; 🕙11am-2pm Tue, to 9pm Wed & Thu, 7:30am-9:30pm Fri & Sat, 8am-2pm Sun), where you can relax amid funky local art as waiters trot out sumptuous weekend breakfasts, sometimes set to a zydeco jam.

Check out the friendly **Tourist Center** (☎337-332-8500; www.breauxbridgelive. com; 318 E Bridge St; 🕙8am-4pm Mon-Fri, to noon Sat), which can hook you up with one of numerous B&Bs in town, like tidy **Maison des Amis** (☎337-507-3399; www. maisondesamis.com; 111 Washington St; r $100-125; P ❄ 🛜) right along Bayou Teche.

Tiny **St Martinville** (www.stmartinville.org), 15 miles southeast of Lafayette, packs a mighty punch. Within one block of the bayou in the town center, visit the **African American Museum & Acadian Memorial**

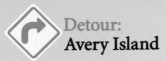

Detour:
Avery Island

Drive southwest of New Iberia along Hwy 329 through cane fields to lush and lovely **Avery Island** (admission per vehicle $1), home of **McIlhenny Tabasco** (☎337-365-8173; tours free; ⏱9am-4pm) and its excellent **wildlife sanctuary** (adult/child $8/5; ⏱9am-5:30pm). The beautiful, manicured paths around the island actually cover a salt dome that extends 8 miles below the surface. Even though the air smells lightly of Tabasco, alligators and egrets bask in the protected sunshine.

At the Tabasco store, you can sample Tabasco-laced grub, including sweet and spicy ice cream and jalapeño soda. Bring lunch and mosquito repellent.

(www.acadianmemorial.org; adult/child $3/free; ⏱10am-4pm) to learn about the diasporas of both Cajuns and African Americans.

One mile north of the town center, **Longfellow-Evangeline State Historic Site** (www.lastateparks.com; 1200 N Main St; adult/child $4/free; ⏱9am-5pm) explains the nuances of Creole and Acadian history, and gives tours of its restored Raised Creole Cottage and replica Acadian farmstead.

MEMPHIS

Memphis, Tennessee, doesn't just attract tourists. It draws pilgrims. Music-lovers come to lose themselves amid the throb of blues guitar on Beale St. Barbecue connoisseurs come to stuff themselves sick on smoky pulled pork and dry-rubbed ribs. Elvis fanatics fly in from London and Reykjavik and Osaka to worship at the altar of the King at Graceland. You could spend days hopping from one museum or historic site to another, stopping only for a spot o' barbecue, and leave happy.

◉ Sights & Activities

Downtown
MUD ISLAND Park, Museum
(www.mudisland.com; park admission free; 125 N Front St; ⏱10am-5pm Tue-Sun Apr-Oct, later Jun-Aug; ♿) A small peninsula jutting into the Mississippi, Mud Island is downtown

Memphis' best-loved green space. Hop the monorail ($4, or free with museum admission) or walk across the bridge to the park, where you can jog, rent bikes, or wade through a super-cool scale model of the Mississippi, which empties into a 1.3-million-gallon 'Gulf of Mexico' where visitors tool around in pedal boats. The park's **Mississippi River Museum** (adult/child $8/5; ⏱10am-5pm Apr-May & Sep-Oct, to 6pm Jun-Aug, closed Mon) has a full-size replica of a packet boat and other historical displays.

Beale Street

The pedestrian-only stretch of Beale St is a 24-hour carnival zone, where you'll find deep-fried funnel cakes, to-go beer counters, and music, music, music.

MEMPHIS ROCK 'N' SOUL MUSEUM Museum
(www.memphisrocknsoul.org; cnr Lt George W Lee Ave & 3rd St; adult/child $11/8; ⏱10am-7pm) The Smithsonian's museum, next to FedEx Forum, examines how African American and white music mingled in the Mississippi Delta to create modern sound.

GIBSON BEALE STREET SHOWCASE Factory Tour
(www.gibson.com; 145 Lt George W Lee Ave; admission $10, no children under 5; ⏱tours 11am-4pm Mon-Sat, noon-4pm Sun) Take the fascinating 45-minute tour of this enormous place to see master craftspeople transform solid blocks of wood into legendary Gibson guitars. Tours leave on the hour.

Don't Miss **Graceland**

If you only make one stop in Memphis, it ought to be here: the sublimely kitschy and gloriously bizarre home of Elvis Presley, the King of Rock and Roll.

Though actually born in Mississippi, Elvis was a true son of Memphis: he was raised in the Lauderdale Courts public housing projects, was inspired by the blues in the Beale St clubs, and was discovered at Sun Studio on Union Ave. In the spring of 1957, the already-famous 22-year-old spent $100,000 on a Colonial-style mansion, which had been named Graceland by its previous owners. Priscilla Presley (who divorced Elvis in 1973) opened Graceland to tours in 1982; now millions come here to pay homage to the King and gawk at the infamous decor. The King himself had the place redecorated in 1974; with a 15ft couch, fake waterfall, yellow vinyl walls and green shag-carpet ceiling – it's a virtual textbook of ostentatious '70s style. Elvis died here (in the upstairs bathroom) from heart failure in 1977. Throngs of fans still weep at his grave, next to the swimming pool out back.

The basic self-guided mansion tour comes with a headset audio narration with the voices of Elvis, Priscilla and Lisa Marie. Buy a package to see the entire estate, or pay extra for additional attractions: several clothing museums, the car museum, and two custom airplanes (check out the blue-and-gold private bathroom on the *Lisa Marie,* a Convair 880 Jet). Parking costs $10. Nondrivers can take bus 43 from downtown, or hop on the free Sun Studio shuttle.

THINGS YOU NEED TO KNOW

📞901-332-3322, 800-238-2000; www.elvis.com; Elvis Presley Blvd/US 51; house-only tours adult/child $31/14, full tour $35/17; ⏱9am-5pm Mon-Sat, to 4pm Sun; shorter hours & closed Tue in winter

RAY LASKOWITZ/LONELY PLANET IMAGES ©

Don't Miss **National Civil Rights Museum**

Housed in the Lorraine Motel (five blocks south of Beale St), where the Reverend Dr Martin Luther King Jr was fatally shot on April 4, 1968, is the gut-wrenching National Civil Rights Museum. The museum's extensive exhibits, detailed timeline and accompanying audioguide chronicle the ongoing struggles for African American freedom and equality in the US. Both Dr King's cultural contribution and his assassination serve as prisms for looking at the Civil Rights movement, its precursors and its indelible and continuing impact on American life. The turquoise exterior of the 1950s motel and two preserved interior rooms remain much as they were at the time of King's death, and serve as a pilgrimage point in their own right. Vintage cars at the Lorraine Motel

THINGS YOU NEED TO KNOW

www.civilrightsmuseum.org; 450 Mulberry St; adult/child $13/9.50; ⊘9am-5pm Mon & Wed-Sat, 1-5pm Sun Sep-May, to 6pm Jun-Aug

---

ORPHEUM THEATRE   Theater
(www.orpheum-memphis.com; 203 S Main St) Originally built for vaudeville, the Orpheum has been restored to its glittering 1928 glory. Today you can catch big comedy and Broadway shows; but beware – the ghost of a pigtailed little girl named Mary is said to giggle eerily between acts.

East of Downtown

SUN STUDIO   Studio Tour
(www.sunstudio.com; 706 Union Ave; adult/child $12/free; ⊘10am-6pm) It doesn't look like much from outside, but this dusty storefront is ground zero for American rock and roll music. Starting in the early 1950s, Sun's Sam Phillips recorded blues artists such as Howlin' Wolf, BB King and Ike Turner, followed by the rockabilly dynasty of Jerry Lee Lewis, Johnny Cash, Roy

Orbison and, of course, the King himself (who started here in 1953). Today, packed 40-minute guided tours through the tiny studio offer a chance to hear original tapes of historic recording sessions.

From here, you can hop on the studio's free shuttle (hourly, starting at 11:15am), which does a loop between Sun Studio, Beale St and Graceland.

Overton Park

Off Poplar Ave in Midtown, stately homes surround Overton Park, a 342-acre rolling green oasis in the middle of this often gritty city.

MEMPHIS ZOO Zoo
(www.memphiszoo.org; 2000 Prentiss Pl; adult/child $15/10; ⊗9am-4pm Mar-Oct, to 4pm Nov-Feb; 👪) At the park's northwestern corner, this world-class zoo hosts two giant panda stars, Ya Ya and Le Le, in a $16-million exhibit on native Chinese wildlife and habitat. Other residents include the full gamut of monkeys, polar bears, penguins, eagles, sea lions and more.

BROOKS MUSEUM OF ART Art Gallery
(www.brooksmuseum.org; 1934 Poplar Ave; adult/child $7/3; ⊗10am-4pm Wed-Sat, to 8pm Thu, 11am-5pm Sun) At the park's western fringe, this well-regarded art museum has an excellent permanent collection encompassing everything from Renaissance sculpture to Impressionists (eg Renoir) to abstract expressionists (eg Robert Motherwell).

South of Downtown

STAX MUSEUM OF AMERICAN SOUL MUSIC Museum
(www.staxmuseum.com; 926 E McLemore Ave; adult/child $12/9; ⊗10am-5pm Mon-Sat, 1-5pm Sun Mar-Oct, closed Mon Nov-Mar) Wanna get funky? Head directly to Soulsville USA, where this 17,000-sq-ft museum sits on the site of the old Stax recording studio. This venerable spot was soul music's epicenter in the 1960s, when Otis Redding, Booker T and the MGs and Wilson Pickett recorded here. Dive into soul-music history with photos, displays of '60s and '70s peacock clothing and, above all, Isaac Hayes' 1972 Superfly Cadillac outfitted with shag-fur carpeting and 24-carat-gold exterior trim.

FULL GOSPEL TABERNACLE CHURCH Church
(www.algreenmusic.com; 787 Hale Rd; ⊗services 11:30am & 4pm Sun) If you're in town on a Sunday, put on your least-wrinkled pants and head to services at South Memphis, where soul music legend turned reverend Al Green presides over a powerful choir. Visitors are welcome, and usually take up about half the pews. Join in the whooping 'hallelujahs,' but don't forget the tithe (about $1 is fine). Green is not around every single weekend, but the services are a fascinating cultural experience nonetheless.

Statue of Elvis Presley, Graceland (p225)
LEE FOSTER/LONELY PLANET IMAGES ©

 Tours

AMERICAN DREAM SAFARI Driving Tour
(901-527-8870; www.americandreamsafari.
com; walking tour per person $15, driving tours per
vehicle from $125) Southern culture junkie
Tad Pierson shows you the quirky, personal side of Memphis – juke joints, gospel
churches, eerie decaying buildings – on
foot or by car (in his pink Cadillac).

Memphis Riverboats Boat Tour
(901-527-5694, 800-221-6197; www.memphis
riverboats.net; adult/child from $20/10)
Sightseeing and dinner cruises on the Mississippi.

 **Sleeping**

Downtown
TALBOT HEIRS Guesthouse $$
(901-527-9772, 800-955-3956; www.talbot
house.com; 99 S 2nd St; ste from $130;)
Inconspicuously located on the 2nd floor
of a busy downtown street, this cheerful
guesthouse is one of Memphis' best kept
and most unique secrets. Suites are more
like studio apartments than hotel rooms,
with Oriental rugs and funky local art-
work, and kitchens stocked with snacks.

PEABODY HOTEL Hotel $$$
(901-529-4000; www.peabodymemphis.com;
149 Union Ave; r from $209;) The
Mississippi Delta's most storied hotel, the
Peabody has been catering to a Who's
Who of Southern gentry since the 1860s.
The hotel's current incarnation, a 13-story
Italian Renaissance Revival–style building, dates to the 1920s. The daily march
of the lobby fountain's resident mallard
ducks is a legendary Memphis tradition.

INN AT HUNT PHELAN B&B $$
(901-525-8225; www.huntphelan.com; 533
Beale St; r from $155;) Outside the
gates are dystopian warehouses and
vacant lots. But inside the gates it's still
1828, the year this aristocratic mansion
was built. Sip complimentary evening

Left: Sun Studio (p226); **Below:** Fried chicken meal at Gus's World Famous Fried Chicken

cocktails by the courtyard fountain and wander the 4.5-acre gardens before retiring to your four-poster bed (or heading to the Beale St bars, just down the road).

 Eating

Downtown

GUS'S WORLD-FAMOUS FRIED CHICKEN
Chicken $

(☎901-527-4877; 310 S Front St; mains $5-9; ⏰11am-9pm Sun-Thu, to 10pm Fri & Sat) Fried-chicken connoisseurs across the globe twitch in their sleep at night, dreaming about the gossamer-light fried chicken at this downtown concrete bunker. On busy nights, waits can top an hour. So worth it.

ALCENIA'S
Southern $

(www.alcenias.com; 317 N Main St; mains $6-9; ⏰11am-5pm Tue-Fri, 9am-3pm Sat) The lunch menu at this funky little gold- and purple-painted cafe rotates daily – look for killer fried chicken and catfish, melt-in-your-mouth spiced cabbage and an exquisite, eggy custard pie.

CHARLIE VERGOS' RENDEZVOUS
Barbecue $$

(☎901-523-2746; www.hogsfly.com; 52 S 2nd St; mains $7-18; ⏰4:30-10:30pm Tue-Thu, 11am-11pm Fri & Sat) Tucked in an alleyway off Union Ave, this subterranean institution sells an astonishing 5 tons of its exquisite dry-rubbed ribs weekly. Friendly service and walls plastered with historic memorabilia make eating here an event. Expect a wait.

East of Downtown

COZY CORNER
Barbecue $

(www.cozycornerbbq.com; 745 N Pkwy; mains $5-16; ⏰10:30am-5pm Tue-Sat, later in summer) Slouch in a torn vinyl booth and devour an entire barbecued Cornish game hen, the house specialty at this pug-ugly cult favorite. Ribs and wings are spectacular too, and the fluffy, silken sweet-potato pie is an A-plus specimen of the classic Southern dessert.

RESTAURANT IRIS New Southern **$$$**
(📞901-590-2828; www.restaurantiris.com; 2146 Monroe Ave; mains $23-34; ⏱5-10pm Mon-Sat, Sun brunch 3rd Sun each month) Chef Kelly English's avant-garde Creole menu sends foodies into paroxysms of delight, with playful dishes like a 'knuckle sandwich' of tarragon-flecked lobster, or an oyster-stuffed steak 'surf n' turf.'

Drinking & Entertainment

Beale St is the obvious spot for live blues, country, rock and jazz. Hip locals head to the Cooper-Young neighborhood for everything from margarita bars to Irish pubs.

Bars

EARNESTINE & HAZEL'S Bar
(531 S Main St) One of the world's greatest dive bars has a 2nd floor full of rusty bed-springs and claw-foot tubs, remnants of its brothel past. The Soul Burger, the bar's only food, is the stuff of legend.

COVE Bar
(www.thecovememphis.com; 2559 Broad Ave) Far from the Beale St crowds, this hipster-ish new dive rocks a nautical theme while serving retro cocktails (sidecars, Singapore Slings) and upscale bar snacks (oysters on the half shell, chips with fresh anchovies).

Live Music

WILD BILL'S Blues
(1580 Vollentine Ave; ⏱10pm-late Fri & Sat) Order a 40oz beer and a basket of wings then sit back to watch some of the greatest blues acts in Memphis. Expect some stares from the locals; it's worth it for the ultra-authentic jams.

HI-TONE CAFE Live music
(www.hitonememphis.com; 1913 Poplar Ave) Near Overton Park, this unassuming little dive is one of the city's best places to hear live local bands and touring indie acts.

🛈 Information

Tennessee State Visitor Center (📞901-543-5333, 888-633-9099; www.memphistravel.com; 119 N Riverside Dr; ⏱9am-5pm Nov-Mar, to 6pm Apr-Oct) Stocked with brochures for the whole state.

🛈 Getting There & Away

AIR Memphis International Airport (MEM; 📞901-922-8000; www.memphisairport.org; 2491 Winchester Rd) is 12 miles southeast of downtown via I-55; taxis to downtown cost about $30.
BUS & TRAIN Greyhound (www.greyhound.com; 203 Union Ave) is right downtown, as is Central Station (www.amtrak.com; 545 S Main St), the Amtrak terminal.

NASHVILLE

Nashville, Tennessee, has many attractions to keep you busy, from the Country Music Hall of Fame and the revered Grand Ole Opry House to rough blues bars, historic buildings and big-name sports. It also has friendly people, a lively university community, excellent fried chicken and an unrivaled assortment of tacky souvenirs.

◉ Sights & Activities

Downtown, the entertainment area called the District runs along Broadway from 2nd Ave to 5th Ave, with divey honky-tonks rubbing up against tourist-grabbers like the Hard Rock Cafe. Midtown/West End is a lively area around Vanderbilt University, with funky shops and restaurants along Broadway, West End Ave, and Elliston Pl. Ten minutes northeast of downtown off Briley Pkwy, Music Valley is a tourist zone full of budget motels, franchise restaurants and outlet stores built around the Grand Ole Opry.

Downtown
The historic 2nd Ave N business area was the center of the cotton trade in the 1870s

RICHARD CUMMINS/LONELY PLANET IMAGES ©

and 1880s, when most of the Victorian warehouses were built; note the cast-iron and masonry facades. Today, it's the heart of the **District**, with shops, restaurants, underground saloons and nightclubs. Two blocks west, **Printers Alley** is a narrow cobblestoned lane known for its nightlife since the 1940s. Along the Cumberland River, Riverfront Park is a landscaped promenade featuring **Fort Nashborough**, a 1930s replica of the city's original outpost.

COUNTRY MUSIC HALL OF FAME & MUSEUM
Museum

(www.countrymusichalloffame.com; 222 5th Ave S; adult/child $22/15; ⊙9am-5pm) 'Honor Thy Music' is the catchphrase of this monumental museum, reflecting the near-biblical importance of country music to Nashville's soul. See case upon case of artifacts including Patsy Cline's cocktail gown, Johnny Cash's guitar, Elvis' gold Cadillac and Conway Twitty's yearbook picture (back when he was Harold Jenkins).

RYMAN AUDITORIUM
Historic Building

(www.ryman.com; 116 5th Ave N; self-guided tour adult/child $13/6.50, backstage tour $17/10.50;

⊙9am-4pm) The so-called 'Mother Church of Country Music' has hosted a laundry list of 20th-century performers, from Martha Graham to Elvis to Katherine Hepburn to Bob Dylan. The *Grand Ole Opry* took place here for 31 years, until it moved out to the Opryland complex in Music Valley in 1974. Today the *Opry* returns to the Ryman during winter.

Midtown

Along West End Ave, starting at 21st Ave, sits prestigious **Vanderbilt University**, founded in 1883 by railway magnate Cornelius Vanderbilt.

PARTHENON
Park, Art Gallery

(www.parthenon.org; 2600 West End Ave; adult/ child $6/4; ⊙9am-4:30pm Tue-Sat, plus Sun in summer) Yes, that is indeed a reproduction Athenian Parthenon sitting in **Centennial Park**. Originally built in 1897 for Tennessee's Centennial Exposition and rebuilt in 1930 due to popular demand, the full-scale plaster copy of the 438-BC original now houses an art museum with a collection of American paintings and a 42ft statue of the Greek goddess Athena.

Plantations

HERMITAGE Museum, Gardens
(www.thehermitage.com; 4580 Rachel's Lane; adult/child $18/12; ◷8:30am-5pm Apr-Oct, 9am-4:30pm Oct-Mar) The former home of seventh president Andrew Jackson lies 15 miles east of downtown. The 1000-acre plantation is a peek into what life was like for a Mid-South gentleman farmer in the 19th century. Tour the Federal-style brick mansion, now a furnished house museum with costumed interpreters, and see Jackson's original 1804 log cabin and the old slave quarters (Jackson was a lifelong supporter of slavery, at times owning up to 150 slaves; a special exhibit tells their stories).

 Tours

NASHTRASH Bus Tour
(☎615-226-7300; www.nashtrash.com; 900 8th Ave N; 90min tour $32) The big-haired 'Jugg Sisters' lead a campy frolic through the risqué side of Nashville history while guests sip BYO booze. Book in advance.

General Jackson Showboat Boat Tour
(☎615-458-3900; www.generaljackson.com; tours from $46) Paddleboat sightseeing cruises of varying length on the Cumberland River, some with music and food.

 Sleeping

Downtown

UNION STATION HOTEL Hotel $$$
(☎615-726-1001; www.unionstationhotelnashville.com; 1001 Broadway; r from $209; P✳︎🛜) This soaring Romanesque stone castle was Nashville's train station back in the days when travel was a grand affair; today it's downtown's most iconic hotel. The vaulted lobby is dressed in peach and gold with inlaid marble floors and a stained-glass ceiling. Rooms are tastefully modern, with flat-screen TVs and deep soaking tubs.

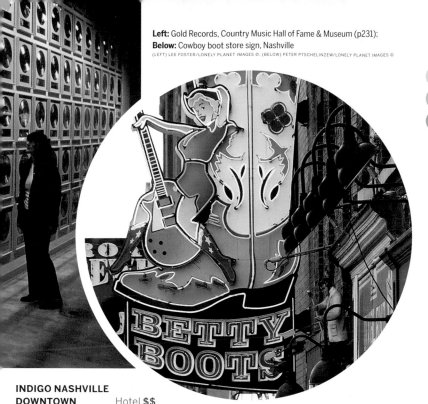

INDIGO NASHVILLE DOWNTOWN   Hotel $$
(☎877-846-3446; www.ichotelsgroup.
com; 301 Union St; r from $139; P ❄ 🗢)
Most of downtown's midprice hotels are
corporate behemoths catering to conven-
tioneers. Not so the newly opened Indigo,
with its mod high-ceiling lobby, space age
violet-and-lime color schemes, and arty
floor-to-ceiling photomurals of Nashville
landmarks.

West End

🖉 HUTTON HOTEL   Hotel $$$
(☎615-340-9333; www.huttonhotel.com;
1808 West End Ave; r from $189; P ❄ @ 🗢)
Nashville's newest hotel is also its slick-
est, riffing on mid-Century Modern design
with bamboo-paneled walls and grown-up
beanbags in the lobby. Rooms decorated
with rust and chocolate palettes have
miniature cactus gardens and a number
of ecofriendly touches.

1501 LINDEN MANOR   B&B $$
(☎615-298-2701; www.nashville-bed-breakfast.
com; 1501 Linden Ave; r from $125; P ❄ 🗢 ☀)
The husband-and-wife owners have
filled this yellow Victorian cottage with
antiques collected through their world
travels – Persian rugs, Asian carvings, old
Victrolas.

Music Valley

GAYLORD OPRYLAND HOTEL   Resort $$$
(☎615-889-1000, 866-972-6779; www.gaylord
hotels.com; 2800 Opryland Dr; r from $199;
P ❄ @ 🗢 ☀) This whopping 2881-room
hotel is a universe unto itself. Why set foot
outdoors when you could ride a paddleboat along an artificial river, eat sushi
beneath a faux waterfall in an indoor
garden or sip Scotch in an antebellum-
style mansion, all *inside* the hotel's three
massive glass atriums?

Eating

PRINCE'S HOT CHICKEN
Chicken $

(123 Ewing Dr; mains $4-8; ☉noon-10pm Tue-Thu, noon-4am Fri & Sat) Cayenne-rubbed 'hot chicken,' fried to succulent perfection and served on white bread with a side of pickles, is Nashville's unique contribution to the culinary universe. Tiny, faded Prince's, in a northside strip mall, is a local legend that's gotten shout-outs everywhere from the *New York Times* to *Bon Appétit*.

CITY HOUSE
New Southern $$

(☎615-736-5838; www.cityhousenashville. com; 1222 4th Ave N; mains $9-24; ☉5pm-10pm Wed-Mon) This signless brick building in Nashville's gentrifying Germantown neighborhood hides one of the South's best new restaurants. The food, cooked in an open kitchen in the warehouselike space, is a crackling bang-up of Italy-meets-New South – local chicken livers with red-onion jam, pizza with house-cured pork belly, root-beer layer cake with buttermilk buttercream.

MONELL'S
Southern $$

(www.monellstn.com; 1235 6th Ave N; all-you-can-eat $16; ☉10:30am-2pm Mon, 10:30am-2pm & 5-8:30pm Tue-Fri, 8:30am-1pm & 5-8:30pm Sat, 8:30am-4pm Sun) In an old brick house just north of the District, Monell's is beloved for down-home Southern food served communally, meaning you sit with strangers and pass the food around the table yourselves.

MARCHÉ ARTISAN FOODS
Bistro $$

(www.marcheartisanfoods.com; 1000 Main St; mains $9-16; ☉8am-9pm Tue-Sat, to 4pm Sun) In rapidly gentrifying East Nashville, this airy bistro has a menu of light French- and Italian-inflected fare, made with seasonal local ingredients. Drop in for a cinnamon brioche at breakfast, or a plate of homemade gnocchi with sweet corn for dinner.

Elliston Place Soda Shop
Diner $

(2111 Elliston Pl; mains $3-6; ☉7am-7pm Mon-Sat) Serving fountain Cokes and meat-and-threes to Vandy students since the 1930s.

Drinking & Entertainment

Bars & Nightclubs

CAFE COCO
Cafe, Bar

(www.cafecoco.com; 210 Louise Ave; ☉24hr) In a ramshackle old cottage just off Elliston Pl, Cafe Coco is like an especially groovy frat house, with a 24-hour whirl of action. Twenty-somethings snack on sandwiches and cake in the front parlor, smoke on the large patio, drink at the bar and tap away on laptops in the old bedrooms (there's free wi-fi).

WHISKEY KITCHEN
Pub

(www.whiskeykitchen.com; 118 12th Ave S) In the Gulch, an up-and-coming patch

Southern cocktails
JERRY ALEXANDER/LONELY PLANET IMAGES ©

LEE FOSTER/LONELY PLANET IMAGES ©

Don't Miss **Grand Ole Opry**

This unassuming modern brick building seats 4400 for the Grand Ole Opry, held on Friday and Saturday from March to November. This boot-stompin' extravaganza pays lavish tribute to classic Nashville country music. In the winter (December to February), shows play at the Ryman Auditorium.

Guided backstage tours are offered daily by reservation – book online up to two weeks ahead. Across the plaza, a small **museum** tells the story of the Opry with wax characters, colorful costumes and dioramas.

The Opry is 10 miles northeast of Downtown at Hwy 155/Briley Pkwy exits 11 and 12B.

THINGS YOU NEED TO KNOW

Grand Ole Opry (☎ 615-871-6779; www.opry.com; 2802 Opryland Dr, Music Valley; adult $28-88, child $18-53); museum (admission free; ☺ 10:30am-6pm Mar-Dec)

---

of rehabbed warehouses adjacent to downtown, this neo-Southern gastropub with a mile-long whiskey menu is one of Nashville's trendiest spots. Expect crowds.

Live Music

TOOTSIE'S ORCHID LOUNGE   Club
(☎ 615-726-7937; www.tootsies.net; 422 Broadway) The most venerated of the downtown honky-tonks, Tootsie's vibrates with boot-stompin' every night of the week. In the 1960s club owner and den mother 'Tootsie'

Bess nurtured the likes of Willie Nelson, Kris Kristofferson and Waylon Jennings.

BLUEBIRD CAFE   Club
(☎ 615-383-1461; www.bluebirdcafe.com; 4104 Hillsboro Rd; cover free-$15; ☺ shows 6pm & 9:30pm) It's in a strip mall in suburban South Nashville, but don't let that fool you: some of the best original singer-songwriters in country music have graced this tiny stage. Steve Earle, Emmylou Harris, and the Cowboy Junkies have all played the Bluebird.

Detour:
Dollywood

Dollywood (www.dollywood.com; 1020 Dollywood Lane, Pigeon Forge, TN; adult/child $57/46; ⏱Apr-Dec) is a self-created ode to the patron saint of East Tennessee, the big-haired, bigger-bosomed country singer Dolly Parton. The park features Appalachian-themed rides and attractions, from the Mystery Mine roller coaster to the bald-eagle sanctuary, to the faux one-room chapel named after the doctor who delivered Dolly.

ROBERT'S WESTERN WORLD   Club
(www.robertswesternworld.com; 416 Broadway) Buy a pair of boots, a beer or a burger at Robert's, a longtime favorite on the strip. Music starts at 11am and goes all night.

STATION INN   Club
(☎615-255-3307; www.stationinn.com; 402 12th Ave S) South of downtown, this unassuming stone building is the best place in town for serious bluegrass. Don't miss the Tuesday-night Doyle and Debbie show.

RYMAN AUDITORIUM   Concert Venue
(☎tickets 615-458-8700, info 615-889-3060; www.ryman.com; 116 5th Ave) The Ryman's excellent acoustics, historic charm and large seating capacity have kept it the premier venue in town.

ℹ Information

Nashville Visitors Information Center (☎615-259-4747; www.visitmusiccity.com; 501 Broadway, Sommet Center; ⏱8:30am-5:30pm) Has free city maps here at the glass tower. Great online resource.

ℹ Getting There & Around

AIR Nashville International Airport (BNS; ☎615-275-1675; www.nashintl.com) is 8 miles east of town. Taxis charge a flat rate of $25 to downtown or Opryland.

Pole act at Dollywood

Scenic Drive: Natchez Trace Parkway

About 25 miles southwest of Nashville off Hwy 100, drivers pick up the Natchez Trace Pkwy, which leads 444 miles southwest to Natchez, MS. This northern section is one of the most attractive stretches of the entire route, with broad-leafed trees leaning together to form an arch over the winding road. There are three primitive campsites along the way, free and available on a first-come, first-served basis. Near the parkway entrance, stop at the landmark **Loveless Cafe**, a 1950s roadhouse famous for its biscuits with homemade preserves, country ham and ample portions of Southern fried chicken.

GREAT SMOKY MOUNTAINS NATIONAL PARK

More than 10 million visitors a year come through this majestic park, one of the world's most biodiverse areas. Land-scapes range from deep, dim spruce forest to sunny meadows carpeted with daisies and Queen Anne's lace to wide, coffee-brown rivers. There's ample hiking and camping, and opportunities for horse-back riding, bike rental and fly-fishing.

The 815-sq-mile park, which straddles the border between Tennessee and North Carolina, is the country's most visited and, while the main arteries and attractions can get crowded, studies have shown that 95% of visitors never venture further than 100yd from their cars, so it's easy to leave the teeming masses behind.

Stop by a visitor center to pick up a park map and the free park newspaper, *Smokies Guide*.

👁 Sights & Activities

Great Smoky Mountains National Park straddles the North Carolina–Tennessee border, which zigzags diagonally through the heart of the park. The north–south Newfound Gap Road/Highway 441 spans the park, connecting the gateway towns of Gatlinburg, Tennessee, on the north-central border and Cherokee, North Carolina, on the south-central border.

The remains of the 19th-century settlement at **Cades Cove** are some of the park's most popular sights, as evidenced by the teeth-grinding summer traffic jams on the loop road.

Mt LeConte has some of the park's best hikes, as well as the only non-camping accommodations, **LeConte Lodge** (☎ 865-429-5704; www.leconte-lodge.com; cabins per person $79). Though the only way to get to the lodge's rustic, electricity-free cabins is via an 8-mile uphill hike, it's so popular you need to reserve up to a year in advance. Dinner and breakfast are available for $37. You can drive right up to the dizzying heights of **Clingmans Dome**, the third-highest mountain east of the Mississippi, with a futuristic observation tower.

ℹ Information

The park's three interior visitor centers are Sugarlands Visitor Center, at the park's northern entrance near Gatlinburg; Cades Cove Visitor Center, halfway up Cades Cove Loop Rd, off Hwy 441 near the Gatlinburg entrance; and Oconaluftee Visitor Center, at the park's southern entrance near Cherokee, NC.

CHARLESTON

Put on your twinset and pearls or your seersucker suit, have a fortifying sip of sherry, and prepare to be thoroughly drenched in Southern charm. Charleston, South Carolina, is a city for strolling, for admiring antebellum architecture, stop-ping to smell the blooming jasmine and

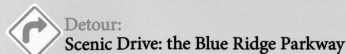

Detour:
Scenic Drive: the Blue Ridge Parkway

Commissioned by president Franklin D Roosevelt as a Depression-era public-works project, the glorious Blue Ridge Parkway traverses the southern Appalachians from Virginia's Shenandoah National Park at Mile 0 to the Great Smoky Mountains National Park at Mile 469. Alpine vistas are unforgettable, particularly during the blooming wildflowers of spring, and autumn's fiery blaze. The National Park Service **campgrounds & visitor centers** (877-444-6777; www.blueridgeparkway.org; tent sites $16) are open May to October. Parkway entrance is free; be aware that restrooms and gas stations are few and far between.

Parkway highlights and campgrounds include the following:

Cumberland Knob (Mile 217.5) NPS visitor center; easy walk to the knob.

Doughton Park (Mile 241.1) Gas, food, trails and camping.

Blowing Rock (Mile 291.8) Small tourist town, named for a craggy, commercialized cliff that offers great views, occasional updrafts and a Native American love story.

Moses H Cone Memorial Park (Mile 294.1) A lovely old estate with pleasant walks and a craft shop.

Grandfather Mountain (Mile 305.1) Hugely popular for its mile-high pedestrian 'swinging bridge.'

Linville Falls (Mile 316.4) Short hiking trails to the falls, and campsites.

Linville Caverns (Mile 317) Limestone cave with neat formations and underground streams; tours $7.

Little Switzerland (Mile 334) Old-style mountain resort.

Mt Mitchell State Park (Mile 355.5) Highest peak east of the Mississippi (6684ft); hiking and camping.

Craggy Gardens (Mile 364) Hiking trails explode with rhododendron blossoms in summer.

Folk Art Center (Mile 382) Local crafts for sale.

Mount Pisgah (Mile 408.8) Hiking and camping.

---

long dinners on the verandah. A tooth-achingly romantic place: everywhere you turn another blushing bride is standing on the steps of yet another charming church.

 Sights & Activities

Historic District
The quarter south of Beaufain and Hasell Sts has the bulk of the antebellum mansions, shops, bars and cafes.

OLD SLAVE MART MUSEUM Museum
(www.nps.gov/nr/travel/charleston/osm.htm; 6 Chalmers St; adult/child $7/5; 9am-5pm Mon-Sat) African men, women and children were once auctioned off here; it's now a museum of South Carolina's shameful past. Text-heavy exhibits illuminate the slave experience; the few artifacts, such as leg shackles, are especially chilling.

OLD EXCHANGE & PROVOST DUNGEON Historic Building
(www.oldexchange.com; 122 E Bay St; adult/child $8/4; 9am-5pm;) Kids love this dungeon, built in 1771 as a customs house

and later used as a prison for pirates. Costumed guides lead tours.

HEYWARD-WASHINGTON HOUSE
Historic Building

(www.charlestonmuseum.org; 87 Church St) Built in 1772, this house belonged to Thomas Heyward Jr, a signer of the Declaration of Independence, and contains some lovely examples of Charleston-made mahogany furniture, as well as the city's only preserved historic kitchen.

City Market
Market

(Market St) The historic market is the crowded center of the district, with vendors hawking junky souvenirs from open-air stalls.

White Point Park
Garden

Sit a spell in this shady park and ponder whether 'rich merchant seaman' is still a viable career.

Rainbow Row
Neighborhood

Around the corner from White Point Park, a stretch of lower E Bay St known as is one of the most photographed areas of town for its candy-colored houses.

Aquarium Wharf

Aquarium Wharf surrounds pretty Liberty Sq and is a great place to stroll around and watch the tugboats guiding ships into the seventh-largest container port in the US. The wharf is the embarkation point for tours to Fort Sumter.

FORT SUMTER
Historic Site

The first shots of the Civil War rang out at Fort Sumter, on a pentagon-shaped island in the harbor. A Confederate stronghold, the fort was shelled to bits by Union forces from 1863 to 1865. A few original guns and fortifications give a feel for the momentous history. The only way to get here is by boat tour (☎843-883-3123; www.nps.gov/fosu; adult/child $17/10; ☺tours 9:30am, noon & 2:30pm summer, fewer winter).

SOUTH CAROLINA AQUARIUM
Aquarium

(www.scaquarium.org; 100 Aquarium Wharf; adult/child $20/13; ☺9am-5pm; ▥) This massive, excellent aquarium showcases the state's diverse aquatic life, from the otters of the Blue Ridge Mountains to the loggerhead turtles of the Atlantic. The highlight is the 42ft Great Ocean Tank, which teems with various sharks and alien-looking puffer fish.

Horsedrawn wagon tour, Charleston's Historic District

DENNIS JOHNSON/LONELY PLANET IMAGES ©

If You Like...
Southern Cooking

If you like the celebrated New South cuisine at Husk (p240), make time to explore these other great Charleston restaurants:

1 FIG
(☏843-805-5900; www.eatatfig.com; 232 Meeting St; mains $28-32; ⏰5:30-10:30pm Mon-Thu, to 11pm Fri-Sun) Foodies swoon over inspired nouvelle-Southern fare like crispy pig's trotters (that means 'feet' – local and hormone-free, of course) with celery-root remoulade in this rustic-chic dining room.

2 S.N.O.B.
(☏843-723-3424; www.mavericksouthern kitchens.com; 192 E Bay St; mains $18-34; ⏰lunch Mon-Fri, dinner nightly) The cheeky name (it stands for 'slightly north of Broad,' as in Broad St) reflects the anything-goes spirit of this upscale-casual spot, which draws raves for its eclectic menu, filled with treats such as house-smoked salmon, and sautéed squab breast over cheese grits.

🛏 Sleeping

B&Bs fill up fast, so try using an agency such as **Historic Charleston B&B** (☏843-722-6606; www.historiccharlestonbedandbreak fast.com; 57 Broad St).

ANSONBOROUGH INN　Hotel $$
(☏800-522-2073; www.ansonboroughinn.com; 1 Maiden Ln; r $149-290; ❄🛜) A central atrium done up with burnished pine, exposed beams and nautical-themed oil paintings makes this intimate Historic District hotel feel like being inside an antique sailing ship. Droll neo-Victorian touches like the Persian-carpeted glass elevator and the closet-sized British pub add a sense of fun. Huge guest rooms mix old and new, with worn leather couches, high ceilings and flat-screen TVs.

VENDUE INN　Inn $$
(☏843-577-7970; www.vendueinn.com; 19 Vendue Range; r incl breakfast $145-255; ❄🛜) This teeny boutique hotel, in the part of downtown known as the French Quarter, is decked out in a trendy mix of exposed brick and eccentric antiques. Rooms have cool amenities like deep soaking tubs and gas fireplaces. Even cooler is the Rooftop bar.

MILLS HOUSE HOTEL　Hotel $$$
(☏843-577-2400; www.millshouse.com; 115 Meeting St; r from $189; ❄🛜🏊) This grand old dame (150 years young, merci) has had an $11-million facelift and is now one of the most opulent choices in the area. Gilded elevators lead from an enormous marble lobby to 214 lushly upholstered rooms. The sun has still not set on the British Empire inside the clubby, wood-paneled Barbadoes Room restaurant.

Eating

HUSK　New Southern $$$
(☏843-577-2500; www.huskrestaurant.com; 76 Queen St; mains $22-26; ⏰11:30am-2:30pm Mon-Sat, 5:30-10pm daily, brunch 10am-2:30pm Sun) Husk was the South's most buzzed-about restaurant when it burst onto the scene in late 2010. Everything on the menu is grown or raised in the South, from the jalapeño marmalade-topped Georgia corn soup to the yuzu-scented Cooper River oysters. The setting, in a two-story mansion, is elegant but un-fussy, and the adjacent speakeasy-style bar is straight-up terrific.

ℹ Information

Visitor center (☏843-853-8000; www. charlestoncvb.com; 375 Meeting St; ⏰8:30am-5pm) Find help with accommodations and tours or watch a half-hour video on Charleston history in this spacious renovated warehouse.

Getting There & Around

AIR Charleston International Airport (CHS; 843-767-7009; www.chs-airport.com; 5500 International Blvd) is 12 miles outside of town in North Charleston.

BUS & TRAIN The Greyhound station (3610 Dorchester Rd) and the Amtrak train station (4565 Gaynor Ave) are both in North Charleston.

PUBLIC TRANSPORTATION City-wide buses are run by CARTA (www.ridecarta.com; fare $1.75); the free DASH streetcars do four loop routes from the visitor center.

SAVANNAH

Like a Southern belle who wears hot pants under her skirt, Georgia's grand historic town revolves around formal antebellum architecture and the revelry of local students from Savannah College of Art & Design. It sits alongside the Savannah River, about 18 miles from the coast, amid Lowcountry swamps and mammoth live oak trees dripping with Spanish moss. With its gorgeous mansions, cotton warehouses, wonderfully beautiful squares and Colonial public buildings, Savannah preserves its past with pride and grace. However, unlike its sister city of Charleston, SC, which retains its reputation as a dignified and refined cultural center, Savannah isn't clean-cut – the town has been described as 'a beautiful lady with a dirty face.'

Sights & Activities

Savannah's Historic District is a rectangle bounded by the Savannah River, Forsyth Park, E Broad St and Martin Luther King Jr Blvd (MLK). In converted cotton warehouses situated along the Savannah River, you'll find a touristy commercial district of bars, restaurants and shops. City Market is an equally touristy district of shops and restaurants near Franklin Sq, and W Broughton St is a cosmopolitan shopping drag with cafes and restaurants. There are hip enclaves around town: on busy MLK by the college and E Park Ave by Forsyth Park.

The Central Park of Savannah is a sprawling rectangular green space called **Forsyth Park**.

Classic buildings in Savannah

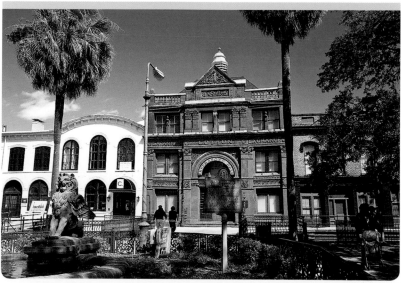

CHARLES COOK/LONELY PLANET IMAGES ©

OWENS-THOMAS HOUSE
Historic Building

(www.telfair.org; 124 Abercorn St; adult/child $15/5; ⊙noon-5pm Mon, 10am-5pm Tue-Sat, 1-5pm Sun) Completed in 1819 by British architect William Jay, this gorgeous villa exemplifies English Regency–style architecture, which is known for its symmetry. The guided tour is fussy, but it delivers interesting trivia about the mansion.

JEPSON CENTER FOR THE ARTS
Art Gallery

(JCA; www.telfair.org; 207 W York St; multivenue ticket adult/child $20/5; ⊙10am-5pm Mon, Wed, Fri & Sat, 10am-8pm Thu, noon-5pm Sun; 🚼) Now over five years old but still looking pretty darn space-age by Savannah's standards, the JCA focuses on 20th- and 21st-century art. Its contents are modest in size but intriguing. There's also a neat interactive area for kids.

TELFAIR MUSEUM OF ART
Art Gallery

(www.telfair.org; 121 Barnard St; multivenue ticket adult/child $20/5; ⊙noon-5pm Mon, 10am-5pm Tue-Sat, 1-5pm Sun) Along with silver from the 1800s and a colossal oil painting depicting a scene from the Hundred Years War, Sylvia Shaw's famous 1936 *Bird Girl* sculpture – the one on the cover of *Midnight in the Garden of Good and Evil* – stands inside this museum.

RALPH MARK GILBERT CIVIL RIGHTS MUSEUM
Museum

(460 Martin Luther King Jr Blvd; adults/child $8/4; ⊙9am-5pm Tue-Sat) Focuses on the local history of segregated schools, hotels, hospitals, jobs and lunch counters. Don't neglect to the push the buttons at the Levy's lunch counter – a dramatization, but no less stinging.

 Sleeping

THUNDERBIRD INN
Motel $$

(☎912-232-2661; www.thethunderbirdinn. com; 611 W Oglethorpe Ave; r $99; P❄🛜) A little dab of Palm Springs, a little dip of

Vegas best describes this renovated vintage-chic 1964 motel. But in a land of stuffy B&Bs, this groovy place is an oasis, made all the better by a fresh coat of soothing paints and local SCAD (Savannah College of Art and Design) student art. The hotel is just outside the tourist area, across from the Greyhound station.

MANSION ON FORSYTH PARK
Hotel $$$

(📞912-238-5158; www.mansiononforsyth-park.com; 700 Drayton St; r weekday/weekend $199/249; ✳@🛜🏊) A choice location and chic design highlight the luxe accommodations on offer at the 18,000-sq-ft Mansion. The best part of the hotel-spa is the amazing local and international art that crowds its walls and hallways, over 400 original pieces in all.

BED & BREAKFAST INN
B&B $$

(📞912-238-0518; www.savannahbnb.com; 117 W Gordon St; r weekday/weekend from $159/179; P✳🛜) Spittin' distance from Savan-nah's most architecturally diverse square (Monterrey), this is a well-loved, well-worn establishment, but the rooms are crisp, unique and tidy. Easy to walk right by on a uniform street of 1850 row houses, the rooms are scattered about six buildings along the street.

Eating

MRS WILKES'
Southern $$

(www.mrswilkes.com; 107 W Jones St; lunch $16; 11am-2pm Mon-Fri) The line outside can begin as early as 8am at this first-come, first served, Southern comfort food institution. Once the lunch bell rings and you are seated family-style, the kitchen unloads on you: fried chicken, beef stew, meatloaf, cheese potatoes, collard greens, black-eyed peas, mac 'n' cheese, rutabaga, candied yams, squash casserole, creamed corn *and* biscuits. It's like Thanksgiving and the Last Supper rolled into one massive feast chased with sweet tea.

OLDE PINK HOUSE   New Southern $$$

(☎912-232-4286; 23 Abercorn St; mains $25-31; ⏰5-10:30pm Sun-Mon, 11am-10:30pm Tue-Thu, 11am-11pm Fri & Sat) There are fancier and trendier restaurants in Savannah but this 1771 National Landmark on Reynolds Sq is rarely trumped for food or experience. The whole place epitomizes antebellum romance and you'll fall in love with the signature crispy scored flounder (though the menu is chock-full of irresistible Southern-bent delights). The service is casually flawless; the dark and cozy downstairs bar is also worthy of a cocktail pop-in.

ANGEL'S BBQ   Barbecue $

(www.angels-bbq.com; 21 West Oglethorpe Ln; pulled-pork sandwich $6; ⏰11:30am-3pm Tue, to 6pm Wed-Sat) Utterly low-brow and hidden down a uneventful lane, Angel's pulled-pork sandwich and sea-salted fries will leave you humbled and thoroughly satisfied.

CHA BELLA   American $$

(www.cha-bella.com; 102 E Broad St; dinner mains $17-32; ⏰5:30-9pm Tue-Thu, to 10pm Fri & Sat, 5:30-9pm Sun) With a commitment to organic, local and well-presented vittles, this welcoming restaurant leaves pretention behind: swings hang on the lovely patio. The Georgia white-shrimp risotto or fish-market special will not leave you unpleased.

🍷 Drinking

ROCKS ON THE ROOF   Bar

(102 West Bay St; ⏰from 11am) The expansive rooftop bar at the new Bohemian Hotel is just what Savannah needed: a breezy, lipstick-red wrap-around rooftop set to an indie-cred soundtrack with lovely river views.

LULU'S CHOCOLATE BAR   Cafe

(www.luluschocolatebar.net; 42 Martin Luther King Jr Blvd) More a place to sink yourself into a sugar coma than catch a buzz, Lulu's is an adorable yet chic neighborhood martini and dessert bar.

Boardwalk trail, Okefenokee Swamp Park

CAROL POLICH/LONELY PLANET IMAGES ©

Detour:
Okefenokee National Wildlife Refuge

Established in 1937, the **Okefenokee National Wildlife Refuge** (www.fws.gov/okefenokee) is a national gem, encompassing 396,000 acres of bog in a giant saucer-shaped depression that was once part of the ocean floor. The swamp, which straddles the Georgia–Florida border, is home to an estimated 9000 to 15,000 alligators, 234 bird species, 49 types of mammal and 60 amphibian species. The **Okefenokee Swamp Park** (www.okeswamp.com; US 1 South, Waycross; adult/child $12/11; ☉9am-5:30pm) maintains around 3000 acres of the refuge and has captive bears and gators on-site, or you can explore the swamp in a canoe or on a boat tour. The ultimate experience is a multiday canoe trip on the swamp's 120 miles of waterways. Call the US Fish & Wildlife Service's **Okefenokee National Wildlife Refuge Wilderness Canoe Guide** (☏912-496-7836; www.fws.gov/okefenokee) if you're considering a trip. Guided boat trips are also available if the water levels are high enough.

GALLERY ESPRESSO   Cafe
(www.galleryespresso.com; 234 Bull St; ☉7:30am-10pm Mon-Fri, 8am-11pm Sat & Sun) Savannah's best coffee shop is cozy, more conveniently located and is near-fiendish regarding its teas. There's also light fare and scrumptious desserts.

❶ Information

Visitor center (☏912-944-0455; www.savannahvisit.com; 301 Martin Luther King Jr Blvd; ☉8:30am-5pm Mon-Fri, 9am-5pm Sat & Sun) Excellent resources and services are available in this center, based in a restored 1860s train station. Many privately operated city tours start here.

❶ Getting There & Away

AIR The Savannah/Hilton Head International Airport (SAV; www.savannahairport.com) is about 5 miles west of downtown off I-16. The visitor center runs shuttles from the airport to Historic District hotels for $25 round-trip.
TRAIN The Amtrak station (2611 Seaboard Coastline Dr) is just a few miles west of the Historic District.

Cumberland Island

An unspoiled paradise, a backpacker's fantasy, a site for day trips or extended stays – it's clear why the Carnegie family used Cumberland as a retreat long ago. Most of this southernmost barrier island off Georgia is now occupied by the **Cumberland Island National Seashore** (www.nps.gov/cuis; admission $4). Almost half of its 36,415 acres consists of marsh, mudflats and tidal creeks. On the ocean side are 16 miles of wide, sandy beach that you might have all to yourself. The island's interior is characterized by a maritime forest. Ruins from the Carnegie estate Dungeness are astounding, as are the wild turkeys, tiny fiddler crabs and beautiful butterflies. Feral horses roam the island and are a common sight.

The only public access to the island is via boat to/from the quirky, lazy town of **St Marys** (www.stmaryswelcome.com). A convenient and pleasant **ferry** (☏912-882-4335; adult/child $20/14; ☉departures 9am & 11:45am) leaves from the mainland at the St Marys dock. Reservations are staunchly recommended well before you arrive, and visitors are required to check in at the **Visitors Center** (☏912-882-4336; ☉8am-4:30pm) at the dock at least 30 minutes prior to departure.

Florida

Blessed with almost year-round sunshine, Florida is a captivating subtropical peninsula famed for its white-sand beaches, aquamarine waters and fiery red sunsets. Surreal, garish, wacky and perpetually self-amused, Florida is a fantasy-filled swampy wonderland of giddy delights, from alligators, mermaids and Mickey Mouse to Miami's hedonistic, art-fueled, celebrity playground.

Florida's gorgeous beaches are its calling card, and you could visit one every day of the year and still not see them all. But the state offers much more: the prehistoric Everglades with its dizzying plant and animal life, Orlando's phantasmagorical theme parks, the art-deco eye-candy of South Beach, Key West's nightly carnival and Key Largo's Technicolored coral reefs. Given its wide-ranging offerings, diversity thrives in Florida: Cubans, retirees, fishermen, environmentalists, Christian fundamentalists and circus performers are all contribute to the ever-mutable social landscape.

Diver and loggerhead sea turtle off the Florida coast   **247**
MICHAEL PATRICK O'NEILL/ALAMY ©

Florida

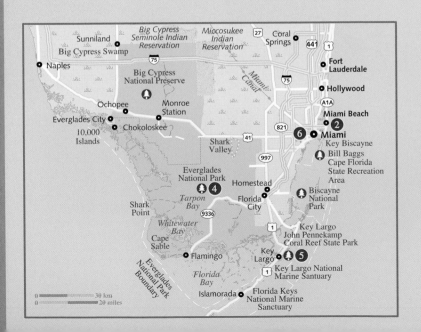

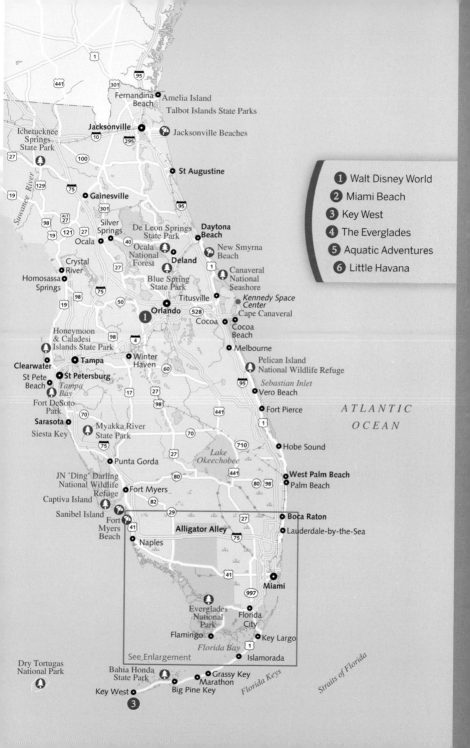

1 Walt Disney World
2 Miami Beach
3 Key West
4 The Everglades
5 Aquatic Adventures
6 Little Havana

Fernandina Beach
Amelia Island
Talbot Islands State Parks
Jacksonville
Jacksonville Beaches
Ichetucknee Springs State Park
St Augustine
Gainesville
Silver Springs
De Leon Springs State Park
Daytona Beach
Ocala
Ocala National Forest
Deland
New Smyrna Beach
Crystal River
Blue Spring State Park
Canaveral National Seashore
Homosassa Springs
Titusville
Kennedy Space Center
Orlando
Cocoa
Cape Canaveral
Honeymoon & Caladesi Islands State Park
Winter Haven
Cocoa Beach
Clearwater
Tampa
Melbourne
St Pete Beach
St Petersburg
Pelican Island National Wildlife Refuge
Tampa Bay
Sebastian Inlet
Fort DeSoto Park
Vero Beach
Sarasota
Myakka River State Park
Fort Pierce
Siesta Key
Suwannee River
ATLANTIC OCEAN
Punta Gorda
Lake Okeechobee
Hobe Sound
JN 'Ding' Darling National Wildlife Refuge
West Palm Beach
Captiva Island
Fort Myers
Palm Beach
Sanibel Island
Fort Myers Beach
Alligator Alley
Boca Raton
Naples
Lauderdale-by-the-Sea
Miami
Everglades National Park
Florida City
Flamingo
Key Largo
Florida Bay
Islamorada
See Enlargement
Dry Tortugas National Park
Bahia Honda State Park
Grassy Key
Marathon
Big Pine Key
Florida Keys
Straits of Florida
Key West

Florida's Highlights

1
Walt Disney World

Walt Disney World (p282) stretches superlatives (and queues, admittedly) like few other places. While the rides are good, when it comes to the sheer variety of parades, light displays and dance shows, this is where the bar is set in the theme-park world.

Need to Know

LINES Arrive 30 minutes before parks open **SNACKS** Save money by bringing your own **DINING** Call ☎407-939-3463 for all Disney restaurant bookings **For more, see p282.**

Walt Disney World Don't Miss List

BY DEWAYNE BEVIL, REPORTER,
COVERING THEME PARKS AND ATTRACTIONS
FOR THE *ORLANDO SENTINEL*

1 MAGIC KINGDOM

No first-time visitor to Walt Disney World should miss Magic Kingdom (p282), the theme park that changed Florida tourism. Nostalgia and classic attractions dominate, but Disney has upgraded favorites such as the Haunted Mansion and the Enchanted Tiki Room, even using interactive features to make the waits on line less tedious. Magic Kingdom is a winner with little princesses, which is unlikely to change with the major expansion of Fantasyland.

2 TOY STORY MIDWAY MANIA

The long, long line leading into this ride is testimony to its extreme popularity. Once inside and aboard, guests are effectively shrunk into a video game with characters from the Pixar movies, and rapid-fire virtual carnival games.

3 WILD AFRICA TREK

Kilimanjaro Safari is a behind-the-scenes tour at Disney's Animal Kingdom (below left; p282) that takes guests beyond the beaten track, with unique angles of rhinos and crocodiles, rope bridges and extended quality time. Only a few dozen folk are allowed each day, so there's a special price – $189 per person, on top of regular admission to Animal Kingdom – but you'll feel special having a snack in a pavilion overlooking wildlife on the savanna.

4 EPCOT INTERNATIONAL FOOD & WINE FESTIVAL

This seasonal event, which kicks off in September, spotlights global cuisine in kiosks scattered throughout the theme park's World Showcase. The food is served up tapas-style during the festival, which lasts six weeks and is a favorite of locals, even those who normally avoid the tourism corridor.

5 FIREWORKS

Major pyrotechnics are a nightly event at Walt Disney World. The 'Wishes' show (far left), complete with real-life Tinker Bell flying out of Cinderella Castle, caps off the day at Magic Kingdom, while 'IllumiNations' is the impressive finale at Epcot. Boat excursions tied to the fireworks shows are also available on select nights.

251

Miami Beach

White sand, deep-blue Atlantic water and sun worshippers from every corner of the globe are all part of the enchanting scenery on lovely Miami Beach (p263). Frolicking in the waves by day, strolling the restaurant-lined Española Way by night, then wandering through its stunning Art Deco Historic District (p258) is a good introduction to the Miami lifestyle. Cocktails, seafood feasts, steamy salsa: it's all part of quintessential Miami.

2

3 Key West

At the end of the road in the continental US, the eccentric-loving island of Key West (p276) has a long, colorful past of pirates, sunken treasures, literary legends and plenty of ghosts. Today, local residents celebrate their free-spirited ethos, while visitors soak up the mellow vibe, share drinks and swap stories with local characters, snorkel the crystal clear waters and reset their internal clocks to 'island time.' Local weaving a sun-hat out of palm fronds

MICAH WRIGHT/LONELY PLANET IMAGES ©

The Everglades

4

With a geologic history dating back to prehistoric times, the Everglades (p269) cover more than 1.5 million acres and is home to a staggering variety of plant and animal life, including 69 species on America's endangered list. Manatees, alligators, Florida panthers, bottlenose dolphins and some 350 bird species inhabit this vast wetland ecosystem. There are many ways to experience it, including by canoe, kayak, bike or on foot. Great blue heron

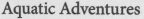

5

Aquatic Adventures

No matter where you are in Florida, you're never more than 60 miles from the shoreline, and there are boundless adventures just beyond the beach. You can head to the Keys (p272) for snorkeling in crystal-clear water that's home to a vibrant coral reef, or book a boat tour or fishing expedition anywhere along the coast. There's also kayaking, windsurfing and a host of other waterside adventures to be had – Miami (p264) is a good place to start.

6

Little Havana

Calle Ocho (Spanish for 'Eighth Street'; p266) is the heart of this thriving Latino community and one of Miami's most vibrant neighborhoods. Here you can watch *tabaqueros* hand-roll cigars, see old-timers throwing bones at Máximo Gómez Park, or have a bang-up meal at a classic Cuban diner. At night, don't miss Cuban jazz and steamy salsa nights – served up with plenty of mojitos, of course.

Florida's Best...

Beaches

○ **South Beach, Miami**
(p263) Home to lovely sands
and the eye-candy that
saunter here.

○ **Fort Zachary Taylor**
(p277) Key West's prettiest
beach, with swaying pines
and calm waters.

○ **Bahia Honda State Park**
(p275) One of Florida's most
beautiful beaches lies some
45 minutes east of Key West.

○ **Sanibel Island** (p273)
Idyllic beaches on this barrier
island are a beachcombers'
paradise.

Activities for Families

○ **Universal Orlando Resort**
(p283) Entertainment galore,
including the movie magic
of Universal Studios and the
celebrated new Wizarding
World of Harry Potter.

○ **SeaWorld** (p280) Close
encounters with sea animals
of all shapes and sizes.

○ **Watson Island** (p262)
Home to the Miami
Children's Museum and the
wildlife-packed Jungle Island.

○ **Everglades by Tram**
(p270) This two-hour tram
tour reveals loads of wildlife,
including ibis, herons and
alligators.

Wildlife Spotting

○ **10,000 Islands** (p271) Spy
wondrous wildlife, including
dolphins and manatees, on
an Everglades cruise.

○ **John Pennekamp
Coral Reef State Park**
(p272) Go eye-to-eye with
iridescent tropical fish and
coral blooms in this vibrant
underwater world.

○ **Grassy Key** (p275) At the
Dolphin Research Center,
you can learn all about our
aquatic cousins and even
take a swim with them.

○ **JN 'Ding' Darling
National Wildlife Refuge**
(p273) A first-rate bird-
watching site on peaceful
Sanibel Island.

Left: Burrowing owl, JN 'Ding' Darling National Wildlife Refuge (p273);
Above: Sanibel Island (p273)

Need to Know

Bars & Nightlife

○ **Nikki Beach Club** (p268) Bask beneath swaying palms at this stylish club in hedonistic South Beach.

○ **Green Parrot** (p279) In drink-loving Key West, this divey classic has been going strong for over a century.

○ **House of Blues** (p285) For a break from the Big Mouse, head to this excellent live-music spot in downtown Disney.

○ **Tobacco Road** (p268) Ramshackle old roadhouse in Miami with a much celebrated indie-rock scene.

ADVANCE PLANNING

○ **Six months before** For Disney-goers, book accommodation and special dining reservations (ie Cinderella's Royal Table). Purchase theme-park tickets to safeguard against future price increases. If you're going to Miami's massive Art Basel, reserve rooms.

○ **Two months before** Book popular Orlando attractions that can sell out (like Discovery Cove). Buy tickets for pro sports and concerts in Miami.

○ **One week before** Book walking and Everglades tours, river cruises and other activities.

RESOURCES

○ **Cool Junkie** (www. cooljunkie.com) Nightlife and other goings-on in Miami.

○ **Beached Miami** (www. beachedmiami.com) Arts, nightlife, music and other happenings in Miami.

○ **Greater Miami & the Beaches** (www.miamiand beaches.com) Official Miami tourism site with events listings.

○ **EvergladesOnline.com** (www.everglades online.com) Handy info for visiting the Everglades and nearby gateways.

○ **Visit Orlando** (www. visitorlando.com) Good resource for trip-planning to Florida's entertainment capital.

○ **Florida Keys & Key West** (www.fla-keys.com) Useful for Keys-bound travelers.

GETTING AROUND

○ **Airports** Miami International Airport (MIA; www.miami-airport.com), Orlando (MCO; www. orlandoairports.net) and Key West (EYW; www. keywestinternational airport.com) are gateways.

○ **Boat** Key West Express (☎888-539-2628; www. seakeywestexpress.com) runs fast catamarans from Miami to Key West.

○ **Train** Amtrak has daily trains between Miami and New York City via Orlando.

BE FOREWARNED

○ **Hurricanes** Official hurricane season lasts from June 1 to November 30.

○ **Traffic** A major headache in Miami and other large Florida cities. Avoid traveling during rush (peak) hour.

○ **Crime** In Miami, be cautious of Little Haiti, stretches of the Miami riverfront and Biscayne Blvd, and deserted South Beach areas below 5th St.

Florida Itineraries

In two weeks, you can explore the world's finest theme parks in Orlando, then head south for rewarding exploration in Miami, the Everglades and the Florida Keys. Great beaches, seafood feasts, wildlife watching and aquatic adventures are all essential experiences.

 5 DAYS

DISNEY WORLD, UNIVERSAL STUDIOS & ORLANDO
Magical Journeys

Spend your first day at the **(1) Magic Kingdom**, Walt Disney World's most famous attraction. Visit Cinderella's Castle, get a dose of yo-ho-ho at Pirates of the Caribbean and take a thrilling ride at Space Mountain. Dine with princesses at Cinderella's Royal Table, then catch the nightly fireworks show.

On day two, head to **(2) Epcot**. At the World Showcase, 'travel' through 11 countries, catch live shows, browse native arts and crafts, and feast on global fare. Stick around for the brilliant Illuminations light show.

Rise early for the **(3) Animal Kingdom**. Go on the Kilimanjaro Safari where you can see elephants, giraffes and other African wildlife. Catch a show inside the 14-story Tree of Life, then have dinner at African-inspired Boma.

On day four, enter Universal Studio's **(4) Islands of Adventure**, with its dazzling rides, shows and interactive amusement. Delve into the worlds of Marvel Super Heroes, Jurassic Park, Doctor Seuss and Harry Potter. Dine in Orlando at the Ravenous Pig.

On your last day, explore the life aquatic at **(5) SeaWorld**. Watch dolphin and whale shows and learn about the world beyond the shore. If you prefer to bliss out on your last day, opt for the tropical idyll of the Discovery Cove.

7 DAYS

MIAMI TO KEY WEST
Beaches, Wetlands & Coral Reefs

Start in **(1) Miami**. On day one, explore the Art Deco Historic District, then sunbake and people-watch on South Beach. That evening, go for Haitian cuisine at Tap Tap and cocktails at the stylish Skybar. On day two, visit Little Havana, gallery-filled Wynwood and the Design District, and Little Haiti. That night catch a show at Tobacco Road.

On day three head for the **(2) Everglades National Park**. Stop at the Ernest Coe Visitor Center for hiking and wildlife-watching, then go deeper to **(3) Flamingo Marina** for a wetlands boat ride. Spend the night in **(4) Key Largo**. In the morning, dive the underwater splendors of **(5) John**

Pennekamp Coral Reef State Park. In the afternoon, take a glass-bottom boat tour.

On day five, enjoy the scenic drive along the **(6) Overseas Hwy**. Have a toes-in-the-sand seafood feast at Morada Bay on **(7) Islamorada**, take a swim off Marathon's **(8) Sombrero Beach** then go for walk in **(9) Bahia Honda State Park**.

Spend your last two days in **(10) Key West**. Visit Hemingway House, watch the sunset from Mallory Sq, take a catamaran trip, bar-hop on Duval St, and get your fill of key lime pie, conch fritters and margaritas.

Art Deco Historic District (p258), Miami Beach
RICHARD CUMMINS/LONELY PLANET IMAGES ©

Discover Florida

A lizard in the Everglades (p269)
MARK NEWMAN / LONELY PLANET IMAGES ©

MIAMI

Miami moves to a different rhythm from anywhere else in the USA. Subtropical beauty and Latin sexiness are everywhere: from the cigar-smoke-filled dance halls where Havana expats dance to *son* music and boleros to the exclusive nightclubs where stiletto-heeled Brazilian models shake to Latin hip-hop. Whether you're meeting avant-garde gallery hipsters or passing the buffed, perfect bodies recumbent along South Beach, everyone can seem oh-so-artfully posed. Meanwhile, street vendors and restaurants dish out flavors of the Caribbean, Cuba, Argentina and Haiti. For travelers, the city can be as intoxicating as a sweaty-glassed mojito.

 Sights

Miami Beach

ART DECO HISTORIC DISTRICT Neighborhood
The well-preserved, pastel-hued Art Deco Historic District verily screams 'Miami.' It's the largest concentration of art deco anywhere in the world, with approximately 1200 buildings lining the streets around Ocean Dr and Collins Ave. For info and **walking tours** (90-min guided tours adult/child $20/free; ◷10:30am Fri-Wed, 6:30pm Thu), make your first stop the **Art Deco Welcome Center** (Map p260; ☏305-531-3484; www.mdpl.org; 1200 Ocean Dr; ◷9:30am-7pm).

BASS MUSEUM OF ART Art Gallery
(off Map p260; www.bassmuseum.org; 2121 Park Ave; adult/child $8/6; ◷noon-5pm Wed-Sun)
The best art museum in Miami Beach has a playfully futurist facade, and the

Greater Miami

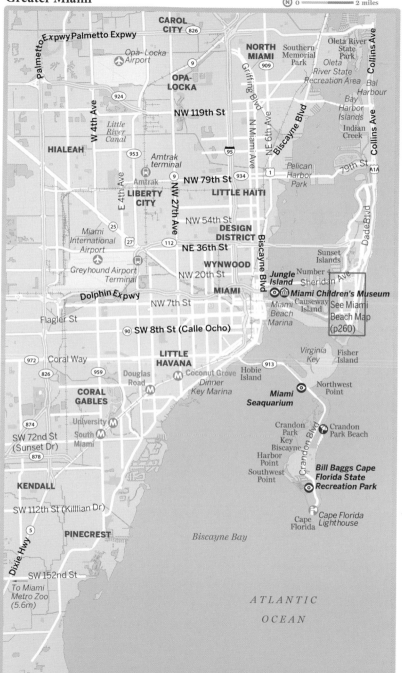

See Miami Beach Map (p260)

Miami Beach

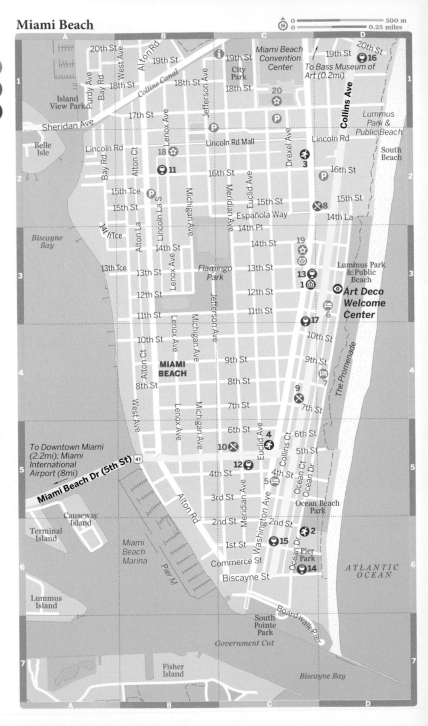

DISCOVER FLORIDA MIAMI

Miami Beach

collection isn't shabby either, ranging from 16th-century European religious works to Renaissance paintings.

WORLD EROTIC ART MUSEUM   Art Gallery
(Map p260; www.weam.com; 1205 Washington Ave; adult $15; ☺11am-10pm, to midnight Fri & Sat) Unfazed by South Beach's bare flesh? Something will get your attention here, with an amazingly extensive collection of naughty and erotic art, and even furniture depicting all sorts of parts and acts.

Design District, Wynwood & Little Haiti

Proving that Miami Beach's 'SoBe' (South Beach) doesn't hold the lease on hip, these two trendy areas north of downtown – all but deserted 25 years ago – have ensconced themselves as bastions of art and design. The **Design District** (www.miamidesign district.net) is a mecca for interior designers, home to dozens of galleries and contemporary furniture, fixture and design showrooms. Just south of the Design District, Wynwood is a notable arts district, with myriad galleries and art studios housed in abandoned factories and warehouses.

View from the lifeguard tower,
South Beach, Miami
RICHARD CUMMINE/LONELY PLANET IMAGES ©

The home of Miami's Haitian refugees, **Little Haiti** is defined by brightly painted homes, markets and *botanicas* (voodoo shops).

LITTLE HAITI CULTURAL CENTER
Art Gallery

(305-960-2969; www.miamigov.com/lhcultural center; 212 NE 59th Tce; 9am-5pm) Miami has the largest community of *Ayisens* (Haitians) in the world outside Haiti, and this cultural center is the place to learn about their story. Time your visit for **Big Night in Little Haiti** (www.bignightlittlehaiti.com), a monthly street celebration on the third Friday of the month from 6pm to 10pm.

Coral Gables & Coconut Grove

Designed as a 'model suburb' by George Merrick in the early 1920s, Coral Gables is a Mediterranean-style village that's centered around the shops and restaurants of the Miracle Mile, a four-block section of Coral Way between Douglas and LeJeune Rds.

VIZCAYA MUSEUM & GARDENS
Historic Building

(www.vizcayamuseum.org; 3251 S Miami Ave; adult/child $12/5; 9:30am-4:30pm Wed-Mon) This Italian Renaissance–style villa in Coconut Grove, the housing equivalent of a Fabergé egg, is Miami's most fairy-tale–like residence. The 70 rooms are stuffed with centuries-old furnishings and art, and the 30-acre grounds contain splendid formal gardens and Florentine gazebos.

VENETIAN POOL
Swimming Pool

(www.coralgablesvenetianpool.com; 2701 DeSoto Blvd; adult/child $11/7; 10am-4:30pm) 'Swimming pool' doesn't even begin to

Miami for Children

The best beaches for kids are in Miami Beach north of 21st St, especially at 53rd St, which has a playground and public toilets, and the dune-packed beach around 73rd St. **Watson Island** houses a few great kid-pleasers, including the Miami Children's Museum and Jungle Island.

Miami Seaquarium (Map p259; 305-361-5705; www.miamiseaquarium.com; 4400 Rickenbacker Causeway; adult/child $38.95/29.95; 9:30am-6pm, last entry 4:30pm) On Key Biscayne, this 38-acre marine-life park is more extensive than the usual aquarium; it also rehabilitates dolphins, manatees and sea turtles, and presents great animal shows. You can also swim with dolphins here.

Miami Children's Museum (Map p259; www.miamichildrensmuseum.org; 980 MacArthur Causeway; admission $15; 10am-6pm) A hands-on museum with fun music and art studios.

Jungle Island (Map p259; www.jungleisland.com; 1111 Parrot Jungle Trail, off MacArthur Causeway; adult/child $33/25; 10am-5pm) Jungle Island is packed with tropical birds, alligators, orangutans, chimps and a liger, a cross between a lion and a tiger.

Miami Metrozoo (off Map p259; www.miamimetrozoo.com; 12400 SW 152nd St; adult/child $16/12; 9:30am-5:30pm, last entry 4pm) A huge zoo with all the exotic Asian and African species.

Monkey Jungle (www.monkeyjungle.com; 14805 SW 216th St; adult/child $30/24; 9:30am-5pm, last entry 4pm) Their tagline – 'Where humans are caged and monkeys run free' – tells you all you need to know. Unforgettable fun.

JON DAVISON/LONELY PLANET IMAGES ©

Don't Miss Miami Beach

Miami Beach (Map p260) has some of the best beaches in the country, with white sand and warm aquamarine water that rival the Bahamas. That movie in your head of art-deco hotels, in-line skating models, preening young studs and cruising cars? That's **Ocean Drive** (from 1st to 11th Sts), with the beach merely a backdrop for strutting peacocks. This confluence of waves, sunshine and exhibitionist beauty is what makes **South Beach** (or 'SoBe') world-famous.

In the evening, stroll down **Española Way**, a *très* European strip lined with restaurants and cafes. Just a few blocks north, **Lincoln Rd** (between Alton Rd and Washington Ave) is blocked off and becomes a pedestrian mall.

describe this spring-fed goblet, made by filling in the limestone quarry used to build Coral Gables. With waterfalls, grottos and an Italianate feel, it looks like a vacation home for rich mermaids.

 **Activities**

Cycling & In-Line Skating

Skating or cycling the strip along Ocean Dr in South Beach is pure Miami; also try the Rickenbacker Causeway to Key Biscayne.

Fritz's Skate Shop   Skating
(Map p260; ☎305-532-1954; www.
fritzmiamibeach.com; 1620 Washington Ave;
☺10am-10pm) Rentals and free in-line skating lessons (10:30am Sunday).

Miami Beach Bicycle Center   Cycling
(Map p260; www.bikemiamibeach.com; 601 5th St; per hr/day $8/24; ☺10am-7pm Mon-Sat, to 5pm Sun) Convenient bike rentals in the heart of SoBe.

NIK WHEELER/CORBIS ©

Don't Miss **Little Havana**

As SW 8th St heads away from downtown, it becomes Calle Ocho. That's when you know you've arrived in **Little Havana**, the most prominent community of Cuban Americans in the US. One of the best times to come is the last Friday of the month during **Viernes Culturales**, or 'Cultural Fridays,' a street fair showcasing Latino artists and musicians.

The jewel of the Little Havana Art District, **Cuba Ocho** functions as a Cuban community center, art gallery and research outpost. Check for events and performances. Or get a sensory-filled taste of old Cuba at **Máximo Gómez Park**, also known as 'Domino Park' – you'll understand why when you see the old-timers throwing bones. Carnival parade along Calle Ocho

THINGS YOU NEED TO KNOW

Map p259; Viernes Culturales (www.viernesculturales.com; ⊙6-11pm); Cuba Ocho (☑305-285-5880; cubaocho.com; 1465 SW 8th St; ⊙9am-6pm); Máximo Gómez Park (cnr Calle Ocho & SW 15th Ave)

Water Sports

Boucher Brothers
Watersports   Water Sports
(Map p260; www.boucherbrothers.com; 161 Ocean Dr; ⊙10:30am-4:30pm) Rentals and lessons for all sorts of water-related activities: kayaking, waterskiing, windsurfing, parasailing, waverunners and boats.

Sailboards Miami   Water Sports
(www.sailboardsmiami.com; 1 Rickenbacker Causeway; ⊙10am-6pm Fri-Tue) The waters off Key Biscayne are perfect for windsurfing, kayaking and kiteboarding; get your gear and lessons here.

Sleeping

South Beach
PELICAN HOTEL   Boutique Hotel $$$
(Map p260; ☑305-673-3373; www.pelican hotel.com; 826 Ocean Dr; r $225-345; ❄ 🛜)
The name and deco facade don't hint

at anything unusual, but the decorators went wild inside with great themes such as 'Best Whorehouse,' 'Executive Zebra' and 'Me Tarzan, You Vain.'

HOTEL ST AUGUSTINE
Boutique Hotel $$$

(Map p260; 305-532-0570; www.hotelst augustine.com; 347 Washington Ave; r $180-280; P ❄ 🗢) Wood that's blonder than Barbie's hair and a crisp-and-clean deco theme combine to create one of South Beach's most elegant yet stunningly modern sleeps. A hip-and-homey standout.

KENT HOTEL
Boutique hotel $$

(Map p260; 305-604-5068; www.thekent hotel.com; 1131 Collins Ave; r $79-220; P ❄ 🗢) The lobby is a kick, filled with fuchsia and electric-orange geometric furniture plus bright Lucite toy blocks. Rooms continue the playfulness.

Northern Miami Beach

CIRCA 39
Boutique hotel $$

(305-538-3900; www.circa39.com; 3900 Collins Ave; r $90-150; P ❄ 🗯) If you love South Beach style but loathe South Beach attitude, Circa has got your back. It combines one of the funkiest lobbies in Miami, hip icy-blue-and-white rooms and a welcoming attitude.

Coral Gables

BILTMORE HOTEL
Hotel $$$

(305-913-3158; www.biltmorehotel.com; 1200 Anastasia Ave; r $240-400; P ❄ 🗢 🗯 🛉) This 1926 hotel is a National Historic Landmark and an icon of luxury. Standard rooms may be small, but public spaces are palatial; its fabulous pool is the largest hotel pool in the country.

HOTEL ST MICHEL
Hotel $$

(305-444-1666; www.hotelstmichel.com; 162 Alcazar Ave; r $125-220; P ❄ 🗢 🛉) You could conceivably think you're in Europe in this vaulted place in Coral Gables, with inlaid floors, old-world charm and just 28 rooms.

 Eating

South Beach

TAP TAP
Haitian $$

(Map p260; 305-672-2898; www.taptap restaurant.com; 819 5th St; mains $9-20; ⏱noon-11pm Mon-Thu, to midnight Fri & Sat) In this tropi-psychedelic Haitian eatery, you dine under bright murals of Papa Legba while enjoying cuisine that's a happy marriage of West Africa, France and the Caribbean: try spicy pumpkin soup, curried goat and a side of their signature *mayi moulen* (cornmeal with beans).

Miami Eats: Latin American Spice

Thanks to its immigrant heritage, Miami is legendary for its authentic fare. For a good introduction to Cuban food, sidle up to a Cuban *loncheria* (snack bar) and order a *pan cubano* (a buttered, grilled baguette stuffed with ham, roast pork, cheese, mustard and pickles). For dinner, order the classic *ropa vieja* (shredded flank steak cooked in tomatoes and peppers), accompanied by fried plantains, black beans and yellow rice.

Other treats to look for include Haitian *griots* (marinated fried pork), Jamaican jerk chicken, Brazilian BBQ, Central American *gallo pinto* (red beans and rice) and *batidos* (a milky, refreshing Latin American fruit smoothie).

OSTERIA DEL TEATRO Italian $$$
(Map p260; 305-538-7850; www.osteriadel
teatromiami.com; 1443 Washington Ave; mains
$16-31; 6-11pm Mon-Thu, to 1am Fri-Sun)
Stick to the specials of one of Miami's
oldest and best Italian restaurants,
and you can't go wrong. Better yet, let
the gracious Italian waiters coddle and
order for you.

PUERTO SAGUA Cuban $
(Map p260; 305-673-1115; 700 Collins Ave;
mains $6-17; 7:30am-2am) Pull up to
the counter for authentic, tasty and
inexpensive *ropa vieja* (shredded beef),
black beans and *arroz con pollo* (rice with
chicken) – plus some of the best Cuban
coffee in town.

Design District & Wynwood

SENORA MARTINEZ Fusion $$$
(305-573-5474; www.sramartinez.com;
4000 NE 2nd Ave; mains $13-30; noon-3pm

Tue-Sun, 6-11pm Tue-Thu, to midnight Fri-Sat, to
10pm Sun;) One of Miami's most exciting top-end restaurants, Senora Martinez
pushes the boundaries of experimenta-
tion and plain good food. The menu is
eclectic – exemplifying Miami itself.

SUSTAIN American $$$
(305-424-9079; www.sustainmiami.com;
3252 NE 1st Ave; mains $13-30; 11:30am-3pm
& 5-10:30pm;) Sustain is one of Miami's
leading – and more affordable – purvey-
ors of locally sourced, organically grown
food.

Little Havana

VERSAILLES Cuban $
(305-444-0240; 3555 SW 8th St; mains
$5-20; 8am-2am) *The* Cuban restaurant
in town is not to be missed. It finds room
for everybody in the large, cafeteria-style
dining rooms.

Left: Domino game in Máximo Gómez Park (p264);
Below: Bengal tiger, Miami Metrozoo (p262)
(LEFT) RICHARD I'ANSON/LONELY PLANET IMAGES ©: (BELOW) MARK NEWMAN/LONELY PLANET IMAGES ©

Drinking & Entertainment

Bars

There are tons of bars along Ocean Dr; a happy-hour meander unearths half-price drinks.

THE ROOM   Bar
(Map p260; www.theotheroom.com; 100 Collins Ave) This dark, atmospheric, boutique beer bar is a gem: hip and sexy as hell but with a low-key attitude. Per the name, it's small and gets crowded.

ABRAXAS   Bar
(Map p260; 407 Meridian Ave) In a classic deco building, Abraxas couldn't be friendlier. Uncrowded and serving fantastic beer from around the world.

ELECTRIC PICKLE   Bar
(www.electricpicklemiami.com; 2826 N Miami Ave) Wynwood's arty hipsters become glamorous club kids in this two-story hot spot.

ABBEY BREWERY   Bar
(Map p260; www.abbeybrewinginc.com; 1115 16th St) The only brewpub in South Beach is packed with friendly folks listening to the Grateful Dead and slinging back the excellent homebrew.

Nightclubs

In South Beach clubs and live music venues, covers range from $20 to $25, and half that elsewhere.

BARDOT   Club
(☎ 305-576-5570; www.bardotmiami.com; 3456 N Miami Ave) In Wynwood, Bardot is a saucy vision of decadent excess, yet the glam local scene is much more laid-back and friendly than in SoBe.

SKYBAR
Club

(Map p260; ☎305-695-3900; Shore Club, 1901 Collins Ave) Sip chic cocktails on the alfresco terrace. Or, if you're 'somebody,' head for the indoor A-list Red Room. Both have a luxurious Moroccan theme and beautiful people-watching.

TWIST
Club

(Map p260; ☎305-538-9478; www.twistsobe.com; 1057 Washington Ave) This (free) gay hangout has serious staying power and a little bit of something for everyone, including dancing, drag shows and go-go dancers.

NIKKI BEACH CLUB
Club

(Map p260; ☎305-538-1111; www.nikkibeach.com; 1 Ocean Dr) Lounge on beds or inside your own tipi in this beach-chic outdoor space that's right on the sand.

MANSION
Club

(Map p260; ☎305-532-1525; www.mansion miami.com; 1235 Washington Ave; cover from $20; ☉Thu-Sun) Prepare for some quality time with the velvet rope and wear fly duds to enter this grandiose, exclusive megaclub, which lives up to its name.

Live Music

TOBACCO ROAD
Bar

(☎305-374-1198; www.tobacco-road.com; 626 S Miami Ave) Old-school roadhouse around since 1912; blues, jazz and occasional impromptu jams by well-known rockers.

Hoy Como Ayer
Live Music

(☎305-541-2631; www.hoycomoayer.us; 2212 SW 8th St) Authentic Cuban music.

Jazid
Lounge

(Map p260; ☎305-673-9372; www.jazid.net; 1342 Washington Ave) Quality jazz in a candlelit lounge; upstairs, DJ-fueled soul and hip-hop.

Theater & Culture

ADRIENNE ARSHT CENTER FOR THE PERFORMING ARTS
Performing Arts

(☎305-949-6722; www.arshtcenter.org; 1300 Biscayne Blvd) Showcases jazz from around the world, as well as theater, dance, music, comedy and more.

NEW WORLD CENTER
Classical Music

(Map p260; ☎305-673-3330; www.nws.edu; 500 17th St) The new home of the acclaimed

Lighthouse, Bill Baggs Cape Florida State Recreation Park, Key Biscayne

AERIAL ARCHIVES/ALAMY ©

Detour:
Key Biscayne

Serene beaches and stunning sunsets can be enjoyed just across the Rickenbacker Causeway (toll $1) at Key Biscayne, where you'll find the boardwalks and bike trails of the beachfront **Bill Baggs Cape Florida State Recreation Park** (Map p259; www.floridastateparks.org/capeflorida; 1200 S Crandon Blvd; car/bicycle $8/2; ⏰8am-dusk). From the park's southern shore you can catch a glimpse of **Stiltsville**, seven colorful houses hovering on pilings in the shallow waters of Biscayne Bay.

New World Symphony is one of the most beautiful buildings in Miami.

COLONY THEATER   Performing Arts
(Map p260; ☎305-674-1040; www.mbculture.com; 1040 Lincoln Rd) Everything – from off-Broadway productions to ballet and movies – plays in this renovated 1934 art-deco showpiece.

Sports

Miami Dolphins   Football
(www.miamidolphins.com; Sun Life Stadium, 2269 Dan Marino Blvd; tickets from $35) NFL football season runs from August to December.

Florida Marlins   Baseball
(www.marlins.mlb.com; Sun Life Stadium, 2269 Dan Marino Blvd; tickets from $15) MLB baseball season is May to September.

Miami Heat   Basketball
(www.nba.com/heat; American Airlines Arena, 601 Biscayne Blvd; tickets from $20) NBA basketball season is November to April.

 # Shopping

Browse for one-of-a-kind and designer items at the South Beach boutiques around Collins Ave between 6th and 9th Sts and along Lincoln Rd mall. For unique items, try Little Havana and the Design District.

 ## Information

Tourist Information

Greater Miami & the Beaches Convention & Visitors Bureau (☎305-539-3000, www.miamiandbeaches.com; 701 Brickell Ave, 27th fl; ⏰8:30am-5pm Mon-Fri)

Miami Beach Chamber of Commerce (☎305-672-1300; www.miamibeachchamber.com; 1920 Meridian Ave; ⏰9am-5pm Mon-Fri)

 ## Getting There & Away

AIR Miami International Airport (MIA; www.miami-airport.com) is about 6 miles west of downtown and is accessible by **SuperShuttle** (☎305-871-8210; www.supershuttle.com), which costs about $26 to South Beach.
TRAIN Amtrak (☎305-835-1222; 8303 NW 37th Ave) has a main Miami terminal.

THE EVERGLADES

Contrary to what you may have heard, the Everglades is not a swamp. Or at least, it's not *only* a swamp. Its complex taxonomy of environments is most accurately characterized as a wet prairie – grasslands that happen to be flooded most of the year. Nor is it stagnant. In the wet season, a horizon-wide river creeps ever-so-slowly beneath the rustling saw grass and around the subtly raised cypress and hardwood hammocks toward

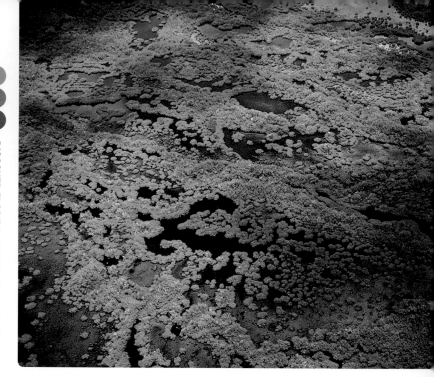

the ocean. The Everglades is indeed filled with alligators – and perhaps a few dead bodies, as *CSI: Miami* would have it. Yet its beauty is not measured in fear or geological drama, but in the timeless, slow Jurassic flap of a great blue heron as it glides over its vast and shockingly gentle domain.

Accordingly, exploring the Everglades by foot, bicycle, canoe and kayak (or camping) is so much more satisfying than by noisy, vibrating airboat. There is an incredible variety of wonderful creatures to see within this unique, subtropical wilderness: all those alligators, bottlenose dolphins, manatees, snowy egrets, herons, anhingas, bald eagles and ospreys.

The Everglades has two seasons: the summer wet season and the winter dry season. Winter (from December to April) is the prime time to visit: the weather is mild and pleasant, and the wildlife is out in abundance. In summer (May through October) it's stiflingly hot, humid and buggy, with frequently afternoon thunderstorms.

Everglades National Park

The park has three main entrances and areas: in the south along Rte 9336 through Homestead and Florida City to Ernest Coe Visitor Center and, at road's end, Flamingo; along the Tamiami Trail/ Hwy 41 in the north out to Shark Valley; and on the Gulf Coast located near Everglades City.

You only need to pay the entrance fee (per car/pedestrian $10/5 for seven days) once to access all points.

Even in winter it's almost impossible to avoid mosquitoes, but they're ferocious in summer: bring *strong* repellent.

 Sights & Activities

SHARK VALLEY VISITOR CENTER Park (305-221-8776; Tamiami Trail; 8:30am-6pm) For a quick Everglades trip from

Left: Aerial view of the wetlands, Everglades National Park;
Below: Red-bellied woodpecker in the Everglades

(LEFT) JIM WARK/LONELY PLANET IMAGES ©; (BELOW) NICHOLAS REUSS/LONELY PLANET IMAGES ©

Miami, come here. On the excellent two-hour **tram tour** (☎305-221-8455; www.sharkvalleytram tours.com; adult/child $18.25/11.50), which runs along a 15-mile asphalt road, you'll see copious numbers of alligators and lots of migratory herons and ibis in winter. The narration by park rangers is both knowledgeable and witty, providing an ideal overview of the Everglades and its inhabitants.

ERNEST COE VISITOR CENTER Park
(☎305-242-7700; www.nps.gov/ever; Hwy 9336; ⏰8am-5pm) Those with a day to give the Glades could start with this visitor center in the south. It has excellent, museum-quality exhibits and tons of activity info: the road accesses numerous short trails and lots of top-drawer canoeing opportunities.

FLAMINGO VISITOR CENTER Park
(☎239-695-2945; ⏰8am-4:15pm) From Royal Palm, Hwy 9336 cuts through

the belly of the park for 38 miles until it reaches the isolated Flamingo Visitor Center, which has maps of canoeing routes and hiking trails. The **Flamingo Marina** (☎239-695-3101) offers backcountry boat tours and kayak/canoe rentals for self-guided trips along the coast.

GULF COAST VISITOR CENTER Park
(☎239-695-3311; 815 Oyster Bar Lane, off Hwy 29, Everglades City; ⏰9am-4:30pm) Those with enough time should consider visiting the northwestern edge of the Everglades, where the mangroves and waterways of the **10,000 Islands** offer incredible canoeing and kayaking opportunities, and great boat tours with a chance to spot dolphins. The visitor center is next to the marina, with rentals (from $13 per hour) and various guided boat trips (from $25).

271

FLORIDA KEYS

Before Henry Flagler completed his railroad in 1912, which connected the Keys to the mainland, this 126-mile string of islands was just a series of untethered bumps of land accessible only by boat. Flagler's railroad was destroyed by a hurricane in 1935, but what remained of its bridges allowed the Overseas Highway to be completed in 1938. Now, streams of travelers swarm down from the mainland to indulge in the alluring jade-green waters, laid-back island lifestyle, great fishing, and idyllic snorkeling and diving.

Upper Keys

The Upper Keys – from Key Largo to Islamorada – are cluttered with touristy shops and motels. At first you can't even see the water from the highway, then – bam – you're in Islamorada and water is everywhere.

Key Largo

Key Largo has long been romanticized in movies and song lyrics, so it can be a shock to arrive and find...no Bogart, no Bacall, no love-sick Sade. Root down side roads for those legendary island idiosyncrasies, and dive underwater for the most amazing coral reef in the continental US.

Sights & Activities

JOHN PENNEKAMP CORAL REEF STATE PARK Park
(305-451-6300; www.pennekamppark. com; MM 102.5 oceanside; car $8, pedestrian or bicycle $2; 8am-sunset) This park has boardwalk trails through mangroves and a cute aquarium, but as the USA's first underwater park, it's true jewel box is beneath the sea, a vast living coral reef that's home to a panoply of sea life (and the oft-photographed statue, *Christ of the Deep*).

Your options for seeing the reef are many: take a 2.5-hour **glass-bottom boat tour** (adult/child $24/17; 9:15am, 12:15pm & 3pm) on a thoroughly modern 38ft catamaran. Dive in with a **snorkeling trip** (adult/child $30/25) or two-tank **diving trip** (305-451-6322; $60); half-day trips leave twice daily, usually around 9am and 1pm. Or go DIY and rent a **canoe or kayak** (per hr single/double $12/17) and journey through a 3-mile network of water trails. Call the park for boat-rental information.

Florida Bay Outfitters Kayaking
(305-451-3018; www. kayakfloridakeys.com; MM 104 bayside; kayak rental per half-day $40) All sorts of guided kayak trips and rentals.

Horizon Divers Diving
(305-453-3535; www. horizondivers.com; 100 Ocean Dr, off MM 100 oceanside; snorkel/scuba trips $50/80) Friendly crew; offers rentals, dive trips and scuba instruction.

Fishing at sunset, Florida Keys
LEE FOSTER/LONELY PLANET IMAGES ©

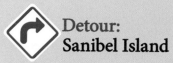

Detour:
Sanibel Island

Located 75 miles northwest of Everglades City and connected to the mainland by a 2-mile causeway, Sanibel Island is upscale but unpretentious, with a carefully managed shoreline that feels remarkably lush and undeveloped. The island is an idyllic, cushy getaway, where bikes are the preferred mode of travel, brilliant shells litter the beaches and romantic meals are a reservation away.

In addition to its fabulous beaches, Sanibel's 6300-acre **JN 'Ding' Darling National Wildlife Refuge** (www.fws.gov/dingdarling; MM2 Sanibel-Captiva Rd; car/bike $5/1; ⏱visitor center 9am-5pm, refuge 7am-7pm Sat-Thu) is a splendid refuge that's home to an abundance of seabirds and wildlife. It has an excellent nature center, a 5-mile Wildlife Drive, narrated tram tours and easy kayaking in Tarpon Bay. For tours and boat rentals, contact **Tarpon Bay Explorers** (☎239-472-8900; www.tarponbayexplorers.com; 900 Tarpon Bay Rd).

Like a mermaid's jewelry box, the **Bailey-Matthews Shell Museum** (www.shellmuseum.org; 3075 Sanibel-Captiva Rd; adult/child $7/4; ⏱10am-5pm) is a natural history of the sea, with covetous displays of shells from around the world.

The five-room **Tarpon Tale Inn** (☎239-472-0939; www.tarpontale.com; 367 Periwinkle Way; r $150-260; ❄@🗟🐾) does a nice imitation of a charming, hammock-strung B&B, but without breakfast.

For romantic gourmet, one excellent choice is **Sweet Melissa's Cafe** (☎239-472-1956; www.sweetmelissascafe.net; 1625 Periwinkle Way; tapas $11-14, mains $26-34; ⏱11:30am-2:30pm Mon-Fri, from 5pm nightly), which offers creative, relaxed refinement.

 ## Sleeping

LARGO LODGE   Hotel **$$**
(☎305-451-0424; www.largolodge.com; MM 102 bayside; cottages $125-195; **P**) These six charming, sunny cottages – family owned since the '50s – have their own private beach and are surrounded by palm trees, tropical flowers and lots of roaming birds. Stay here for a taste of Florida in the good old days.

KEY LARGO HOUSE BOATEL   Houseboat **$$**
(☎305-766-0871; www.keylargohouseboatel.com; Shoreland Dr, MM 103.5 oceanside; houseboats from $75-150) These five houseboats are a steal. The largest is incredibly spacious, sleeping six people comfortably. The boats are right on the docks, so there's no possibility of being isolated from land (or booze).

 ## Eating & Drinking

KEY LARGO CONCH HOUSE   Fusion **$$**
(☎305-453-4844; www.keylargocoffeehouse.com; MM 100.2 oceanside; mains $8-25; ⏱7am-10pm) Now *this* feels like the islands: conch architecture, tropical foliage, a parrot, and crab and conch dishes that ease you off the mainland.

MRS MAC'S KITCHEN   American **$$**
(MM 99.4 bayside; mains $7-18; ⏱7am-9:30pm Mon-Sat) This cute roadside diner bedecked with rusty license plates serves classic highway food such as burgers and fish baskets.

FISH HOUSE   Seafood **$$**
(☎305-451-4665; www.fishhouse.com; MM 102.4 oceanside; mains $12-28; ⏱11:30am-10pm) Delivers on its name, serving fish, fish and more fish that's as fresh as it gets.

ALABAMA JACK'S
Bar

(58000 Card Sound Rd; mains $5-25; ⏰11am-7pm) On the back road between Key Largo and Florida City, this funky open-air joint draws an eclectic booze-hungry crowd of genuine Keys characters. Try the rave-worthy conch fritters.

Islamorada

Things finally get pretty around Islamorada, which is actually a long string of several islands (from MM90 to MM74); the epicenter is Upper Matecumbe Key. Several little nooks of beach are easily accessible, providing scenic rest stops.

Sights & Activities

Billed as 'the Sportfishing Capital of the World,' Islamorada is an angler's paradise.

ROBBIE'S MARINA
Marina

(☎305-664-9814; www.robbies.com; MM 77.5 bayside; ⏰8am-6pm) This marina/roadside attraction offers the buffet of boating options: fishing charters, jet skiing, party boats, ecotours, snorkeling trips, kayak rentals and more. Come here to visit the area's island parks.

LIGNUMVITAE KEY STATE BOTANICAL PARK
Island

(☎305-664-2540; www.floridastateparks.org/lignumvitaekey; ⏰9am-5pm Thu-Mon) It'll feel like just it's you and about a jillion mosquitoes on this bayside island park, with virgin tropical forests and the 1919 Matheson House. Come for the ship-wrecked isolation. Robbie's Marina offers boat rentals and tours.

🛏 Sleeping & Eating

CASA MORADA
Boutique Hotel $$$

(☎305-664-0044; www.casamorada.com; 136 Madeira Rd, off MM 82.2; ste summer $239-459, winter $299-659; P❄🛜🏊) Come for a welcome dash of South Beach sophistication mixed with laid-back Keys style. The slick bar is a great oceanside sunset perch.

RAGGED EDGE RESORT
Resort $$

(☎305-852-5389; www.ragged-edge.com; 243 Treasure Harbor Rd; apt $69-259; P❄🏊) Swim off the docks at this happily unpretentious oceanfront complex off MM 86.5. It has 10 spotless and popular efficiencies and apartments, and a happily comatose vibe.

Relaxing on the beach, Islamorada

PETER PTSCHELINZEW/LONELY PLANET IMAGES ©

MORADA BAY
American $$$

(☎305-664-0604; www.moradabay-restaurant.com; MM 81.6 bayside; lunch $10-15, dinner $21-29; ⏱11:30am-10pm) Grab a table under a palm tree on the white-sand beach and sip a rum drink with your fresh seafood for a lovely, easy-going Caribbean experience. Don't miss the monthly full-moon party.

Middle Keys
Grassy Key

Sedate Grassy Key was once the village-like heart of the Keys. Today, the main reason for travelers to pause here is the **Dolphin Research Center** (☎305-289-1121; www.dolphins.org; MM 59 bayside; adult/child $20/15, swim program $180-650; ⏱9am-4pm). Of all the dolphin swimming spots in the Keys, this is preferred simply because the dolphins are free to leave the grounds and a lot of marine-biology research goes on behind the scenes.

Marathon

Halfway between Key Largo and Key West, Marathon is the most sizable town between them; it's a good base and a hub for commercial fishing and lobster boats.

⊙ Sights & Activities

CRANE POINT MUSEUM Museum
(www.cranepoint.net; MM 50.5 bayside; adult/child $12.50/8.50; ⏱9am-5pm Mon-Sat, from noon Sun) Escape all the development at this 63-acre reserve, where you'll find a vast system of nature trails and mangroves, a raised boardwalk and a rare early-20th-century Bahamian-style house. Kids will enjoy pirate and wreck exhibits, a walk-through coral reef tunnel and the bird hospital.

PIGEON KEY NATIONAL HISTORIC DISTRICT Island
(☎305-743-5999; www.pigeonkey.net; adult/child $12/9; ⏱tours 10am, 11:30am, 1pm & 2:30pm) On the Marathon side of Seven Mile Bridge, this tiny key served as a camp for the workers who toiled to build the Overseas Hwy in the 1930s. You can tour the historic structures or just sun and snorkel on the beach. Reach it by ferry, included in admission.

Sombrero Beach Beach
(Sombrero Beach Rd, off MM 50 oceanside) One of the few white-sand, mangrove-free beaches in the Keys; good swimming.

Marathon Kayak Kayaking
(☎305-395-0355; www.marathonkayak.com; 6363 Overseas Hwy/MM 50 oceanside) Kayak instruction and three-hour guided ecotours (from $45 per person).

Sleeping & Eating

SEASCAPE Motel $$
(☎305-743-6212; 1275 76th St, btwn MM 51 & 52; r from $125; [P][✳][🛜][♿][👤]) The classy, understated luxury in this B&B manifests in the nine rooms, which all have a different feel, from old-fashioned cottage to sleek boutique. Seascape also has a waterfront pool, kayaks for guest use and includes breakfast.

KEYS FISHERIES Seafood $
(☎305-743-4353; 35th St, off MM 49 bayside; mains $7-16; ⏱11:30am-9pm) Shoo the seagulls from your picnic table on the deck and dig in to fresh seafood in a down-and-dirty dockside atmosphere.

HURRICANE American $$
(www.hurricaneblues.com; MM 49.5 bayside; mains $12-19; ⏱11am-midnight) As well as being a favorite Marathon bar, the Hurricane also serves an excellent menu of creative South Florida–inspired goodness, like snapper stuffed with crabmeat and conch sliders jerked in Caribbean seasoning.

Lower Keys

The Lower Keys (MM 46 to MM 0) are fierce bastions of conch culture in all its variety. One of Florida's most acclaimed beaches – and certainly the best in the Keys for its shallow, warm and eminently wade-able water – is at **Bahia Honda State Park** (www.bahiahondapark.com; MM 36.8 oceanside; per car/bicycle $5/2; ⏱8am-sunset), a 524-acre park with nature trails, ranger-led programs and water-sports rentals. Snorkel some of the best coral reefs outside Key Largo.

It's hard to miss the jumbo shrimp statue that marks your arrival at the **Good Food Conspiracy** (305-872-3945; MM 30 oceanside; mains $7-10; 9:30am-7pm Mon-Sat, 11am-5pm Sun), where you'll find healthy hippie food along with your classic Keys photo op.

Key West

Key West is an eccentric frontier town that fosters and promotes its own brand of funky insanity. Perhaps this is a quirk of geography: Key West is the literal end of the road on the map of the continental US, closer to Cuba than the rest of America and a welcoming port for all sorts of global wayfarers. Or perhaps, as a local saying goes, 'They shook the United States and all the nuts fell to the bottom.'

Artists, renegades and other free spirits have long made Key West their own. It's impossible to tease apart high and low culture: on one side are expensive art galleries, literary festivals, Caribbean villas and Hemingway's legacy. On the other are S&M fetish parades,

frat boys toppling over dead drunk and 30-something women tossing their bras to the rafters.

◉ Sights

Key West has more than its fair share of historic homes, buildings and districts (like the colorful Bahama Village); it's a walkable town that rewards exploring.

MALLORY SQUARE   Square
Sunset at Mallory Square, at the end of Duval St, is a bizzaro attraction of the highest order. It takes all those energies, subcultures and oddities of Keys life – the hippies, the rednecks, the foreigners and the tourists – and focuses them into one torchlit, playfully edgy (but still family-friendly) street party.

DUVAL STREET   Street
Key West locals have a love–hate relationship with their island's most famous road. Duval, Old Town Key West's main drag, is a miracle mile of booze, tacky everything

Left: South Beach, Key West;
Below: Great white heron, Florida Keys
(LEFT) KKR/IMAGEBROKER ©: (BELOW) LEE FOSTER/LONELY PLANET IMAGES ©

and awful behavior that still manages, somehow, to be fun.

HEMINGWAY HOUSE — House
(☎305-294-1136; www.hemingwayhome.com; 907 Whitehead St; adult/child $12.50/6; ◷9am-5pm) Ernest Hemingway lived in this Spanish-Colonial house from 1931 to 1940 – to write, drink and fish, if not always in that order. Tours run every half-hour, and as you listen to docent-spun yarns of Papa, you'll see his studio, his unusual pool, and the descendents of his six-toed cats languishing in the sun, on furniture and pretty much wherever they feel like.

FREE FLORIDA KEYS ECO-DISCOVERY CENTER — Museum
(☎305-809-4750; www.eco-discovery.com/ecokw.html; 35 East Quay Rd; ◷9am-4pm Tue-Sat) This excellent nature center pulls together all the plants, animals and habitats that make up the Keys' unique ecosystem and presents them in fresh, accessible ways.

FORT EAST MARTELLO MUSEUM & GARDENS — Museum
(☎305-296-3913; www.kwahs.com/martello.htm; 3501 S Roosevelt Blvd; adult/child $7/5; ◷9:30am-4:30pm) This fortress preserves interesting historical artifacts and some fabulous folk art by Mario Sanchez and 'junk' sculptures by Stanley Papio. Yet Martello's most famous resident – Robert the Doll – is a genuinely creepy, supposedly haunted, 19th-century doll that's kept in a glass case to keep him from making mischief.

Activities

FORT ZACHARY TAYLOR — Beach
(www.floridastateparks.org/forttaylor; per car/pedestrian $6/2; ◷8am-sunset) Key West has three city beaches, but they aren't special; most head to Bahia Honda. That said, Fort Zachary Taylor has the best beach on Key West, with white sand, decent swimming

277

and some near-shore snorkeling; it's great for sunsets and picnics.

DIVE KEY WEST Diving
(☎305-296-3823; www.divekeywest.com) Key West generally doesn't have great reefs for snorkeling, but it does have some notable wreck diving, such as a massive WWII ship that was sunk for the purpose in 2009. Dive Key West arranges trips.

Subtropic Dive Center Diving
(☎305-296-9914; www.subtropic.com) Arranges wreck-diving trips.

Charter Boat Key West Fishing
(www.charterboatkeywest.com) Fishing and cruising charters.

Reelax Charters Kayaking
(☎305-304-1392; www.keyskayaking.com; MM 17 Sugarloaf Key Marina; kayak trips $200) Runs guided kayaks from nearby Sugarloaf Key.

Jolly II Rover Cruise
(☎305-304-2235; www.schoonerjollyrover.com; cnr Greene & Elizabeth Sts, Schooner Wharf; cruise $39) Book a sunset cruise on a pirate ship.

Sleeping

CURRY MANSION INN Hotel $$$
(☎305-294-5349; www.currymansion.com; 511 Caroline St; r winter $240-365, summer $195-285; P ❄ 📶 🏊) In a city full of stately 19th-century homes, the Curry Mansion is especially handsome. It's a pleasing mix of aristocratic American elements, but especially the bright Floridian rooms with canopied beds. Enjoy bougainvillea and breezes on the verandah.

MERMAID & THE ALLIGATOR Guesthouse $$$
(☎305-294-1894; www.kwmermaid.com; 729 Truman Ave; r winter $218-298, summer $148-198; P ❄ @ 📶 🏊) Book way ahead: with only nine rooms, this place's charm exceeds its capacity. It's chock-a-block with treasures collected from the owners' travels, giving it a worldly flair that's simultaneously European and Zen.

L'HABITATION Guesthouse $$
(☎305-293-9203; www.lhabitation.com; 408 Eaton St; r $109-179; ❄ 📶) At this beautiful classic Keys cottage, the friendly, bilingual

Key West is famous for its key lime pie

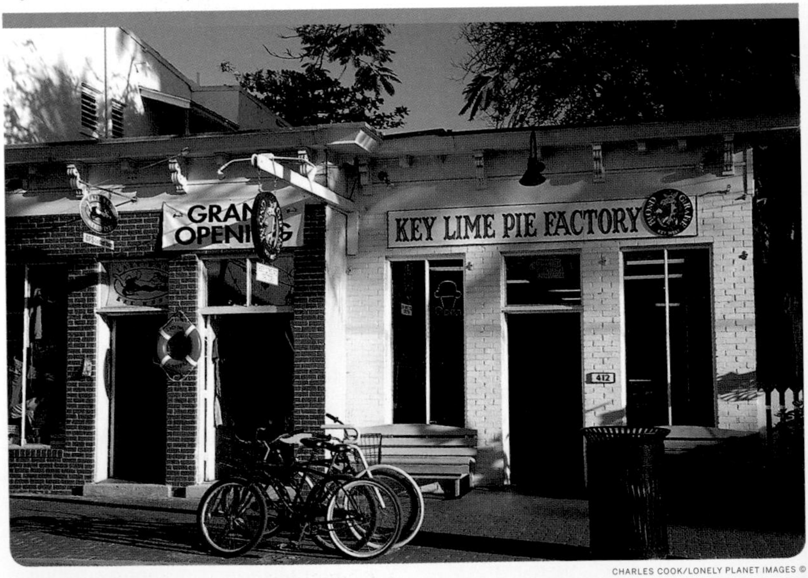

CHARLES COOK/LONELY PLANET IMAGES ©

owners welcome guests in English or French. The cute rooms come kitted out in light tropical shades, with lamps that look like contemporary art pieces and skittles-bright quilts.

CARIBBEAN HOUSE Guesthouse $
(305-296-0999; www.geocities.com/carib beanhousekw; 226 Petronia St; r from $85; P ❄ @) In the heart of Bahama Village, rooms are tiny, but they're clean, cozy and cheery. Add free breakfast and welcoming hosts and you get a rare find in Key West: a bargain.

Eating

You aren't technically allowed to leave the island without sampling the conch fritters or the key lime pie, made with key limes, sweetened condensed milk, eggs and sugar on a Graham-cracker crust.

CAFÉ SOLÉ French $$$
(305-294-0230; www.cafesole.com; 1029 Southard St; lunch $5-11, dinner $25-32; ⏰5:30-10pm) Conch carpaccio with capers? Yellowtail fillet and foie gras? Oh yes. This locally and critically acclaimed venue is known for its cozy back-porch ambience and innovative menus, the result of a French-trained chef exploring island ingredients.

MO'S RESTAURANT Caribbean $$
(www.salsalocakeywest.com; 1116 White St; mains $11-16; ⏰11am-10pm Mon-Sat) If the phrase 'Caribbean home cooking' makes you drool, don't hesitate to dine here. The dishes are mainly Haitian, and they're delicious.

BLUE HEAVEN American $$$
(305-296-8666; http://blueheavenkw. homestead.com; 729 Thomas St; dinner $19-38; ⏰8am-3pm & 5-10pm) One of the island's quirkiest venues, where you dine in an outdoor courtyard with a flock of chickens. Customers gladly wait, bemusedly, for Blue Heaven's well-executed, Southern-fried interpretation of Keys cuisine.

♥ If You Like... Nightlife

If you like the Green Parrot and the nightly revelry that is Key West's biggest drawcard, check out these other great nightspots.

1 LA TE DA
(www.lateda.com; 1125 Duval St) Look for drag queens to mark your arrival. The complex has three bars and a cabaret space famous for its drag shows.

2 PORCH
(429 Caroline St) Escape the Duval St frat-boy bars and head to the Porch, where knowledgeable bartenders dispense artisan beers.

3 GARDEN OF EDEN
(224 Duval St) You can make like Adam and Eve at this clothing-optional rooftop bar; the fig leaf is also optional.

4 CAPTAIN TONY'S SALOON
(www.capttonyssaloon.com; 428 Greene St) This former icehouse, morgue and Hemingway haunt is built around the town's old hanging tree. The eclectic decor includes women's bras and signed dollar bills.

EL SIBONEY Cuban $$
(900 Catherine St; mains $10-16; ⏰11am-9:30pm) Key West is only 90 miles from Cuba, so this awesome rough-and-ready corner establishment is quite literally the closest you can get to real Cuban food in the US. Cash only.

Drinking

Another way to think of Key West is as a floating bar. You can crawl along Duval St till about 3am, when most bars close.

GREEN PARROT Bar
(www.greenparrot.com; 601 Whitehead St) This rogue's cantina has the longest tenure of any bar on the island (since 1890). It's a fabulous dive drawing a lively mix of locals and out-of-towners, with a century's

worth of strange decor. Men, don't miss the urinal.

Information

In town, get maps and brochures at **Key West Chamber of Commerce** (☎305-294-2587; www.keywestchamber.org; 510 Greene St; ☉8am-6:30pm Mon-Sat, to 6pm Sun).

❶ Getting There & Away

AIR You can fly into **Key West International Airport** (EYW; www.keywestinternationalairport.com) with frequent flights from major cities, most going through Miami.

BOAT Take a fast catamaran from Fort Myers or Miami; call the **Key West Express** (☎888-539-2628; www.seakeywestexpress.com) for schedules and fares.

ORLANDO

Like Las Vegas, Orlando is almost entirely given over to fantasy. It's a place to come when you want to imagine you're somewhere else: Hogwarts, perhaps, or Cinderella's Castle, Dr Seuss' world or an African safari. And like Vegas' casinos, Orlando's theme parks work hard to be constantly entertaining thrill rides where the only concern is your pleasure. Even outside the theme parks, Orlando can exhibit a hyper atmosphere of fiberglass-modeled, cartoon-costumed pop culture amusement.

◎ Sights & Activities

International Drive

Like a theme park itself, International Dr (I-Dr) is shoulder to shoulder with high-energy amusements: sprinkled among the major theme, wildlife and water parks, smaller attractions shout for attention: Ripley's Believe It or Not, the upside-down WonderWorks and an indoor skydiving experience. Chain restaurants and hotels also crowd the thoroughfare.

SEAWORLD   Amusement Park, Aquarium
(☎407-351-3600; www.seaworld.com; 7007 SeaWorld Dr; 2-day ticket $72; ☉from 9am)
A peculiarly Floridian blend of marine animal shows and thrill rides, SeaWorld is home to both Shamu the killer whale and Kraken the floorless roller coaster. While the rides provide jolts of adrenaline, the real draws are the up-close sea life encounters (with manta rays, sharks, penguins and beluga whales) and the excellent dolphin, sea lion and killer whale shows.

DISCOVERY COVE   Water Park
(☎407-370-1280; www.discoverycove.com; 6000 Discovery Cove Way; admission $129-169, incl dolphin swim $199-319; ☉8:30am-5:30pm)
Attendance is limited, ensuring Discovery Cove retains the feel of an exclusive tropical resort, complete with beaches, a fish-filled reef and an aviary. There's no high-speed thrills or frantic screaming here, just blessed relaxation and the chance to swim with dolphins. The price is steep, but everything is included: buffet lunch, beer, towels, parking and even a day pass to SeaWorld.

 Sleeping

In addition to the Walt Disney World resorts, Orlando has countless lodging options.

EO INN & SPA   Boutique Hotel $$
(☎407-481-8485; www.eoinn.com; 227 N Eola Dr; r $139-229; P❄☎✿) Sleek and understated, this downtown boutique hotel overlooks Lake Eola near Thornton Park, with neutral-toned rooms that are elegant in their simplicity.

VERANDA BED & BREAKFAST   B&B $$
(☎407-849-0321; www.theverandabandb.com; 115 N Summerlin Ave; r $110-270; P❄☎✿)
Ideal for wandering Thornton Park and Lake Eola, this European-style B&B has big antique beds and is a lovely retreat from all the bustle.

Eating

RAVENOUS PIG American **$$$**
(☎ 407-628-2333; 1234 Orange Ave, Winter Park; mains $14-29; ⏱ 11:30am-2pm & 5:30-9:30pm Tue-Thu, to 10:30pm Fri & Sat) One of Orlando's most talked-about foodie destinations, this bustling hot spot serves designer cocktails and creative, delicious versions of shrimp and grits, and lobster tacos. Reservations recommended.

DESSERT LADY CAFÉ Cafe **$**
(☎ 407-999-5696; 120 W Church St; mains $5-10; ⏱ 11:30am-11pm Tue-Thu, to midnight Fri, 4pm-midnight Sat) There's a bordello atmosphere and a bistro menu of pulled-pork sliders, chicken salad, soups and quiches to go with the sinful desserts, from fruit cobbler to bourbon pecan pie.

DANDELION COMMUNITEA CAFÉ
Vegetarian $

(407-362-1864; www.dandelioncommunitea. com; 618 N Thornton Ave; mains $5-10; 11am-10pm Mon-Sat, to 5pm Sun;) Unabashedly crunchy and definitively organic, this pillar of creative, sustainable, locavore vegetarianism is genuinely delicious, with tons of community spirit. Look for events.

ℹ Information

For city information, good multilingual guides and maps, visit Orlando's Official Visitor Center (407-363-5872; www.visitorlando.com; 8723 International Dr; 8:30am-6:30pm).

ℹ Getting There & Around

AIR Orlando International Airport (MCO; www. orlandoairports.net) has buses and taxis to major tourist areas.

PUBLIC TRANSPORTATION I-Ride Trolley (www.iridetrolley.com; adult/child $1/free; 8am-10:30pm) buses run along I-Dr.

Walt Disney World Resort

Covering 40 sq miles, **Walt Disney World** (WDW; http://disneyworld.disney.go.com) is the largest theme park resort in the world. It includes four separate theme parks, two water parks, a sports complex, five golf courses, two dozen hotels, 100 restaurants and two shopping and nightlife districts – proving that it's not such a small world, after all. Naturally, expectations run high, and even the self-proclaimed 'happiest place on earth' doesn't always live up to its billing. Still, it always happens: Cinderella curtsies to your little Belle, your own Jedi knight vanquishes Darth Maul, or you tear up on that corny ride about our tiny planet, and you're swept up in the magic.

Sights & Activities

Anytime school is out – during summer and holidays – is when WDW will be the most crowded. The least crowded times are January to February, mid-September through October and early December.

MAGIC KINGDOM
Theme Park

When people think of WDW, they picture the Magic Kingdom, from the iconic Cinderella's Castle to Space Mountain, the Haunted Mansion and Pirates of the Caribbean (now including Johnny Depp's Jack Sparrow). This is where the fireworks and nighttime light parade illuminate **Main Street, USA**. For Disney mythology, it doesn't get better, and rides and shows aim squarely at young kids and their parents and grandparents.

DISNEY HOLLYWOOD STUDIOS
Theme Park

Formerly Disney-MGM Studios, this is the least-charming of Disney's parks. However, it does have two of WDW's most exciting rides: the unpredictable elevator in the **Twilight Zone Tower of Terror** and the Aerosmith-themed **Rock 'n' Roller Coaster**. Wannabe singers can audition for the American Idol Experience, kids can join the Jedi Training Academy, and various programs present Walt Disney himself and how Disney's movies are made.

EPCOT
Theme Park

An acronym for 'Experimental Prototype Community of Tomorrow,' Epcot was Disney's vision of a high-tech city when it opened in 1982. It's divided into two halves: **Future World**, with rides and corporate-sponsored interactive exhibits, and **World Showcase**, providing an interesting toe-dip into the cultures of 11 countries. Epcot is much more soothingly low-key than other parks, and it has some of the best food and shopping.

ANIMAL KINGDOM
Theme Park

This sometimes surreal blend of African safari, zoo, rides, costumed characters, shows and dinosaurs establishes its own distinct tone. It's best at animal encounters and shows, with the 110-acre **Kilimanjaro Safaris** as its centerpiece. The iconic **Tree of Life** houses the fun It's Tough to Be a Bug! show, and **Expedition Everest** and **Kali River Rapids** are the top thrill rides.

Don't Miss Universal Orlando Resort

Smaller, easier to navigate with kids in tow and more pedestrian-friendly than Walt Disney World, **Universal Orlando** is everything you wish Disney could be. Universal features two theme parks, a water park, three hotels and an entertainment district. The megaplex is as absorbingly themed as Disney, but it replaces Snow White and the Seven Dwarves with Spider-Man, the Simpsons and – to widespread acclaim in 2010 – the boy wizard himself, Harry Potter.

For good ol' scream-it-from-the-rooftops, no-holds-barred, laugh-out-loud fun, explore the multiple worlds within **Islands of Adventure**, which is packed with adrenaline rides. **Marvel Super Hero Island** is a sensory overload of comic book characters; there's dino-happy **Jurassic Park**; the ersatz-mystical **Lost Continent**; and the kid-friendly **Toon Lagoon** and **Seuss Landing**. But most famous of all is the **Wizarding World of Harry Potter** (above), which brings to life Hogwarts and Hogsmeade in exquisite, rib-tickling detail.

At **Universal Studios**, the central question is: would you like to *live* the movies? Do battle with the Terminator? Go *Back to the Future?* Escape Jaws, Beetlejuice, the Mummy, *Men in Black* aliens and a *Twister* tornado? Do Lucille Ball, Curious George, Shrek and the Simpsons amuse you? With a Hollywood backlot feel, Universal Studio's simulation-heavy rides are dedicated to silver screen and TV icons.

Review multiple ticket options online, which can include add-ons like Express Plus line-skipping and a dining plan; resort hotel guests also get nice park perks.

THINGS YOU NEED TO KNOW

☎ 407-363-8000; www.universalorlando.com; 1000 Universal Studios Plaza; 1-4 day adult pass single park $85-146, both parks $120-156; ⏱ from 9am

Sleeping

WDW has two dozen family-friendly sleeping options, from camping to deluxe resorts; Disney guests receive great perks (extended park hours, discount dining, free transportation and airport shuttles).

For the most amenities, choose a roomy **Deluxe Villa (villas $540-1600)**, the only properties with full kitchen and in-room washer/dryer. **Value Resorts (r $120-150)** are the least-expensive option (besides camping); quality is equivalent to basic chain hotels, and (fair warning) they are favored by school groups.

Eating

Theme park food ranges from OK to awful; far and away the most interesting food is served in Epcot's World Showcase. Sit-down meals are best, but *always* make reservations; seats can be impossible to get without one. For any and all dining,

you can call **central reservations (☎407-939-3463)** up to 180 days in advance.

Disney has three dinner shows (a luau, country-style BBQ and vaudeville show) and about 15 character meals, which are insanely popular (see website for details). Book them the minute your 180-day window opens. The most sought-after meal is **Cinderella's Royal Table (adult $33-45, child $24-28)** where you dine with Disney princesses in the Magic Kingdom's castle.

Sci-Fi Dine-In Theater American **(Hollywood Studios; mains $11-21)** Dine in Cadillacs and watch classic sci-fi flicks.

California Grill American **(Contemporary Resort; mains $15-38)** Dine with great views of the Magic Kingdom's fireworks.

O'Hana Hawaiian **(Polynesian Resort; mains $15-30)** Great South Pacific decor and interactive Polynesian-themed luau shenanigans.

Boma Buffet **(Animal Kingdom Lodge; adult/child breakfast $17/10, dinner $27/13)** Pleasant African-inspired

eatery with a buffet several notches above the rest.

Victoria and Albert American
(Grand Floridian; prix fixe $125-200) A true jacket-and-tie, crystal-goblet romantic gourmet restaurant – no kidding, and no kids under 10.

Entertainment

In addition to theme park events like Magic Kingdom parades and fireworks and Epcot's IllumiNations, Disney has two entertainment districts – Downtown Disney and Disney's Boardwalk – with eats, bars, music, movies, shops and shows.

Cirque du Soleil Circus
(☎ 407-939-7600; www.cirquedusoleil.com; adult $76-132, child $61-105; ⊙ 6pm & 9pm Tue-Sat) Exquisite acrobatics in WDW's best live show.

House of Blues Live Music
(☎ 407-934-2583; www.houseofblues.com) Top acts visit this national chain; Sunday's Gospel Brunch truly rocks.

Information

The simple logic behind Disney World ticket options is the longer you stay, the less you pay per day. Tickets allow entrance to one park per day, and can range from one to 10 days: adults from $82 to $262, and children aged three to nine from $74 to $239. Check online for packages. For discounts, check out www.mousesavers.com and www.undercovertourist.com.

Getting There & Around

Most hotels in Orlando – and all Disney properties – offer free transportation to WDW. Disney-owned resorts also offer free transportation from the airport. Drivers can reach all four parks via I-4 and park for $14. The Magic Kingdom lot is huge; trams get you to the entrance.

Within WDW, a complex network of monorails, boats and buses get you between the parks, resorts and entertainment districts.

The Grand Canyon & the Southwest

Breathtaking beauty and the allure of adventure merge seamlessly in the Southwest. It's a captivating mix that has drawn dreamers and explorers for centuries. Pioneers staked their claims beside lush riverbanks, prospectors dug into mountains for untold riches and religious refugees built cities across empty deserts, while astronomers and rocket builders peered into star-filled skies.

For travelers, beauty and adventure still loom large in this land of mountains, deserts and wide-open spaces that sprawl across Arizona, Nevada, Utah and New Mexico. You can hike past red rocks, mountain-bike over wild landscapes, raft through canyons and roll the dice under the mesmerizing lights of Vegas. But remember, beauty and adventure here can also loom small. Study that saguaro up-close. Ask a Hopi artist about his craft. Savor some green chile stew. It's the tap-you-on-the-shoulder moments you may just cherish the most.

View from Mather Point, Grand Canyon South Rim (p300) **287**

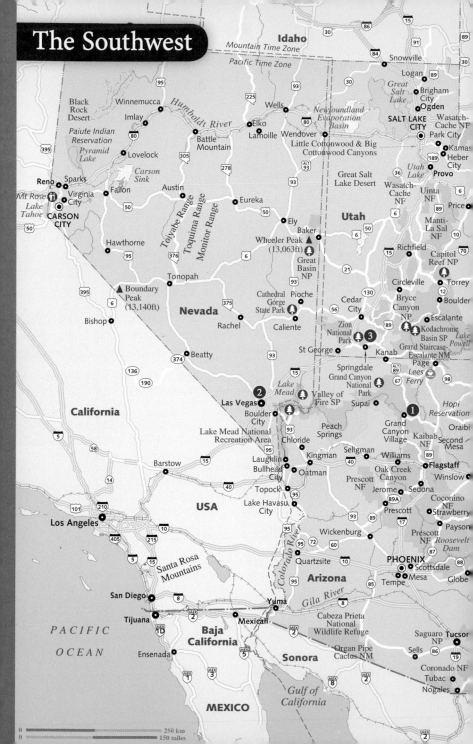

The Southwest

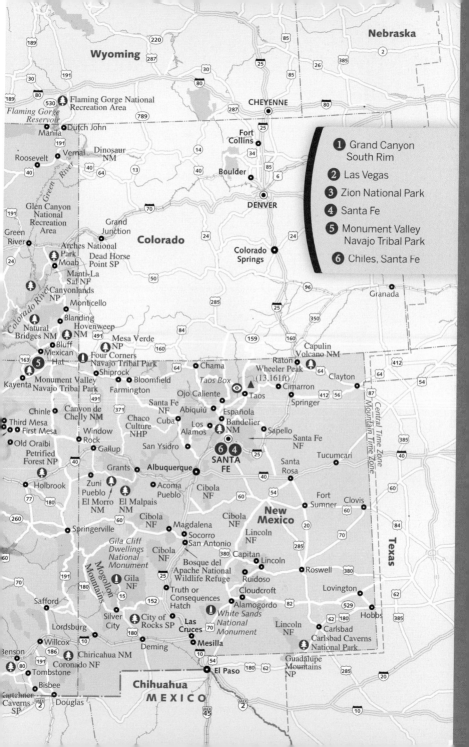

The Grand Canyon & the Southwest's Highlights

① Grand Canyon South Rim

It took two billion years to create the canyon, but change is afoot on the South Rim (p300), with new interpretative exhibits opening at lightning-speed pace. But don't worry. Beyond the rim, the view remains the same: an immense, mesmerizing tableau that still shares the earth's geologic treasures layer by dramatic layer.

Need to Know

TOP TRAFFIC TIP In summer, ride the free Tusayan shuttle to avoid entrance-gate jams **TOP SURVIVAL TIP** Acclimatize before long hikes; wear layers **For more, see p298**.

Grand Canyon South Rim Don't Miss List

BY JUDY HELLMICH-BRYAN, CHIEF OF INTERPRETATION, GRAND CANYON NATIONAL PARK

1 GRAND CANYON VISITOR CENTER & PLAZA

The visitor center, with its all-new interpretative exhibits, is really the place to start your visit. In the plaza area we've done a lot of very soft interpretations of the canyon – a series of little medallions have a poem, like a Dr Seuss poem, so that you get a sense of discovery: there are etchings of reptile footprints and little critter footprints, and there's a condor silhouette that's been etched into the rock so you can see how big the condor is.

2 GRAND CANYON: A JOURNEY OF WONDER

We recently finished production of a park orientation film. It's 20-minutes long and screens every half-hour. It takes visitors on a rim-to-river trip through the canyon, so you're learning about all the different aspects of the canyon, about geology and Native American history. It's high definition. It's beautiful. Peter Coyote narrated it.

3 TRAIL OF TIME

The Trail of Time is a timeline trail that extends from Yavapai Geology Museum into Grand Canyon Village. Every meter represents a million years in the history of the earth. As you walk, there are samples of rocks from within the canyon that you can touch, and there are wayside exhibits that explain the different processes that formed the canyon.

4 TUSAYAN RUIN & MUSEUM

This is a wonderful **exhibit** (Desert View Dr, about 20 miles east of Grand Canyon Village; admission free; ⊙9am-5pm) on past and present native cultures that existed at the Grand Canyon and had ties to the canyon. It's an 800-year-old Ancestral Puebloan ruin (above left) and people tend to drive right by it and not stop.

5 RIM TRAIL

The Rim Trail is the easy trail. On sections of it you can get away from big crowds of people, especially if you walk between Mather Point and the Village. The other really nice section is west of Hermit interchange. The walk out to Hermits Rest is spectacular.

Las Vegas

Vegas (p309) is Hollywood for the rest of us, where you get to play the leading role instead of watching someone else do it. It's the only place in the world where you can see ancient hieroglyphics, the Eiffel Tower, the Brooklyn Bridge and the canals of Venice, all in a few short hours. Sure, they're reproductions, but in a slice of desert that's transformed into one of the most lavish places on earth, nothing is done halfway – not even the illusions.

3 Zion National Park

This spectacular red-rock canyon (p317) offers some of the Southwest's most breathtaking scenery, with stunning clifftop panoramas, and soaring massifs that look like ancient carved cathedrals. Over 100 miles of trails take you through dramatic canyons and up to vertiginous heights. Those seeking to revel in the experience can book a night at the beautifully sited Zion Lodge.

Santa Fe ④

Sitting at the base of the Sangre de Cristo range, Santa Fe (p322), at 7000ft, is the highest state capital in the US. It's also one of America's oldest cities, with roots dating back to the early 17th century. It's home to fascinating pueblo architecture, a burgeoning gallery scene and excellent restaurants and farmers markets, while outdoor adventures – such as hiking, mountain biking and skiing – are available in its backyard.

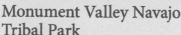

⑤ Monument Valley Navajo Tribal Park

Towering sandstone monoliths rise like ancient sentinels over an endless expanse of desert. The stark beauty of Monument Valley (p321) has been immortalized in road movies and old westerns, and remains a deep source of pride for the Navajo Nation that has lived here for generations. Taking a scenic drive is the best way to see the fiery beauty of this unchanged landscape.

⑥ Chiles

An essential ingredient in many regional dishes, the locally-grown chile pepper transforms everything from tacos to cheeseburgers into gastronomic works of art. Chile stew (beef, beans, potatoes and, of course, chile) is a perennial favorite at down-home San Marcos Café (p326) in Santa Fe. If asked 'red or green?', say which kind of chile sauce you want. For both, just ask for 'Christmas style.'

The Grand Canyon & the Southwest's Best...

Geologic Wonders

○ **Carlsbad Caverns National Park** (p331) Magnificent subterranean kingdom.

○ **Arches National Park** (p319) Photogenic sandstone arches and curiosities such as Balanced Rock.

○ **Canyonlands National Park** (p320) Gallery of ancient wonders – arches, buttes, mesas, spires and canyons.

○ **Bryce Canyon National Park** (p316) Fantastic red-rock park famed for its hoodoos (spire-like rock formations).

Hiking

○ **Santa Fe** (p324) Just outside of town, you'll find superb hiking in the Pecos Wilderness and Santa Fe National Forest.

○ **Moab** (p318) Outdoors-loving town that's a gateway to adventure.

○ **South Kaibab** (p300) Spectacular scenery along one of the Grand Canyon's loveliest trails.

○ **Angels Landing Trail** (p317) Gasp your way to the top of this narrow overlook in Zion National Park for awe-inspiring views.

Museums & Galleries

○ **Heard Museum** (p307) Home to one of the nation's finest Native American art collections.

○ **Georgia O'Keeffe Museum** (p322) Santa Fe has a fabulous collection of the Southwest's most famous painter.

○ **Atomic Testing Museum** (p312) Decode the mysteries and horrors of the atomic age at this fascinating Las Vegas attraction.

○ **Canyon Road** (p322) Scores of art galleries and studios line this vibrant stretch of Santa Fe.

Left: Petroglyphs, Canyon de Chelly National Monument (p320);
Above: Mesa Arch, Canyonlands National Park (p320).
(LEFT) JOHN ELK III/LONELY PLANET IMAGES ©: (ABOVE) WITOLD SKRYPCZAK/LONELY PLANET IMAGES ©

Need to Know

Native American Sites

○ **Acoma Pueblo**
(p309) One of the oldest continuously inhabited settlements in North America.

○ **Canyon de Chelly National Monument** (p320) Home to ancient clifftop dwellings on Navajo lands.

○ **Wheelwright Museum of the American Indian**
(p323) Fantastic collection of Navajo works in Santa Fe.

○ **Bandelier National Monument** (p328) Haunting site of Ancestral Puebloans who lived among the cliffs.

ADVANCE PLANNING

○ **Nine months before**
If you're planning on taking a mule trip into the Grand Canyon, reserve well ahead. Also reserve in advance for Grand Canyon, Zion and other national park accommodation.

○ **One month before**
Buy tickets for upcoming festivals and events.

○ **Two weeks before**
Reserve a table at top restaurants in Santa Fe and Taos. Book tours and outdoor excursions, including hiking, kayaking and mountain biking.

RESOURCES

○ **American Southwest**
(www.americansouthwest. net) Covers parks and natural landscapes.

○ **National Park Service**
(www.nps.gov/grca) Has a downloadable trip planner, maps and seasonal guides.

○ **Visit Las Vegas** (www. visitlasvegas.com) Official city tourism site.

○ **Las Vegas Weekly**
(www.lasvegasweekly. com) Vegas food and entertainment listings.

○ **Santa Fe Reporter**
(www.sfreporter.com) Santa Fe dining, arts and entertainment.

GETTING AROUND

○ **Airports** Main airports include Phoenix (PHX; www.skyharbor. com), which has free bus transport to/from downtown; and Las Vegas (LAS; www.mccarran. com), a $7 shuttle ride to hotels on the Strip.

○ **Bus** Greyhound (www. greyhound.com) provides service between major towns.

○ **Hire car** Essential for exploring the Southwest on your own.

○ **Train** Amtrak stops in Flagstaff, Arizona and Lamy, New Mexico (20 miles south of Santa Fe) on its Chicago–LA run.

BE FOREWARNED

○ **Crowds** Expect big crowds (and sweltering heat) if visiting the Grand Canyon during summer. For a more sedate experience, visit the North Rim rather than the South Rim.

○ **Heat** Temperatures soar in summer (climbing regularly above 90 degrees). Whether hiking or driving, be prepared and take plenty of water.

○ **Respect** Be respectful when interacting with Native Americans; ask permission before taking photos and don't pry about cultural practices.

The Grand Canyon & the Southwest Itineraries

Few places on earth rival the dramatic beauty of the American Southwest. These two itineraries take in canyons, red-rock deserts and alpine scenery, as well as more urbane diversions in Las Vegas and Santa Fe.

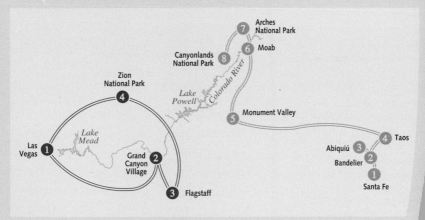

5 DAYS

SIN CITY & WONDROUS CANYONS
Las Vegas & the Grand Canyon

Spend your first day in **(1) Las Vegas**. Take a surreal trip around the world without leaving the Strip, hopping between Encore, the Bellagio, the Venetian and Caesar's Palace. That night catch a show (perhaps Cirque du Soleil), followed by cocktails at sky-high Mix.

On day two, make the five-hour drive east to **(2) Grand Canyon Village**, on the South Rim of the Grand Canyon. Gaze at the mesmerizing abyss from the Rim Trail, then enjoy more great vistas over dinner at El Tovar. Spend the night and rise early for a scenic day-hike along the Bright Angel Trail. Afterwards, head 80 miles south to

(3) Flagstaff. Go stargazing at the Lowell Observatory, then kick up your heels at the honky-tonk Museum Club.

On day four, drive five hours northwest to **(4) Zion National Park**. Gear up for a magnificent hike on Angels Landing Trail, with dramatic views over the red-rock landscape. Spend the night in perfectly sited Zion Lodge. On your last day, make the three-hour drive back to Vegas. Celebrate the big journey over a memorable meal at Sage, try to win back your travel expenses at the Cosmopolitan, then indulge in a touch of Vegas' decadence at the Gold Lounge.

7 DAYS

SANTA FE TO MOAB
Road Trip Around the Southwest

Start by spending two days in **(1) Santa Fe**, taking in the artful vibe of this history-rich town – visit the shops and art galleries of Canyon Road, the stellar Georgia O'Keeffe Museum and the fascinating Wheelwright Museum of the American Indian. On day three, explore the countryside around Santa Fe: visit the ancient clifftop dwellings of **(2) Bandelier**, then soak up the scenery that inspired Georgia O'Keeffe in **(3) Abiquiú**. On the next morning, drive to nearby **(4) Taos**. Visit the photogenic Taos Pueblo, take a hike amid mountain scenery and overnight in an ecofriendly Earthship rental. On day five, drive seven hours west

beneath the big skies of Native American country to **(5) Monument Valley**. Catch the flaming red buttes at sunset, and spend the night in the Navajo-run View Hotel. In the morning, head three hours northeast to **(6) Moab**, an adventure-loving town ringed by mountains. Use it as a base for exploring the sandstone formations of **(7) Arches National Park** and awe-inspiring **(8) Canyonlands National Park**. On your last day, go kayaking, rafting or horseback riding with one of Moab's many outfitters.

Angels Landing Trail, Zion National Park (p317)
GEORGE H.H. HUEY/CORBIS ©

Discover the Grand Canyon & the Southwest

At a Glance

- **Grand Canyon** (p298) One of earth's great wonders.

- **Flagstaff** (p305) Easy-going town and gateway to Grand Canyon.

- **Phoenix** (p307) Largest urban hub of the Southwest.

- **Las Vegas** (p309) Over-the-top casinos and extravagant nightlife.

- **Zion & Southern Utah** (p316) Dazzling red-rock scenery.

- **Monument Valley** (p320) Spectacular scenery in Navajo country.

- **Santa Fe** (p322) Artful town set against a stunning backdrop.

- **Taos** (p328) Eccentric village nestled in the mountains.

View from Inspiration Point, Bryce Canyon National Park (p316)
ROBERTO GEROMETTA/LONELY PLANET IMAGES ©

GRAND CANYON NATIONAL PARK

Why do folks become giddy when describing the Grand Canyon? One peek over the edge of this Arizona landmark makes it clear. The canyon captivates travelers because of its sheer immensity; it's a tableau that reveals the earth's history in a dramatic palette of colorful layers. Mother Nature adds artistic details – rugged plateaus, crumbly spires and shadowed ridges – that flirt and catch your eye as the sun crosses the sky.

Snaking along the canyon's floor are 277 miles of the Colorado River, whose waters have carved out the canyon over the past six million years and exposed rocks up to two billion years old – half the age of the earth.

The two rims of the Grand Canyon offer quite different experiences; they lie more than 200 miles apart by road and are rarely visited on the same trip. Most visitors choose the South Rim with its easy access, wealth of services and vistas that don't disappoint. The quieter North Rim has its own charms; at 8200ft elevation (1000ft higher than the South Rim), its cooler temperatures support wildflower meadows and tall, thick stands of aspen and spruce.

ℹ️ Information

The park's most developed area is Grand Canyon Village, 6 miles north of the South Rim Entrance Station. The only entrance to the North Rim lies 30 miles south of Jacob Lake on Hwy 67. The North Rim and South Rim are 215 miles apart by car and 21 miles on foot through the canyon.

Grand Canyon National Park

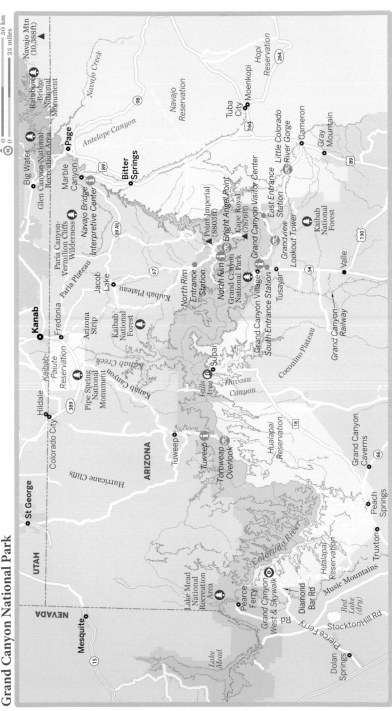

June is the driest month, July and August the wettest. January has average overnight lows of 13°F (-11°C) to 20°F (-7°C) and daytime highs around 40°F (4°C). Summer temperatures inside the canyon regularly soar above 100°F (38°C). While the South Rim is open year-round, most visitors come between late May and early September. The North Rim is open from mid-May to mid-October.

Tourist Information

The **park entrance ticket** (vehicles $25, cyclists & pedestrians $12) is valid for seven days and can be used at both rims.
SOUTH RIM Grand Canyon Visitor Center (📞928-638-7644; 🕐8am-5pm) Three hundred yards behind Mather Point, a large plaza encompasses this visitor center and the Books & More Store. On the plaza, bulletin boards display information about ranger programs, the weather, tours and hikes.
TUSAYAN National Geographic Visitor Center (📞928-638-2468; www.explorethecanyon.com; Hwy 64, Tusayan; adult/child $13/10; 🕐8am-10pm) In Tusayan, 7 miles south of Grand Canyon Village, you can pay your $25 vehicle entrance fee and spare yourself a potentially long wait at the park entrance, especially in summer. The IMAX

theater screens the terrific 34-minute film *Grand Canyon: The Hidden Secrets*.
NORTH RIM North Rim Visitor Center (📞928-638-7864; www.nps.gov/grca; 🕐8am-6pm, closed mid-Oct–mid-May) Adjacent to the Grand Canyon Lodge, with maps, books, trail guides and current conditions.

South Rim

To escape the throngs, visit during fall or winter, especially on weekdays. You'll also gain some solitude by walking a short distance away from the viewpoints on the Rim Trail or by heading into the canyon itself.

 Sights & Activities

Driving & Hiking

A **scenic drive** follows the rim on the west side of the village along Hermit Rd. Closed to private vehicles March through November, the road is serviced by the free park shuttle bus; cycling is encouraged because of the relatively light traffic. Stops offer spectacular views,

Panorama Point, South Kaibab Trail

JOHN ELK III/LONELY PLANET IMAGES ©

and interpretive signs explain canyon features.

Hiking along the South Rim is among park visitors' favorite pastimes, with options for every skill level. The **Rim Trail** is the most popular, and easiest, walk in the park. It dips in and out of the scrubby pines of Kaibab National Forest and connects a series of scenic points and historical sights over 12 miles. Portions are paved, and every viewpoint is accessed by one of the three shuttle routes.

Desert View Drive starts to the east of Grand Canyon Village and follows the canyon rim for 26 miles to Desert View, the east entrance of the park. Pullouts offer spectacular views, and interpretive signs explain canyon features and geology.

The most popular of the corridor trails is the beautiful **Bright Angel Trail**. The steep and scenic 8-mile descent to the Colorado River is punctuated with four logical turnaround spots. Summer heat can be crippling; day hikers should either turn around at one of the two resthouses (a 3- to 6-mile round-trip) or hit the trail at dawn to safely make the longer hikes to Indian Garden and Plateau Point (9.2 and 12.2 miles round-trip respectively). Hiking to the river in one day should not be attempted. The trailhead is just west of Bright Angel Lodge.

The **South Kaibab** is arguably one of the park's prettiest trails, combining stunning scenery and unobstructed 360-degree views with every step. Steep, rough and wholly exposed, summer ascents can be dangerous: during this season rangers discourage all but the shortest day hikes – otherwise it's a 6-mile, grueling round-trip. Turn around at **Cedar Ridge**, perhaps the park's finest short day hike.

Cycling

BRIGHT ANGEL BICYCLES   Bicycle Rental
(☎ 928-814-8704; www.bikegrandcanyon.com; full day adult/child $35/25; ⏰ 8am-6pm May-Sep, 10am-4:30pm Mar-Apr & Oct-Nov, weather

Detour: Route 66

Running for 2400 miles from Chicago to Los Angeles, Route 66 (aka the 'Mother Road') was the first cross-country highway to be paved in 1937. Families fled west on it during the Dust Bowl; after WWII, they got their kicks road-tripping. The route was bypassed by Interstate 40 in 1985, but some original parts remain, including approximately 875 miles across New Mexico and Arizona. Some highlights: the Grand Canyon, classic diners and kitschy delights like the Wigwam Motel in Holbrook, Arizona. Check the **Historic Route 66 Association of Arizona** (www.azrt66.com) and **Historic Route 66** (www.historic66. com) websites for more details.

permitting) Renting 'comfort cruiser' bikes, the friendly folks here custom-fit each bike to the individual.

Rafting

Rafting the Colorado is an epic, truly adrenaline-pumping adventure. The biggest single drop at Lava Falls plummets 37ft in just 300yd. But the canyon's true grandeur is best grasped looking up from the river, not down from the rim. Its cultural history comes alive in ruins, wrecks and rock art.

Commercial trips vary from three days to three weeks and in the type of watercraft used. At night you'll be camping under stars on sandy beaches (gear provided). It takes about two or three weeks to run the entire 279 miles of river through the canyon. Shorter sections of around 100 miles take four to nine days.

ARIZONA RAFT ADVENTURES Rafting

(✆928-786-7238, 800-786-7238; www.azraft.com; 6-day Upper Canyon hybrid trips/paddle trips $1940/2040, 10-day Full Canyon motor trips $2830)

ARIZONA RIVER RUNNERS Rafting

(✆602-867-4866, 800-477-7238; www.raftarizona.com; 6-day Upper Canyon oar trips $1795, 12-day Full Canyon motor trips $2695)

 Tours

XANTERRA Horseback Riding

(✆303-297-2757; www.grandcanyonlodges.com/mule-rides-716.html) Park tours are run by Xanterra, which has information desks at Bright Angel, Maswik and Yavapai Lodges. Various daily bus tours (tickets from $20) are offered.

Rather than going below the rim, three-hour day trips ($119) now take riders along the rim, through the ponderosa and piñon and juniper forest to the Abyss overlook. Overnight trips (one/two people $482/850) and two-night trips (one/two people $701/1170) still follow the Bright Angel Trail to the river, travel east on the River Trail and cross the river on the Kaibab Suspension Bridge. Riders spend the night at Phantom Ranch.

🛏 **Sleeping**

Advance or same-day reservations are required for the South Rim's six lodges, which are operated by **Xanterra** (✆888-297-2757; www.grandcanyonlodges.com). Use this phone number to make advance reservations (highly recommended) at any of the places (including Phantom Ranch) listed here. If you can't find accommodations in the national park, try Tusayan (at South Rim Entrance Station), Valle (31 miles south), Cameron (53 miles east) or Williams (about 60 miles south).

EL TOVAR HOTEL Lodge $$$

(d $178-273, ste $335-426; ❄ 🔊) Wide, inviting porches wreathe the rambling wooden structure, offering pleasant spots to people-watch and admire canyon

El Tovar Hotel

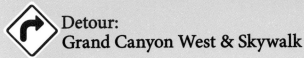

Detour:
Grand Canyon West & Skywalk

Grand Canyon West is not part of the national park, which is about 215 driving miles to the east. Run by the Hualapai Nation, the remote site is 70 miles northeast of Kingman, and the last 9 miles are unpaved and unsuitable for RVs. The Grand Canyon **Skywalk** (☎928-769-2636; www.grandcanyonwest.com; per person $71; ⏰7am-7pm Apr-Sep, 8am-5pm Oct-Mar) is the main draw. A slender, see-through glass horseshoe levitates over a 4000ft chasm of the Grand Canyon. The only way to visit is to purchase a package tour. A hop-on, hop-off shuttle travels the loop road to scenic points along the rim. Tours can include lunch, horse-drawn wagon rides from an ersatz Western town, and informal Native American performances.

views – even if you're not a guest. The public spaces show the lodge-like, genteel elegance of the park's heyday. The standard rooms are small but first-class.

BRIGHT ANGEL LODGE   Lodge $
(d with/without private bath $92/81, cabins $113-178; ❄@🛜) Built in 1935, the log-and-stone Bright Angel offers historic charm and refurbished rooms, the cheapest of which have shared bathrooms. Don't expect a TV in these very basic rooms (think university dorm room), but the rim cabins have better views than a TV.

Eating & Drinking

EL TOVAR DINING ROOM   International $$$
(☎928-638-2631, ext 6432; El Tovar; mains $18-31; ⏰6:30-11am, 11:30am-2pm & 5-10pm) A stone's throw from the canyon's edge, it has the best views of any restaurant of the state, if not the country. The grand stone and dark-oak dining room warms the soul like an upscale lodge of yore, and the food, especially the steaks, makes the trip worthwhile.

BRIGHT ANGEL LOUNGE   Bar $$
(Bright Angel Lodge, mains $10-26; ⏰11:30am-3pm Mar-Oct & 4:30-10pm Mar-Dec) Perfect for those who want to unwind with a burger and a beer without cleaning up

too much; a fun place to relax at night when the lack of windows and dark decor aren't a big deal.

Arizona Room   American $$
(Bright Angel Lodge; mains $8-28; ⏰11:30am-3pm Mar-Oct & 4:30-10pm Mar-Dec) Antler chandeliers hang from the ceiling and picture windows overlook the canyon. Mains include steak, chicken and fish dishes. No reservations; there's often a wait.

 Getting There & Around

Under the new Park-n-Ride program, summer visitors can buy a park ticket at the National Geographic Visitor Center (p300), park their vehicle at a designated lot, then hop aboard a free park shuttle that follows the Tusayan Route (⏰8am-9:30pm mid-May–early Sep) to the Grand Canyon Visitor Center inside the park.

Inside the park, free park shuttles operate along three routes: around Grand Canyon Village, west along Hermits Rest Route and east along Kaibab Trail Route. Buses typically run at least twice per hour, starting from one hour before sunset to one hour afterward.

North Rim

Head here for blessed solitude in nature's bountiful bosom; only 10% of park visitors make the trek. Meadows are thick with wildflowers and dense clusters of willowy aspen and spruce trees, and the air is often crisp, the skies big and blue.

Sights & Activities

The short and easy paved trail (0.5 miles) to **Bright Angel Point** is a canyon must. Beginning from the back porch of Grand Canyon Lodge, it goes to a narrow finger of an overlook with fabulous views.

The **North Kaibab Trail** is the North Rim's only maintained rim-to-river trail and connects with trails to the South Rim. The first 4.7 miles are the steepest, dropping 3050ft to **Roaring Springs** – a popular all-day hike. If you prefer a shorter day hike below the rim, walk just 0.75 miles down to **Coconino Overlook** or 2 miles to the **Supai Tunnel** to get a flavor for steep inner-canyon hiking. The 28-mile round-trip to the Colorado River is a multiday affair.

Canyon Trail Rides (☎435-679-8665; www.canyonrides.com; Grand Canyon Lodge; ☾mid-May–mid-Oct) offers one-hour ($40) and half-day ($75, minimum age 10 years) mule trips.

Sleeping

Accommodations are limited to one lodge and one campground. If these are booked, try your luck 80 miles north in Kanab, UT, or 84 miles northeast in Lees Ferry.

GRAND CANYON LODGE   Historic Hotel **$$**
(☎928-638-2611/12 same-day reservations, 480-337-1320 reservations outside the USA; www.gandcanyonlodgenorth.com; r $116, cabins $121-170; ☾mid-May–mid-Oct; 🛜👨) Made of wood, stone and glass, the lodge is the kind of place you imagine should be perched on the rim. Rustic yet modern cabins make up the majority of accommodations. The most expensive cabins offer two rooms, a porch and beautiful rim views. Reserve far in advance.

Left: Grand Canyon Skywalk (p303);
Below: Claret cup cactus, Desert Botanical Garden (p307)

(LEFT) NATIONAL GEOGRAPHIC IMAGE COLLECTION/ALAMY ©;
(BELOW) RICHARD CUMMINS/LONELY PLANET IMAGES ©

Eating & Drinking

The Grand Canyon Lodge will also prepare sack lunches ($11), ready for pickup at 6:30am, for those wanting to picnic on the trail.

**GRAND CANYON LODGE
DINING ROOM** American $$
(☎928-638-2611; mains $12-24; ☻6:30-10am, 11:30am-2:30pm & 4:45-9:45pm mid-May–mid-Oct) The windows are so huge that you can sit anywhere to get a good view. The menu includes several vegetarian options and Western treats such as Utah Ruby trout and bison flank steak.

**Grand Canyon Cookout
Experience** American $$
(☎928-638-2611; adult $30-35, child $12-22; ☻6-7:45pm Jun-Sep; 🚼) This chuck-wagon-style cookout featuring barbecue and cornbread is more of an event than a meal.

Kids love it. Make arrangements at the Grand Canyon Lodge.

🛈 Getting There & Around

The Transcanyon Shuttle (☎928-638-2820; www.trans-canyonshuttle.com; one-way/round-trip $80/150; ☻7am mid-May–mid-Oct) departs daily from Grand Canyon Lodge for the South Rim (five hours) and is perfect for rim-to-rim hikers. Reserve at least one or two weeks in advance.

FLAGSTAFF

The laid-back charms of Flagstaff, Arizona, are myriad, from its pedestrian-friendly historic downtown crammed with eclectic vernacular architecture and vintage neon to its high-altitude pursuits such as skiing and hiking.

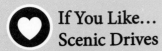

If You Like...
Scenic Drives

If you like the magnificent Desert View Drive along the Grand Canyon's South Rim (p300), don't miss these other scenic drives.

1 OAK CREEK CANYON, ARIZONA
A thrilling plunge past swimming holes, rock slides and crimson canyon walls on Hwy 89A between Flagstaff and Sedona.

2 KAYENTA-MONUMENT VALLEY, ARIZONA
Become the star of your own Western on an iconic loop past cinematic red rocks in Navajo Country just off Hwy 163.

3 HIGHWAY 12, UTAH
Arguably Utah's most diverse and stunning route, **Hwy 12 Scenic Byway** (www.scenicbyway12.com) winds through rugged canyon land on a 124-mile journey west of Bryce Canyon to near Capitol Reef. The section between Escalante and Torrey traverses a moonscape of sculpted slickrock, crosses narrow ridgebacks and climbs over an 11,000ft-high mountain.

4 BILLY THE KID SCENIC BYWAY, NEW MEXICO
This mountain-and-valley **loop** (www.billybyway.com) in southeastern New Mexico swoops past Billy the Kid's stomping grounds, Smokey Bear's gravesite and the orchard-lined Hondo Valley. From Roswell, take Hwy 380 west.

5 HIGH ROAD TO TAOS, NEW MEXICO
The back road between Santa Fe and Taos passes through sculpted sandstone desert, fresh pine forests and rural villages with historic adobe churches and horse-filled pastures. The 13,000ft Truchas Peaks soar above. From Santa Fe, take Hwy 84/285 to Hwy 513 then follow the signs.

 Sights

MUSEUM OF NORTHERN ARIZONA
Museum
(www.musnaz.org; 3101 N Fort Valley Rd; adult/student $7/4; ⊙9am-5pm) If you have time for only one sight in Flagstaff, head to the Museum of Northern Arizona. It features exhibits on local Native American archaeology, history and customs, as well as geology, biology and the arts.

LOWELL OBSERVATORY
Observatory
(☏928-774-3358; www.lowell.edu; 1400 W Mars Hill Rd; adult/child $6/3; ⊙9am-5pm Mar-Oct, noon-5pm Nov-Feb, night hr vary) This observatory witnessed the first sighting of Pluto in 1920. Weather permitting, there's nightly stargazing, helped by the fact that Flagstaff is the first International Dark Sky city in the world. Day tours are offered between 10am and 4pm in summer, with reduced hours in winter.

 Sleeping

WEATHERFORD HOTEL
Historic Hotel $$
(☏928-779-1919; www.weatherfordhotel.com; 23 N Leroux St; r without bath $49-79, r with bath $89-139; ❄ 🛜) This atmospheric hotel offers 11 charmingly decorated rooms with turn-of-the-20th-century feel. Since the Weatherford's three bars often feature live music, it can get noisy.

HOTEL MONTE VISTA
Historic Hotel $$
(☏928-779-6971; www.hotelmontevista.com; 100 N San Francisco St; d $65-130, ste $120-175; ❄ 🛜) Feather lampshades, vintage furniture, bold colors and eclectic decor – things are historically frisky in the 50 rooms and suites here, which are named for the film stars who slept in them.

 Eating

 CRIOLLO LATIN KITCHEN
Fusion $$
(☏928-774-0541; www.criollolatinkitchen.com; 16 N San Francisco St; mains $13-30; ⊙11am-10pm Mon-Thu, 11am-11pm Fri, 9am-11pm Sat,

9am-2pm & 4-10pm Sun) This Latin fusion spot has a romantic, industrial setting for cozy cocktail dates and delectable late-night small plates.

BEAVER STREET BREWERY
Pub $$

(www.beaverstreetbrewery.com; 11 S Beaver St; mains $8-12; ⏱11am-11pm Sun-Thu, 11am-midnight Fri & Sat; ♿) Beaver Street Brewery is a bustling place to go for a bite to eat with a pint of local microbrew.

🍷 Drinking & Entertainment

MUSEUM CLUB
Roadhouse

(☎928-526-9434; 3404 E Rte 66; ⏱11am-2am) Yee-haw! Kick up your heels at this honky-tonk roadhouse where the country dancing is nightly.

ℹ️ Information

Visitor center (☎928-774-9541; www.flagstaffarizona.org; 1 E Rte 66; ⏱8am-5pm Mon-Sat, 9am-4pm Sun) Inside the historic Amtrak train station.

ℹ️ Getting There & Around

TRAIN Operated by **Amtrak** (☎928-774-8679; www.amtrak.com; 1 E Route 66; ⏱3am-10:45pm), the *Southwest Chief* stops at Flagstaff on its daily run between Chicago and Los Angeles.
PUBLIC TRANSPORTATION Arizona Shuttle (☎928-226-8060; www.arizonashuttle.com) has shuttles that run to the park, Williams and Phoenix Sky Harbor Airport.

PHOENIX

Anchoring nearly 2000 sq miles of suburbs, strip malls and golf courses, Phoenix, Arizona, is the largest urban area in the Southwest. The beige sprawl does little to inspire travelers upon arrival, but if you look a little closer there's an interesting mix of upscale pampering and sunbaked weirdness.

👁 Sights

HEARD MUSEUM
Museum

(www.heard.org; 2301 N Central Ave; adult/child $15/7.50; ⏱9:30am-5pm Mon-Sat, 11am-5pm Sun; ♿) This engaging museum houses one of the best Native American collections in the entire world.

DESERT BOTANICAL GARDEN
Gardens

(☎480-941-1225; www.dbg.org; 1201 N Galvin Pkwy; adult/child $18/8; ⏱8am-8pm Oct-Apr, 7am-8pm May-Sep) This inspirational garden is a refreshing place to reconnect with

Hotel Monte Vista

If You Like...
Native American Culture & History

If you like the fascinating clifftop dwellings at Bandelier National Monument (p328) outside of Santa Fe, don't miss these other spots to get a taste of Native American culture.

1 WALNUT CANYON NATIONAL MONUMENT, ARIZONA

(☎928-526-3367; www.nps.gov/waca; admission $5; ☺8am-5pm May-Oct, 9am-5pm Nov-Apr) Sinagua cliff dwellings are set in the nearly vertical walls of a small limestone butte amid a forested canyon at this worth-a-trip monument. It's 11 miles southeast of Flagstaff off I-40 exit 204.

2 ACOMA PUEBLO, ARIZONA

The dramatic mesa-top 'Sky City' sits 7000ft above sea level and 367ft above the surrounding plateau. One of the oldest continuously inhabited settlements in North America, this place has been home to pottery-making people since the later part of the 11th century. Guided **tours** (adult/child $20/12; ☺hourly 10am-3pm Fri-Sun mid-Oct–mid-Apr, 9am-3:30pm daily mid-Apr–mid-Oct) leave from the **visitor center** (☎800-747-0181; http://sccc. acomaskycity.org) at the bottom of the mesa. From I-40, take exit 102, which is about 60 miles west of Albuquerque, then drive 12 miles south.

3 NEWSPAPER ROCK RECREATION AREA, UTAH

This tiny recreation area showcases a single, large sandstone-rock panel packed with more than 300 petroglyphs attributed to Ute and Ancestral Puebloan groups during a 2000-year period. The red-rock figures etched out of a black 'desert varnish' surface make for great photos. It's located 50 miles south of Moab, east of Canyonlands National Park on Hwy 211.

nature and offers a great introduction to desert plant life.

PHOENIX ART MUSEUM   Art Gallery
(☎602-257-1222; www.phxart.org; 1625 N Central Ave; adult/child $10/4, admission free Wed 3-9pm; ☺10am-9pm Wed, 10am-5pm Thu-Sat, noon-5pm Sun) The Phoenix Art Museum is Arizona's premier repository of fine art.

 Sleeping

CLARENDON HOTEL & SUITES   Hotel $$
(☎602-252-7363; www.theclarendon.net; 401 W Clarendon Ave, Phoenix; r $160-199; P ❄ @ �🛜 ✇) The Clarendon's finger-snapping, minimalist cool manages to be both welcoming and hip. Ride up to the breezy skydeck for citywide views.

ALOFT PHOENIX-AIRPORT   Hotel $$
(☎602-275-6300; www.aloftphoenixairport .com; 4450 E Washington St, Phoenix; r $129-160; P ❄ @ �🛜 ✇) Rooms blend a pop-art sensibility with the cleanest edges of modern design.

 Eating & Drinking

DICK'S HIDEAWAY   Mexican $$
(☎602-265-5886; www.richardsonsnm. com; 6008 N 16th St; breakfast $8-16, lunch $12-16, dinner $17-37; ☺7am-midnight) Grab a table beside the bar or join the communal table in the side room and settle in for hearty servings of savory, chile-slathered enchiladas, tamales and other New Mexican cuisine.

POSTINO WINECAFÉ ARCADIA   Wine Bar $$
(www.postinowinecafe.com; 3939 E Campbell Ave, at 40th St, Phoenix; ☺11am-11pm Mon-Thu, 11am-midnight Fri & Sat, 11am-10pm Sun) This convivial, indoor-outdoor wine bar is a perfect gathering spot for a few friends ready to enjoy the good life, but solos will do fine too.

ℹ Information

Downtown Phoenix Visitor Information Center (☎602-254-6500; www.visitphoenix. com; 125 N 2nd St, Suite 120; ☺8am-5pm Mon-

Fri) Offers the Valley's most complete source of tourist information.

 Getting There & Around

Sky Harbor International Airport (www.skyharbor.com; 📶) is 3 miles southeast of downtown Phoenix .

LAS VEGAS

Las Vegas is the ultimate escape. Here on the edge of the Nevada desert, time is irrelevant. There are no clocks, just never-ending buffets and ever-flowing drinks. This is a city of multiple personalities, constantly reinventing itself since the days of the Rat Pack. Sin City aims to infatuate, and its reaches are all-inclusive. Hollywood bigwigs gyrate at A-list ultralounges, while college kids seek cheap debauchery and grandparents whoop it up at the penny slots. Sip designer martinis and sample the apex of world-class cuisine or wander the casino floor with a 3ft-high cocktail tied around your neck.

Sights

The Strip, aka Las Vegas Blvd, is the center of Sin City. Whether you're walking or driving, distances on the Strip are deceiving: a walk to what looks like a nearby casino usually takes longer than expected.

Downtown Las Vegas is the original town center and home to the city's oldest hotels and casinos: expect a retro feel, cheaper drinks and lower table limits. Its main drag is fun-loving Fremont St, four blocks of which are a covered pedestrian mall that runs a groovy light show every night.

Casinos

COSMOPOLITAN Casino
(www.cosmopolitanlasvegas.com; 3708 Las Vegas Blvd S) Like the new Hollywood 'It girl,' the Cosmo looks good at all times of the day or night, full of ingenues and entourages, plus regular folks who enjoy contemporary design.

ENCORE Casino
(www.encorelasvegas.com; 3121 Las Vegas Blvd S) Filled with indoor flower gardens, a

Las Vegas skyline

RICHARD CUMMINS/LONELY PLANET IMAGES ©

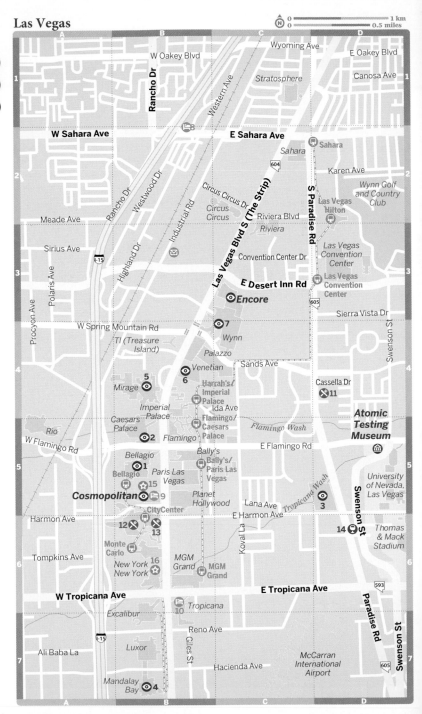

Las Vegas

0   1 km
0   0.5 miles

W Oakey Blvd
E Oakey Blvd
Wyoming Ave
Canosa Ave
Stratosphere

Rancho Dr
Western Ave

W Sahara Ave
E Sahara Ave
Sahara
Sahara
Karen Ave
604
Wynn Golf and Country Club
Circus Circus Dr
Las Vegas Hilton
Las Vegas Blvd S (The Strip)
Circus Circus
Riviera Blvd
Riviera
S Paradise Rd
Meade Ave
Rancho Dr
Westwood Dr
Industrial Rd
Las Vegas Convention Center
Convention Center Dr
Sirius Ave
Highland Dr
I-15
Las Vegas Convention Center
3
605
Polaris Ave
E Desert Inn Rd
Encore
Sierra Vista Dr
Swenson St
Procyon Ave
7
W Spring Mountain Rd
Wynn
Palazzo
TI (Treasure Island)
Venetian
Sands Ave
6
Cassella Dr
Mirage
5
11
Harrah's/ Imperial Palace
Atomic Testing Museum
Imperial Palace
Ida Ave
Caesars Palace
Flamingo/ Caesars Palace
Flamingo Wash
Rio
2
Flamingo
Bellagio
E Flamingo Rd
W Flamingo Rd
Bellagio
1
Paris Las Vegas
Bally's/ Paris Las Vegas
Bally's
University of Nevada, Las Vegas
Cosmopolitan
15
9
Planet Hollywood
Lana Ave
Tropicana Wash
3
Swenson St
Harmon Ave
CityCenter
E Harmon Ave
12
13
Koval La
14
Thomas & Mack Stadium
Monte Carlo
Tompkins Ave
New York New York
16
MGM Grand
MGM Grand
W Tropicana Ave
E Tropicana Ave
Paradise Rd
Swenson St
593
Excalibur
Tropicana
10
Reno Ave
Ali Baba La
I-15
Luxor
Giles St
McCarran International Airport
605
Hacienda Ave
Mandalay Bay
4

Las Vegas

butterfly motif and a dramatically luxe casino, it's an oasis of bright beauty. Encore is attached to its sister property, the $2.7-billion **Wynn Las Vegas** (www.wynnlasvegas.com; 3131 Las Vegas Blvd S). The entrance is obscured from the Strip by a $130-million artificial mountain, which rises seven stories tall in some places. Inside, the Wynn resembles a natural paradise – with mountain views, tumbling waterfalls, fountains and other special effects.

HARD ROCK   Casino
(www.hardrockhotel.com; 4455 Paradise Rd) Beloved by SoCal visitors, this trés hip casino hotel is home to one of the world's most impressive collections of rock and roll memorabilia, including Jim Morrison's handwritten lyrics to one of the Door's greatest hits, and leather jackets from a who's who of famous rock stars.

BELLAGIO   Casino
(www.bellagio.com; 3600 Las Vegas Blvd S) The Bellagio dazzles with Tuscan architecture and an 8-acre artificial lake, complete with don't-miss choreographed dancing fountains. The **Bellagio Gallery of Fine Art** (adult/child $13/free; ◷10am-6pm Sun, Mon, Tue & Thu, 10am-7pm Wed, Fri & Sat) showcases temporary exhibits by top-notch artists. The **Bellagio Conservatory & Botanical Gardens** (admission free; ◷daily) features changing exhibits throughout the year.

VENETIAN
(www.venetian.com; 3355 Las Vegas Blvd S) Hand-painted ceiling frescoes, roaming mimes, gondola rides, and full-scale reproductions of famous Venice landmarks are found at the romantic Venetian.

CAESARS PALACE   Casino
(www.caesarspalace.com; 3570 Las Vegas Blvd S) Quintessentially Las Vegas, Caesars Palace is a Greco-Roman fantasyland featuring marble reproductions of classical statuary, including a not-to-be-missed 4-ton Brahma shrine near the front entrance.

MIRAGE   Casino
(www.mirage.com; 3400 Las Vegas Blvd S) With a tropical setting replete with a huge atrium filled with jungle foliage and soothing cascades, the Mirage

captures the imagination. Don't miss the 20,000-gallon saltwater aquarium, with 60 species of critters hailing from Fiji to the Red Sea. Out front in the lagoon, a fiery faux volcano erupts hourly after dark until midnight.

MANDALAY BAY Casino
(M-Bay; www.mandalaybay.com; 3950 Las Vegas Blvd S) Not trying to be any one fantasy, the tropically themed Mandalay Bay is worth a walk-through. Standout attractions include the multilevel **Shark Reef** (www.sharkreef.com; adult/child $18/12; 10am-8pm Sun-Thu, 10am-10pm Fri & Sat;), an aquarium home to thousands of submarine beasties with a shallow pool where you can pet pint-sized sharks.

Other Attractions

ATOMIC TESTING MUSEUM Museum
(www.atomictestingmuseum.org; 755 E Flamingo Rd; adult/child $14/11; 10am-5pm Mon-Sat, noon-5pm Sun) Recalling an era when the word 'atomic' conjured modernity and mystery, the Smithsonian-run Atomic Testing Museum remains an intriguing testament to the period when the fantastical – and destructive – power of nuclear energy was tested just outside of Las Vegas.

FREMONT STREET EXPERIENCE Street
(www.vegasexperience.com; Fremont St; 7pm-midnight hourly) A four-block pedestrian mall topped by an arched steel canopy and filled with computer-controlled lights, the Fremont Street Experience, between Main St and Las Vegas Blvd, has brought life back to downtown. Every evening, the canopy is transformed into a six-minute light-and-sound show enhanced by 550,000 watts of wraparound sound.

Sleeping

The Strip

MANDALAY BAY Casino Hotel **$$**
(702-632-7777; www.mandalaybay.com; 3950 Las Vegas Blvd S; r $100-380;) The ornately appointed rooms here have a South Seas theme, and amenities include floor-to-ceiling windows and luxurious bathrooms. Swimmers will swoon over the sprawling pool complex, with a sand-and-surf beach.

TROPICANA Casino Hotel **$**
(702-739-2222; www.troplv.com; 3801 Las Vegas Blvd S; r/ste from $40/140;) As once-celebrated retro properties go under, the Tropicana – keeping the Strip tropical vibe going since 1953 – just got (surprise!) cool again. The multimillion-dollar renovation shows, from the airy casino to the lush, relaxing gardens with their newly unveiled pool and beach club.

Atomic Testing Museum
RICHARD CUMMINS/LONELY PLANET IMAGES ©

COSMOPOLITAN   Casino Hotel **$$$**
(702-698-7000; www.cosmopolitanlasvegas.com; 3708 Las Vegas Blvd S; r $200-400; ❄@🛜🏊) The rooms are impressive exercises in mod design, but the real delight of staying here is to stumble out of your room at 1am to play some pool in the upper lobbies before going on a mission to find the 'secret' pizza joint.

Caesars Palace   Casino Hotel **$$**
(866-227-5938; www.caesarspalace.com; 3570 Las Vegas Blvd S; r from $99; ❄@🏊) Send away the centurions and decamp in style – Caesars' standard rooms are some of the most luxurious you will find in town.

Downtown & Off the Strip
HARD ROCK   Casino Hotel **$$**
(702-693-5000; www.hardrockhotel.com; 4455 Paradise Rd; r $69-450; @🛜🏊) Everything about this boutique hotel spells stardom. French doors reveal skyline and palm tree views, and brightly colored Euro-minimalist rooms feature souped-up stereos and plasma-screen TVs. The hottest action revolves around the lush Beach Club.

ARTISAN HOTEL   Boutique Hotel **$**
(800-554-4092; www.artisanhotel.com; 1501 W Sahara Ave; r from $40; ❄@🛜🏊) A Gothic baroque fantasy with a decadent dash of rock and roll, each suite is themed around the work of a different artist. Yet with one of Vegas' best after-parties raging on weekend nights downstairs (a fave with the local alternative set), you may not spend much time in your room.

 Eating

The Strip
SAGE   American **$$$**
(877-230-2742; www.arialasvegas.com; Aria, 3730 Las Vegas Blvd S; mains $25-42; 5-11pm Mon-Sat) Acclaimed chef Shawn McClain meditates on the seasonally sublime with global inspiration and artisanal, farm-to-table ingredients and inspired cocktails in one of Vegas' most drop-dead gorgeous dining rooms.

DOCG ENOTECA   Italian **$$**
(702-698-7920; Cosmopolitan, 3708 Las Vegas Blvd S; mains $13-28; 10am-5pm) Order to-die-for fresh pasta or a wood-fired pizza in the stylish *enoteca* (wine shop)–inspired room that feels like you've joined a festive dinner party. Or head next door to sexy **Scarpetta**, which offers a more intimate, upscale experience by the same fantastic chef, Scott Conant.

SOCIAL HOUSE   Japanese **$$$**
(702-736-1122; www.socialhouselv.com; Crystals at CityCenter, 3720 Las Vegas Blvd S; mains $24-44; 5-10pm Mon-Thu, noon-11pm Fri & Sat, noon-10pm Sun) Watermarked scrolls, wooden screens and loads of dramatic red and black conjure visions of Imperial Japan, while the sushi and steaks are totally contemporary.

Downtown & Off the Strip
FIREFLY   Tapas **$$**
(www.fireflylv.com; 3900 Paradise Rd; small dishes $4-10, large dishes $11-20; 11:30am-2am Sun-Thu, to 3am Fri & Sat) Nosh on traditional Spanish tapas, while the bartender pours sangria and flavor-infused mojitos.

Pink Taco   Mexican **$$**
(www.hardrockhotel.com; Hard Rock, 4455 Paradise Rd; mains $8-24; 7am-11am Mon-Thu, to 3am Fri & Sat) Whether it's the 99-cent taco and margarita happy hour, the leafy poolside patio, or the friendly rock-and-roll clientele, Pink Taco always feels like a worthwhile party.

Drinking

The Strip
MIX   Lounge
(www.mandalaybay.com; 64th fl, Mandalay Bay, 3950 Las Vegas Blvd S; cover after 10pm $20-25) *The* place to grab sunset cocktails. The glassed-in elevator has amazing views, and that's before you even glimpse the mod interior design and soaring balcony.

GOLD LOUNGE   Lounge, Club
(www.arialasvegas.com; Aria, 3730 Las Vegas Blvd S; cover after 10pm $20-25) You won't find watered-down Top 40 at this luxe ultralounge, but you will find gold, gold and more gold. Make a toast in front of the giant portrait of Elvis.

Downtown & Off the Strip

Want to chill out with the locals? Head to one of their go-to favorites.

DOUBLE DOWN SALOON   Bar
(www.doubledownsaloon.com; 4640 Paradise Rd; no cover; ⊙24hr) You can't get more punk rock than a dive where the tangy, blood-red house drink is named 'Ass Juice'. The jukebox vibrates with New Orleans jazz, British punk, Chicago blues and surf-guitar king Dick Dale.

FRANKIE'S TIKI ROOM   Theme Bar
(www.frankiestikiroom.com; 1712 W Charleston Blvd; ⊙24hr) At the only round-the-clock tiki bar in the US, the drinks are rated in strength by skulls and the top tiki sculp-

tors and painters in the world have their work on display.

 Entertainment

Nightclubs & Live Music

MARQUEE   Club
(www.cosmopolitanlasvegas.com; Cosmopolitan, 3708 Las Vegas Blvd) When someone asks what the coolest club in Vegas is, Marquee is the undisputed answer. Celebrities (we spotted Macy Gray as we danced through the crowd), an outdoor beach club, hot DJs, and that certain *je ne sais quoi* that makes a club worth waiting in line for.

TRYST   Club
(www.trystlasvegas.com; Wynn Las Vegas, 3131 Las Vegas Blvd S) All gimmicks aside, the flowing waterfall makes this place ridiculously (and literally) cool. Blood-red booths and plenty of space to dance

Left: Bellagio Casino (p311);
Below: An Elvis impersonator on the Strip
(LEFT) RICHARD CUMMINS/LONELY PLANET IMAGES ©; (BELOW) DOUG MCKINLAY/LONELY PLANET IMAGES ©

ensure that you can have a killer time even without splurging for bottle service.

STONEY'S ROCKIN' COUNTRY
Live Music

(www.stoneysrockincountry.com; 9151 Las Vegas Blvd S; cover $5-10; ⊙7pm-late Thu-Sun) An off-Strip place that's worth the trip. Friday and Saturday features all-you-can-drink draft beer specials and free line-dancing lessons. The mechanical bull is a blast.

Production Shows

Steel Panther
Live Music

(☎702-617-7777; www.greenvalleyranchresort.com; Green Valley Resort, 2300 Paseo Verde Pkwy, Henderson; admission free; ⊙11pm-late Thu) A hair-metal tribute band makes fun of the audience, themselves and the 1980s with sight gags, one-liners and drug and sex references.

LOVE
Performing Arts

(☎702-792-7777; www.cirquedusoleil.com; tickets $99-150) At the Mirage is a popular addition to the Cirque du Soleil lineup; locals who have seen many a Cirque production come and go say it's the best one yet.

Zumanity
Performing Arts

(☎702-740-6815; www.cirquedusoleil.com; tickets $69-129) A sensual and sexy adults-only Cirque du Soleil show at New York New York

❶ Getting There & Around

AIR McCarran International Airport (www.mccarran.com) has direct flights from most US cities, and some from Canada and Europe. Bell Trans (☎702-739-7990; www.bell-trans.com) offers airport shuttle service (from $6.50) to the Strip and downtown.

PUBLIC TRANSPORT The monorail (www.lvmonorail.com; one-way $5; ⊙7am-2am Mon-Thu, to 3am Fri-Sun) connects the Sahara to the MGM Grand, stopping at major Strip megaresorts along the way.

ZION & SOUTHERN UTAH

Southern Utah red-rock country is defined by soaring Technicolor cliffs, spindles and spires that defy gravity, and seemingly endless expanses of sculpted sandstone desert. Interspersed throughout it all you'll find Native American rock-art sites and well-organized little towns with pioneer buildings dating back to the state's founding.

Springdale

Positioned at the main (south) entrance to Zion National Park, Springdale, Utah, is a perfect little park town. Stunning red cliffs form the backdrop to eclectic cafes, restaurants are big on organic ingredients, and artist galleries are interspersed with indie motels and B&Bs.

In addition to hiking trails in the national park, you can take outfitter-led **climbing** and **canyoneering** trips (from $150 per half-day) on adjacent BLM lands. All the classes and trips with terrific **Zion Rock & Mountain Guides** (☎435-772-3303; www.zionrockguides.com; 1458 Zion Park Blvd) are private. Singles can save money by joining an existing group with **Zion Adventure Company** (☎435-772-1001; www.zionadventures.com; 36 Lion Blvd).

Springdale has an abundance of good restaurants and nice lodging options. The updated motorcourt rooms at **Canyon Ranch Motel** (☎435-772-3357; www.canyonranchmotel.com; 668 Zion Park Blvd; s $84-94, d $94-99, r with kitchenette $114-125; ❄ 🤖 🏊) ring a shady lawn with picnic tables and swings. From colorful tractor reflectors to angel art, the owners' collections enliven every corner of the 1930s bungalow that is **Under-the-Eaves Bed & Breakfast** (☎435-772-3457; www.under-the-eaves.com; 980 Zion Park Blvd; r incl breakfast $95-185; ❄ 🤖).

Bryce Canyon National Park

The Grand Staircase, a series of steplike, uplifted rock layers elevating north from the Grand Canyon, culminates at this rightly popular **national park** (www.nps.gov/brca; Hwy 63; 7-day pass per vehicle $25; ⏱24hr, visitor center 8am-8pm May-Sep, 8am-4:30pm Nov-Mar, 8am-6pm Oct & Apr) in Utah's Pink

Navajo Loop Trail, Bryce Canyon National Park

DAVID TOMLINSON/LONELY PLANET IMAGES ©

Don't Miss Zion National Park

Entering Zion National Park from the east along Hwy 9, the route rolls past yellow sandstone, and **Checkerboard Mesa**, before reaching an impressive gallery-dotted tunnel and 3.5 miles of switchbacks going down in red-rock splendor. More than 100 miles of park trails here offer everything from leisurely strolls to wilderness backpacking and camping.

If you have time for only one activity, the 6-mile **Scenic Drive**, which pierces the heart of Zion Canyon, is it. From April through October, you'll need to take a free **visitors shuttle** from the visitor center, but you can hop off and on at any of the scenic stops and trailheads along the way. The famous **Angels Landing Trail** is a strenuous, 5.4-mile vertigo-inducer (1400ft elevation gain, with sheer drop-offs), but the views of Zion Canyon are phenomenal. Allow four hours for a round-trip.

Smack in the middle of the scenic drive, rustic **Zion Lodge** has 81 well-appointed motel rooms and 40 cabins with gas fireplaces. All have wooden porches with stellar red-rock cliff views, but no TVs. The lodge's full-service dining room, **Red Rock Grill** has similarly amazing views. Just outside the park, the town of Springdale offers many more services.

THINGS YOU NEED TO KNOW

Zion National Park (www.nps.gov/zion; Hwy 9; 7-day pass per vehicle $25; ⏰24hr); Zion Canyon Visitor Center (⏰8am-7pm May-Sep, 8am-6pm Apr & Oct, 8am-5pm Nov-Mar); vistors shuttle (⏰6:45am-10pm); Zion Lodge (☎435-772-7700; www.zionlodge.com; r & cabins $160-180; ❄@🛜); Red Rock Grill (Zion Lodge; breakfasts $10-15, lunch $8-20, dinner $15-30; ⏰7am-10pm Apr-Nov, hours vary Dec-Mar)

Cliffs formation. It's full of wondrous, sorbet-colored pinnacles and points, steeples and spires, and totem-pole-shaped 'hoodoo' formations. The canyon is actually an amphitheater eroded from the cliffs. From Hwy 12, turn south on Hwy 63; the park is 50 miles southwest of Escalante.

Rim Road Scenic Drive (8000ft) travels 18 miles one-way, roughly following the canyon rim past the visitor center, the lodge, incredible overlooks (don't miss **Inspiration Point**) and trailheads, ending at **Rainbow Point** (9115ft). From May through September, a free **shuttle bus** (8am-6pm) runs from just north of the park to as far south as **Bryce Amphitheater**.

The 1920s **Bryce Canyon Lodge** (435-834-8700; www.brycecanyonforever.com; Hwy 63; r $135-180; Apr-Oct; @) exudes rustic mountain charm. The lodge **restaurant** (breakfasts $6-10, lunch & dinner mains $12-40; 6:30-10:30am, 11:30am-3pm & 5-10pm Apr-Oct) is excellent, if expensive.

Just north of the park boundaries, **Ruby's Inn** (435-834-5341; www.rubysinn.com; 1000 S Hwy 63; campsites $25-40, r $89-199;) is a town as much as it is a motel complex.

Eleven miles east on Hwy 12, the small town of Tropic has additional food and lodging.

Moab

Southeastern Utah's largest community (population 5121) bills itself as the state's recreation capital – and man, does it deliver. Scads of rafting and riding outfitters (mountain bike, horse, 4WD) base here for forays into surrounding public lands. You can hike Arches or Canyonlands National Parks during the day, then come back to a comfy bed, a hot tub and your selection of surprisingly good restaurants at night.

Activities

Area outfitters offer half-day to multiday adventures (from $50 for four hours) that include transport, the activity, and sometimes meals.

Sheri Griffith Expeditions Rafting
(435-259-8229; www.griffithexp.com; 2231 S Hwy 191) Highly rated rafting outfitter; some multisport adventures.

Canyon Voyages Adventure Sports
(435-259-6007; www.canyonvoyages.com; 211 N Main St) River running, raft-hike-bike-4WD combos available; kayak and canoe rentals too.

Poison Spider Bicycles Cycling, Mountain Biking
(435-259-7882; www.poisonspiderbicycles.com; 497 N Main St) Mountain- and road-bike rentals and tours; superior service.

Red Cliffs Lodge Horseback Riding
(435-259-2002; www.redcliffslodge.com/tours-activities; Mile 14, Hwy 128) Half-day trail rides.

Sleeping

CALI COCHITTA B&B **$$**
(435-259-4961; www.moabdreaminn.com; 110 S 200 East; cottages incl breakfast $125-160;) Make yourself at home in one of the charming brick cottages a short walk from downtown. The patio's long wooden table is a welcome setting for community breakfasts.

Delicate Arch, Arches National Park
EDDIE BRADY/LONELY PLANET IMAGES ©

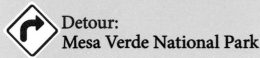

Detour:
Mesa Verde National Park

Shrouded in mystery, **Mesa Verde** (📞 970-529-4461; www.nps.gov/meve; 7-day park entry per vehicle $15, cyclists, hikers & motorcyclists $8) is a fascinating, if slightly eerie, national park to explore. It is here that a civilization of Ancestral Puebloans left in AD 1300, leaving behind cliff dwellings, some accessed by sheer climbs.

Mesa Verde rewards travelers who set aside a day or more to take the ranger-led tours of Cliff Palace and Balcony House, explore Wetherill Mesa or participate in one of the campfire programs. But if you only have time for a short visit, check out the Chapin Mesa Museum and walk through the Spruce Tree House, where you can climb down a wooden ladder into the cool chamber of a *kiva* (ceremonial structure, usually partly underground). The park is in southwestern Colorado, a three-hour drive from Moab.

REDSTONE INN   Motel **$**
(📞 435-259-3500; www.moabredstone.com; 535 S Main St; r $79-99; ❄ 📶) Great budget digs: simple, pine-paneled rooms have refrigerator, microwave, coffeemaker and free wired internet access. Hot tub on-site, pool privileges at sister hotel across street.

 Eating

LOVE MUFFIN   Cafe **$**
(139 N Main St; mains $6-8; ⊙ 7am-2pm; 📶) The largely organic menu at this vibrant cafe includes creative sandwiches, breakfast burritos and inventive egg dishes such as 'Verde,' with brisket and slow-roasted salsa.

JEFFREY'S STEAKHOUSE   Steakhouse **$$$**
(📞 435-259-3588; 218 N 100 West; mains $22-40; ⊙ 5-10pm) A historic sandstone building serves as home to one of the latest stars of the local dining scene. Jeffrey's is serious about beef, which comes grain-fed, Wagyu-style and in generous cuts.

MOAB BREWERY   American **$$**
(686 S Main St; mains $8-18; ⊙ 11:30am-10pm Mon-Thu, 11:30am-11pm Fri & Sat) Choosing among the list of microbrews made in the vats just behind the bar area may be easier than deciding what to eat off the vast and varied menu.

ⓘ Information

Moab Information Center (cnr Main & Center Sts; ⊙ 8am-8pm) An excellent source of information on area parks, trails, activities, camping and weather.

Arches National Park

One of the Southwest's most gorgeous parks, **Arches** (www.nps.gov/arch; 7-day pass per vehicle $10; ⊙ 24hr, visitor center 7:30am-6:30pm Apr-Oct, 8am-4:30pm Nov-Mar) boasts the world's greatest concentration of sandstone arches – more than 2000 ranging from 3ft to 300ft wide at last count. Nearly one million visitors make the pilgrimage here, in Utah just 5 miles north of Moab on Hwy 191, every year. Many noteworthy arches are easily reached by paved roads and relatively short hiking trails; much of the park can be covered in a day. To avoid crowds, consider a moonlight exploration, when it's cooler and the rocks feel ghostly.

Highlights include **Balanced Rock**, oft-photographed **Delicate Arch** (best captured in the late afternoon), spectacularly elongated **Landscape Arch**, and popular **Windows Arches**. Reservation are necessary for the twice-daily ranger-led hikes into the fins of the **Fiery Furnace** (adult/child $10/5; ⊙ Apr-Oct). Book in person or online at www.recreation.gov.

Canyonlands National Park

Red-rock fins, bridges, needles, spires, craters, mesas, buttes – **Canyonlands** (www.nps.gov/cany; 7-day per vehicle $10; ⏱24hr), in Utah, is a crumbling, decaying beauty, a vision of ancient earth. Roads and rivers make inroads to this high-desert wilderness stretching 527 sq miles, but much of it is still an untamed environment. You can hike, raft (Cataract Canyon offers some of the wildest white water in the West) and 4WD here, but be sure that you have plenty of gas, food and water.

The canyons of the Colorado and Green Rivers divide the park into three districts. **Island in the Sky** (☎435-259-4712; ⏱visitor center 9am-4:30pm Nov-Apr, 9am-6:30pm Mar-Oct) is most easily reached and offers amazing overlooks. Our favorite short hike is the half-mile loop to oft-photographed **Mesa Arch**, a slender, cliff-hugging span framing a picturesque view of Washer Woman Arch and Buck Canyon. Drive a bit further to reach the **Grand View Overlook** trailhead. The path follows the canyon's edge and ends at a praise-your-maker precipice. This park section is 32 miles from Moab; head north along Hwy 191 then southwest on Hwy 313.

MONUMENT VALLEY & NAVAJO NATION

Amid the isolation of some of North America's most spectacular scenery you'll find Monument Valley, Arizona, a place where cultural pride remains strong and many still speak Navajo as their first language. The Navajo rely heavily on tourism; visitors can help keep their heritage alive by staying on reservation land or purchasing their renowned crafts.

Canyon de Chelly National Monument

This many-fingered canyon (pronounced *duh-shay*) contains several beautiful Ancestral Puebloan sites important to Navajo history, including ancient cliff dwellings. Families still farm the land, wintering on the rims, then moving to hogans on the canyon floor in spring and summer. The Arizona canyon is private Navajo property administered by the NPS. Enter hogans only with a guide and don't photograph people without their permission. Most of the bottom of the canyon is off-limits to visitors unless you hire a guide. **Thunderbird Lodge** (☎928-674-5841; www.tbirdlodge.com; d Mar-Oct $115-171, Nov-Feb $66-95; ❄@🛜) is the place to book a tour (from $46/35 per adult/child) into the canyon. The lodge also boasts comfortable rooms, an ATM and an inexpensive

Cliff dwelling, Canyon de Chelly National Monument
JOHN ELK III/LONELY PLANET IMAGES ©

Don't Miss Monument Valley Navajo Tribal Park

With flaming-red buttes and impossibly slender spires reaching to the heavens, the Monument Valley landscape off Hwy 163 has starred in countless Hollywood Westerns and looms large in many a road-trip daydream.

For up-close views of the towering formations, you'll need to visit the **Monument Valley Navajo Tribal Park**, where a rough and unpaved scenic driving loop covers 17 miles of stunning valley views.

Inside the tribal park is the **View Hotel at Monument Valley**. It's been built in harmony with the landscape, and most of the 96 rooms have private balconies facing the monuments. The Navajo-based specialties at the adjoining restaurant (mains $13 to $23, no alcohol served) are mediocre, but the red-rock panorama is stunning.

The historic **Goulding's Lodge**, just across the border in Utah, offers lodge rooms, camping and small cabins.

THINGS YOU NEED TO KNOW

Monument Valley Navajo Tribal Park (435-727-5874; www.navajonationparks.org; admission $5; 6am-8pm May-Sep, 8am-4:30pm Oct-Apr); View Hotel at Monument Valley (435-727-5555; www. monumentvalleyview.com; Hwy 163; r $219-229, ste $299-319; @); Goulding's Lodge (435-727-3235; www.gouldings.com; r $185-205, cabins $79, RV sites $25-44, tent sites $25;   )

cafeteria serving tasty Navajo and American meals ($5 to $21).

The Canyon de Chelly **visitor center** (928-674-5500; www.nps.gov/cach; 8am-5pm) is three miles from Rte 191 in the small village of Chinle.

Four Corners Navajo Tribal Park

Don't be shy: do a spread eagle at the **four corners marker** (928-871-6647; www. navajonationparks.org; admission $3; 7am-8pm May-Aug, 8am-5pm Sep-Apr), the middle-of-nowhere landmark that's looking spiffy after a 2010 renovation of the central plaza. The only spot in the US where you can straddle four states – Arizona, New Mexico, Colorado, Utah – it makes a good photograph, even if it's not 100% accurate.

SANTA FE

Walking among the historic adobe neighborhoods or even around the tourist-filled plaza, there's no denying that Santa Fe, New Mexico, has a timeless, earthy soul. Founded around 1610, Santa Fe is the second-oldest city and oldest state capital in the USA. Yet the city is synonymous with contemporary chic, and boasts the second-largest art market in the nation, gourmet restaurants, great museums, spas and a world-class opera.

 Sights

GEORGIA O'KEEFFE MUSEUM   Art Gallery
(☎505-946-1000; www.okeeffemuseum.org; 217 Johnson St; adult/child $10/free; ⊙10am-5pm, to 8pm Fri) Possessing the world's largest collection of her work, the Georgia O'Keeffe Museum features the artist's paintings of flowers, bleached skulls and adobe architecture. Tours of O'Keeffe's house (p327) require advance reservations.

CANYON ROAD   Neighborhood
(www.canyonroadarts.com) The epicenter of the city's upscale art scene. More than 100 galleries, studios, shops and restaurants line the narrow historic road. Look for Santa Fe School masterpieces,

Santa Fe

rare Native American antiquities and wild contemporary work.

FREE WHEELWRIGHT MUSEUM OF THE AMERICAN INDIAN
Museum

(www.wheelwright.org; 704 Camino Lejo; ◷10am-5pm Mon-Sat, 1-5pm Sun) In 1937, Mary Cabot established the Wheelwright Museum of the American Indian, part of Museum Hill, to showcase Navajo ceremonial art. While its strength continues to be Navajo exhibits, it now includes contemporary Native American art and historical artifacts as well.

MUSEUM OF NEW MEXICO
Museum

(www.museumofnewmexico.org; adult admission 1 museum $9, 4-day pass to all 4 museums $20, child admission free; ◷10am-5pm Sat-Thu, 10am-8pm Fri, closed Mon winter) The Museum of New Mexico celebrated its centennial in 2009. It administers the following four museums around town:

Palace of the Governors
(www.nmhistorymuseum.org; 105 W Palace Ave) On the plaza, this 400-year-old abode was once the seat of the Spanish colonial government. It displays a handful of regional relics, but most of its holdings are now shown in an adjacent exhibit space called the **New Mexico History Museum** (113 Lincoln Ave), a glossy, 96,000-sq-ft expansion that opened in 2009.

New Mexico Museum of Art
(www.nmartmuseum.org; 107 W Palace Ave) Just off the plaza, there are more than 20,000 pieces of fine art here, mostly by Southwestern artists.

Museum of Indian Arts & Culture
(www.indianartsandculture.org; 710 Camino Lejo) Over on Museum Hill, this is one of the most complete collections of Native American arts and crafts anywhere – and a perfect companion to the nearby Wheelwright Museum.

Museum of International Folk Art
(www.internationalfolkart.org; 706 Camino Lejo;) Also on Museum Hill, the galleries here are at once whimsical and mind-blowing – featuring the world's largest collection of

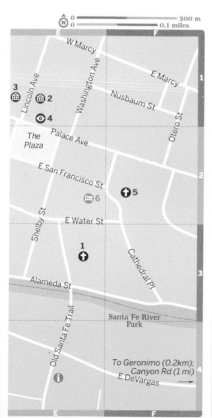

traditional folk art. Try to hit the incredible folk art market, held each June.

St Francis Cathedral
Church

(131 Cathedral Pl; ◷8:30am-5pm) Houses the oldest Madonna statue in North America.

Loretto Chapel
Church

(207 Old Santa Fe Trail; admission $3; ◷9am-5pm Mon-Sat, 10:30am-5pm Sun) Famous for its 'miraculous' spiral staircase that appears to be supported by thin air.

 Activities

The **Pecos Wilderness** and **Santa Fe National Forest**, east of town, have more than 1000 miles of hiking trails, several of which lead to 12,000ft peaks. Summer storms are frequent, so prepare for hikes by checking weather reports. For maps and details, contact the **Public Lands Information Center** (☏877-851-8946; www.publiclands.org). If mountain biking is your

thing, drop into **Mellow Velo** (☏505-995-8356; www.mellowvelo.com; 621 Old Santa Fe Trail), which rents bikes and has loads of information about regional trails.

Busloads of people head up to the Rio Grande and Rio Chama for white-water river running on day and overnight trips. Contact **New Wave Rafting** (☏505-984-1444; www.newwaverafting.com) and stay cool on trips through the Rio Grande Gorge (adult/child half-day $57/50, full day $95/85), the wild Taos Box (p330) (full day $116) or the Rio Chama Wilderness (three days $525).

10,000 WAVES
Spa

(☏505-982-9304; www.tenthousandwaves.com; 3451 Hyde Park Rd; communal tubs $19, private tubs per person $29-49; ◷2-10:30pm Tue, 9am-10:30pm Wed-Mon Jul-Oct, hr vary Nov-Jun) The Japanese-style 10,000 Waves, with landscaped grounds concealing eight attractive tubs in a smooth Zen design, offers waterfalls, cold plunges, massage, and hot and dry saunas.

Left: Old adobe house, Santa Fe;
Below: Native American handicrafts for sale at a street stall, Santa Fe
(LEFT) RICHARD CUMMINS/LONELY PLANET IMAGES ©; (BELOW) JOHN HAY/LONELY PLANET IMAGES ©

🛏 Sleeping

SANTA FE MOTEL & INN   Hotel **$$**
(☎ 505-982-1039; www.santafemotel.com;
510 Cerrillos Rd; r $89-155, casitas $119-169;
P ❄ @ 🛜) It's the aesthetic and techno-
logical attention to detail that make this
downtown-adjacent motel a great pick.
Bright tiles, clay sunbursts, LCD TVs
and a welcoming chile pepper carefully
placed atop your towels are just a few
memorable pluses.

SILVER SADDLE MOTEL   Motel **$**
(☎ 505-471-7663; www.silversaddlemotelllc.
com; 2810 Cerrillos Rd; r incl continental break-
fast from $45; P ❄ @ 🛜) Shady wooden
arcades outside and rustic cowboy-
inspired decor inside, including some
rooms with attractively tiled kitchen-
ettes. For a bit of kitschy Southwestern
fun, request to stay in the Kenny Rogers
or Wyatt Earp room.

LA FONDA   Historic Hotel **$$$**
(☎ 505-982-5511; www.lafondasantafe.
com; 100 E San Francisco St; r $210-400, ste
$430-800; P ❄ @ 🛜 ≈) Claiming to be
the original 'Inn at the end of the Santa
Fe Trail,' here since 1610, La Fonda has
always offered some of the best lodging
in town. The hotel today seamlessly
blends modern luxury with folk-art
touches; it's authentic, top-shelf Santa
Fe style.

EL REY INN   Historic Hotel **$$**
(☎ 505-982-1931; www.elreyinnsantafe.com;
1862 Cerrillos Rd; r incl breakfast $99-165, ste
from $150; P ❄ @ 🛜 ≈) A highly recom-
mended classic courtyard hotel, with
super rooms, a great pool and hot tub,
and even a kids' playground scattered
around 5 acres of greenery.

Eating

SAN MARCOS CAFÉ
New Mexican, American **$**
(☎505-471-9298; www.sanmarcosfeed.com; 3877 Hwy 14; mains $7-10; ⊙8am-2pm) About 10 minutes' drive south on Hwy 14, this spot is well worth the trip. Aside from the down-home feeling and the best red chile you'll ever taste, turkeys and peacocks strut and squabble outside and the whole place is connected to a feed store, giving it some genuine Western soul.

TUNE-UP CAFÉ
International **$$**
(☎505-983-7060; www.tuneupcafe.com; 1115 Hickox St; mains $7-14; ⊙7am-10pm Mon-Fri, 8am-10pm Sat & Sun) Santa Fe's newest favorite restaurant is casual, busy and does food right. The chef, from El Salvador, adds a few twists to classic New Mexican and American dishes, while also serving Salvadoran *pupusas* (stuffed corn tortillas), huevos and other specialties.

HORSEMAN'S HAVEN
New Mexican **$**
(4354 Cerrillos Rd; mains $6-12; ⊙8am-8pm Mon-Sat, 8:30am-2pm Sun) Hands down the hottest green chile in town! Service is friendly and fast, and the enormous 3-D burrito might be the only thing you need to eat all day.

COWGIRL HALL OF FAME
Barbecue **$$**
(www.cowgirlsantafe.com; 319 S Guadalupe St; mains $8-18; ⊙11am-midnight Mon-Fri, 10am-midnight Sat, 10am-11pm Sun, bar open later) Two-step up to the cobblestoned courtyard and try the salmon tacos, butternut-squash casserole or the BBQ platter – all served with Western-style feminist flair.

GERONIMO
Modern American **$$$**
(☎505-982-1500; 724 Canyon Rd; dishes $28-44; ⊙5:45-10pm Mon-Thu, 5:45-11pm Fri & Sat) Housed in a 1756 adobe, Geronimo is among the finest and most romantic restaurants in town. The short but diverse menu includes fiery sweet chile and honey-grilled prawns and peppery elk tenderloin with applewood-smoked bacon.

Cabin at Ghost Ranch, Abiquiú

WITOLD SKRYPCZAK/LONELY PLANET IMAGES ©

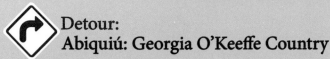

Detour:
Abiquiú: Georgia O'Keeffe Country

The tiny community of Abiquiú (sounds like 'barbecue'), New Mexico, on Hwy 84 (about a 45-minute drive northwest of Santa Fe) is famous for the renowned artist Georgia O'Keeffe, who lived and painted here from 1949 until her death in 1986. With the Chama River flowing through farmland and spectacular rock landscape, the ethereal setting continues to attract artists, and many live and work in Abiquiú. O'Keeffe's adobe house is open for limited visits, and the Georgia O'Keeffe Museum (p322) offers one-hour **tours** (☏505-685-4539; www.okeeffemuseum.org; tours $35-45; ☺Tue, Thu & Fri Mar-Nov, plus Sat Jun-Oct) that are often booked out months in advance.

Ghost Ranch (☏505-685-4333; www.ghostranch.org), a retreat center on 21,000 Technicolor acres that obviously inspired O'Keeffe's work (and was a shooting location for the movie *City Slickers*), has free hiking trails, a **dinosaur museum** (☺9am-5pm Mon-Sat, 1-5pm Sun) and offers horseback rides (from $40), including instruction for kids as young as four years ($20).

The lovely **Abiquiú Inn** (☏505-685-4378; www.abiquiuinn.com; Hwy 84; RV sites $18, r $140-200, ste $170, 4-person casitas $190; ✳☏) is a sprawling collection of shaded faux adobes; spacious casitas have kitchenettes.

Drinking & Entertainment

SANTA FE BREWING
COMPANY   Brewery, Live Music
(www.santafebrewing.com; 35 Fire Pl) Santa Fe's original microbrewery covers the full beer spectrum, from pilsner to porter to stout. Big-name bands play here surprisingly often.

EVANGELO'S   Bar, Live Music
(200 W San Francisco St) There's foot-stompin' live music nightly at Evangelo's and the sounds of rock, blues, jazz and Latin combos spill into the street.

SANTA FE OPERA   Opera
(☏800-280-4654; www.santafeopera.org; tickets $26-188; ☺Jul & Aug) Opera fans (and those who've never attended an opera in their lives) come to Santa Fe for this alone: an architectural marvel, with views of wind-carved sandstone wilderness crowned with sunsets and moonrises, and at center stage internationally renowned vocal talent performing masterworks of aria and romance.

Bell Tower Bar   Bar
(100 E San Francisco St) At La Fonda hotel, ascend five floors to the Bell Tower and watch one of those patented New Mexico sunsets.

Information

New Mexico Tourism Department (☏505-827-7400; www.newmexico.org; 491 Old Santa Fe Trail; ☺8:30am-5:30pm; ☏) Offers brochures, a hotel reservation line, free coffee and free internet access.

Getting There & Around

AIR American Eagle (☏800-433-7300; www.aa.com) flies in and out of **Santa Fe Municipal Airport** (wwwsantafenm.gov; 121 Aviation Dr).
BUS Sandia Shuttle Express (www.sandiashuttle.com) runs between Albuquerque's airport (Sunport) and Santa Fe ($27).
TAXI If you need a taxi, call **Capital City Cab** (☏505-438-0000).
TRAIN Amtrak (☏800-872-7245; www.amtrak.com) stops at Lamy; buses continue 17 miles to Santa Fe.

Bandelier National Monument

Ancestral Puebloans dwelt in the cliffsides of beautiful Frijoles Canyon, now preserved within **Bandelier** (www.nps.gov/band; admission per vehicle $12; ⏱8am-6pm summer, 9am-5:30pm spring & fall, 9am-4:30pm winter). The adventurous can climb four ladders to reach ancient caves and kivas used until the mid-1500s. There are also almost 50 sq miles of canyon and mesalands offering scenic backpacking trails.

TAOS

Taos is a place undeniably dominated by the power of its landscape: 12,300ft snowcapped peaks rise behind town; a sage-speckled plateau unrolls to the west before plunging 800ft straight down into the Rio Grande Gorge.

 Sights

MILLICENT ROGERS MUSEUM Museum (www.millicentrogers.org; 1504 Millicent Rogers Museum Rd; adult/child $10/6; ⏱10am-5pm, closed Mon Nov-Mar) Filled with pottery, jewelry, baskets and textiles, this has one of the best collections of Native American and Spanish Colonial art in the US.

HARWOOD MUSEUM OF ART Art Gallery (www.harwoodmuseum.org; 238 Ledoux St; adult/child $8/7; ⏱10am-5pm Tue-Sat, noon-5pm Sun) Housed in a historic mid-19th-century adobe compound, the Harwood Museum of Art features paintings, drawings, prints, sculpture and photography by northern New Mexico artists, both historical and contemporary.

TAOS HISTORIC MUSEUMS Museum (www.taoshistoricmuseums.com; adult/child individual museums $8/4, both museums $12; ⏱10am-5pm Mon-Sat, noon-5pm Sun) Runs two great houses: the **Blumenschein**

Cave rooms, Bandelier National Monument

RICHARD CUMMINS/LONELY PLANET IMAGES ©

ANDREW MARSHALL & LEANNE WALKER/LONELY PLANET IMAGES ©

Don't Miss Taos Pueblo

Taos Pueblo, believed to be the oldest continuously inhabited community in the US (it was built around AD 1450), is the largest existing multistoried pueblo structure in the country, and one of the best surviving examples of traditional adobe construction. It roots the town in a long history with a rich cultural legacy – including conquistadors, Catholicism and cowboys.

In the 20th century this New Mexico icon became a magnet for artists, writers and creative thinkers, from DH Lawrence to Dennis Hopper. It remains a relaxed and eccentric place, with classic adobe architecture, fine-art galleries, quirky cafes and excellent restaurants.

THINGS YOU NEED TO KNOW

📞575-758-1028; www.taospueblo.com; Taos Pueblo Rd; adult/child $10/5, photography or video permit $6; 🕑8am-4pm, closed for 6 weeks around Feb & Mar

Home (222 Ledoux St), a trove of art from the 1920s by the Taos Society of Artists, and the **Martínez Hacienda** (708 Lower Ranchitos Rd), a 21-room colonial trader's former home dating from 1804.

SAN FRANCISCO DE ASÍS
CHURCH Church
(St Francis Plaza; 🕑9am-4pm Mon-Fri) Four miles south of Taos in Ranchos de Taos, the San Francisco de Asís Church, famed

for the angles and curves of its adobe walls, was built in the mid-18th century but didn't open until 1815. It's been memorialized in Georgia O'Keeffe paintings and Ansel Adams photographs.

RIO GRANDE GORGE
BRIDGE Bridge, Canyon
Standing 650ft above the Rio Grande, the steel Rio Grande Gorge Bridge is the second-highest suspension bridge in the

US; the view down is eye-popping. For the best pictures of the bridge itself, park at the rest area on the western end of the span.

EARTHSHIPS Neighborhood
(www.earthship.net; Hwy 64; adult/child $5/free; 10am-4pm) Just 1.5 miles west of the bridge is the fascinating community of Earthships, with self-sustaining, environmentally savvy houses built with recycled materials that are completely off the grid. You can also rent one out for accommodations.

Activities

During summer, white-water rafting is popular in the **Taos Box**, the steep-sided cliffs that frame the Rio Grande. Day-long trips begin at around $100 per person; contact the visitor center for local outfitters, where there's also good info about hiking and mountain-biking trails.

Sleeping

EARTHSHIP RENTALS Bungalow **$$**
(575-751-0462; www.earthship.net; Hwy 64; r $120-160) Experience an off-grid overnight in a boutique-chic, solar-powered dwelling. A cross between organic Gaudí architecture and space-age fantasy, these sustainable dwellings are put together using recycled tires, aluminum cans and sand, with rain catchment and gray-water systems to further minimize their footprint.

HISTORIC TAOS INN Historic Hotel **$$**
(575-758-2233; www.taosinn.com; 125 Paseo del Pueblo Norte; r $75-275; P) Even though it's not the plushest place in town, it's still fabulous, with a cozy lobby, a garden for the restaurant, heavy wooden furniture, a sunken fireplace and lots of live local music at its famed Adobe Bar. Parts of this landmark date to the 1800s – the older rooms are actually the nicest.

Stalagmites in the Hall of Giants, Carlsbad Caverns National Park

HOLGER LEUE/LONELY PLANET IMAGES ©

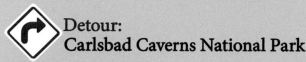

Detour:
Carlsbad Caverns National Park

In the southeast corner of New Mexico (a six hour drive from Santa Fe), you'll find scores of caves hidden under the hills at this unique 73-sq-mile **national park** (☎575-785-2232, bat sightings info 505-785-3012; www.nps.gov/cave; 3225 National Parks Hwy; adult/child $6/free; ⊙caves 8:30am-4pm late May–early Sep, 8:30am-3:30pm early Sep–late May). The cavern formations are an ethereal wonderland of stalactites and fantastical geological features. You can ride an elevator from the visitor center (which descends the length of the Empire State Building in under a minute) or take a 2-mile subterranean walk from the cave mouth to the Big Room, an underground chamber 1800ft long, 255ft high and more than 800ft below the surface.

Guided tours of additional caves are available (adult $7 to $20, child $3.50 to $10), and should be reserved well in advance (call ☎877-444-6777 or visit www.recreation.gov). Bring long sleeves and closed shoes; it gets chilly.

The cave's other claim to fame is the 300,000-plus Mexican free-tailed bat colony that roosts here from mid-May to mid-October. Be here by sunset, when they cyclone out for an all-evening insect feast.

SUN GOD LODGE Motel **$**
(☎575-758-3162; www.sungodlodge.com; 919 Paseo del Pueblo Sur; r from $55; P❈🛜)
The hospitable folks at this well-run two-story motel can fill you in on local history as well as what's the craziest bar in town. Rooms are clean – if a bit dark – and decorated with low-key Southwestern flair. The highlight here is the lush-green courtyard dappled with twinkling lights, a scenic spot for a picnic or enjoying the sunset.

 Eating

TRADING POST CAFE International **$$$**
(☎575-758-5089; www.tradingpostcafe.com; Hwy 68, Ranchos de Taos; mains lunch $8-14, dinner $16-32; ⊙11:30am-9:30pm Tue-Sat, 5-9pm Sun) A longtime favorite, the Trading Post is a perfect blend of relaxed and refined. The food, from paella to pork chops, is always great.

LOVE APPLE Organic **$$**
(☎575-751-0050; www.theloveapple.net; 803 Paseo del Pueblo Norte; mains $13-18; ⊙5-9pm Tue-Sun) Housed in the 19th century adobe Placitas Chapel, the understated rustic-sacred atmosphere is as much a part of this only-in-New-Mexico restaurant as the food is. From the posole with shepherd's lamb sausage to the grilled trout with chipotle cream, every dish is made from organic or free-range regional foods.

 Drinking

ADOBE BAR Bar, Live Music
(Historic Taos Inn, 125 Paseo del Pueblo Norte) Everybody's welcome in 'the living room of Taos.' And there's something about it: the chairs, the Taos Inn's history, the casualness, the tequila. The packed street-side patio has some of the state's finest margaritas, along with an eclectic lineup of great live music and never a cover.

 Information

Visitor center (☎575-758-3873; 1139 Paseo del Pueblo Sur; ⊙9am-5pm; @🛜)

The Pacific Northwest

As much a state of mind as a geographical region, the US's northwest corner is a land of subcultures and new trends. It's a place where evergreen trees frame snow-dusted volcanoes and inspired ideas scribbled on the back of napkins become tomorrow's business start-ups. You can't peel off the history in layers here, but you *can* gaze wistfully into the future in fast-moving, innovative cities such as Seattle and Portland, both sprinkled with food carts, streetcars, microbrews, green belts, coffee connoisseurs and weird urban sculpture.

Ever since the days of the Oregon Trail, the Northwest has had a hypnotic lure for risk takers and dreamers, and the metaphoric carrot still dangles. There's the air, so clean they ought to bottle it; the trees, older than many of Rome's renaissance palaces; and the end-of-the-continent coastline, holding back the force of the world's largest ocean. Cowboys take note; it doesn't get much more 'wild' or 'west' than this.

Cannon Beach, Oregon (p365)
JORDAN SIEMENS/AURORA OPEN/CORBIS ©

The Pacific Northwest

1. Pike Place Market
2. Space Needle
3. Portland
4. Mt Rainier
5. San Juan Islands
6. Olympic National Park

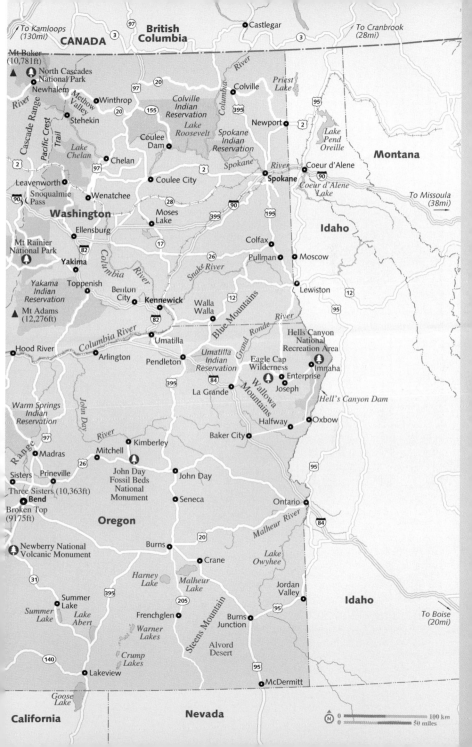

The Pacific Northwest's Highlights

1

Pike Place Market

Seattle's soul lies not in its sleek downtown skyscrapers, but in charismatic Pike Place Market (p344). Spread over 9 acres, this vivacious 'town within a city' has been exuding its manic energy since 1907. Today, you'll find local farmers, entertaining street theatre, and small glimpses of small-town life beneath the urban veneer.

Need to Know

HOURS 9am to 6pm Monday to Saturday, 9am to 5pm Sunday: arrive before 8am to watch things wake up **NEAREST STATION** Westlake (4th Ave and Pine St) **For more, see p344.**

Pike Place Market Don't Miss List

BY SCOTT DAVIES,
PUBLIC INFORMATION SPECIALIST

1 RACHEL THE PIG

The market's unofficial mascot is a life-sized bronze statue of a Whidbey Island pig called Rachel (below left). She has stood here since 1986 and acts as a giant piggy bank, raking in over $10,000 a year for the market's social services. The area around Rachel is called the Main Arcade and is famous for its entertaining fish-throwing fishmongers.

2 ORIGINAL STARBUCKS

The famous global coffee franchise's first ever store still stands in Pike Place's North End. In accordance with market rules, the shop has to display its original brown logo and is not permitted to serve any food or snacks. Buskers are a regular feature in the street outside. Look out for Johnny Hahn who has been wheeling his makeshift piano out into the street for 25 years.

3 DELAURENTI

The largest food outlet inside the market is a specialty food and wine store that displays cured meats, nearly 2000 wines, and a deli counter stuffed with over 200 different kinds of cheese. It's been in business since the 1940s and also has an on-site cafe and espresso bar.

4 NORTH ARCADE

The North Arcade is where the farmers and craftspeople sell their wares. Look out for the numerous flower sellers, many of whom are Hmong people originally from Laos and Thailand. Opposite, in the market's North End, are some of Pike Place's best restaurants and takeouts including the ever-popular Russian bakery, Piroshky Piroshky, and artisan cheese-maker Beechers, both of which make their products from scratch in their front windows.

5 SPECIALTY SHOPS

Most of the specialty shops are in the market's 'down under' section. The bulk of them are mom-and-pop-run places specializing in comic books, movie memorabilia, coins, magic tricks, you name it. One of my favourites is Tenzing Momo, an herbal apothecary that sells herbs, oils, incense and teas. It reminds me of something out of Diagon Alley from the Harry Potter books.

Space Needle

Don't leave Seattle without heading to the top of the needle (p345), the city's most distinctive symbol and landmark. From more than 500ft up, you'll get sweeping 360-degree views of downtown and Puget Sound, and up to the Cascades and Mt Rainier. There's a pricey rotating restaurant up top, but the best thing is the 'top of the world' feeling you get as the city slowly spins around you.

Portland

It's easy to fall for Portland (p358). After all, everyone loves this city. It's as friendly as a big town and home to a mix of students, artists, cyclists, hipsters, young families, old hippies, ecofreaks and everything in between. There's great food, a relentless music scene and plenty of culture, plus adventures in the great outdoors lies right on Portland's doorstep. Crowd-surfing at a Portland music festival

ANTHONY PIDGEON/LONELY PLANET IMAGES ©

Mt Rainier

When the skies are clear, Mt Rainier (p359) looms high over Seattle, creating an amazing backdrop to the emerald city. Still very much an active volcano, the 14,411ft peak is the shining centerpiece of a lush national park, which harbors a rare inland temperate rainforest. The hiking here is stunning, whether you opt for a short meander through alpine meadows strewn with wildflowers or the more challenging 93-mile Wonderland Trail. Climber on Emmons Glacier, Mt Rainier

San Juan Islands

Leafy hedgerows, sleepy settlements and winding lanes jammed with more cyclists than cars – this serene archipelago feels like a world removed from the mainland. Comprising some 450 islands, the San Juan Islands (p356) are a great place to reconnect with nature while cycling, sea kayaking and exploring state parks. There are peaceful island getaways and scenic spots for sea-gazing – keep an eye out for breaching orcas. Killer whale breaching off San Juan Island

Olympic National Park

This vast and pristine wonderland (p354) is home to Tolkien-esque valleys, rugged shorelines and misty, old-growth Pacific rainforest. Lakes, hot springs and glacial-capped peaks are a few of the prime attractions of this stellar peninsular park. There's great hiking, kayaking and skiing, and idyllic lodges for relaxing after taking in one of the great wilderness gems of the Northwest. Sol Duc Falls, Olympic National Park

The Pacific Northwest's Best...

Outdoor Activities

○ **Ecola State Park** (p365) Surfing, hiking, beachcombing and spectacular sea views from the headlands.

○ **Olympic National Park** (p354) Hiking amid pristine beauty in one of the world's only temperate rainforests.

○ **Mt Rainier National Park** (p359) Making the challenging four-day ascent up Mt Rainier.

○ **Portland** (p358) Kayaking and cycling in this adventure-loving city.

Wildlife Watching

○ **San Juan Islands** (p356) Prime destination for spotting orcas.

○ **Oregon Coast** (p365) Spot migrating gray whales in spring and winter.

○ **Hoh River Rainforest** (p355) Home to Northern Spotted Owls, Roosevelt elk and Olympic black bears.

○ **Wonderland Trail** (p359) The chance to see great herds of elk, mountain goat and deer, plus over 100 bird species.

Seafood

○ **Shiro's Sushi Restaurant** (p352) Uber-fresh delicacies at one of Seattle's top sushi restaurants.

○ **Jake's Famous Crawfish** (p363) An old-fashioned classic serving up some of Portland's best seafood.

○ **Steelhead Diner** (p352) A top-notch Seattle spot for Pacific oysters, Quinault River Coho salmon and Dungeness crab cakes.

○ **Lowells** (p351) Some of the best fish and chips in the Pacific Northwest are served at this spot in Pike Place Market.

Live Music

○ **Crocodile** (p353) A reborn Seattle spot that played a major role in the grunge scene.

○ **Doug Fir Lounge** (p364) This slick nightspot in South Burnside hosts some of Portland's most promising talent.

○ **Crystal Ballroom** (p364) Historic Portland spot to catch a live show, with a fun, bouncy dancefloor.

○ **Seattle Symphony** (p353) Hear some of the world's greatest compositions inside acoustically brilliant Benaroya Concert Hall.

Left: The Seattle Symphony Orchestra (p353);
Above: Hiking in Olympic National Park (p354)

ADVANCE PLANNING

○ **Three months before** Book accommodations ahead for travel from June to August.

○ **One month before** Browse upcoming festivals and events; buy tickets if needed.

○ **Two weeks before** Reserve at top restaurants in Seattle and Portland. Book tours and outdoor excursions, including hiking, kayaking, mountain biking and climbing.

RESOURCES

○ **Seattle.Gov** (www.seattle.gov) The city's official website.

○ **Seattle Weekly** (www.seattleweekly.com) Free weekly with news and entertainment listings.

○ **Washington State** (www.experiencewa.com) Washington state's official tourism site.

○ **Travel Portland** (www.travelportland.com) Key lowdown on Portland.

○ **Willamette Week** (www.wweek.com) Free Portland weekly with loads of entertainment listings.

○ **Travel Oregon** (www.traveloregon.com) Lots of tips on Oregon travel, state wide.

GETTING AROUND

○ **Airports** Seattle-Tacoma International Airport (www.portseattle.org/seatac), aka 'Sea-Tac,' is linked to downtown by Link Light Rail (30 minutes); taxis are about $35. Portland International Airport (www.flypdx.com) has downtown connections via Max Light Rail (40 minutes); taxis are around $30.

○ **Bus** Greyhound (www.greyhound.com) provides service between major towns.

○ **Hire car** Great for exploring national parks and the coast.

○ **Train** Amtrak runs south to California, linking Seattle, Portland and other major urban centers with the Cascades and Coast Starlight routes. The famous Empire Builder heads east to Chicago from Seattle and Portland (meeting in Spokane, WA).

BE FOREWARNED

○ **Weather** Expect cold temperatures and plenty of rain if traveling from November to March; high passes can be blocked with snow.

○ **Hiking** Be prepared when heading into the wilderness; bring warm, weatherproof gear; heed posted warnings about wildlife; be mindful of ticks.

The Pacific Northwest Itineraries

Lush forests, snow-capped peaks and wild coastlines are highlights of the Northwest. Eco-conscious urban hubs Seattle and Portland are famed for global cuisine, coffeehouses, microbreweries and indie culture.

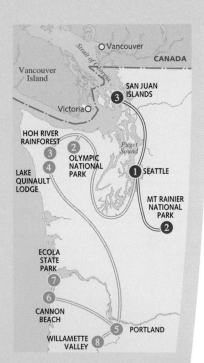

5 DAYS

SEATTLE TO THE SAN JUAN ISLANDS
The Emerald City & Around

Spend the first two days in **(1) Seattle**. Go early to beat the crowds at the iconic Pike Place Market, where you can sip world-class coffee and shop and snack on diverse temptations. Afterwards, hit the sprawling galleries of the nearby Seattle Museum. In the evening, head to trendy Belltown for dinner and drinks. On day two, visit the historic district of Pioneer Square, enjoy a sublime view from the Space Needle, ride the futuristic (a la 1962) monorail and rock out at the Experience Music Project. Day three, make a two-hour drive southeast to **(2) Mt Rainier National Park**, where you can hike among glaciers, wildflower-filled alpine meadows and old-growth forests on a visit to one of Washington's most captivating national parks. On day four, drive 90 minutes north of Seattle to Anacortes and take a ferry to the lovely **(3) San Juan Islands**. Spend your last two days exploring idyllic San Juan Island and neighboring Orcas Island: go bike riding and sea kayaking, watch whales from Lime Kiln Point State Park, sip wine at San Juan vineyards and take in the views from Orcas' Mt Constitution.

Top Left: A pod of Killer whales off the San Juan Islands (p356);
Top Right: Organic beer at Hopworks Urban Brewery (p363)

SEATTLE TO PORTLAND

Pacific Northwest Explorer

Start off in **(1) Seattle**, exploring downtown, the waterfront and Seattle Center. On day two, head 90 miles west to the wilderness wonderland of **(2) Olympic National Park**. It's well worth spending two days taking in the wild and rugged coastal scenery, hiking through the unbelievably lush **(3) Hoh River Rainforest** and relaxing at one of the park's peaceful inns, like the beautifully set **(4) Lake Quinault Lodge**. On day four, drive 240 miles south to **(5) Portland**, known for its roses, bridges, beer and progressive politics. Spend two days here. Visit downtown landmarks like Pioneer Courthouse Square; wander through the boutiques and galleries of the Pearl District; and stroll along the Willamette River. Take frequent breaks for coffee and/or microbrews. Eat at food trucks and Paley's Place, and catch a show at Doug Fir Lounge. On day five, head to the coast. Base at picturesque **(6) Cannon Beach**, while exploring the dreamlike scenery of nearby **(7) Ecola State Park** with its crashing waves and wild beaches backed by rolling forests. On day six, take a tour (by car or bicycle) through the picturesque vineyards of the **(8) Willamette Valley**, home to some of the country's finest pinot noir.

Discover the Pacific Northwest

Hoh River Rainforest (p355)
JOHN ELK III/LONELY PLANET IMAGES ©

SEATTLE

Surprisingly elegant in places and coolly edgy in others, Seattle, Washington, is notable for its strong neighborhoods, top-rated university, monstrous traffic jams and proactive city mayors who harbor green credentials. Although it has fermented its own pop culture in recent times, it has yet to create an urban mythology befitting of Paris or New York, but it does have 'the Mountain.' Better known as Rainier to its friends, Seattle's unifying symbol is a 14,411ft mass of rock and ice, which acts as a perennial reminder to the city's huddled masses that raw wilderness and potential volcanic catastrophe are never far away.

 Sights

Downtown

PIKE PLACE MARKET   Market
(www.pikeplacemarket.org) Take a bunch of small-time businesses and sprinkle them liberally around a spatially challenged waterside strip amid crowds of bohemians, restaurateurs, tree-huggers, bolshie students, artists, vinyl lovers and artisans. The result: Pike Place Market, a cavalcade of noise, smells, personalities, banter and urban theater that's almost London-like in its cosmopolitanism. In operation since 1907, Pike Place Market is famous for many things, not least its eye-poppingly fresh fruit and vegetables, its anarchistic shops and its loquacious fish-throwing fishmongers. Improbably, it also spawned the world's first Starbucks, which is still there (if you can get past the tourists) knocking out the old 'joe' from under its original brown logo.

RICHARD CUMMINS/LONELY PLANET IMAGES ©

Don't Miss **Seattle Center**

The remnants of the futuristic 1962 World's Fair (subtitled 'Century 21 Exposition') hosted by Seattle are now into their sixth decade at the Seattle Center. And what remnants! The fair was a major success, attracting 10 million visitors, running a profit (rare for the time) and inspiring a skin-crawlingly kitsch Elvis movie, *It Happened at the World's Fair* (1963).

Standing apart from the rest of Seattle's skyscrapers, the **Space Needle** is the city's undisputed modern symbol. Built for the World's Fair, it was the highest structure in Seattle at the time, topping 605ft, though it has since been easily usurped. Visitors make for the 520ft-high observation station, which has a revolving restaurant.

Floating like a low-flying spaceship through Belltown, Seattle's **monorail** is a 1.5-mile experiment in mass transit that was so ahead of its time that some American cities have still to cotton on to it. The slick, raised trains run every 10 minutes from downtown's Westlake Center to a station next to the **Experience Music Project**, the brainchild of Microsoft co-founder Paul Allen. This modern architectural marvel – or monstrosity, depending on your view – is a dream fantasy to anybody who has picked up an electric guitar and plucked the opening notes to 'Stairway to Heaven.' The ultramodern Frank Gehry building houses 80,000 music artifacts, many of which pay homage to Seattle's local music icons.

THINGS YOU NEED TO KNOW

Space Needle (www.spaceneedle.com; adult/child $18/11; ☺9:30am-11pm Sun-Thu, to 11:30pm Fri & Sat); Monorail (www.seattlemonorail.com; adult/child $4/1.50; ☺9am-11pm); Experience Music Project (EMP; www.empmuseum.org; 325 5th Ave N; adult/child $15/12; ☺10am-5pm Sep-May, to 7pm Jun-Aug)

Seattle

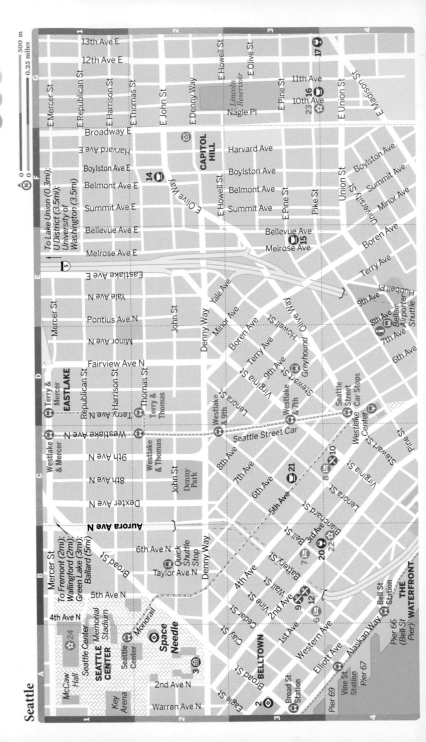

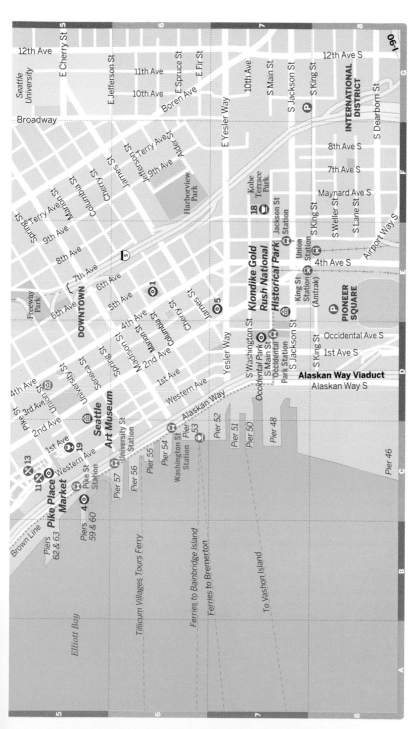

I-90

12th Ave

E Cherry St S

Seattle
University

E Jefferson St

11th Ave

10th Ave

E Spruce St

E Fir St

Boren Ave

Broadway

Terry Ave

9th Ave

Alder

James St

Jefferson St

Columbia St

Cherry St

Marion

Terry Ave

8th Ave

9th Ave

Spring St

Spring St

Freeway
Park

6th Ave

7th Ave

DOWNTOWN

6th Ave

5th Ave

5th Ave

4th Ave

Madison St

Marion St

2nd Ave

Columbia St

Cherry St

James St

Harborview
Park

E Yesler Way

10th Ave

Kobe
Terrace
Park

18

Klondike Gold
Rush National
Historical Park

Jackson St
Station

Union
Station

King St
Station
(Amtrak)

S Main St

S Jackson St

S King St

12th Ave S

INTERNATIONAL
DISTRICT

S Dearborn St

8th Ave S

7th Ave S

Maynard Ave S

S Weller St

S Lane St

S King St

Airport Way S

4th Ave S

PIONEER
SQUARE

Occidental Ave S

1st Ave S

S King St

Yesler Way

S Washington St

Occidental Park

S Main St

Occidental
Park Station

S Jackson St

1

5

Seattle
Art Museum

University St

University St
Station

Spring St

Seneca St

1st Ave

Western Ave

Alaskan Way

Alaskan Way Viaduct

Alaskan Way S

Pike St

3rd Ave

Union St

4th Ave

2nd Ave

1st Ave

Western Ave

Pike St
Station

13

11

Pike Place
Market

4

Piers
59 & 60

Piers
62 & 63

Brown Line

19

Pier 57

Pier 56

Pier 55

Pier 54

Washington St
Station

Pier
53

Pier 52

Pier 51

Pier 50

Pier 48

Pier 46

Elliott Bay

Tillicum Villages Tours Ferry

Ferries to Bainbridge Island

Ferries to Bremerton

To Vashon Island

347

Seattle

SEATTLE ART MUSEUM   Art Gallery
(www.seattleartmuseum.org; 1300 1st Ave; adult/
child $15/12; ⌚10am-5pm Wed-Sun, to 9pm Thu
& Fri) Extensively renovated and expanded
in 2007, Seattle's world-class art museum
now has 118,000 sq ft extra space. Above
the ticket counter hangs Cai Guo-Qiang's
Inopportune: Stage One, a series of white
cars exploding with neon. Between the
two museum entrances (one in the old
building and one in the new) is the 'art
ladder,' a free space with installations cascading down a wide stepped hallway. The
museum's John H Hauberg Collection is
an excellent display of masks, canoes,
totems and other pieces from Northwest
coastal tribes.

BELLTOWN   Neighborhood
Where industry once fumed, glassy
condos now rise in the thin walkable strip
of Belltown. The neighborhood gained a
reputation for trend-setting nightlife in
the 1990s and two of its bar/clubs – the
Crocodile and Shorty's – can still claim
legendary status. Then there are the
restaurants – over 100 of them – and not
all are prohibitively expensive.

FREE **OLYMPIC SCULPTURE PARK**   Park
(2901 Western Ave; ⌚sunrise-sunset) After
sharing lattes with the upscale condo
crowd in Belltown, you can stroll over
to the experimental new sculpture park
(an outpost of the Seattle Art Museum)
overlooking Elliott Bay.

Pioneer Square

Pioneer Square is Seattle's oldest quarter,
which isn't saying much if you're visiting
from Rome or London. Most of the buildings here date from just after the 1889
fire (a devastating inferno that destroyed
25 city blocks, including the entire central
business district), and are referred to
architecturally as Richardson Roman-
esque, a red-brick revivalist style in vogue
at the time.

   The quarter today mixes the historic
with the seedy, while harboring art
galleries, cafes and nightlife. Its most
iconic building is the 42-story **Smith
Tower** (cnr 2nd Ave S & Yesler Way; observation
deck adult/child $7.50/5; ⌚10am-dusk),
completed in 1914 and, until 1931, the
tallest building west of the Mississippi.

FREE **KLONDIKE GOLD RUSH NATIONAL HISTORICAL PARK** Museum
(www.nps.gov/klse; 117 S Main St; ⏲9am-5pm)
A shockingly good museum with exhibits, photos and news clippings from the years of the 1897 Klondike gold rush, when a Seattle-on-steroids acted as a fueling and supply depot for prospectors bound for the Yukon in Canada.

Capitol Hill

Millionaires mingle with goth musicians in irreverent Capitol Hill, a well-heeled but liberal neighborhood rightly renowned for its fringe theater, alternative music scene, indie coffee bars, and vital gay and lesbian culture. You can take your dog for a herbal bath here, go shopping for ethnic crafts on Broadway, or blend in (or not) with the young punks and the old hippies on the eclectic Pike-Pine Corridor. The junction of Broadway and E John St is the nexus from which to navigate the quarter's various restaurants, brewpubs, boutiques and dingy but not dirty dive bars.

Higher than the Space Needle

Everyone makes a rush for the iconic Space Needle, but it's neither the tallest nor the cheapest of Seattle's glittering viewpoints. That honor goes to the sleek, tinted-windowed **Columbia Center (701 5th Ave)**, built in 1985, which at 932ft high is the loftiest building in the Pacific Northwest. From the plush **observation deck** (adult/child $5/3; ⏲8:30am-4:30pm Mon-Fri) on the 73rd floor you can look down on ferries, cars, islands, roofs and – ha, ha – the Space Needle!

Ballard

Six miles northwest of downtown, Ballard, despite its recent veneer of hipness, still has the feel of an old Scandinavian fishing village – especially around the locks, the marina and the Nordic Heritage Museum. The old town has become a nightlife hot

Seattle Art Museum

JOHN ELK III/LONELY PLANET IMAGES ©

Seattle for Children

Make a beeline for the Seattle Center, preferably on the monorail, where food carts, street entertainers, fountains and green space will make the day fly by. One essential stop is the **Pacific Science Center** (www.pacsci.org; 200 2nd Ave N; adult/child $14/9, plus IMAX show $4; ⊙10am-5pm Mon-Fri, to 6pm Sat & Sun), which entertains and educates with virtual-reality exhibits, laser shows, holograms, an IMAX theater and a planetarium – parents won't be bored either.

Downtown on Pier 59, **Seattle Aquarium** (www.seattleaquarium.org; 1483 Alaskan Way, at Pier 59; adult/child $19/12; ⊙9:30am-5pm) is a fun way to learn about the natural world of the Pacific Northwest. The centerpiece of the aquarium is a glass-domed room where sharks, octopuses and other deepwater denizens lurk in the shadowy depths.

spot, but even in the daytime, its historic buildings and cobblestoned streets make it a pleasure to wander through.

HIRAM M CHITTENDEN LOCKS Locks (3015 NW 54th St; ⊙24hr) Here, the waters of Lake Washington and Lake Union flow through the 8-mile-long Lake Washington Ship Canal and into Puget Sound. Construction of the canal began in 1911; today 100,000 boats a year pass through the locks, about a half-mile west of Ballard, off NW Market St. On the southern side of the locks you can watch from underwater glass tanks or from above as salmon navigate a **fish ladder** on their way to spawning grounds in the Cascade headwaters of the Sammamish River, which feeds Lake Washington.

🛏 Sleeping

BELLTOWN INN Hotel $$ (☎206-529-3700; www.belltown -inn.com; 2301 3rd Ave; s/d $109/119; P❄@☎) Can it be true? The Belltown is such a bargain and in such a prime location that it's hard not believe it hasn't accidently floated over from a smaller, infinitely cheaper city. But no, those clean functional rooms, handy kitch-enettes, roof terrace, free bikes and – vitally important – borrow-and-

Seattle Aquarium
JOHN ELK III/LONELY PLANET IMAGES ©

return umbrellas are all yours for the price of a posh dinner.

HOTEL ANDRA Boutique Hotel **$$**
(206-448-8600; www.hotelandra.com; 2000 4th Ave; r $189-229; P ❄ 📶) It's in Belltown (so it's trendy), and it's Scandinavian-influenced (so it has lashings of minimalist style), plus the Andra's fine location is complemented by leopard-skin fabrics, color accents, well-stocked bookcases, fluffy bathrobes, Egyptian-cotton bed linen and a complimentary shoe-shine.

ACE HOTEL Hotel **$$**
(206-448-4721; www.acehotel.com; 2423 1st Ave; r with shared/private bath $99/190; P 📶) Emulating (almost) its hip Portland cousin, the Ace sports minimal, futuristic decor (everything's white or stainless steel, even the TV), antique French army blankets, condoms instead of pillow mints and a Kama Sutra in place of the Bible.

MEDITERRANEAN INN Hotel **$$**
(206-428-4700; www.mediterranean-inn. com; 425 Queen Anne Ave N; r from $119; P ❄ @) There's something about the surprisingly un-Mediterranean Med Inn that just clicks. Maybe it's the handy cusp-of-downtown location, or the genuinely friendly staff, or the kitchenettes in every room, or the small downstairs gym, or the surgical cleanliness in every room.

 Eating

LOLA Greek **$$$**
(206-441-1430; www.tomdouglas.com; 2000 4th Ave; mains $22-32) Seattle's ubiquitous cooking maestro, Tom Douglas, goes Greek in this new Belltown adventure and delivers once again with gusto. Stick in trendy clientele, some juicy kebabs, heavy portions of veg, shared meze dishes and pita with dips, and you'll be singing Socratic verse all the way home.

♥ If You Like…
Cafes

If you like Bauhaus (p352), don't miss these other great Seattle coffeehouses – the perfect retreats when the rain arrives.

1 B&O ESPRESSO
(204 Belmont Ave E; 🕒7am-late Mon-Thu, 8am-late Fri-Sun) Full of understated swank, this Capitol Hill legend (open since 1976) is the place to go for Turkish coffee – if you can get past the pastry case up front.

2 CAFFÉ VITA
(1005 E Pike St; 🕒6am-11pm) The laptop fiend, the radical student, the homeless hobo, the business guy on his way to work; watch the neighborhood pass through this Capitol Hill institution (one of four in Seattle) with its own on-site roasting room.

3 PANAMA HOTEL TEA & COFFEE HOUSE
(607 S Main St; 🕒8am-7pm Mon-Sat, 9am-7pm Sun) The Panama, a historic 1910 building containing the only remaining Japanese bathhouse in the US, doubles as a memorial to the neighborhood's Japanese residents forced into internment camps during WWII.

LA VITA É BELLA Italian **$$**
(www.lavitaebella.us; 2411 2nd Ave; pasta $10-14) As any Italian food snob will tell you, it's very hard to find authentic home-spun Italian cuisine this side of Sicily. Thus extra kudos must go to La Vita é Bella for trying and largely succeeding in a difficult field. Judge the pizza margherita as a good yardstick, though the *vongole* (clams), desserts and coffee are also spot on.

LOWELLS Diner **$**
(www.eatatlowells.com; 1519 Pike Pl; mains $6-9) Fish and chips is a simple meal often done badly, but not here. Slam down your order for Alaskan cod at the front entry and take it up to the top floor for delicious views over Puget Sound.

Right: Seattle is famous for its coffee (p351);
Below: Detail of Native American totem pole, Pioneer Square (p348)

(LEFT) RICHARD CUMMINS/LONELY PLANET IMAGES ©: (BELOW) IMAGE BROKER/LONELY PLANET IMAGES ©

SHIRO'S SUSHI RESTAURANT
Japanese $$$
(www.shiros.com; 2401 2nd Ave; dinners $27; ⏱5:30-9:45pm) There's barely room for all the awards and kudos that cram the window in this sleek Japanese joint. Grab a pew and watch the experts concoct delicate and delicious Seattle sushi.

STEELHEAD DINER
Seafood $$
(☎206-625-0129; www.steelheaddiner.com; 95 Pine St; sandwiches $9-13, mains $15-33; ⏱11am-10pm Tue-Sat, 10am-3pm Sun) Homey favorites such as fish and chips, grilled salmon or braised short ribs and grits become fine cuisine when they're made with the best of what Pike Place Market has to offer.

 Drinking

You'll find cocktail bars, dance clubs and live music on Capitol Hill. The main drag in Ballard has brick taverns, old and new, filled with the hard-drinking older set in daylight hours and indie rockers at night. Belltown has gone from grungy to shabby chic but has the advantage of many drinking holes neatly lined up in rows.

Coffeehouses

BAUHAUS
Cafe
(www.bauhauscoffee.net; 301 E Pine St; ⏱6am-1am Mon-Fri, from 7am Sat, from 8am Sun) Drink coffee, browse books, nibble pastries, stay awake...until 1am! Bauhaus positively encourages lingering with its mezzanine bookshelves, Space Needle view and lazy people-watching opps.

TOP POT HAND-FORGED DOUGHNUTS
Cafe
(www.toppotdoughnuts.com; 2124 5th Ave; ⏱6am-7pm) Top Pot is to doughnuts what champagne is to wine – a different class. And its cafes – this one in an old car showroom with floor-to-ceiling library shelves and art-deco signage – are equally legendary.

Bars

SHORTY'S Bar
(www.shortydog.com; 2222 2nd Ave) A cross between a pinball arcade and the Korova Milk Bar out of the film *A Clockwork Orange,* Shorty's is a Belltown legend where you can procure cheap beer, hot dogs, alcohol slushies and a back room of pinball heaven.

PIKE PUB & BREWERY Brewery
(www.pikebrewing.com; 1415 1st Ave) Leading the way in the microbrewery revolution, this brewpub opened in 1989 underneath Pike Place Market. Today it still serves great burgers and brews in a neo-industrial multilevel space that's a beer nerd's heaven.

ELYSIAN BREWING COMPANY Brewery
(www.elysianbrewing.com; 1221 E Pike St) On Capitol Hill, the Elysian's huge windows are great for people-watching – or being watched, if your pool game's good enough.

 Entertainment

CROCODILE Live Music
(www.thecrocodile.com; 2200 2nd Ave) Re-opened in March 2009 after a year in the doldrums, the sole survivor of Belltown's once influential grunge scene (formerly known as the Crocodile Café) will have to work hard to reclaim an audience who grew up listening to Nirvana, Pearl Jam and REM at this hallowed music venue.

NEUMO'S Live Music
(www.neumos.com; 925 E Pike St) A punk/hip-hop/alternative music venue that counts Radiohead and Bill Clinton (not together) among its former guests, Neumo's (formerly known as Moe's) fills the big shoes of its original namesake.

Seattle Symphony Classical Music
(www.seattlesymphony.org) A major regional ensemble. It plays at the Benaroya Concert Hall, which you'll find downtown at 2nd Ave and University St.

RICHARD CUMMINS/LONELY PLANET IMAGES ©

ⓘ Information

Seattle Convention & Visitors Bureau (www.visitseattle.org; cnr 7th Ave & Pike St; ◷9am-5pm Mon-Fri) Located inside the Washington State Convention and Trade Center; it opens weekends June to August.

ⓘ Getting There & Away

AIR Seattle-Tacoma International Airport (SEA; www.portseattle.org/seatac), aka 'Sea-Tac,' is 13 miles south of Seattle on I-5.

BOAT Victoria Clipper (www.victoriaclipper.com) operates several high-speed passenger ferries to the San Juan Islands.

TRAIN Amtrak (www.amtrak.com) serves Seattle's **King Street Station** (303 S Jackson St; ◷6am-10:30pm, ticket counter 6:15am-8pm).

ⓘ Getting Around

TO/FROM THE AIRPORT Seattle's brand new light-rail train, **Sound Transit** (www.soundtransit.org), runs between Sea-Tac Airport and downtown (Westlake Center) every 15 minutes between 5am and midnight.

TAXI The following offer reliable taxi service:

Orange Cab Co (☎206-444-0409; www.orangecab.net)

Yellow Cab (☎206-622-6500; www.yellowtaxi.net)

OLYMPIC NATIONAL PARK

Declared a national monument in 1909 and a national park in 1938, the 1406-sq-mile **Olympic National Park** (www.nps.gov/olym) is one of North America's last great wilderness, sheltering one of the world's only temperate rainforests and a 57-mile strip of Washington's Pacific coastal wilderness (added in 1953). Opportunities for independent exploration abound, with visitors enjoying such diverse activities as hiking, fishing, kayaking and skiing.

Eastern Entrances

The graveled Dosewallips River Rd follows the river from US 101 (turn off approximately 1km north of Dosewallips State Park) for 15 miles to **Dosewallips Ranger**

Station, where the trails begin. Even hiking smaller portions of the two long-distance paths – with increasingly impressive views of heavily glaciated **Mt Anderson** – is reason enough to visit the valley.

Northern Entrances

The park's easiest (and most popular) entry point is at **Hurricane Ridge**, 18 miles south of Port Angeles. At the road's end, an interpretive center overlooks a stupendous view of Mt Olympus (7965ft) and dozens of other peaks. The 5200ft altitude can mean inclement weather and the winds here can be ferocious. Aside from various summer trekking opportunities, the area maintains one of only two US national park–based ski runs, operated by the small, family-friendly **Hurricane Ridge Ski & Snowboard Area** (www.hurricaneridge.com).

Popular for boating and fishing is **Lake Crescent**, the site of the park's oldest and most reasonably priced **lodge** (☑360-928-3211; www.olympicnationalparks.com; 416 Lake Crescent Rd; lodge r with shared bath $76, cottages $142-224; ☉May-Oct; P ✳ ☎). Delicious sustainable food is served in the lodge's ecofriendly restaurant. From **Storm King Information Station** (☑360-928-3380; ☉May-Sep) on the lake's south shore, a 1-mile hike climbs through old-growth forest to Marymere Falls.

Along the Sol Duc River, the **Sol Duc Hot Springs Resort** (☑360-327-3583; www.northolympic.com/solduc; 12076 Sol Duc Hot Springs Rd, Port Angeles; RV sites $33, r $131-189; ☉late Mar-Oct; ✳ ☎) has lodging, dining, massage and, of course, hot-spring pools (adult/child $10/7.50), as well as great day hikes.

Western Entrances

Isolated by distance and one of the US' rainiest microclimates, the Pacific side of the Olympics remains its wildest. Only US 101 offers access to its noted temperate rainforests and untamed coastline. The **Hoh River Rainforest**, at the end of the 19-mile Hoh River Rd, is a Tolkienesque maze of dripping ferns and moss-draped trees.

A little to the south lies **Lake Quinault**, a beautiful glacial lake surrounded by forested peaks. **Lake Quinault Lodge** (☑360-288-2900; www.visitlakequinault.com; 345 S Shore Rd; lodge r $134-167, cabins $125-243; ✳ ☎ ☎), a luxury classic of 1920s 'parkitecture,' has a heated pool and sauna, a crackling fireplace and a

The Twilight Zone

Forks, a small lumber town on Hwy 101, was little more than a speck on the Washington state map when Stephanie Meyer set the first of her now famous *Twilight* vampire novels here in 2003. Forks has apparently seen a 600% rise in tourism since the *Twilight* film franchise began in 2008, the bulk of the visitors comprising gawky, wide-eyed, under-15-year-old girls, who are more than a little surprised to find Forks for what it really is – chillingly ordinary (and wet).

A fresh bit of color was needed and it was provided in November 2008 with the opening of **Dazzled by Twilight** (www.dazzledbytwilight.com; 11 N Forks Ave; ☉10am-6pm), which runs two *Twilight* merchandise shops in Forks (and another in Port Angeles) as well as the Forks **Twilight Lounge** (81 N Forks Ave). The lounge hosts a downstairs restaurant along with an upstairs music venue that showcases regular live bands and a blood-curdling 5pm to 8pm Saturday-night tweens karaoke. The company also runs four daily **Twilight Tours** (adult/child $39/25; ☉8am, 11:30am, 3pm & 6pm), visiting most of the places mentioned in Meyer's books. Highlights include the Forks High School, the Treaty Line at the nearby Rivers Resort and a sortie out to the tiny coastal community of La Push. (Ecola State Park was also a stand-in for La Push Beach.)

memorable dining room noted for its sweet-potato breakfast pancakes.

ℹ Information

The park entry fee is $5/15 per person/vehicle, valid for one week, payable at park entrances.

ℹ Getting There & Away

CAR From Seattle, drive to the Seattle Ferry Terminal and cross Puget Sound on the **Washington State Ferry System** (206-464-6400; www.wsdot.wa.gov) to Bainbridge Island (1 hour, car and driver from $13). Once across take the 305 N to the 3 N, to the 104 W, to the 101 N, which leads to the northern entrance.

SAN JUAN ISLANDS

Take the ferry west out of Anacortes and you'll feel like you've dropped off the edge of the continent. Street crime here barely registers, fast-food franchises are a nasty mainland apparition, and cars – those most essential of US travel accessories – are best left at home.

There are 172 landfalls in this expansive Washington archipelago but unless you're rich enough to charter your own yacht or seaplane, you'll be restricted to seeing the big four – San Juan, Orcas, Shaw and Lopez Islands – all served daily by Washington State Ferries. Communally, the islands are famous for their tranquility, whale-watching opportunities, sea kayaking and seditious nonconformity.

The best way to explore the San Juans is by sea kayak or bicycle. Kayaks are available for rent on Lopez, Orcas and San Juan Islands. Expect a guided half-day trip to cost $45 to $65.

ℹ Getting There & Around

BOAT **Washington State Ferries** (www.wsdot. wa.gov/ferries) leave Anacortes for the San Juans. Ferries run to Lopez Island (45 minutes), Orcas Landing (60 minutes) and Friday Harbor on San Juan Island (75 minutes).

Left: Woman feeding horses, San Juan Island;
Below: Kayaking off the coast of San Juan Island

(LEFT) LAWRENCE WORCESTER/LONELY PLANET IMAGES ©; (BELOW) TOM BOYDEN/LONELY PLANET IMAGES ©

PUBLIC TRANSPORTATION
Shuttle buses ply Orcas and San
Juan Island in the summer months.

Lopez Island

If you're going to Lopez – or 'Slow-pez,'
as locals prefer to call it – take a bike.
With its undulating terrain and saluta-
tion-offering locals (who are famous
for their three-fingered 'Lopez wave'),
this is the ideal cycling isle. A leisurely
pastoral spin can be tackled in a day with
good overnight digs available next to
the marina in the **Lopez Islander Resort**
(☎ 360-468-2233; www.lopezislander.com;
2864 Fisherman Bay Rd; d from $120; P ❀ ☲),
which has a restaurant, gym and pool
and offers free parking in Anacortes
(another incentive to dump the car). If
you arrive bikeless, call up **Lopez Bicycle
Works** (www.lopezbicycleworks.com; 2847 Fisherman Bay Rd; ☾10am-6pm May-Sep), which
can deliver a bicycle to the ferry terminal
for you.

San Juan Island

San Juan Island is the archipelago's
unofficial capital, a harmonious mix of low
forested hills and small rural farms that
resonate with a dramatic and unusual
19th-century history.

 Sights & Activities

FREE **SAN JUAN ISLAND NATIONAL
HISTORICAL PARK**   Historic Site
(www.nps.gov/sajh; ☾8:30am-4pm) San Juan
Island hides one of the 19th-century's
oddest political confrontations, the so-
called 'Pig War' between the USA and Britain. This curious 19th-century cold war
stand-off is showcased in two separate
historical parks on either end of the island
that once housed opposing American and
English military encampments.

357

LIME KILN POINT STATE PARK — Park

(🕐8am-5pm mid-Oct–Mar, 6:30am-10pm Apr–mid-Oct) Clinging to the island's rocky west coast, this beautiful park overlooks the deep Haro Strait and is, reputedly, one of the best places in the world to view whales from the shoreline.

SAN JUAN VINEYARDS — Winery

(www.sanjuanvineyards.com; 3136 Roche Harbor Rd; 🕐11am-5pm) Washington's unlikeliest winery has a tasting room next to an old schoolhouse built in 1896. Open-minded tasters should try the Siegerrebe and Madeleine Angevine varieties.

 ## Sleeping & Eating

There are hotels, B&Bs and resorts scattered around the island, but Friday Harbor has the best concentration.

EARTHBOX MOTEL & SPA — Boutique Motel $$

(📞360-378-4000; www.earthboxmotel.com; 410 Spring St; r from $197; P 🛜 ♿) Reaching out to retro-lovers, Earthbox styles itself as a 'boutique motel,' a hybrid of simplicity and sophistication in a former motor inn embellished with features more commonly associated with a deluxe hotel.

🌿MARKET CHEF — Deli $

(225a St; 🕐10am-6pm) The 'Chef's' specialty is deli sandwiches and very original ones at that. Join the queue and watch staff prepare the goods with fresh, local ingredients.

Orcas Island

Precipitous, unspoiled and ruggedly beautiful, Orcas Island is the San Juans' emerald icon, excellent for hiking and, more recently, gourmet food. The ferry terminal is at Orcas Landing, 8 miles south of the main village, Eastsound. On the island's eastern lobe is **Moran State Park** (🕐6:30am-dusk Apr-Sep, from 8am Oct-Mar), dominated by Mt Constitution (2409ft), with 40 miles of trails and an amazing 360-degree mountain-top view.

Kayaking in the calm island waters is a real joy here. **Shearwater** (www.

shearwaterkayaks.com; 138 North Beach Rd, Eastsound) has the equipment and know-how. Three hour guided trips start at $69.

 ## Sleeping

ROSARIO RESORT & SPA — Resort $$$

(📞360-376-2222; www.rosario-resort.com; 1400 Rosario Rd, Eastsound; r $188-400; P ❄️ 🛜 ♿) A magnificent seafront mansion built by former shipbuilding magnate Robert Moran in 1904 and now converted into an exquisite, upscale resort and spa.

OUTLOOK INN — Hotel $$

(📞360-376-2200; www.outlookinn.com; 171 Main St, Eastsound; r with shared/private bath $89/119; P ❄️ 🛜) Eastsound village's oldest building (1888) is an island institution that has kept up with the times by expanding into a small bayside complex. Also on-site is the rather fancy New Leaf Café.

 ## Eating

🌿ALLIUM — International $$$

(📞360-376-4904; www.alliumonorcas.com; 310E Main St, Eastsound; dinner mans $30; 🕐10am-2pm Sat & Sun, 5-8pm Thu-Mon) Orcas got a destination restaurant in 2010 with the opening of the illustrious Allium, where the secret is very simple: 'simplicity' (local ingredients, limited opening hours and only five mains on the menu). The result: food worth visiting the island for.

PORTLAND

If you want to see what the future looks like, come to Portland, Oregon, a city 10 years ahead of its time and as definitive of its age as the Rome of Caesar or the Paris of Haussmann. What Portland lacks in Coliseums and baroque opera houses, it makes up for in innovation and ideas that start from the ground up. Urban growth boundaries (which have prevented ugly suburban sprawl) were established in 1973, a light-rail network was instituted in 1986, and the first community bike

JOHN ELK III/LONELY PLANET IMAGES ©

Don't Miss Mt Rainier National Park

The USA's fourth-highest peak (outside Alaska), majestic Mt Rainier is also one of Washington's most beguiling sights. Encased in a 368-sq-mile national park (the world's fifth national park when it was inaugurated in 1899), the mountain's snowcapped summit and forest-covered foothills harbor numerous hiking trails, huge swaths of flower-carpeted meadows and an alluring conical peak that presents a formidable challenge for aspiring climbers.

The park has four entrances. Nisqually, on Hwy 706 via Ashford (near the park's southwest corner) is the busiest and most convenient gate; it's open year-round.

The park's two main nexus points are Longmire and Paradise. Longmire, 7 miles inside the Nisqually entrance, has a **museum & information center**, a number of important trailheads and the rustic **National Park Inn**, complete with an excellent restaurant. More hikes and interpretive walks can be found 12 miles further east at loftier Paradise, which is served by the informative **Henry M Jackson Visitor Center** and the vintage **Paradise Inn**. The **Wonderland Trail** is a 93-mile path that completely circumnavigates Mt Rainier via a well-maintained unbroken route.

For more information on the park, check out its official website, which includes downloadable maps and descriptions of 50 park trails.

THINGS YOU NEED TO KNOW

Mt Rainier National Park (www.nps.gov/mora; entry pedestrian/car $5/15); museum & information center (admission free; ⏰9am-6pm Jun-Sep, to 5pm Oct-May); National Park Inn (☎360-569-2275; www.guestservices.com/rainier; r with shared/private bath $104/139, units $191; P ❄); Henry M Jackson Visitor Center (⏰10am-7pm daily Jun-Oct, to 5pm Sat & Sun Oct-Dec); Paradise Inn (☎360-569-2275; www.mtrainierguestservices.com; r with shared/private bath $105/154; ⏰May-Oct; P ❄ 🛜)

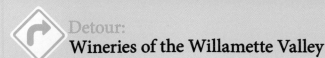

Detour:
Wineries of the Willamette Valley

Beer, coffee and wine; Portland excels at all three. For the latter you'll have to venture a little out of town to the wineries that embellish the Willamette Valley, in particular those around the towns of Dundee and McMinnville along Hwy 99W. **Willamette Valley Wineries Association** (www.willamettewines.com) is a good information portal for this alluring region.

For a decent overview of the area's many wineries, visit **Ponzi Vineyards** (14665 SW Winery Lane, Beaverton; ⊙10am-5pm), 30 minutes southwest of downtown Portland, where you can taste current releases and visit the historic cellars and vineyards.

Wine in Oregon is all about its premier grape variety – pinot noir. One of the earliest planters was **Erath Winery** (www.erath.com; 9409 NE Worden Hill Rd, Dundee; ⊙11am-5pm), who have been sowing the stuff since 1969.

Meandering through plush green hills from one wine-tasting room to another is a delightful way to spend an afternoon (just make sure you designate a driver). Alternatively, Portland-based **Pedal Bike Tours** (http://pedalbiketours.com; tour $89) runs five-hour spins from the town of Dundee on Hwy 99W.

projects hit the streets in 1994. Prone to becoming daring rather than depressed during economic downturns, Portland's pugnacious DIY attitude has charitably endowed the metro area (and, in some cases, the nation) with food carts, microbreweries, hard-core punk rock, bike culture, indie 'zines and a traffic-calmed downtown that feels more small town than big city.

 Sights

Downtown

TOM MCCALL WATERFRONT PARK   Park
Sinuous, 2-mile-long Tom McCall Waterfront Park flanks the west bank of the Willaette River and is both an unofficial training ground for lunchtime runners and a commuter path for the city's avid army of cyclists. The east side of the river is embellished by the **Eastbank Esplanade**, a path that tracks below the roaring overpasses that carry traffic north and south.

**PIONEER COURTHOUSE
SQUARE**   Landmark
Portland's downtown hub is Pioneer Courthouse Square, a red-bricked people-friendly square with minimal traffic interference where you'll find chess

players, sunbathers, lunching office workers, buskers and the odd political activist.

PORTLAND ART MUSEUM   Art Gallery
(www.portlandartmuseum.org; 1219 SW Park Ave; adult/child under 17yr $10/free; ⊙10am-5pm Tue, Wed & Sat, to 8pm Thu & Fri, noon-5pm Sun) Excellent exhibits here include Native American carvings and Asian and American art.

AERIAL TRAM   Cable Car
(www.gobytram.com; 3303 SW Bond Ave; round-trip $4; ⊙5:30am-9:30pm Mon-Fri, 9am-5pm Sat) Portland's aerial tram runs a three-minute trip from a south Waterfront streetcar stop to Marquam Hill, traveling 3300ft with a vertical ascent of 500ft.

Old Town

The core of rambunctious 1890s Portland, the once-notorious Old Town still exhibits a slightly seedy, if innocuous, underbelly.

SHANGHAI TUNNELS   Historic Site
(www.shanghaitunnels.info; adult/child $13/8) Back in the 1850s, unscrupulous people would kidnap, or 'shanghai', drunken men through this series of underground tunnels running under the streets of Old Town, then sell them to sea captains as indentured workers. Tours run Fridays and Saturdays at 6:30pm and 8pm.

Saturday Market

Market

(www.portlandsaturday
market.com; ⏱10am-5pm Sat, 11am-4:30pm
Sun Mar-Dec) Hit the river walk on a weekend
to catch the famous market, which showcases
handicrafts, street entertainers and food carts.

Northwest Portland

PEARL DISTRICT   Neighborhood
(www.explorethepearl.com) Slightly to the
northwest of downtown, the Pearl Distict
is an old industrial quarter that has transformed its once grotty warehouses into
expensive lofts, upscale boutiques and
creative restaurants. Don't miss the block-
wide **Powell's City of Books** (www.powells.
com; 1005 W Burnside St; ⏱9am-11pm), the largest independent bookstore in the USA.

NOB HILL   Neighborhood
Nob Hill – or 'Snob Hill' to its detractors –
has its hub on NW 23rd Ave, a trendy
neighborhood thoroughfare that brims
with clothing boutiques, home decor
shops and cafes. The restaurants –
including some of Portland's finest – lie
mostly along NW 21st Ave.

West Hills

FOREST PARK   Park
Not many cities have 5100 acres of
temperature rainforest within their
limits, but then not many cities are
like Portland. Abutting the more
manicured Washington Park to
the west (to which it is linked
by various trails) is the far
wilder Forest Park, whose
dense foliage harbors
plants, animals and an
avid hiking fraternity.

**WASHINGTON
PARK**   Park
West of Forest Park,
the more tamed
Washington Park
contains a good
half-day's worth of
attractions within its
400 acres of greenery.

Hoyt Arboretum (www.hoytarboretum.org;
4000 Fairview Blvd; admission free; ⏱trails
6am-10pm, visitor center 9am-4pm Mon-Fri,
to 3pm Sat) showcases more than 1000
species of native and exotic trees and
has 12 miles of walking trails. It's prettiest
in the fall. The **International Rose Test
Gardens** (www.rosegardenstore.org; admission
free; ⏱sunrise-sunset) is the centerpiece
of Portland's famous rose blooms; there
are 400 types on show here, plus great
city views. Further uphill is the **Japanese
Garden** (www.japanesegarden.com; 611 SW
Kingston Ave; adult/child $9.50/6.75; ⏱noon-
7pm Mon, from 10am Tue-Sun; P), another
oasis of tranquility.

Activities

Cycling

For bike rental, try **Waterfront Bicycles**
(www.waterfrontbikes.com; 10 SW Ash St),
where the ballpark price for day rental
is $35. Some hotels (eg Ace Hotel) offer
bikes free of charge.

Powell's City of Books, Portland
ANTHONY PIDGEON/LONELY PLANET IMAGES ©

Sleeping

ACE HOTEL   Boutique Hotel **$$**
(☎503-228-2277; www.acehotel.com; 1022
SW Stark St; d with shared/private bath from
$107/147; ❄ @ 🛜) The reception area
is a good indication of what's to come:
big sofas, retro-industrial decor, the
Ramones on the sound system and the
comforting aroma of Stumptown coffee
wafting in through the connecting door.
If you make it upstairs you'll find chic
minimalist rooms (some with shared
bath) kitted out with wonderfully com-
fortable beds.

CRYSTAL HOTEL   Hotel **$$**
(☎503-972-2670, www.mcmenamins.com; 303
SW 12th Ave; r $105-165; 🛜) Room furnish-
ings that blend Grateful Dead–inspired
psychedelia with the interior of a Victorian boudoir can only mean one thing.
Welcome to the latest McMenamins
hotel, an action-packed accommodations option, bar, cafe and restaurant

that shares a name and ownership with
the famous Ballroom across the road.

JUPITER HOTEL   Boutique Motel **$$**
(☎503-230-9200; www.jupiterhotel.com;
800 E BurnsideSt; d $114-149; P ❄ @ 🛜)
The Jupiter has hijacked America's
most ubiquitous cheap-sleep idea and
personalized it with retro furnishings,
chalkboard doors (on which you can
write instructions to the room maid) and
vivid color accents.

Eating

Food carts have a huge presence in Port-
land. Check out www.foodcartsportland.
com for an online guide.

PALEY'S PLACE   French, Fusion **$$$**
(☎503-243-2403; www.paleysplace.net; 1204
NW 21st Ave; mains $20-32; ⏱5:30-10pm
Mon-Thu, to 11pm Fri & Sat, 5-10pm Sun) It
takes a special kind of talent to win a
Food Network *Iron Chef*. Luckily for
Portland, Vitaly Paley, recent recipient
of the honor, had been serving up top-
drawer duck confit, Kobe burger and veal
sweetbreads long before reality TV came
knocking.

ANDINA   South American **$$$**
(☎503-228-9535; www.andinarestau
rant.com; 1314 NW Glisan St;
mains $25-30) Always the
trend-setter, Portland's
restaurant-of-the-moment
is not French, Italian or
Thai but...novo-Peruvian.
The hook? Take locally
grown ingredients and
inject them with flavors
reminiscent of the High
Andes. The result?
Food that's daring,
delicious and – above
all – different.

Food cart dining, Portland
ANTHONY PIDGEON/LONELY PLANET IMAGES ©

SILK
Vietnamese $$

(1012 NW Glisan St; mains $9-14; 🕙11am-3pm & 5-10pm Mon-Sat) An interesting modern take on Vietnamese cuisine, for Silk read Slick. The clean-lined minimalist decor offers sit-down or cocktail-bar options, but the atmosphere is laid-back (lots of single diners) and the prices are very reasonable.

JAKE'S FAMOUS CRAWFISH
Seafood $$$

(📞503-226-1419; 401 SW 12th Ave; mains $17-32; 🕙11am-11pm Mon-Thu, to midnight Fri, noon-midnight Sat, 3-11pm Sun) Portland's best seafood lies within this elegant old-time venue, which serves up divine oysters, revelatory crab cakes and a horseradish salmon made in heaven.

 # Drinking

Coffeehouses

STUMPTOWN COFFEE
Cafe

(www.stumptowncoffee.com; 📶) Ace Hotel (1022 SW Stark St); Belmont (3356 SE Blmont St); Division (3377 SE Division St); Downtown (128 SW 3rd Ave) The godfather of the micro-roasting revolution still takes some beating. The Ace Hotel location is the coolest nook, where trendy baristas compare asymmetrical haircuts over an Iggy Pop soundtrack.

BARISTA
Cafe

(www.baristapdx.com) Pearl District (539 NW 13th Ave); Alberta (1725 NE Alberta St) Pro baristas serve made-to-perfection coffee with charm at these two newish locations that showcase different roasts every week and get their fresh pastries from a nearby Pearl district bakery.

PUBLIC DOMAIN COFFEE
Cafe

(www.publicdomaincoffee.com; 603 SW Broadway, cnr Alder St; 6am-7pm Mon-Fri from 7am Sat & Sun) A swanky new downtown outlet owned by long-time indie roasters Coffee Bean International.

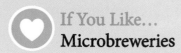

If You Like…
Microbreweries

It's enough to make a native Brit jealous. Portland has about 30 brewpubs within its borders – more than any other city on earth. If you like Bridgeport Brewpub (p363), try some of these other renowned spots.

1 LUCKY LABRADOR BREWING COMPANY
(www.luckylab.com) Hawthorne (915 SE Hawthorne Blvd); Pearl District (1945 NW Quimby St) The name's no joke. Dogs are welcome at this mild-mannered and mild-beered pub; there's even a dog-friendly back patio at the Hawthorne branch where movies are shown in summer.

2 DESCHUTES BREWERY
(www.deschutesbrewery.com; 210 NW 11th Av) Proof that not all good ideas start in Portland is Deschutes, an import from Bend that serves great pub grub and beer from its swanky perch in the Pearl District. The beer is brewed on-site.

3 HOPWORKS URBAN BREWERY
(www.hopworksbeer.com; 2944 SE Powell Blvd) One of the newer kids on the brewpub block has furnished Portland with its first 100% ecobrewery, featuring organic ales, local ingredients, on-site composting and even a 'bicycle bar.'

Bars & Brewpubs

BRIDGEPORT BREWPUB
Brewery

(www.bridgeportbrew.com; 1313 NW Marshall St) This huge, relaxing unpretentious ba (which also sells great food) hides a small piece of history. This is where the micro-brewing industry in the US was kick-started in 1984. And yes, it's still here working the magic.

SAUCEBOX
Bar

(www.saucebox.com; 214 SW Broadway) Trendy downtowners slink into this ubersleek downtown restaurant with pretty bar staff serving upscale Asian-fusion cuisine; but entertainment-seeking out-of-towners are welcome to pop by for a creative cocktail. DJs fire up at 10pm.

Entertainment

DOUG FIR LOUNGE — Live Music
(www.dougfirlounge.com; 830 E Burnside St)
Since the closing of the egendary Satyr-icon nightclub in the late 2000s, Portland's musical baton has been passed onto the Doug Fir, a bar/lounge with a personality that's more middle-aged rock star than angry young punk. But, true to form, the Fir still delivers where it matters, luring edgy, hard-to-get talent into a venue that pits tattooed youths against suburban yuppies.

LIVING ROOM THEATER — Cinema
(www.livingroomtheaters.com; 341 SW 10th Ave)
These six movie theaters with cutting-edge digital technology screen art-house, foreign and retro films, while the staff bring you drinks and tapas to enjoy in front of the big screen.

CRYSTAL BALLROOM — Live Music
(www.mcmenamins.com; 1332 W Burnside St)
Opened in 1914, the Crystal saw it all – jazz, Beat poets and psychedelic – until a 1968 closure led to it becoming the city's favorite squat. The McMenamin

brothers rescued it from oblivion in 1997 and it's back to its '50s high water mark, complete with a 'floating' dancefloor that bounces at the slightest provocation.

ℹ Information

Portland Oregon Visitors Association (www.travelportland.com; 701 SW 6th Ave; ⏰ 8:30am-5:30pm Mon-Fri, 10am-4pm Sat, 10am-2pm Sun) Super-friendly volunteers staff this office in Pioneer Courthouse Sq.

ℹ Getting There & Away

Portland International Airport (PDX; www.flypdx.com) has daily flights all over the US, as well as to four international destinations.

ℹ Getting Around

To/From the Airport
Tri-Met's MAX light-rail train runs between PDX airport and downtown ($2.35, 45 minutes). Taxis from the airport cost about $30.

Bus, Light Rail & Streetcar
The city runs standard local buses, a MAX light-rail system – run by Tri-Met with an **information**

Outdoor music festival at Cathedral Park, Portland

Detour:
Mt Hood

If the Cascade Mountains were people, Mt Hood – Oregon's highest peak at 11,239ft – would be the congenial, easy-to-get-to-know one. There are plenty of reasons to admire its ethereal snowcapped beauty.

Hood is rightly revered for its skiing. There are six ski areas on the mountain, including **Timberline** (lift tickets adult/child $48/30), which lures Canadians and Californians (as well as Oregonians) with the only year-round skiing in the US.

The **Mt Hood National Forest** protects an astounding 1200 miles of hiking trails. A Northwest Forest Pass ($5) is required at most trailheads.

Stanley Kubrick fans will have no trouble recognizing the historic 1937 **Timberline Lodge** (☏800-547-1406; www.timberlinelodge.com; d $115-290; 🛜🈂️) as the fictional Overlook Hotel from the film *The Shining* (exterior shots only). 'All work and no play makes Jack a dull boy,' typed Jack Nicholson repeatedly in the movie – if only he'd known about the year-round skiing, the hikes, the cozy fires and the hearty restaurant.

Mt Hood is about a one-hour drive from Portland along US-26 East.

center (www.trimet.org; 🕗8:30am-5:30pm Mon-Fri) at Pioneer Courthouse Sq – and a streetcar (tram) introduced in 2001, which runs from Portland State University, south of downtown, through the Pearl District to NW 23rd Ave.

OREGON COAST

While Washington's coast is speckled with islands and inland seas, Oregon's 362 miles gets full exposure to the crashing waves of the Pacific. This magnificent littoral is paralleled by view-hugging US 101, a scenic highway that winds its way through towns, resorts, state parks (over 70 of them) and wilderness areas.

Cannon Beach

Cannon Beach is a sensitively laid-out small resort where upmarket serenity is juxtaposed against thunderous Pacific breakers and fickle weather. Immense basalt promontories and a sweeping sandy beach have given the town its tourist-brochure wrapping paper, but Cannon Beach is uniquely beautiful and far from spoiled. The town itself is replete with small art galleries and esoteric shops.

The coast to the north, protected inside **Ecola State Park**, is the Oregon you may have already visited in your dreams: sea stacks, crashing surf, hidden beaches and gorgeous pristine forest.

The **Cannon Beach Hotel** (☏503-436-1392; www.cannonbeachhotel.com; 1116 S Hemlock St; d $132-242; @🛜) is a classy joint with small but meticulously turned-out rooms in a historic wooden arts-and-crafts building dating from 1914.

Oregon Dunes National Recreation Area

Stretching for 50 miles between Florence and Coos Bay, the Oregon Dunes form the largest expanse of coastal dunes in the USA. The dunes tower up to 500ft and undulate inland as far as 3 miles to meet coastal forests, harboring curious ecosystems that sustain an abundance of wildlife. Hiking trails, bridle paths, and boating and swimming areas are available, but avoid the stretch south of Reedsport as noisy dune buggies dominate this area. Inform yourself at the Oregon Dunes National Recreation OArea's **headquarters** (☏541-271-3495; www.fs.fed/us/r6/sius law; 855 Highway Ave; 🕗8am-4:30pm Mon-Fri, to 4pm Sat & Sun) in Reedsport.

California

With its dramatic coastlines, sun-dappled vineyards and snow-covered peaks, California soars beyond any expectations sold on Hollywood's silver screens.

More than anything, California is iconic. It was here that the hurly-burly gold rush kicked off in the mid-19th century, where naturalist John Muir rhapsodized about the Sierra Nevada's 'range of light,' and Jack Kerouac and the Beat Generation defined what it really means to hit the road. California's multicultural melting pot has been cookin' since this bountiful, promised land was staked out by Spain and Mexico. Waves of immigrants still look today to find their own American dream on these palm tree–studded Pacific shores. It's time for you to join them.

Redwood trees, Muir Woods National Monument (p413)
LEE FOSTER/LONELY PLANET IMAGES ®

California

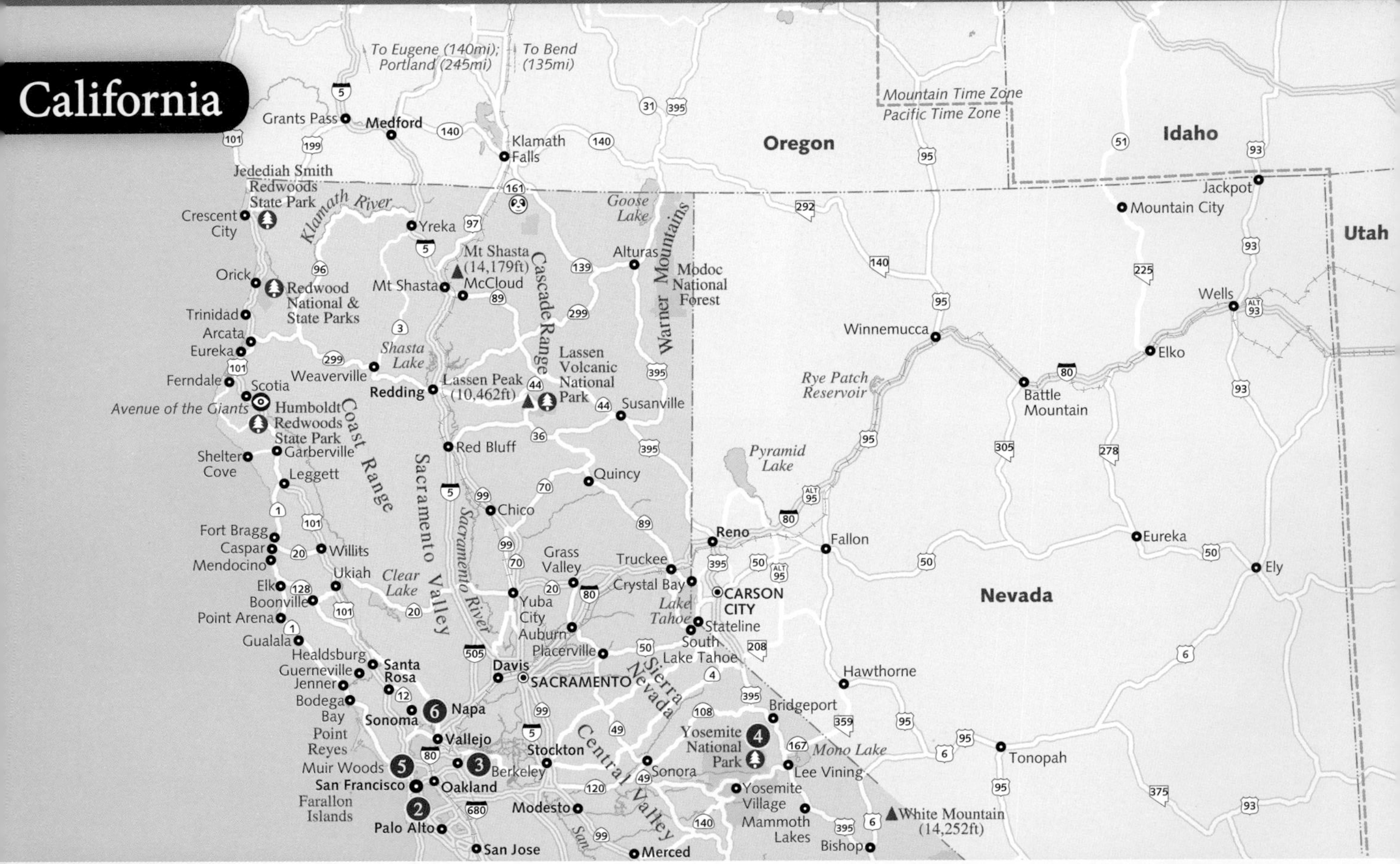

Utah

Idaho

Oregon

Nevada

Mountain Time Zone
Pacific Time Zone

Jackpot
Mountain City
Wells
Elko
Eureka
Ely
Battle Mountain
Winnemucca
Rye Patch Reservoir
Fallon
Tonopah
White Mountain (14,252ft)
Bishop
Mammoth Lakes
Hawthorne
Pyramid Lake
Bridgeport
Mono Lake
Lee Vining
Yosemite Village
Reno
CARSON CITY
Stateline
South Lake Tahoe
Crystal Bay
Truckee
Lake Tahoe
Yosemite National Park
Sonora
Merced
To Bend (135m)
Klamath Falls
To Eugene (140mi); Portland (245m)
Grants Pass
Medford
Modoc National Forest
Warner Mountains
Alturas
Goose Lake
Susanville
Quincy
Grass Valley
Yuba City
Auburn
Placerville
SACRAMENTO
Stockton
Modesto
San Jose
Palo Alto
Jedediah Smith Redwoods State Park
Crescent City
Klamath Falls
Yreka
Mt Shasta (14,179ft)
McCloud
Cascade Range
Lassen Volcanic National Park
Lassen Peak (10,462ft)
Red Bluff
Chico
Davis
Berkeley
Oakland
San Francisco
Farallon Islands
Orick
Trinidad
Arcata
Eureka
Ferndale
Scotia
Redwood National & State Parks
Shasta Lake
Weaverville
Redding
Sacramento River
Sacramento Valley
Clear Lake
Napa
Vallejo
Santa Rosa
Sonoma
Muir Woods
Humboldt Redwoods State Park
Garberville
Shelter Cove
Avenue of the Giants
Coast Range
Ukiah
Willits
Healdsburg
Guerneville
Jenner
Bodega Bay
Point Reyes
Fort Bragg
Caspar
Mendocino
Point Arena
Gualala
Leggett
Elk
Boonville
Sierra Nevada
Central Valley

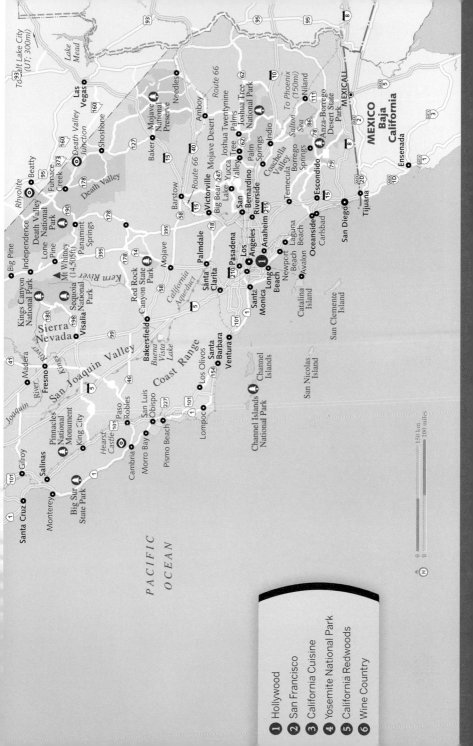

California's Highlights

① Hollywood

Hollywood (p381) has been synonymous with motion pictures since Cecil B DeMille shot one of the world's first full-length feature films in a 'Hollywoodland' barn in 1914. LA took center stage in the world of popular culture and has been there ever since.

Need to Know

STUDIO TOURS Book two weeks in advance **TRANSPORTATION** Metro Rail's Red Line follows Hollywood Blvd; alight at Vine or Highland **For more, see p381.**

Hollywood Don't Miss List

BY LERON GUBLER,
MASTER OF CEREMONIES,
HOLLYWOOD WALK OF FAME

1 HOLLYWOOD MUSEUM

The **Hollywood Museum** (above left; ☎323-464-7776; www.thehollywoodmuseum.com; 1660 N Highland Ave; admission $15; ⏰10am-5pm Wed-Sun) is a great place to spend a few hours looking at movies costumes, posters, memorabilia, celebrity cars like Cary Grant's Rolls Royce and film sets including Hannibal Lecter's cell from *Silence of the Lambs*. It's in the historic Max Factor Building – a former speakeasy – and the ground-floor rooms each have a unique color scheme that was designed to complement the hair colors of different actresses.

2 MOVIE PALACES

There are many fantastic restored motion-picture palaces in Hollywood. Disney has its premieres at the El Capitan, which also has a Wurlitzer pipe organ. The Egyptian, the first themed movie palace, began the concept of dazzling premieres with klieg lights. The Pantages has a spectacular lobby, with grand ceilings and art-deco chandeliers. And of course there's Grauman's Chinese Theatre (below left; p381).

3 STUDIO TOURS

For the real flavor of what Hollywood's all about, do a studio tour (p385) at Paramount Pictures or Warner Brothers. You get to see working studios in action, and the groups are small. The guides take you around to the prop shop, and you can watch shows being filmed. You also tour the backlots and find out about the movies filmed there.

4 HOLLYWOOD WALK OF FAME

It's free! We currently have 2449 stars on the Walk (far left; p381), and average about 24 new ones each year. Besides the stars, 46 buildings along Hollywood Blvd and Vine have historic markers detailing what happened there.

5 SUNSET RANCH

This stable (www.sunsetranchhollywood.com) has been in business for over 70 years – very 'old Hollywood'. Sunset horseback rides through Griffith Park to Burbank are a fun experience because the views are just great. You have all kinds of vistas, including the Hollywood sign, the Griffith Observatory and Downtown LA.

San Francisco

Rattling cable cars, fog-draped hillsides, picture-book Victorians and stunning views are all part of the scenery of this captivating city by the bay. Sometimes elegant and other times bohemian, San Francisco (p400) has fascinatingly diverse neighborhoods lined with eclectic shops and boutiques, old-world cafes, hipster-filled nightspots and amber-lit restaurants serving fare from every corner of the globe. Walkable, green and utterly disarming, San Francisco is an easy city to love.

California Cuisine

In the 1970s and '80s, star chefs – like Alice Waters of Berkeley's now legendary Chez Panisse (p411) – pioneered 'California cuisine' by incorporating the best local ingredients into simple yet delectable preparations. Since then the locavore scene has exploded, with a magnificent pairing of cheesemakers, organic growers, winemakers and the innovative chefs who help bring the produce to life. California is bursting with first-rate restaurants serving market-fresh fare.

Yosemite National Park

The head turner of America's national parks, Yosemite (p416) garners the devotion of all who enter. From the waterfall-striped granite walls buttressing emerald-green Yosemite Valley to the towering giant sequoias standing like ancient sentinels at Mariposa Grove, you feel a sense of awe and reverence that so much natural beauty exists in one place. This paradise for hikers, landscape artists and photographers should not be missed. Mist Trail and Vernal Falls

California Redwoods

Just off the coast stands one of the state's most extraordinary sights: the magnificent redwood, standing in towering groves with root structures dating back many centuries. Muir Woods National Monument (p413) is one of the best places to see these ancient sentinels.

Napa Valley

Vineyards litter this scenic, fertile state, and you won't have to travel far for a memorable quaff. One of the finest wine-growing regions, though, lies just north of San Francisco. Amid rolling verdure (with more than a passing resemblance to Tuscany), you'll find the sun-dappled vineyards of the Napa Valley (p414). Tour the fields, sample spicy zinfandels and refreshing sauvignon blancs and drink up the pastoral beauty.

California's Best...

Beaches

○ **Malibu** (p384)
Spectacular SoCal beauty with great surfing and celebrity appeal.

○ **Santa Monica** (p385)
LA's hippest beach, within strolling distance to galleries and great restaurants.

○ **Huntington Beach** (p392) Bonfires, beach volleyball and rolling waves in 'Surf City USA.'

○ **Coronado Island** (p394)
Hop on the ferry to reach this head-turner in ever-sunny San Diego.

Activities for Kids

○ **Disneyland** (p391)
Journey into imaginary worlds and give Mickey a high-five at this famed theme park.

○ **San Diego Zoo** (p394)
Budding wildlife lovers will love this sprawling zoo, home to more than 800 animal species.

○ **SeaWorld** (p396) Take in whale and dolphin shows, rides, penguins, sharks and much more.

○ **Alcatraz** (p409) Take a scenic boat ride, then wander the spooky cells of this former island prison.

Restaurants

○ **Chez Panisse** (p411)
Legendary birthplace of California cuisine.

○ **Benu** (p408) Magnificent fusion cuisine in San Francisco.

○ **Bazaar** (p388) Molecular gastronomy by renowned chef José Andrés in a Philippe Starck-designed interior. What could be more LA?

○ **Ad Hoc** (p415) Superb farm-to-table cooking – and a menu that changes daily – in the food- and wine-loving Napa Valley.

Architecture

- **California Academy of Sciences** (p407) A $500 million San Francisco masterpiece with LEED platinum credentials (including a 'Living Roof') designed by Renzo Piano.

- **Walt Disney Concert Hall** (p379) Frank Gehry's surreal and futuristic hall that has become an LA icon.

- **Old Town** (p395) Adobe buildings showcase San Diego's early Spanish settlement.

- **Golden Gate Bridge** (p408) Run it, bike it or just sit on San Francisco's Crissy Field gazing at this captivating icon.

Left: Wildflowers in Malibu (p384);
Above: Golden Gate Bridge (p408)

Need to Know

ADVANCE PLANNING

- **Two months before** Book tickets to big-name concerts, pro games and shows. Reserve accommodations, transportation and/or rental car if need be.

- **One month before** Reserve a table at top restaurants like Chez Panisse.

- **One week before** Browse entertainment and restaurant listings for top tips when you're in town.

RESOURCES

- **San Francisco Bay Guardian** (www.sfbg.com) Free weekly covering entertainment listings, reviews and local gossip for San Francisco.

- **San Francisco Chronicle** (www.sfgate.com) News, entertainment and event listings from Northern California's largest daily.

- **Napa Valley.com** (www.napavalley.org) Overview of wineries, restaurants, spas, shops and lodging.

- **ExperienceLA.com** (www.experiencela.com) Cultural calendar packed with LA goings-on.

- **Los Angeles Times (www.latimes.com)** Arts, dining and entertainment from this respected paper.

GETTING AROUND

- **Airports** Los Angeles (LAX) and San Francisco (SFO) are major international airports. Transport to/from LAX to Downtown or West Hollywood is via shuttle ($16 to $25) or taxi ($30 to $50). SFO has fast BART trains to downtown San Francisco.

- **Bus** Greyhound (www.greyhound.com) provides service between major towns.

- **Hire car** Essential for taking the epic road trip along the coast.

- **Train** Amtrak trains can take you from Seattle to San Francisco and LA, then on to San Diego. Other routes link Chicago with either SF or LA, and New Orleans with LA.

BE FOREWARNED

- **Traffic** Prepare for mind-numbing traffic if driving in LA, San Diego or the San Francisco Bay area. Avoid driving at peak times – and that includes visiting popular getaways (Marin County, Wine Country, Lake Tahoe) on weekends.

- **Cold summer** Expect foggy, chilly days if you visit San Francisco in summer. Wear layers and save the shorts for Southern California.

California Itineraries

With beaches, vineyards and urban adventures aplenty, you could spend months exploring California. These two itineraries let you delve into two of America's finest cities, followed by a cinematic drive up the Pacific Coast Highway.

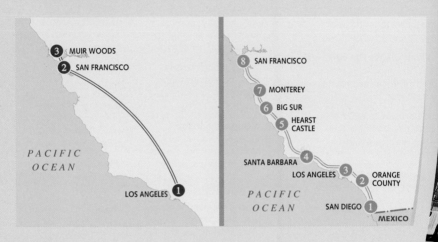

5 DAYS

SOUTH VS NORTH
Los Angeles & San Francisco

Start in **(1) Los Angeles**. Go star-searching on the Hollywood Walk of Fame, then have lunch at the Ivy. Drive to the lofty Getty Center before heading west to the Venice Boardwalk for the seaside sideshow. Watch the sunset over the ocean in Santa Monica.

On day two, visit Downtown LA, historic El Pueblo de Los Angeles and futuristic Walt Disney Concert Hall. Grab food in Chinatown and rooftop cocktails at the Standard.

Catch a morning flight to **(2) San Francisco**. Take a bay-front stroll from the Ferry Building to Fisherman's Wharf, then ferry it to Alcatraz. Hop a cable car to North Beach and stroll through Chinatown. Browse exhibits at the San Francisco Museum of

Modern Art (SFMOMA), and have dinner at Frances, followed by a SoMa club.

Start day four in the Mission, checking out murals, window-shopping along Valencia, and burrito-feasting at a real-deal taquería. Head to the Haight for vintage boutiques, then to Golden Gate Park for a walk inside the California Academy of Sciences rainforest dome. Later, have a market-fresh feast at Commonwealth.

On your last day head across the Golden Gate Bridge for a wander among the redwoods of **(3) Muir Woods**. On the way back stop for a scenic walk at Crissy Field. In the evening, have dinner in North Beach and hear a band at the Fillmore.

CRUISING THE PACIFIC COAST HIGHWAY

San Diego to San Francisco

7 DAYS

Start in **(1) San Diego**. Spend the morning exploring the sights of Balboa Park and the afternoon basking on comely Coronado beach. In the evening, have dinner and drinks in the Gaslamp Quarter. On day two, drive north to **(2) Orange County** and spend the day hopping between Huntington Beach, Newport Beach and Laguna Beach. Rise early to beat the traffic up to **(3) Los Angeles** for an exploration of Venice, Santa Monica and Malibu. Spend the night in nightlife-loving Hollywood. On your fourth day take a 90-minute drive to **(4) Santa Barbara**, a lovely town with a Mediterranean vibe. Breathe in the scent of jasmine, then continue three hours north to **(5) Hearst Castle** for a glimpse of palatial extravagance, circa 1920s. Another 65 miles north is **(6) Big Sur**, a great spot to break your journey (reserve ahead). Spend day five, exploring the stunning scenery here, stopping in Partington Cove, lunching at clifftop Nepenthe and hiking at Andrew Molera State Park. Next up is **(7) Monterey**, known for its excellent aquarium and historic downtown. On your last day, hightail it up to **(8) San Francisco** and toast the journey's end with a bang-up meal in the city.

Rainforest exhibit, California Academy of Sciences (p407)
SABRINA DALBESIO/LONELY PLANET IMAGES ©

Discover California

Facade detail, Grauman's Egyptian Theatre (p371)
RICHARD CUMMINS/LONELY PLANET IMAGES ©

LOS ANGELES

If you think you've already got LA figured out – celebrity culture, smog, traffic, Botox babes and wannabes – think again. Although it's the world's entertainment capital, the city's truths aren't delivered on movie screens or reality shows; rather, in small portions of everyday experiences. Chances are, the more you explore, the more you'll enjoy.

Now is an exciting time to visit the City of Angels. Hollywood and Downtown LA are undergoing an urban renaissance, and art, music, fashion and food are all in high gear.

Sights

Downtown

EL PUEBLO DE LOS ANGELES & AROUND

Compact, colorful and car-free, this historic district is an immersion in LA's Spanish-Mexican roots. Its spine is **Olvera Street**, a festive tack-o-rama where you can chomp on tacos and stock up on handmade candy, folkloric trinkets and bric-a-brac.

FREE AVILA ADOBE   Historic Building
(Map p382; ☎213-628-1274, Olvera St; ⏰9am-4pm) This 1818 ranch home claims to be the city's oldest existing building. It's decorated with period furniture, and a video gives history and highlights of the neighborhood.

LA PLAZA DE CULTURA Y ARTES
Museum

(Map p382; www.lapca.org; 501 Main St; adult/child $9/5; ⏱noon-7pm Wed-Sun; P) This new museum (opened 2010) chronicles the Mexican-American experience in Los Angeles, in exhibits about city history from the Zoot Suit Riots to the Chicana movement.

CIVIC CENTER & GRAND AVENUE CULTURAL CORRIDOR

FREE WALT DISNEY CONCERT HALL
Cultural Building

(Map p382; www.laphil.com; 111 S Grand Ave) Architect Frank Gehry's now-iconic 2003 structure is a gravity-defying sculpture of curving and billowing stainless-steel walls, and walkways encircling the maze-like roof and exterior. It's home base for the Los Angeles Philharmonic, now under the baton of Venezuelan phenom Gustavo Dudamel. Free tours are available subject to concert schedules.

MUSEUM OF CONTEMPORARY ART
Art Gallery

(MoCA; Map p382; www.moca.org; 250 S Grand Ave; adult/child $10/free, 5-8pm Thu free; ⏱11am-5pm Mon & Fri, to 8pm Thu, to 6pm Sat & Sun) MoCA offers headline-grabbing special exhibits; its permanent collection presents heavy hitters from the 1940s to the present.

FREE CATHEDRAL OF OUR LADY OF THE ANGELS
Church

(Map p382; www.olacathedral.org; 555 W Temple St; ⏱6:30am-6pm Mon-Fri, from 9am Sat, 7am-6pm Sun) Architect José Rafael Moneo mixed Gothic proportions with bold contemporary design for the main church of LA's Catholic Archdiocese.

LITTLE TOKYO

Little Tokyo swirls with shopping malls, Buddhist temples, public art, traditional gardens, authentic sushi bars and *izakaya* (Japanese pubs).

JAPANESE AMERICAN NATIONAL MUSEUM
Museum

(Map p382; www.janm.org; 369 E 1st St; adult/child $9/5; ⏱11am-5pm Tue, Wed & Fri-Sun, to 8pm Thu) Get an in-depth look at the Japanese immigrant experience, including the painful chapter of the WWII internment camps.

Walt Disney Concert Hall, designed by Frank Gehry

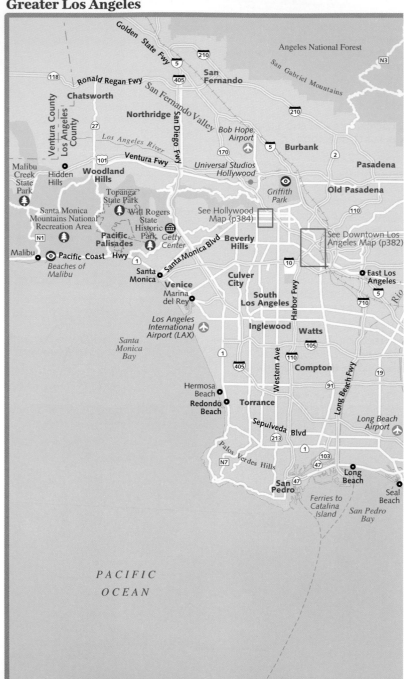

Angeles National Forest

San Gabriel Mountains

Golden State Fwy

Ronald Regan Fwy

San Fernando

San Fernando Valley

Chatsworth

Ventura County
Los Angeles County

Northridge

Los Angeles River

Ventura Fwy

San Diego Fwy

Bob Hope Airport

Burbank

Pasadena

Old Pasadena

Malibu Creek State Park

Hidden Hills

Woodland Hills

Topanga State Park

Will Rogers State Historic Park

Getty Center

Universal Studios Hollywood

Griffith Park

See Hollywood Map (p384)

See Downtown Los Angeles Map (p382)

Santa Monica Mountains National Recreation Area

Pacific Palisades

Santa Monica Blvd

Beverly Hills

Malibu

Pacific Coast Hwy

Beaches of Malibu

Santa Monica

Venice

Marina del Rey

Culver City

South Los Angeles

East Los Angeles

Rio

Los Angeles International Airport (LAX)

Inglewood

Watts

Harbor Fwy

Santa Monica Bay

Compton

Western Ave

Long Beach Fwy

Hermosa Beach

Redondo Beach

Torrance

Sepulveda Blvd

Long Beach Airport

Palos Verdes Hills

San Pedro

Ferries to Catalina Island

Long Beach

Seal Beach

San Pedro Bay

PACIFIC OCEAN

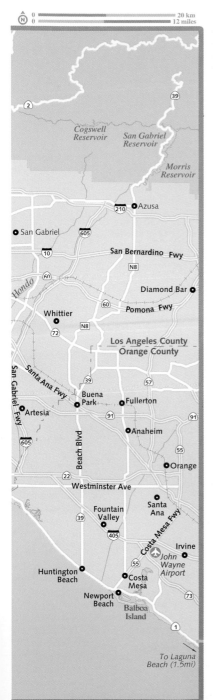

SOUTH PARK

GRAMMY MUSEUM · Museum

(Map p382; www.grammymuseum.org; 800 W Olympic Blvd; adult/child $13/11; ⏱11:30am-7:30pm Mon-Fri, from 10am Sat & Sun) Opened in 2008, with mind-expanding interactive displays of the history of American music and plenty of listening opportunities.

EXPOSITION PARK & AROUND

NATURAL HISTORY MUSEUM · Museum

(www.nhm.org; 900 Exposition Blvd; adult/child $12/5; ⏱9:30am-5pm) Dinos to diamonds, bears to beetles, hissing roaches to an ultra-rare megamouth shark – this old-school museum will take you around the world and back millions of years in time.

FREE CALIFORNIA SCIENCE CENTER · Museum

(www.californiasciencecenter.org; 700 State Dr; ⏱10am-5pm) A simulated earthquake, hatching baby chicks and a giant techno-doll named Tess bring out the kid in all of us at this great, hands-on science museum.

Hollywood

Just as aging movie stars get the occasional facelift, so has central Hollywood. While it still hasn't recaptured its Golden Age glamour of the 1920s, '30s and '40s, much of its late-20th-century seediness is gone.

GRAUMAN'S CHINESE THEATRE · Cinema

(Map p384; 6925 Hollywood Blvd) Even the most jaded visitor may thrill in the Chinese's famous forecourt, where generations of screen legends have left their imprints in cement: feet, hands, dreadlocks (Whoopi Goldberg) and even magic wands (the young stars of the *Harry Potter* films). Actors dressed as Superman, Marilyn Monroe and the like pose for photos (for tips), and you may be offered free tickets to TV shows. The theater is on the **Hollywood Walk of Fame** (p371), which honors more than 2000 celebrities with stars embedded in the sidewalk.

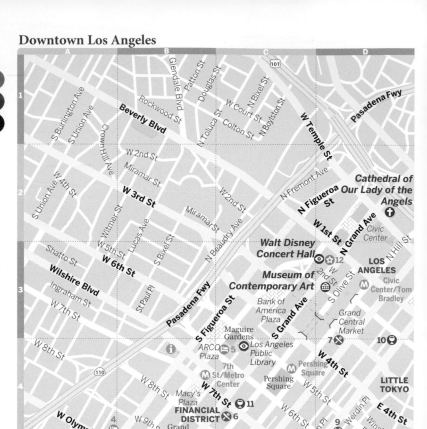

KODAK THEATRE Theater
(Map p384; www.kodaktheatre.com; adult/child $15/10; ⏱10:30am-4pm) Real-life celebs sashay along the Kodak's red carpet for the Academy Awards – columns with names of Oscar-winning films line the entryway. Pricey 30-minute tours take you inside the auditorium, VIP room and past an actual Oscar statuette. Cirque du Soleil presents **Iris** (www.cirquedusoleil.com; **tickets $43-253**) here, a new film-themed show.

Griffith Park, Silver Lake & Los Feliz

FREE **GRIFFITH PARK** Park
(Map p380; www.laparks.org/dos/parks/griffith pk; ⏱6am-10pm, trails close at dusk; P)
America's largest urban park is five times the size of New York City's Central Park. It embraces an outdoor theater, zoo, observatory, museum, antique trains, golf, tennis, playgrounds, bridle paths, 53 miles of hiking trails, Batman's caves and the Hollywood Sign.

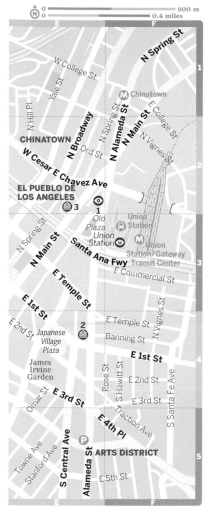

Downtown Los Angeles

◎ **Top Sights**

Cathedral of Our Lady of the
Angels..D2
Grammy Museum...............................A5
Museum of Contemporary Art..........D3
Walt Disney Concert Hall..................D3

◎ **Sights**

1 Avila Adobe.. E2
2 Japanese American National
Museum.. E4
3 La Plaza de Cultura y Artes.................E2

🛏 **Sleeping**

4 Figueroa Hotel A4
5 Standard Downtown LA C4

🍴 **Eating**

6 Bottega Louie..C4
7 Grand Central Market D4
8 LA Live...A5
9 Nickel Diner...D4

🍷 **Drinking**

10 Edison..D4
11 Seven Grand C4

🎭 **Entertainment**

12 Los Angeles Philharmonic D3
13 Staples Center A5

Mid-City

Some of LA's best museums line Museum
Row, a short stretch of Wilshire Blvd just
east of Fairfax Ave.

**LOS ANGELES COUNTY
MUSEUM OF ART**   Art Gallery

(LACMA; www.lacma.org; 5905 Wilshire Blvd;
adult/child under 17yr $15/free; ☉noon-8pm
Mon, Tue & Thu, to 9pm Fri, 11am-8pm Sat & Sun)
One of the country's top art museums
and the largest in the western USA. The
collection in the Renzo Piano–designed
Broad Contemporary Art Museum
(B-CAM) includes seminal pieces by
Jeff Koons, Roy Lichtenstein and Andy
Warhol, and two gigantic works in rusted
steel by Richard Serra.

GRIFFITH OBSERVATORY
                    Observatory, Planetarium
(www.griffithobservatory.org; 2800 Observatory
Rd; observatory free, planetarium shows adult/
child $7/3; ☉noon-10pm Tue-Fri, from 10am
Sat & Sun, closed occasional Tue; P) Above
Los Feliz loom the iconic triple domes of
this 1935 observatory, which boasts a
super-techie planetarium and films in
the Leonard Nimoy Event Horizon
Theater.

Hollywood

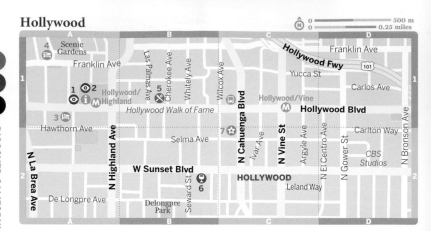

Hollywood

◎ **Sights**
1 Grauman's Chinese Theatre............... A1
2 Kodak Theatre A1

▢ **Sleeping**
3 Hollywood Roosevelt Hotel................. A1
4 Magic Castle Hotel A1

⊗ **Eating**
5 Musso & Frank Grill B1

◉ **Drinking**
6 Cat & Fiddle... B2

◉ **Entertainment**
7 Hotel Cafe C2

LA BREA TAR PITS   Archaeological Site www.tarpits.org; 5801 Wilshire Blvd; adult/child $11/5, 1st Tue each month free; ◔9:30am-5pm Between 10,000 and 40,000 years ago, a giant pool of tarlike, bubbling crude oil here trapped saber-toothed cats, mammoths and other now-extinct ice-age critters, the remains of which are still being excavated at the La Brea Tar Pits. Check out their fossilized remains at the on-site **Page Museum**.

Beverly Hills

No trip to LA would be complete without a saunter along pricey, pretentious **Rodeo Drive**, that famous three-block ribbon of style.

PALEY CENTER FOR MEDIA   Broadcasting Museum (www.paleycenter.org; 465 N Beverly Dr; suggested donation adult/child $10/5; ◔noon-5pm Wed-Sun) TV and radio addicts can indulge their passion at this mind-boggling archive of TV and radio broadcasts from 1918 through the internet age. Pick your faves, grab a seat at a private console and enjoy.

Westwood & Around

FREE **GETTY CENTER**   Art Gallery (Map p380; www.getty.edu; 1200 Getty Center Dr; ◔10am-5:30pm Sun & Tue-Thu, to 9pm Fri & Sat) Triple delights: a stellar art collection, Richard Meier's fabulous architecture and Robert Irwin's ever-changing gardens. On clear days, add breathtaking views of the city and ocean to the list.

Malibu

Hugging 27 spectacular miles of Pacific Coast Hwy, Malibu has long been synonymous with surfing, stars and a hedonistic lifestyle, but it actually looks far less posh than the glossy mags make it sound. Still, it's been celebrity central since the 1930s.

Malibu's twin natural treasures are the Santa Monica Mountains National Recreation Area and its beaches, including the aptly named Surfrider.

Santa Monica

Santa Monica is the belle by the beach, mixing urban cool with a laid-back vibe. Tourists, teens and street performers make car-free, chain-store-lined **Third Street Promenade** the most action-packed zone.

For some more local flavor, shop along celeb-favored **Montana Avenue** or down-homey **Main Street**, backbone of the neighborhood once nicknamed 'Dogtown' and known as the birthplace of skateboard culture.

SANTA MONICA PIER　Amusement Park (www.santamonicapier.org) Kids love the venerable pier, where attractions include a quaint carousel, a solar-powered Ferris wheel and tiny aquarium with touch tanks.

BERGAMOT STATION ARTS CENTER　Art Gallery (2525 Michigan Ave; ◷10am-6pm Tue-Sat; P) Art fans gravitate inland toward this avant-garde center, a former trolley stop that now houses 35 galleries and the progressive **Santa Monica Museum of Art** (www.smmoa.org; 2525 Michigan Ave; suggested donation $5; ◷11am-6pm Tue-Sat).

Activities

Swimming & Surfing

Top beaches for swimming are Malibu's **Zuma**, **Santa Monica State Beach** and **Hermosa Beach**. **Surfrider Beach** in Malibu is a legendary surfing spot.

 # Sleeping

For seaside life, base yourself in Santa Monica or Venice. Cool-hunters and party people will be happiest in Hollywood or WeHo; culture-vultures, in Downtown.

Downtown

STANDARD DOWNTOWN LA　Hotel $$ (Map p382; ☏213-892-8080; www.standard hotel.com; 550 S Flower St; r from $165; ❄@ ☞ ☰) This 207-room design-savvy hotel in a former office building goes for a young, hip and shag-happy crowd – the rooftop bar fairly pulses – so don't come here with kids or to get a solid night's sleep.

FIGUEROA HOTEL　Historic Hotel $$ (Map p382; ☏213-627-8971; www.figueroahotel. com; 939 S Figueroa St; r $148-184, ste $225-265; ❄@ ☞ ☰) A rambling, 1920s oasis

---

Touring the Studios

Half the fun of visiting Hollywood is hoping you'll see stars. Up the odds by being part of the studio audience of a sitcom or game show, which usually tape between August and March. For free tickets, contact **Audiences Unlimited** (☏818-260-0041; www.tvtickets.com).

For an authentic behind-the-scenes look, take a small group tour in an open-sided shuttle at **Paramount Pictures** (☏323-956-1777; www.paramount.com; 5555 Melrose Ave, Hollywood; tours $40, minimum age 12yr; ◷10am-2pm Mon-Fri) or **Warner Bros Studios** (☏818-972-8687; www.wbstudiotour.com; 3400 Riverside Dr, Burbank, San Fernando Valley; tours $45, minimum age 8yr; ◷8:30am-4pm Mon-Fri; P), or a walking tour of **Sony Pictures Studios** (☏310-244-8687; 10202 W Washington Blvd, Culver City; tours $33, minimum age 12yr; ◷tours 9:30am, 10:30am, 12:30pm, 1:30pm & 2:30pm Mon-Fri; P).

across from LA Live, the Fig welcomes guests with a richly tiled Spanish-style lobby that segues to a sparkling pool and buzzy outdoor bar. Rooms are furnished in a world-beat mash-up of styles (Morocco, Mexico, Zen...), and are comfy but varying in size and configuration.

Hollywood

HOLLYWOOD ROOSEVELT HOTEL
Hotel $$$

(Map p384; ☏ 323-466-7000; www.hollywood roosevelt.com; 7000 Hollywood Blvd; r from $269; ❄ @ 🗢 ≋) This venerable hotel has hosted elite players since the first Academy Awards were held here in 1929. It pairs a palatial Spanish lobby with sleek Asian contemporary rooms, a busy pool scene and rockin' restos. Parking is $33.

MAGIC CASTLE HOTEL
Apartment $$

(Map p384; ☏ 323-851-0800; www.magic castlehotel.com; 7025 Franklin Ave; r $154-304; ❄ 🗢 ≋ ♠) The walls are thin, but this renovated former apartment building around a courtyard boasts contemporary furniture, attractive art, comfy bathrobes

and fancy bath amenities. For breakfast: freshly baked goods and gourmet coffee on your balcony or poolside.

West Hollywood & Mid-City

STANDARD HOLLYWOOD
Hotel $$

(☏ 323-650-9090; www.standardhotel.com; 8300 W Sunset Blvd; r $165-250, ste from $350; ❄ @ 🗢 ≋) This white-on-white property on the Sunset Strip is a scene, with Astroturf-fringed pool with a view across LA and sizable shagadelic rooms with silver beanbag chairs, orange-tiled bathrooms and Warhol poppy-print curtains. Parking is $29.

Santa Monica & Venice

HOTEL ERWIN
Hotel $$

(☏ 310-452-1111; www.jdvhotels.com; 1679 Pacific Ave, Venice; r from $169; ❄ @ 🗢) A worthy emblem of Venice. Rooms aren't the biggest and in most there's a low traffic hum, but you're steps from the beach and your room features graffiti- or anime-inspired art and an honor bar containing sunglasses and '70s-era soft drinks. The rooftop bar offers spellbinding coastal vistas.

EMBASSY HOTEL APARTMENTS
Boutique Hotel $$

(☏ 310-394-1279; www.embassyhotelapts.com; 1001 3rd St, Santa Monica; r $169-390; P @) This hushed 1927 Spanish-Colonial hideaway delivers charm by the bucket. A rickety elevator takes you to units oozing old-world flair and equipped with internet. Kitchens make many rooms well suited to do-it-yourselfers. No air con.

 Eating

LA's culinary scene is one of the world's most vibrant and eclectic, from celebrity chefs whipping up farmers-market-fab to authentic international cooking.

View from Griffith Observatory (p383)
EDDIE BRADY/LONELY PLANET IMAGES ©

HANAN ISACHAR/LONELY PLANET IMAGES ©

Don't Miss Venice

The **Venice Boardwalk** (Ocean Front Walk) is a freak show, a human zoo, a wacky carnival and an essential LA experience. This cauldron of counterculture is the place to get your hair braided, enjoy a *qi gong* back massage, pick up cheap sunglasses or buy a woven bracelet. Encounters with bodybuilders, hoop dreamers, a Speedo-clad snake charmer or a roller-skating Sikh minstrel are pretty much guaranteed, especially on hot summer afternoons. (Alas, the vibe gets a bit creepy after dark.)

To escape the hubbub, meander inland to the **Venice Canals**, a vestige of Venice's early days when gondoliers poled visitors along quiet, artificial waterways. Today ducks preen and locals lollygag in rowboats in this serene, flower-festooned neighborhood.

The hippest Westside strip is funky, sophisticated **Abbot Kinney Boulevard**, a palm-lined mile of restaurants, yoga studios, art galleries and eclectic shops selling mid-century furniture and handmade fashions.

Downtown

Downtown's restaurant scene has exploded. Great neighborhoods for browsing include 7th St east of Grand Ave, Little Tokyo (not just for Japanese cuisine anymore), **LA Live** (Map p382; www.lalive.com; 800 W Olympic Blvd) and the food stalls of the **Grand Central Market** (Map p382; 317 S Broadway; ⏰9am-6pm).

BOTTEGA LOUIE   Italian **$$**
(Map p382; ☎213-802-1470; www.bottegalouie.com; 700 S Grand Ave; mains $11-18; ⏰10:30am-

11pm Mon Fri, Sat & Sun from 9am) The wide marble bar has become a magnet for the artsy loft set and office workers alike. The open-kitchen crew, in chef's whites, grills housemade sausage and wood-fires thin-crust pizzas in the white-on-white, big-as-a-gym dining room. Always busy, always buzzy.

NICKEL DINER   Diner **$**
(Map p382; ☎213-623-8301; 524 S Main St; mains $8-14; ⏰8am-3:30pm Tue-Sun, 6-11pm Tue-Sat) In Downtown's boho historic

district, this red vinyl joint feels like a throwback to the 1920s. Ingredients are 21st century, though: artichokes stuffed with quinoa salad, burgers piled with poblano chilies.

Hollywood

OSTERIA MOZZA & PIZZERIA MOZZA
Italian $$$
(323-297-0100; www.mozza-la.com; 6602 Melrose Ave, Mid-City; mains Osteria $17-29, Pizzeria $10-18; lunch & dinner) Reserve weeks ahead at LA's hottest Italian eatery, run by celebrity chefs Mario Batali and Nancy Silverton. Two restaurants share the same building: a wide-ranging menu at the Osteria, and precision-made pizzas baked before your eyes at the **Pizzeria** (323-297-0101, 641 N Highland Ave).

MUSSO & FRANK GRILL
Bar & Grill $$
(Map p384; 323-467-7788; 6667 Hollywood Blvd; mains $12-35; 11am-11pm Tue-Sat) Hollywood history hangs thickly in the air at the boulevard's oldest eatery. Waiters balance platters of steaks, chops, grilled liver and other dishes harking back to the days when cholesterol wasn't part of our vocabulary. The service is as smooth as the martinis.

West Hollywood, Mid-City & Beverly Hills

BAZAAR
Modern Spanish $$$
(310-246-5555; 465 S La Cienega Blvd; dishes $8-18; 6-11pm, brunch 11am-3pm Sat & Sun) In the SLS Hotel, the Bazaar dazzles with over-the-top design by Philippe Starck and 'molecular gastronomic' tapas by José Andrés. Caprese salad pairs cherry tomatoes with mozzarella balls that explode in your mouth, or try cotton-candy foie gras or a Philly cheesesteak on 'air bread.'

THE IVY
Californian $$$
(310-274-8303; 113 N Robertson Blvd; mains $20-38; 11:30am-11pm Mon-Fri, from 11am Sat, from 10am Sun) In the heart of Robertson's fashion frenzy, the Ivy's picket-fenced porch and rustic cottage are *the* power lunch spot. Chances of catching A-lister babes nibbling on a carrot stick or studio execs discussing sequels over the lobster omelet are excellent.

ORIGINAL FARMERS MARKET
Market $
(www.farmersmarketla.com; cnr 3rd St & Fairfax Ave) The market hosts a dozen worthy,

Library Alehouse, Santa Monica

DEEDEE DEGELIA/LONELY PLANET IMAGES ©

LA: So Gay

'Boystown,' centred on Santa Monica Blvd in West Hollywood (WeHo), is LA's gay ground zero. Silver Lake, LA's original gay enclave, has evolved from a largely leather and Levi's scene to encompass cute multiethnic hipsters.

WEHO

The Abbey (www.abbeyfoodandbar.com; 692 N Robertson Blvd; mains $9-24; ⏰9am-2am) LA's essential gay bar and restaurant.

Eleven (www.eleven.la; 8811 Santa Monica Blvd; mains $13-29; ⏰6-10pm Tue-Sun, 11am-3pm Sat & Sun) This glam spot occupies a historic building, serves New American cuisine and offers different theme nights.

SILVER LAKE

Akbar (www.akbarsilverlake.com; 4356 W Sunset Blvd) Best jukebox in town, a Casbah atmosphere, and a crowd that's been known to change from hour to hour.

MJ's (www.mjsbar.com; 2810 Hyperion Ave) Popular contempo hangout for dance nights, 'porn star of the week' and cruising.

---

budget-priced eateries, most *al fresco*. Try the classic diner Du-par's, Cajun-style cooking at the Gumbo Pot, ¡Loteria! Mexican grill or Singapore's Banana Leaf.

Santa Monica & Venice

LIBRARY ALEHOUSE   Pub $$
(☎310-399-7892; www.libraryalehouse.com; 2911 Main St; mains $12-20; ⏰11:30am-midnight) Locals gather as much for the food as the 29 beers on tap at this wood-paneled gastropub with a cozy outdoor back patio. Angus burgers, fish tacos and hearty salads sate the 30-something regulars.

 **Drinking**

EDISON   Bar
(Map p382; www.edisondowntown.com; 108 W 2nd St, off Harlem Alley, Downtown; ⏰Wed-Sat) *Metropolis* meets *Blade Runner* at this industrial-chic basement boîte, where you'll be sipping mojitos surrounded by turbines and other machinery from its days as a boiler room. Don't worry: it's all tarted up nicely with cocoa leather couches, three cavernous bars and a dress code.

SEVEN GRAND   Bar
(Map p382; ☎213-614-0737; 515 W 7th St, Downtown) It's as if hipsters invaded Mummy and Daddy's hunt club, with tartan-patterned carpeting and deer heads on the walls.

CAT & FIDDLE   Pub
(Map p384; www.thecatandfiddle.com; 6530 W Sunset Blvd; ⏰11:30am-2am; P) Morrissey to Frodo, you never know who might be popping by for Boddingtons or Sunday-night jazz. Still, this Brit pub with leafy beer garden is more about friends and conversation than faux-hawks and deal-making.

DRESDEN   Retro Bar, Live Music
(1760 N Vermont Ave, Los Feliz) Dresden's answer to Bogey & Bacall is the campy songster duo Marty & Elayne. They're an institution: you saw them crooning 'Stayin' Alive' in *Swingers*.

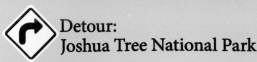

Detour: Joshua Tree National Park

Like figments from a Dr Seuss book, the whimsical Joshua trees (actually tree-sized yuccas) welcome visitors to this 794,000 acre (321,000 hectare) **national park** (☏760-367-5500; www.nps.gov/jotr) located at the convergence of the Sonora and Mojave Deserts. It's popular with rock climbers and day hikers, especially in spring, when the trees each send up a single huge, cream-colored flower. The boulder-strewn landscape has inspired many artists, most famously the band U2.

The park's northern half harbors most of the attractions, including all of the Joshua trees. Entry permits ($15 per vehicle) are valid for seven days and come with a map and newspaper guide. There are no park facilities aside from restrooms, but you can get gas and stock up in the trio of desert communities linked by Twentynine Palm Hwy (Hwy 62) along its northern boundary. (Route I-10 borders the park to the south.) Of these, Yucca Valley has the most facilities and arty Joshua Tree the best eating options.

 **Entertainment**

Live Music

SPACELAND   Live Music
(www.clubspaceland.com; 1717 Silver Lake Blvd, Silver Lake) Beck played some early gigs at what is still LA's best place for indie and alterna-sounds.

HOTEL CAFE   Live Music
(Map p384; www.hotelcafe.com; 1623½ N Cahuenga Blvd; tickets $10-15) The 'it' place for handmade music sometimes features big-timers such as Suzanne Vega, but it's really more of a stepping stone for message-minded newbie balladeers.

Classical Music

LOS ANGELES PHILHARMONIC   Orchestra
(Map p382; ☏323-850-2000; www.laphil.org; 111 S Grand Ave, Downtown) The world-class LA Phil performs classics and cutting-edge works at the Walt Disney Concert Hall, under the baton of Venezuelan phenom Gustavo Dudamel.

HOLLYWOOD BOWL   Amphitheater
(☏323-850-2000; www.hollywoodbowl.com; 2301 N Highland Ave, Hollywood; ☉late Jun-Sep) This historic natural amphitheater is the LA Phil's summer home and also a stellar place to catch big-name rock, jazz, blues and pop acts. Come early for a preshow picnic (alcohol is allowed).

Sports

DODGER STADIUM   Baseball
(www.dodgers.com; 1000 Elysian Park Dr, Downtown) LA's Major League Baseball team plays from April to October in this legendary stadium.

STAPLES CENTER   Spectator Sports
(Map p382; www.staplescenter.com; 1111 S Figueroa St, Downtown) All the high-tech trappings fill this flying-saucer-shaped home to the Lakers, Clippers and Sparks basketball teams, and the Kings ice hockey team. Headliners – Britney Spears to Katy Perry – also perform here.

ⓘ Information

Discover Los Angeles (☏323-467-6412; www.discoverlosangeles.com; Hollywood & Highland complex, 6801 Hollywood Blvd; ☉10am-10pm Mon-Sat, to 7pm Sun)

ⓘ Getting There & Away

AIR LA's main gateway is Los Angeles International Airport (LAX; ☏310-646-5252; www.lawa.org/lax), one of the world's five busiest. BUS The main Greyhound bus terminal (☏213-629-8401; 1716 E 7th St) is in an unsavory part of Downtown, so avoid arriving after dark. Some buses go directly to the **Hollywood terminal** (323-466-6381; 1715 N Cahuenga Blvd).

TRAIN Amtrak trains roll into Downtown's historic Union Station (📞800-872-7245; www.amtrak.com; 800 N Alameda St).

❶ Getting Around

To & From the Airport

At LAX, door-to-door shared-ride vans operated by Prime Time (📞800-473-3743; www.primetime shuttle.com) and Super Shuttle (📞310-782-6600; www.supershuttle.com) leave from the lower level of all terminals. Typical fares to Santa Monica, Hollywood or Downtown are $20, $25 and $16, respectively.

Curbside dispatchers will summon a taxi for you. There's a flat fare of $46.50 to Downtown LA. Otherwise, metered fares ($2.85 at flagfall plus $2.70 per mile) average $30 to Santa Monica, $42 to Hollywood and up to $90 to Disneyland.

Taxi

Checker (📞800-300-5007)

Independent (📞800-521-8294)

Yellow Cab (📞800-200-1085)

Crescent Bay, Laguna Beach (p393)

DISNEYLAND & ORANGE COUNTY

◎ Sights & Activities

DISNEYLAND RESORT
Amusement Parks

(📞714-781-4565, 714-781-4400; www.disneyland.com; 1313 Harbor Blvd, Anaheim; 1-day pass either park adult/child 3-9yr $80/74, both parks $105/99) The 'merriest place on earth' offers two parks for kids of all ages: Disneyland Park and Disney's California Adventure (combined passes are available).

DISNEYLAND PARK Amusement Park
Spotless, wholesome Disneyland Park is still laid out according to Walt's original plans. **Main Street USA**, a pretty thoroughfare lined with old-fashioned ice-cream parlors and shops, is the gateway into the park. At the far end of the street is **Sleeping Beauty Castle**, an obligatory photo op and a central landmark worth noting – its towering blue turrets are visible from many areas of the park. The

ANGUS OBORN/LONELY PLANET IMAGES ©

sections of Disneyland radiate from here like spokes on a wheel.

Fantasyland is your best bet for meeting princesses and other characters in costume; it's also home to a few notable rides like the famous spinning teacups of Mad Tea Party, Peter Pan's Flight and It's a Small World. For something a bit more fast-paced, head to the exhilarating Space Mountain roller coaster in **Tomorrowland** or the popular Indiana Jones Adventure ride in **Adventureland**. Nearby **New Orleans Square** offers several worthwhile attractions, too – the Haunted Mansion (not too scary for older kids) and the otherworldly Pirates of the Caribbean cruise, where cannons shoot across the water, wenches ply piratical rascals with rum and the mechanical Jack Sparrow character is creepily lifelike. Find Big Thunder Mountain Railroad, another popular roller coaster, in the Old West–themed **Frontierland**. If you've got little ones in tow, you'll likely spend time in kid-focused **Critter Country** and **Mickey's Toontown**, too.

DISNEY'S CALIFORNIA ADVENTURE *Amusement Park*
Disneyland resort's larger but less crowded park, California Adventure celebrates the natural and cultural glories of the Golden State but lacks the density of attractions and depth of imagination of Disneyland Park. The best rides are Soarin' Over California, a virtual hang-glide, and the famous Twilight Zone Tower of Terror, which drops you 183ft down an elevator chute. Cars Land is the newest addition.

DOWNTOWN DISNEY *Plaza*
Disney's open-air pedestrian mall, sandwiched between the two parks, offers plenty of opportunities to drop even more cash in its stores, restaurants and entertainment venues.

Sleeping

DISNEY'S GRAND CALIFORNIAN HOTEL & SPA *Luxury Hotel* $$$
(☎714-635-2300; http://disneyland.disney. go.com/grand-californian-hotel; 1600 S Disneyland Dr; d $384-445; P❄☎☲♨) Along the promenade of Downtown Disney, you'll see the entrance to this splurge-worthy arts-and-crafts-style hotel which offers family-friendly scavenger hunts, swimming pools bordered by private cabanas and a private entrance to California Adventure.

❶ Getting There & Away

The Disneyland Resort is just off I-5 (Santa Ana Fwy), about 30 miles southeast of Downtown LA.

Orange County Beaches

Hummer-driving hunks and Botoxed beauties mix it up with surfers and artists to give Orange

Gaslamp Quarter, San Diego
RICHARD CUMMINS/LONELY PLANET IMAGES ©

County's beach towns their distinct vibe. Just across the LA–OC county-line, **Seal Beach** is refreshingly noncommercial with its pleasantly walkable downtown, while gentrified **Huntington Beach** (aka Surf City, USA) epitomizes the California surfing lifestyle. Fish tacos and happy-hour specials abound along Main St.

Next up is the ritziest of the OC's beach communities: **Newport Beach**, portrayed in *The OC* and nirvana for luxe shoppers. Families should steer toward Balboa Peninsula for its beaches, vintage wooden pier and quaint amusement center. Near the Ferris wheel on the harbor side, the **Balboa Island Ferry** (www.balboaislandferry. com; 410 S Bayfront; car & driver/adult/child $2/1/50¢; ☉6:30am-midnight) shuttles passengers across the bay to ritzy **Balboa Island** for ice-cream cones, strolls past historic beach cottages, and the boutiques along Marine Ave.

Laguna Beach is the OC's most cultured and charming seaside town, where secluded beaches, glassy waves and eucalyptus-covered hillsides create a Riviera-like feel. Art galleries dot the Pacific Coast Hwy here, and Laguna's summer arts festivals are institutions.

SAN DIEGO

San Diegans shamelessly yet endearingly promote their hometown as 'America's Finest City.' Smug? Maybe, but it's easy to see why. The weather is practically perfect, with coastal high temperatures hovering around 72°F (22°C) all year, and beaches or forests are rarely more than 10 minutes' drive away.

 Sights

Downtown

Downtown's main street, 5th Ave, was once a notorious strip of saloons, gambling joints and bordellos known as Stingaree. These days, Stingaree has been beautifully restored as the thumping heart of

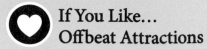

If You Like...
Offbeat Attractions

If you like the wacky freakshow of Venice Boardwalk (p387) and want to explore more of the surreal side of California, pay a visit to these other fascinating spots.

1 HEARST CASTLE
(☏800-444-4445; www.hearstcastle.org; tours adult/child from $25/12; ☉daily, call for opening hours) Around 200 miles south of San Francisco near the coast, hilltop Hearst Castle is California's most famous monument to wealth and ambition. William Randolph Hearst, the newspaper magnate, entertained Hollywood stars and royalty at this fantasy estate dripping with European antiques, accented by shimmering pools and surrounded by flowering gardens.

2 SALTON SEA
(www.saltonsea.ca.gov) East of Anza-Borrego and south of Joshua Tree awaits a most unexpected sight: the Salton Sea, California's largest lake in the middle of its biggest desert, created in 1905 when the Colorado River breached its banks.

3 SALVATION MOUNTAIN
(www.salvationmountain.us) An even stranger sight near Salton's eastern shore is Salvation Mountain, a 100ft-high hill blanketed in colorful paint and found objects and inscribed with religious messages. It's in Niland, about 3 miles off Hwy 111, via Main St.

4 RHYOLITE
(www.rhyolitesite.com; Hwy 374; admission free; ☉sunrise-sunset) Four miles west of Beatty, NV, look for the turn-off to the ghost town of Rhyolite, which epitomizes the hurly-burly, boom-and-bust story of so many Western gold-rush mining towns. Don't overlook the 1906 'bottle house' or the skeletal remains of a three-story bank.

downtown San Diego and rechristened the **Gaslamp Quarter**, a playground of restaurants, bars, clubs, shops and galleries.

In northern downtown, **Little Italy** (www.littleitalysd.com) has evolved into one of the city's hippest places to live, eat and shop. India St is the main drag.

WILLIAM HEATH DAVIS HOUSE
Historic Building

(📞619-233-4692; www.gaslampquarter.org; 410 Island Ave; adult/child $5/4; ⊙10am-6pm Tue-Sat, 9am-3pm Sun) For a full historical picture, peruse the exhibits inside this museum; the saltbox house was the onetime home of William Heath Davis, the man credited with starting the development of modern San Diego.

MARITIME MUSEUM
Museum

(📞619-234-9153; www.sdmaritime.com; 1492 N Harbor Dr; adult/child $14/8; ⊙9am-8pm, to 9am late May-early Sep) The 1863 *Star of India* is one of seven historic sailing vessels open to the public at the Maritime Museum. Don't miss the B-39 Soviet attack submarine. Metered parking and $10 day lots are nearby.

Coronado Island
The main draw here is the **Hotel del Coronado**, famous for its buoyant Victorian architecture and illustrious guest book, which includes Thomas Edison, Brad Pitt and Marilyn Monroe (its exterior stood in for a Miami hotel in the classic film *Some Like It Hot*).

Coronado is also home to one of San Diego's prettiest **beaches**, and often tops lists among California's best shorelines.

CORONADO FERRY
Ferry

(📞619-234-4111; www.sdhe.com; ferry each way $4.25; ⊙9am-10pm) Hourly ferries shuttle between Broadway Pier on San Diego's Embarcadero and the Coronado Ferry Landing at the foot of 1st St.

Balboa Park & Around
Balboa Park is an urban oasis brimming with more than a dozen museums, gorgeous gardens and architecture, performance spaces and the famous zoo. Early 20th-century beaux arts and Spanish-Colonial buildings (the legacy of world's fairs) are grouped around plazas along the east–west El Prado promenade.

SAN DIEGO ZOO
Zoo

(📞619-231-1515; www.sandiegozoo.org; 2920 Zoo Dr; adult/child with guided bus tour & aerial

Left: San Diego coastline at sunset;
Below: Flamingo, San Diego Zoo
(LEFT) RICHARD CUMMINS/LONELY PLANET IMAGES © (BELOW) RICHARD CUMMINS/LONELY PLANET IMAGES ©

tram ride $40/30; ⏱from 9am)
If it slithers, crawls, stomps,
swims, leaps or flies, chances are
you'll find it in this world-famous zoo
in northern Balboa Park. It's home to
3000-plus animals representing 800-
plus species in a beautifully landscaped
setting, including the giant Panda Canyon and the 7.5-acre Elephant Odyssey.
For a wildlife viewing experience that's
closer to the real thing, get a combination ticket to the affiliated **San Diego Zoo
Safari Park**.

Old Town & Mission valley

**MISSION BASILICA
SAN DIEGO DE ALCALÁ**   Church
(☎619-281-8449; www.missionsandiego.com;
10818 San Diego Mission Rd; adult/child $3/1;
⏱9am-4:45pm) Secluded in a corner of
what's now called Mission Valley, the
'Mother of the Missions' was founded by
Junípero Serra in 1769. Come at sunset
for glowing views over the valley and the
ocean beyond.

**OLD TOWN STATE
HISTORIC PARK**   Historic Site
(☎619-220-5422; www.parks.ca.gov; San Diego
Ave, at Twiggs St; ⏱visitor center 10am-5pm;
🅿) Preserves five original adobe buildings and several re-created structures
from the first pueblo, including a schoolhouse and a newspaper office. Most now
contain museums, shops or restaurants.
The visitor center operates free tours
daily at 11am and 2pm.

Mission Bay & Beaches

San Diego's three major beaches are
ribbons of hedonism where armies of
tanned, taut bodies frolic in the sand and
surf. South of Mission Bay, hippie-flavored
Ocean Beach (OB) has a fishing pier,
beach volleyball, sunset BBQs and good
surf. Newport Ave is chockablock with
bohemian bars, eateries and shops selling
beachwear, surf gear and antiques.

West of Mission Bay, **Mission Beach** (MB) and its northern neighbor, **Pacific Beach** (PB), are connected by the car-free **Ocean Front Walk**, which swarms with skaters, joggers and cyclists year-round.

SEAWORLD

Amusement Park, Aquarium (☎619-226-3901; www.seaworld.com; 500 SeaWorld Dr; adult/child 3-9yr $70/62; ⏰9am-10pm Jul–mid-Aug, to 11pm Fri-Sun, shorter hours rest of year) It's easy to spend a day here; the biggest draws are live animal shows like Blue Horizons, a bird and dolphin extravaganza, and One Ocean, featuring Shamu and his killer whale amigos leaping, diving and gliding.

Sleeping

Downtown

LITTLE ITALY INN B&B $$
(☎619-230-1600; www.littleitalyhotel.com; 505 W Grape St; r with shared/private bath $89/109, apt from $149; 📶) The 23-room

Victorian-style inn boasts comfortable beds, cozy bathrobes in each room, a casual European-style breakfast and wine socials on weekend evenings.

🖋**HOTEL INDIGO** Boutique Hotel $$
(☎619-727-4000; www.hotelsandiegodowntown.com; 509 9th Ave; r from $146; 🅿❄@📶♨) The first LEED-certified hotel in San Diego, Hotel Indigo is smartly designed and ecofriendly.

Beaches

🖋**INN AT SUNSET CLIFFS** Hotel $$
(☎619-222-7901; www.innatsunsetcliffs.com; 1370 Sunset Cliffs Blvd, Point Loma; r from $175; 🅿❄@📶♨) Hear the surf crashing onto the rocky shore at this breezy charmer wrapped around a flower-bedecked courtyard.

🖋**LA VALENCIA** Luxury Hotel $$$
(☎858-454-0771; www.lavalencia.com; 1132 Prospect St, La Jolla; r from $285; 🅿❄@📶♨) This 1926 landmark, the Mediterranean-style 'Pink Lady,' was designed by William Templeton Johnson. Its 116 rooms are rather compact, but it wins for Old Hollywood romance; recent ecofriendly efforts add to the charm.

Eating

Downtown & Embarcadero

C LEVEL Seafood $$$
(☎619-298-6802; www.islandprime.com; 880 Harbor Island Dr; mains $14-30; ⏰from 11am) The bay views are stunning from this airy, elegant eatery; well-prepared seafood dishes include the popular seared Hawaiian 'ahi tuna, lobster truffle mac 'n' cheese and Japanese-style sesame salmon.

Cheetah, San Diego Zoo Safari Park
MARK NEWMAN/LONELY PLANET IMAGES ©

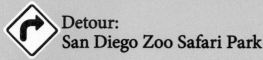

Detour:
San Diego Zoo Safari Park

Take a walk on the 'wild' side at this 1800-acre open-range **safari park** (760-747-8702; www.sandiegozoo.org; 15500 San Pasqual Valley Rd, Escondido; general admission incl tram adult/child $40/30, with San Diego Zoo $76/56; from 9am). Giraffes graze, lions lounge and rhinos romp more or less freely on the valley floor. For that instant safari feel, board the Journey to Africa tram ride, which tours you around the second-largest continent in under half an hour.

The park is in Escondido, about 35 miles north of downtown San Diego. Take I-15 Fwy to the Via Rancho Pkwy exit and then follow the signs.

OCEANAIRE SEAFOOD ROOM
Seafood **$$$**

(619-858-2277; www.theoceanaire.com; 400 J St; mains $24-40; 5-10pm Sun-Thu, to 11pm Fri & Sat) The look is art-deco ocean liner and the service is just as refined, with an oyster bar (get them for a buck during happy hour, 5pm to 6pm Monday to Friday) and inventive creations such as Maryland blue crab cakes and horseradish-crusted Alaskan halibut.

Balboa Park & Old Town

PRADO
Mediterranean **$$**

(619-557-9441; www.pradobalboa.com; 1549 El Prado, Balboa Park; mains lunch $10-15, dinner $21-34; 11:30am-3pm Mon-Fri, from 5pm Tue-Sun, 11am-3pm Sat & Sun;) This classic lunch spot in the museum district of Balboa Park serves up fresh Mediterranean cuisine like steamed mussels, shrimp paella and grilled portobello sandwiches.

OLD TOWN MEXICAN CAFÉ
Mexican **$**

(619-297-4330; www.oldtownmexcafe.com; 2489 San Diego Ave, Old Town; mains $4-15; 7am-2am;) Watch the staff turn out fresh tortillas in the window while waiting for a table. Besides breakfast (great *chilaquiles* – soft tortilla chips covered with mole), there's *pozole* (spicy pork stew), avocado tacos and margaritas at the festive central bar.

Beaches

GEORGE'S AT THE COVE
Modern American **$$**

(858-454-4244; www.georgesatthecove.com; 1250 Prospect St, La Jolla; mains $11-48; 11am-11pm) Chef Trey Foshee's Euro-Cal cusine is as dramatic as this eatery's oceanfront location. Three venues allow you to enjoy it at different price ranges: **George's Bar** (mains lunch $9-16), **Ocean Terrace** (mains lunch $11-18) and **George's California Modern** (mains dinner $28-48).

 **Drinking**

WINE STEALS
Wine Bar

(619-295-1188; www.winestealssd.com; 1243 University Ave, Hillcrest) Laid-back wine tastings (go for a flight or choose a bottle off the rack in the back), live music, gourmet pizzas and cheese platters bring in a nightly crowd to this low-lit wine bar.

TIPSY CROW
Bar, Lounge

(www.thetipsycrow.com; 770 5th Ave, Downtown) There are three distinct levels at this historic Gaslamp building that's been turned into an atmospheric watering hole: the main floor with its long mahogany bar, the lounge-like 'Nest' (thought to be the site of a former brothel), and the brick-walled 'Underground,' with a dancefloor and live music acts.

Below: Colorful house, San Diego;
Right: Mojave Desert near Death Valley National Park
(LEFT) RICHARD CUMMINS/LONELY PLANET IMAGES ©; (BELOW) WITOLD SKRYPCZAK/LONELY PLANET IMAGES ©

 Entertainment

ANTHOLOGY   Live Music
(☏619-595-0300; www.anthologysd.com; 1337 India St, Downtown; cover free-$60) Near Little Italy, Anthology presents live jazz, blues and indie music in a swank supper-club setting, from both up-and-comers and big-name performers.

CASBAH   Live Music
(☏619-232-4355; www.casbahmusic.com; 2501 Kettner Blvd, Little Italy; cover free-$20) Liz Phair, Alanis Morissette and the Smashing Pumpkins all rocked the funky Casbah on their way up the charts; catch local acts and headliners like Bon Iver.

❶ **Information**

Tourist information

Balboa Park Visitors Center (☏619-239-0512; www.balboapark.org; 1549 El Prado;

⏱9:30am-4:30pm) In the House of Hospitality, the visitor center sells park maps and the Passport to Balboa Park (adult/child $45/24, with zoo admission $77/42), which allows one-time entry to 14 of the park's museums within seven days.

San Diego Visitor Information Center (☏619-236-1212; www.sandiego.org; cnr W Broadway & Harbor Dr; ⏱9am-5pm Jun-Sep, to 4pm Oct-May)

❶ **Getting There & Away**

AIR San Diego International Airport (Lindbergh Field; ☏619-400-2404; www.san.org) sits about 3 miles west of Downtown. A taxi fare to Downtown from the airport is $10 to $15.
BUS Greyhound (☏619-515-1100; 120 W Broadway, Downtown) has hourly direct buses to Los Angeles (one way/round-trip $19/31, two to three hours).
TRAIN Amtrak (☏800-872-7245; www.amtrak. com) runs the *Pacific Surfliner* several times daily to Los Angeles ($36, three hours) and Santa Barbara ($41, 5½ hours) from the Santa Fe Depot (1055 Kettner Blvd, Downtown).

DEATH VALLEY NATIONAL PARK

The name itself evokes all that is harsh and hellish – a punishing, barren and lifeless place of Old Testament severity. Yet closer inspection reveals that in Death Valley nature is putting on a spectacular show – of water-sculpted canyons, singing sand dunes, palm-shaded oases, eroded mountains and plenty of endemic wildlife. It's a land of superlatives, holding the US records for hottest temperature (134°F, or 57°C), lowest point (Badwater, 282ft below sea level) and largest national park outside Alaska (over 5000 sq miles). Peak tourist season comes when spring wildflowers bloom. Furnace Creek is the park's commercial hub.

 Sights & Activities

Drive up to **Zabriskie Point** at sunrise or sunset for spectacular valley views across golden badlands eroded into waves, pleats and gullies. Some 20 miles further south, at **Dante's View**, you can simultaneously see the highest (Mt Whitney, 14,505ft) and lowest (Badwater) points in the contiguous USA. En route, consider detouring along the bone-rattling scenic one-way loop through **Twenty Mule Team Canyon**.

Badwater, a timeless landscape of crinkly salt flats, is a 17-mile drive south of Furnace Creek. Along the way, narrow **Golden Canyon** and **Natural Bridge** are both easily explored on short hikes. On the **Devil's Golf Course**, crystallized salt has piled up into saw-tooth mini mountains. A 9-mile detour along **Artist's Drive** is best in the late afternoon when eroded hillsides erupt in fireworks of color.

North of Furnace Creek, near Stovepipe Wells, you can scramble along the smooth marble walls of **Mosaic Canyon** or roll down the Saharan-esque **Mesquite Flat sand dunes** – magical during a full moon.

Another 36 miles north is whimsical **Scotty's Castle** (☏760-786-2392; adult/child $11/6; ⊙tours 9am-5pm Nov-Apr, to 4pm May-Oct), where costumed guides bring to life the strange tale of con-man Death Valley Scotty.

Sleeping & Eating

FURNACE CREEK RANCH   Resort $$
(760-786-2345; www.furnacecreekresort.com;
cabins $130-162, r $162-213; ❄ 🖧 ☕ 🛗) Tailor-
made for families, this rambling resort
has been subjected to a vigorous facelift
resulting in rooms dressed in desert-
color decor, updated bathrooms and
porches with comfortable patio furniture.
The grounds encompass a playground,
spring-fed swimming pool, tennis courts
and the Forty-Niner Café (mains $12 to
$25), which cooks up decent American
standards.

ℹ Information

Entry permits ($20 per vehicle) are valid for
seven days and sold at self-service pay stations
throughout the park. For a free map and
newspaper, show your receipt at the **visitor
center** (🕽760-786-3200; www.nps.gov/deva;
🕐8am-5pm) in Furnace Creek, which has a
general store, gas station, post office, ATM,
internet access, lodging and restaurants.

SAN FRANCISCO

Psychedelic drugs, newfangled technol-
ogy, gay liberation, green ventures, free
speech and culinary experimentation
all became mainstream long ago in San
Francisco. After 160 years of booms and
busts, losing your shirt has become a
favorite local pastime at the clothing-op-
tional Bay to Breakers race, Pride Parade
and hot Sundays on Baker Beach. This is
no place to be shy: out here among ec-
centrics of every stripe, no one's going to
notice a few tan lines. So long, inhibitions;
hello, San Francisco.

Sights

Let San Francisco's 43 hills and more
than 80 arts venues stretch your legs
and imagination while you take in some
(literally) breathtaking views. The 7 x 7–
mile city is laid out on a staid grid, but
its main street is a diagonal contrar-
ian streak called Market St. Downtown
sights are within walking distance of
Market St, but keep your city smarts and
wits about you, especially around South
of Market (SoMa) and the Tenderloin
(5th to 9th Sts). SF's most historic
landmarks are in the Mission, while
exciting new destinations are inside
Golden Gate Park.

Financial District
**FERRY
BUILDING**   Landmark
(🕽415-983-8000, www.ferry
buildingmarketplace.com;
🕐10am-6pm Mon-Fri,
from 9am Sat, 11am-5pm
Sun) Hedonism is alive
and well at this transit
hub turned gourmet
emporium, where food-
ies happily miss their
ferries slurping local
oysters and bubbly. Star
chefs are frequently spot-
ted at the **farmers market**

Cable car on Nob Hill, San Francisco
THOMAS WINZ/LONELY PLANET IMAGES ©

SABRINA DALBESIO/LONELY PLANET IMAGES ©

Don't Miss San Francisco Museum of Modern Art

Bold moves have set the San Francisco Museum of Modern Art (SFMOMA) apart since 1935, with curatorial gambles on then-controversial contemporary painters like Diego Rivera and Frida Kahlo, and history-making works by local photographers Dorothea Lange, Eadweard Muybridge, Ansel Adams and Edward Weston. The museum moved into architect Mario Botta's light-filled brick box just in time for the tech boom in 1995, making room for new media mavericks such as San Franciscan Matthew Barney, who debuted his dazzling Vaseline-smeared videos at SFMOMA. Today installations fill the atrium, sculpture sprouts from the rooftop garden and a $480 million expansion is under way to accommodate 1100 major modern works donated by the Fisher family (local founders of the Gap clothing chain) alongside emerging niches: conceptual architecture, wall-drawing installations and relational art. Go Thursday night after 6pm for half-price admission and the most artful flirting in town.

THINGS YOU NEED TO KNOW

415-357-4000; www.sfmoma.org; 151 3rd St; adult/child $18/free; 1st Tue of month free; 11am-6pm Fri-Tue, to 9pm Thu

(10am-2pm Tue & Thu, from 8am Sat) that wraps around the building year-round.

Civic Center

ASIAN ART MUSEUM   Museum
(415-581-3500; www.asianart.org; 200 Larkin St; adult/child $12/7; 10am-5pm Tue, Wed, Fri-Sun, to 9pm Thu) Your imagination will race from ancient Persian miniatures to cutting-edge Japanese fashion through three floors spanning 6000 years of Asian arts. Besides the largest collection outside Asia – 17,000 works – the Asian offers excellent programs for all ages, from shadow-puppet shows and yoga for kids to monthly over-21 Matcha mixers with cross-cultural cocktails and DJ mashups.

401

Downtown San Francisco

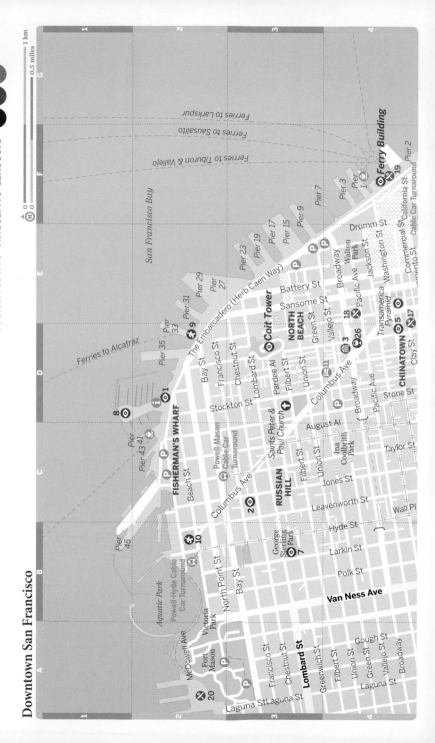

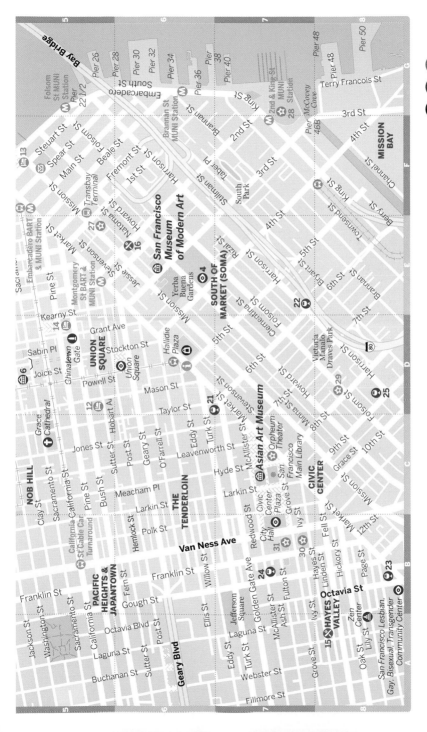

Downtown San Francisco

Chinatown

Since 1848 this community has survived riots, earthquakes, bootlegging gangsters and politicians' attempts to relocate it down the coast.

CHINESE HISTORICAL SOCIETY OF AMERICA   Museum

(CHSA; ☏415-391-1188; www.chsa.org; 965 Clay St; adult/child $5/2; 1st Tue of month free; ⊙noon-5pm Tue-Fri, 11am-4pm Sat) Picture what it was like to be Chinese in America during decades past at the nation's largest Chinese-American historical institute. Rotating exhibits are across the courtyard in CHSA's graceful red-brick, green-tile-roofed landmark building.

CHINESE CULTURE CENTER Art Gallery

(☏415-986-1822; www.c-c-c.org; 3rd fl, Hilton Hotel, 750 Kearny St; donation requested; ⊙10am-4pm Tue-Sat) On the 3rd floor of the Hilton, this cultural center hosts exhibits of traditional Chinese artists, cutting-edge art installations and Art at Night, mixing art, jazz and food.

North Beach

COIT TOWER   Landmark

(☏415-362-0808; elevator rides $5; ⊙10am-6pm) An exclamation mark on the SF cityscape, Coit Tower offers views worth shouting about – especially after you climb the giddy, steep Filbert St steps to get here.

BEAT MUSEUM   Museum

(☏800-537-6822; www.thebeatmuseum.org; 540 Broadway; admission $5; ⊙10am-7pm Tue-Sun) Beat writers Jack Kerouac, Allen Ginsberg and Lawrence Ferlinghetti made North Beach the proving ground for free spirits and free speech in the 1950s, as shown in this rambling, shambling museum of literary curios and vintage video.

Russian Hill & Nob Hill

Drivers test their mettle on the crooked 1000 block of Lombard St, but many obliviously roll past one of the city's best sunset bay vista points at **George Sterling Park**, and a splendid Diego Rivera mural at the nearby **Art Institute** (☏415-771-7020; www.sfai.edu; 800 Chestnut St; ⊙9am-7:30pm).

Fisherman's Wharf

PIER 39   Landmark

(www.pier39.com) The Wharf may not be the 'real San Francisco', but it's always lively and still retains some authenticity and a few surprises. Stick near the waterfront, where sea lions bray, street performers scare passersby, and an aquarium and carousel entice wide-eyed kids. After you've eaten the obligatory clam chowder from a sourdough bowl, consult mechanical fortune tellers at Musée Mécanique.

The Marina & Presidio

EXPLORATORIUM   Museum

(415-561-0360; www.exploratorium.edu; 3601 Lyon St; adult/child $15/10, incl Tactile Dome $10; 10am-5pm Tue-Sun) Budding Nobel Prize winners swarm this award-winning, hands-on discovery museum, learning the scientific secrets to skateboarding and groping through the Tactile Dome (ages seven and up). The Exploratorium is outgrowing its picturesque Palace of Fine Arts location and moving to the piers in 2013. Meanwhile, ducklings march past the Exploratorium through Bernard Maybeck's faux-Roman 1915 rotunda.

CRISSY FIELD   Waterfront, Beach

(415-561-7690; www.crissyfield.org) The Presidio's army airstrip has been stripped of asphalt and reinvented as a haven for coastal birds, kite-fliers and windsurfers enjoying sweeping views of Golden Gate Bridge.

BAKER BEACH   Beach

(sunrise-sunset) Unswimmable waters (except when the tide's coming in) but unbeatable views of the Golden Gate make this former Army beachhead SF's tanning location of choice, especially the clothing-optional north end – at least until the afternoon fog rolls in.

The Mission

MISSION DOLORES   Church

(415-621 8203; www.missiondolores.org; cnr Dolores & 16th Sts; adult/child $5/3; 9am-4pm) The city's oldest building and its namesake, the whitewashed adobe Missión San Francisco de Asís was founded in 1776 and rebuilt in 1782 with conscripted Ohlone and Miwok labor – note the ceiling patterned after Native American baskets.

View of downtown San Francisco from North Beach

THOMAS WINZ/LONELY PLANET IMAGES ©

BALMY ALLEY   Street
(off 24th St, near Folsom St) Mission activist artists set out in the 1970s to transform the political landscape, one mural-covered garage door at a time. Today, a one-block walk down Balmy Alley leads past three decades of murals, from an early memorial for El Salvador activist Archbishop Óscar Romero to an homage to the golden age of Mexican cinema.

Dolores Park   Park
(cnr Dolores & 18th Sts) Sunshine and politics come with the Mission territory: protests are held here almost every weekend, alongside soccer, tennis and hillside tanning.

The Castro

Rainbow flags fly high over **Harvey Milk Plaza** (Castro & Market Sts) in San Francisco's historic out-and-proud neighborhood, home of the nation's first openly gay official. Milk's former camera storefront is now home to civil-rights advocacy group Human Rights Campaign (HRC).

GLBT HISTORY MUSEUM   Museum
(415-621-1107; www.glbthistory.org/museum; 4127 18th St; admission $5, 1st Wed of month free; 11am-7pm Tue-Sat, noon-5pm Sun-Mon)

America's first gay-history museum captures proud moments and historic challenges: Harvey Milk's campaign literature, interviews with trailblazing bisexual author Gore Vidal, matchbooks from long-gone bathhouses and pages of the 1950s penal code banning homosexuality.

The Haight

Better known as the hazy hot spot of the Summer of Love, the Haight has hung onto its tie-dyes, ideals and certain habits – hence the high density of medical marijuana dispensaries (sorry, dude: prescription required). Fanciful 'Painted Lady' Victorian houses surround **Alamo Square Park** (Hayes & Scott Sts) and the corner of Haight and Ashbury Sts, where Jimi Hendrix, Janis Joplin and the Grateful Dead crashed during the Haight's hippie heyday.

Golden Gate Park & Around

San Francisco was way ahead of its time in 1865, when the city voted to turn 1017 acres of sand dunes into the world's largest city park.

Toward Ocean Beach, the park's scenery turns quixotic, with bison stampeding in their paddock toward

A musical gathering in Golden Gate Park

Gay/Les/Bi/Trans San Francisco

Doesn't matter where you're from, who you love or who's your daddy: if you're here, and queer, welcome home. The intersection of 18th and Castro Sts is the heart of the gay cruising scene, but dancing queens and slutty boys head South of Market (SoMa) for thump-thump clubs.

Some top GLBT venues:

Stud (☎415-252-7883; www.studsf.com; 399 9th St; admission $5-8; ⏰5pm-3am) Rocking the gay scene since 1966, and branching out beyond leather daddies with rocker-grrl Mondays, Tuesday drag variety shows, raunchy comedy/karaoke Wednesdays, Friday art-drag dance parties, and performance-art cabaret whenever hostess/DJ Anna Conda gets it together.

Rebel Bar (☎415-431-4202; 1760 Market St; ⏰5pm-3am Mon-Thu, to 4am Fri, 11am-4am Sat & Sun) Funhouse southern biker disco.

Aunt Charlie's (☎415-441-2922; www.auntcharlieslounge.com; 133 Turk St; ⏰9am-2am) Total dive, with the city's best classic drag show Fridays and Saturdays at 10pm.

Endup (☎415-646-0999; www.theendup.com; 401 6th St; admission $5-20; ⏰10pm-4am Mon-Thu, 11pm-11am Fri, 10pm Sat-4am Mon) Home of Sunday 'tea dances' (gay dance parties) since 1973.

Lexington Club (☎415-863-2052; 3464 19th St; ⏰3pm-2am) The baddest lesbian bar in the West, with pool, pinball and grrls galore.

windswept windmills. At the north end of Ocean Beach, the recently restored **Cliff House** (☎415-386-3330; www.cliffhouse.com; 1090 Pt Lobos Ave) restaurant overlooks the splendid ruin of **Sutro Baths**, where Victorian ladies and dandies once converged by the thousands for bracing baths in rented itchy wool bathing suits. Follow the partly paved hiking trail above Sutro Baths around **Lands End** for end-of-the-world views of Marin and the Golden Gate Bridge.

CALIFORNIA ACADEMY OF SCIENCES   Aquarium, Wildlife Reserve
(☎415-379-8000; www.calacademy.org; 55 Concourse Dr; adult/child $30/25, $3 discount with Muni ticket, 6-10pm Thu $10 (age 21+ only); ⏰9:30am-5pm Mon-Sat, from 11am Sun) Architect Renzo Piano's 2008 landmark LEED-certified green building houses 38,000 weird and wonderful animals in a four-story rainforest and split-level aquarium under a 'living roof' of California wildflowers.

MH DE YOUNG FINE ARTS MUSEUM   Art Gallery
(☎415-750-3600; www.famsf.org/deyoung; 50 Hagiwara Tea Garden Dr; adult/child $10/free, $2 discount with Muni ticket, 1st Tue of month free; ⏰9:30am-5:15pm Tue-Sun, to 8:45pm Fri) Follow sculptor Andy Goldsworthy's artificial fault line in the sidewalk into Herzog & de Meuron's sleek, copper-clad building that's oxidizing green to blend into the park. Don't be fooled by the de Young's camouflaged exterior: shows here boldly broaden artistic horizons from Oceanic ceremonial masks and Balenciaga gowns to sculptor Al Farrow's cathedrals built from bullets.

CALIFORNIA PALACE OF THE LEGION OF HONOR   Art Gallery
(☎415-750-3600; http://legionofhonor.famsf. org; 100 34th Ave; adult/child $10/6, $2 discount with Muni ticket, 1st Tue of month free; ⏰9:30am-5:15pm Tue-Sun) Featured artworks range from Monet water lilies to John Cage soundscapes, Iraqi ivories to R Crumb comics – part of the Legion's Achenbach collection of 90,000 graphic artworks.

OCEAN BEACH
Beach

(415-561-4323; www.parksconservancy.org; ☼sunrise-sunset) The park ends in this blustery beach, too chilly for bikini-clad clambakes but ideal for wet-suited pro surfers braving rip tides (casual swimmers beware).

San Francisco Bay

GOLDEN GATE BRIDGE
Bridge

(www.goldengatebridge.org) Imagine a squat concrete bridge striped black and caution yellow spanning the San Francisco Bay – that's what the US Navy initially had in mind. Luckily, engineer Joseph B Strauss and architects Gertrude and Irving Murrow insisted on the soaring art-deco design and 'International Orange' paint of the 1937 Golden Gate Bridge. Cars pay a $6 toll to cross from Marin to San Francisco; pedestrians and cyclists stroll the east sidewalk for free.

Sleeping

Union Square & Civic Center
HOTEL REX
Boutique Hotel $$

(415-433-4434; www.jdvhotels.com; 562 Sutter St; r $169-279; P❄@🛜) Noir-novelist chic, with 1920s literary lounge and compact rooms with hand-painted lampshades, local art and sumptuous beds piled with down pillows.

ORCHARD GARDEN HOTEL
Boutique Hotel $$

(415-399-9807; www.theorchardgardenhotel.com; 466 Bush St; r $179-249; ❄@🛜) SF's first all-green-practices hotel has soothingly quiet rooms with luxe touches, like Egyptian-cotton sheets, plus an organic rooftop garden.

Financial District & North Beach
HOTEL BOHÈME
Boutique Hotel $$

(415-433-9111; www.hotelboheme.com; 444 Columbus Ave; r $174-194; @🛜) A love letter to North Beach's Beat era, with vintage photos, retro orange, black and sage-green color schemes, and Chinese parasols for lampshades (but no elevator).

HOTEL VITALE
Luxury Hotel $$$

(415-278-3700; www.hotelvitale.com; 8 Mission St; d $239-379; ❄@🛜) SF's sexiest splurge is the shagadelic-chic Vitale, with roof-top hot tubs at the on-site spa, silky 450-threadcount linens on sumptuous beds and some sweeping bay views.

The Mission

INN SAN FRANCISCO
B&B $$

(415-641-0188; www.innsf.com; 943 S Van Ness Ave; r incl breakfast $175-285, with shared bath $120-145, cottage $335; P@🛜) Impeccably maintained and packed with antiques, this 1872 Italianate-Victorian mansion has a redwood hot tub in the English garden, genteel guestrooms with fresh-cut flowers and featherbeds, and limited parking.

The Castro

PARKER GUEST HOUSE
B&B $$

(415-621-3222; www.parkerguesthouse.com; 520 Church St; r incl breakfast $149-229; P@🛜) SF's best gay B&B has cushy rooms in adjoining Edwardian mansions, a steam room and garden.

The Haight

RED VICTORIAN
B&B $

(415-864-1978; www.redvic.net; 1665 Haight St; r incl breakfast $149-229, with shared bath $89-129; 🛜) Peace, love and nature worship live on in themed rooms at the tripped-out Red Vic. Four of 18 rooms have baths, but all include organic breakfasts; wi-fi and meditation pillows are available in the lobby.

Eating

SOMA, Union Square & Civic Center

BENU
Californian Fusion $$$

(415-685-4860; www.benusf.com; 22 Hawthorne St; mains $25-40; ⊙5:30-10pm Tue-Sat) SF has refined fusion cuisine over 150

DISCOVER CALIFORNIA SAN FRANCISCO

JOHNNY HAGLUND/LONELY PLANET IMAGES ©

Don't Miss Alcatraz

For 150 years, the name has given the innocent chills and the guilty cold sweats. Alcatraz was the nation's first military prison, a maximum-security penitentiary housing A-list criminals like Al Capone, as well as hotly disputed Native American territory. No prisoners escaped Alcatraz alive, but since importing guards and supplies cost more than putting up prisoners at the Ritz, the prison was closed in 1963. Native American leaders occupied the island from 1969 to '71 to protest US occupation of Native lands; their standoff with the FBI is commemorated in a dockside museum and 'This is Indian Land' water-tower graffiti.

Day visits include captivating audio tours, with prisoners and guards recalling life on 'the Rock,' while night tours are led by a park ranger; reserve tickets at least two weeks ahead. Ferries depart Pier 33 every half-hour from 9am to 3:55pm, plus 6:10pm and 6:45pm.

THINGS YOU NEED TO KNOW

☏ 415-981-7625; www.nps.gov/alcatraz, www.alcatrazcruises.com; adult/child day $26/16, night $33/19.50; ⏱ call center 8am-7pm

years, but no one rocks it quite like chef Corey Lee, who remixes local fine-dining staples and Pacific Rim flavors with a SoMa DJ's finesse.

🔪 **BAR JULES**   Californian $$
(☏ 415-621-5482; www.barjules.com; 609 Hayes St; mains $10-26; ⏱ 6-10pm Tue, 11:30am-3pm

& 6-10pm Wed-Sat, 11am-3pm Sun) Small and succulent is the credo at this corridor-sized neighborhood bistro, where the short daily menu packs a wallop of local flavor – think duck breast with cherries, almonds and arugula. Waits are a given, but so is unfussy, tasty food.

Financial District, Chinatown & North Beach

COTOGNA Italian $$
(📞415-775-8508; www.cotognasf.com; 470 Pacific Av; mains $14-24; 🕐noon-3pm & 7-10pm Mon-Sat; 🖊) No wonder chef-owner Michael Tusk won the 2011 James Beard Award: his rustic Italian pastas and toothsome pizzas magically balance a few pristine, local flavors.

CITY VIEW Chinese $
(📞415-398-2838; 662 Commercial St; small plates $3-5; 🕐11am-2:30pm Mon-Fri, from 10am Sat & Sun) Dim sum aficionados used to cramped quarters and surly service will be wowed by impeccable shrimp and leek dumplings, tender black-bean asparagus and crisp Peking duck, all served with a flourish in a spacious, sunny room.

The Marina

OFF THE GRID Food Trucks $
(www.offthegridsf.com; Fort Mason parking lot; dishes under $10; 🕐5-10pm Fri) Some 30 food trucks circle their wagons at SF's largest mobile-gourmet hootenanny (other nights/locations attract fewer than a dozen trucks; see website). Take your dinner to nearby docks for Golden Gate Bridge sunsets. Cash only.

The Mission

LA TAQUERÍA Mexican $
(📞415-285-7117; 2889 Mission St; burritos $6-8; 🕐11am-9pm Mon-Sat, to 8pm Sun) No debatable tofu, saffron rice, spinach tortillas or mango salsa here: just classic tomatillo or mesquite salsa, marinated, grilled meats and flavorful beans inside a flour tortilla – the optional housemade spicy pickles and sour cream are highly recommended.

COMMONWEALTH Californian $$
(📞415-355-1500; www.commonwealthsf.com; 2224 Mission St; small plates $5-16; 🕐5:30-10pm Tue-Thu & Sun, to 11pm Fri & Sat; 🖊) California's most imaginative farm-to-table dining isn't in some quaint barn, but the converted cinderblock Mission dive where chef Jason Fox serves crispy hen with toybox carrots cooked in hay (yes, hay), and sea urchin floating on a bed of farm egg and organic asparagus that looks like a tide pool and tastes like a dream.

A North Beach cafe

ORIEN HARVEY/LONELY PLANET IMAGES ©

DISCOVER CALIFORNIA SAN FRANCISCO

San Francisco for Children

Besides **Golden Gate Park** (p406), the **Exploratorium** (p405) and the **California Academy of Sciences** (p407), try these other kid-friendly favorites:

Children's Creativity Museum (☎415-820-3320; www.zeum.org; 221 4th St; admission $10; ⊙11am-5pm Tue-Sun) Technology that's too cool for school: robots, live-action video games, DIY music videos and 3D animation workshops.

Aquarium of the Bay (☎415-623-5300; www.aquariumofthebay.com; Pier 39; adult/child $17/8; ⊙9am-8pm summer, 10am-6pm winter) Glide through glass tubes underwater on conveyor belts as sharks circle overhead.

Fire Engine Tours (☎415-333-7077; www.fireenginetours.com; Beach St at the Cannery; adult/child $50/30; ⊙tours depart 1pm) Hot stuff: a 75-minute, open-air vintage fire-engine ride over Golden Gate Bridge.

The Castro

FRANCES   Californian $$
(☎415-621-3870; www.frances-sf.com; 3870 17th St; mains $14-27; ⊙5-10.30pm Tue-Sun) Daily menus showcase bright, seasonal flavors and luxurious textures: cloud-like sheep's-milk ricotta gnocchi with crunchy breadcrumbs and broccolini, grilled calamari with preserved Meyer lemon, and artisan Wine Country vino served by the ounce.

The Haight

🍃MAGNOLIA BREWPUB   Californian $$
(☎415-864-7468; www.magnoliapub.com; 1398 Haight St; mains $11-20; ⊙noon-midnight Mon-Thu, to 1am Fri, 10am-1am Sat, 10am-midnight Sun) Organic pub grub and homebrew samplers keep conversation flowing at communal tables, while grass-fed Prather Ranch burgers satisfy stoner appetites in side booths – it's like the Summer of Love is back, only with better food.

Berkeley

CHEZ PANISSE   American $$$
(☎restaurant 510-548-5525, cafe 510-548-5049; 1517 Shattuck Ave; restaurant mains $60-95, cafe mains $18-29; ⊙restaurant dinner Mon-Sat) Genuflect at the temple of Alice Waters: the birthplace of California cuisine remains at the pinnacle of Bay Area dining. Book one month ahead for its legendary prix-fixe

meals (no substitutions); or book upstairs at the less-expensive, à la carte cafe. It's located across the bay in Berkeley.

 **Drinking**

SMUGGLER'S COVE   Theme Bar
(www.smugglerscovesf.com; 650 Gough St; ⊙5pm-2am) Yo-ho-ho and a bottle of rum... or make that 200 at this Barbary Coast shipwreck of a tiki bar. With tasting flights and 70 historic cocktail recipes gleaned from rum-running around the world, you won't be dry-docked for long.

ZEITGEIST   Bar
(www.zeitgeistsf.com; 199 Valencia St; ⊙9am-2am) When temperatures rise, bikers and hipsters converge on Zeitgeist's huge outdoor beer garden for 40 brews on tap and late-night tamales.

TORONADO   Pub
(www.toronado.com; 547 Haight St) Glory hallelujah, beer-lovers: 50-plus microbrews, with hundreds more in bottles. Stumble next door to Rosamunde for sausages.

TOSCA CAFE   Cocktail Bar
(www.toscacafesf.com; 242 Columbus Ave; ⊙5pm-2am Tue-Sun) With red vinyl booths and a jukebox of opera and Sinatra, Tosca is classic North Beach.

⭐ Entertainment

Live Music

FILLMORE
Live Music

(www.thefillmore.com; 1805 Geary Blvd; tickets from $20) Hendrix, Zeppelin, Janis – they all played the Fillmore, where the 1250 capacity means you're close to the stage. Don't miss the psychedelic poster-art gallery upstairs.

YOSHI'S
Jazz

(www.yoshis.com; 1300 Fillmore St; tickets $12-50; ⊙most shows 8pm) San Francisco's definitive jazz club draws the world's top talent, and adjoins a pretty good sushi restaurant.

SLIM'S
Live Music

(☎415-255-0333; www.slims-sf.com; 333 11th St; tickets $11-28; ⊙5pm-2am) Guaranteed good times by Gogol Bordello, Tenacious D and AC/DShe (a hard-rocking female tribute band) fill the bill at this mid-sized club, where Prince and Elvis Costello have shown up to play sets unannounced.

CAFÉ DU NORD
Live Music

(www.cafedunord.com; 2170 Market St) The historic speakeasy in the basement of the Swedish-American Hall with glam-rock, afrobeats, retro-rockabilly and indie-record-release parties almost nightly.

Nightclubs

CAT CLUB
Club

(www.catclubsf.com; 1190 Folsom St; admission after 10pm $5; ⊙9pm-3am Tue-Sun) Thursday's '1984' is a euphoric bi/straight/gay party scene from a lost John Hughes movie; other nights vary from Saturday power pop to Bondage-a-Go-Go.

EL RIO
Club

(☎415-282-3325; www.elriosf.com; 3158 Mission St; admission $3-8; ⊙5pm-2am Mon-Thu, from 4pm Fri, from noon Sun) 'Salsa Sundays' are legendary: arrive at 3pm for lessons. Other nights: oyster happy hours, eclectic music and pan-sexual crowd flirting on the patio.

111 MINNA
Club

(www.111minnagallery.com; 111 Minna St) Street-wise art gallery by day, after-work lounge and club after 9pm, when '90s and '80s dance parties take the back room by storm.

Classical Music, Opera & Ballet

WAR MEMORIAL OPERA HOUSE
Opera, Ballet

(301 Van Ness Ave) Rivaling City Hall's grandeur is this 1932 opera house, home to **San Francisco Opera** (www.sfopera.com), whose season runs from June to December, and **San Francisco Ballet** (www.sfballet.org), performing January to May.

DAVIES SYMPHONY HALL
Classical Music

(☎415-864-6000; www.sfsymphony.org; 201 Van Ness Ave) Home of the nine-time Grammy-award-winning SF Symphony, conducted with verve by Michael Tilson Thomas. The season runs September to July.

Cinema

CASTRO THEATRE
Cinema

(www.thecastrotheatre.com; 429 Castro St; adult/child $10/7.50) The city's grandest movie place screens vintage, foreign, documentary and new films.

Sports

San Francisco Giants
Baseball

(www.sfgiants.com; AT&T Park; tickets $5-135) Watch and learn how the World Series is won – bushy beards, women's underwear and all.

San Francisco 49ers
Football

(☎415-656-4900; www.sf49ers.com; Candlestick Park) Head to this bayside stadium for NFL football, beer and garlic fries.

ℹ Information

San Francisco's Visitor Information Center (☎415-391-2000; www.onlyinsanfrancisco.com; lower level, Hallidie Plaza; ⊙9am-5pm Mon-Fri, to 3pm Sat & Sun)

Don't Miss Marin County

Majestic redwoods cling to coastal hills just across the Golden Gate Bridge in woodsy, wealthy, laid-back **Marin** (www.visitmarin.org).

The windswept, rugged **Marin Headlands** are laced with hiking trails, providing stunning views of San Francisco and the Golden Gate. To reach the **visitor center**, take the Alexander Ave exit from the Golden Gate Bridge, turn left under the freeway, and then turn right on Conzelman Rd and follow signs. Attractions include the **Point Bonita Lighthouse**, climbable Cold War–era bunkers and **Rodeo Beach**.

Or you can wander among an ancient stand of the world's tallest trees in 550-acre **Muir Woods National Monument** (above), 12 miles north of the Golden Gate. The easy 1-mile Main Trail Loop leads past 1000-year-old redwoods at Cathedral Grove and returns via Bohemian Grove. Come midweek to avoid crowds, otherwise arrive in the early morning or late afternoon. Take Hwy 101 to the Hwy 1 exit, and follow the signs.

THINGS YOU NEED TO KNOW

Marin Headlands Visitor Center (☎ 415-331-1540; www.nps.gov/goga/marin-headlands.htm; ⊙ 9:30am-4:30pm); Point Bonita Lighthouse (⊙ 12:30-3:30pm Sat-Mon); Muir Woods National Monument (☎ 415-388-2595; www.nps.gov/muwo; adult/child $5/free)

---

❶ Getting There & Away

AIR San Francisco International Airport (SFO; www.flysfo.com) is 14 miles south of downtown San Francisco off Hwy 101 and is accessible by Bay Area Rapid Transit (BART).

TRAIN Amtrak (☎ 800-872-7245; www.amtrakcalifornia.com) The *Coast Starlight*'s spectacular 35-hour train service runs from Los Angeles to Seattle, and stops in Oakland. Amtrak runs free shuttle buses to San Francisco's Ferry Building and CalTrain station.

ⓘ Getting Around

To/From San Francisco International Airport

BART (www.bart.gov; one way $8.10) Offers a fast, direct ride to downtown San Francisco.

Taxi To downtown San Francisco costs $35 to $50.

Public Transportation

MUNI (Municipal Transit Agency; www.sfmuni. com) Two cable-car lines leave from Powell and Market Sts; a third leaves from California and Markets Sts. Standard fare for buses or streetcars is $2; cable-car fare is $6.

Taxi

DeSoto Cab (☏415-970-1300)

Green Cab (☏415-626-4733; www.626green. com) Fuel-efficient hybrids; worker-owned collective.

Luxor (☏415-282-4141)

Yellow Cab (☏415-333-3333)

WINE COUNTRY

A patchwork of vineyards stretches from sunny inland Napa to chilly coastal Sonoma – America's premier wine-growing region. Napa has art-filled tasting rooms by big-name architects, with prices to match; in down-to-earth Sonoma, you'll drink in sheds and probably meet the vintner's dog. NB: there are three Sonomas – the town, the valley and the county.

Napa Valley

Some 230 wineries crowd 30-mile-long Napa Valley along three main routes. Main Hwy 29 is lined with blockbuster wineries; it jams on weekends. Parallel-running Silverado Trail moves faster; it's lined with boutique wineries, bizarre architecture and cult-hit cabs. Hwy 121 (aka Carneros Hwy) runs west toward Sonoma, with landmark wineries specializing in sparkling wines and pinot noir.

Traveling south to north, **Downtown Napa** – the valley's workaday hub – lacks rusticity, but has trendy restaurants, tasting rooms and mansions reinvented as B&Bs. Picky picnickers head to **Oxbow**

Wine tasting at a Sonoma Valley vineyard

Public Market; bargain hunters hit **Napa Valley Welcome Center** (707-260-0107; wwww.legendarynapavalley.com; 600 Main St; 9am-5pm) for spa deals, wine-tasting passes and winery maps.

Formerly a stagecoach stop, tiny **Yountville** – home of the famous French Laundry restaurant – has more Michelin-starred eateries per capita than anywhere else in America.

Folksy **Calistoga**, Napa's least-gentrified town, has hot-spring spas and mud-baths that use volcanic ash from adjacent Mt St Helena. To find spas, contact **Calistoga Visitors Center** (707-942-6333; www.calistogavisitors.com; 1133 Washington St; 9am-5pm).

 Sleeping & Eating

 MOUNTAIN HOME RANCH B&B, Resort **$$**
(707-942-6616; www.mountainhomeranch.com; 3400 Mountain Home Ranch Rd, Calistoga; r $109-119, cabins $69-144; @ 🛜 👪) Secluded, rustic 1913 guest ranch on 340 acres, with hiking, canoeing and farm animals.

 OXBOW PUBLIC MARKET Market **$**
(707-226-6529; www.oxbowpublicmarket.com; 610 & 644 1st St, Napa; 9am-7pm Mon-Sat, 10am-5pm Sun) Oxbow showcases sustainably produced artisanal foods by multiple vendors.

AD HOC American **$$$**
(707-944-2487; www.adhocrestaurant.com; 6476 Washington St, Yountville; 5-9pm Wed-Mon, 10:30am-2pm Sun brunch) Don't ask for a menu at Thomas Keller's most innovative restaurant since French Laundry: chef Dave Cruz dreams up his four-course, $48 market menu daily.

Sonoma Valley

More casual, less commercial than Napa, Sonoma Valley has 70 wineries around Hwy 12 – and unlike Napa, most welcome picnicking.

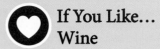

If You Like… Wine

If you like sipping the fine produce of Napa Valley (p413) and exploring picturesque countryside, don't miss these other great wine-loving retreats.

1 RUSSIAN RIVER VALLEY
More than 90 wineries dot the Russian River, Dry Creek and Alexander Valleys within a 30-mile radius of Healdsburg, where upscale eateries, wine-tasting rooms and stylish inns surround the Spanish-style plaza. For tasting passes and maps, hit the **Healdsburg Visitors Center** (www.healdsburg.org; 217 Healdsburg Ave).

2 SANTA YNEZ & SANTA MARIA VALLEYS
(www.sbcountywines.com) A scenic backcountry drive north of Santa Barbara follows Hwy 154, where you can go for the grape in the Santa Ynez and Santa Maria Valleys. For eco-conscious vineyard tours, check **Sustainable Vine** (805-698-3911; www.sustainablevine.com; all-day tour $125).

👁 Sights & Activities

SONOMA PLAZA Square
(Napa, Spain & 1st Sts, Sonoma) The state's largest town square looks stately with chic boutiques, historical buildings and stone **visitor center** (707-996-1090; www.sonomavalley.com; 453 1st St E; 9am-5pm), but it gets lively during summer evenings and **farmers markets** (9am-noon Fri, 5:30-8pm Tue Apr-Oct).

🛏 Sleeping & Eating

BELTANE RANCH Ranch **$$**
(707-996-6501; www.beltaneranch.com; 11775 Hwy 12; r incl breakfast $150-240; 🛜) Surrounded by pasturelands, Beltane's cheerful 1890s ranch house occupies 100 acres and has double porches lined with swinging chairs and white wicker and five guest rooms. No phones or TVs.

FIG CAFE & WINEBAR
Californian $$

(☎707-938-2130; www.thefigcafe.com; 13690 Arnold Dr, Glen Ellen; mains $15-20; ⊙10am-2:30pm Sat & Sun, 5:30-9pm daily) Sonoma's take on comfort food – organic salads, Sonoma duck cassoulet and free corkage on Sonoma wines – in a convivial room with vaulted wooden ceilings.

ℹ️ Getting There & Around

Wine Country begins 75 minutes north of San Francisco, via Hwy 101 or I-80.

Napa Valley Wine Train (☎707-253-2111; www.winetrain.com; per person from $89-189) offers cushy, touristy three-hour trips with an optional winery stop.

YOSEMITE NATIONAL PARK

There's a reason why everybody's heard of it: the granite-peak heights are dizzying, the mist from thunderous waterfalls drenching, the Technicolor wildflower meadows amazing, and the majestic, hulking silhouettes of El Capitan and Half Dome almost shocking against a crisp blue sky. It's a landscape of dreams, relentlessly surrounding us oh-so-small people on all sides. While staggering crowds can't be ignored, these rules will shake most of 'em:

● Avoid summer in the valley. Spring's best, especially when waterfalls gush in May. Autumn is blissfully peaceful, and snowy winter days can be magical, too.

● Park your car and leave it – simply by hiking a short distance up almost any trail, you'll lose the car-dependent majority of visitors.

● Get up early, or go for moonlit hikes and do some unforgettable stargazing.

👁️ Sights

Yosemite's entrance fee ($20 per car, $10 on bicycle, motorcycle or foot) is valid for seven days and includes a free map and helpful newspaper guide. The primary entrances are Arch Rock (Hwy 140), South Entrance (Hwy 41), Big Oak Flat (Hwy 120 west) and Tioga Pass (Hwy 120 east).

Yosemite Valley

From the ground up, this dramatic valley cut by the meandering Merced River is song-inspiring: rippling green meadow-grass; stately pines; cool, impassive pools reflecting looming granite monoliths and cascading, glacier-cold whitewater ribbons.

You can't ignore monumental **El Capitan** (7569ft), an El Dorado for rock climbers, while toothed **Half Dome** (8842ft) is Yosemite's spiritual

Half Dome, Yosemite National Park
GLENN VAN DER KNIJFF/LONELY PLANET IMAGES ©

Detour: Lake Tahoe

Shimmering in myriad blues and greens, Lake Tahoe is the nation's second-deepest lake. Driving around its spellbinding 72-mile scenic shoreline gives you quite a workout behind the wheel. The north shore is quiet and upscale; the west shore, rugged and old-timey; the east shore, undeveloped; and the south shore, tacky and busy with aging motels and flashy casinos. The horned peaks surrounding the lake, which straddles the California–Nevada state line, are four-seasons playgrounds.

Hwy 89 threads northwest along the thickly forested west shore to **Emerald Bay State Park** (www.parks.ca.gov; per car/campsites $8/35; ☉late May-Sep), where granite cliffs and pine trees frame a fjordlike inlet, truly sparkling green. A steep 1-mile trail leads down to **Vikingsholm Castle** (tours adult/child $5/3; ☉10:30am-4:30pm). From this 1920s Scandinavian-style mansion, the 4.5-mile **Rubicon Trail** ribbons north along the lakeshore past an old lighthouse and petite coves to **DL Bliss State Park** (www.parks.ca.gov; entry per car $8, campsites $35-45; ☉late May-Sep), offering sandy beaches. Further north, **Tahoma Meadows B&B Cottages** (☏530-525-1553; www.tahomameadows.com; 6821 W Lake Blvd, Tahoma; d incl breakfast $109-269) rents darling country cabins.

Tahoe gets packed in summer, on winter weekends and holidays, when reservations are essential.

---

centerpiece. The classic photo-op is up Hwy 41 at **Tunnel View**. Sweat it out and you'll get better views – sans crowds – from the **Inspiration Point Trail** (2.6 miles round-trip), starting near the tunnel. Early or late in the day, head up the 2-mile round-trip trail to **Mirror Lake** to catch the ever-shifting reflection of Half Dome in the still waters, full only in spring and early summer.

Spring snowmelt turns the valley's famous waterfalls into thunderous cataracts; most are reduced to a mere trickle by late summer. **Yosemite Falls** is North America's tallest, dropping 2425ft in three tiers. A wheelchair-accessible trail leads to the bottom of this cascade or, for solitude and different perspectives, you can trek the grueling switchback trail to the top (7.2 miles round-trip).

Glacier Point & Wawona

Rising 3200ft above the valley floor, dramatic **Glacier Point** (7214ft) practically puts you at eye level with Half Dome. It's about an hour's drive from Yosemite Valley up Glacier Point Rd (usually open late May to mid-November) off Hwy 41, or a strenuous hike along the **Four Mile Trail** (actually, 4.8 miles one way) or the less-crowded, waterfall-strewn **Panorama Trail** (8.5 miles one way). To avoid backtracking, reserve a seat on the hikers' shuttle bus.

Sleeping & Eating

Concessionaire **Delaware North Companies** (DNC; ☏801-559-4884; www.yosemitepark.com) has a monopoly on park lodging and eating establishments. Lodging reservations (available up to 366 days in advance) are essential from May to September. In summer, DNC sets up simple canvas-tent cabins at riverside **Housekeeping Camp** (cabins $93) in Yosemite Valley, busy **Tuolumne Meadows Lodge** (cabins $107) and serene **White Wolf Lodge** (cabins $99-120) off Tioga Rd. Tuolumne Meadows is about a 90-minute drive northeast of the valley, while White Wolf is an hour away.

YOSEMITE LODGE AT THE FALLS
Motel $$

(Yosemite Valley; r $191-218; @ 🛜 🏊) Spacious motel-style rooms have patios or balconies overlooking Yosemite Falls, meadows or the parking lot. Fork into grass-fed steaks, river trout and organic veggies at the lodge's Mountain Room (dinner mains $17 to $35), open nightly (no reservations).

WAWONA HOTEL
Historic Hotel $$

(Wawona; r without/with bath incl breakfast $147/217; 🛜 🏊) Filled with character, this Victorian-era throwback has wide porches, manicured lawns and a golf course. Half of the thin-walled rooms share baths. The romantic dining room with vintage details serves three meals a day (dinner mains $19 to $30). Wawona is about a 45-minute drive south of the valley.

ⓘ Information

Yosemite Valley Visitor Center (📞 209-372-0299; www.nps.gov/yose; Yosemite Village; 🕙9am-7:30pm, shorter hours in winter) Smaller visitor centers at Wawona, Tuolumne Meadows and Big Oak Flat are open seasonally.

ⓘ Getting Around

Free shuttle buses loop around Yosemite Valley and, in summer, the Tuolumne Meadows and Wawona areas.

Bike rentals (per hour/day $10/28) are available at Yosemite Lodge and Curry Village, both in the valley.

PACIFIC COAST HIGHWAY

No trip to California would be worth its salt without a jaunt along the surreally scenic Central Coast. Make your escape from those tangled, traffic-jammed freeways and cruise in the slow lane. Snaking for over 1000 miles along dizzying sea cliffs, California's legendary coastal highways connect the dots between star-powered Los Angeles, surfin' San Diego and bohemian San Francisco. In between, you'll uncover hidden beaches and surf breaks, rustic seafood shacks and wooden piers – perfect for catching sunsets over boundless Pacific horizons.

Big Sur coastline

DOUGLAS STEAKLEY/LONELY PLANET IMAGES ©

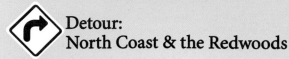

Detour:
North Coast & the Redwoods

The North Coast is a land of towering redwoods, hoppy microbrews and the ever-present crash of waves along the craggy shoreline. Hippies and finely cultivated gardens of marijuana have long lent this enclave its bohemian vibe.

Road-tripping in this part of California is best if you just keep driving: the winding coastal drive gets more rewarding with every gorgeous, white-knuckled mile of road. Tree huggers will want to stop off at these places:

○ **Standish-Hickey State Recreation Area** Nine miles of hiking trails in virgin and second-growth redwoods (look for the 225ft-tall Miles Standish tree).

○ **Richardson Grove State Park** 1400 acres of virgin redwoods; camp sites available.

○ **Humboldt Redwoods State Park** Home to three-quarters of the world's tallest 100 trees (rivaling those in Redwood National Park).

○ **Avenue of the Giants** A 32-mile, two-lane road parallel to Hwy 101. Don't miss the drive-through tree.

○ **Redwood National & State Parks** Contain almost half the remaining old-growth redwood forests in California.

Big Sur

Much ink has been spilled extolling the raw beauty and energy of this 100-mile stretch of craggy coastline shoehorned south of the Monterey Peninsula. When the sun goes down, the moon and stars provide the only illumination – if summer fog hasn't extinguished them. Lodging, food and gas are all scarce and pricey. Demand for rooms is high year-round, so book ahead. The free, info-packed newspaper *Big Sur Guide* (www.bigsurcalifornia.org) is available everywhere along the way. The $10 parking fee at Big Sur's state parks is valid for same-day entry to all.

Heading north up the coast, some 42 miles south of Big Sur, you'll pass Gorda, home of **Treebones Resort** (☎ 877-424-4787; www.treebonesresort.com; 71895 Hwy 1; d with shared bath incl breakfast $169-199; 🛜🏊), which offers back-to-nature clifftop yurts, some with ocean-view decks. Don't expect much privacy, though.

Three miles north, **Julia Pfeiffer Burns State Park** harbors California's only coastal waterfall, 80ft-high McWay Falls,

which is reached via a quarter-mile stroll. Two more miles north, a steep dirt trail descends from a hairpin turn on Hwy 1 to **Partington Cove**, a raw and breathtaking spot where crashing surf salts your skin – truly scenic, but swimming isn't safe.

Around 8 miles further north, the beatnik **Henry Miller Memorial Library** (☎ 831-667-2574; www.henrymiller.org; Hwy 1; ⏰ 11am-6pm Wed-Mon; @ 🛜) is the art and soul of Big Sur bohemia, with a jam-packed bookstore, live-music concerts and DJs, open-mic nights and outdoor film screenings. Opposite, food takes a backseat to dramatic ocean views at clifftop **Nepenthe** (☎ 831-667-2345; 48510 Hwy 1; mains $14-39; ⏰ 11:30am-10pm), meaning 'no sorrow.' Its Ambrosia burger is mighty famous.

Heading north, USFS rangers at **Big Sur Station** (☎ 831-667-2315; ⏰ 8am-4pm Wed-Sun Nov-Mar, daily Apr-Oct) can clue you in about hiking trail conditions and camping options. Across the road, turn onto obscurely marked Sycamore Canyon Rd, which drops two narrow, twisting miles to crescent-shaped **Pfeiffer Beach**

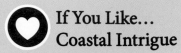

If You Like...
Coastal Intrigue

If you like the stunning ocean scenery at Big Sur (p419), don't miss these other great waterfront charmers.

1 **SANTA BARBARA**
Life is certainly sweet in this coastal Shangri-La, where the air is redolent with citrus and jasmine, bougainvillea drapes whitewashed buildings with Spanish-esque red-tiled roofs, and it's all cradled by pearly beaches. State St, the main drag, abounds with bars, cafes, theaters and boutique shops.

2 **SANTA CRUZ**
SoCal beach culture meets NorCal counterculture in Santa Cruz. The UCSC student population makes this old-school, radical town youthful, hip and lefty-political. It's also a surfer's paradise.

3 **MENDOCINO**
Some 160 miles north of San Francisco, Mendocino is a salt-washed historical gem perched on a gorgeous headland. A headland walk passes berry bramble and wildflowers, where cypress trees stand guard over dizzying cliffs. Nature's power is evident everywhere, from driftwood-littered fields and cave tunnels to the raging surf.

(per car $5; ⏱9am-8pm), with a towering offshore sea arch and strong currents too dangerous for swimming.

Most of Big Sur's commercial activity is concentrated along the next 2 miles, including a post office, shops, gas stations, private campgrounds, motels and restaurants. At **Glen Oaks Motel** (☎831-667-2105; www.glenoaksbigsur.com; Hwy 1; d $175-350; 📶), a chic, redesigned 1950s redwood-and-adobe motor lodge, snug rooms and woodsy cabins all have gas fireplaces.

Heading north, many visitors overlook **Andrew Molera State Park**, a trail-laced pastiche of grassy meadows, waterfalls, ocean bluffs, rugged beaches and wildlife watching. Learn all about endangered California condors at the park's **Discovery Center** (☎831-620-0702; www.ventanaws.org;

admission free; ⏱9am-4pm Fri-Sun late May–mid-Sep) and the on-site bird-banding lab.

Six miles before the famous Bixby Bridge, take a tour of 1889 **Point Sur Lightstation** (☎831-625-4419; www.pointsur.org; tour adult/child from $10/5).

Monterey

Working-class Monterey is all about the sea. Today it lures visitors with a top-notch aquarium that's a veritable temple to Monterey Bay's underwater universe. A National Marine Sanctuary since 1992, the bay begs for exploration by kayak, boat, scuba or snorkel. Meanwhile, downtown's historic quarter preserves California's Spanish and Mexican roots.

Give yourself at least half a day for the **Monterey Bay Aquarium** (☎831-648-4800; tickets 866-963-9645; www.montereybayaquarium.org; 886 Cannery Row; adult/child $30/20; ⏱10am-5pm Sep-May, 9:30am-6pm Mon-Fri, to 8pm Sat & Sun Jun-Aug), where you can see sharks and sardines play hide-and-seek in kelp forests, observe the antics of frisky otters and meditate upon ethereal jellyfish.

Downtown, Old Monterey has a cluster of lovingly restored 19th-century brick-and-adobe buildings, including novelist Robert Louis Stevenson's one-time boarding house and the Cooper-Molera Adobe, a sea captain's house. Pick up walking-tour maps and check schedules at the **Pacific House Museum** (☎831-649-7118; 20 Custom House Plaza; ⏱10am-4:30pm), which has in-depth period exhibits on California's multinational history.

The **Asilomar Conference Grounds** (☎831-372-8016; www.visitasilomar.com; 800 Asilomar Ave, Pacific Grove; r incl breakfast $115-175; 📶🏊🚶) has buildings designed by architect Julia Morgan, of Hearst Castle fame. Historic rooms are small and thin-walled, but charming nonetheless.

Passionfish (☎831-655-3311; www.passionfish.net; 701 Light house Ave, Pacific Grove; mains $17-26; ⏱5-10pm) is a chef-owned seafood restaurant where the sustainable fish is dock-fresh, every preparation fully flavored and the wine list more than affordable.

The Best of the Rest

Hawaii (p422)
An island getaway with idyllic beaches, mighty volcanoes and magical sunsets.

Alaska (p426)
Rugged and beautiful with soaring peaks, massive glaciers and awe-inspiring wildlife.

The Rocky Mountains (p429)
Grizzlies, geysers, alpine meadows, snow-covered mountains and farm-fresh food.

Texas (p433)
Historic sites, world-class barbecue and one of America's finest live music scenes.

Philadelphia (p436)
Colonial history, heritage buildings, excellent museums and a burgeoning dining scene.

Niagara Falls (p438)
Dramatic views of thundering waterfalls dividing New York from Canada.

Mount Rushmore (p440)
Four-faced icon of America's great presidents gazing proudly over South Dakota.

Above: Bear cubs, Denali National Park & Preserve (p427);
Below: Castle Geyser, Yellowstone National Park (p431)

Hawaii

It's true: this string of emerald islands in the cobalt-blue Pacific, more than 2000 miles from any continent, takes work to get to. But it's so worth it. Hawaii is diving coral-reef cities in the morning and listening to slack-key guitar at sunset. It's slurping chin-dripping passion fruit with hibiscus flowers in your hair. It's Pacific Rim cuisine, fiery volcanoes and breaching whales. The islands are an expression of nature at its most divine, blessed with a multicultural society rooted in Polynesia, Asia, America and even Europe.

O'ahu

O'ahu is the *ali'i* (chief) of Hawaii's main islands – so much so that others are referred to as 'Neighbor Islands.' O'ahu is the center of Hawaii's government, commerce and culture, while Waikiki's beaches gave birth to the whole tiki-craze Hawaii fantasia. If you want to take the measure of Hawaii's diversity, O'ahu offers the full buffet in one tidy package: in the blink of an eye you can go from crowded metropolis to turquoise bays teeming with sea life – and surfers.

Honolulu & Waikiki

Among its many museums and cultural offerings, Honolulu has the USA's only royal palace. Saunter over to Waikiki Beach to lounge on the sand, play in the water and hear Hawaiian music and watch hula dancers sway after sunset.

◉ Sights & Activities

Immediately north of downtown Honolulu, **Chinatown** is an intriguing quarter that lends itself to exploring.

'IOLANI PALACE　　Historic Building
(☏808-538-1471, tour reservations 808-522-0832/0823; www.iolanipalace.org; 364 S King St; adult/child 5-12yr from $13/6; ◷9am-4pm Mon-Sat) In the heart of downtown Honolulu, this historical site where the monarchy was overthrown offers a unique glimpse into the Kingdom of Hawai'i's late-19th-century history.

HIGHLIGHTS

❶ Haleakalā National Park (p425) Catching dawn over Maui's 'house of the rising sun'.

❷ Hanauma Bay (p423) Snorkeling with tropical fish in stunning O'ahu.

❸ Road to Hana (p425) Driving Maui's twisting seaside highway past jungle valleys and waterfalls.

❹ Waikiki (p423) Frolicking in the waves and strolling the powdery sands.

Waikiki Beach, O'ahu
ANN CECIL/LONELY PLANET IMAGES ©

BISHOP MUSEUM　　　　Museum
(808-847-3511; www.bishopmuseum.org;
1525 Bernice St; adult/child 4-12yr $18/15;
9am-5pm Wed-Mon;) Considered the
world's finest Polynesian anthropological
museum, impressive cultural displays
here include the regal Hawaiian Hall.

BEACHES　　　　Beaches
It's all about looooong **Waikiki Beach**.
Catamarans and outrigger canoes offering rides pull right up onto the sand,
while concession stands rent surfboards,
kayaks and windsurfing gear and offer
lessons.

Sleeping & Eating

HOTEL RENEW　　Boutique Hotel **$$**
(808-687-7700, 888-485-7639; www.hotel
renew.com; 129 Pa'oakalani Ave; r incl breakfast
$150-225; P ✳ @ 🤶) Located just a half-
block from the beach, this ecoconscious,
gay-friendly boutique hotel will satisfy
sophisticated urbanites nursing romantic
island dreams with its stylish, design-
savvy rooms, attentive staff and lots of
little niceties.

ROY'S—WAIKIKI BEACH　　Fusion **$$$**
(808-923-7697; www.roysrestaurant.com; 226
Lewers St; mains $28-45; 11am-10pm) Ground-
breaking Hawaii chef Roy Yamaguchi
doesn't actually cook here, but his signature *misoyaki* butterfish, blackened 'ahi
(tuna), macnut-encrusted mahimahi and
deconstructed sushi rolls are always on the
menu. Reservations essential.

Diamond Head & Southeast O'ahu

O'ahu's glamorous southeast coast
abounds in dramatic scenery and offers
plenty of activities. For windy panoramas,
make the 0.8-mile climb up **Diamond
Head** (www.hawaiistateparks.org; off Diamond
Head Rd; pedestrian/car $1/5; 6am-6pm, last
trail entry 4:30pm), the 760ft extinct volcano
crater visible from Waikiki Beach.

The best place on O'ahu to go eyeball
to eyeball with tropical fish is at **Hanauma
Bay Nature Preserve** (www.honolulu.gov/
parks/facility/hanaumabay; Hwy 72, Hawai'i
Kai; adult/child under 13yr $7.50/free; 6am-
7pm Wed-Mon Apr-Oct, to 6pm rest of yr;),
a gorgeous turquoise bathtub set in a
rugged volcanic ring. You can rent snorkel
gear on-site. Parking costs $1; when the

Hanauma Bay Nature Preserve, O'ahu

lot fills, often by mid-morning, visitors arriving by car will be turned away.

Hale'iwa & North Shore

O'ahu's North Shore is legendary for the massive, 30ft winter swells that thunder against its beaches. The gateway to the North Shore, **Hale'iwa** is the region's only real town – along its main road you'll find a funky surf museum, shops selling surf gear and bikinis, and rusty pickup trucks with surfboards tied to the roof. **Hale'iwa Ali'i Beach Park**, right in town, gets towering swells.

The North Shore's most popular beach, **Waimea Bay Beach Park**, flaunts a dual personality. In summer the water can be as calm as a lake and ideal for swimming and snorkeling; in winter it rips with the island's highest waves.

Team Real Estate (☎808-637-3507; www.teamrealestate.com; 1-/2-/3-bedroom apt from $100/150/200) rents everything from studio apartments to beachfront luxury homes, along the North Shore; book well in advance.

 Getting There & Around

Honolulu International Airport (HNL; http://hawaii.gov/hnl) is a major Pacific air hub. Fares from California start at around $400.

Roberts Hawaii (☎808-441-7800; www.robertshawaii.com) runs 24-hour airport shuttles to/from Waikiki (one way/round-trip $9/15).

Maui

According to some, you can't have it all. Perhaps those folks haven't been to Maui, which consistently lands atop travel-magazine reader polls as one of the world's most romantic islands. And why not? With its sandy beaches, deluxe resorts, gourmet cuisine, fantastic luau and world-class windsurfing, whale-watching, snorkeling, diving and hiking, it leaves most people a little more in love than when they arrived.

Lahaina & West Maui

For the megahotel and resort experience, bunk down in West Maui, with its prime sunset beaches. For historical atmos-phere, entertainment and dining out, make time for Lahaina, a 19th-century whaling town rich in well-preserved period architecture.

 Sights & Activities

The focal point of Lahaina is its bustling small-boat harbor, backed by the historic **Pioneer Inn** and Banyan Tree Sq, the latter home to the largest **banyan tree** in the US. The main tourist drag is oceanside Front St, lined with shops, galleries and restaurants.

As for those world-famous beaches, head north and keep going: between Ka'anapali and Kapalua, one impossible perfect strand follows another. Three top-ranked gems are **Kahekili Beach Park, Kapalua Beach** and **DT Fleming Beach Park**.

Sleeping & Eating

PLANTATION INN   Boutique Hotel $$$
(☎808-667-92255; www.theplantationinn.com; 174 Lahainaluna Rd; r/ste incl breakfast from $159/239; ❄️🛜⛵) Forget cookie-cutter resorts – if you want an authentic taste of Old Hawaii, book a romantic (if small) room at this genteel oasis, furnished with antiques and Hawaiian quilts on four-poster beds.

NAPILI SURF   Apartments $$
(☎808-669-8002, 888-627-4547; www.napilisurf.com; 50 Napili Pl; studio/1BR condo from $125/250; ⛵🛜) On a curving bay perfectly poised between Ka'anapali and Kapalua, staying at this low-slung oceanfront complex feels like staying with *ohana* (family and friends), especially during Wednesday night mai-tai parties. No credit cards.

MALA OCEAN TAVERN   Seafood, Hawaiian $$$
(☎808-667-9394; www.malaoceantavern.com; 1307 Front St; dinner mains $23-39; ⏱11am-9:30pm Mon-Fri, 9am-9:30pm Sat, 9am-9pm Sun) Looking for Lahaina's best waterfront fine dining? Stop searching. Mala features nouveau Hawaii cuisine using organic, farm-fresh ingredients and a bounty of just-caught seafood.

Scenic Drive: Road to Hana

One of Hawaii's most spectacular scenic drives, the **Hana Highway** (Hwy 360) winds its way past jungle valleys and back out above a rugged coastline. The road is a real cliff-hugger, with 54 one-lane bridges, roadside waterfalls and head-spinning views. Gas up and buy snacks and drinks in Pa'ia before starting out.

Swimming holes, heart-stopping vistas and awesome hikes call out almost nonstop. Detour to explore the ancient coastal trails and black-sand beach at **Wai'anapanapa State Park**, offering basic tent camping ($18) and cabins ($90); for overnight reservations (required), contact the **Division of State Parks** (📞808-984-8109; www.hawaiistateparks.org).

⭐ Entertainment

Around sunset, catch a free torch-lighting and cliff-diving ceremony at Pu'u Keka'a (Black Rock), at the north end of Ka'anapali Beach.

OLD LAHAINA LU'AU Luau
(📞808-667-1998; www.oldlahainaluau.com; 1251 Front St; adult/child 2-12yr $95/65; ⏱5:45-8:45pm; 🚼) For a night to remember, this beachside luau is unsurpassed for its authenticity and all-around aloha – the hula is first-rate and the feast darn good. Book far ahead.

Haleakalā National Park

No trip to Maui is complete without visiting this sublime **national park** (www.nps.gov/hale; 3-day entry pass per car $10), containing East Maui's mighty volcano. From the towering volcano's rim near the summit, there are dramatic views of a lunarlike surface and multicolored cinder cones. For an unforgettable (and chilly) experience, arrive in time for sunrise – an event Mark Twain called the 'sublimest spectacle' he'd ever seen.

ⓘ Getting There & Around

Most visitors arrive on US mainland or interisland flights at Kahului International Airport (OGG; http://hawaii.gov/ogg).

From the airport, bio-diesel Speedi Shuttle (📞877-242-5777; www.speedishuttle.com) charges $35 to Kihei, $50 to Lahaina.

The Seven Sacred Pools,
Haleakalā National Park, Maui
JOHN ELK III/LONELY PLANET IMAGES ©

Alaska

HIGHLIGHTS

1 **Denali National Park & Preserve (p427)** Viewing wildlife and blazing your own trails off the Park Road.

2 **Anchorage (p426)** Exploring culture-rich museums and hiking scenic trails outside of town.

3 **River Rafting (p428)** Taking in the stunning scenery on an adrenaline-charged white-water trip in Denali.

Ski-plane in front of Mt Foraker, Denali National Park & Preserve
GRANT DIXON/LONELY PLANET IMAGES ©

Big, beautiful and wildly bountiful. Far away, rurally isolated and very expensive. Alaska is a traveler's dilemma. No one can deny there are few places in the world with such grandeur and breathtaking beauty.

Anchorage

Anchorage offers the comforts of a large US city but is only a 30-minute drive from the Alaskan wilderness.

Sights & Activities

ANCHORAGE MUSEUM   Museum
(www.anchoragemuseum.org; 625 C Street; adult/child $12/7; ☺9am-6pm; 👬) Spend an afternoon viewing paintings by Alaskan masters such as Sydney Laurence on the 1st floor and learning Alaska's fascinating history on the 2nd.

ALASKA NATIVE HERITAGE CENTER   Cultural Building
(www.alaskanative.net; 8800 Heritage Center Dr; adult/child $25/17; ☺9am-5pm) This cultural center, spread over 26 acres, has studios with artists carving baleen or sewing skin-boats, a small lake and five replica villages.

FLATTOP MOUNTAIN   Hiking
A three- to five-hour, 3.4-mile round-trip of Alaska's most-climbed peak starts from a trailhead on the outskirts of Anchorage. Maps are available at the **Alaska Public Lands Information Center** (www.alaska centers.gov); the **Flattop Mountain Shuttle** (☎907-279-5293; www.hike-anchor age-alaska.com; round-trip adult/child $22/15) will run you to the trailhead.

TONY KNOWLES COASTAL TRAIL   Hiking
Beginning at the west end of 2nd Ave on the other side of the creek from Flattop Mountain trail, this 11-mile trail is the most scenic of the city's 122 miles of paved path.

Tours

Rust's Flying Service   Scenic Flight
(☎907-243-1595; www.flyrusts.com; 4525 Enstrom Circle) Has 30-minute tours ($100), a

Wildlife Watching

Because hunting has never been allowed in the park, professional photographers refer to animals in Denali as 'approachable wildlife.' That means bear, moose, Dall sheep and caribou aren't as skittish here as in other regions of the state. For this reason, and because Park Rd was built to maximize the chances of seeing wildlife by traversing high open ground, the national park is an excellent place to view a variety of animals.

On board the park shuttle buses, your fellow passengers will be armed with binoculars and cameras to help scour the terrain for animals, most of which are so accustomed to the rambling buses that they rarely run and hide. When someone spots something and yells, 'Stop!' the driver will pull over for viewing and picture taking. The best wildlife watching is on the first morning bus.

three hour flight to view Mt McKinley in Denali National Park ($375) and a 1½-hour tour of Knik Glacier ($225).

 ## Sleeping & Eating

COPPER WHALE INN   Inn $$$
(☎ 907-258-7999; www.copperwhale.com; W 5th Ave & L St; r $185-220; @ 🛜) An ideal downtown location, recently remodeled rooms and a bright and elegant interior make this gay-friendly inn one of the best top-end places in Anchorage. Many rooms and the breakfast lounge give way to views of Cook Inlet.

SNOW CITY CAFÉ   Cafe $$
(www.snowcitycafe.com; 1034 W 4th Ave; breakfast $7-15; lunch $9-13; ⏱7am-3pm Mon-Fri, to 4pm Sat & Sun; 🛜🍽) This hip and busy cafe serves up healthy all-day breakfast and lunch grub, with vegan and gluten-free options on offer as well. The walls are adorned with local art that changes monthly.

 ## Getting There & Away

The vast majority of visitors to Alaska fly into **Ted Stevens Anchorage International Airport** (ANC; www.dot.state.ak.us/anc).

Denali National Park & Preserve

For many travelers, Denali National Park & Preserve is the beginning and end of their Alaskan adventure, and why not? Here is probably your best chance in the Interior (if not in the entire state) to see a grizzly bear, moose or caribou, and maybe even a fox or wolf. And unlike most wilderness areas in the country, you don't have to be a backpacker to view this wildlife. The window of the park bus will do just fine for a close look at these magnificent creatures roaming free in their natural habitat.

At the center of it all is the icy behemoth of **Mt McKinley** (20,320ft), known to most Alaskans as Denali and to native Athabascans as the Great One. This is North America's highest peak, and rightly celebrated as an icon of all that is awesome and wild in the state.

There's only one road through the park: the 92-mile, unpaved Park Rd, which is closed to private vehicles after Mile 14. The park entrance area, where most visitors congregate, lies 1.5 miles up Park Rd. It's here you'll find the park headquarters, visitor center and main campground, as well as the Wilderness Access Center (WAC), where you pay the park entrance fee and arrange shuttle bus bookings to take you further into the park. If you're not booking a shuttle bus ticket or paying for a campground, pay your entrance fee at the visitor center.

There are few places to stay within the park, excluding campgrounds, and only one restaurant. The majority of visitors base themselves in the nearby communities of Canyon, McKinley Village, Carlo Creek and Healy.

 Tours

DENALI AIR SCENIC FLIGHTS Scenic Flights
(907-683-2261; www.denaliair.com; airstrip Mile 229.5 George Parks Hwy) Charges $250 to $350 for narrated flights of about an hour around the mountain. Flights leave from the company's airstrip.

DENALI OUTDOOR CENTER Rafting
(907-683-1925; www.denalioutdoorcenter. com; Mile 238.9 George Parks Hwy) Considered one of the finest rafting outfits, with good equipment, a 'safety first' philosophy and friendly guides.

 **Sleeping**

CAMP DENALI Lodge $$$
(907-683-2290; www.campdenali.com; s/d cabins without bath for 3 nights $1645/3090) Think of it as luxury camping, with gourmet meals, guided hikes, free bicycle and canoe rentals, killer views of the mountain, and staff so devoted to Denali that you'll come away feeling like the beneficiary of a precious gift. Located at the end of the 92-mile Park Rd, near Wonder Lake. Minimum stay is three nights.

CROW'S NEST Lodge $$$
(907-683-2723, 888-917-8130; www.denali crowsnest.com; Mile 238.5 George Parks Hwy; cabins $202;) Rustic but proud might describe the feel of the Nest's rooms, arranged in terraced rows that afford better and better views the higher up you go.

① Information

Denali Visitor Center (www.nps.gov/dena; Mile 1.5 Park Rd; ⊙8am-6pm). Park entrance fee is $10 per person, good for seven days. Vehicles are an extra $20.

① Getting There & Around

The most enjoyable way to travel between Anchorage and the park is aboard the Alaska Railroad (907-265-2494; www.alaskarailroad.com). Inside the park, shuttle buses ferry wildlife watchers and day hikers. Costs range from $27 to $50 for one-way fares and from $67 to $159 for narrated tours. Buses depart from the Wilderness Access Center.

Caribou antlers on the tundra, Denali National Park & Preserve
MARK NEWMAN/LONELY PLANET IMAGES ©

The Rocky Mountains

The high backbone of the lower 48, the Rockies is nature on steroids, with rows of snowcapped peaks, rugged canyons and wild rivers running buckshot all over Western states. With its beauty and vitality, it's no wonder that a hundred years ago ailing patients came here with last-ditch hopes to be cured. The Rocky Mountains' healing powers persist, whether tranquility or adrenaline is the balm you're after. Locals love a good mud-spattered adventure and, with plenty of climbing, skiing and white-water paddling, it's easy to join in.

Denver

Spirited, urbane and self-aware, Denver is the West's cosmopolitan capital. The gleaming skyscrapers of Denver's Downtown and historic LoDo districts sit packed with breweries and the best culinary scene between Chicago and California.

HIGHLIGHTS

1 **Denver (p429)** Window-shopping along 16th street, followed by dinner in one of the city's culinary gems.

2 **Rocky Mountain National Park (p431)** Taking in the sweeping views from a soaring mountain peak.

3 **Yellowstone National Park (p431)** Seeing geysers, alpine scenery and an awesome variety of wildlife.

Dancers by Jonathan Borofsky, downtown Denver
RICHARD CUMMINS/LONELY PLANET IMAGES ©

 **Sights & Activities**

16TH STREET MALL & LODO   Neighborhood
The **16th Street Mall**, a pedestrian-only strip of downtown, is lined with shops, restaurants and bars. The funkier **LoDo**, around Larimer Sq, is the best place to have a drink or browse the boutiques.

DENVER ART MUSEUM   Museum
(720-865-5000; www.denverartmuseum.org; 100 W 14th Ave; adult/student $13/10; 1st Sat of month free; 10am-5pm Tue-Thu, Sat & Sun, to 8pm Fri) The DAM is home to one of the largest Native American art collections in the US and puts on special avant-garde multimedia exhibits.

 **Sleeping**

QUEEN ANNE BED & BREAKFAST INN   B&B $$
(303-296-6666; www.queenannebnb.com; 2147 Tremont Pl; r incl breakfast $135-215; P ❄ 🛜) Earthy, cool and modern, this outstanding B&B is also cutting-edge sustainable.

HOTEL MONACO
Boutique Hotel **$$$**

(☎303-296-1717; www.monaco-denver.com; 1717 Champa St; r from $199; P ❄ @ 🛜) This ultrastylish boutique joint is a favorite with the celebrity set. Modern rooms blend French and art deco – think bold colors and fabulous European-style feather beds.

CAPITOL HILL MANSION B&B
B&B **$$**

(☎303-839-5221; www.capitolhillmansion.com; 1207 Pennsylvania St; r incl breakfast $119-219; P ❄ @ 🛜) Stained-glass windows, original 1890s woodwork and turrets make this delightful, gay- and family-friendly Romanesque mansion a special place to stay.

Eating & Drinking

STEUBEN'S FOOD SERVICE
American **$$**

(☎303-803-1001; www.steubens.com; 523 E 17th Ave; mains $8-21; ⏰11am-11pm Sun-Thu, to midnight Fri & Sat; 🚼) Although styled as a mid-century drive-in, the upscale treatment of comfort food (mac 'n' cheese, fried chicken, lobster rolls) and the solar-powered kitchen demonstrate Steuben's contemporary smarts.

LOLA
Mexican **$**

(☎720-570-8686; www.loladenver.com; 1575 Boulder St; mains $4-12; ⏰5pm-close Mon-Fri, 10am-2pm & 2:30-5pm Sat & Sun) Bringing costal Mexican to a landlocked town, LoLa pleases with fresh, smoky, chili-infused fare, best paired with a fantastic cocktail – try the hibiscus tea with citrus-infused tequila.

GREAT DIVIDE BREWING COMPANY
Brewpub

(www.greatdivide.com; 2201 Arapahoe St; ⏰2-8pm Mon-Tue, to 10pm Wed-Sat) An excellent local brewery focused on crafting exquisite beer. Belly up to the bar and try the spectrum of seasonal brews.

🛈 Getting There & Away

AIR Denver International Airport, 24 miles east of downtown, has numerous flights. An hourly SkyRide service connects the airport with downtown Denver ($9 to $13, one hour).

TRAIN Amtrak (www.amtrak.com) runs the *California Zephyr* service daily between Chicago and San Francisco via Denver. Trains arrive and depart from a temporary station (1800 21st St) behind Coors Field until light-rail renovations at Union Station finish in 2014.

Maroon Lake, Rocky Mountain National Park

GREG GAWLOWSKI/LONELY PLANET IMAGES ©

Rocky Mountain National Park

Rocky Mountain National Park showcases classic alpine scenery, with wildflower meadows and serene mountain lakes set under snowcapped peaks. Elk are the park's signature mammal – you will even see them grazing hotel lawns – but also keep an eye out for bighorn sheep, moose, marmots and black bears.

 Activities

TRAILS
Hiking

The bustling **Bear Lake Trailhead** offers easy hikes to several lakes and beyond. Another busy area is **Glacier Gorge Junction Trailhead**.

Forested Fern Lake, 4 miles from the **Moraine Park Trailhead**, is dominated by craggy Notchtop Peak. You can complete a loop to the Bear Lake shuttle stop in about 8.5 miles for a rewarding day hike. The strenuous **Flattop Mountain Trail** is the only cross-park trail, linking Bear Creek on the east side with either **Tonahutu Creek Trail** or the **North Inlet Trail** on the west side.

Trail Ridge Rd crosses the **Continental Divide** at Milner Pass (10,759ft), where trails head 4 miles (and up 2000ft!) southeast to Mt Ida for fantastic views.

 Sleeping & Eating

The following options are in nearby Estes Park.

STANLEY HOTEL
Hotel **$$$**

(☎970-586-3371; www.stanleyhotel.com; 333 Wonderview Ave; r from $199; P 🗐 🏊 ♿) The inspiration for Stephen King's famous novel *The Shining*, this white Georgian Colonial Revival is the grand dame of Rocky Mountain resort hotels.

YMCA OF THE ROCKIES – ESTES PARK CENTER
Resort **$$**

(☎970-586-3341; www.ymcarockies.org; 2515 Tunnel Rd; r & d/cabins from $109/129; P ❄ 🗐 ♿) This very kid-friendly resort sits in a serene and ultra-pristine location in the mountains just outside town. The 860-acre plot is home to cabins and motel rooms, along with lots of wide-open spaces dotted with forests and fields of wildflowers.

ED'S CANTINA & GRILL
Mexican **$$**

(☎970-586-2919; www.edscantina.com; 390 E Elkhorn Ave; mains $9-15; ⊙11am-late daily, from 8am Sat & Sun) With an outdoor patio right on the river, Ed's is a great place to kick back with a margarita and one of the daily $3 blue-plate specials (think fried, rolled tortillas with shredded pork and guacamole).

ℹ Information

Entry to the park (vehicles $20, hikers and cyclists $10) is valid for seven days.

ℹ Getting There & Around

There are two entrance stations on the east side, Fall River (US 34) and Beaver Meadows (US 36). The Grand Lake Station (also US 34) is the only entry on the west side.

The majority of visitors enter the park in their own cars, using the long and winding Trail Ridge Rd (US 34) to cross the Continental Divide. In summer a free shuttle bus operates from the Estes Park Visitor Center multiple times daily, bringing hikers to a park-and-ride location where you can pick up other shuttles.

Yellowstone National Park

They grow their critters and geysers big up in Yellowstone, America's first national park and Wyoming's flagship attraction. From shaggy grizzlies to oversized bison and magnificent packs of wolves, this park boasts the lower 48's most enigmatic concentration of wildlife. Throw in half the world's geysers, the country's largest high-altitude lake and a plethora of blue-ribbon rivers and waterfalls, all sitting pretty atop a giant supervolcano, and you'll quickly realize you've stumbled across one of Mother Nature's most fabulous creations.

Sights & Activities

Yellowstone is split into five distinct regions, each with unique attractions. All the visitor centers have information desks staffed by park rangers, who can help you tailor a hike to your tastes, from great photo spots to best chance of spotting a bear.

GEYSER COUNTRY   Geysers, Hiking
With the densest collection of geothermal features in the park, Upper Geyser Basin contains 180 of the park's 250-odd geysers. The most famous is **Old Faithful**, which spews from 3700 to 8400 gallons of water 100ft to 180ft into the air every 1½ hours or so. For an easy walk, check out the predicted eruption times at the brand new visitor center and then follow the easy boardwalk trail around the Upper Geyser Loop.

MAMMOTH COUNTRY   Springs, Hiking
Known for the geothermal terraces and elk herds of historic **Mammoth** and the hot springs of **Norris Geyser Basin**, Mammoth Country is North America's most volatile and oldest-known continuously active thermal area. The peaks of the Gallatin Range rise to the northwest, towering above the area's lakes, creeks and numerous hiking trails.

ROOSEVELT COUNTRY   Wildlife, Hiking
Fossil forests, the commanding **Lamar River Valley** and its tributary trout streams, **Tower Falls** and the Absaroka Mountains' craggy peaks are the highlights of Roosevelt Country – the park's most remote, scenic and undeveloped region.

CANYON COUNTRY   Viewpoints, Hiking
A series of scenic overlooks linked by hiking trails highlight the colorful beauty and grandeur of the Grand Canyon of the Yellowstone and its impressive **Lower Falls**.

LAKE COUNTRY   Lakes, Boating
Yellowstone Lake, the centerpiece of Lake Country and one of the world's largest alpine lakes, is a watery wilderness lined with volcanic beaches and best explored by boat or sea kayak.

Sleeping

Reservations are essential in summer. Contact the park concessionaire **Xanterra** (☎ 307-344-7311; www.yellowstone nationalparklodges.com) to reserve a spot at its campsites, cabins or lodges.

OLD FAITHFUL INN   Hotel **$$**
(Geyser Country; d without bath $96, with bath $126-236) Built right next to the signature geyser, it's little surprise Old Faithful is the most requested lodging in the park. There's a good restaurant here.

LAKE YELLOWSTONE HOTEL   Hotel **$$**
(Lake Country; cabins $130, r $149-223) Oozing grand 1920s Western ambience, this romantic, historic hotel is a classy option. It offers big picture windows with lake views, lots of natural light and a live string quartet serenading in the background. The dining room is the best in the park.

Information

Park entrance permits (hiker/vehicle $12/25) are valid for seven days. Summer-only visitor centers are evenly spaced every 20 to 30 miles along Grand Loop Rd.

Albright Visitors Center (☎ 307-344-2263; www.nps.gov/yell; Mammoth; ☺8am-7pm Jun-Sep, 9am-5pm Oct-May) Serves as park headquarters. The park website is a fantastic resource.

Getting There & Away

The airport (WYS) in West Yellowstone, MT, is usually open June to September. It's often more affordable to fly into Billings, Montana (170 miles), Salt Lake City, Utah (390 miles), or Denver, Colorado (563 miles; p429), then rent a car.

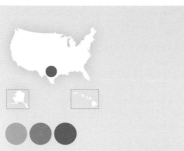

Texas

Cue the theme music, and make it something epic: Texas is as big and sweeping a state as can be imagined – if it were a country, it would be the 40th largest in the world. Cattle ranches, pick-up trucks, cowboy boots and thick Texan drawls – all of those are part of the culture, to be sure, but an Old West theme park it is not. With a state this big, there's room for Texas to be whatever you want it to be.

Austin

Austin is about the experience. Bars, restaurants and even grocery stores and the airport have live music. And there are outdoor activities galore. A full day might also include shopping for some groovy vintage clothes, sipping a margarita at a patio cafe and lounging on the shores of Barton Springs.

💿 Sights & Activities

At dusk bazillions of bats fly out from under Congress Avenue Bridge – it's quite a spectacle.

BOB BULLOCK TEXAS STATE HISTORY MUSEUM   Museum
(www.thestoryoftexas.com; 1800 Congress Ave; adult/child $9/6, Texas Spirit film $5/4; ⏰9am-6pm Mon-Sat, noon-6pm Sun) Big, glitzy and still relatively new, it shows off the Lone Star State's history, all the way from when it used to be part of Mexico up to the present, with high-tech interactive exhibits and fun theatrics.

BARTON SPRINGS POOL   Swimming
(2201 Barton Springs Rd; adult/child $3/2; ⏰9am-10pm Fri-Wed mid-Apr–Sep) Even when the temperature hits 100°F (38°C), you'll be shivering in a jiff after you jump into this icy-cold, natural spring pool.

ZILKER PARK   Park
(www.ci.austin.tx.us/zilker; 2200 Barton Springs Rd) Barton Springs forms the centerpiece of this 351-acre park, which has trails, a nature center and botanical gardens. Rent kayaks at **Zilker Park Boat Rentals** (2100 Barton Springs Rd; www.zilkerboats.com;

HIGHLIGHTS

1 **Austin (p433)** Taking in the fabled live music scene of Texas' free-spirited capital.

2 **San Antonio (p435)** Sauntering along the riverfront and visiting the famed Alamo.

3 **Lockhart (p435)** Feasting on tender morsels of perfection in the state's celebrated Barbecue capital.

Texas barbecue meal
PHILLIP KOSCHEL/CORBIS ©

per hr/day $12/40; ⊙10am-dark daily May-Oct) and paddle from the park out onto Lady Bird Lake.

 Sleeping

HOTEL SAN JOSÉ Hotel $$
(☎512-444-7322; www.sanjosehotel.com; 1316 S Congress Ave; r with shared bath $105, with private bath $175-360; P❄🛜🖨) Local hotelier Liz Lambert revamped a 1930s-vintage motel into a chic SoCo (South Congress) retreat, with minimalist rooms, native Texas gardens and a very Austin-esque hotel bar in the courtyard that's known for its celebrity-spotting potential.

DRISKILL HOTEL Historic Hotel $$$
(☎512-474-5911, 800-252-9367; www.driskill hotel.com; 604 Brazos St; r $185-275, ste $300-900; P🛜) Built from native stone by a wealthy cattle baron in the 1800s, this hotel is pure Texas, from the leather couches to the mounted longhorn head on the wall. (Not to worry, the elegant rooms are taxidermy-free.)

Eating

MOONSHINE PATIO BAR & GRILL American $$
(☎512-236-9599; 303 Red River St; lunch $9-14, dinner $11-21; ⊙11am-10pm Mon-Thu, to 11pm Fri & Sat, 9:30am-2:30pm & 5-10pm Sun) Dating from the mid-1850s, this historic building is a remarkably well preserved homage to Austin's early days. Within its exposed limestone walls, you can enjoy upscale comfort food, half-price appetizers at happy hour or a lavish Sunday brunch buffet ($16.95).

SHADY GROVE RESTAURANT American $$
(1624 Barton Springs Rd; mains $7-12; ⊙11am-10:30pm Sun-Thu, to 11pm Fri & Sat) Outdoors under the pecan trees is prime real estate for enjoying everything from chili cheese fries to the vegetarian Hippie Sandwich.

Entertainment

CONTINENTAL CLUB Live Music
(www.continentalclub.com; 1315 S Congress Ave) No passive toe-tapping here: this 1950s-era lounge has a dance floor that swings with some of the city's best local acts.

BROKEN SPOKE Live Music
(www.brokenspokeaustintx.com; 3201 S Lamar Blvd; ⊙11am-midnight Tue-Thu, to 1am Fri & Sat) With sand-covered floors and wagon-wheel chandeliers that George Strait once hung from, Broken Spoke is a true Texas honky-tonk.

ℹ Getting There & Away

Austin-Bergstrom International Airport (AUS; www.ci.austin.tx.us/austinairport) is off Hwy 71, southeast of downtown.

Cowboy boots for sale, San Antonio

Lockhart Barbecue

In 1999 the Texas Legislature adopted a resolution naming Lockhart the Barbecue Capital of Texas. Of course, that means it's the Barbecue Capital of the *world*. You can eat very well for under $10 at these places:

Black's Barbecue (215 N Main St; ⊙10am-8pm Sun-Thu, to 8:30pm Fri & Sat) A longtime Lockhart favorite since 1932, with sausage so good Lyndon Johnson had Black's cater a party at the nation's capital.

Kreuz Market (619 N Colorado St; ⊙10:30am-8pm Mon-Sat) Serving Lockhart since 1900, the barnlike Kreuz Market uses a dry rub, so don't insult them by asking for barbecue sauce – Kreuz doesn't serve it, and the meat doesn't need it.

Chisholm Trail Bar-B-Q (1323 S Colorado St; ⊙11am-8:30pm) Like Black's and Kreuz Market, Chisholm Trail has been named one of the top 10 barbecue restaurants in the state by *Texas Monthly* magazine.

The downtown **Amtrak station** (www.amtrak.com; 250 N Lamar Blvd) is served by the *Texas Eagle* that extends from Chicago to Los Angeles.

San Antonio

In most large cities, downtown is bustling with businesspeople dressed for office work hurrying to their meetings and luncheons. Not so in San Antonio, located 81 miles southwest of Austin. Instead, downtown is filled with tourists in shorts consulting their maps. In fact, many people are surprised to find that two of the state's most popular destinations – the Riverwalk and the Alamo – are right smack dab in the middle of downtown, surrounded by historical hotels, tourist attractions and souvenir shops.

 **Sights & Activities**

FREE THE ALAMO — Mission (www.thealamo.org; 300 Alamo Plaza; ⊙9am-5:30pm Mon-Sat, from 10am Sun) The folks who valiantly fought for Texas' independence from Mexico would never have imagined the Alamo as it is today, surrounded by tacky tourist attractions and having its picture taken every 17 seconds by people exclaiming how much smaller it looks in real life. But it's more than just a photo op.

Go on in and find out why the story of the Alamo can rouse a Texan's sense of state pride as few other things can.

RIVERWALK — Riverfront Development (www.thesanantonioriverwalk.com) An essential part of the San Antonio experience, this charming canal and pedestrian street is the main artery at the heart of San Antonio's tourism efforts. Restaurant after restaurant and bar after bar vie for your attention.

RIO SAN ANTONIO CRUISES — Boat Tour (www.riosanantonio.com; adult/child 5 & under $8.25/2; ⊙9am-9pm) Narrated cruises ply the entire river daily, offering a nice visual overview along with a light history lesson. Buy tickets across the water from the Hilton near Market and S Alamo Sts.

MISSION TRAIL — Historic Buildings Spain's missionary presence can best be felt at the ruins of the four missions south of town. Together, Missions Concepción (1731), San José (1720), San Juan (1731) and Espada (1745–56) make up **San Antonio Missions National Historical Park** www.nps.gov/saan). Stop first at **Mission San José** (6701 San José Dr; admission free; ⊙9am-5pm), which is also the location of the main **visitor center**. Known in its time as the Queen of the Missions, it's certainly the largest and arguably the most beautiful.

Sleeping

RIVERWALK VISTA B&B $$
(☎210-223-3200, 866-898-4782; 262 Losoya St;
www.riverwalkvista.com; d incl breakfast $120-210,
ste $180-270; ❄@) Soaring ceilings with
enormous windows, exposed brick walls,
crisp, white bedding – simplicity done right.

**OMNI LA MANSION
DEL RIO** Historic Hotel $$$
(☎210-518-1000; www.lamansion.com; 112 Col-
lege St; d $219-399; P❄@☎) This fabulous
downtown property was born out of
19th-century religious school buildings in
the Spanish-Mexican hacienda style. On a
quiet stretch of the Riverwalk, its discreet
oasis attracts stars and other notables.

Eating & Drinking

PALOMA BLANCA Tex-Mex $$
(☎210-822-6151; 5800 Broadway St; lunch $8-10,
mains $10-18; ⊙11am-9pm Mon-Wed, to 10pm Thu
& Fri, 10am-10pm Sat, 10am-9pm Sun) Of all the
great Mexican choices around, this place
sets itself apart with sleek and stylish am-
bience and food that lives up to the decor.

**BLUE STAR BREWING
COMPANY** American, Brewpub $$
(1414 S Alamo St; mains $7-13; ⊙11am-10pm
Mon-Thu, to 11pm Fri & Sat, 10am-9pm Sun) Attracting a casual, creative crowd (thanks
to its location in the Blue Star Arts
Complex) this brewpub and restaurant
is a relaxed place to hang out for a bite
served with one of its craft brews.

Getting There & Around

AIR San Antonio International Airport is 8
miles north of downtown. Bus 5 runs between the
airport and downtown ($1.10, 30 min).
TRAIN Amtrak (www.amtrak.com) trains on the
Florida–California and San Antonio–Chicago runs
stop here several times a week.
PUBLIC TRANSPORT San Antonio's historic
streetcars ($1.10) are handy for getting around
downtown.

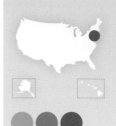

Philadelphia

HIGHLIGHTS

❶ **Independence National Historic
Park (p437)** Peering back in
time at Revolutionary War-era
Philadelphia.

❷ **Philadelphia Museum of Art
(p437)** Climbing up the steps like
Rocky, then exploring the galleries
of Philly's superb art showcase.

❸ **Reading Terminal Market (p438)**
Browsing, shopping and eating to
your heart's content.

Independence Hall
BRIAN CRUICKSHANK/LONELY PLANET IMAGES ©

Philadelphia

Although it may seem like a little sibling to NYC, which is less than 90 miles away, Philadelphia is more representative of what East Coast city living is like. And in the minds of many, it offers every upside of urban life – burgeoning food, music and art scenes; neighborhoods with distinct personalities; copious parkland and, maybe equally importantly, relatively affordable real estate. The older, preserved buildings in historic Philadelphia provide a picture of what colonial American cities once looked like, based on a grid with wide streets and public squares.

Sights & Activities

INDEPENDENCE NATIONAL
HISTORIC PARK — Historic Site
(☏ 215-597-1785; www.nps.gov/inde) This L-shaped 45-acre park, along with Old City, has been dubbed 'America's most historic square mile.' Once the backbone of the United States government, today it's the backbone of Philadelphia's tourist trade. Stroll around and you'll see the storied buildings in which the seeds for the Revolutionary War were planted and the US government came into bloom. You'll also find beautiful, shaded urban lawns dotted with large groups of schoolchildren and costumed actors.

PHILADELPHIA
MUSEUM OF ART — Museum
(☏ 215-763-8100; www. philamuseum.org; cnr Benjamin Franklin Pkwy & 26th St; adult/child $16/free; ⏱10am-5pm Tue-Sun, to 8:45pm Fri) It's one of the nation's largest and most important museums, featuring some

excellent collections of Asian art, Renaissance masterpieces, postimpressionist works and modern pieces by Picasso, Duchamp and Matisse.

 Sleeping

MORRIS HOUSE
HOTEL — Boutique Hotel $$$
(☏ 215-922-2446; www.morrishousehotel.com; 225 S 8th St; r incl breakfast from $189; ❄🖥) This upscale, colonial-era boutique hotel, in a Federal-era building, has the friendly charm and intimacy of an elegant B&B and the professionalism and good taste of a designer-run 21st-century establishment.

HOTEL PALOMAR — Boutique Hotel $$
(☏ 888-725-1778; www.hotelpalomar-phila delphia.com; 117 S 17th St; r from $149; ❄🖥) Marble and dark-wood accents add warmth to the hip and stylish room furnishings. On offer are wine and snacks, hot chocolate (in winter), a gym and an attached restaurant.

Historic houses in the Old City district
RICHARD CUMMINS/LONELY PLANET IMAGES ©

Eating

CUBA LIBRE Cuban $$
(☎215-627-0666; 10 S 2nd St; dinner $13-31;
🕙11:30am-10pm Mon-Fri, from 10:30am Sat &
Sun, to 11:30pm Fri & Sat) Colonial America
couldn't feel further away at this festive,
multistoried Cuban eatery and rum bar.

SILK CITY DINER Diner $$
(435 Spring Garden St; mains $13; 🕙4pm-1am,
from 10am Sat & Sun) Cocktails have re-
placed milkshakes at this classic-looking
diner on the edge of the Old City and
Northern Liberties.

READING TERMINAL MARKET Market $
(cnr 12th & Arch Sts; dishes $3-10; 🕙8am-6pm
Mon-Sat, 9am-5pm Sun) Take your pick, from
fresh Amish cheeses and Thai desserts
to falafel, cheesesteaks, salad bars, sushi,
Peking duck, great Mexican and cups of
fresh-roasted java.

ℹ️ Information

Independence Visitor Center (☎800-537-7676;
www.independencevisitorcenter.com; 6th St at
Market St; 🕙8:30am-5:30pm) Run by the NPS,
the center distributes useful visitor guides and
maps, and sells tickets for the various official
tours that depart from nearby locations.

ℹ️ Getting There & Away

Bus

Greyhound (www.greyhound.com; 1001 Filbert
St) and Peter Pan Bus Lines (www.peterpanbus.
com; 1001 Filbert St) are the major bus carriers;
Bolt Bus (www.boltbus.com) and Mega Bus
(www.us.megabus.com) are popular and
comfortable competitors.

Train

Beautiful 30th St Station is one of the biggest
train hubs in the country. Amtrak (www.amtrak.
com) provides service.

Niagara Falls

HIGHLIGHTS

① **Horseshoe Falls (p439)** Cross
the border and get a photogenic
panorama from the Canadian side.

② **Goat Island (p440)** Gaze over the
thundering falls from this superb
vantage point.

③ **Maid of the Mist (p440)** Take a
memorable (and wet!) boat ride
around the base of the falls.

The American Falls in winter
JOHN PENNOCK/LONELY PLANET IMAGES ©

Canadian Niagara Falls

When people say they are visiting the falls they usually mean the Canadian side, which is naturally blessed with superior views. Canada's **Horseshoe Falls** are wider and especially photogenic from Queen Victoria Park; at night they're illuminated with a colored light show. The **Journey Behind the Falls** (adult/ child US$15/7; ☺9am-8:30pm Mon-Fri) gives access to a spray-soaked viewing area beneath the falls. **Niagara on the Lake**, 15km to the north, is a small town full of elegant B&Bs and a famous summertime theater festival.

River Rd is lined with B&Bs, but **Chestnut Inn** (☏905-374-7623; www.chestnutinn bb.com; 4983 River Rd; r from US$90; ❄), a tastefully decorated colonial home with a wrap-around porch, stands above the rest.

Niagara Falls

There are honeymooners and heart-shaped Jacuzzis, arcades, tacky shops and kitschy, boardwalk-like sights, but as long as your attention is focused nothing can detract from the majestic sight. The closer to the falls you get the more impressive they seem, and the wetter you become. For good reason, the Canadian side is where almost everyone visits, though it's easy to stroll back and forth between the two.

 ## Sights & Activities

The falls are in two separate towns: Niagara Falls, New York (USA) and Niagara Falls, Ontario (Canada). The towns face each other across the Niagara River, which is spanned by the Rainbow Bridge (accessible for both cars and pedestrians). You can see views of the **American Falls** and their western portion, the **Bridal Veil Falls**, which drop 180ft, from

Maid of the Mist boat tour at Canada's Horseshoe Falls

the **Prospect Point Observation Tower** (admission $1, ⏱9:30am-5pm Mon-Thu, to 7pm Fri & Sat, to 6pm Sun).

Cross the small bridge to **Goat Island** for close-up viewpoints, including **Terrapin Point**, which has a fine view of Horseshoe Falls and pedestrian bridges to the Three Sisters Islands in the upper rapids. From the north corner of Goat Island, an elevator descends to the **Cave of the Winds** (☎716-278-1730; adult/child $6/4; ⏱9am-5pm), where walkways go within 25ft of the cataracts (raincoats provided).

The **Maid of the Mist** (☎716-284-8897; www.maidofthemist.com; tours adult/child $13.50/8; ⏱10am-5pm Mon-Fri, to 6pm Sat & Sun May-Sep; 👶) boat trip around the bottom of the falls has been a major attraction since 1846 and is highly recommended. Boats leave from the base of the Prospect Park Observation Tower on the US side and from the bottom of Clifton Hill on the Canadian side.

Sleeping

GIACOMO Boutique Hotel **$$**
(☎716-299-0200; www.thegiacomo.com; 220 First St; r from $150; P ❄ 🛜) While the majority of floors are taken up by high-end condos, the three dozen spacious rooms are luxuriously appointed and the 19th-floor lounge offers spectacular falls views.

ℹ Getting There & Around

The Amtrak train station (27th St at Lockport Rd) is about 2 miles northeast of downtown. From Niagara Falls, daily trains go to New York City ($60, nine hours).

Mount Rushmore

HIGHLIGHTS

❶ **Presidential Trail (p441)** Go eye-to-eye (or eye-to-nose rather) with four legendary statesmen.

❷ **Visitor Center (p441)** Learn about the massive effort to create one of America's icons.

❸ **Jewel Cave (p441)** Wander through the sparkling chambers of this subterranean wonder.

Mount Rushmore
JOHN ELK III/LONELY PLANET IMAGES ©

Mount Rushmore

America's awe-inspiring mountainside sculpture is well worth a visit to the Black Hills of South Dakota. George Washington, Thomas Jefferson, Abraham Lincoln and Theodore Roosevelt look proudly down from 60ft-tall glory. Fans of *North by Northwest* will instantly recognize the cinematic backdrop, which played a starring role in Hitchcock's suspense-filled thriller.

You pass through an avenue of all 50 state flags before reaching a terrace, underneath which is the **visitor center** (www.nps.gov/moru; admission free, parking $11; ⏱8am-10pm summer, to 5pm rest of year). Displays give an overview for the massive physical effort of the team (led by sculptor Gutzon Borglum) who created the memorial between 1927 and 1941.

Although summertime crowds pack the monument, with a little walking you can escape the pack and fully appreciate this magnificent work. The **Presidential Trail** loop leads near the monument for some fine nostril views and past the fascinating sculptors' studio. A **nature trail** to the right as you face the entrance connects the viewing and parking areas, passing through a pine forest.

🛌 Sleeping

In Hill City, 13 miles northwest of Mt Rushmore, the **Lantern Inn** (☎605-574-2582; www. lanterninn.com; 580 E Main St; r $65-130; ❄🛜🏊) is an 18-room motel-style place spread over two stories, fronting attractive grounds.

ℹ Getting There & Away

Rapid City Airport, 32 miles northeast of Mt Rushmore, has regional connections. Once here, you'll need a car, as there's no public transport to Mt Rushmore.

Jewel Cave National Monument

Another of the Black Hills' many fascinating caves is Jewel Cave, 13 miles west of Custer on US 16, so named because calcite crystals line nearly all of its walls. Currently 145 miles have been surveyed, making it the second-longest known cave in the world, but it is presumed to be the longest. **Tours** (reservations ☎605-673-8300; adult $4-27, child free-$4) range in length and difficulty; reservations (seven days in advance max) are recommended. Make arrangements at the **visitor center** (www.nps.gov/jeca; ⏱8am-5:30pm).

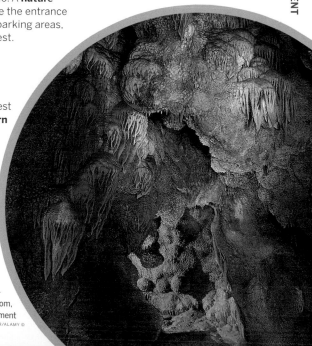

The Formation Room,
Jewel Cave National Monument
CLINT FARLINGER/ALAMY ©

USA
In Focus

Bull elk, Yellowstone National Park (p431)
KRAIG LIEB/LONELY PLANET IMAGES ©

USA Today

> *Recycling, energy efficiency and renewable energy are the buzzwords of the moment*

Greenmarket Farmers Market (p70), New York City

belief systems
(% of population)

51	24	2	2	21
Protestant	Roman Catholic	Mormon	Jewish	Other

if the USA were 100 people

65 would be white
15 would be Hispanic
13 would be African American
4 would be Asian American
3 would be other

population per sq mile

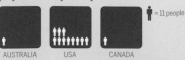

♂ ≈ 11 people

AUSTRALIA   USA   CANADA

Economic Woes

The 21st century has certainly been a tumultuous one for the USA. The boom days of peace and prosperity in the 1990s seems more and more of a distant memory as America hurtles into the future. These are, after all, unprecedented times economically, with the US in the largest financial crisis since the Great Depression. What started as a collapse of the US housing bubble in 2007 spread to the banking sector, with the meltdown of major financial institutions. The shockwave quickly spread across the globe, and by 2008 many industrialized nations around the world were experiencing a recession in one form or another. By 2011, the economy was still limping along, despite the ambitious $800 billion stimulus package passed by Congress in 2009.

Big-City Appeal

While pundits wring their hands over America's sluggish growth and unwavering unemployment (over 9% in 2011), on other fronts

HUW JONES/LONELY PLANET IMAGES ©

and Jamie Oliver's quest to change diets in America's 'fattest city' were constant reminders that something has gone deeply wrong. Fast food, soft drinks and too much TV have all been vilified in recent years; whether this brings substantive change – or just higher ratings for weight-loss shows – remains to be seen.

Sustainable Agriculture

Diet, of course, isn't just about dieting, and awareness of problems in American agriculture is growing in leaps and bounds. The documentary *Food, Inc.*, by Robert Kenner, and books by Michael Pollan (*The Omnivore's Dilemma*), Eric Schlosser (*Fast Food Nation*) and others have shined a light on the disheartening way food is produced in America, and its enormous unseen costs on society – from both a health and environmental perspective. As a result, more Americans are eating organic food and supporting local farmers markets. Big corporations are getting in on the act – even WalMart sells organic food now – though regulation of the organic industry leaves unanswered questions.

Greener Lifestyles

Speaking of sustainability, the word 'green' seems to be on everyone's mind – recycling, energy efficiency and renewable energy are the buzzwords of the moment. Owing in part to high gas prices, Americans are less eager to buy vehicles that aren't fuel-efficient. And big projects are underway, with large solar and wind-power plants in the works, greener cities (environmentally friendly architecture and infrastructure, more parks) and electric cars soon to bring great changes to the American landscape.

great changes continue to unfold across the county, affecting many spheres of life. The city, once regarded as a place of crime and urban decay, is now seen as a place where multiculturalism, the arts and great restaurants flourish. Indeed cities have become greener, more livable and more appealing (shorter commutes, mostly car-free living). Americans – not just singles, but families, too – are moving back into the city. Some suburban areas, meanwhile, are beginning to adopt elements of urban living – many Americans want more than just a house in a sidewalk-free gated community. They want farmers markets, entertainment options and cultural attractions, and a better sense of community.

Changing Eating Habits

In terms of diet, Americans are doing some soul-searching. No one could deny that many in America struggle with obesity. Shows like *The Biggest Loser*

History

MARK NEWMAN/LONELY PLANET IMAGES

Demagogues, visionaries and immigrants all contribute to the American story. Early colonists arrive in the 1600s, planting the seeds of independence, which later blossom into full nationhood. Westward expansion follows, along with bloody Civil War and the emancipation of slaves. In modern times, America struggles through the Great Depression and horrific wars, and enacts great changes during the Civil Rights movement. After the USSR's demise, America becomes the world's leading superpower.

Enter the Europeans

In 1492, the Italian explorer Christopher Columbus, backed by the monarchy of Spain, voyaged west by sea, looking for the East Indies. He found the Bahamas. With visions of gold, Spanish explorers quickly followed: Hernán Cortés conquered much of today's Mexico; Francisco Pizarro conquered Peru; Juan Ponce de León wandered through Florida looking for the fountain of youth. Not to be left out, the French explored Canada

8000 BC

Widespread extinction of Ice Age mammals. Indigenous peoples hunt smaller game and start gathering native plants.

and the Midwest, while the Dutch and English cruised North America's eastern seaboard.

Of course, they weren't the first ones on the continent. When Europeans arrived, approximately two to 18 million Native American people occupied the lands north of present-day Mexico and spoke over 300 languages. European explorers left in their wake diseases to which indigenous peoples had no immunity. More than any other factor – war, slavery or famine – disease epidemics devastated indigenous populations by anywhere from 50% to 90%. By the 17th century, Native North Americans numbered only about one million, and many of the continent's once-thriving societies were in turmoil and transition.

In 1607, English noblemen established North America's first permanent European settlement in Jamestown, Virginia. Eventually, the colony came to be run by a representative assembly of citizens, and it brought the first African slaves to the continent to work the tobacco fields.

In 1620, a boatload of radically religious Puritans established a colony at Plymouth, Massachusetts. Their settlement – intended to be a religious and moral beacon to the world – was notable for its 'Mayflower Compact,' an agreement to govern themselves by consensus. Sadly, the harmony did not extend to the colonists' relationships with local Native American tribes, and their eventual falling out led to bloody warfare.

Thus, at Jamestown and Plymouth, the seeds of the 'American paradox' were sown: white political and religious freedom would come to be founded through the enslavement of blacks and the displacement of Native Americans.

The American Revolution

For the next 150 years, European powers – particularly England, France, Portugal and Spain – competed for position and territory, bringing all their Old World political struggles to the new one. In the south, English businessmen developed a cotton and tobacco plantation economy that became entirely dependent on the use of forced labor, and slavery was eventually legalized into a formal institution. By 1800, one out of every five persons in America was a slave.

The Best... Colonial Sites

1 Independence National Historic Park (p437), Philadelphia

2 Freedom Trail (p156), Boston

3 Strawbery Banke Museum (p188), Portsmouth, NH

4 Boston's North End (p168)

IN FOCUS HISTORY

7000 BC–100 AD

During 'Archaic period,' the agricultural 'three sisters' (corn, beans, squash) and permanent settlements become well established.

1492

Italian explorer Christopher Columbus 'discovers' America, eventually making three voyages throughout the Caribbean.

1607

Jamestown is founded, though life there is grim: 80 of 108 settlers die the first year.

The Best... Historic Homes

1 Mount Vernon (p119), Alexandria, VA

2 Paul Revere House (p168), Boston

3 Heyward-Washington House (p239), Charleston, SC

4 Hearst Castle (p393), California

Meanwhile, in the 1760s – after winning the Seven Years' War with France and finally gaining control of the eastern seaboard – England started asking their American colonies to chip in to the Crown's coffers. Up to then, Britain had mostly left the colonists alone to govern themselves, but now England raised new taxes and stationed a permanent army.

This didn't sit well, to put it mildly. Colonists protested and boycotted English policies (arguing for 'no taxation without representation'), and openly questioned the benefits of monarchy. Who needed a king imposing rules from abroad when they were doing quite well without one?

In 1774, fired by increasing conflict and the era's Enlightenment ideas of individualism, equality and liberty, the colonists convened the First Continental Congress in Philadelphia to decide what to do. Before they could agree, in April 1775, British troops skirmished with armed colonists in Massachusetts, and both sides were at war.

It wasn't until July 4, 1776, that the Revolutionary War's ultimate treasonous goal – independence from England – was first articulated in the Declaration of Independence. Unfortunately, the Continental army, led by George Washington, was underfunded, poorly armed, badly trained and outnumbered by Britain's troops, who were the largest professional army in the world. If not for a 1778 alliance with France, who provided the materials and sea power that eventually won the war for the colonists, America might very well have been a very short-lived experiment.

Westward Expansion

After winning their independence, the Founding Fathers came to the hard part: fashioning a government. The US Constitution wasn't adopted till 1787. While the democratic government it created amounted to a radical political revolution, economic and social relationships were not revolutionized: rich landholders kept their property, including slaves; Native Americans were excluded from the nation; and women were excluded from politics. As a result, following the ratification of the Constitution, US life has pulsed with the ongoing struggle to define 'all' and 'equal' and 'liberty' – to take the universal language of America's founding and either rectify or justify the inevitable disparities that bedevil any large society.

1620
The *Mayflower* lands at Plymouth with 102 English Pilgrims. Local Indians save them from starvation.

1773
Bostonians protest British taxes by dumping tea into the harbor, called the 'Boston Tea Party.'
Statue of Sam Adams, Boston

RICHARD CUMMINS/LONELY PLANET IMAGES ©

However, it would be 70 years before the first real troubles surfaced. In the meantime, America looked west, and its ambitions grew to continental size. Believers in 'Manifest Destiny' felt that it was divinely fated that the United States should occupy all the land from sea to shining sea – and through wars, purchase and outright theft, they succeeded. Particularly after the discovery of gold in California in 1848 (the Spanish explorers just hadn't known where to look), groaning wagon trains brought fevered pioneers west, a motley collection of miners, farmers, entrepreneurs, immigrants, outlaws and prostitutes, all seeking their fortunes on the frontier. This made for exciting, legendary times, but throughout loomed a troubling question: as new states joined the USA, would they be slave states or free states? The nation's future depended on the answer.

The Civil War

The US Constitution hadn't ended slavery, but it had given Congress the power to approve (or not) slavery in new states. Public debates raged constantly over the expansion of slavery, particularly since this shaped the balance of power between the industrial North and the agrarian South.

Since the founding, Southern politicians had dominated government and defended slavery as 'natural and normal,' which an 1856 New York Times editorial called 'insanity.' The Southern pro-slavery lobby enraged Northern abolitionists. But even many Northern politicians feared that ending slavery would be ruinous. Limit slavery, they reasoned, and in the competition with industry and free labor, slavery would wither without inciting a violent slave revolt – a constantly feared possibility. Indeed, in 1859, radical abolitionist John Brown tried unsuccessfully to spark an uprising to free the slaves at Harpers Ferry, West Virginia.

The economics of slavery were undeniable. In 1860, there were over four million slaves in the US, most held by Southern planters, who grew 75% of the world's cotton, accounting for over half of US exports. Thus, the Southern economy supported the nation's economy, and it required slaves. The 1860 presidential election became a referendum on this issue, and the election was won by a young politician who favored limiting slavery: Abraham Lincoln.

In the South, even the threat of federal limits was too onerous to abide, and as President Lincoln took office, 11 states eventually seceded from the union and formed the Confederate States of America. Lincoln faced the nation's greatest moment of crisis. He had two choices: let the Southern states secede and dissolve the union, or wage war to keep the union intact. He chose the latter.

The war began in April 1861, when the Confederacy attacked Fort Sumter in Charleston, South Carolina, and raged on for the next four years in the most gruesome combat that the world had known up to that time. By the end, over 600,000 soldiers – nearly an entire generation of young men – were dead, and

1775
Paul Revere warns colonial militia men that British troops are coming. The Revolutionary War begins.

1781
General Washington leads his ragtag troops to victory at Yorktown as the British surrender.

1787
US Constitution establishes a democratic form of government, with power vested in the hands of the people.

Southern plantations and cities (most notably Atlanta) lay sacked and burned. The North's industrial might provided an advantage, but its victory was not preordained; it unfolded battle by bloody battle.

As fighting progressed, Lincoln recognized that if the war didn't end slavery outright, victory would be pointless. In 1863, his Emancipation Proclamation expanded the war's aims and freed all slaves. In April 1865, Confederate General Robert E Lee surrendered to Union General Ulysses S Grant in Appomattox, Virginia. The Union had been preserved, but at a staggering cost.

Immigration & Industrial Revolution

The Civil War ended an economic system of forced labor. But American society remained largely, and often deeply, racist. During Reconstruction (1865–77), the civil rights of ex-slaves were protected by the federal government, which also extracted reparations from Southern states, creating Civil War grudges that lingered for a century.

Charging Bull sculpture, Wall Street, New York City
ROB BLAKERS/LONELY PLANET IMAGES ©

1803–6
France sells the US the Louisiana Purchase; Lewis and Clark then trailblaze west through it to reach the Pacific Ocean.

1849
An epic cross-country gold rush sees 60,000 'Forty-Niners' flock to California's Mother Lode.

1865
The Civil War ends, though celebration is curtailed by President Lincoln's assassination five days later.

After Reconstruction, Southern states developed a labor system of indentured servitude (called 'sharecropping') and enacted laws aimed at keeping whites and blacks 'separate but equal.' The South's segregationist 'Jim Crow' laws (which remained in place until the 1960s Civil Rights movement) effectively disenfranchised African Americans in every sphere of daily life.

Meanwhile, with the rapid, post–Civil War settlement of the West, the US appeared like a mythic 'land of opportunity' to immigrants, who flooded in from Europe and Asia. In total, about 25 million people arrived between 1880 and 1920. Poles, Germans, Irish, Italians, Russians, Eastern Europeans, Chinese and more fed an urban migration that made the late 19th century the age of cities. New York was transformed into a buzzing, multi-ethnic 'melting pot,' and the nation's undisputed capital of commerce and finance.

America's industrialists became so rich, and so effective at creating monopolies in steel, oil, banking and railroads, they became known as 'robber barons,' and not always disparagingly. These paragons of capitalism fueled the industrial revolution, even as choking factories and sweatshops consigned many to lives of poverty and pain. Through the turn of the century, the rise of labor unions and progressive reformers, like President Woodrow Wilson, led to new laws that broke up the monopolies and softened workplace abuses.

After America's brief involvement in WWI, the prosperity of the 'roaring' 1920s led to a wave of optimism and good times. The Jazz Age bloomed: flappers danced the Charleston, radio and movies captivated millions, and stock prices went up, up, up.

Great Depression, the New Deal & World War II

In October 1929, investors, worried about a gloomy global economy, started selling stocks – seeing all the selling, everyone panicked until they'd sold everything. The stock market crashed, and the US economy collapsed like a house of cards.

Thus began the Great Depression. Frightened banks called in their dodgy loans, people couldn't pay, and the banks folded. Millions lost their homes, farms, businesses and savings, and as much as 50% of the American workforce became unemployed in certain parts of the country (the overall rate at its peak was nearly 33%).

In 1932, Democrat Franklin D Roosevelt was elected president on the promise of a 'New Deal' to rescue the US from its crisis, which he did with resounding success. When war once again broke out in Europe in 1939, the isolationist mood in America was as strong as ever. However, the extremely popular President Roosevelt, elected to an unprecedented third term in 1940, understood that the US couldn't sit by and allow victory for fascist, totalitarian regimes. Roosevelt sent aid to Britain and persuaded a skittish Congress to go along with it.

1880–1920

Millions of immigrants flood in to the cities from Europe and Asia, fueling a new age of urban living.

1917

President Woodrow Wilson plunges US into WWI, pledging 'the world must be made safe for democracy.'

1920

The 19th Amendment is passed, giving American women the right to vote.

Americans Get a New Deal

America reached its lowest point in history during the Great Depression. By 1932, nearly one-third of all American workers were unemployed. National output fell by 50%, hundreds of banks shuttered, and great swaths of the country seemed to disappear beneath enormous dust storms.

Franklin D Roosevelt, elected president in 1932, helped rescue the nation from collapse. He bailed out banks, saved homeowners from foreclosure and added millions of jobs. He created massive projects like the Civilian Conservation Crops, which planted more than two billion trees, and the Works Progress Administration, a 600,000-strong workforce that built bridges, dams and other infrastructure.

Then, on December 7, 1941, Japan launched a surprise attack on Hawaii's Pearl Harbor, killing over 2000 Americans and sinking several battleships. As US isolationism transformed overnight into outrage, Roosevelt suddenly had the support he needed. Germany declared war on the US, and America joined the Allied fight against Hitler and the Axis powers, putting almost its entire will and industrial prowess into the war effort.

Initially, neither the Pacific nor European theaters went well for America. Fighting in the Pacific didn't turn around until the US unexpectedly routed the Japanese navy at Midway Island in June 1942. In Europe, the US dealt the fatal blow to Germany with its massive D-Day invasion of France on June 6, 1944; Germany surrendered the following year.

Nevertheless, Japan continued fighting. Rather than invade the country, President Harry Truman chose to drop experimental atomic bombs (created by the government's top-secret Manhattan Project) on Hiroshima and Nagasaki in August 1945, destroying both cities. Japan surrendered, and the nuclear age was born.

The Red Scare, Civil Rights & the Wars in Asia

The US enjoyed unprecedented prosperity in the decades after WWII, but little peace.

Formerly wartime allies, the communist Soviet Union and the capitalist USA soon engaged in a running competition to dominate the globe. The superpowers engaged in proxy wars – notably the Korean War (1950–53) and Vietnam War (1959–75) – with only the mutual threat of nuclear annihilation preventing direct war. The UN, founded in 1945, couldn't overcome this worldwide ideological split and was largely ineffectual in preventing Cold War conflicts.

1920s

The Harlem Renaissance inspires a burst of African American literature, art, music and cultural pride.

Jazz musician, New Orleans

1941–45

US enters WWII, deploying over 16 million troops and suffering around 400,000 deaths.

Meanwhile, with its continent unscarred and its industry bulked up by WWII, the American homeland entered an era of growing affluence. In the 1950s, a mass migration left the inner cities for the suburbs, where affordable single-family homes sprang up. Americans drove cheap cars using cheap gas over brand-new interstate highways. They relaxed with the comforts of modern technology, swooned over TV, and got busy, giving birth to a 'baby boom.'

Middle-class whites did, anyway. African Americans remained segregated, poor and generally unwelcome at the party. Echoing 19th-century abolitionist Frederick Douglass, the Southern Christian Leadership Coalition (SCLC), led by African American preacher Martin Luther King Jr, aimed to end segregation and 'save America's soul': to realize color-blind justice, racial equality and fairness of economic opportunity for all.

Beginning in the 1950s, King preached and organized nonviolent resistance in the form of bus boycotts, marches and sit-ins, mainly in the South. White authorities often met these protests with water hoses and batons, and demonstrations sometimes dissolved into riots, but with the 1964 Civil Rights Act, African Americans spurred a wave of legislation that swept away racist laws and laid the groundwork for a more just and equal society.

Meanwhile, the 1960s saw further social upheavals: rock and roll spawned a youth rebellion and drugs sent Technicolor visions spinning in their heads. President John F Kennedy was assassinated in Dallas in 1963, followed by the assassinations in 1968 of his brother, Senator Robert Kennedy, and of Martin Luther King Jr. Americans' faith in their leaders and government was further tested by the bombings and brutalities of the Vietnam War, as seen on TV, which led to widespread student protests.

Yet President Richard Nixon, elected in 1968 partly for promising an 'honorable end to the war,' instead escalated US involvement and secretly bombed Laos and Cambodia. Then, in 1972, the Watergate scandal broke: a burglary at the Democratic Party offices was, through dogged journalism, tied to 'Tricky Dick,' who, in 1974, became the first US president to resign from office.

The tumultuous 1960s and '70s also witnessed the sexual revolution, women's liberation, struggles for gay rights, energy crises over the supply of crude oil from the Middle East and, with the 1962 publication of Rachel Carson's *Silent Spring,* the realization that the USA's industries had created a polluted, diseased environmental mess.

The Best...
Ethnic &
Cultural Sites

1 Ellis Island (p62), NYC

2 National Civil Rights Museum (p226), Memphis

3 Taos Pueblo (p329), Taos, NM

4 La Plaza de Cultura y Artes (p379), Los Angeles

1954

In Brown v. Board of Education, the Supreme Court ends segregation in public schools.

1963

President John F Kennedy is assassinated while riding in a motorcade in Dallas, Texas.

1959–75

The US fights the Vietnam War, in which it supports South Vietnam against communist North Vietnam.

Pax Americana & the War on Terror

In 1980, Republican California governor and former actor Ronald Reagan campaigned for president by promising to make Americans feel good about America again. The affable Reagan won easily, and his election marked a pronounced shift to the right in US politics.

Reagan wanted to defeat communism, restore the economy, deregulate business and cut taxes. To tackle the first two, he launched the biggest peacetime military build-up in history, and dared the Soviets to keep up. They went broke trying, one of the many factors that led to the eventual dissolution of the USSR at the end of the decade.

Reagan's military spending and tax cuts created enormous federal deficits, but these were largely erased during the 1990s high-tech internet boom, which seemed to augur a 'new US economy' based on white-collar telecommunications. These hopes and surpluses vanished in 2000, when the high-tech stock bubble burst. That year, after one of the most divisive elections in modern US politics, President George W Bush enacted tax cuts that returned federal deficits to amounts greater than before.

Then, on September 11, 2001, Islamic terrorists flew hijacked planes into New York City's World Trade Center and the Pentagon in Washington, DC. This catastrophic

Spherical sculpture from the World Trade Center, Battery Park, New York City

1974
President Richard Nixon resigns after being connected to the Watergate burglary of Democratic headquarters.

1989
The 1960s-era Berlin Wall is torn down, marking the official end of the decades-long Cold War.

1990s
The internet revolution creates the biggest boom and bust since the Great Depression.

The Civil Rights Movement

Beginning in the 1950s, a movement was underway in African American communities to fight for equality. Rosa Parks, who refused to give up her seat to a white passenger on a bus, inspired the Montgomery bus boycott. There were sit-ins at lunch counters where blacks were excluded; massive demonstrations led by Martin Luther King Jr in Washington, DC; and harrowing journeys by 'freedom riders' aiming to end bus segregation. The work of millions paid off: in 1964, President Johnson signed the Civil Rights Act, which banned discrimination and racial segregation by federal law.

attack united Americans behind their president, as he vowed revenge and declared a 'war on terror.' But finding and fighting the Al-Qaeda terrorists, who belonged to no nation, proved elusive and challenging.

US forces attacked Afghanistan in an unsuccessful hunt for the terrorists, and subsequently invaded Iraq in 2003 and toppled its anti-US dictator, Saddam Hussein Eventually, both wars dragged on, losing much popular support. In 2011, President Obama announced a major withdrawal, with the majority of troops scheduled to return home before the end of the year.

In 2005, the USA's most expensive natural disaster occurred when Hurricane Katrina devastated the Gulf Coast, including New Orleans. When federal relief efforts were slow to arrive and then proved inadequate, a sour mood once again settled over the nation, reminiscent of the 1970s.

Promising hope and change, Democrat Barack Obama was elected as the nation's first African American president in 2008, in itself a hopeful sign that America's long-standing racial divides were healing. However, Obama's New Deal–style initiatives – such as a massive economic stimulus bill and an overhaul of the broken US health-care system – were met with widespread protests from a growing anti-government, conservative 'tea party' movement. So far in the new millennium, America remains a politically divided nation.

2001
The September 11 terrorist attacks destroy NYC's World Trade Center and kill nearly 3000 people.

2005
Hurricane Katrina ruptures levees, flooding New Orleans and killing over 1800 people.

2008–12
Financial mismanagement and a housing market crash fuel America's worst recession since the Great Depression.

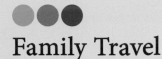

Family Travel

The amusement park on Santa Monica Pier (p385)

The USA generally welcomes families with young travelers. From coast to coast, you'll find superb attractions for all ages: theme parks, zoos, eye-popping aquariums, natural history exhibits and hands-on science museums. There's also bucket-and-spade fun to be had at the beach, hikes in wilderness reserves and plenty of other activities likely to wow the young ones. Wherever you go, traveling with children can bring an exciting new dimension to the American experience.

Planning

Weather and crowds are all-important considerations when planning a US family getaway. The peak travel season across the country is from June to August, when schools are out and the weather is warmest. Expect high prices and abundant crowds, meaning long lines at amusement and water parks, fully booked resort areas and heavy traffic on the roads; you'll need to reserve well in advance for popular destinations. The same holds true for winter resorts during the high season of January to March.

Lodging

Motels and hotels typically have rooms with two beds, which are ideal for families. Some also have roll-away beds or cribs that can be brought into the room for an extra charge, but keep in mind these are usually 'Pack 'n' Plays', which not all children sleep well in. Some hotels offer 'kids stay free' programs for children up to 12 or even sometimes 18 years old. Be wary of B&Bs, as many don't allow children; ask when booking.

Dining with Children

The US restaurant industry seems built on family-style service: children are not just accepted almost everywhere, but are usually catered to, with special children's menus offering smaller portions and lower prices. In some restaurants children under a certain age even eat for free. Some restaurants may also offer crayons and puzzles, and occasionally live performances by cartoon-like characters.

Restaurants without children's menus don't necessarily discourage kids, though higher-end restaurants might; however, even at the nicer places, if you show up early enough (right at dinner-time opening hours), you can usually eat without too much stress – and you'll likely be joined by other foodie couples with kids. You can ask if the kitchen will make a smaller order of a dish (also ask how much it will cost). Chinese, Mexican and Italian restaurants are the best bet for finicky young eaters.

Farmers markets are widespread in the USA, and every sizeable town has at least one a week. This is a good place to assemble a first-rate picnic, sample the local specialities and support independent growers in the process. After getting your stash, head to a park or waterfront, at least one of which will probably be nearby.

The Best... Theme Parks & Animal Spotting

1 Walt Disney World (p282), Florida

2 Universal Orlando (p283), Florida

3 Disneyland (p391), California

4 SeaWorld (p280), Florida

5 San Diego Zoo (p394), California

6 Monterey Bay Aquarium (p420), California

Driving

Every car rental agency should be able to provide an appropriate child seat, since these are required in every state, but you need to request it when booking and expect to pay around $10 more per day.

Be particularly conservative planning road trips. Distances in the USA can be long, and kids often need extra 'transition time' when traveling. With kids, it can be hard to hit the road early, drive far without stopping and to keep to regular mealtimes – all of these things can throw off a trip schedule. So keep distances short, don't string driving days together, and always try to arrive an hour before mealtime, so everyone can unwind.

Planes & Trains

Domestic airlines don't charge for children under two. Those aged two and over must have a seat, but discounts are unlikely. Very rarely, some resort areas (like Disneyland) offer a 'kids fly free' promotion. Amtrak and other train operators occasionally run similar deals (with kids up to 15 years old riding free) on various routes.

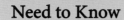

Need to Know

- **Change facilities** Found in most public buildings and restaurants.
- **Cots** Available at most hotels.
- **High chairs** Available at most restaurants, as are booster seats.
- **Diapers (Nappies)** Widely available.
- **Health** Pack basic medicines; standard of hospital care is excellent.
- **Children's menus** Sometimes available, though many restaurants are willing to improvise to make a kid-friendly meal.
- **Strollers** Bring an umbrella stroller.
- **Transport** Major car-rental firms can supply car seats.

Discounts

Child concessions often apply for tours, admission fees and transport, with some discounts as high as 50% off the adult rate. However, the definition of 'child' can vary from under 6 to under 16 years. Some popular sights also have discount rates for families, which will save a few dollars compared to buying individual tickets. Most sights also offer free admission to children under two years.

Helpful Resources

Family Travel Files (www.thefamilytravelfiles.com) Ready-made vacation ideas, destination profiles and travel tips.

Kids.gov (www.kids.gov) Eclectic, enormous national resource; download songs and activities, or even link to the CIA Kids' Page.

Travel with Children For all-around information and advice, check out Lonely Planet's *Travel with Children*.

Local Tips

To find family-oriented sights and activities, accommodations, restaurants and entertainment throughout this guide, just look for the child-friendly icon (👪). Major cities in this guide also have a special 'For Children' box.

Food & Drink

California cuisine: shrimp kebabs with tomato and zucchini

Long before the dawn of competitive cooking shows, molecular gastronomy and organic farm stands, Wampanoag tribes people brought food to help the Pilgrims stave off certain famine over the winter of 1620, thus kicking off the very first Thanksgiving. Since then Americans have mixed myriad food cultures to create their own distinct culinary traditions, based in part on the rich bounty of the continent.

STAPLES & SPECIALTIES

These days you can get almost every type of food nearly everywhere in America, but regional specialties are always best, and sometimes unrecognizably better, in the places where they originated.

NYC: Culinary Powerhouse

They say that you could eat at a different restaurant every night of your life in New York City and not exhaust the possibilities. Considering that there are over 23,000 restaurants in the five boroughs, with constant openings and closings, it's true. Owing to its huge immigrant population and an influx of 49 million tourists annually, New York captures the title of America's greatest restaurant city, hands down. Its diverse neighborhoods serve up authentic Italian food and thin crust-style pizza, all manner

The Best... Local Temptations

1 Boston clam chowder

2 Maine lobsters

3 Cajun crawfish

4 Memphis barbecue

5 Chicago deep-dish pizza

6 Santa Fe chili stew

of Asian food, French *haute cuisine*, and classic Jewish deli food, from bagels to piled-high pastrami on rye. But the list goes around the globe: Moroccan, Indian, Vietnamese, Russian, Cuban, Brazilian and more. Plus, Manhattan boasts street-cart dining that puts some city restaurant-scenes to shame.

New England: Clam Bakes & Lobster Boils

New England's claim to have the nation's best seafood is hard to beat, because the North Atlantic offers up clams, mussels, oysters and huge lobsters, along with shad, bluefish and cod. New Englanders love a good chowder (seafood stew) and a good clambake, an almost ritual meal where the shellfish are buried in a pit fire with corn, chicken, potatoes and sausages. Fried clam fritters and lobster rolls (lobster meat with mayonnaise served in a bread bun) are served throughout the region. There are excellent cheeses made in Vermont, cranberries (a Thanksgiving staple) harvested in Massachusetts and maple syrup from New England's forests. Maine's coast is lined with lobster shacks, while baked beans and brown bread are Boston specialties.

Mid-Atlantic: Global Cooking, Crabcakes & Cheesesteaks

Washington, DC, has a wide array of global fare – not surprising given its ethnically diverse population. In particular, you'll find some of the country's best Ethiopian fare. DC also makes fine use of its position near the Chesapeake Bay and you'll find top crab cakes and seafood here. In Philadelphia, you can gorge on 'Philly cheese steaks': thin, sautéed beef, fried onions and melted cheese on a bun.

The South: Barbecue, Biscuits & Gumbo

No region is prouder of its food culture than the South, which has a long history of mingling Anglo, French, African, Spanish and Native American foods in dishes such as slow-cooked barbecue, which has as many meat and sauce variations as there are towns in the South. Southern fried chicken is crisp outside and moist inside. In Florida, dishes made with alligator, shrimp and conch incorporate hot chili peppers and tropical spices. Breakfasts are as big as can be, and treasured dessert recipes tend to produce big layer cakes or pies made with pecans, bananas and citrus. Light, fluffy biscuits are served hot and well buttered, and grits (ground corn cooked to a porridge-like consistency) are a passion among Southerners, as are refreshing mint julep cocktails.

Louisiana's legendary cuisine is influenced by colonial French and Spanish cultures, Afro-Caribbean cooking and Choctaw Indians' traditions. Cajun food is found in the bayou country and marries native spices such as sassafras and chili peppers with provincial French cooking. Creole food is more urban, and centered on New Orleans, where dishes such as shrimp remoulade, crabmeat ravigote, crawfish étouffée and beignets are ubiquitous.

The Southwest: Chili, Steak & Smokin' Hot Salsa

Two ethnic groups define Southwestern food culture: the Spanish and Mexicans, who controlled territories from Texas to California until well into the 19th century. While there is little actual Spanish food today, the Spanish brought cattle to Mexico, which the Mexicans adapted to their own corn-and-chili-based gastronomy to make tacos, tortillas, enchiladas, burritos, chimichangas and other dishes made of corn or flour pancakes, and filled with everything from chopped meat and poultry to beans. Don't leave New Mexico without trying a bowl of spicy green-chili stew. Steaks and barbecue are always favorites on Southwestern menus, and beer is the drink of choice for dinner and a night out. For a cosmopolitan foodie scene, visit Las Vegas, where top chefs from NYC, LA and even Paris are sprouting satellite restaurants.

Vegetarian & Vegan Dining

Some of the most highly regarded American restaurants cater exclusively to vegetarians and vegans. Vegetarian and vegan restaurants abound in major US cities, though not always in small towns and rural areas away from the coasts. Eateries that have a good selection of vegetarian options are noted throughout this book using the 🖋 icon. Browse the online directory at www.happycow.net.

California: Farm-to-Table Restaurants & Taquerías

Owing to its vastness and variety of microclimates, California is truly America's cornucopia for fruits and vegetables, and a gateway to myriad Asian markets. The state's natural resources are overwhelming: wild salmon, Dungeness crab, and oysters from the ocean; robust produce year-round; and artisanal products such as cheese, bread, olive oil, wine and chocolate. Starting in the 1970s and '80s, star chefs such as Alice Waters and Wolfgang Puck pioneered 'California cuisine' by incorporating the best local ingredients into simple yet delectable preparations. The influx of Asian immigrants, especially after the Vietnam War, enriched the state's urban food cultures with Chinatowns, Koreatowns and Japantowns, along with huge enclaves of Mexican Americans who maintain their own culinary traditions across the state. Don't miss the fist-sized burritos in San Francisco's Mission District and the fish tacos in San Diego.

Pacific Northwest: Salmon & Starbucks

The cuisine of the Pacific Northwest region draws on the traditions of the local tribes of Native Americans, whose diets traditionally centered on game, seafood – especially salmon – and foraged mushrooms, fruits and berries. Seattle spawned the modern international coffeehouse craze with Starbucks, while the beers and wines from both Washington and Oregon are of an international standard, especially the pinot noirs and rieslings.

WINE, BEER & BEYOND

Go ahead, crack open that beer: work-hard, play-hard Americans are far from teetotalers. About 67% of Americans drink alcohol, with the majority preferring beer to wine. Though the country's attitudes have come a long way from its early Puritan roots and days of Prohibition, the strongest predictor that an American adult abstains from alcohol is – unsurprisingly or not – church attendance.

Craft & Local Beer

Microbrewery and craft beer production is rising meteorically, accounting for 11% of the domestic market in 2010. There are over 1500 craft breweries across the USA, with Vermont boasting the most microbreweries per capita. In recent years, it has become possible to 'drink local' all over the country as microbreweries pop up in urban centers, small towns and unexpected places.

Wine

American wines have made an even more dramatic impact: the nation is the world's fourth largest producer of wine, behind Italy, France and Spain. Today almost 90% of US wine comes from California, and Oregon, Washington and New York wines have achieved international status. According to the *LA Times*, 2010 marked the first year that the US actually consumed more wine than France.

Wine isn't cheap in the US, as it's considered a luxury rather than a staple – go ahead and blame the Puritans for that. But it's possible to procure a perfectly drinkable bottle of American wine at a liquor or wine shop for around $10.

Wine Regions

Without a doubt, the country's hotbed of wine tourism is in Northern California, just outside of the Bay Area in the Napa and Sonoma Valleys. As other regions, such as Oregon's Willamette Valley, have evolved as wine regions, they've spawned an entire industry of B&B tourism that seems to go hand-in-hand with the quest to find the perfect pinot noir.

So what are the best American wines? There are many excellent 'new world' wines that have flourished in the rich American soil. The most popular white varietals are chardonnay and sauvignon blanc; best-selling reds include cabernet sauvignon, merlot, pinot noir and zinfandel.

The Hard Stuff

You might know him by his first name: Jack. (Hint: his last name is Daniels.) Good ol' Jack Daniels remains the most well-known brand of American whiskey around the world, and is also the oldest continually operating US distillery, going strong since 1870.

While whiskey and bourbon are the most popular American exports, rye, gin and vodka are also crafted in the USA. Bourbon, made from corn, is the only native spirit and is traditionally made in Kentucky.

Cocktails were invented in America before the Civil War. Born in New Orleans, an appropriately festive city to launch America's contribution to booze history, the first cocktail was the Sazerac – a mix of rye whiskey or brandy, simple syrup, bitters and a dash of absinthe (before absinthe was banned in 1912, that is). American cocktails created at bars in the late-19th and early-20th centuries include such long-standing classics as the martini, the Manhattan, and the old-fashioned.

The Vintage Cocktail Craze

Inspired by vintage recipes featuring natural and homemade spirits and elixirs, a new breed of retro-modern cocktails – complete with ingredients like small-batch liqueurs, whipped egg whites, hand-chipped ice and fresh fruits – are lovingly concocted by nattily dressed bartenders who regard their profession as somewhere between an art and a science. Also quite the rage are 'speakeasies' – which are really just unsigned bars carefully concealed to evade the average passerby.

The Great Outdoors

Whitewater rafting, Grand Canyon National Park (p298)

Towering redwoods, alpine lakes, rolling hills, chiseled peaks, lunarlike deserts and a dramatic coastline of unrivaled beauty: the USA has no shortage of spectacular settings for a bit of outdoor adventure – and so far, we've described just one state (California). In the other 49 lie an astounding collection of natural wonders, from red-rock canyons and lush rainforests to snow-covered mountains and vast stretches of wilderness devoid of people but full of endless possibility.

The Land

The USA is big, no question. Covering over 3.5 million sq miles, it's the world's third-largest country, trailing only Russia, and its friendly neighbor to the north, Canada. The continental USA is made up of 48 contiguous states ('the lower 48'), while Alaska, its largest state, is northwest of Canada, and the volcanic islands of Hawaii, the 50th state, lie 2600 miles southwest of the mainland in the Pacific Ocean.

It's more than just size, though. America feels big because of its incredibly diverse topography, which began to take shape around 50 to 60 million years ago.

National Parks

National parks are America's big backyards. Every cross-country road trip connects the dots between the USA's big-shouldered cities, but not always its national parks. There

Top National Parks

- **Acadia, ME** Rocky coastlines and end-of-the-world Atlantic islands.
- **Everglades, FL** Home to crocs, panthers, manatees and more.
- **Grand Canyon, AZ** Ancient, colorful chasm carved by the Colorado River.
- **Great Smoky Mountains, TN** Southern Appalachian woodland with thickly forested ridges.
- **Mt Rainier, WA** Alpine meadows, high-elevation snowfields and a glacier-covered, rumbling giant.
- **Olympic, WA** Primeval rainforests, mist-clouded mountains and wild Pacific Coast beaches.
- **Rocky Mountain, CO** Jagged mountain peaks, lakes, streams and pine forests.
- **Yellowstone, WY** North America's largest intact ecosystem.
- **Yosemite, CA** Verdant valleys featuring thunderous waterfalls and Sierra Nevada peaks.
- **Zion, UT** Stunning desert oasis in the heart of red-rock country.

you'll encounter remarkable places, rich in unspoiled wilderness, rare wildlife and rich history.

Some parks look much the same as they did centuries ago, when this nation was just starting out. From craggy islands off the Atlantic Coast, to prairie grasslands and buffalo herds across the Great Plains, to the Rocky Mountains raising their jagged teeth along the Continental Divide, and onward to the tallest trees on earth – coastal redwoods – standing sentinel on Pacific shores, you'll be amazed by the natural bounty.

Wildlife

The USA is home to creatures both great and small, from the ferocious grizzly bear to the industrious beaver, with colossal bison, snowy owls, soaring eagles, howling coyotes and doe-eyed manatees all part of the great American menagerie. The nation's varied geography – coastlines along two oceans, mountains, deserts, rainforests and massive bay and river systems – harbor ecosystems where an extraordinary array of plant and animal life can flourish.

Wildlife Watching: USA's Endangered Species

Currently, over 1300 plants and animals are listed in the USA as either endangered or threatened. Although all endangered species are vital to the ecosystem, if it's brag-worthy animals that you're keen to see (and photograph), here are places to spot them before (gulp) it's too late:

- **Bighorn sheep** Zion National Park, UT
- **California condor** Big Sur, CA & Grand Canyon National Park, AZ
- **Florida panther** Everglades National Park, FL
- **Gray wolf** Yellowstone National Park, WY
- **Manatee** Everglades National Park, FL

Hiking

Fitness-focused Americans take great pride in their formidable network of trails – literally tens of thousands of miles – and there's no better way to experience the countryside up close and at your own pace.

The wilderness is amazingly accessible for easy exploration. National parks are ideal for short and long hikes; if you long for nights in remote places beneath star-filled skies, plan on securing a backcountry permit in advance, especially in places like the Grand Canyon, where spaces are limited, particularly during summer.

Beyond the parks, you'll find troves of trails in every state. Almost anywhere you go will have great hiking and backpacking within easy distance. Just bring a sturdy pair of shoes (sneakers or hiking boots) and a water bottle.

Hiking Resources

○ **American Hiking Society** (www.americanhiking.org) Find local hiking clubs and 'volunteer vacations' building trails.

○ **Backpacker** (www.backpacker.com) Premier national magazine for backpackers, from novices to experts.

○ **Rails-to-Trails Conservancy** (www.railstotrails.org) Converts abandoned railroad corridors into hiking and biking trails; publishes free trail reviews at www.traillink.com.

The Best...
Jaw-Dropping Scenery

1 Grand Canyon National Park (p298)

2 Yosemite National Park (p416)

3 Acadia National Park (p193)

4 Zion National Park (p317)

5 Olympic National Park (p354)

6 Death Valley National Park (p399)

Morning Glory Pool, Yellowstone National Park (p431).

JOHN ELK III/LONELY PLANET IMAGES ©

- **Survive Outdoors** (www.surviveoutdoors.com) Dispenses safety and first-aid tips, plus helpful photos of dangerous critters.

- **Wilderness Survival** (Gregory Davenport; Stackpole Books, 2006) Easily the best book on surviving nearly every contingency.

Cycling

Cycling's popularity grows by the day in the USA, with many cities (including New York) adding more cycle lanes and becoming more bike-friendly, and an increasing number of greenways dotting the countryside. You'll find die-hard enthusiasts in every town, and numerous outfitters offering guided trips for all levels and durations. For the best advice on rides and rentals, stop by a local bike shop or Google the area you plan to visit.

Top Cycling Towns

- **San Francisco, CA** A pedal over the Golden Gate Bridge lands you in the stunningly beautiful, and stunningly hilly, Marin Headlands.

- **Austin, TX** This indie-rock-loving town has nearly 200 miles of trails and great weather year-round.

- **Portland, OR** A trove of great cycling (on- and off-road) in the Pacific Northwest.

Mountain Biking

Mountain-biking enthusiasts will find trail nirvana in Moab, UT and Marin, CA, where Gary Fisher and friends bunny-hopped the sport forward by careening down the rocky flanks of Mt Tamalpais on home-rigged bikes.

A few great rides include the following:

- **Kokopelli's Trail, UT** One of the premier mountain-biking trails in the Southwest, the trail stretches 140 miles on mountainous terrain between Loma, CO, and Moab, UT. Other nearby options include the 206-mile, hut-to-hut ride between Telluride, CO, and Moab, UT.

- **Sun Top Loop, WA** A 22-mile ride with challenging climbs and superb views of Mt Rainier and surrounding peaks on the western slopes of Washington's Cascade Mountains.

- **Porcupine Rim, UT** A 30-mile loop from Moab, this venerable high-desert romp features stunning views and hairy downhills.

Scuba Diving & Snorkeling

On the continental USA, Florida has the lion's share of great diving, with more than 1000 miles of coastline subdivided into 20 unique undersea areas. There are hundreds of sites and countless dive shops offering equipment and guided excursions. South of West Palm Beach, you'll find clear waters and fantastic year-round diving with ample reefs. In the Panhandle (the northern part of the state), you can scuba in the calm and balmy waters of the Gulf of Mexico; off Pensacola and Destin, there are fabulous wreck dives; and you can dive with manatees near Crystal River.

The Florida Keys, a curving string of 31 islets, are the crown jewel; expect a brilliant mix of marine habitats, North America's only living coral garden and the occasional shipwreck. Key Largo is home to the John Pennekamp Coral Reef State Park, with over 200 miles of underwater bliss.

There's also terrific diving and snorkeling (and much warmer water) just off the mangrove swamps of the Florida Keys, boasting the world's third-largest coral system.

Top Hiking Trails in the USA

Ask 10 people for their top hiking trails and no two answers will be alike. The country is so varied and the distances so enormous, there's little consensus. That said, you can't go wrong with the following all-star sampler.

Appalachian Trail (www.appalachiantrail.org) Completed in 1937, the country's longest footpath is over 2100 miles long, crosses six national parks, traverses eight national forests and hits 14 states from Georgia to Maine.

Pacific Crest Trail (PCT; www.pcta.org) Follows the spines of the Cascades and Sierra Nevada, traipsing 2650 miles from Canada to Mexico, passing through six of North America's seven ecozones.

John Muir Trail (Yosemite National Park, CA) 222 miles of scenic bliss, from Yosemite Valley up to Mt Whitney.

Enchanted Valley (Olympic National Park, WA) Magnificent mountain views, roaming wildlife and lush rainforests – all on a 13-mile out-and-back trail.

South Kaibab/North Kaibab Trail (Grand Canyon National Park, AZ) A multiday cross-canyon tramp down to the Colorado River and back up to the rim.

Tahoe Rim Trail (Lake Tahoe, CA) This 165-mile all-purpose trail circumnavigates the lake from high above, affording glistening Sierra views.

Surfing

The best surf in continental USA breaks off the coast of California. There are loads of options – from the funky and low-key Santa Cruz, CA, to San Francisco's Ocean Beach (a tough spot to learn!) and bohemian Bolinas, 30 miles north. South, you'll find strong swells and Santa Ana winds in San Diego, La Jolla, Malibu and Santa Barbara, all sporting warmer waters, fewer sharks of the great white variety, and a saucy SoCal beach scene. The best conditions are from September to November. Along the coast of Oregon and Washington, you'll find miles and miles of crowd-free beaches and pockets of surfing communities.

Top Surfing Spots

Huntington Beach, CA – aka Surf City, USA – is the quintessential surf capital, with perpetual sun and a 'perfect' break, particularly during winter when the winds are calm. Other fine breaks:

○ **Black's Beach, San Diego, CA** This 2-mile sandy strip at the base of 300ft cliffs in La Jolla is known as one of the most powerful beach breaks in SoCal, thanks to an underwater canyon just offshore.

○ **Huntington Beach, CA** A great place to take in the scene, or even some lessons.

○ **Rincon, Santa Barbara, CA** Arguably one of the planet's top surfing spots; nearly every major surf champion on the globe has taken Rincon for a ride.

○ **Steamer Lane & Pleasure Point, Santa Cruz, CA** There are 11 world-class breaks, including the point breaks over rock bottoms, at these two sweet spots.

○ **Coast Guard Beach, Eastham, MA** Part of the Cape Cod National Seashore, this family-friendly beach is known for its consistent shortboard/longboard swell all summer long.

Rock Climbing

Scads of climbers flock to **Joshua Tree National Park**, an otherworldly shrine in southern California's sun-scorched desert. There, amid craggy monoliths and the country's oldest trees, they pay pilgrimage on more than 8000 routes, tackling sheer vertical, sharp edges and bountiful cracks with aplomb. Or not. Fortunately, the top-notch **Joshua Tree Rock Climbing School** (www.joshuatreerockclimbing.com) offers classes for all levels, with local guides leading beginners to experts on 7000 different climbs in the park.

In **Zion National Park, UT**, multiday canyoneering classes teach the fine art of going *down*: rappelling off sheer sandstone cliffs into glorious, red-rock canyons filled with trees. Some of the sportier pitches are made in dry suits, down the flanks of roaring waterfalls into ice-cold pools.

Horseback Riding

Horseback riding is a mighty pleasurable way to survey the landscape, and particularly west of the Mississippi River, many national parks are serviced by outfitters offering trail rides. Most last an hour or two; overnight pack trips require reservations. Some great places to saddle up include **Grand Canyon National Park**, **Zion National Park**, **Bryce Canyon National Park**, **Yellowstone National Park** and **Rocky Mountains National Park**.

Water Sports

In summer, national parks are great places for getting your feet wet in rivers and lakes. At Maine's **Acadia National Park** and Washington's **San Juan Islands**, sea kayaking is one of the highlights. Meanwhile, **Everglades National Park** offers unforgettable canoeing.

Surfer on a San Diego beach
RICHARD CUMMINS/LONELY PLANET IMAGES ©

The People

Native American dancer

JOHN ELK III/LONELY PLANET IMAGES ©

Many people point to the election of President Barack Obama as proof of America's multicultural achievements. It's not just his personal story (white mother, black father, Muslim name), or that he's the first African American to be elected president – it's the belief that America is a land of possibility where if you apply yourself you can achieve your dreams. As simplistic as it sounds, it's the core of the national psyche.

Population

'The times they are a-changin', Bob Dylan famously sang – it could be the theme song for America's demographics. During the next four decades the country's population will undergo two major shifts: it will become significantly older, and it will become far more Hispanic/Latino.

The total US population is well over 310 million, making it the world's third-most populous country (behind China and India). Broken down by ethnicity, the USA is 66% white, 15% Hispanic, 13% African American, 5% Asian and 1% Native American, according to 2007–08 census data. But by 2050, census demographers project that Hispanics, African Americans and Asians will make up more than 50% of the population – the minorities will become the majority.

The other big change will be the nation's elderly population: it will more than double in size by 2050. One in five Americans will be

Unbreakable Code

The Navajo's Athabascan tongue is the most spoken Native American language, despite its notorious complexity. In the Pacific Theater during WWII, Navajo 'code talkers' sent and received military messages in Navajo; Japan never broke the code, and the code talkers were considered essential to the US victory.

aged over 65 by then, creating a new challenge: how will the country take care of all these older citizens?

Multiculturalism

From the get-go, America was called a 'melting pot,' which presumed that newcomers came and blended into the existing American fabric. The country hasn't let go of that sentiment completely. On one hand, diversity is celebrated (Cinco de Mayo, Martin Luther King Jr Day and Chinese New Year all get their due), but on the other hand, Americans from all different backgrounds celebrate Independence Day and Thanksgiving.

Immigration is at the crux of the matter. Immigrants currently make up about 12% of the population. About 470,000 newcomers enter the US legally each year, with the majority from Mexico, followed by Asia and Europe. Another 11 million or so are in the country illegally. This issue makes many Americans edgy, especially as it gets politicized.

Religion

When the Pilgrims (early settlers to the US who had fled their European homeland to escape religious persecution) came ashore, they were adamant that their new country would be one of religious tolerance. They valued the freedom to practice religion so highly they refused to make their Protestant faith official state policy. What's more, they forbade the government from doing anything that might sanction one religion or belief over another. Separation of church and state became the law of the land.

Today, Protestants are on the verge of becoming a minority in the country they founded. According to the Pew Research Center, Protestant numbers have declined steadily to just over 50% of the population. Meanwhile, other faiths have held their own or seen their numbers rise. Catholics represent about 25% of the country, with the denomination receiving a boost from the many Hispanics who have immigrated here. Those practicing non-Christian 'world religions' – Islam, Buddhism, Hindu, Judaism – have grown collectively to represent 5% of the country. Mormons comprise about 2%.

Interestingly, one of the fastest-growing categories is 'unaffiliated.' The proportion of those who say they have 'no religion' is now around 16%. Some in this catch-all category disavow religion altogether (around 4%), but the majority sustain spiritual beliefs that simply fall outside the box. What's more, the country is in a period of exceptional religious fluidity. Forty-four percent of American adults have left the denomination of their childhood for another denomination, another faith or no faith at all, according to Pew.

Culture Wars

America's biggest schism isn't between religions or even between faith and skepticism: it's between fundamentalist and progressive interpretations within each faith. At the forefront are questions on abortion, contraception, gay rights, stem-cell research, the teaching of evolution, school prayer and government displays of religious icons. The country's Religious Right (the oft-used term for evangelical Christians) has pushed these issues onto center stage. This effort has prompted a slew of court cases, testing the nation's principles on separation of church and state. The fundamentalist-progressive divide remains one of America's biggest culture wars, and it plays a prominent role in politics, especially during elections.

Native Americans

Today, there are over three million Native Americans (a fraction of their pre-Columbian numbers) from 500 tribes, speaking some 175 languages and residing in every region of the United States. Not surprisingly, North America's indigenous people are an extremely diverse bunch with unique customs and beliefs, molded in part by the landscapes they inhabit – from the Inuit living in the frozen tundra of Alaska, to the many tribes of the arid, mountainous Southwest.

Native Americans today follow equally diverse paths, as they inherit a legacy left by both their ancestors and the cultures that invaded from outside. Some may be weavers who live on reservations, others may be web designers living in Phoenix. Some plant corn and squash, others seek to harvest the sun in solar-energy farms.

Culturally speaking, America's tribes today grapple with questions about how to prosper in contemporary America while protecting their traditions from erosion and their lands from further exploitation, and how to lift their people from poverty and a variety of social and health problems while still maintaining their sense of identity and ties to sacred culture.

The Best... Places to See Native American Art

1 American Indian Museum (p105), Washington, DC

2 Heard Museum (p307), Phoenix

3 Wheelwright Museum of the American Indian (p323), Santa Fe

4 Acoma Pueblo (p309), Arizona

The Tribes

The Cherokee, Navajo, Chippewa and Sioux are the largest tribal groupings in the lower 48 (ie barring Alaska and Hawaii). Other well-known tribes include the Choctaw (descendants of a great mound-building society originally based in the Mississippi River Valley), the Apache (a nomadic hunter-gatherer tribe that fiercely resisted forced relocation) and the Hopi (a Pueblo people with Southwest roots dating back 2000 years). The Navajo Nation in Arizona is by far the largest reservation by size, though the highest percentage of Native Americans (about 25%) live in California and Oklahoma.

Art & Crafts

Encyclopedias have been written about the artistic traditions of America's indigenous peoples, which span from ancient rock art to contemporary paintings and literature. In places like the Southwest, Native American art is as integral to the landscape as sagebrush and slot canyons.

An essential feature of most Native American crafts is that everyday function and spiritual beliefs are intertwined. Decoration is not merely pretty, but woven with ceremonial meaning. This is in keeping with Native American religions, which see the entire natural world as infused with living spirit. Some of the most famous crafts include Navajo rugs and turquoise-and-silver jewelry, Southwestern pueblo pottery, Hopi katchinas, Zuni fetishes, Sioux beadwork, Inuit sculptures and Cherokee wood carvings, to name a few.

Arts & Culture

Jack Kerouac St, North Beach (p404), San Francisco

JACK KEROUA STREET

On January 25, 198 The City of San Franc approved a proposal t CITY LIGHTS BOC to rename 12 streets f S.F. writers and artis including this alle

RICHARD CUMMINS/LONELY PLANET IMAGES ©

America has always been a chaotic, democratic jumble of high and low cultures; of Frank Lloyd Wright and Frank Sinatra; of Georgia O'Keefe and A Chorus Line; *of* The Great Gatsby *and* Star Wars. *Like so much else, America's arts are a pastiche, a crazy mix-and-match quilt of cultures and themes, of ideas borrowed and stolen to create something new, often leaving dramatic new paradigms along the way.*

Music

No other American art has been as influential as American popular music, which is the nation's heartbeat. Blues, jazz, country, rock and roll, hip-hop: download them to your iPod and you've got the soundtrack of America's 20th century. The rest of the world has long returned the love, and American music today is a joyful, multicultural feast, a freewheeling blend of genres and styles.

The South is the mother of American music, most of which has roots in the frisson and interplay of black-white racial relations. Blues was the first – the seminal sound – and nearly all subsequent American music has tapped this deep well. It developed out of the work songs of African slaves, and out of black spiritual songs and their 'call-and-response' pattern, both of which were adaptations of African music. Famous musicians include Robert

Johnson, Bessie Smith, Muddy Waters, BB King, John Lee Hooker and Buddy Guy.

The birthplace of jazz is New Orleans, where ex-slaves combined African-influenced rhythms with the reed, horn and string instruments played by the city's Creole musicians. Over the years, this fertile cross-pollination has produced a steady stream of innovative sounds: ragtime, Dixieland jazz, big-band swing, bebop and numerous jazz fusions. Major artists include Duke Ellington, Louis Armstrong, Billie Holiday, John Coltrane, Miles Davis and Charles Mingus.

True fiddle-and-banjo country music developed in the Appalachian Mountains, the product of Scottish, Irish and English immigrants. In the Southwest, 'western' music was distinguished by steel guitars and larger bands. These styles merged into 'country-and-western' music in the 1920s, becoming centered on Nashville, Tennessee, while bluegrass music mixed country with jazz and the blues. For the originals, listen to Bill Monroe, Hank Williams, Johnny Cash, Patsy Cline and Loretta Lynn.

Rock and roll, meanwhile, combined guitar-driven blues, black rhythm and blues (R&B), and country-and-western music. Most say rock and roll was born when Elvis Presley started singing, but from the 1950s on, it evolved into the anthem for a nationwide social revolution in youth culture. Today, it is probably the most malleable and well-known American music.

Finally, hip-hop emerged from 1970s New York, as DJs spun and mixed records, calling out rhymes with a microphone, to spur dance parties. Synonymous with urban street culture, it became the defining rebel sound of American pop culture by the 1990s.

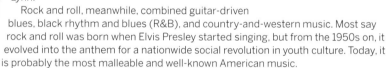

The Best... Live Music Scenes

IN FOCUS ARTS & CULTURE

Literature

Not so long ago, the nation's imagination stirred when critics heralded the next Great American Novel. Not everyone cared, but for over a century the novel was the vital engine of US culture and art, and literature was how America first articulated a unique vision of itself. In the internet age, this exclusive position no longer remains, but American writers still get their say as they feverishly digest and define what life in the United States is all about.

James Fenimore Cooper is credited with creating the first truly American literature with *The Pioneers* (1823), which celebrated frontier wilderness, 'everyman' humor and individualism. Other vital 19th-century writers were Herman Melville (*Moby Dick*, 1851), Nathaniel Hawthorne (*The Scarlet Letter*, 1850) and Edge Allan Poe, who is credited with inventing the mystery story, the horror story and science fiction, all enduring genres in America.

However, poet Walt Whitman (*Leaves of Grass*, 1855), still perhaps the greatest American writer, was the first to encapsulate the heart of the new nation in his rebellious free verse, which were songs of individualism, democracy and joyous optimism.

The greatest American novel, the one against which all others are measured, remains *Huckleberry Finn* (1884), written by Samuel Clemens (aka Mark Twain), whose satirical humor and vernacular style came to define American letters.

After WWI, American novelists came into their own. They were revolutionary in voice and style, and became often sharp critics of a newly industrialized, and later suburbanized, 20th-century American society. There are too many excellent, important writers to name, but a short list of those who are essential for understanding American literature include Ernest Hemingway (*The Sun Also Rises*, 1926), John Steinbeck (*The Grapes of Wrath*, 1939), William Faulkner (*The Sound and the Fury*, 1929), Zora Neale Hurston (*Their Eyes Were Watching God*, 1937), Flannery O'Connor (*Wise Blood*, 1952), Allen Ginsberg (*Howl*, 1956), Jack Kerouac (*On the Road*, 1957) and Toni Morrison (*The Bluest Eye*, 1970). Notable contemporary writers include Don DeLillo, Dave Eggers, Jonathan Lethem and Michael Chabon.

Film & TV

What would America be without movies and TV? They are like the nation's mirror, where America checks its hair and profile before going out. That's fitting, as both mediums were essentially invented here.

Classic American Films

WESTERN

- *High Noon* (1952), Fred Zinnemann
- *The Searchers* (1956), John Ford

MUSICAL

- *42nd Street* (1933), Lloyd Bacon
- *Singin' in the Rain* (1952), Stanley Donen & Gene Kelly

GANGSTER

- *The Maltese Falcon* (1941), John Huston
- *The Godfather trilogy* (1972–90), Francis Ford Coppola
- *Goodfellas* (1990), Martin Scorsese
- *Pulp Fiction* (1994), Quentin Tarantino

DRAMA

- *Gone with the Wind* (1939), Victor Fleming
- *Citizen Kane* (1941), Orson Welles
- *Rear Window* (1954), Alfred Hitchcock
- *Rocky* (1976), John Avildsen

COMEDY

- *The Gold Rush* (1925), Charlie Chaplin
- *Some Like It Hot* (1959), Billy Wilder
- *Dr Strangelove* (1964), Stanley Kubrick
- *Annie Hall* (1977), Woody Allen

Though France was developing similar technology, Thomas Edison is credited with creating the first motion pictures and the first movie studio in New Jersey, in the 1890s. Early American films like *The Great Train Robbery* (1903) and *Birth of a Nation* (1915) introduced much of cinema's now-familiar language, such as the fade, the close-up and the flashback. Then in the 1920s, Hollywood established itself as the home of the film studios, and the rest, as they say, is history – very glamorous, celebrity-studded, Cinemascope-size history. However, what's interesting nowadays is that the rest of the world has caught up, and Hollywood films are increasingly the product of an internationalized cinema, one that emulates Hollywood even as it redefines it.

The first commercial TV set, meanwhile, was introduced at the 1939 New York World's Fair. By the 1950s and 1960s, TV was so big that it outshone the movies, nearly killing the film studios, and by the 1990s, the handful of original stations had multiplied into hundreds. For a long time, TV was looked down on as the doughy middle of American culture – the 'boob tube,' as it was called – yet today some TV programs exhibit depth and storytelling that can surpass that of cinema.

The Best...
Art
Museums

1 Metropolitan Museum of Art (p79), NYC

2 Museum of Modern Art (p75), NYC

3 National Gallery of Art (p105), Washington, DC

4 Art Institute of Chicago (p134)

5 Museum of Fine Arts (p170), Boston

6 Los Angeles County Museum of Art (p383)

Visual Arts

While America's 19th-century painters – like Thomas Cole and Frederick Remington – helped romanticize America's frontier, painting in America did not draw much worldwide or even national attention until the advent of abstract expressionism. Exposed to the shockwaves of European modernism in the early 20th century, America's artists found their voice after WWII and began to lead movements.

New York painters Franz Kline, Jackson Pollock and Mark Rothko pushed abstract expressionism to its extremes, throwing color and movement across epic canvases. In the 1960s, America's other definitive style – pop art – developed in response to this: Jasper Johns, Robert Rauschenberg and Andy Warhol playfully blurred the line between art and commerce and often reduced the artist to an assembly-line mechanic. Pop art co-opted media images, comics, advertising and product packaging in a self-conscious ironic wink that is now the media age America lives and breathes.

Minimalism followed this, swinging back toward abstraction and emphasizing mixed media and installation art; major artists included Sol LeWitt, James Turrell, Richard Serra and Richard Tuttle.

By the 1980s, civil rights, feminism and AIDS activism had made inroads in visual culture; artists not only voiced political dissent through their work but embraced a range of once-marginalized media, from textiles and graffiti to video, sound and performance. To get the pulse of contemporary art in the US, check out works by artists like Jenny Holzer, Kara Walker, Chuck Close, Martin Puryear and Frank Stella.

Sports

A Boston Red Sox baseball player at bat, Fenway Park (p175)

LOU JONES/LONELY PLANET IMAGES

What really draws Americans together — sometimes slathered in blue body paint or crowned with foam-rubber cheese wedges atop their heads — is sports. It provides an important social glue, so whether a person is conservative or liberal, married or single, Mormon or pagan, chances are come Monday at the office they'll be chatting about the weekend performance of their favorite team.

Seasons

The fun and games go on all year long. In spring and summer there's a baseball game nearly every day. In fall and winter, a weekend or Monday night doesn't feel right without a football game on, and through the long days and nights of winter, there's plenty of basketball to keep the adrenaline going.

Baseball

Despite high salaries and its biggest stars being dogged by steroid rumors, baseball remains America's favorite pastime. It may not command the same TV viewership (and subsequent advertising dollars) as football, but baseball teams have 162 games over a season, versus 16 for football.

Besides, baseball isn't about seeing it on TV – it's all about the live version: being at the ballpark on a sunny day, sitting in the bleachers with a beer and hot dog and indulging in the seventh-inning stretch, when the entire park erupts in a communal sing-along of 'Take Me Out to the Ballgame.' The final play-offs, held every October, still deliver excitement and unexpected champions. The New York Yankees, Boston Red Sox and Chicago Cubs continue to be America's favorite teams, even when they're abysmal (the Cubs haven't won a World Series in over 100 years).

Tickets are relatively inexpensive – seats average about $14 at most stadiums – and are easy to get for most games. Minor-league baseball games cost half as much, and can be even more fun, with lots of audience participation, stray chickens and dogs running across the field and wild throws from the pitcher's mound. For more information, go to www.minorleaguebaseball.com.

Football

Football is big, physical and rolling in dough. With the shortest season and least number of games of any of the major sports, every match takes on the emotion of an epic battle, where the results matter and an unfortunate injury can deal a lethal blow to a team's play-off chances.

Football's also the toughest because it's played in fall and winter in all manner of rain, sleet and snow. Some of history's most memorable matches have occurred at below-freezing temperatures. Green Bay Packers fans are in a class by themselves when it comes to severe weather. Their stadium in Wisconsin, known as Lambeau Field, was the site of the infamous Ice Bowl, a 1967 championship game against the Dallas Cowboys where the temperature plummeted to 13°F below zero – mind you, that was with a wind-chill factor of -48°F.

Different teams have dominated different decades: the Pittsburgh Steelers in the 1970s, the San Francisco 49ers in the 1980s, the Cowboys in the 1990s and the New England Patriots in the 2000s. The pro league's official website (www.nfl.com) is packed with information. Tickets are expensive and hard to get, which is why many fans congregate in bars to watch televised games instead.

The Best...
Places to See
a Pro Game

1 Fenway Park (p175), Boston

2 Wrigley Field (p141), Chicago

3 Dodger Stadium (p390), Los Angeles

4 Yankee Stadium (p89), NYC

5 Sun Life Stadium (p269), Miami

6 Nationals Park (p120), Washington, DC

Start Your Engines

Nascar – officially, the National Association for Stock Car Auto Racing – has played an unusual role in American culture. It flew under the radar for years, mostly thrilling fans in the Southeast, where it originated. Money started to flow in during the 1990s, and it burst onto the national scene in a big way in 2002. The Sprint Cup is the top-tier tour, with the Daytona 500 being the year's biggest race, attracting over 180,000 spectators.

Even college and high-school football games enjoy an intense amount of pomp and circumstance, with cheerleaders, marching bands, mascots, songs and mandatory pre- and postgame rituals, especially 'tailgating' – a full-blown beer-and-barbecue feast that takes place over portable grills in parking lots where games are played.

The rabidly popular Super Bowl is pro football's championship match, held in late January or early February. The other 'bowl' games (such as the Rose Bowl and the Orange Bowl) are college football's title matches, held on and around New Year's Day.

Basketball

The teams bringing in the most fans these days include the Chicago Bulls (thanks to the lingering Michael Jordan effect), the Detroit Pistons (a rowdy crowd where riots have broken out), the Cleveland Cavaliers, the San Antonio Spurs and last but not least, the Los Angeles Lakers, who won five championships between 2000 and 2010. Small-market teams like Philadelphia and Portland have true-blue fans, and such cities can be great places to take in a game.

College-level basketball also draws millions of fans, especially every spring when March Madness rolls around. This series of college play-off games culminates in the Final Four, when the four remaining teams compete for a spot in the championship game. The games are widely televised, and bet upon – this is when Las Vegas bookies earn their keep – and their Cinderella stories and unexpected outcomes rival the pro league for excitement.

The Washington Redskins football team (p120)

Survival
Guide

Cyclists cross the Willamette River, Portland (p358)
ANTHONY PIDGEON/LONELY PLANET IMAGES ©

A-Z
Directory

Accommodations

For all but the cheapest places and the slowest seasons, reservations are advised. In high-season tourist hot spots, hotels can book up months ahead. Online travel booking, bidding and comparison websites (see p488) are another good way to find discounted hotel rates – but are usually limited to chain hotels; also check out **Hotels.com** (www.hotels.com) and **Hotwire** (www.hotwire.com).

B&BS

In the USA, many B&Bs are high-end romantic retreats in restored historic homes that are run by personable, independent innkeepers who serve gourmet breakfasts. These B&Bs often take pains to evoke a theme – Victorian, rustic, Cape Cod and so on – and amenities range from merely comfortable to indulgent. Rates normally top $100, and the best-run are $200 to $300. Some B&Bs have minimum-stay requirements, and some exclude young children.

Some online resources:

Bed & Breakfast Inns Online (www.bbonline.com)

Bed and Breakfast.com (www.bedandbreakfast.com)

BnB Finder (www.bnbfinder.com)

Pamela Lanier's Bed & Breakfast Inns (www.lanierbb.com)

Select Registry (www.selectregistry.com)

HOTELS

Hotels in all categories typically include in-room phones, cable TV, alarm clocks, private baths and a simple continental breakfast. Many midrange properties provide minibars, microwaves, hairdryers, internet access, air-conditioning and/or heating, swimming pools and writing desks, while top-end hotels add concierge services, fitness and business centers, spas, restaurants, bars and higher-end furnishings.

Even if hotels advertise that children 'sleep free,' cots or rollaway beds may cost extra. Always ask about the hotel's policy for telephone calls; all charge an exorbitant amount for long-distance and international calls, but some also charge for dialing local and toll-free numbers.

MOTELS

Motels – distinguishable from hotels by having rooms that open onto a parking lot – tend to cluster around interstate exits and along main routes into town. Some remain smaller, less-expensive 'mom-and-pop' operations; breakfast is rarely included, and amenities might top out at a phone and a TV (maybe with cable). However, motels often have a few rooms with simple kitchenettes.

Book Your Stay Online

For more accommodations reviews by Lonely Planet authors, check out http://hotels.lonelyplanet.com/USA. You'll find independent reviews, as well as recommendations on the best places to stay. Best of all, you can book online.

Business Hours

Reviews won't list operating hours unless they deviate from the following normal opening times:

○ Bars: 5pm-midnight Sun-Thu, to 2am Fri & Sat

○ Banks: 8:30am-4:30pm Mon-Thu, to 5:30pm Fri (and possibly 9am-noon Sat)

○ Nightclubs: 10pm-2am Thu-Sat

○ Post offices: 9am-5pm Mon-Fri

○ Shopping malls: 9am-9pm

○ Stores: 10am-6pm Mon-Sat, noon-5pm Sun

○ Supermarkets: 8am-8pm, some open 24hr

Customs Regulations

For a complete list of US customs regulations, visit the official website for **US Customs and Border Protection** (www.cbp.gov).

Duty-free allowance per person is as follows:

○ 1L of liquor (provided you are at least 21 years old)

○ 100 cigars and 200 cigarettes (if you are at least 18 years old)

○ $100 worth of gifts and purchases ($800 if a returning US citizen)

○ If you arrive with $10,000 in cash (US or foreign currency), it must be declared.

There are heavy penalties for attempting to import illegal drugs. Other forbidden items include drug paraphernalia, lottery tickets, items with fake brand names, and most goods made in Cuba, Iran, North Korea, Myanmar (Burma), Angola and Sudan. Any fruit, vegetables, or other food or plant material must be declared (whereby you'll undergo a time-consuming search) or discarded in the bins in the arrival area.

Discount Cards

The following passes can net you savings on museums, accommodations and some transport (including Amtrak): **International Student Identity Card** (ISIC; www.isiccard.com), for international nonstudents under 26; **Student Advantage Card** (www.studentadvantage.com), for US and foreign travelers; the **American Association of Retired Persons** (AARP; www.aarp.org) for US travelers age 50 and older. Membership in the **American Automobile Association** (AAA; www.aaa.com) and reciprocal clubs in the UK, Australia and elsewhere can also earn discounts.

Climate

New York City

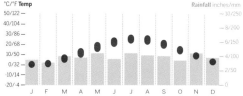

New Orleans

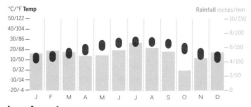

Los Angeles

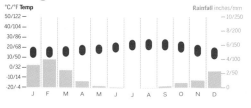

Electricity

120V/60Hz

120V/60Hz

Food

Price ranges for main meals in Eating reviews are:

○ **$** less than $10

○ **$$** $10 to $20

○ **$$$** more than $20

482

Gay & Lesbian Travelers

It's never been a better time to be gay in the USA. GLBT travelers will find lots of places where they can be themselves without thinking twice. Beaches and big cities are typically the gayest destinations.

HOT SPOTS

Manhattan (NYC) is too crowded and cosmopolitan to worry about who's holding hands. Other East Coast cities good for GLBT travelers are Boston, Philadelphia, Washington, DC and Massachusetts' Provincetown.

In Florida, Miami and the 'Conch Republic' of Key West support thriving gay communities. Of course, everyone gets their freak on in New Orleans.

In the Midwest, seek out Chicago. You've probably heard of San Francisco, the happiest gay city in America, and gays and lesbians will also find plenty to do in Los Angeles and Las Vegas.

Lastly, for an island idyll, Hawaii is generally gay-friendly, especially in Waikiki.

ATTITUDES

Most major US cities have a visible and open GLBT community that's easy to connect with.

Levels of acceptance vary nationwide. In some places, there is absolutely no tolerance whatsoever, and in others acceptance is predicated on GLBT people not 'flaunting' their sexual orientation or identity.

Sadly, bigotry still exists. In rural areas and extremely conservative enclaves, it's unwise to be openly out, as violence and verbal abuse can sometimes occur.

RESOURCES

Gay Travel (www.gaytravel.com) Online guides to dozens of US destinations.

OutTraveler (www.outtraveler.com) Has useful online city guides and travel articles about various US and worldwide destinations.

Purple Roofs (www.purpleroofs.com) Lists gay-owned and gay-friendly B&Bs and hotels nationwide.

Gay & Lesbian National Help Center (📞 888-843-4564; www.glnh.org; 🕐 1-9pm PST Mon-Fri, 9am-2pm PST Sat) A national hotline for counseling, information and referrals.

Gay Yellow Network (www.gayyellow.com) Yellow-page listings for more than 30 US cities. Also available as an app for iOS and Android phones.

Health

The USA offers possibly the finest health care in the world. The problem is that unless you have good insurance, it can be prohibitively expensive. It's essential to purchase travel health insurance if your regular policy doesn't cover you when you're abroad.

Bring any medications you may need in their original

containers, clearly labeled. A signed, dated letter from your physician that describes all medical conditions and medications, including generic names, is also a good idea.

If your health insurance does not cover you for medical expenses abroad, consider supplemental insurance. Check the Travel Services section of the **Lonely Planet** (www.lonelyplanet.com) website for more information. Find out in advance if your insurance plan will make payments directly to providers or reimburse you later for overseas health expenditures. For more information on insurance, see below.

Practicalities

o **Electricity** AC 110/120V is standard; buy plug adapters to run most non-US electronics (must be dual-voltage).

o **Newspapers & Magazines** National newspapers include the *New York Times, Wall Street Journal* and *USA Today*. For mainstream news magazines try *Time, Newsweek* and *US News & World Report*.

o **Radio & TV** Radio news: National Public Radio (NPR), lower end of FM dial. Broadcast TV: ABC, CBS, NBC, FOX, PBS (public broadcasting). Major cable channels: CNN (news), ESPN (sports), HBO (movies), Weather Channel.

o **Video Systems** NTSC standard (incompatible with PAL or SECAM). DVDs coded for Region 1 (US and Canada only).

o **Weights & Measures** The US uses imperial measurements. Weight: ounces (oz), pounds (lb), tons. Liquids: oz, pints, quarts, gallons (gal). Distance: feet (ft), yards (yd), miles (mi).

AVAILABILITY & COST OF HEALTH CARE

In general, if you have a medical emergency, your best bet is to find the nearest hospital and go to its emergency room. If the problem isn't urgent, you can call a nearby hospital and ask for a referral to a local physician, which is usually cheaper than a trip to the emergency room.

Pharmacies are abundantly supplied, but you may find that some medications that are available over-the-counter in your home country require a prescription in the USA and, as always, if you don't have insurance to cover the cost of prescriptions, they can be shockingly expensive.

Insurance

No matter how long or short your trip, make sure you have adequate travel insurance, purchased before departure. At a minimum, you need coverage for medical emergencies and treatment, including hospital stays and an emergency flight home if necessary. Medical treatment in the USA is of the highest caliber, but the expense could kill you.

If you will be driving in the USA, it's essential that you have liability insurance. Car rental agencies offer insurance that covers damage to the rental vehicle and separate liability insurance, which covers damage to people and other vehicles. See p491 for details.

Worldwide travel insurance is available at www.lonelyplanet.com/bookings/insurance.do. You can buy, extend and claim online anytime – even if you're already on the road.

Internet Access

Travelers will have few problems staying connected in the tech-savvy USA.

This guide uses an internet icon (@) when a place has a net-connected computer for public use and the wi-fi icon (⌀) when it offers wireless internet access, whether free or fee-based. These days, most hotels and some motels have either a public computer terminal or wi-fi (sometimes free, sometimes for a surcharge of $10 or more per day); ask when reserving.

Big cities have a few internet cafes, but in smaller towns, you may have to head to the public library or a copy center to get online if you're not packing a laptop or other web-accessible device.

If you're not from the US, remember that you will

need an AC adapter for your laptop, plus a plug adapter for US sockets; both are available at larger electronics shops, such as **Best Buy** (📞 888-237-8289; www. bestbuy.com).

Legal Matters

In everyday matters, if you are stopped by the police, bear in mind that there is no system of paying traffic or other fines on the spot. For traffic offenses, the police officer or highway patroller will explain the options to you.

If you are arrested, you have a legal right to an attorney, and you are allowed to remain silent. There is no legal reason to speak to a police officer if you don't wish, but never walk away from an officer until given permission to do so. Anyone who is arrested is legally allowed to make one phone call. If you can't afford a lawyer, a public defender will be appointed to you free of charge. Foreign visitors who don't have a lawyer, friend or family member to help should call their embassy; the police will provide the number upon request.

As a matter of principle, the US legal system presumes a person innocent until proven guilty. Each state has its own civil and criminal laws, and what is legal in one state may be illegal in others.

DRINKING

Bars and stores will usually ask you for photo ID to prove that you are of legal drinking

age: 21 years or older. Being 'carded' is standard practice; don't take it personally. The sale of liquor is subject to local government regulations; some counties prohibit liquor sales on Sunday, after midnight or before breakfast. In 'dry' counties, liquor sales are banned altogether.

DRIVING

In all states, driving under the influence of alcohol or drugs is a serious offense, subject to stiff fines and even imprisonment. For more information on driving in the USA and road rules, see p493.

DRUGS

Recreational drugs are prohibited by federal and state laws. Some states, such as California and Alaska, treat possession of small quantities of marijuana as a misdemeanor, though it is still punishable with fines and/or imprisonment.

Possession of any illicit drug, including cocaine, ecstasy, LSD, heroin, hashish or more than an ounce of pot, is a felony potentially punishable by lengthy jail sentences.

SMOKING

As of 2011, about half the states, the District of Columbia and many municipalities across the US were entirely smoke-free in restaurants, bars and workplaces. You may still encounter smoky lobbies in chain hotels and budget-minded inns, but most other accommodations are smoke-free. For more on smoking, see www.cdc.gov.

Money

See p49 for exchange rates and costs.

Most locals do not carry large amounts of cash for everyday use, relying instead on credit cards, ATMs and debit cards. If coming from overseas, don't plan to rely exclusively on credit cards, as some machines (notably at many gas stations) won't accept foreign cards.

ATMS

ATMs are available 24/7 at most banks, and in shopping centers, airports, grocery stores and convenience shops. Most ATMs charge a service fee of $2.50 or more per transaction, and your home bank may impose additional charges.

CREDIT CARDS

Major credit cards are almost universally accepted. In fact, it's nearly impossible to rent a car or make phone reservations without one (though some airlines require your credit card billing address to be in the USA – a hassle if you're booking domestic flights once there). Visa and MasterCard are the most widely accepted.

If your credit cards are lost or stolen, contact the issuing company immediately:

American Express (📞 800-528-4800; www.americanexpress.com)

Diners Club (📞 800-234-6377; www.dinersclub.com)

Discover (📞 800-347-2683; www.discovercard.com)

MasterCard (☎ 800-627-8372; www.mastercard.com)

Visa (☎ 800-847-2911; www.visa.com)

CURRENCY EXCHANGE

Banks are usually the best places to exchange foreign currencies. Most large city banks offer currency exchange, but banks in rural areas may not.

TAXES

Sales tax varies by state and county. Hotel taxes vary by city.

TIPPING

Tipping is *not* optional; only withhold tips in cases of outrageously bad service.

Airport & hotel porters $2 per bag, minimum $5 per cart

Bartenders 10–15% per round, minimum $1 per drink

Hotel maids $2–4 per night, left under the card provided

Restaurant servers 15–20%, unless a service charge is already on the bill

Taxi drivers 10–15%, rounded up to the next dollar

Valet parking attendants At least $2 (when they hand you back your keys)

Public Holidays

On the following national public holidays, banks, schools and government offices (including post offices) are closed, and transportation, museums and other services operate on a Sunday schedule. Holidays falling on a weekend are usually observed the following Monday.

New Year's Day January 1

Martin Luther King Jr Day Third Monday in January

Presidents Day Third Monday in February

Memorial Day Last Monday in May

Independence Day July 4

Labor Day First Monday in September

Columbus Day Second Monday in October

Veterans Day November 11

Thanksgiving Fourth Thursday in November

Christmas Day December 25

During spring break, high school and college students get a week off from school so they can overrun beach towns and resorts. These occur throughout March and April. For students of all ages, summer vacation runs from June to August.

Safe Travel

Despite its seemingly Babylonian list of dangers – guns, violent crime, riots, earthquakes, tornadoes – the USA is actually a pretty safe country to visit. The greatest danger for travelers is posed by car accidents (buckle up – it's the law).

CRIME

For the traveler, petty theft is the biggest concern, not violent crime. When possible, withdraw money from ATMs during the day, or at night in well-lit, busy areas. When driving, don't pick up hitchhikers, and lock valuables in the trunk of your car before arriving at your destination. In hotels, you can secure valuables in room or hotel safes.

Telephone

The US phone system comprises regional service providers, competing long-distance carriers and several mobile-phone and pay-phone companies. Overall, the system is very efficient, but it can be expensive. Avoid making long-distance calls on a hotel phone or on a pay phone. It's usually cheaper to use a regular landline or cell phone.

CELL PHONES

In the USA mobile phones use GSM 1900 or CDMA 800, operating on different frequencies from other systems around the world. The only foreign phones that will work in the USA are GSM tri- or quad-band models. If you have one of these phones, check with your service provider about using it in the USA. Ask if roaming charges apply, as these will turn even local US calls into pricey international calls.

It might be cheaper to buy a compatible prepaid SIM card for the USA, like those sold by AT&T, T-Mobile or Cingular, which you can insert into your international mobile phone to get a local phone number and voicemail.

If you don't have a compatible phone, you can buy inexpensive, no-contract (pre-paid) phones with a local number and a set number of minutes, which can be topped up at will. Virgin Mobile, T-Mobile, AT&T and other providers offer phones starting at $15, with a package of minutes starting around $40 for 400 minutes. Electronics stores such as Radio Shack and Best Buy sell these phones.

Huge swaths of the rural US, including many national parks and recreation areas, won't pick up a signal. Check your provider's coverage map.

DIALING CODES

All phone numbers within the USA consist of a three-digit area code followed by a seven-digit local number; many areas require you to dial ☏1 first.

☏1 – the international country code for the USA if calling from abroad (the same as Canada, but international rates apply between the two countries).

☏011 – to make an international call from the USA (followed by country code, area code and phone number)

☏00 – for assistance making international calls

☏411 – directory assistance nationwide

☏800-555-1212 – directory assistance for toll-free numbers

PAY PHONES

Pay phones are an endangered species in an ever-expanding mobile-phone world. Local calls at pay phones that work (listen for a dial tone before inserting coins) cost 35¢ to 50¢ for the first few minutes; talking longer costs more.

PHONE CARDS

A prepaid phone card is a good solution for travelers on a budget. Phone cards are easy to find in larger towns and cities, where they are sold at newsstands, convenience stores, supermarkets and major retailers.

Time

The USA uses Daylight Saving Time (DST). On the second Sunday in March, clocks are set one hour ahead ('spring forward'). Then, on the first Sunday of November, clocks are turned back one hour ('fall back'). Just to keep you on your toes, Arizona (except the Navajo Nation), Hawaii and much of Indiana don't follow DST.

The US date system is written as month/day/year. Thus, 8 June 2013 becomes 6/8/13.

Tourist Information

There is no national office promoting US tourism. However, visit the federal government's official web portal (www.usa.gov), go to the 'Travel and Recreation' topic page, and you'll find links to every US state and territory tourism office and website, plus more links to indoor and outdoor recreation, from museums and historical landmarks to scenic byways and national parks.

In this book, state tourism offices are listed in the Information section at the end of relevant sections.

Travelers with Disabilities

If you have a physical disability, the USA can be an accommodating place. The Americans with Disabilities Act (ADA) requires that all public buildings, private buildings built after 1993 (including hotels, restaurants, theaters and museums) and public transit be wheelchair accessible. However, call ahead to confirm what is available. Some local tourist offices publish detailed accessibility guides.

Telephone companies offer relay operators, available via teletypewriter (TTY) numbers, for the hearing impaired. Most banks provide ATM instructions in Braille and via earphone jacks for hearing-impaired customers. All major airlines, Greyhound buses and Amtrak trains will assist travelers with disabilities; just describe your needs when making reservations at least 48 hours in advance. Service animals (guide dogs) are allowed to accompany passengers, but bring documentation.

Some car rental agencies – such as Budget and Hertz – offer hand-controlled vehicles and vans with wheelchair lifts at no extra charge, but you must reserve them well in advance. **Wheelchair Getaways** (☎ 800-642-2042; www.wheelchairgetaways. com) rents accessible vans throughout the USA. In many cities and towns, public buses are accessible to wheelchair riders and will 'kneel' if you are unable to use the steps; just let the driver know that you need the lift or ramp. Cities with underground transport have elevators for passengers needing assistance; DC has the best network (every station has an elevator), but NYC's elevators are few and far between.

Many national and some state parks and recreation areas have wheelchair-accessible paved, graded dirt or boardwalk trails. US citizens and permanent residents with permanent disabilities are entitled to a free 'America the Beautiful' Access Pass (www.nps.gov/findapark/passes.htm), which gives free entry to all federal recreation lands (eg national parks).

Some helpful resources for travelers with disabilities:

Access-Able Travel Source (☎ 303-232-2979; www.access-able.com) General travel website with useful tips and links.

Disabled Sports USA (☎ 301-217-0960; www.dsusa.org) Offers sports and recreation programs for those with disabilities and publishes *Challenge* magazine.

Flying Wheels Travel (☎ 507-451-5005, 877-451-5006; www.flyingwheelstravel.com) A full-service travel agency.

Mobility International USA (☎ 541-343-1284; www.miusa.org) Advises disabled travelers on mobility issues and runs educational international-exchange programs.

Moss Rehabilitation Hospital (☎ 215-663-6000; www.mossresourcenet.org/travel.htm) Extensive links and tips for accessible travel.

Society for Accessible Travel & Hospitality (☎ 212-447-7284; www.sath.org) Advocacy group provides general information for travelers with disabilities.

Visas

Warning: all of the following information is highly subject to change. US entry requirements keep evolving as national security regulations are modified. All travelers should double-check current visa and passport regulations *before* coming to the USA.

The **US State Department** (www.travel.state.gov/visa) maintains the most comprehensive visa information, providing downloadable forms, lists of US consulates abroad and even visa wait times calculated by country.

VISA APPLICATIONS

Apart from most Canadian citizens and those entering under the Visa Waiver Program, all foreign visitors will need to obtain a visa from a US consulate or embassy abroad.

VISA WAIVER PROGRAM

Under the current Visa Waiver Program (VWP), citizens of the following countries may enter the USA without a visa for stays of 90 days or fewer: Andorra, Australia, Austria, Belgium, Brunei, Czech Republic, Denmark, Estonia, Finland, France, Germany, Greece, Hungary, Iceland, Ireland, Italy, Japan, Latvia, Liechtenstein, Lithuania, Luxembourg, Malta, Monaco, the Netherlands, New Zealand, Norway, Portugal, San Marino, Singapore, Slovakia, Slovenia, South Korea, Spain, Sweden, Switzerland and the UK.

If you are a citizen of a VWP country, you do not need a visa *only if* you have a passport that meets current US standards (see p488) *and* you have gotten approval from the Electronic System for Travel Authorization (ESTA) in advance. Register online with the Department of Homeland Security at https://esta.cbp.dhs.gov at least 72 hours before arrival; once travel authorization is approved, your registration is valid for two years. The fee, payable online, is $14.

Visitors from VWP countries must still produce at the port of entry all the same evidence as for a nonimmigrant visa application. They must demonstrate that their trip is for 90 days or less, and that they have a round-trip or onward ticket, adequate funds to cover the trip and binding obligations abroad.

Transport

Getting There & Away

Flights and tours can be booked online at www.lonely-planet.com/booking.

ENTERING THE USA

If you are flying to the US, the first airport that you land in is where you must go through immigration and customs, even if you are continuing on the flight to another destination. Upon arrival, all international visitors must register with the US-VISIT program, which entails having your fingerprints scanned and a digital photo taken.

Once you go through immigration, you collect your baggage and pass through customs (see p481). If you have nothing to declare, you'll probably clear customs without a baggage search, but don't assume this. If you are continuing on the same plane or connecting to another one, it is your responsibility to get your bags to the right place. There are usually airline representatives just outside the customs area who can help you.

PASSPORTS

Every visitor entering the USA from abroad needs a passport. Your passport must be valid for at least six months longer than your intended stay in the USA. Also, if your passport does not meet current US standards, you'll be turned back at the border. If your passport was issued before October 26, 2005, it must be 'machine readable' (with two lines of letters, numbers and <<< at the bottom); if it was issued between October 26, 2005, and October 25, 2006, it must be machine readable and include a digital photo; and if it was issued on or after October 26, 2006, it must be an e-Passport with a digital photo and an integrated RFID chip containing biometric data.

 AIR

AIRPORTS

The US has more than 375 domestic airports, but only a baker's dozen are the main international gateways, including:

Boston Logan International (BOS; www.massport.com/logan)

Chicago O'Hare International (ORD; www.flychicago.com)

Honolulu (HNL; www.honoluluairport.com)

Los Angeles (LAX; www.lawa.org/lax)

Miami (MIA; www.miami-airport.com)

New York John F Kennedy International (JFK; www.panynj.gov)

Newark Liberty International (EWR; www.panynj.gov)

San Francisco (SFO; www.flysfo.com)

Seattle Seattle-Tacoma International (SEA; www.portseattle.org/seatac)

Washington, DC Dulles International (IAD; www.metwashairports.com/dulles)

TICKETS

Flying midweek and in the off-season (normally, fall to spring, excluding holidays) is always less expensive, but fare wars can start anytime. To ensure you've found the cheapest possible ticket for the flight you want, check every angle: compare several online travel booking sites with the airline's own website. Engage a living, breathing travel agent if your itinerary is complex.

Keep in mind your entire itinerary. Some deals for travel within the USA can only be purchased overseas in conjunction with an international air ticket, or you may get discounts for booking air and car rental together. Or, you may find domestic flights within the USA are less expensive when added on to your international airfare.

For a good overview of online ticket agencies, visit **Airinfo** (http://airinfo.aero), which also lists travel agencies worldwide. The big three US travel-booking websites are **Travelocity** (www.travelocity.com), **Orbitz** (www.orbitz.com) and **Expedia** (www.expedia.com). Similar to these and worth trying are **Cheap Tickets** (www.

cheaptickets.com) and **Lowest Fare** (www.lowestfare.com). Typically, these sites don't include budget airlines such as Southwest.

Meta sites like **Kayak** (www.kayak.com) and **Mobissimo** (www.mobissimo.com).are good for price comparisons, as they gather from many sources (but don't provide direct booking).

Bidding for travel can be very successful, but read the fine print carefully before bidding. Try **Hotwire** (www.hotwire.com), **Skyauction** (www.skyauction.com) and **Priceline** (www.priceline.com).

Getting Around

 AIR

When time is tight, book a flight. The domestic air system is extensive and reliable, with dozens of competing airlines, hundreds of airports and thousands of flights daily.

Main 'hub' airports in the USA include all international gateways plus many other large cities. Most cities and towns have a local or county airport, but you usually have to travel via a hub airport to reach them.

AIRLINES IN THE USA

Overall, air travel in the USA is very safe (much safer than driving out on the nation's highways); for comprehensive details by carrier, check out **Airsafe.com** (www.airsafe.com).

The main domestic carriers:

AirTran Airways (☎ 800-247-8726; www.airtran.com) Atlanta-based airline; primarily serves the South, Midwest and eastern US.

Alaska Airlines/ Horizon Air (☎ 800-252-7522/547-9308; www.alaskaair.com) Serves Alaska and the western US, with flights to the East Coast and Hawaii.

American Airlines (☎ 800-433-7300; www.aa.com) Nationwide service.

Continental Airlines (☎ 800-523-3273; www.continental.com) Nationwide service.

Delta Air Lines (☎ 800-221-1212; www.delta.com) Nationwide service.

Frontier Airlines (☎ 800-432-1359; www.frontierairlines.com) Denver-based airline with nationwide service, including to Alaska.

Hawaiian Airlines (☎ 800-367-5320; www.hawaiianair.com) Serves the Hawaiian Islands and West Coast, plus Las Vegas and Phoenix.

JetBlue Airways (☎ 800-538-2583; www.jetblue.com) Nonstop connections between eastern and western US cities, plus Florida, New Orleans and Texas.

Southwest Airlines (☎ 800-435-9792; www.southwest.com) Service across the continental USA.

Climate Change & Travel

Every form of transport that relies on carbon-based fuel generates CO_2, the main cause of human-induced climate change. Modern travel is dependent on airplanes, which might use less fuel per mile per person than most cars but travel much greater distances. The altitude at which aircraft emit gases (including CO_2) and particles also contributes to their climate change impact. Many websites offer 'carbon calculators' that allow people to estimate the carbon emissions generated by their journey and, for those who wish to do so, to offset the impact of the greenhouse gases emitted with contributions to portfolios of climate-friendly initiatives throughout the world. Lonely Planet offsets the carbon footprint of all staff and author travel.

Spirit Airlines (☎ 800-772-7117; www.spiritair.com) Florida-based airline; serves many US gateway cities.

United Airlines (☎ 800-864-8331; www.united.com) Nationwide service.

US Airways (☎ 800-428-4322; www.usairways.com) Nationwide service.

Virgin America (☎ 877-359-8474; www.virginamerica.com) Flights between East and West Coast cities and Las Vegas.

BICYCLE

Regional bicycle touring is popular. It means coasting winding backroads (because bicycles are often not permitted on freeways), and calculating progress in miles per day, not miles per hour. Cyclists must follow the same rules of the road as automobiles, but don't expect drivers to respect your right of way. **Better World Club** (p491) offers a bicycle roadside assistance program.

For highlights of the USA's cycling and mountain-biking trails, see p466. For epic cross-country journeys, get the support of a tour operator; it's about two months of dedicated pedaling coast to coast.

For advice, and lists of local bike clubs and repair shops, browse the **League of American Bicyclists website** (www.bikeleague. org). If you're bringing your own bike to the USA, visit the **International Bicycle Fund website** (www.ibike.org), which lists bike regulations by airline and has lots of advice. In the past, most international and domestic airlines have carried bikes as checked baggage without charge when they're in a box; recently, many have changed their regulations and imposed or increased fees (from $50 to upwards of $250 each way). Amtrak trains and Greyhound buses will transport bikes within the USA, sometimes charging extra.

It's not hard to buy a bike once you're here and resell it before you leave. Every city and town has bike shops; if you prefer a cheaper, used bicycle, try garage sales, bulletin boards at hostels and colleges, or the free classified ads at **Craigslist** (www.craigslist.org). These are also the best places to sell your bike, though stores selling used bikes may also buy from you.

Long-term bike rentals are also easy to find; recommended rental places are listed throughout this guide. Rates run from $100 per week and up, and a credit card authorization for several hundred dollars is usually necessary as a security deposit.

🚌 BUS

To save money, travel by bus, particularly between major towns and cities. Gotta-go middle-class Americans prefer to fly or drive, but buses let you see the countryside and meet folks along the way. As a rule, buses are reliable, cleanish and comfortable, with air-conditioning, barely reclining seats, onboard lavatories and no smoking on board.

Greyhound (📞 800-231-2222; www.greyhound.com) is the major long-distance bus company, with routes throughout the USA and Canada. To improve efficiency and profitability, Greyhound has recently stopped service to many small towns; routes generally trace major highways and stop at larger population centers. To reach country towns on rural roads, you may need to transfer to local or county bus systems; Greyhound can usually provide their contact information.

Competing with Greyhound are the 75-plus franchises of **Trailways** (📞 703-691-3052; www.trailways.com). Upstart long-distance bus lines that may offer cheaper fares include **Megabus** (📞 877-462-6342; www.megabus.com), primarily operating routes in the Northeast and Midwest.

The frequency of bus services varies widely, depending on the route. Despite the elimination of many tiny destinations,

Bus Fares

Here are some sample standard one-way adult fares and trip times on Greyhound:

SERVICE	PRICE	DURATION (HR)
Boston–Philadelphia	$55	7
Chicago–New Orleans	$133	23
Los Angeles–San Francisco	$55	8
New York–Chicago	$108	18
New York–San Francisco	$252	72
Washington, DC–Miami	$160	28

nonexpress Greyhound buses still stop every 50 to 100 miles to pick up passengers, and long-distance buses stop for meal breaks and driver changes.

Many bus stations are clean and safe, but some are in dodgy areas; if you arrive in the evening, it's worth spending the money on a taxi. Some towns have just a flag stop. If you are boarding at one of these, pay the driver with exact change.

COSTS

For lower fares on Greyhound, purchase tickets at least seven days in advance (purchasing 14 days in advance will save even more). Round trips are also cheaper.

RESERVATIONS

Tickets for some Trailways and other buses can only be purchased immediately prior to departure. Greyhound bus tickets can be bought over the phone or online. You can print tickets at home or pick them up at the terminal using 'Will Call' service.

Seating is normally first-come, first-served. Greyhound recommends arriving an hour before departure to get a seat.

CAR & MOTORCYCLE

For maximum flexibility and convenience, and to explore rural America and its wide-open spaces, having a car is essential. Although gas (petrol) prices are high, you can often score fairly inexpensive rentals (NYC excluded), with rates as low as $20 per day.

For recommended driving routes, look for Scenic Drives

boxed texts throughout the regional chapters.

AUTOMOBILE ASSOCIATIONS

The **American Automobile Association** (AAA; ☎ 800-874-7532; www.aaa.com) has reciprocal membership agreements with several international auto clubs (check with AAA and bring your membership card from home). For its members, AAA offers travel insurance, tour books, diagnostic centers for used-car buyers and a wide-ranging network of regional offices. AAA advocates politically for the auto industry.

A more ecofriendly alternative, the **Better World Club** (☎ 866-238-1137; www.betterworldclub.com) donates 1% of revenue to assist environmental cleanup, offers ecologically sensitive choices for every service it provides and advocates politically for environmental causes.

In either organization, the primary member benefit is 24-hour emergency roadside assistance anywhere in the USA. Both also offer trip planning, free travel maps, travel agency services, car insurance and a range of travel discounts (eg on hotels, car rentals, attractions).

DRIVER'S LICENSE

Foreign visitors can legally drive a car in the USA for up to 12 months on their home driver's license, but an International Driving Permit (IDP) will have more credibility with US traffic police, especially if your home license doesn't have a photo or isn't in English. Your automobile association at home can issue an IDP, valid

for one year, for a small fee. Always carry your home license together with the IDP.

To drive a motorcycle in the USA, you will need either a valid US state motorcycle license or an IDP specially endorsed for motorcycles.

INSURANCE

Rental-car companies will provide liability insurance, but most charge extra. Rental companies almost never include collision-damage insurance for the vehicle. Instead, they offer an optional Collision Damage Waiver (CDW) or Loss Damage Waiver (LDW), usually with an initial deductible cost of $100 to $500. For an extra premium, you can usually get this deductible covered as well. Paying extra for some or all of this insurance increases the cost of a rental car by as much as $30 a day.

Many credit cards offer free collision damage coverage for rental cars if you rent for 15 days or less and charge the total rental to your card. This is a good way to avoid paying extra fees to the rental company, but note that if there's an accident, sometimes you must pay the rental car company first and then seek reimbursement from the credit-card company. There may be exceptions that are not covered, too, such as 'exotic' rentals (eg 4WD Jeeps, convertibles).

RENTAL

Car

Car rental is a competitive business in the USA. Most rental companies require that you have a major credit

Driving Distances & Times

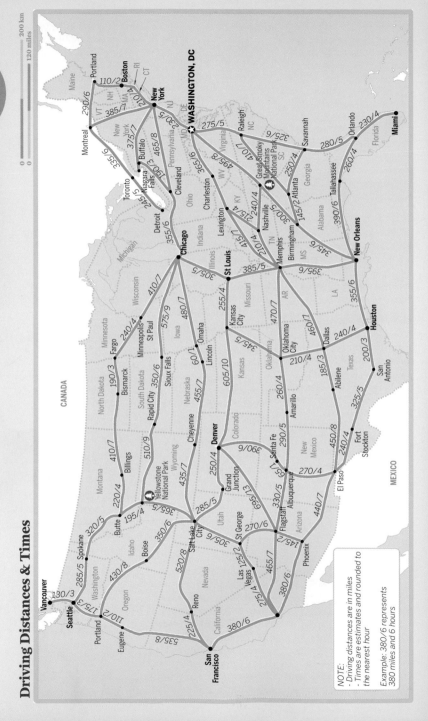

NOTE:
- Driving distances are in miles
- Times are estimates and rounded to
the nearest hour

Example: 380/6 represents
380 miles and 6 hours

card, be at least 25 years old and have a valid driver's license. Some major national companies may rent to drivers between the ages of 21 and 24 for an additional charge of around $25 per day. Those under 21 are usually not permitted to rent at all.

Major national car-rental companies:

Alamo (☎ 877-222-9075; www.alamo.com)

Avis (☎ 800-230-4898; www.avis.com)

Budget (☎ 800-527-0700; www.budget.com)

Dollar (☎ 800-800-3665; www.dollar.com)

Enterprise (☎ 800-261-7331; www.enterprise.com)

Hertz (☎ 800-654-3131; www.hertz.com)

National (☎ 877-222-9058; www.nationalcar.com)

Rent-a-Wreck (☎ 877-877-0700; www.rentawreck.com)

Thrifty (☎ 800-847-4389; www.thrifty.com)

Car-rental prices vary wildly. The average daily rate for a small car ranges from $30 to $75, or $200 to $500 weekly.

ROAD CONDITIONS & HAZARDS

America's highways are legendary ribbons of unblemished asphalt, but not always. Road hazards include potholes, city commuter traffic, wandering wildlife and, of course, cell-phone-wielding, kid-distracted and enraged drivers. Caution,

foresight, courtesy and luck usually gets you past them.

In places where winter driving is an issue, many cars are fitted with steel-studded snow tires; snow chains can sometimes be required in mountain areas. Driving off-road, or on dirt roads, is often forbidden by rental-car companies, and it can be very dangerous in wet weather.

In deserts and range country, livestock sometimes graze next to unfenced roads. These areas are signed as 'Open Range' or with the silhouette of a steer. Where deer and other wild animals frequently appear roadside, you'll see signs with the silhouette of a leaping deer. Take these signs seriously, particularly at dusk and dawn.

ROAD RULES

In the USA, cars drive on the right-hand side of the road. The use of seat belts and child safety seats is required in every state. Most car rental agencies rent child safety seats for around $12 per day, but you must reserve them when booking. In some states, motorcyclists are required to wear helmets.

On interstate highways, the speed limit is sometimes raised to 75mph. Unless otherwise posted, the speed limit is generally 55mph or 65mph on highways, 25mph to 35mph in cities and towns and as low as 15mph in school zones (strictly enforced during school hours). It's forbidden to pass a school bus when its lights are flashing.

Unless signs prohibit it, you may turn right at a red light after first coming to a full stop – except in NYC,

where turning on right on red is illegal. At four-way stop signs, cars should proceed in order of arrival; when two cars arrive simultaneously, the one on the right has the right of way. When in doubt, just politely wave the other driver ahead. When emergency vehicles (ie police, fire or ambulance) approach from either direction, pull over safely and get out of the way.

Most states have laws against (and hefty fines for) littering along the highway. In an increasing number of states, it is illegal to talk on a handheld cell (mobile) phone while driving; use a hands-free device instead.

The maximum legal blood-alcohol concentration for drivers is 0.08%. Penalties are very severe for Driving Under the Influence (DUI) of alcohol and/or drugs. Police can give roadside sobriety checks to assess if you've been drinking or using drugs. If you fail, they'll require you take a breath test, urine test or blood test to determine the level of alcohol or drugs in your body. Refusing to be tested is treated the same as if you'd taken the test and failed.

In some states it is illegal to carry 'open containers' of alcohol in a vehicle, even if they are empty.

HITCHHIKING

Hitchhiking in the USA is potentially dangerous and definitely not recommended. Indeed, drivers have heard so many lurid reports they tend to be just as afraid of those with their thumbs out. Hitchhiking on freeways is prohibited. You'll see more people hitchhiking in rural areas and in Alaska and Hawaii, but these places aren't safer than anywhere else, and with sparse traffic, you may well get stranded. In and around national parks, hitching to and from trailheads is common, but a safer bet is to check ride-share boards at hostels, park visitor centers and wilderness information stations.

LOCAL TRANSPORTATION

Except in large US cities, public transportation is rarely the most convenient option for travelers, and coverage can be sparse to outlying towns and suburbs. However, it is usually cheap, safe and reliable. For details, see the Getting Around sections for the main cities and towns covered in the On the Road chapters. In addition, more than half the states in the nation have adopted ☎511 as an all-purpose help line for local transportation.

AIRPORT SHUTTLES

Shuttle buses provide inexpensive and convenient transport to/from airports in most cities. Most are 12-seat vans; some have regular routes and stops (which include the main hotels) and some pick up and deliver passengers 'door to door' in their service area. Costs average $15 to $30 per person.

BICYCLE

Some cities are more suited to bicycle riding than others, but most have at least a few dedicated bike lanes and paths, and bikes can usually be carried on public transportation. See p489 for more on bicycling in the USA, including rentals.

BUS

Most cities and larger towns have dependable local bus systems, though they are often designed for commuters and provide limited service in the evening and on weekends. Costs range from free to between $1 and $3 per ride.

SUBWAY & TRAIN

The largest systems are in New York, Chicago, Boston, Philadelphia, Washington, DC, Chicago, Los Angeles and the San Francisco Bay Area. Other cities may have small, one- or two-line rail systems that mainly serve downtown.

TAXI

Taxis are metered, with flagfall charges of around $2.50 to start, plus $1.50 to $2 per mile. They charge extra for waiting and handling baggage, and drivers expect a 10% to 15% tip. Taxis cruise the busiest areas in large cities; otherwise, it's easiest to phone and order one.

TOURS

Hundreds of companies offer all kinds of organized tours of cities or regions of the USA. See Tours in the city sections throughout this book for more recommendations.

Backroads (☎ 510-527-1555, 800-462-2848; www.backroads.com) Designs a range of active, multisport and outdoor-oriented trips for all abilities and budgets.

Gray Line (☎ 800-966-8125; www.grayline.com) For those short on time, Gray Line offers a comprehensive range of standard sightseeing tours across the country.

Green Tortoise (☎ 415-956-7500, 800-867-8647; www.greentortoise.com) Offering budget adventures for independent travelers, Green Tortoise is famous for its sleeping-bunk buses. Most trips leave from San Francisco, traipsing through the West and nationwide.

Road Scholar (800-454-5768; www.roadscholar.org) For those aged 55 and older, this venerable nonprofit offers 'learning adventures' in all 50 states.

🚆 TRAIN

Amtrak (☎ 800-872-7245; www.amtrak.com) has an extensive rail system throughout the USA, with Amtrak's Thruway buses providing connections to and from the rail network to some smaller centers and national parks. Compared with other modes of travel, trains are rarely the quickest, cheapest, timeliest or most convenient option, but they turn the journey into a relaxing, social and scenic all-American experience.

Amtrak has several long-distance lines traversing the nation east to west, and even more running north to south. These connect all of America's biggest cities and many of its smaller ones. Long-distance services (on named trains) mostly operate daily on these routes, but some run only three to five days per week. See Amtrak's website for detailed route maps, as well as the Getting There & Away sections in this guide's regional chapters.

Commuter trains provide faster, more frequent services on shorter routes, especially the northeast corridor from Boston, MA, to Washington, DC. Amtrak's high-speed Acela Express trains are the most expensive, and rail passes are not valid on these trains. Other commuter rail lines include those serving the Lake Michigan shoreline near Chicago, major cities on the West Coast and the Miami area.

CLASSES & COSTS

Amtrak fares vary according to the type of train and seating; on long-distance lines, you can travel in coach seats (reserved or unreserved), business class, or 1st class, which includes all sleeping compartments. Sleeping cars include simple bunks (called 'roomettes'), bedrooms with en suite bathrooms and suites sleeping four with two bathrooms. Sleeping-car rates include meals in the dining car, which offers everyone sit-down meal service (pricey if not included). Food service on commuter lines, when it exists, consists of sandwich and snack bars. Bringing your own food and drink is recommended on all trains.

Various one-way, round-trip and touring fares are available from Amtrak, with discounts of 15% for seniors aged 62 and over and for students with a 'Student Advantage' card ($20) or an International Student Identity Card (ISIC), and 50% discounts for children aged two to 15 when accompanied by a paying adult. AAA members get 10% off. Web-only 'Weekly Specials' offer deep discounts on certain undersold routes.

Generally, the earlier you book, the lower the price.

Train Fares

Sample standard, one-way, adult coach-class fares and trip times on Amtrak's long-distance routes:

SERVICE	PRICE	DURATION (HR)
Chicago–New Orleans	$112	20
New York–Chicago	$88	19
New York–Los Angeles	$248	68
Seattle–Oakland, CA	$154	23
Washington, DC–Miami	$125	27

To get many of the standard discounts, you need to reserve at least three days in advance. If you want to take an Acela Express or Metroliner train, avoid peak commute times and aim for weekends.

Amtrak Vacations (☎ 800-268-7252; www. amtrakvacations.com) offers vacation packages that include rental cars, hotels, tours and attractions. Air-Rail packages let you travel by train in one direction, then return by plane the other way.

RESERVATIONS

Reservations can be made any time from 11 months in advance up to the day of departure. Space on most trains is limited, and certain routes can be crowded, especially during summer and holiday periods, so it's a good idea to book as far in advance as you can; this also gives you the best chance of fare discounts.

TRAIN PASSES

Amtrak's USA Rail Pass offers coach-class travel for 15 ($389), 30 ($579) or 45 ($749) days, with travel limited to eight, 12 or 18 one-

way 'segments,' respectively. A segment is *not* the same as a one-way trip. If reaching your destination requires riding more than one train (for example, getting from New York to Miami with a transfer in Washington, DC) that one-way trip will actually use two segments of your pass.

Present your pass at an Amtrak office to pick up your ticket(s) for each trip. Reservations should be made by phone (call ☎ 800-872-7245, or ☎ 215-856-7953 from outside the USA) as far in advance as possible. Each segment of the journey must be booked. At some rural stations, trains will only stop if there's a reservation. Tickets are not for specific seats, but a conductor on board may allocate you a seat. Business-class, 1st-class and sleeper accommodations cost extra and must be reserved separately.

All travel must be completed within 180 days of purchasing your pass. Passes are not valid on the Acela Express, Auto Train, Thruway motorcoach connections or the Canadian portion of Amtrak routes operated jointly with Via Rail Canada.

Behind the Scenes

Author Thanks

REGIS ST LOUIS

Thanks go to Suki and my talented co-authors who did such a stellar job bringing America to life. Thanks to Eve and friends for top tips in Washington and to the Krishna friends at New Vrindaban for a magical visit. Big hugs to Cassandra, Magdalena and Genevieve for joining on the big Southern road trip. Lastly, thank you to the Kaufman gang for letting us join in the Wrightsville Beach holiday.

Acknowledgments

Climate map data adapted from Peel MC, Finlayson BL & McMahon TA (2007) 'Updated World Map of the Köppen-Geiger Climate Classification', *Hydrology and Earth System Sciences,* 11, 163344.

Cover photographs: Front: Statue of Liberty, New York City, Richard Cummins/Lonely Planet Images © 2012; Back: Monument Valley Navajo Tribal Park, Arizona, Douglas Steakley/Lonely Planet Images © 2012. Many of the images in this guide are available for licensing from Lonely Planet Images: www.lonelyplanetimages.com.

This Book

This 1st edition of *Discover USA* was coordinated by Regis St Louis. See Our Writers for a list of authors who researched and wrote the book. This guidebook was commissioned in Lonely Planet's Oakland office, and produced by the following:

Commissioning Editor Suki Gear
Coordinating Editor Ali Lemer
Coordinating Cartographer Mark Griffiths
Coordinating Layout Designer Jessica Rose
Managing Editors Bruce Evans, Anna Metcalfe
Managing Cartographer Alison Lyall
Managing Layout Designer Chris Girdler
Assisting Editors Gabrielle Innes, Catherine Naghten, Dianne Schallmeiner
Assisting Cartographer Valeska Cañas
Assisting Layout Designer Wibowo Rusli
Cover Research Brendan Dempsey
Internal Image Research Sabrina Dalbesio
Thanks to Ryan Evans, Martin Heng, Yvonne Kirk, Gerard Walker

SEND US YOUR FEEDBACK

Index

000 Map pages

000 Map pages

N

P

O

T

How to Use This Book

These symbols will help you find the listings you want:

- ◉ Sights
- 🏖 Beaches
- ➕ Activities
- ⟲ Courses
- 📷 Tours
- ✴ Festivals & Events
- ▦ Sleeping
- ✕ Eating
- 🍸 Drinking
- ★ Entertainment
- 🅐 Shopping
- ℹ Information/Transport

These symbols give you the vital information for each listing:

- ☏ Telephone Numbers
- ⊘ Opening Hours
- P Parking
- ⊖ Nonsmoking
- ✳ Air-Conditioning
- @ Internet Access
- 🛜 Wi-Fi Access
- ⊠ Swimming Pool
- 🍴 Vegetarian Selection
- 📖 English-Language Menu
- 👪 Family-Friendly
- 🐾 Pet-Friendly
- 🚌 Bus
- ⛴ Ferry
- Ⓜ Metro
- Ⓢ Subway
- ⊖ London Tube
- 🚊 Tram
- 🚉 Train

Reviews are organised by author preference.

Look out for these icons:

- FREE — No payment required
- 🌿 — A green or sustainable option

Our authors have nominated these places as demonstrating a strong commitment to sustainability – for example by supporting local communities and producers, operating in an environmentally friendly way, or supporting conservation projects.

Map Legend

Sights
- 🏖 Beach
- 🛕 Buddhist
- 🏰 Castle
- ✝ Christian
- 🕉 Hindu
- ☪ Islamic
- ✡ Jewish
- 🗿 Monument
- 🏛 Museum/Gallery
- 🏚 Ruin
- 🍇 Winery/Vineyard
- 🐾 Zoo
- ◉ Other Sight

Activities, Courses & Tours
- 🤿 Diving/Snorkelling
- 🛶 Canoeing/Kayaking
- 🎿 Skiing
- 🏄 Surfing
- 🏊 Swimming/Pool
- 🚶 Walking
- 🏄 Windsurfing
- ➕ Other Activity/Course/Tour

Sleeping
- ▦ Sleeping
- ⛺ Camping

Eating
- ✕ Eating

Drinking
- 🍸 Drinking
- ☕ Cafe

Entertainment
- ★ Entertainment

Shopping
- 🅐 Shopping

Information
- ✉ Post Office
- ℹ Tourist Information

Transport
- ✈ Airport
- ⊗ Border Crossing
- 🚌 Bus
- 🚠 Cable Car/Funicular
- 🚲 Cycling
- ⛴ Ferry
- Ⓜ Metro
- 🚝 Monorail
- P Parking
- Ⓢ S-Bahn
- 🚕 Taxi
- 🚉 Train/Railway
- 🚊 Tram
- ⊖ Tube Station
- Ⓤ U-Bahn
- ● Other Transport

Routes
- Tollway
- Freeway
- Primary
- Secondary
- Tertiary
- Lane
- Unsealed Road
- Plaza/Mall
- Steps
-)= = Tunnel
- Pedestrian Overpass
- Walking Tour
- Walking Tour Detour
- Path

Boundaries
- ––– International
- –––– State/Province
- – – Disputed
- – – Regional/Suburb
- Marine Park
- Cliff
- Wall

Population
- ✪ Capital (National)
- ◉ Capital (State/Province)
- ● City/Large Town
- ● Town/Village

Geographic
- 🛖 Hut/Shelter
- 🗼 Lighthouse
- 👁 Lookout
- ▲ Mountain/Volcano
- ◉ Oasis
- ⊕ Park
-)(Pass
- 🛑 Picnic Area
- ◉ Waterfall

Hydrography
- River/Creek
- Intermittent River
- Swamp/Mangrove
- Reef
- Canal
- Water
- Dry/Salt/Intermittent Lake
- Glacier

Areas
- Beach/Desert
- Cemetery (Christian)
- Cemetery (Other)
- Park/Forest
- Sportsground
- Sight (Building)
- Top Sight (Building)

ANDREA SCHULTE-PEEVERS

California Andrea fell in love with California – its pizzazz, people and sunshine – almost the instant she landed in the Golden State. She grew up in Germany, lived in London and traveled the world before getting a degree from UCLA and embarking on a career in travel writing. Andrea has written or contributed to some 60 Lonely Planet books, including several editions of this one, as well as the guides *California* and *Los Angeles & Southern California*.

RYAN VER BERKMOES

Best of the Rest Ryan first drove across the Great Plains with his family in the 1960s. Among the treasured memories are a pair of Wild West six-shooters he got at Wall Drugs in South Dakota and which he still has (in a box someplace *not* under his pillow). Through the years he never passes up a chance to wander the backroads of America's heartland, finding beauty and intrigue where he least expects it. Find more at www.ryanverberkmoes.com.

Read more about Ryan at:
lonelyplanet.com/members/ryanverberkmoes

JOHN A VLAHIDES

California John A Vlahides co-hosts the TV series *Lonely Planet: Roads Less Travelled,* screening on National Geographic Channels International. John studied cooking in Paris, with the same chefs who trained Julia Child, and is a former luxury-hotel concierge and member of Les Clefs d'Or, the international union of the world's elite concierges. He lives in San Francisco, where he sings tenor with the San Francisco Symphony, and spends his free time skiing the Sierra Nevada. For more, see JohnVlahides.com and Twitter.com/JohnVlahides.

Read more about John at:
lonelyplanet.com/members/johnvlahides

KARLA ZIMMERMAN

Chicago As a lifelong Midwesterner, Karla is well-versed in the region's beaches, ballparks, breweries and pie shops. When she's not home in Chicago watching the Cubs or writing for newspapers, books and magazines, she's out exploring. Karla has written for several Lonely Planet guidebooks covering the USA, Canada, the Caribbean and Europe.

Read more about Karla at:
lonelyplanet.com/members/karlazimmerman

BRIDGET GLEESON

California A journalist who divides her time between California and Argentina, Bridget has written about food, wine, hotels and adventure travel for *Budget Travel*, *Afar*, *Delta Sky*, *Jetsetter*, *Continental*, *Tablet Hotels* and *Mr & Mrs Smith*. Follow her travels at www.bridgetgleeson.com.

MICHAEL GROSBERG

New York City, Best of the Rest Growing up, Michael spent family holidays crisscrossing New York, New Jersey and Pennsylvania with his large NYC family and grew to know their neighborhoods as if they were his own. After several long overseas trips and many careers, some abroad, Michael returned to New York City for graduate school and taught literature in NYC colleges. He's lived in three of the five boroughs and takes every opportunity to hit the road and explore.

BETH KOHN

California A lucky long-time resident of San Francisco, Beth lives to be playing outside or splashing in big puddles of water. For this guide, she hiked and biked Bay Area byways, lugged a bear canister along the John Muir Trail and selflessly soaked in hot springs – for research purposes, of course. An author of Lonely Planet's *Yosemite, Sequoia & Kings Canyon National Parks* and *California* guides, you can see more of her work at www.bethkohn.com.

MARIELLA KRAUSE

Best of the Rest Although she currently lives in California, Mariella will always consider Texas home. She lived in Austin for 15 years and still sprinkles her language with Texanisms whenever possible, much to the amusement of those who don't consider 'ya'll' a proper pronoun. Fresh off last year's *Texas* guide, Mariella is as proud as a kitten in a pickup to once again share her favorite places in the Lone Star state.

EMILY MATCHAR

New Orleans & the South A native Tarheel, Emily lives and works in Chapel Hill, North Carolina (when she's not bopping around the globe, that is). Though she doesn't have a Southern accent, she does know how to smoke a hog, hotwire a pickup truck and bake a mean coconut cake. She writes about culture, food and travel for a variety of national magazines and newspapers, and has contributed to a dozen Lonely Planet guides.

BRADLEY MAYHEW

Best of the Rest An expat Brit, Bradley currently calls southeastern Montana home. Half a lifetime of travels through Central Asia, Tibet and Mongolia has made him feel quite at home in Big Sky country. He is the coordinating author of a dozen Lonely Planet guides, including *Tibet*, *Bhutan*, *Nepal*, *Central Asia* and *Yellowstone & Grand Teton National Parks* and he hikes nearby Yellowstone Park and the Beartooth Mountains every chance he gets. See what he's up to at www.bradleymayhew.blogspot.com.

CAROLYN MCCARTHY

Best of the Rest Author Carolyn McCarthy became enamored of the Rockies as an undergraduate at Colorado College. She studied, skied and hiked her way through the region, even working as a boot fitter. In the last seven years she has contributed to over a dozen Lonely Planet titles, and has written for *National Geographic*, *Outside*, *Lonely Planet Magazine* and other publications. You can follow her Americas blog at www.carolynswildblueyonder.blogspot.com.

KEVIN RAUB

New Orleans & the South Kevin Raub grew up in Atlanta and started his career as a music journalist in New York, working for *Men's Journal* and *Rolling Stone* magazines. The rock 'n' roll lifestyle took its toll, so he took up travel writing while ditching the States for Brazil. This is Kevin's 14th Lonely Planet guide. You can find him at www.kevinraub.net.

BRENDAN SAINSBURY

The Pacific Northwest UK-born Brendan lives in White Rock, Canada, within baseball-pitching distance (well, almost) of the USA and the Pacific Northwest. He has been researching the area for Lonely Planet since 2007 and his forays across the border have included fine-dining in the San Juan Islands, hitchhiking in western Montana and running 100 miles unassisted across the Cascade Mountains in a so-called endurance race. Brendan is also a co-author of Lonely Planet's current *Washington, Oregon & the Pacific Northwest* guidebook.

SARA BENSON

California, Best of the Rest After graduating from college in Chicago, Sara jumped on a plane to California with just one suitcase and $100 in her pocket. She has bounced around the Golden State ever since, in between stints living in Asia and Hawaii and working as a national park ranger. The author of 50 travel and nonfiction books, Sara dodged avalanches in Lake Tahoe and rockslides along Big Sur's splendid coast while writing this guide. Follow her adventures online at www.indietraveler.blogspot.com and www.twitter.com/indie_traveler.

Read more about Sara at:
lonelyplanet.com/members/Sara_Benson

ALISON BING

California After 18 years in San Francisco, Alison has done everything you're supposed to do in the city and some things you're definitely not, including falling in love on the Haight St bus and eating a Mission burrito in one sitting. Alison holds degrees in art history and international relations and regularly contributes to newspapers, magazines, TV, radio and books, including various Lonely Planet guides to Venice, Morocco, the USA, California and San Francisco.

JEFF CAMPBELL

Florida, In Focus Jeff Campbell is the great-grandson of Florida pioneers who cleared the pines, mined the phosphate, and paved the roads in central Florida. As a child, he remembers searching for alligators in the local lake, and riding Space Mountain the year it opened. As an adult, he's been a travel writer for Lonely Planet since 2000; he has been the coordinating author of *Florida* and three editions of *USA*, among other US titles.

NATE CAVALIERI

California A native of central Michigan, Nate Cavalieri lives in Northern California and has crisscrossed the region's back roads on a tireless search for the biggest trees, the best camping and the hoppiest pints of craft beer. Besides authoring guides on California and Latin America for Lonely Planet, he writes about jazz and pop music and is the Jazz Editor at Rhapsody Music Service. Photos from his travels in Northern California and other writing can be found at www.natecavalieri.com.

Read more about Nate at:
lonelyplanet.com/members/natecavalieri

SARAH CHANDLER

The Grand Canyon & the Southwest, In Focus Long enamored of Sin City's gritty enchantments, Sarah jumped at the chance to sharpen her blackjack skills while delving into the atomic mysteries of rural Nevada. In Vegas, Sarah learned the secret art of bypassing velvet ropes, bounced from buffets to pool parties, and explored the seedy vintage glamour of downtown. Sarah is currently based between the US and Amsterdam, where she works as a writer, actress, and lecturer at Amsterdam University College. When in doubt, she always doubles down.

Read more about Sarah at:
lonelyplanet.com/members/sarahchandler

JIM DUFRESNE

Best of the Rest Jim has lived, worked and wandered across Alaska. As the Sports & Outdoors Editor of the *Juneau Empire*, he was the first Alaskan sportswriter to win a national award from Associated Press. As a guide for Alaska Discovery he has witnessed the Hubbard Glacier shed icebergs the size of pickup trucks off its 8-mile-wide face. Jim now lives in Michigan writing for www.MichiganTrailMaps.com and regularly returns to the Far North to update Lonely Planet's *Alaska*.

LISA DUNFORD

The Grand Canyon & the Southwest As one of the possibly thousands of great-great-granddaughters of Brigham Young, ancestry first drew Lisa to Utah. But it's the incredible red rocks that keep her coming back. Driving the remote backroads outside Bluff, she was once again reminded how here the earth seems at its most elemental. Before becoming a freelance Lonely Planet author 10 years ago, Lisa was a newspaper editor and writer in South Texas. Lisa co-authored Lonely Planet's *Zion & Bryce Canyon National Parks*.

NED FRIARY & GLENDA BENDURE

Boston & New England Ned and Glenda hail from Cape Cod, their home since the 1980s. Ocean swims, long bike rides and road trips around New England are favorite pastimes. The highlight of their latest trip was a climb to the summit of Acadia Mountain in Acadia National Park, where the jaw-dropping views reminded them just how wildly diverse New England is. They've written extensively on the region and are co-authors of Lonely Planet's *New England* and *Discover USA's Best National Parks* guides.

Our Story

A beat-up old car, a few dollars in the pocket and a sense of adventure. In 1972 that's all Tony and Maureen Wheeler needed for the trip of a lifetime – across Europe and Asia overland to Australia. It took several months, and at the end – broke but inspired – they sat at their kitchen table writing and stapling together their first travel guide, *Across Asia on the Cheap*. Within a week they'd sold 1500 copies. Lonely Planet was born.

Today, Lonely Planet has offices in Melbourne, London and Oakland, with more than 600 staff and writers. We share Tony's belief that 'a great guidebook should do three things: inform, educate and amuse'.

Our Writers

REGIS ST LOUIS

Coordinating Author, Plan Your Trip, Washington, DC, In Focus, Survival Guide A Hoosier by birth, Regis grew up in a sleepy riverside town where he dreamed of big-city intrigue. In 2001, he settled in New York, which had all that and more. He has also lived in San Francisco and Los Angeles and has crossed the country by train, bus and car, while visiting remote corners of America. Favorite memories from his most recent trip include chasing the bluegrass scene across southern Virginia, chanting with Krishna devotees in West Virginia and crab feasting all over Maryland. Regis has contributed to more than 30 Lonely Planet titles, including *Washington, DC*, and *New York City*.

Read more about Regis at:
lonelyplanet.com/members/regisstlouis

AMY C BALFOUR

The Grand Canyon & the Southwest Amy has hiked, biked, skied and gambled her way across the Southwest, finding herself returning again and again to Flagstaff, Monument Valley and, always, the Grand Canyon. On this trip she fell hard for Bisbee and Chiricahua National Monument. When she's not daydreaming about red rocks and green-chile hamburgers, she's writing about food, travel and the outdoors. Amy has authored or co-authored 11 guidebooks for Lonely Planet, including *Los Angeles Encounter*, *California*, *Hawaii* and *Arizona*.

Read more about Amy at:
lonelyplanet.com/members/amycbalfour

MICHAEL BENANAV

The Grand Canyon & the Southwest Michael came to New Mexico in 1992 and quickly fell under its spell; soon after, he moved to a rural village in the Sangre de Cristo foothills, where he still lives. A veteran international traveler, he can't imagine a better place to come home to after a trip. Aside from his work for Lonely Planet, he's authored two nonfiction books and writes and photographs for magazines and newspapers. His website is www.michaelbenanav.com.

Read more about Michael at:
lonelyplanet.com/members/mbenanav

ANDREW BENDER

California Two decades ago, this native New Englander packed up the car and drove cross-country to work in film production, and eventually realized that the joy was in the journey (and writing about it). His work has since appeared in the *Los Angeles Times*, *Forbes*, over two dozen Lonely Planet titles, and on his blog, www.wheres-andy-now.com. Current obsessions: discovering LA's next great ethnic enclave, and winter sunsets over the bike path in Santa Monica.

More Writers

Published by Lonely Planet Publications Pty Ltd
ABN 36 005 607 983
1st edition – May 2012
ISBN 978 1 74220 001 9
© Lonely Planet 2012   Photographs © as indicated 2012
10 9 8 7 6 5 4 3 2 1
Printed in China

Although the authors and Lonely Planet have taken all reasonable care in preparing this book, we make no warranty about the accuracy or completeness of its content and, to the maximum extent permitted, disclaim all liability arising from its use.